A HERZEN READER

A

HERZEN

READER

Edited and translated from the Russian
with an introduction by Kathleen Parthé

With a critical essay by Robert Harris

NORTHWESTERN UNIVERSITY PRESS
EVANSTON, ILLINOIS

Northwestern University Press
www.nupress.northwestern.edu

 transcript

This book was published under the auspices of the Mikhail Prokhorov Foundation
TRANSCRIPT Programme to Support Translations of Russian Literature.

Printed in the United States of America

10 9 8 7 6 5 4 3 2 1

Library of Congress Cataloging-in-Publication Data

Herzen, Aleksandr, 1812–1870.
    [Selections. English. 2012]
    A Herzen reader / edited and translated from the Russian with an introduction by
Kathleen Parthe ; with a critical essay by Robert Harris.
        p. cm.
    Includes bibliographical references.
    ISBN 978-0-8101-2847-7 (pbk. : alk. paper)
    1. Herzen, Aleksandr, 1812–1870. 2. Russia—History—1801–1917. 3. Russia—
Politics and government—1801–1917. 4. Socialism—Russia—History—19th
century. 5. Intellectuals—Soviet Union. I. Parthé, Kathleen. II. Harris, Robert
(Robert Neil) III. Title.
DK189.H42 2012
947.073—dc23

                                                          2012026561

CONTENTS

Critical Essay

ACKNOWLEDGMENTS

A Herzen Reader owes its greatest debt to Russian scholars who worked on the thirty-volume edition of Herzen's collected works (*Sobranie sochinenii v tridtsati tomakh*). Information about the translated documents not otherwise attributed comes from their notes to the original texts. The five-volume chronicle (*Letopis' zhizni i tvorchestva A. I. Gertsena*) of Herzen's life and works is another valuable source; references to it indicate the volume and page number (e.g., *Let* 2:37). For over a century, members of the Herzen family in Europe and the United States have been extraordinarily generous with materials in their possession, and the result has been a steady increase in the availability of important documents to the editors of the works mentioned above and to the scholars who organized Herzen volumes for *Literaturnoe nasledstvo* (*Literary Heritage*). Their generosity also helped furnish the house-museum on Sitsev Vrazhek in Moscow, whose existence is due in no small measure to the efforts of scholar Irena Zhelvakova. Alexander Herzen was no great fan of jubilees, but he was eager to make his observations about Russia available to readers in his homeland and abroad, and to stimulate further discussion, and it is with this goal that we offer *A Herzen Reader* to the public. We are grateful to the University of Rochester (Kathleen Parthé) and New College, Oxford (Robert Harris), and to Northwestern University Press for helping us to complete this project.

INTRODUCTION

> He awaits his readers in the future.
>
> —Tolstoy's 1905 diary entry on Herzen

There was a time when Russian readers were divided into followers of Alexander Herzen—willing to take considerable risks to acquire and discuss his works—and his implacable enemies, who saw in him a traitor to the nation. There was a time when leading European liberals and radicals engaged him in a lively and prolonged debate, while Marx and Engels treated Herzen and his friend Mikhail Bakunin as unwelcome distractions in the lead-up to their revolution. During his life (1812–1870), Herzen survived the dogged pursuit of the tsarist secret police at home and abroad, and after his death, he overcame Lenin's embrace to reemerge in the post-Stalin era as a beacon of individual conscience, free speech, and national self-determination. Despite Herzen's enduring reputation outside Russia as the author of *Past and Thoughts* and *From the Other Shore*, Isaiah Berlin was still moved to tell an interviewer that Herzen remained an unknown thinker "because he was not translated."[1] In his early twenties, Herzen wrote to Natalya Zakharina, his future wife, that he wished to see part of his soul present in every piece of writing: "let their sum total serve as my biography in hieroglyphics."[2] Two centuries after this illegitimate son of a wealthy nobleman was born in the momentous year of 1812, Herzen's political writing and his personal correspondence remain largely unavailable in English. *A Herzen Reader* will add to the Herzen narrative, with a selection of one hundred essays and editorials written between 1850 and 1867.

As the *Reader* begins, two years have elapsed since Herzen saw for himself the turbulent Europe of 1848 and learned of the official reaction to these events in Nicholas I's Russia. Having left his homeland for an indefinite period in 1847, Herzen was from time to time ordered to return, and then forbidden from returning. The Third Section (political police) debated the merits of kidnapping him or having the Russian government request his extradition, and more than one European state made him feel unwelcome. Both Herzen and his mother, Louisa Haag, were denied income from their properties until intervention by the Paris branch of the Rothschild banking family forced the tsar to relent. For Herzen, wealth meant the freedom to accomplish his political goals, and he also saw no great virtue in real or assumed poverty, and he enjoyed good wine, expensive cigars, and French snuff. Generous toward his family and friends, he resisted the entreaties of fellow Russians (and other political émigrés), who requested—or demanded—loans, responding matter-of-factly that "money is one of my weapons, and it should not be squandered."[3]

The desire to please the Russian authorities and keep revolution at bay led Swiss officials to threaten the expulsion of Herzen's mother and his deaf six-year-old son Nikolay, who attended a special school in Switzerland. Herzen countered with a European-wide publicity campaign that shamed the officials into reversing their decision.[4] In the turbulence of post-revolutionary Europe, even the cosmopolitan Herzen needed to be a citizen somewhere, and the Swiss canton of Freiburg finally obliged in March 1851, after substantial funds were deposited in a local bank.[5] Rather than initiating a peaceful stage of his life, this turned out to be the beginning of a period of personal tragedy; in rapid succession, Herzen lost his mother and young son, and then his wife.

Isaiah Berlin claimed *Past and Thoughts* to be the "ark" in which Herzen saved himself, but, for all that, it was still only the "accompaniment to Herzen's central activity: revolutionary journalism."[6] After his August 1852 move to England, the forty-year-old Herzen spent several months in isolation while he decided what to do with the rest of his life, wishing to avoid the Russian pattern of beginning many projects and finishing none of them.[7] For several years Herzen had worked to acquaint Europeans with progressive Russian literature (Doc. 1). Resolved to henceforth address Russia directly, he began writing his memoir in a more organized way, and established the Free Russian Press.[8] In Berlin's terms, Herzen attempted, simultaneously, to save himself and his country. His memoir *Past and Thoughts* provides a general background to the work of the press and the personality of its chief writer, although the richest source of Herzen's thoughts about the purpose of *The Polestar* (*Poliarnaia zvezda*) and *The Bell* (*Kolokol*) can be found in the periodicals themselves and in his private correspondence.

In the memoir, we meet the Polish exiles who welcomed Herzen to London and worked tirelessly on the printing and distributing of Russian publications. We experience the early London years, when there were few customers and virtually no response from what was still a very rigid Nicholaevan Russia. The death of Nicholas I in 1855 led Herzen to launch the almanac *Polestar*, which was printed with Cyrillic type acquired from the same Parisian firm that supplied official Russian printers, leading Herzen to humorously call his enterprise "The Imperial and Revolutionary Press."[9]

It took two additional years and the stimulus of poet Nikolay Ogaryov's arrival in London before activity reached an even higher level.

Herzen credited Ogaryov (1813–1877) with the idea of a newspaper supplement to *The Polestar,* which soon assumed its independent existence as *The Bell.*[10] Friends since childhood, they were linked by their early oath on the Moscow hills to avenge the Decembrists. Presenting a united front to the outside world, their personal correspondence reveals substantial differences in tactics, priorities, judgments of people, and work habits. This decades-long relationship was, strangely enough, not weakened by the widower Herzen's liason with Ogaryov's second wife, Natalya Tuchkova-Ogaryova, with whom he had three children. By the mid-1860s, both men had tired of her difficult personality, and preferred each other's company to hers. What Herzen wrote from jail in 1834 remained true for the rest of their lives: "The worst thing for me is to be parted from Ogaryov . . . without him I am but a single volume of an unfinished epic, a mere excerpt."[11]

At the beginning of the reform era, Russians started sending Herzen fresh material and showing up at his door, as the newspaper grew in popularity and influence. Yakov Rostovtsev, who presided over the main Emancipation Committee, suggested that members read *The Bell* for its useful ideas. "While cursing us," Herzen wrote to his eldest son, the government "implements half of what we have been advocating."[12] Officials from various government agencies read the paper in order to "know the enemy"; one way or another, keeping up with its contents was a necessity, and it was printed on lightweight paper to make easier its safe and prompt transport to readers.[13] What Herzen calls the paper's "apogee" was not long-lived; the authorities saw how Russia was increasingly unsettled by the talk of emancipation, and they began to persecute Herzen's visitors, correspondents, and even his readers. This repression took a far more serious turn after the Polish uprising of 1863 and the first attempt on the tsar's life in 1866.

Even as the weakness of the reform program became clear by 1862, Herzen refused to alter his moderately socialist principles and embrace the violent agenda of the newest group of Russian radicals. He subsequently refused to abandon the Poles in 1863 to satisfy his own generation of Russian liberals, proud to furnish "living proof" of protest against the "extermination of an entire people."[14] Toward the end of *Past and Thoughts,* while wandering from one picturesque European "purgatory" to the next with no place to call his own, Herzen stoically embraced homelessness, serving out the Russian government's 1850 sentence of "perpetual exile."[15] A veteran of decades of political struggle, he contemplated, with his "essential aloofness,"[16] fellow exiles, including the latest Russian revolutionaries, who "throw themselves into the stream with a handbook on swimming."[17] Publication of *The Polestar, The Bell,* and *Past and Thoughts,* all of which began on such a high note, came to an indeterminate and somewhat melancholy end two years before Herzen's death. At times, Herzen had considered going back to Russia, prompting Ogaryov to ask whether he would really take such a terrible risk "for a view of the fields and Staraya Konyushennaya street?"[18] It was just a thought, and Herzen never acted on it. He had decided early on that his only return home would be through the Free Russian Press (Doc. 52). Scarcely a month after Herzen's death, Bakunin wrote to Herzen's oldest daughter Tata and Natalya Tuchkova-Ogaryova that the deceased was the last Russian "to act in isolation," and that the time had come for *"clear thinking* and *collective action."*[19] One of Bakunin's chosen partners in this "clear thinking and collective action" was Sergey Nechaev, whom Herzen had never trusted and who turned out to be a fake revolutionary but a real murderer.

During his twenty-three years abroad, the prolific Herzen "poured out a mass of articles, letters, essays, proclamations, the best of which are original masterpieces of both journalism and art."[20] The essays translated for this volume are less personal than his memoirs, and less abstractly philosophical than the longer analyses, but they are no less reflective of Herzen's experiences and values, and carry a greater sense of urgency about abuses that needed to be publicized and corrected. Most of the translations from *The Bell* are editorials, a genre that Herzen virtually introduced to Russian journalism. As lead articles, they set the tone for the issue, and constituted its primary response to news from Russia. Because they are specific reactions to specific events, no two of these editorials are alike; they draw the reader in with their unique set of facts and their spirited, but logical, argumentation.[21] Herzen also wrote lead articles that summarized the events of the year that had just ended (Docs. 25, 67) or that examined a longer period, from five to thirty years, in the life of the Free Russian Press or of Russia itself (Docs. 28, 52, 54, 100).

Herzen was, of course, one of Russia's first and most successful investigative journalists, and most of *The Bell*'s 245 issues are "accusatory documents," which give an impression of "unrelieved political, cultural and moral darkness, with shocking revelations of systematic injustice, cruelty, oppression, and continuous abuses and misgovernment, some of which were actually remedied as a result of these revelations."[22] He was obliged to depend on others for on-site reports, but he turned this raw material into brilliantly constructed attacks on public officials and their private supporters. Using publicity as a kind of "anti-police" force, he called to account those who punished the Russian people and who threatened him personally.[23] It is hardly surprising that the Russian authorities and other opponents of meaningful reform were incensed by what appeared in the Free Russian Press, but Herzen was also criticized in print and in person by Boris Chicherin, a liberal professor, and by Dobrolyubov and Chernyshevsky, the progressive voices of *The Contemporary* (*Sovremennik*), the most important thick journal of the reform years. Faced with conservatives who found him despicable, liberals who thought him immoderate, and the radical intelligentsia who called him naive, Herzen did not waver from positions which accorded with his openly stated values; he was happy to be corrected on facts, but never altered his principles.

Herzen defended the many exposés of government misconduct in *The Bell*, with some of his most explicit arguments presented in 1858–59 (Docs. 20–22). When Chernyshevsky was arrested in 1862, Herzen, himself a former political prisoner, dropped their quarrel and focused on the shame that Russia brought on itself through its treatment of a man who only wished the best for the Russian people (Doc. 64). He was appalled that Russia's liberals failed to offer the fallen man their support. In their private correspondence, Herzen and Ogaryov frequently debated the function of their paper; for Herzen, its role was "uncompromising propaganda," a profound sermon which "could be transformed into political agitation, but was not itself agitation."[24]

During the second half of the 1850s, while the reforms were under discussion, Herzen's essays offered a nuanced picture of Alexander II. At the beginning of the new tsar's reign in 1855, Herzen had made it clear that it should not matter whence liberation came; Herzen was principled, but not rigid or dogmatic. His letters to the tsar were respectful and positive, understanding that change from above was the preferred nonviolent alternative. Still, there was ample evidence by 1858 that conservative figures surrounding Alexander II continued to influence the censorship, the universities, and other institutions. When Herzen's elaborately planned London celebration of the March 1861 emancipation announcement was ruined by news of bloody repression in Poland, it was rightly seen as a poor omen. The government's subsequent response to fires in St. Petersburg, upheaval among students and peasants, and the Polish uprising of 1863 bore no signs of a progressive spirit. For the 1867 essay "Our System of Justice" (Doc. 94) one of *The Bell*'s correspondents provided evidence that even when the criminal chamber recommended moderate sentences, the State Senate substantially increased them, while military tribunals routinely handed out corporal punishment and even death sentences. The exalted tone often used by memoirists and historians to describe the Russian judicial reforms of the 1860s is absent from Herzen's account, especially when the inauguration of a modern court system coincided with the closed proceedings and vindictive atmosphere surrounding the case of Dmitry Karakozov.

A dozen of the hundred essays in this volume are reflections on this first assassination attempt against Alexander II on April 4, 1866. Herzen's initial reaction (Doc. 80) was disapproval of such individual "surprises" as a way of changing history. "The shot was insane, but what is the moral condition of a state when its fate can be altered by chance actions, which cannot be foreseen or prevented, exactly because they are insane?" (Doc. 82). Three years earlier, a group of young Russians visiting England had offered to kill the tsar, but Herzen convinced them to abandon the plan.[25] He called Karakozov a "fanatic" who did much more harm than good by bringing the reform era to an abrupt conclusion. That the peasant Komissarov, who reportedly deflected the shot, was elevated to the nobility seemed absurd to Herzen. He reminds his reader that while the tsar escaped harm, Nikolay Serno-Solovyovich, the founder of the first Land and Liberty group and a member of *The Contemporary*'s editorial staff, lay dying in Siberian exile. Having resolved early on to put information-gathering above ideological abstractions, Herzen developed the ability to vividly juxtapose facts and events, which became one of his greatest strengths as a political analyst.

Herzen's main point in the essays on Karakozov from 1866 and 1867 is that *there was no conspiracy*, no matter how hard the Investigative Commission tried to manufacture one (Docs. 82, 84, 86, 91). Therefore, no justification existed for the widespread repression in the wake of the April 4 shot (Docs. 85, 88, 92). He deplored the efforts of the formerly liberal Mikhail Katkov to whip up enthusiasm for Karakozov's execution; the rhetoric in *The Moscow Gazette* may remind modern readers of Katkov's professional descendants during the 1930s (Docs. 87, 88). Herzen asks "who can fail to see that we were right in pointing out all the absurdity of bringing socialism, nihilism, positivism, realism, materialism, journal articles, student dissertations, etc. into the Karakozov case?" He even laments the split in the conservative forces, pitting Moscow against Petersburg, because political truth and national unity suffered as a result. "Won't this enormous empire—whose peripheries are held together by lead and blood . . . crack at its very center?" (Doc. 89).

At the time, only an incomplete record of the investigation and trial was available even to pro-government journalists; a more thorough recent study of the archives in Claudia Verhoeven's *The Odd Man Karakozov* adds interesting details to the picture painted by Herzen. While the lengthy secret dossier points to the Russian Free Press as one of the foreign stimuli for Karakozov's act, the condensed version published at the time left out Herzen's name; in Russia, he could not be mentioned officially even to cast blame.[26] *The Moscow Gazette* still felt free to speculate on the failed assassin as an agent of the Russian revolutionaries Herzen, Ogaryov, and Bakunin, with their links to radical Polish circles, while government officials spread a rumor that Ogaryov was the young villain's relation.[27] The numerous searches carried out in the hunt for co-conspirators turned up illegal Russian publications and photos of the heroic editors.[28] At the end of her monograph, Verhoeven focuses on the "odd" nature of Karakozov's act. When asked by the tsar what he wanted, his answer was "Nothing," underscoring the terrorists' belief that the tsar had no power to act; Karakozov's vision on April 4, 1866, was of "power's void."[29] In "Order Triumphs!" one of Herzen's final essays on the subject, a similar observation is made: "The echo of Karakozov's shot exposed a terrifying vacuum in the Winter Palace" (Doc. 92).

The translated essays from *The Bell* are presented in chronological order, but out of their original context, since the biweekly issues carried material by Ogaryov and others, along with reports and letters from Russia. The commentary at the beginning of each essay addresses the question of reading in context, but for Herzen the articles were also contributions to an ongoing discussion with fellow Russians, a vigorous debate that began in student groups of the 1830s, continued most famously in Moscow and its environs in the 1840s, and never ceased while he drew breath. He even refused to have his memoir called a chronicle, insisting to Ivan Turgenev that it was a conversation, full of "facts, and tears, and theory."[30] In an 1868 letter he told his daughter Tata that "nothing is as boring as a monologue," and Herzen dreaded boredom most of all.[31] He enjoyed leaping from topic to topic, from Russian peasants to Polish rebels, and from ridiculous government ceremonies to the censorship, all the while deftly parrying blows from the right and left. Along with the Russian government's weak commitment to reform, Herzen addressed the desert-like sterility of homegrown Russian journalism.[32] Accused by some of trying to dominate political discourse, he responded that while demanding and exercising freedom of speech, he did not claim an exclusive "concession on Russian speech in foreign lands" (Doc. 21).

The strength of the essays in *A Herzen Reader* comes from astute political commentary married to the formidable literary talent of a man with a deeply personal approach to history; Thomas Masaryk saw this as an unusual and unbeatable combination that could not fail to attract attention.[33] Dostoevsky characterized Herzen as, in all things, first and foremost a poet.[34] Herzen's "lyrical journalism" was sufficiently distinctive to make unworkable a proposal to publish several essays in Russia under a pseudonym; it was clear that the author's "voice" was easily recognizable, and everyone knew the identity behind the pseudonym Iskander.[35] The unique Herzen style comes through in all genres, but it is perhaps strongest in his lead articles, where the goal is more immediate and the timing precise, resembling to a degree the telegrams that were altering the speed—and even the nature—of mid-nineteenth-century communication.[36] He placed a great value on precision, even "terseness," which was for many a welcome change from the "opaque, intractable atmosphere of so much Russian thought."[37] For Herzen, who funded the Free Russian Press from his inheritance, and who placed at risk himself and others involved in its publication and distribution networks, every word counted and cost; the editorial was never a leisurely literary form. Each comparison and ironic twist, each well-chosen foreign expression, was there to address a weighty matter.

"Vivos voco" (I summon the living) serves as the epigraph to Herzen's announcement in *The Polestar* of a supplement called *The Bell* that would commence in mid-1857 (Docs. 9, 10). *The Polestar* offered hitherto repressed manuscripts and had a retrospective orientation, looking back to the Nicholaevan era and, in particular, the martyred Decembrists; in 1855 Herzen called its goal "a continuation of the legend and the work" (Doc. 4). In contrast, *The Bell* was entirely forward-looking; the Russia of both the bullying Nicholas I and the soft-spoken historian Timofey Granovsky had passed away, and the possibilities for change were palpable, even from faraway London. Herzen's use of the phrase "Vivos voco" can stand on its own, but he could safely assume that educated readers would recognize this as a borrowing from Friedrich Schiller's 1798 poem "The Song of the Bell" ("Das Lied von der Glocke"). Schiller himself had appropriated the Latin phrase traditionally inscribed on church bells (he apparently knew it from a fifteenth-century church bell in Schaffhausen, Switzerland). In full, the inscription reads:

Vivos voco.	I summon the living.
Mortuous plango.	I weep for the dead.
Fulgura frango.	I shatter the lightning.

This epigraph perfectly describes the "voice" of *The Bell,* with its unrelenting insistence on greater participation in the process of bringing change to Russia. In the 1857 announcement "summoning the living," Herzen explains that *The Polestar* came out too rarely, while "events in Russia are moving quickly, and they must be caught on the fly and discussed right away." An urgent tone entered Herzen's style and remained there for as long as he published this newspaper. He reiterates the general principles governing the two publications: "everywhere, in all matters, to be on the side of freedom against coercion, the side of reason against prejudice, the side of science against fanaticism, and the side of advancing peoples against backward governments." The urgent and necessary steps are announced in capital letters:

FREEDOM OF EXPRESSION FROM CENSORSHIP
FREEDOM OF THE SERFS FROM THE LANDOWNERS
FREEDOM FROM CORPORAL PUNISHMENT

The editor would not limit himself, though, and *"The Bell . . .* will *ring out* from whatever touches it—absurd decrees or the foolish persecutions of religious dissidents, theft by high officials or the senate's ignorance. The comical and the criminal, the evil and the ignorant—all of these come under *The Bell.*" He asks fellow countrymen who share his love for Russia "not only to listen to our *Bell* but to take their own turn in ringing it."

In reading the essays selected for *A Herzen Reader*—and in comparing them to other Herzen writing that appeared in *The Bell*—what is striking is the forcefulness of the style and the frequent mood swings, offering indignation, outrage, irony, sarcasm, satire (Docs. 11, 36, 43, 99), bitter scorn, wistfulness, and sympathy, alongside encouragement, civic prayers, and priceless puns (Docs. 27, 34, 57). In 1947, Ioann Novich spoke of the "assorted literary references, analogies, and comparisons" familiar to Herzen's readers, and goes on to say that the author's expressiveness was found in "the clash of naturally contrasting attributes, images and juxtapositions."[38] The somewhat "extravagant vocabulary" was full of foreign words and phrases, but often no more than one would expect in the speech of an educated Russian member of the gentry who grew up in a trilingual household and spent long years in Europe—what was different was the cause they served.[39] Herzen felt at home in other languages, but Engels, at least, complained that Herzen's French was "totally repulsive."[40] For the most part, the journalism translates with relative ease, although the title of a lead article (Doc. 33) from the April 15, 1861, issue posed a challenge. In the end, the English version of " 'Kolokol,' Kovalevskii, Kostomarov, kopiia, kannibaly" preserved most, but not all, of the alliteration ("*The Bell,* Kovalevsky, Kostomarov, a Copy, and Cannibals").

Herzen's laughter is "no mere diversion," but "his alternative to doctrinal or pedagogical fervor."[41] In *Rabelais and His World*, Mikhail Bakhtin remarked on the way that Herzen was drawn to the power of laughter, although, as he notes, "Herzen was not acquainted with the laughing Middle Ages."[42] Bakhtin's first chapter begins with an epigraph from "A Letter Criticizing *The Bell*" (Doc. 14), stating the need for a history of laughter.

Laughter is one of the most powerful weapons against something
that is obsolete but is still propped up by God knows what. . . . I
repeat what I said previously [in *Letters from France and Italy*]: "what
a man cannot laugh about without falling into blasphemy or fearing
the pangs of conscience is a fetish. . . ."
    Laughter is no joking matter, and we will not give it up. . . . It
would be extraordinarily interesting to write the history of laughter.
. . . Laughter is a leveler, and people don't want that, afraid of being
judged according to their individual merits.

Later in the same chapter Bakhtin refers to other "profound" comments on
the subject by Herzen in the essay 'VERY DANGEROUS!!!" (Doc. 22).

Laughter is convulsive, and if, during the first minute a man laughs
at everything, during the second moment he blushes and despises
his laughter and that which caused it. . . . Without a doubt, laughter
is one of the most powerful means of destruction. . . . From laughter
idols fall. . . . With its revolutionary leveling power, laughter is terribly popular and catchy; having begun in a modest study, it moves in
widening circles to the limits of literacy.

Herzen exploited a number of comic possibilities in his writing, "from a
brilliant joke to cruel sarcasm."[43] At times he offered skilled parody of the
bombastic style (*vysprennyi slog*) of official communiqués (Doc. 27). Irony
was by far his favorite verbal weapon, a form of "controlled intensity."[44]
In notebook entries on irony from 1970–71, Bakhtin described a kind of
laughter that "lifts the barrier and clears the path," which was Herzen's
aim, to make a more open political debate work for Russia's future.[45] His
style in *The Bell* is remarkable for the "purposefulness" and "accuracy" of
his rage.[46] Rejecting the "false monastic theory of passivity" that he saw
in some of his fellow Russians in the early 1840s, Herzen boldly declared
that he "loved" his anger as much as they loved a sense of peace.[47] Herzen professed an interest in the further development of "our own native
irony, irony-the-consoler and the avenger" (*rodnaia nasha ironiia—ironiia
uteshitel'nitsa, mstitel'nitsa*).[48] In the midst of the public debate with Boris
Chicherin, Herzen proclaimed his goal to be "not just Russia's revenge, but
its irony" (Doc. 21).
    Herzen's use of irony is bound up with his awareness of the pain (*bol'*)
experienced by a Russian people yearning for liberty. In "Ends and Beginnings," a series of open letters to Turgenev from the early 1860s, he characterized the preliminary nature of work that he and Ogaryov had undertaken.

> Consciousness . . . is a very different thing from practical applica-
> tions. Pain does not give treatment but calls for it. The pathology may
> be good, but the therapy may be bad. . . . To demand medicine from
> a man who points out some evil is exceedingly precipitate. . . . We are
> not the doctors, we are the pain; what will come of our moaning and
> groaning we do not know; but the pain has been declared.[49]

Isaiah Berlin, who valued the Russian intelligentsia's passion for thrash-
ing ideas out in spontaneous discussion, acknowledged Herzen as a "vigorous" presence in his life, with his "wit, malice, imagination."[50] While many
admired Herzen's targeted witticisms in his own time and afterward and
refer to his hearty and infectious laughter, even his friends encouraged him
to show some restraint, and his ideological opponents attributed his verbal
humor to a lack of basic decency and even of emotional balance.[51] Ivan
Aksakov spoke for many when he complained of Herzen's "morbid desire
to be witty at all times," and an article about the intelligentsia in *The News*
(*Vesti*) mentioned Herzen's high-spirited sarcasm, while adding that he
was a poor philosopher and an even worse political thinker.[52]

When government officials considered in late 1857 the possibility of
launching a specifically anti-Herzen magazine, the head of the Third Department reminded the minister of enlightenment that it would be difficult
to achieve the same level of popularity with a public that voraciously read
"reprimands, abuse, and mockery. . . . But what would prevent an opposing
sexton from ringing out sharply, amusingly, and cleverly in answer to this?
Those who read the London *Bell*—or at least half of them—will be curious
about finding out what his rival has to say."[53] A successful journalistic challenge to *The Bell* would have to come from one or more equally formidable
writers who would be free to speak their minds. This proposal by the poet
and censor Fyodor Tyutchev was rebuffed by the head of the Third Department, who said that it was the equivalent of killing oneself out of a fear of
being killed.[54] Another suggestion, to reprint articles from *The Bell* in order
to refute them, was also judged unworkable.[55] In the end, the decision was
made not to try matching Herzen's approach, but to find a way of stopping
him, whether by bribery, threats, or some other means.[56]

For Herzen, nothing leisurely or long-winded could be permitted in the
printed messages sent back to Russia. In a letter to Ogaryov, Herzen insisted
that in *publitsistika* "one must sharply cut, throw out, and, most importantly,
one must compress phrases." This remark conveys the energy of Herzen's
writing, by means of which he launched phrases like missiles in order to
strike the enemy.[57] Vasily Rozanov wrote bitterly in pre-revolutionary years
of Herzen's introduction of "a whole stream of expressions into Russia,"

of being the "founder of political nonsense," and a bad influence on high-school students.[58] Alexander Solzhenitsyn, in a newspaper article of 1965, noted that in Herzen "we find a great number of bold formations which firmed the step of Russian letters and reached out for the unexpected, concise, and energetic control of words."[59] Brevity and well-aimed wit become strategies, with each phrase and punctuation mark playing a role in his journalism. There is a decided preference for the exclamation, which appears in the titles of Herzen essays (e.g., "St. George's Day! St. George's Day!" "Forward! Forward!" "Down with Birch Rods!", "Russian Blood Is Flowing!" "A Giant is Awakening!" "Order Triumphs!"), and even more frequently within the body of his essays.[60]

Herzen's style is both emphatic and interrogative, as he poses numerous questions, some genuine, others with the goal of rhetorically engaging his readers. One feels the presence of a masterful prosecutor, arguing his case before the court of public opinion, as well as an inspired preacher trying to get the faithful to sit up in their seats and pay close attention, because the stakes were so high. To sustain a style whose essence was more oral than written, Herzen required "supporters, opponents, conversationalists, and readers."[61] The author's acceptance of multiple voices and of dialogue over monologue was already evident in his essay *From the Other Shore,* something that had impressed the otherwise skeptical Dostoevsky. In the process of gathering material for what eventually became the novel *Demons,* Dostoevsky found Herzen to be essential reading.[62] His own publication *Diary of a Writer* (1873–81) carried on *The Bell*'s practice of reacting to specific events in a passionately political, and yet still very literary voice.[63] Dostoevsky lacked Herzen's gift for irony, but took his sarcasm to a much higher level.

Herzen mistrusted oratory and rhetoric, but he understood the power of direct address and saved its impact for his public letters to the tsar and, on one famous occasion, to the empress (Doc. 19). In these letters he exercised considerable control over his style, muting any strong emotion except deep concern for the Russian people. His conservative foes criticized the brazen inappropriateness of unsolicited advice to the imperial family, while radicals resented the respectful tone and the implication that reform was preferable to revolution. For his first letter to Alexander II (Doc. 5), Herzen took as his epigraph an 1823 poem of encouragement to the five-year-old Alexander Nikolaevich, who would likely assume the throne one day. This was hardly an innocent gesture, since the poet, Kondraty Ryleev, had taken part in the Decembrist rebellion two years later and died as one of the five martyrs of 1826. Despite this provocative beginning, the letter itself is conciliatory in tone.[64]

. . . there is one thing in common between your banner and mine—
namely that love for the people about which we speak.

And in its name I am prepared to make a huge sacrifice. . . .

I am prepared to wait, to step back a bit, to speak about something
else, as long as I have a real hope that you will do something for Russia.

Your majesty, grant freedom to the Russian word. . . .

Give land to the peasants. It already belongs to them. . . .

Hurry! Save the serf from future crimes, save him from the blood
that he will have to spill. . . .

Your majesty, if these lines reach you, read them without malice,
alone, and then think about them. You do not often get to hear the
sincere voice of a free Russian man.

Ten years later, the letter of May 2, 1865 (Doc. 68), at first addressed the
tsar with empathy on the death of the heir, Nikolay Alexandrovich; Herzen,
after all, had ample experience of personal tragedy. After a few sentences,
however, Herzen compares the tsar's loss to that of Polish families whose
sons died in the 1863 rebellion. Alexander is praised for the emancipation,
and then reminded of the sins he committed against his own and other
peoples, for which he must atone.

Forgiveness is not needed for your innocent victims or the suffering martyrs. *It is necessary for you.* You cannot go forward in a
humane way without an amnesty from them.

Sovereign, be worthy of it!

The following year saw a final letter to Alexander II (Doc. 84), prompted
by the government's frenzied search for conspirators after Karakozov's attempt on the tsar's life.

. . . let them call me crazy and weak, but I am writing to you because
it is so difficult for me to abandon the idea that you have been drawn
by others to this . . . terrible injustice that is going on around you. . . .

In all likelihood this is my last letter to you, Sovereign. Read it. Only
endless and agonizing grief about the destruction of youthful, fresh
strength under the impure feet of profane old men . . . only this pain
could make me stop you once more on the road and once more raise
my voice.

The number of the "living" summoned by Herzen with *The Bell* fluctu-
ated during the 1860s and the great bell went silent a few years before

the writer's death, not, he explained, because of his enemies, but the result of being abandoned by his friends.[65] In a civilization that responded to the bold gesture and the heroic deed (*podvig*), Herzen had reached across great distances to project his ideas back to Russia, and had "stylistically conquered fate."[66] He wrote in *Past and Thoughts* that when he returned from administrative exile in 1839 "any action was impossible . . . but, to make up for this, great was the power of speech."[67] In a 1938 letter, Isaiah Berlin speculated that "if anyone were alive now who talked as he must have done . . . one would never listen to anyone else."[68] Herzen preferred discussions among a small circle of close associates and visitors at home and abroad, and spoke only infrequently in public. He was able, however, to bring not just his political analysis but his confident *voice* to the lead articles that made *The Bell* so controversial and so influential.

Despite the many decades it took before Herzen's works were easily and legally available in his homeland, interest in him never flagged for long, as each generation found new reasons to listen to his vigorous commentary on Russia. The greatest response to his 1861 call to the intelligentsia to "go to the people" (Doc. 39) came in 1873, three years after his death. Russians traveling to Europe took the opportunity to find his forbidden writings and immerse themselves in his thought before returning home to a still-authoritarian state. Once there had been a stream of visitors to his London residence; now the pilgrims went to his grave in Nice. Fyodor Rodichev (1854–1933), an aristocrat who became a liberal leader in the Duma, "discovered" Herzen in Berlin in 1872, and what he read inspired him for a lifetime.[69] Characters in Russian novels were said to keep copies of *The Bell* at home in order to give themselves a progressive air; what could not be a subject of serious public debate could appear as a slightly risqué object. The revolutionary year of 1905 and the four Dumas that followed brought his works before a more politicized public that was looking for immediate answers about Russia's future direction. In Tolstoy's opinion, the intelligentsia was so degraded that they were unfit to understand Herzen's writings.[70] Trotsky gave Herzen his due for the emphasis on the peasants' "collectivist traditions," but any "cult" was out of the question, because all authority must be subject to "constant reexamination."[71] Gorky was more enthusiastic, calling Herzen "an entire province, a country amazingly rich in ideas."[72] The authors of the seminal *Landmarks* (*Vekhi*) anthology of 1909 found Herzen a frequent point of reference in charting the intelligentsia's political and spiritual evolution. The man who was deemed by many to be a guide for troubled times was excoriated by writer Vasily Rozanov as the villain who helped destroy a millennium-old civilization.

The events of 1917 elevated Herzen to even greater heights, as the new nation grew into a land dotted with "Herzen streets" and "Herzen institutes." In 1920, the fiftieth anniversary of his death received substantial attention, and during an evening dedicated to the *iubilei,* the Soviet commissar of enlightenment, Anatoly Lunacharsky, declared that Herzen had ceased being just a tourist attraction for Russians in Europe, and was now a living and healing spring for his homeland. Toward the end of his remarks, Lunacharsky made serious use of the sacred cadences so beloved of the militantly atheist regime, calling Herzen a life-giving prophet. "We summon you to help us, O great writer, great heart and great mind; we summon you to rise out of the grave and help us, to aid us in this time of mighty events."[73] A book from that same year referred to Herzen as a new Moses, and demanded that his precious remains be returned to "red Moscow." The author did, however, object to the series of "ridiculous" letters Herzen had written to the imperial family, an unsurprising comment, seeing that the descendants of the addressees had recently been executed.[74]

The early Soviet era brought the first substantial edition in Russia of Herzen's writings, assembled and edited by M. K. Lemke. In the years that followed, dedicated scholars organized their archival discoveries into multiple issues of *Literary Heritage* (*Literaturnoe nasledstvo*), and published a second edition of his collected works as well as a five-volume chronology of his life. The scholarly work was often of high quality, despite the fact that its sanction came from Lenin's pre-revolutionary essay on the occasion of Herzen's centenary, one of numerous tributes made that year.[75] For Lenin, Herzen was not the perfect revolutionary ancestor, but he was more useful and less troublesome than Bakunin and the anarchists.

In Russian circles abroad, those who fled Lenin and Stalin's Russia saw Herzen as "the first to look on emigration as a base from which one could try to influence intellectual and political developments at home" and the "father of political emigration."[76] A Herzen Foundation in Amsterdam published oppositional political materials for transport back to the Soviet Union, and, during its early years, Radio Liberty featured broadcasts on the contributions of Herzen, Korolenko, and others to Russia's pre-1917 democratic heritage. In a reversal of circumstances, by the mid-1980s, a different set of émigrés at Radio Liberty placed blame for the violence of Bolshevism squarely at the feet of Herzen and Chernyshevsky.[77]

Memoirs of the Soviet era, the best of which only became available after 1985, reveal an unofficial side to readership in the Soviet Union. Irina Paperno found that scores of Soviet memoirists, especially those who wrote "for the drawer," saw in Herzen's "story of intimate life embedded in catastrophic history" the inspiration for their own narratives.[78] In August 1941, poet Vera Inber spoke by radio to inhabitants of a blockaded Leningrad; she rallied them with Herzen's tales of an 1812 Moscow under siege and of the Battle of Borodino, tales he heard repeatedly as a child, becoming his *Iliad* and *Odyssey* and the focus of the first chapter of his memoirs. Inber told listeners that Russia "was creating for future generations new Odysseys, new Iliads," and that they would be the heroes of these epics.[79]

Lidiya Chukovskaya's reminiscences preserve conversations with Anna Akhmatova about their mutual love of Herzen's style and their respect for his honesty. When Chukovskaya stopped by Akhmatova's apartment after work, the poet noticed a portfolio of Herzen materials and demanded that her friend open it at random and read aloud, so that Akhmatova could commit to memory the "sound" of his prose.[80] Although they both loved *Past and Thoughts* (minus the maudlin passages about Herwegh), they also regretted the neglect by Soviet readers of the rest of his work. Granted access to Vyacheslav Molotov's abandoned library, Rachel Polonsky discovered the Lemke edition of Herzen, begun before the Revolution and completed afterward; the only reader's notations she found were in the index and a volume of the memoirs.[81]

Chukovskaya called *The Bell* "a collection of articles that were epics, articles that were poetry, epigrams, laments, funeral orations, prayers for the dead, prophetic songs, and formulas that were so concise that they read like proverbs," most of them as relevant to the Russia of 1962 as they had been a century earlier.[82] In a conversation about how people behaved during the 1937 purges, Akhmatova recalled Herzen's 1867 reproach to those who not only failed to find words of support for political prisoners but who could not even remain silent at such moments (*dazhe ne nashli molchaniia*).[83] Herzen's call for conscience and decency was heard in the years after Stalin's death. In *Zhivago's Children,* a study of the post-Stalinist intelligentsia, Vladislav Zubok charts Herzen's influence during the Thaw. While politically aware young people read widely from the nineteenth-century canon, "their main inspiration came from Alexander Herzen and other Russian socialists," and they concluded that "the existing regime was a horrible deviation from revolutionary ideals."[84] A monograph on the final year of Herzen's life written in Moscow by Raisa Orlova, the wife of Lev Kopelev and active in dissident circles, could only be published abroad.[85]

Herzen remained a rich source of inspiration for the dissident movement in the 1960s, with his example of a successful end run around censorship and border controls sending a quite different message than the regime could possibly have wished. In Solzhenitsyn's novel *The First Circle,* Innokenty Volodin's uncle asks the well-educated young man whether he has ever read Herzen "properly," restating the crucial question of conscience, whether there are limits to patriotism, and whether it extends to aiding the government in the destruction of its people.[86] When a small group of Russians protested the Soviet invasion of Czechoslovakia in 1968, they were inspired by Herzen's slogan in support of the Poles: "To Your Freedom and Ours."[87] Alexander Yanov credits his 1974 *Young Communist* article—with its repeated references to Herzen's political courage in countering pseudo-patriotism—with contributing to his own expulsion from the country.[88]

Herzen and Ogaryov composed a joint letter in 1863 to the impatient Bakunin, saying that they saw their role as holding firm to the banner until the dawn of a better day. Six years later, Herzen wrote to Ogaryov that he did not believe that they had always been effective. "Sometimes we were right on target, but at other times we were working for the 20th century."[89] In the end, Herzen's confidence in the long-term impact of their publications appears to have been more than justified.

In February 1837, Herzen wrote to his beloved Natalya from exile in Vyatka: "I'm already 24 years old, and I still don't know what to do. . . . *To write* or *to serve.* The literary world is unsatisfying because it isn't real life, and government service—how much humiliation would there be before I reached a point where my service would be of use? These . . . are the questions I have been preoccupied with lately."[90] His guiding principles involved greater honesty than was possible in government service, and more practical goals than could be presented effectively in fiction or literary criticism.[91] Herzen obviously found a way to combine writing and service to the people; practically speaking, this was only possible in exile, on another shore, where he could openly serve the "second government" that Russian literature had become.

Unlike many Russian writers and critics of the mid-nineteenth century, Herzen rejected the lure of inserting politics between the lines, believing that under well-formed governments, writers seek not to mask their thoughts, but to express them clearly.[92] When Herzen was still being taught at home, his tutor brought him forbidden verses by Pushkin and Ryleev. "I used to copy them in secret. . . . (and now I print them openly!)."[93] In an 1844 diary entry, he mentions an article by Mikhail Bakunin that had arrived from abroad. "Here is the language of a free man, which seems quite strange to us. . . . We are used to allegory, to a bold word *intra muros,* and we are amazed by the daring speech of a Russian man, like a person sitting in a dark hovel is startled by the light."[94] He also rejected de Custine's popular myth of Russia as a mysterious, undecipherable land; Herzen strove to make sense of it for both Europeans and for the Russians themselves. In remembering the "Remarkable Decade," Pavel Annenkov said that in Russia, where keeping a low profile was the wisest strategy, Herzen's values and criticisms were "undisguised."[95] As his work abroad wound down in 1868, Herzen summed it up in a typically matter-of-fact way: "It wasn't a conspiracy, it was a printing press."[96]

With *Past and Thoughts* Alexander Herzen created one of literature's great memoirs. *From the Other Shore,* "The Russian People and Social- ism," "On the Development of Revolutionary Thought in Russia," and other essays made a significant contribution to European thought between the French and Russian revolutions. Articles in *The Polestar* and editorials in *The Bell* are major documents in the history of nineteenth-century Rus- sian political journalism, not part of a conspiracy, but one very eloquent Russian's service to his country, an interactive "encyclopedia of civic free- dom."[97] It is a pleasure to introduce these previously untranslated writ- ings to a new audience, which, as Tolstoy said in 1905, Herzen so richly deserves.

Notes

The original Russian in the introduction's epigraph is "On uzhe ozhidaet svoikh chi- tatelei vperedi," Oct. 12, 1905, L. N. Tolstoi, *Sobranie sochinenii v dvadtsati tomakh* (Mos- cow: Khudozhestevnnaia literatura, 1960–65), 20:224, 506–7. On Oct. 18, 1905, Tolstoy wrote to Vladimir Stasov from Yasnaya Polyana, thanking him for the suggestion to re- read Herzen. In this turbulent year, Stasov had felt that Herzen's writings allowed him to once again "see the sun and warm himself" (Tolstoi, *Sobranie sochinenii,* 18:368–70).

1. Ramin Jahanbegloo, *Conversations with Isaiah Berlin: Recollections of an Historian of Ideas* (London: Phoenix, 1992), 175.

2. A. I. Gertsen, *Sobranie sochinenii v tridtsati tomakh* (Moscow: ANSSSR, 1954–66), 21:76.

3. Gertsen, *Sobranie sochinenii,* 21:300–303, 314; 26:13. The young radical Alexander Serno-Solovyovich complained that, while turning down the pleas from destitute émi- grés, Herzen could discuss socialism as he dined on caviar and champagne. As cited in: Martin Miller, *The Russian Revolutionary Emigres* (Baltimore: The Johns Hopkins University Press, 1986), 141.

4. *Let* 1:522–31, 540–42 (this refers to the first of five volumes chronicling Herzen's life and work; see the entry under *Letopis' zhizni i tvorchestva A. I. Gertsena* in the bibliography).

5. *Let* 3:19.

6. Introduction to the four-volume edition of Alexander Herzen, *My Past and Thoughts* (London: Chatto and Windus, 1968), 1:xxvi, xxxvii.

7. Herzen, *My Past and Thoughts,* 2:996–97, 3:1023–26.

8. *Let* 2:119–24.

9. Irena Zhelvakova, *Gertsen* (Moscow: Molodaia gvardiia, 2010), 386.

10. Gertsen, *Sobranie sochinenii,* 27:bk. 1, 265. The most recent account of the founda- tion of the Press can be found in Françoise Kunka, *Alexander Herzen and the Free Russian Press in London 1852 to 1866* (Saarbrücken: LAP Lambert Academic Publishers, 2011).

11. Gertsen, *Sobranie sochinenii,* 21:28.

12. Gertsen, *Sobranie sochinenii,* 27:bk. 2, 416.

13. *Let* 3:53.

14. Gertsen, *Sobranie sochinenii,* 27:bk. 2, 449.

15. *Let* 1:589; *Let* 2:20, 48. In a March 10 (Feb. 26) 1867 letter to Ogaryov from Italy, Herzen said that a visit from his friend would be welcome, but hardly possible, since he

had no set residence of his own ("'u menia' net u menia"), Gertsen, *Sobranie sochinenii*, 29:bk. 1, 58.

16. E. Lampert, *Studies in Rebellion* (London: Routledge and Kegan Paul, 1957), 179.

17. Herzen, *My Past and Thoughts*, 3:1441, 1453. This comment is reminiscent of his earlier criticism of the Petrashevtsy, a Petersburg progressive group arrested in 1849 that included a young Dostoevsky: "They wanted to have harvests in return for the intention to sow" (*My Past and Thoughts*, 2:978).

18. Andrei Root, *Gertsen i traditsii Vol'noi russkoi pressy* (Kazan: Izdatel'stvo Kazanskogo universiteta, 2001), 214.

19. The letter was dated Feb. 21, 1870, and is cited in Michael Confino, *Daughter of a Revolutionary: Natalie Herzen and the Bakunin-Nechayev Circle*, trans. Hilary Sternberg and Lydia Bott (LaSalle, Ill.: Library, 1973), 163–64.

20. Isaiah Berlin, "A Revolutionary Without Fanaticism," in *The Power of Ideas*, ed. Henry Hardy (Princeton, N.J.: Princeton University Press, 2000), 93.

21. Root, *Gertsen i traditsii Vol'noi russkoi pressy*, especially chapter 2, "Pervaia russkaia svobodnaia gazeta 'Kolokol' (1857–1867): Dvizhenie publitsisticheskoi mysli Gertsena," which carefully analyzes both the shorter editorials and the longer summary articles. Lampert compared Herzen, who "never said the same thing twice," to Bakunin, who constantly repeated himself (Lampert, *Studies in Rebellion*, 195).

22. Lampert, *Studies in Rebellion*, 187.

23. *Let* 3:255.

24. Gertsen, *Sobranie sochinenii*, 27:bk. 1, 316–18.

25. *Let* 3:595; *Literaturnoe nasledstvo*, vols. 41–42:419–25.

26. Claudia Verhoeven, *The Odd Man Karakozov: Imperial Russia, Modernity, and the Birth of Terrorism* (Ithaca, N.Y.: Cornell University Press, 2009), 23.

27. *Let* 4:254.

28. Verhoeven, *The Odd Man Karakozov*, 21, 45, 84, 118.

29. Ibid., 178–79.

30. *Let* 2:316–18.

31. Gertsen, *Sobranie sochinenii*, 29: 272.

32. Gertsen, *Sobranie sochinenii*, 27:bk. 2, 449.

33. Thomas Garrigue Masaryk, *The Spirit of Russia*, trans. Eden Paul and Cedar Paul (London: George Allen and Unwin, 1961), 1:384–85, 409, 426.

34. From an April 5, 1870, letter to Strakhov, cited in Raisa Orlova, *Poslednii god zhizni Gertsena* (New York: Chalidze, 1982), 21–22. Irena Zhelvakova refers to a list of more than 300 literary references in *The Bell*, which was compiled for the facsimile edition of the newspaper. See Zhelvakova, *Gertsen (Zhizn' zamechatel'nykh liudei)* (Moscow: Molodaia gvardiia, 2010), 434.

35. Orlova, *Poslednii god*, 3; *Let* 5:259.

36. In an 1857 letter to Alexander II about a book that defamed the Decembrists, Herzen characterized modern authoritarian states with unreformed political institutions as "Chinghiz Khan plus the telegraph." See Gertsen, *Sobranie sochinenii*, 13:38.

37. Lampert, *Studies in Rebellion*, 190, 195. Lampert makes much of the resemblance to Voltaire, whom Herzen read in his father Ivan Yakovlev's library. He notes that, unlike Voltaire, Herzen was "saddened by what he knew" (191). For another characterization of Herzen's style, see Miller, *The Russian Revolutionary Emigres*, 180.

38. Ioann Novich, *A. I. Gertsen: Stenogramma publichnoi lektsii, prochitannoi 4 aprelia 1947 goda v Dome Soiuzov v Moskve* (Moscow, 1947), 21.

39. Lampert, *Studies in Rebellion*, 196. Turgenev judged Herzen's style as "monstrously incorrect," although lively and appropriate to the message (Lampert, 196). Herzen, in turn, criticized the politics of Turgenev's novels, in private and in public.

40. *Let* 5:171. From a January 1869 letter to Marx.

41. Lampert, *Studies in Rebellion*, 174.

42. M. M. Bakhtin, "Rabelais in the History of Laughter," chapter 1 of *Rabelais and His World*, trans. Hèléne Iswolsky (Bloomington: Indiana University Press, 1984), 59, 92.

43. Iakov El'sberg, *Gertsen: Zhizn' i tvorchestvo*, 4th rev. ed. (Moscow: Khudozhestvennaia literatura, 1963), 537–38. Given El'sberg's sinister reputation, it is fairly certain that Herzen would have felt uncomfortable in his critical embrace.

44. Lampert, *Studies in Rebellion*, 190. For some key examples of irony, see Docs. 55, 78, and 86.

45. Mikhail Bakhtin, *Speech Genres and Other Essays*, trans. Vern McGee, ed. Caryl Emerson and Michael Holquist (Austin: University of Texas Press, 1986), 135.

46. El'sberg, *Gertsen*, 539, 543.

47. Gertsen, *Sobranie sochinenii*, 22:98.

48. From his preface to his 1858 publication of works by Prince Mikhail Shcherbatov and Alexander Radishchev that had been banned in Russia. Gertsen, *Sobranie sochinenii*, 13:272. His comments on "native irony" refer to Radishchev's *Journey from Petersburg to Moscow*.

49. Herzen, *My Past and Thoughts*, 4:1698. See also 2:628, 808, 3:1065, and 1070. The theme came up often in Herzen's writing, in comments about Chicherin, Proudhon, and others, who seemed surer than he was of the most effective remedies for achieving political health. This well-known formula was a favorite of Yuri Trifonov. See the record of a 1980 conversation with critic Lev Anninsky: Iurii Trifonov, *Kak nashe slovo otzovetsia* (Moscow: Sovetskaia Rossiia, 1985).

50. Isaiah Berlin, *Flourishing: Letters 1928–1946*, ed. Henry Hardy (London: Chatto and Windus, 2004), 68, 239, 258, 269.

51. *Let* 3:238, 449.

52. The first observation was cited by Michael Katz in the introduction to *Who Is to Blame? A Novel in Two Parts*, his translation of Herzen's 1846 novel (Ithaca, N.Y.: Cornell University Press, 1984), 35. The second dates from 1869; see *Let* 5:195–96.

53. *Let* 2:384.

54. *Let* 3:382.

55. *Let* 3:286.

56. *Let* 2:450.

57. Novich, *A. I. Gertsen*, 21.

58. Vasily Rozanov, "Fallen Leaves," in *The Apocalypse of Our Times and Other Writings*, trans. Robert Payne and Nikita Romanoff (New York: Praeger, 1977), 205.

59. Aleksandr Solzhenitsyn, "Ne obychai degtem shchi belit', na to smetana," *Literaturnaia Gazeta*, Nov. 4, 1965. Translated by Donald Fiene for *Russian Literature Triquarterly* 11 (1975): 264–69.

60. Docs. 3, 7, 29, 35, 39, and 92, respectively.

61. Orlova, *Poslednii god*, 29. Martin Miller reminds us that in *The Polestar* for 1855, Herzen issued a warm invitation to his readers, saying that the doors were wide open and all arguments were summoned (*The Russian Revolutionary Emigres*, 179).

62. Let 4:390–96.

63. See Gary Saul Morson, *The Boundaries of Genre: Dostoevsky's "Diary of a Writer" and the Traditions of Literary Utopia* (Austin: University of Texas Press, 1981), as well as his introductions to the full and condensed versions of the *Diary*'s translation: "Introductory Study: Dostoevsky's Great Experiment," in Fyodor Dostoevsky, *A Writer's Diary*, 2 vols., trans. and annotated Kenneth Lantz, 1–117 (Evanston, Ill.: Northwestern University Press, 1993); and "Editor's Introduction: The Process and Composition of a *Writer's Diary*," in Fyodor Dostoevsky, *A Writer's Diary*, one-volume abridged edition, trans. and annotated Kenneth Lantz, xix–lxiii (Evanston, Ill.: Northwestern University Press, 2009).

64. In 1837, the heir to the throne visited Vyatka, to which Herzen had been exiled. Herzen was detailed to guide the tsarevich and his tutor, the poet Zhukovsky, through an exhibit of local products; soon afterward, Zhukovsky was able to bring about Herzen's transfer to Vladimir. See *My Past and Thoughts*, 1:278–82.

65. *Let* 5:172.

66. This was said of the rural writer Viktor Astaf'ev after his death; from an unsigned obituary in *Kul'tura*, December 2001.

67. Herzen, *My Past and Thoughts*, 4:1763.

68. Berlin, *Flourishing*, 280.

69. Kermit McKenzie, "The Political Faith of Fedor Rodichev," in *Essays on Russian Liberalism*, ed. Charles E. Timberlake (Columbia: University of Missouri Press, 1972), 49. The Russian-Jewish writer S. An-sky called an early journalistic effort *The Bells of Vitebsk* (*Vitebsker gleklekh*) in Herzen's honor. See Gabriella Safran, *Wandering Soul* (Cambridge, Mass.: Harvard University Press, 2010), 17–18.

70. This is part of the same passage quoted in the epigraph.

71. Robert Service, *Trotsky: A Biography* (Cambridge, Mass.: Harvard University Press, 2009), 64.

72. Maksim Gorkii, "Iz istorii russkoi literatury," in *Izbrannye literaturno-kriticheskie stat'i* (Moscow: Khudozhestvennaia Literatura, 1941), 70.

73. Anatolii Lunacharskii, "Aleksandr Ivanovich Gertsen," in *Sobranie sochinenii* (Moscow: Khudozhestvennaia literatura, 1963), 1:142–51.

74. Iurii M. Steklov, *A. I. Gertsen (Iskander) 1812–1870 g.* (Moscow: Gosudarstvennaia Izdatel'stvo, 1920), 37, 43, 64. Nikolay Ogaryov's remains were repatriated in the mid-1960s.

75. For example: Georgii Plekhanov, "Rech' na mogile A. I. Gertsena v Nitstse: 7 aprelia 1912," in *Sochinenii* (Moscow: Gosudarstvennaia Izdatel'stvo, 1926), 23:453–56; and Lunacharskii, "Aleksandr Ivanovich Gertsen," 1:129–42.

76. S. V. Utechin, *Russian Political Thought: A Concise History* (New York: Frederick A. Praeger, 1964), 117.

77. James Crichtlow, *Radio Hole-in-the-Head: Radio Liberty, An Insider's Story of Cold War Broadcasting* (Washington, D.C.: American University Press, 1995), 19, 85, 171–72. Ludmilla Alekseyeva, *U.S. Broadcasting to the Soviet Union* (New York: Helsinki Watch Committee, 1986), 29–30.

78. Irina Paperno, *Stories of the Soviet Experience: Memoirs, Diaries, Dreams* (Ithaca, N.Y.: Cornell University Press, 2009), 9–12.

79. Cited by Harrison Salisbury, *The 900 Days: The Siege of Leningrad* (New York: Harper and Row, 1969), 253. See Vera Inber, *Pochti tri goda* (Leningrad: Sovetskii pisatel', 1946), 7–8.

80. Lidiia Chukovskaia, *Zapiski ob Anne Akhmatovoi v trekh tomakh* (Moscow: So-glasie, 1997), 2:544 (Nov. 4, 1962).

81. Rachel Polonsky, *Molotov's Magic Lantern: A Journey Through Russian History* (London: Faber and Faber, 2010), 77–80. For a variety of bicentennial week assessments of Herzen, see: *Literaturnaia gazeta*, April 4, 2012.

82. Chukovskaia, *Zapiski ob Anne Akhmatovoi*, 2:577 (Dec. 29, 1962).

83. Chukovskaia, *Zapiski ob Anne Akhmatovoi*, 2:264 (Sept. 14, 1957). The Herzen quote is from "Otvet I. S. Aksakovu," which appeared in *Kolokol* no. 240 (May 1, 1867), and was republished in Gertsen, *Sobranie sochinenii*, 19:244–55. Other Herzen scholars of a liberal cast included Natan Eidelman and Lidiya Ginzburg.

84. Vladislav Zubok, *Zhivago's Children: The Last Russian Intelligentsia* (Cambridge, Mass.: Harvard University Press, 2009), 67. Zubok goes on to mention an underground group at the Leningrad Institute of Technology called the Bell, whose members were soon arrested by the KGB (156).

85. Orlova, *Poslednii god zhizni Gertsena*. In her *Memoirs* (New York: Random House, 1983), Orlova recalled an August 1968 discussion of the Soviet invasion, during which Solzhenitsyn said that what the Soviet Union needed at that moment was "a new Herzen" to shame intellectuals into action (317).

86. Aleksandr Solzhenitsyn, *The First Circle*, trans. Harry T. Willetts (New York: Harper, 2009), chap. 61, pp. 448–49.

87. Ludmilla Alexeyeva and Paul Goldberg, *The Thaw Generation: Coming of Age in the Post-Stalin Era* (Boston: Little, Brown, 1990), 220.

88. Aleksandr Ianov, "Al'ternativa," *Molodoi Kommunist* 1974: 1 (70–77). See also Yanov's book *The Origins of Autocracy: Ivan the Terrible in Russian History*, trans. Stephen Dunn (Berkeley: University of California Press, 1981), 261–62.

89. *Let* 5:180; Gertsen, *Sobranie sochinenii*, 30:33–34. In an essay from 1923, "On Literature, Revolution, Entropy, and Other Matters," Yevgeny Zamyatin commented on the usefulness of heresy that fights entropy and is right "150 years later." See *A Soviet Heretic*, ed. and trans. Mirra Ginsburg (Chicago: University of Chicago Press, 1970). 109.

90. Gertsen, *Sobranie sochinenii*, 21:142–43.

91. Gertsen, *Sobranie sochinenii*, 21:154.

92. *Let* 1:263, 333. For an analysis of the "dangerous texts" paradigm, see Kathleen Parthé, *Russia's Dangerous Texts: Politics Between the Lines* (New Haven, Conn.: Yale University Press, 2004).

93. Herzen, *My Past and Thoughts*, 1:52.

94. Gertsen, *Sobranie sochinenii*, 2:409. When addressing Europeans (Doc. 1), Herzen acknowledged efforts by Russian writers, especially during the decade after the Decembrist revolt, to make veiled references to political subjects and to encourage readers to be attentive. However, by 1860 he writes in *The Bell* that "we have no secrets, and we passionately want to show the sovereign all there is to know," while the tsar's closest aides "conceal everything except harmful gossip" (Doc. 25).

95. Cited by Isaiah Berlin in chap. 4 of *Russian Thinkers*, ed. Henry Hardy and Aileen Kelly (New York: Penguin, 1979), 200.

96. "U nas byl ne zagovor, a tipografiia." Gertsen, *Sobranie sochinenii*, 20:420. This is from the 1868 essay "K nashim vragam."

97. Zhelvakova, *Gertsen*, 533.

A NOTE ON THE TEXT

For bibliographical entries and for the citation of Russian words, a standard Library of Congress transliteration is employed. In other usages, modifications have been made for ease of pronunciation (e.g., Murav'ev/Muravyov, Arsen'ev/Arseniev, Nikolai/Nikolay, Elena/Yelena). For a small number of prominent figures, the most familiar form of their names has been chosen (e.g., Nicholas I, Alexander II). In the text of the primary documents, Herzen's frequent use of three closely spaced dots, indicating a pause for emphasis, or two dots plus a question mark or an exclamation point, as is common in Russian, has been preserved; any omissions made by the translator in Herzen's writing are indicated by three widely spaced dots in brackets.

All volume and page numbers for the originals of the Herzen documents translated in *A Herzen Reader* refer to Aleksandr I. Gertsen, *Sobranie sochinenii v tridtsati tomakh,* 30 vols. (Moscow: ANSSSR, 1954–66) and are given in a source note following the text. Page numbers indicate first the document itself, then the notes at the back of each volume. For *Poliarnaia zvezda,* the year and book are indicated (kn.), and for *Kolokol,* the issue number (l.) and the date.

A HERZEN READER

→ 1 ←

On the Development of Revolutionary Ideas in Russia was written in 1850, at the dawn of a particularly turbulent period in Herzen's life, so it is fitting that one of the first places it is mentioned is in a letter to the German poet George Herwegh, soon to be revealed as a serious rival for Natalya Herzen's affections. Herzen tells Herwegh that he is writing a "brief note about the development of liberalism and opposition in Russian literature," but a few weeks later admits that it has turned out to be much more political than literary (*Let* 2:572–74). After three years abroad, Herzen felt completely cut off from everything Russian; at best, his letters were answered with expressions of passivity and despair, and at worst, they were returned to him (Zhelvakova, *Gertsen*, 337). Natan Eidelman saw this as the moment when Herzen summed up past Russian thought and sketched the "contours of a new 'program.'" Herzen had not yet seen some of the most important eighteenth-century Russian documents, but as they came to his attention, he published them in London (Eidel'man, *Svobodnoe slovo*, 450–51). The treatise on revolutionary ideas, comprising an introduction, six chapters, an epilogue, and a supplement, was published in German and French in 1851; the translation below is from the French. The appearance of the French edition led to Herzen being thrown out of Nice, which still belonged to the Kingdom of Sardinia, in June of that year. By October 1851, it was on the list of foreign publications that were "absolutely" forbidden in Russia (*Let* 2:25, 51).

Herzen's analysis of Russia's historical development elicited strong reactions across the political spectrum. The first Russian readers were members of the ruling circles who were permitted to receive foreign publications otherwise banned by the censorship committee. Based on rumors emanating from those quarters, and in the wake of the 1849 Petrashevsky trial, Herzen's Moscow acquaintances feared that the pamphlet could provoke additional attacks on progressive circles. Timofey Granovsky, whose friendship Herzen treasured, wrote disapprovingly to the author—before he had read the essay—about the dangers to which Herzen was exposing liberals. In an apologetic letter two years later he admitted that at the time he had been influenced by gossip. Pavel Annenkov believed that Herzen's essay put Granovsky in real peril; the government saw revolution everywhere and was just waiting for the beloved professor to make a mistake (Annenkov, *Extraordinary Decade*, 250–51; Annenkov, *Literaturnye vospominaniia*, 529–31).

The actor Mikhail Shchepkin was delegated by Moscow acquaintances to ask Herzen in person to stop writing and move to America, at least until things had calmed down in Russia. Petr Chaadaev, on the other hand, sent thanks to Herzen for having mentioned his role in the struggle for freedom. It turns out that Chaadaev had also written to the political police, expressing his indignation at receiving the praise of such a scoundrel; he later explained to his puzzled nephew that he had to save himself (Berlin, *Russian Thinkers*, 15). Encouraged by Herzen's bold approach, students at Moscow University later illegally printed their own translation.

3

Nikolay Gogol was frightened by the essay's claim that in his earlier works he depicted noblemen and officials negatively, and Shchepkin said that when he and Turgenev met Gogol at the end of October, the latter was torn between feeling offended and questioning his own wisdom in having published *Selected Passages from Correspondence with Friends* (*Let* 2:51). The critic Vladimir Botkin, a liberal frightened into conservatism by the 1848 revolutions, labeled Herzen's survey a "denunciation." When the minister of state properties, Kiselev, observed that it could not endanger anyone, since it only spoke of the dead, the Third Department's Count Orlov replied that "if we really wanted to, we could use the dead to reach the living"; another conservative journalist, Nikolay Grech, called Herzen a "swine" who led young people to drink the poison of "unbelief and disrespect for sacred things and state power" (*Let* 2:45).

Among the essay's better-known European readers, Friedrich Engels particularly objected to Herzen's elevation of the peasant commune and his association with such figures as Proudhon and Bakunin. In an 1853 letter to an associate about the possibility of revolution in Russia, Engels complained that Herzen had hedged his bets in a Hegelian manner by describing a republic that was simultaneously democratic, socialist, communist, *and* Proudhonian (*Let* 2:139–40). The historian Jules Michelet, with whom Herzen enjoyed long conversations, was very impressed with the article, which he called a "heroic" work by a Russian patriot, and he subsequently cited Herzen's ideas in his own analysis of Russia. Revised versions of *Revolutionary Ideas* were published in French and German in subsequent years, and arrangements were made with William Linton for a translation into English. The 1858 French version, published in London, was the basis of two different Russian translations later commissioned for twentieth-century editions of Herzen's works. An 1860 discussion of Herzen by Nikolay Sazonov for *La gazette du Nord* called *Revolutionary Ideas* a survey, however incomplete, of Russia's "moral and intellectual history . . . distinguished by a remarkable intelligence and a correct assessment of the foundations of Russian life" (Ivanova, *A. I. Gertsen*, 155).

In chapter 5 below, Herzen makes a strong argument for the significance of Russian literature in spreading new and liberating ideas, and provides an impressive "martyrology of Russian literature" (Zhelvakova, *Gertsen*, 341). Free of tsarist censorship, he was able to expand upon views held by the critic Vissarion Belinsky (1811–1848) and other progressive figures, and to introduce them to Europeans, who, based on existing information, had a poor understanding of the country's problems, and who knew virtually nothing of Russia's potential for reform. The Marquis de Custine's travelogue *Lettres de Russie en 1839* had come out to great acclaim in 1843, and *La Russie et les Russes* by the Decembrist émigré Nikolay Turgenev (1799–1871) made its appearance four years later. The former heard only the silence emanating from frightened Russians, while the latter, who was abroad in December 1825 and never returned to his homeland, took little notice of the common people. Herzen heard the voices of both remarkable individuals and the Russians as a whole, and was therefore more hopeful than others in 1850 about Russia's future prospects (Walicki, *Legal Philosophies*, 336–37).

ON THE DEVELOPMENT OF REVOLUTIONARY IDEAS IN RUSSIA

Chapter V. Literature and Public Opinion in Russia After December 14, 1825

[1851/1858]

The twenty-five years since the 14 (26) of December are harder to character-ize than all the time that has elapsed since the age of Peter the Great. Two opposing tendencies—one on the surface, the other in depths where it can barely be seen—make observation difficult. Russia appears to remain im-mobile, even to have retreated a bit, but in essence, everything has taken on a new appearance; the questions are more complex and the answers less simple.

On the surface of official Russia, "the empire of façades," only the losses have been visible—the cruel reaction, the inhuman persecution, the strengthening of despotism. Surrounded by mediocrity, by soldiers on pa-rade, Baltic Germans, and brutal conservatives, one sees Nicholas, suspi-cious, cold, stubborn, pitiless, absent any greatness of soul—as mediocre as his entourage. And, immediately below him, high society, which lost its barely acquired sense of honor and dignity when the first clap of thunder broke over its head after December 14. The Russian aristocracy did not re-cover during the reign of Nicholas, its bloom had faded, and all that was noble and good in it languished in the mines or in Siberia. The nobles who remained and kept the monarch's favor descended to a degree of vileness and servility known to us from de Custine's description.[1]

Then there were the guards officers; formerly brilliant and well-educated, they turned increasingly into dull soldiers. Before 1825, everyone wearing civilian clothes acknowledged the superiority of epaulets. To be *comme il faut,* one had to serve for a couple of years in the guards, or at least in the cavalry. Officers were the heart and soul of any gathering, the heroes of holiday celebrations and balls, and, to be truthful, there was a good reason for this. Officers were more independent and conducted themselves with more dignity than groveling bureaucrats. Circumstances changed, and the guards shared the fate of the aristocracy; the best of the officers were exiled, many others left the military, unable to bear the coarse and insolent tone adopted by Nicholas. Their places were quickly taken by diligent soldiers or pillars of the barracks and the stable. Officers lost the favorable opinion of society and civilian dress gained an advantage—the uniform prevailed only in small provincial towns and at court, the chief guardroom of the empire. Members of the imperial family, along with its head, showed the military a preference that was exaggerated and inappropriate in their position. The public's coldness toward men in uniform did not extend to admitting civilian government employees into society. Even in the provinces, they were treated with an unconquerable disdain, which did not prevent the growth of the bureaucracy's influence. After 1825, the whole administration, formerly aristocratic and ignorant, became petty and mean. Ministries turned into offices, and their heads and senior officials into businessmen or clerks. In their attitude toward the civil service they were exactly like the dull new members of the guards. Consummate experts on every sort of formality, cold and unquestioning in carrying out orders from above, their devotion to the government came from a love of extortion. Nicholas was in need of such officers and administrators.

The barracks and the chancellery were the chief supports of Nicholas's political system. Blind discipline devoid of common sense combined with the dead formalism of Austrian tax officials—those were the foundations of the celebrated mechanism of power in Russia. What a poor concept of governance, what prosaic autocracy and pitiful banality! This is the simplest and most brutal form of despotism.

Add to this Count Benkendorf, chief of the gendarmes—that armed inquisition, that political Masonic order, with members in all corners of the empire, from Riga to Nerchinsk, listening and eavesdropping—heading the Third Department of His Majesty's chancellery (such is the name of the main office for espionage), sitting in judgment over everything, altering court decisions, and interfering in everything but especially in matters concerning political criminals. From time to time in front of this office-tribunal there appeared civilization in the form of a writer or student who was exiled or locked up, his place soon to be taken by another.

In a word, looking at official Russia one could only despair; on the one hand there was Poland, divided and martyred with amazing regularity; on the other hand, the insanity of a war which continued throughout the reign, swallowing up armies without advancing by a single step our domination of the Caucasus; and, in the center, general degradation and governmental incompetence.

But to make up for it, within Russia great work was going on, work that was muffled and mute but active and continuous; everywhere discontent grew, revolutionary ideas gained more territory during those twenty-five years than during the entire previous century, and yet they did not penetrate through to the people.

The Russian people still kept itself far away from political life, having little reason to take part in the work going on at other levels of society. Long-term suffering forced upon them their own sense of dignity; the Russian people had suffered too much to agitate for a minor improvement in their position—better to remain a beggar in rags than to change into something patched together from scraps. But if it took no part in the movement of ideas occupying other classes, this does not at all mean that nothing was transpiring in its soul. The Russian people breathed more heavily than before, and its countenance was sadder; the injustice of serfdom and pilfering by civil servants became more and more unbearable. The government had disturbed the calm of the village commune with its compulsory organization of labor, and, with the introduction of rural police [*stanovye pristavy*] even the repose of the peasant in his own hut was restricted and supervised. There was a major increase in cases brought against arsonists, those who killed landowners, and participants in peasant uprisings. There was grumbling among the large number of religious dissenters; oppressed and exploited by the clergy and the police, they were far from making any major move, and yet one heard from time to time in these dead seas vague sounds heralding fierce storms. The Russian people's discontent of which we have been speaking is scarcely visible to a superficial glance. Russia always seems so tranquil that one would have difficulty believing that anything was going on. Few people know what is happening under the shroud in which the government wraps the dead—the bloodstains, the military executions—when it is said, hypocritically and arrogantly, that there was no blood and no corpse under the shroud. What do we know of the Simbirsk arsonists, and the massacre of landowners simultaneously organized by a number of villages? What do we know of local uprisings, which broke out in connection with Kiselev's new administration?[2] What do we know of the destruction in Kazan, Vyatka, and Tambov, where one had to resort to cannon?

The intellectual effort of which we spoke was not taking place at the highest levels of the state nor at its base, but in between the two, that is to say, between the lower and middle nobility. The facts we will introduce may not seem to have great importance, but it must not be forgotten that propaganda, like all education, is not flashy, especially when it does not dare to show itself in the light of day.

The influence of literature has noticeably increased, and penetrates much more deeply than before; it has not changed its mission and retains its liberal and educational character, to the extent possible under censorship.

A thirst for education is taking hold of the entire younger generation; civilian and military schools, gymnasia, lycées, and academies overflow with students; the children of the poorest parents strive to get into various institutes. The government, which as recently as 1804 enticed children into the schools with various privileges, now uses every effort to hold back the tide; difficulties are created at admission time and during exams; tuition payment is demanded; the education minister issues an order restricting the education of serfs. Nevertheless, Moscow University has become a ca-

thedral of Russian civilization; the emperor detests it, sulks over it, and
each year exiles a batch of its students. He never visits it when in Moscow,
but the University flourishes and its influence grows; in bad repute, it expects nothing, continuing its work and becoming a genuine force. The elite
among the youth in neighboring provinces come to the University, and
each year an army of graduates spreads throughout the country as civil servants, doctors, and teachers.

In the depths of the provinces, and even more so in Moscow, there is a
visibly growing class of independent people not pursuing public service,
who occupy themselves with their properties, science, and literature; they
demand nothing of the government except to be left alone. This is in contrast to Petersburg nobles, who cling to government service and the court,
are consumed by servile ambition, expect everything from the government,
and live only through it. To ask for nothing, to remain independent, not
to seek a position—under a despotic regime this counts as being in opposition. The government looked suspiciously at these idlers and was not
pleased. They constituted a core of educated people poorly disposed toward
the Petersburg regime. Some spent entire years abroad, bringing back with
them liberal ideas; others came to Moscow for a few months, spending the
rest of the year on their estates, reading everything new and acquainting
themselves with intellectual developments in Europe. Among provincial
landowners, reading was in fashion. People bragged about their libraries,
and at the very least ordered new French novels, the *Journal des Débats* and
the Augsburg newspaper; to possess banned books was to be in style. I do
not know of a single well-kept house where one could not find de Custine's
book about Russia, which was specifically banned by Nicholas. Denied the
possibility of action, constantly menaced by the secret police, young people
plunged into their reading with great fervor. The mass of ideas in circulation grew and grew.

But what new ideas and tendencies arose after the 14th of December?[3]

The first years following 1825 were terrible. It took people a dozen years
to realize how servile and persecuted was their lot. Profound despair and
general low spirits took hold. High society, with a haste that was cowardly
and mean, renounced all humane feelings and all civilized thoughts. There
was virtually no aristocratic family without a relative among the exiles, and
almost none of them dared to dress in mourning or express their sorrow.
Turning away from this sad spectacle of servility, immersed in reflection in
order to find some source of advice or hope, one came up against a terrible
thought, which made the blood run cold.

Illusions were impossible: the people were indifferent spectators on the
14th of December. Every clear-thinking person saw the terrible result of the

complete rupture between national Russia and Europeanized Russia. Every living link had been broken between these two parties and they had to be renewed, but how? That was the great question. Some thought that nothing would be achieved by allowing Russia to be pulled along by Europe; they placed their hopes not on the future, but on a return to the past. Others saw in the future only unhappiness and ruin. They cursed the mongrelized civilization and its apathetic people. A great sadness came over the hearts of all thinking people.

Only Pushkin's resonant and broad song echoed across a landscape of slavery and anguish; this song preserved the past epoch, filled the present with its manly sounds, and sent its voice far into the future. Pushkin's poetry was a pledge and a comfort. Amidst poets who live in times of despair and decadence you don't find these types of songs, which do not go well with burials.

Pushkin's inspiration did not deceive him. The blood that had rushed to a heart struck by terror could not stop there; it soon began to make itself known.

Already a journalist had courageously raised his voice to rally the timid.[4] This man, who had spent all his youth in his Siberian homeland, took up trade, which quickly bored him; he then devoted himself to reading. Without any formal education, he learned French and German on his own, and went to live in Moscow. There, without colleagues, without acquaintances, and without a name in literature, he came up with the idea of editing a monthly journal. He soon astonished his readers with the encyclopedic variety of his articles. He wrote boldly of jurisprudence and music, of medicine and Sanskrit. Russian history was one of his specialties, which did not prevent him from writing stories, novels and, finally, reviews, in which he achieved great success.

In Polevoy's writing one would look in vain for great erudition, for philosophical depth, but with each question he was able to discern its humanitarian side; his sympathies were liberal. His journal *The Moscow Telegraph* enjoyed great influence, and we must acknowledge the service he rendered by publishing in such a dismal age. What could be written the day after the uprising, or on the eve of the executions? Polevoy's position was very difficult. He was saved from persecution by his very obscurity. One wrote very little in that epoch; half of the literary world was in exile, and the other half kept silent. A small number of renegades, like the siamese twins Grech and Bulgarin,[5] allied themselves with the government, having smoothed over their part on the 14th December with denunciations against their friends and by suppressing the person who had set type for revolutionary proclamations on Grech's printing press. They alone dominated journalism in

Petersburg, but it was in their role as police agents, not as literary figures. Polevoy was able to hold out against all reactionary forces without betraying his cause until 1834; we must not forget this.

Polevoy began to democratize Russian literature, bringing it down from its aristocratic heights, making it more popular, or at least more bourgeois. His greatest enemies were literary authorities whom he attacked with piti-less irony. He was completely correct in thinking that any destruction of authority was a revolutionary act, and that a man who was able to free him-self from the oppression of great names and pedants could not fully remain either a religious or civil slave. Before Polevoy, critics occasionally dared, amidst allusions and excuses, to make some slight observations about Der-zhavin, Karamzin, or Dmitriev,[6] all the while acknowledging that their greatness was incontestable. From the very first day, Polevoy stood on an equal footing and began to take on these great masters, who were so seri-ous and dogmatic. Old Dmitriev, poet and former Minister of Justice, spoke with sadness and horror at the literary anarchy introduced by Polevoy, with his lack of respect for people whose services were acknowledged by the entire nation.

Polevoy not only attacked literary authorities, but also scholars; he dared to challenge their research, he, the minor Siberian merchant who had never pursued formal studies. Scholars *ex officio* allied themselves with gray-haired literary eminences to begin a proper war against the insurgent journalist.

Polevoy, knowing the public's taste, destroyed his enemies with biting articles.

He replied in a joking manner to the scholars' observations, treating their tedious judgments with an impertinence that made people laugh out loud. It is hard to describe the curiosity with which the public followed the course of this polemic. They seemed to understand that in attacking literary authorities, Polevoy had in mind other authorities. He made use of every occasion to touch on delicate political questions, and did this with admi-rable skill. He said almost everything, without ever leaving himself open to attack. It must be said that censorship really helped the development of style and the art of mastering one's own speech. A man who is irritated by an obstacle he finds offensive wishes to vanquish it and almost always suc-ceeds. Circumlocution carries in it traces of emotion, of battle; it is more impassioned than a simple utterance. An implied word is stronger under its veil, always transparent for one who wishes to understand. Constrained speech has a more concentrated meaning, it is sharp; to speak in a way that the thought is clear, but the words seem to come from the reader himself, that is the best way to be convincing. Implications increase the force of the expression, while nakedness constrains the imagination. The reader who knows the extent to which the writer must be careful will read attentively; a secret bond is established between him and the author: the one conceals what he writes, the other what he understands. The censorship is a spider web that catches small flies but is torn by the large ones. Characters and allusions may perish under *red ink;* energetic thoughts and genuine poetry pass with disdain through this cloakroom, having allowed themselves, at most, to be brushed a bit.[7]

With *The Telegraph,* journals began to dominate Russian literature. They absorbed all intellectual movement. Few books were bought, while the best poetry and stories saw the light of day in journals, and something had to be out of the ordinary—a poem by Pushkin or a novel by Gogol—to otherwise attract the attention of a public as scattered as were the readers of Russia. In no country other than England was the influence of journals so great. This was in fact the best means of spreading enlightenment over such a great expanse. *The Telegraph, The Messenger of Moscow, The Telescope, The Library for Reading, Fatherland Notes,* and their illegitimate son *The Contemporary,* in spite of different tendencies, have spread a great deal of information and many concepts and ideas over the past twenty-five years. They gave the inhabitants of the Omsk and Tobolsk provinces the possibility of reading novels by Dickens and George Sand two months after they had appeared in London or Paris. Even the fact that they appeared as installments was useful, stimulating lazy readers.

Polevoy managed to keep *The Telegraph* going until 1834. However, the persecution of ideas was redoubled after the rebellion in Poland. Victorious absolutism lost all false modesty, all shame. Schoolboy pranks were punished like armed uprisings, and children of 15–16 were exiled or sent away as soldiers for life. A student of Moscow University, Polezhaev,[8] already known for his verse, composed several liberal poems. Without having him tried, Nicholas sent for the young man, ordered him to read the verses aloud, kissed him, and sent him away as a simple soldier; the idea of such an absurd punishment could only arise in the mind of a government that had lost its senses, and that saw the Russian army as a reformatory or a prison. *Eight years* later, the soldier Polezhaev died in a military hospital. A year after that, the Kritsky brothers, also Moscow students, were sent to prison because—if I am not mistaken—they broke a bust of the emperor. Since that time, no one has heard anything about them. In 1832, on the pretext that it was a secret society, a dozen students were arrested and immediately sent to the Orenburg garrison, soon to be joined by a Lutheran pastor's son, Jules Kolreif, who was not a Russian citizen, had only occupied his time with music, but who dared to say that he did not consider it his duty to denounce his friends. In 1834 my friends and I were thrown into prison and, after eight months, sent away as clerks in the chancelleries of distant provinces. We were accused of *intending* to form a secret society and wishing to spread Saint-Simon's ideas; as a bad joke, we were read a death sentence, and then were told that the emperor, with the unpardonable benevolence so typical of him, had only sentenced us to a corrective term in exile. That punishment lasted more than five years.

The Telegraph was suspended that same year of 1834. Polevoy, having lost his journal, was quite at sea. His literary essays no longer enjoyed success; embittered and disappointed he quit Moscow to live in St. Petersburg. A sad astonishment greeted the first issues of his new journal (*Son of the Fatherland*). He became submissive and fawning. It was sad to see this bold fighter, this tireless worker, who was able to get through the most difficult times without deserting his post, come to terms with his enemies as soon as his journal was shut down. It was sad to hear the name of Polevoy coupled with those of Grech and Bulgarin, sad also to be present at the productions of his plays, which were applauded by secret agents and official lackeys.

Polevoy was aware of his own decline, he suffered because of it and was depressed. He wanted to escape his false position, to justify himself, but he lacked the strength and he merely compromised himself with the government, without gaining anything vis-à-vis the public. His nature was more noble than his conduct and could not sustain this struggle for very long. He died soon afterward, leaving his affairs in complete disarray. All his concessions had brought him nothing.

There were two men who continued Polevoy's work—Senkovsky and Belinsky.[9]

Senkovsky, a Russified Pole, an orientalist and academic, was a witty writer, a hard worker without any opinions of his own, unless one calls a profound disdain for people and things, convictions and theories, an opinion. Senkovsky was a true representative of the *direction* which the mentality of the public had taken since 1825, with a luster that was brilliant but cold, a disdainful smile which often hid remorse, a thirst for pleasure stimulated by the uncertainty which hovered over everyone's fate, a materialism that was mocking and therefore melancholy, the constrained jesting of a man in prison.

The antithesis of Senkovsky, Belinsky was a type of studious Moscow youth, a martyr to his doubts and thoughts, an enthusiast, a poet of dialectics, vexed by everything that surrounded him, consumed by torment. This man trembled with indignation and shook with rage at the eternal spectacle of Russian absolutism.

Senkovsky established his magazine as one establishes a commercial enterprise. All the same, we do not share the opinion of those who see a governmental tendency in it. It was read eagerly throughout Russia, which never happened with a journal or book written in the interests of power. *The Northern Bee,* enjoying the protection of the police, only seemed to be an exception to this rule: it was the *sole* unofficial political newspaper allowed, which explains its success; but as soon as the official newspapers had a tolerable staff, *The Northern Bee* was abandoned by its readers. There is no fame, no reputation that can withstand the deadly and degrading government connection. Everyone who reads in Russia detests power; all who love it do not read or only read French trifles. Russia's greatest celebrity—Pushkin—was at one point abandoned because of the congratulations he sent Nicholas after the cholera epidemic and for two political poems. Gogol, the idol of Russian readers, fell instantly into the most profound disgrace because of a servile pamphlet. Polevoy was eclipsed the day he made an alliance with the government. In Russia one does not forgive a turncoat.

Senkovsky spoke with disdain of liberalism and science, but then he had no respect for anything else. He imagined himself eminently practical because he preached a theoretical materialism but, like all theoreticians, he was surpassed by other theoreticians who were much more abstract but had intense convictions, which is infinitely more practical and closer to action than *practology.*

Ridiculing everything which men hold most sacred, Senkovsky, without wishing it, demolished monarchism in people's minds. Preaching comfort and sensual pleasures, he led people to the simple thought that it is impossible to enjoy oneself while constantly thinking about the secret police, denunciations, and Siberia, that fear is not comfortable, and that no man can dine well if he does not know where he will spend the night.

Senkovsky was wholly a man of his time; in sweeping near the entrance to a new era, he mixed together valuable objects with dust, but he cleared the ground for another age which he did not understand. He felt this himself, and as soon as something new and lively broke through in literature, Senkovsky furled his sails and soon completely faded away.

Senkovsky was surrounded by a circle of young men of letters whom he ruined by corrupting their taste. They introduced a style which seemed at first brilliant, but which was, at a second glance, dubious. In the poetry from Petersburg, or rather from Vassilevsky Island,[10] there is nothing living or real in hysterical images that conjure up Kukolniks, Benediktovs, Timofeevs,[11] and others. Such flowers can only bloom at the foot of the imperial throne and in the shadow of the Peter Paul Fortress.

In Moscow, the journal that replaced the suppressed *Telegraph* was *The Telescope;* this did not last as long as its predecessor, but its death was most glorious. This was the one that published the celebrated letter by Chaadaev.[12] The journal was immediately suppressed, the censor pensioned off, and the editor-in-chief exiled to Ust-Sysolsk. The publication of this letter was a momentous event. It was a challenge, a sign of an awakening; it broke the ice after the 14th of December. At last a man appeared whose soul overflowed with bitterness. He found a terrible language with which to express—with funereal eloquence, with an overwhelming serenity— everything acrimonious that had accumulated in the heart of civilized Russia during those ten years. This letter was the testament of a man who gave up his rights not out of love for his descendants, but from disgust; severe and cold, the author demanded an accounting from Russia for all the pain with which it drenched a man who dared to emerge from the savage state. He wanted to know what we had bought at that price, what we had done to merit this situation; he analyzed it with an inexorable, hopeless depth, and, having finished his vivisection, he turned away in horror, cursing the country in its past, in its present, and in its future. Yes, the somber voice sounded only to tell Russia that it had never existed in a normal human way, that it represented "only a gap in human intelligence, only an instructive example for Europe." He told Russia that its past was useless, its present superfluous, and that it had no future.

Without agreeing with Chaadaev, we understand perfectly what led him to this dark and despairing point of view, all the more so since up to the present the facts speak for him and not against him. We believe; for him it was enough to point a finger. We hope; for him it was enough to open the page of a journal to prove that he was right. The conclusion at which Chaadaev arrived could not hold up against any criticism, and that is hardly where one would find the importance of this publication; it is through the lyricism of its austere indignation, which shakes the soul and for a long time leaves it under a painful impression, that it maintains its significance. The author was reproached for his harshness, but it is that which is his greatest achievement. One must not humor us; we forget too quickly our position, we are too accustomed to be distracted within prison walls.

A cry of anguish and astonishment greeted this article, it frightened people, it wounded even those who shared these feelings, and all the same it merely stated what was vaguely agitating each of our souls. Who among us has not had such moments of anger, in which he hated this country that responds to all generous human aspirations with torment, which hastens to wake us up in order to torture us. Who among us has not wished to break away forever from this prison which occupies a quarter of the earthly sphere, from this monstrous empire where every police superintendent is a sovereign and the sovereign is a crowned superintendent of police? Who among us has not indulged in all the temptations to forget this frozen hell, to achieve a few moments of drunkenness and distraction? We see things now in a different way, we envisage Russian history in a different manner, but there is no reason to recant or repent of those moments of despair; we paid too dearly for them to yield them up; they are our right, our protest, they saved us.

Chaadaev went silent but he did not leave us in peace. The Petersburg aristocrats—those Benkendorfs and Kleinmikhels[13]—were offended for Russia. A sober-minded German, Vigel, the chief—evidently Protestant—of the department for religious congregations, protested on behalf of Russian Orthodoxy. The emperor had it announced that Chaadaev suffered a mental breakdown. This tasteless joke brought even his enemies to Chaadaev's side, and his influence in Moscow increased. Even the aristocracy bowed their heads before this thinker and surrounded him with respect and attention, thus giving lie to the imperial joke.

Chaadaev's letter was a sounding trumpet; the signal had been given and from all sides new voices were heard; young fighters entered the arena, giving evidence of the silent work that had taken place during these ten years.

The 14 (26) December had too deeply cut off the past for the literature that preceded it to be able to continue in the same way. Right after this great day, a young man full of the fantasies and ideas of 1825, Venevitinov,[14] could appear. Despair, like the ache after a wound, did not come immediately. But hardly had he pronounced a few noble words when he disappeared like the flowers of a more gentle sky, which expire from the icy breath of the Baltic.

Venevitinov was not viable in the new Russian atmosphere. In order to tolerate the air of that sinister epoch a different constitution was required, and it was necessary from childhood to get used to that ever-present harsh north wind, to become acclimated to insoluble doubts, to the bitterest truths, to one's own weakness, to daily insults; the habit must be ingrained from earliest childhood to conceal everything that disturbs the soul but not to lose any of what has been buried there; on the contrary, to ripen in quiet anger all that has deposited itself in the heart. It was necessary to know how to hate out of love, to despise for humanity's sake, to have unlimited pride in order to raise one's head high while shackled hand and foot.

Every chapter of *Onegin*, which appeared after 1825, was more and more profound. The poet's original plan was light and serene, he had sketched it out in a different time; he was surrounded then by a world which enjoyed this ironic, friendly, and playful laughter. The first chapters of *Onegin* remind us a lot of the sharp but robust comedy of Griboedov.[15] Tears and laughter—everything changed.

The two poets we have in mind who convey the new era in Russian poetry are Lermontov and Koltsov.[16] These two strong voices come from opposite sides. Nothing can demonstrate with greater clarity the change brought about in people's minds since 1825 than a comparison between Pushkin and Lermontov. Pushkin, often dissatisfied and sad, offended and full of indignation, was, however, ready to make his peace. He desired it, and did not despair of it; a chord of remembrance from the times of the emperor Alexander did not cease to resonate in his heart. Lermontov was so used to despair, to antagonism, that not only did he not look for a way out, he could not conceive of the possibility of either a battle or an accommodation. Lermontov never learned to hope, he never sacrificed himself because there was nothing to call forth such a sacrifice. He did not hold his head with pride in the noose, like Pestel and Ryleev,[17] because he could not see the usefulness of sacrifice; he flung himself to the side and died for nothing.

The pistol shot that killed Pushkin aroused Lermontov's soul. He wrote an energetic ode in which, branding the vile intrigues which preceded the duel, intrigues carried out by literary ministers and spying journalists, he cried out with the indignation of a young man: "Vengeance, emperor, vengeance!" The poet paid for this single act of defiance with exile to the Caucasus. This took place in 1837; in 1841, Lermontov's body was placed in a grave at the foot of the Caucasus Mountains.

> And what you said before your death,
> None among those present understood...
>   ...your final words
> Their profound and bitter meaning
> Is lost...[18]

Fortunately, we have not lost what Lermontov wrote during the last four years of his life. He belonged entirely to our generation. All of us were too young to take part on the 14th of December. Awakened by that great day, we saw only executions and banishments. Reduced to a forced silence, suppressing our tears, we learned to retire within ourselves, to prepare our thoughts in secret, and what were those thoughts? These were no longer ideas of a civilizing liberalism, ideas of progress; they were doubts, negations, and thoughts full of fury. Used to such sentiments, Lermontov could not save himself in lyricism the way Pushkin had done. He dragged a ball and chain of skepticism through all his fantasies and all his pleasures. A manly and melancholy thought never left his face and broke through to all his poetry. It was not an abstract thought that sought to adorn itself with poetic flowers; no, Lermontov's meditation is his poetry, his torment, his strength. He had deep feelings for Byron, which Pushkin did not share. To the misfortune of too much insight, he added another, the boldness of saying a great many things without varnish or discretion. Weak creatures, bruised by this, never forgive such sincerity. One spoke of Lermontov as a spoiled child from an aristocratic house, like one of those idle creatures who perish in boredom and excess. One did not wish to see how much this man had struggled, how much he had suffered before daring to express his thoughts. People accept with greater indulgence insults and ill-will than a certain maturity of thought and an alienation which desires to share neither hopes nor fears and which dares to speak openly of this rupture. When Lermontov left Petersburg for a second period of exile in the Caucasus he was quite weary and he told his friends that he would attempt to die as quickly as possible. He kept his word.

What, in the end, is this monster that calls itself Russia, which needs so many victims and which permits its children only the sad alternative of either losing themselves morally in a setting hostile to all that is human, or of dying at the dawn of their life? It is a bottomless abyss, where the best oarsmen will perish, where the greatest efforts, the greatest talents, the greatest minds will be swallowed up before having succeeded at anything.

And yet, can one doubt of the existence of embryonic forces, when one sees from the depths of the nation a voice rise up like that of Koltsov?

For a century, even a century and a half, the people had only sung the old songs, or some made-up monstrosities from the middle of Catherine II's reign. There were a few fairly successful imitations from the beginning of our century, but these artificial pieces lack truthfulness; they were capricious efforts. It was from these same depths of village Russia that new songs came. A herdsman driving his animals across the steppe was inspired to compose them. Koltsov was a genuine son of the people. Born in Voronezh, he studied in a parish school until he was ten, learning only to read and to write without spelling rules. His father, a cattle dealer, made him take up the trade. Koltsov took herds of cattle over hundreds of versts, and became used to a nomadic life, which is reflected in the majority of his lyrics. The young cattle dealer loved to read, and he continually reread one or another poet whom he took as his model, and his attempts at imitation warped his poetic instinct. His true talent finally broke through and he wrote popular songs, which, though few in number, were masterpieces. These were genuine songs of the Russian people. One found in them a melancholy that was their characteristic trait, a heartrending sadness, and an overflowing of life. Koltsov had shown how much poetry was hidden in the soul of the Russian people, and, that after a long and deep sleep, there was something stirring in its chest. We have other poets, statesmen, and artists who have come from the people, but they have emerged in the literal sense of the word, breaking all ties with them. Lomonosov was the son of a White Sea fisherman. He fled the paternal home to study, entered a church school, and then went to Germany, where he ceased to be a man of the people. He had nothing in common with agricultural Russia, except for that which unites all people of the same race. Koltsov remained in the midst of the herds and the business of a father who detested him, and who, along with other relatives, made his life so hard that he died in 1842. Koltsov and Lermontov made their debut and died in the midst of the same era. After them, Russian poetry went silent.

But in prose, activity accelerated and took a different direction.

Gogol, without being by origin a man of the people like Koltsov, was one by his tastes and his turn of mind. Gogol is completely independent of any foreign influence. He did not become familiar with any literature until he had already made his name. He was more in sympathy with the life of the people than with that of the court, which is natural on the part of a Little Russian.

The Little Russian, even when ennobled, does not break so thoroughly with the people as does a Russian. He loves his country, his dialect, the Cossack traditions and the hetmen. The independence of Ukraine, savage and warlike, but republican and democratic, was maintained through the centuries until Peter I. The Little Russians, pestered by the Poles, the Turks, and the Muscovites, and involved in an eternal war against the Crimean Tartars, had never succumbed. Little Russia, in a voluntary union with Great Russia, negotiated significant rights for itself. Tsar Alexey cursed the need to observe them. Peter I, using as a reason Mazeppa's betrayal, kept only a mere shadow of these privileges;[19] Elizabeth and Catherine introduced serfdom. The poor country protested, but could it oppose this fatal avalanche that came down from the North to the Black Sea, and covered all that bore the Russian name with the same shroud of uniform and icy slavery? Ukraine suffered the fate of Novgorod and Pskov, but much later, and a single century of servitude has not been able to efface all that was independent and poetic in this brave people. There is more individual development and more local color than with us; among us, the same miserable garment covers all folk life. People are born to bow down before an unjust fate and die without a trace, leaving their children to begin the same desperate life. Our people do not know their own history, while every village in Little Russia has its own legend. The Russian people know only Pugachev and 1812.

The stories with which Gogol made his debut formed a series of genuinely beautiful tableaux of the customs and landscapes of Little Russia, full
of gaiety, grace, liveliness, and love. Stories like this are impossible in Great
Russia for lack of a plot and a character. With us, popular scenes take on
a somber and tragic appearance, which oppresses the reader; I say tragic,
only in the meaning of Laocoon. It is the tragic of a fate to which man suc-
cumbs without a fight. Suffering changes into rage and grief, laughter into
bitter and spiteful irony. Who can read without shaking in indignation and
shame the magnificent novel *Anton Goremyka*,[20] and Turgenev's master-
piece *Notes of a Hunter?*

As Gogol left Little Russia and approached central Russia, the naive and
gracious images disappeared. There is no further half-wild hero of the type
in *Taras Bulba,* no debonair and patriarchal old man like the one he portrayed in *Old-World Landowners.* Under the Moscow sky, everything in him
turned gloomy, somber, and hostile. He still laughed, he laughed more
than he had done before, but it was a different laughter, and only people
who were very hard-hearted or very simple could allow themselves to be
taken in by this laughter. Passing from Little Russians and Cossacks to
Russians, he left the side of his people and gave himself over to his two
most implacable enemies: the official and the nobleman. Before him no
one had ever given such a complete course of lectures on the anatomy and
pathology of the Russian bureaucrat. With laughter on his lips, he penetrated indiscreetly into the deepest recesses of this impure and malicious
soul. Gogol's comedy *The Inspector General* and his novel *Dead Souls* are
a terrible confession of contemporary Russia, on the scale of Koshikhin's
revelations in the 17th century.[21]

The emperor Nicholas split his sides with laughter when he attended a
production of *The Inspector General!!!*

The poet, in despair from having produced only this majestic hilarity and
the conceited laughter of bureaucrats who exactly resembled those he had
depicted, though they were better protected by the censorship, felt obliged
to explain in an introduction that his comedy was not only very funny, but
also very sad, and that "there are warm tears under its smile."

After *The Inspector General,* Gogol turned to the provincial gentry and
brought into the light this unknown population which had remained behind the scenes, far from roads and large cities, buried deep in the countryside, this Russia of petty squires, who in quietly taking care of their lands
bred a corruption deeper than that of the West. Thanks to Gogol, we finally
saw them leave their manor houses, their lordly homes, and parade before
us without mask or makeup, forever drunk and greedy, slaves of power with
no dignity, and tyrants without compassion toward their serfs, draining the

life and blood of the people with the lack of constraint and the naïveté of a child who nurses at his mother's breast.

Dead Souls roused all Russia.

Such an accusation was necessary for contemporary Russia. It is the story of an illness, written by the hand of a master. Gogol's poetry is a cry of terror and shame, uttered by a man degraded by the vulgarity of life, who suddenly sees in the mirror his own brutalized features. But for such a cry to break loose from a chest there must be healthy parts and the strength for recovery. A person who frankly confesses his weaknesses and faults senses that they do not form the main part of his being, that they do not absorb him entirely, and that there is in him something that escapes and resists the fall; that he can redeem the past, not simply to raise his head again, but to be transformed, as in Byron's tragedy, from Sardanapal the womanish to Sardanapal the hero.

Here we come face to face once more with this great question: where is the evidence that the Russian people can rise up again, and what is the evidence to the contrary? This question, as we have seen, had preoccupied all thinking men without any of them finding an answer.

Polevoy, who encouraged others, believed in nothing; would he have otherwise allowed himself to become discouraged so quickly, and gone over to the enemy at the first setback? *The Library for Reading* leaped right over this problem, circumventing the question without having made an effort to answer it. The solution offered by Chaadaev was no solution at all.

Poetry, prose, art, and history demonstrate for us the formation and development of this absurd milieu, these harmful ways, this monstrous power, but no one points to a way out. Must one become acclimated, as Gogol did later on, or rush toward one's doom like Lermontov? It is impossible to become acclimated; and yet we are loath to perish; something tells us from the bottom of our heart that it is too early to die, it seems there are still some living souls behind *the dead souls*.

The questions have reappeared with greater intensity, and all that is still hopeful demands a solution at any cost.

After 1840, two opinions absorbed the public's attention. From a scholastic controversy they soon passed into literature, and from there into society.

We are speaking of Muscovite pan-Slavism and Russian Europeanism.

The battle between these two opinions was ended by the revolution of 1848.

This was the last spirited polemic that occupied the public, and for that very reason it had real importance. We therefore dedicate the following chapter to it. [. . .]

Epilogue

[. . .] Behind the visible state in Russia there exists no invisible state which could presumably serve as the apotheosis and transformation of the present order of things; there is no unattainable ideal that never coincides with reality, although forever promising to do so. There is nothing behind the stockades where superior force holds us captive. The question of revolution in Russia comes down to a question of material force. That is why, without considering causes other than the ones we have mentioned, this country is the best possible place for a social regeneration.

We have said that after 1830, with the appearance of Saint-Simonism, socialism made a strong impression on minds in Moscow. Accustomed as we were to communes, land partition, and workers' cooperatives, we saw in this doctrine an expression of sentiments that were closer to us than what was found in political doctrines. Having witnessed the most terrible abuses, we were less bothered by socialism than the Western bourgeoisie.

Little by little, literary works were imbued with socialist tendencies and inspirations. Novels, stories, and even Slavophile manuscripts protested against contemporary society from more than simply a political point of view. It is sufficient to mention Dostoevsky's *Poor Folk*.

In Moscow, socialism marched alongside Hegelian philosophy. The alliance of modern philosophy and socialism is not difficult to imagine, but it is only recently that the Germans acknowledged the close ties between science and revolution, not because they had not formerly understood this, but because socialism, like all things practical, simply didn't interest them. Germans can be profoundly radical in science while remaining conservative in their actions—poets on paper and bourgeois in life. Such a dualism is unacceptable to us. Socialism seems to us to be the most natural syllogism, the application of logic to government.

We must note that in Petersburg socialism assumed a different character. Revolutionary ideas were always more practical there than in Moscow; theirs is the cold fanaticism of mathematicians. In Petersburg, they love order, discipline, and practical applications. Whereas in Moscow they argue, in Petersburg they form groups. In the latter city you will find the most passionate adherents of the Masonic movement and mysticism, and *The Messenger of Zion*, the organ of the Bible Society, was published there. The conspiracy of December 14th ripened in Petersburg; in Moscow it never developed sufficiently to go out onto the public square. In Moscow it is difficult to come to any understanding; individuals there are too capricious and too expansive. In Moscow there are more poetic elements, more erudition and, along with that, more nonchalance, greater carelessness, more use-less words and a greater divergence of opinions. Saint-Simonism—vague, religious, and at the same time analytic—goes remarkably well with Musco-vites. Having studied it, they passed naturally on to Proudhon, just as they went from Hegel to Feuerbach.

Fourierism suited the students of Petersburg more than Saint-Simonism. Fourierism values an immediate realization and seeks a practical applica-tion, but it also dreams, basing its dreams on mathematical calculations, concealing its poetry under the name of production, and its love of freedom under the union of workers in brigades—Fourierism was likely to find a response in Petersburg. The phalanstery is nothing more than a Russian commune and a workers' barracks, a military colony on a civilian basis, and an industrial regiment. It has been observed that an opposition openly battling with a government always has something of its character, but in an inverse sense. And I am sure that there is a basis for the fear of com-munism experienced by the Russian government: communism is Russian autocracy turned inside out.

Petersburg is outstripping Moscow, thanks to these sharp—perhaps limited—but active and practical views. The honor of taking the initiative belongs to it and Warsaw, but if tsarism falls, the center of freedom will be in the heart of the nation, in Moscow.

The complete failure of the revolution in France, the unfortunate out-come of the revolution in Vienna, and the comic finale of the revolution in Berlin served as a basis for a renewed reaction in Russia. Once again, every-thing was paralyzed; the plan to free the serfs was abandoned and replaced by a decision to close all universities. Censorship was doubled and more difficulties were put in the way of issuing foreign passports. Newspapers, books, words, clothing, women, and children were all persecuted.

In 1848 a new phalanx of heroic young people were sent to prison, and from there to hard labor in Siberia.[22] An oppressive wave of terror cut down all the new shoots and forced everyone to yield; intellectual life once again hid itself, and, if it revealed itself, then only fearfully, only in mute despair, and, since then, every bit of news coming out of Russia has filled the soul with sorrow and deep sadness. [. . .]

No matter what people say, the methods employed by the Russian gov-ernment—cruel methods—are not, however, sufficient to choke all the new shoots of progress. They cause many to perish in terrible moral suffering, but we must be prepared for this, and there are doubtless more people aroused than disarmed by these measures.

In order to actually choke off the revolutionary principle in Russia—the consciousness of our position and the desire to get out of it—Europe itself must assimilate more deeply the Petersburg government's principles and paths so that its return to absolutism is complete. One must wipe the word *République* from France's façade—that terrible word, even if it is only a lie and a taunt. In Germany the right to free expression—imprudently given— must be taken away. The day after a Prussian gendarme, with the aid of a Croat, has broken up the last printing presses which were dragged in the mud by des Frères Ignorantins[23] against the pedestal of Gutenberg's statue, or when an executioner in Paris, with the pope's blessing, has burned the works of French philosophers on la place de la Révolution—on the follow- ing day the all-powerful tsar will have reached his apogee.

Could this be possible?

Who can say these days what is and isn't possible? The battle is not over, the struggle continues.

The future of Russia has never been more closely linked to the future of Europe than it is at present. Our hopes are well known to all, but our reluctance in answering does not come from childlike vanity, or from a fear of the future catching us in a lie, but because of the impossibility of seeing any aspect of this issue whose resolution does not depend completely on internal conditions.

On the one hand, the Russian government is not Russian, just generally despotic and retrograde. As the Slavophiles say, it is more German than Rus- sian, and that explains the good disposition and love toward it shown by other states. Petersburg is a new Rome, the Rome of universal enslavement, and the capital of absolutism; that is why the Russian emperor fraternizes with the emperor of Austria and helps him to oppress Slavs. The principle of power is not national, and absolutism is more cosmopolitan than the revolution.

On the other hand, the hopes and aspirations of revolutionary Russia coincide with the hopes and aspirations of revolutionary Europe and antici- pate their alliance in the future. The national element that Russia adds is the freshness of youth and a natural tendency toward socialist institutions.

The European states have clearly reached an impasse. They must make a decisive surge forward or they will fall even further back than now. The contradictions are too irreconcilable and the issues are too acute and have ripened too much through suffering and hatred to be able to stop at half- solutions and peaceful negotiations between power and freedom. But if there is no salvation for states in their current form of existence, the man- ner of their death can differ greatly. Death can come by means of rebirth or decay, through revolution or reaction. Conservatism, having no goal other than the preservation of an outdated status quo, is just as destructive as revolution. It annihilates the old order, not with the hot flame of rage, but with the slow flame of senility.

If conservatism gets the upper hand in Europe, imperial power in Russia will not only crush civilization, but will annihilate an entire class of civilized people, and then...

And then—here we find ourselves standing before an entirely new question and a mysterious future. Autocracy, having triumphed over civilization, finds itself face to face with a peasant insurrection, with an enormous revolt in the manner of Pugachev. Half of the strength of the Petersburg government is based on civilization and on the deep divide it has engendered between the civilized classes and the peasants. The government continually leans on the former, and it is primarily in the noble sphere that it finds the means, the people, and counsel. On breaking with his own hands such an essential instrument, the emperor has once again become the *tsar*, but it is not enough for him to let his beard grow and wear a *zipoun*.[24] The house of Holstein-Gottorp[25] is too German, too pedantic, and too sophisticated to throw itself unreservedly into the arms of a half-savage nationalism in order to remain at the head of a popular movement which has wanted from the very beginning to settle accounts with the nobility and to spread the customs of the rural commune to all estates, cities, and the entire nation.

We have seen a monarchy surrounded by republican institutions, but our imagination cannot conceive of an emperor of Russia surrounded by communist institutions.

Before this distant future can be realized, a number of things must occur, and the influence of imperial Russia will be no less pernicious for reactionary Europe than the latter's influence will be for Russia. It is this barracks-room Russia that desires, by means of bayonets, to put an end to the questions that are agitating the world. It is this Russia that is roaring and moaning like the sea at the doors of the civilized world, always ready to overflow its banks, always trembling with a desire for conquest, as if it had nothing to do at home, as if pangs of conscience and bouts of madness disturb the minds of its rulers.

Only reaction can open these doors, with the Hapsburgs and Hohenzollerns requesting fraternal assistance from the Russian army and leading it into the heart of Europe.

Then the great party of order will see what a *strong government* and respect for power are like. We advise the German princelings to acquaint themselves now with the fate of the grand dukes of Georgia, who were given a little money in Petersburg, the title of highness, and the right to have a royal crown on their carriage. But revolutionary Europe cannot be defeated by imperial Russia. It will save Russia from a terrible crisis, and will itself be saved from Russia.

The Russian government, after laboring for twenty years, has managed to link Russia by unbreakable ties with revolutionary Europe.

There are no borders between Russia and Poland.

Of course Europe knows about Poland, this nation that the entire world has abandoned to an unequal struggle, having shed since that time rivers of blood on all the fields of battle where there was any question of winning a people's freedom. Everyone knows this nation, which, having succumbed to numerical superiority, traveled across Europe, more like a conqueror than a victim, and has been dispersed among other peoples in order to teach them—alas, unsuccessfully—the art of bearing defeat without yielding, degrading themselves, or losing faith. One can destroy Poland, but not conquer it, one can carry out the threat made by Nicholas to leave only a sign and a pile of stones where Warsaw once stood, but it is impossible to turn them into slaves like the Baltic provinces.

Having united Poland with Russia, the government has erected an enormous bridge for the solemn passage of revolutionary ideas, a bridge that begins at the Vistula River and ends at the Black Sea.

Poland is thought to be dead, but every time the roll is called it answers "Present," as the speaker of a Polish deputation did in 1848. They should not take a step without assuring themselves of their western neighbors, because they have had enough of Napoleon's sympathy and the celebrated words of Louis-Philippe: "The Polish nationality will not perish."

We have no doubts about Poland or Russia. But we do have doubts about Europe. If we had some confidence in the peoples of Europe, we would enthusiastically tell the Poles:

"Brothers, your fate is worse than ours and you have suffered much, but be patient a little longer; there is a great future at the end of your misfortunes. You will extract a sublime revenge and will bring about the liberation of the people whose hands forged your chains. In your enemies—the tsar and autocracy—you will recognize your brothers in the name of independence and freedom."

Notes

Source: *Du développement des idées révolutionnaires en Russie.* V. "La littérature et l'opinion publique après le 14 décembre 1825," 1851; 7:79–100, 412–33; translation into Russian, 209–30.

1. The account by Astolphe, Marquis de Custine (1790–1857), remains one of the most powerful books written about Russia by a foreigner. Banned in Russia, it was read widely, including in the Winter Palace.

2. Count Pavel D. Kiselev (1788–1872), minister of government property, carried out a reform in the management of state peasants.

3. Herzen comments: "It is not without a degree of fear that I embark on this section of my survey. The reader will understand that I cannot say everything, or name all the people in many cases; to speak of a Russian one must be certain that he is buried or in Siberia. Only after serious reflection did I decide on this publication; silence sustains despotism, things one dare not express only half-exist."

4. Nikolay A. Polevoy (1796–1846), historian, writer, and editor of the progressive *Moscow Telegraph*, later became much more conservative in his views.

5. Nikolay I. Grech (1787–1867) and Faddey V. Bulgarin (1789–1859) were conservative journalists; the latter was, in addition, an agent of the Third Department.

6. Gavrila R. Derzhavin (1743–1816) was a renowned pre-romantic poet and a government official. Nikolay M. Karamzin (1766–1826) wrote poetry, stories, and travel memoirs, all of which strongly influenced the evolution of Russian prose style, but is best known as the author of the officially praised *History of the Russian State*. Ivan I. Dmitriev (1760–1837) was a poet in the sentimentalist style who held a number of high government posts.

7. Herzen: "After the revolution of 1848, censorship became an obsession of Nicholas. Not content with the regular censorship and the two offices set up outside the country in Jassy and Bucharest, where Russian is not being written, he created a second censorship office in Petersburg; we are inclined to hope that this double censorship will be more useful than simple censorship. One will wind up printing books outside of Russia, which is already being done, and one will find out who is more the ingenious, free expression or the emperor Nicholas."

8. Herzen: "This episode is discussed at greater length in *Past and Thoughts*."

9. Osip I. Senkovsky (1800–1858) was a founding editor of *The Library for Reading* and also published under the name "Baron Brambeus." Vissarion G. Belinsky (1819–1848) was the most influential Russian critic of his age, intensely engaged with the political and social issues of the day.

10. Herzen: "A sort of Latin Quarter, mostly inhabited by literary and artistic people who are *unknown* in other parts of the city."

11. Nestor V. Kukolnik (1809–1868) was a dramatist and novelist on patriotic themes. Vladimir G. Benediktov (1807–1873) and Alexey V. Timofeev (1812–1883) were poets, the former popular for his highly ornamented verse, which was disparaged by Belinsky.

12. Petr Ya. Chaadaev (1794–1856) was an officer in the 1812 war, a friend and correspondent of Pushkin, and author of *The Philosophical Letters* and *Apology of a Madman*. Herzen speaks eloquently of Chaadaev in *Past and Thoughts*.

13. Count Alexander Khr. Benkendorf (1783–1844), from a Baltic German family, a hero of the 1812 war, warned Alexander I in 1821 about the growing danger from the secret societies; under Nicholas I he founded the political police and directed them from 1826 to 1844. Count Petr A. Kleinmikhel (1793–1869), another high tsarist official of German descent, was dismissed as minister of communications (which included the inadequate road system) by Alexander II at the beginning of the reform era.

14. Dmitry V. Venevitinov (1805–1827) was a romantic poet and philosopher and founder of the group "Lovers of Wisdom" (*liubomudry*).

15. Alexander S. Griboedov (1795–1829), diplomat and writer, is best known for his satiric play *Woe from Wit*, phrases from which became a staple of the language of the intelligentsia.

16. Mikhail Yu. Lermontov (1814–1841) wrote romantic poetry, sometimes with political implications, and a novel (*A Hero of Our Time*) as well as serving as a career officer in the Russian army; he is considered one of Russia's greatest nineteenth-century poetic talents. Alexey V. Koltsov (1809–1842) was a poet whose work received critical support from Pushkin, Belinsky, and others, as well as popular acclaim.

17. Pavel I. Pestel (1793–1826) and Kondraty F. Ryleev (1795–1826) were two of five executed Decembrists; Ryleev was a romantic poet who preferred historical themes and heroes. His almanac *The Polestar* inspired Herzen's publication of the same name.

18. Herzen: "Verses that Lermontov addressed to the memory of Prince Odoevsky, who died as a soldier in the Caucasus, one of those sentenced after the 14th of December."

19. Ivan Mazeppa (1639–1709) was a well-educated Ukrainian Cossack hetman who went over to the Swedish side during the Battle of Poltava, and was forever after seen as a traitor to the Russians and a hero of Ukraine.

20. Written by Dmitry V. Grigorovich (1822–1899) and published in *The Contemporary* in 1847, which, along with his earlier work *The Village*, gained recognition for their sympathetic description of the serfs.

21. Herzen: "A Russian diplomat at the time of Alexey, father of Peter I, who emigrated to Sweden, fearing persecution by the tsar, and was beheaded in Stockholm for murder."

22. Herzen: "We have in mind the Petrashevsky society. Young people gathered at his place to debate social questions. This club had existed for several years, when, at the beginning of the Hungarian campaign, the government decided to declare it a major conspiracy and increase the number of arrests. Where they sought a criminal plot, they found only opinions, but this did not keep them from condemning *all* the accused to death in order to give themselves a merciful air. The tsar replaced execution with hard labor, exile, or conscription. Among the condemned are Speshnev, Grigoriev, Dostoevsky, Kashkin, Golovinsky, Mombelli, and others."

23. A religious order founded in the late seventeenth century. It refused admission to priests with theological training, while offering a free education to the children of the poor.

24. A homespun coat.

25. Through dynastic alliances, the Romanov dynasty became highly Germanicized during the eighteenth century. Peter III (reigned 1761–1762) was the son of Peter the Great's daughter Anna and Duke Karl Friedrich Holstein-Gottorp.

⇥ 2 ⇤

The announcement below was published as a separate lithographed sheet by the printing house that Herzen established in London in order to challenge the heavily censored press at home. It was also published in a Polish newspaper in May 1853 (where the Russian government took note of it) and in an abridged form in the French newspaper *La Nation* on June 19 of that year. Both a declaration of intent and a call for participation, it stimulated little response until after Nicholas I died in 1855. Eagerly awaiting a response, and yet aware of the fear experienced in Russia even by liberals, Herzen asked a friend to tell him which of their acquaintances had burned the sheet to avoid compromising themselves (*Let* 2:139). In an 1863 publication celebrating the first decade of the Free Press, Herzen refers to the year 1853 as the beginning of uncensored Russian-language publications abroad. This is an excellent example of the author's disciplined writing and barely suppressed emotion. A phrase that he borrowed from the 1830 Polish rebellion—"For our freedom and yours"—appeared on banners displayed in Red Square by Soviet dissidents in August 1968 in support of Czechoslovakia after it was invaded by Warsaw Pact troops.

The Free Russian Press in London
[1853]

To Our Brothers in Russia

Why are we silent?

Do we really have nothing to say?

Or are we really silent because we dare not speak?

At home there is no place for free Russian speech, but it can ring out elsewhere if only its time has come.

I know how hard it is for you to keep silent, what it costs you to conceal every feeling, every thought, every impulse.

Open and free speech is a great thing; without free speech a man cannot be free. Not for nothing do people give their lives, leave their homeland and abandon their property. Only that which is weak, fearful, and immature hides itself. "Silence is a sign of consent" and it clearly speaks of renunciation, hopelessness, a bowing of the head, an acknowledged desperation.

Openness of expression is a solemn declaration, a transition to action.

It seems to us that the time has come to publish in Russian outside of Russia. You will show us whether we are right or wrong.

I will be the first to remove the fetters of a foreign language and once again take up my native tongue.

The desire to speak with foreigners has passed. We told them as best we could about Rus and the Slavic world; what could be done was done.

For whom are we printing in Russian from abroad, and how can forbidden works be sold in Russia?

If we are going to sit with our arms folded and be content with futile grumbling and noble indignation, if we wisely back down in the face of any sort of danger, and, having come up against an obstacle, stop without trying to either step over it or go around it, then it will be a long time before Russia sees any radiant days.

Nothing happens all by itself, without effort and will, without sacrifice and work. The human will, the will of a single steadfast person, is incredibly great.

Ask what is being done by our Polish brothers, who are more oppressed than us. Haven't they sent everything they wanted to Poland for the past twenty-five years, avoiding the lines of police and the nets of informers?

And now, true to their great banner on which is written: "*For our freedom and yours,*" they extend a hand to us; they relieve us of three-quarters of the task, and the rest you can do yourselves.

The Polish democratic brotherhood in London, in a sign of its brotherly union with free Russian people, is offering you the means to get books in Russia and send manuscripts to us from there.

It is your job to come up with material and get involved.

Send what you wish, and everything written in a spirit of freedom will be printed, from scientific and fact-based articles on statistics and history to novels, stories, and verse.

We are even ready to print these materials for free.

If you have nothing ready of your own, send forbidden verses by Pushkin, Ryleev, Lermontov, Polezhaev, Pecherin,[1] et al., which are making the rounds.

Our invitation applies just as much to the pan-Slavists as to all free-thinking Russians. We have even more of a right to expect something from them, because they are exclusively involved with Rus and the Slavic peoples.

Our door is open. Whether you want to make use of it or not will be on your conscience.

If we receive nothing from Russia it will not be our fault. If tranquility is dearer to you than free speech—keep silent.

But I don't believe that—up till now no one has printed anything in Russian abroad, because there was no free printing press. From the first of May 1853 the press will be up and running. In the meantime, while waiting in the hope of receiving something from you, I will publish my own manuscripts.

In 1849 I was already thinking of publishing Russian books in Paris; but, driven from country to country, haunted by a series of terrible calamities, I could not carry out this undertaking. And in addition I was distracted; I sacrificed a lot of time, emotion, life, and means to Western developments. Now I feel superfluous in that sphere.

To be your outlet, your free, uncensored speech is my single goal.

I don't want so much to tell you my new ideas as to use my position to give publicity to your unspoken thoughts and your hidden aspirations, to convey them to your brothers and friends, who are lost in the mute distances of the Russian kingdom.

Together we will find the means and the solutions so that the terrible events that are coming in the West do not catch us unawares or sleeping.

At one time you loved my writing. What I will tell you now is not as youthful nor so warmed by that radiant and joyous flame and that clear faith in the near future which broke through the censor's bars. An entire life has been buried between those times and the present; but after so much loss one's thought has become more mature, and though little faith remains, what is there is firm.

Meet me, as youthful friends meet a warrior returning from his service, aged, wounded, but who has honorably preserved his standard in captivity and abroad—and with the former boundless affection extends his hand to you in honor of our erstwhile alliance in the name of *Russian and Polish freedom.*

London, 21 February, 1853

Note

Source: "Vol'noe russkoe knigopechatanie v Londone. Brat'iam na Rusi," 1853; 12:62–64, 511–12.

1. Vladimir S. Pecherin (1807–1885) was a poet and professor of Greek philosophy at Moscow University in the 1830s, after which he emigrated, eventually entering a monastery.

→ *3* ←

Written in June 1853, this is the first proclamation issued by the Russian Free Press. It was sent directly to senior government officials in St. Petersburg, who informed the tsar; plans were quickly formulated to prevent its distribution, and to henceforth pay the strictest attention to books and other printed materials brought into Russia. Tsarist authorities in Poland received an anonymous letter from a Polish acquaintance of Herzen in London offering to serve as an informant. Nicholas I forwarded a copy of "St. George's Day!" to Count Orlov at the Third Department with a sarcastic note about what "nice" reading it made (*Let* 2:152–54, 163). Herzen received a letter from actor Mikhail Shchepkin—who was staying in Paris—lamenting that Herzen had summoned the ruling class to a sacred deed that they would prove unable and unwilling to perform. Herzen believed that it was Shchepkin's past life as a serf that made him uncomfortable in the presence of free speech and prone to exaggerate its dangers (*Let* 2:167).

In Muscovite Russia, St. George's Day (November 26) was the only day of the year when dependent peasants had the right to move from one overlord to another, a right that was gradually restricted until it completely disappeared during the seventeenth century. This proclamation apparently marks the first time Herzen used the word *topor* (axe) to signify a peasant uprising. The essay retained its power for progressive youth, and it was still being illegally lithographed along with other Herzen essays in Moscow in 1861 (*Let* 3:204).

—◦—

ST. GEORGE'S DAY! ST. GEORGE'S DAY!
[1853]

To the Russian Nobility

Let the first free Russian word from abroad be addressed to you.

It was in your midst that a demand for independence, a striving for freedom, and all the intellectual activity of the past century arose.

Amongst you can be found that self-sacrificing minority which redeems Russia in the eyes of other nations and in its own eyes.

From your ranks came Muravyov and Pestel, Ryleev and Bestuzhev.[1]

From your ranks came Pushkin and Lermontov.

And, finally, we who left the homeland so that at least from abroad there would sound out free Russian speech came from your ranks.

Therefore we turn to you first.

Not with a word of reproach, not with a call to a battle that is at this moment impossible, but with a friendly speech about our common grief and our common shame, and with some fraternal advice.

It is sorrowful and shameful to be slaves, but it is much more sorrowful and shameful to realize that our slavery is necessary, that it is in the order of things, and that it is a natural consequence.

There is a great sin on our soul; we inherited it and are not guilty, but we wrongly hold onto that inheritance, it drags us down like a heavy stone to the bottom, and with it on our neck we will not rise to the surface.

We are slaves because our forefathers sold their human dignity for inhuman rights, and we enjoy these rights.

We are slaves because we are masters.

We are servants because we are landowners, and landowners without faith in our rightness.

We are serfs because we keep in bondage our brothers, who are like us by birth, by blood, and by language.

There is no freedom for us while the curse of serfdom hangs over us, while in our midst there continues to exist the vile, shameful, completely unjustified slavery of the peasants.

Russia's new life will begin with St. George's day, and with St. George's day our emancipation will begin.

It is impossible to be a free person and have servants bought like a product and sold like a herd.

It is impossible to be a free person and have the right to flog peasants and send servants to jail.

It is impossible to even speak of human rights as the owner of human souls.

Might not the tsar say to you: "You want to be free, but whatever for? Take the quit-rent from your peasants, take their labor, take their children, assess their land, sell them, resettle them, flog them—and, if you tire of that, send them to me in the police station and I will be willing to flog them for you. Isn't that enough for you? Understand what's appropriate! Our ancestors ceded to you a portion of our autocracy; by placing free people in bondage to you they tore off the edge of their royal mantle and flung it over the poverty of your forefathers; you did not reject it, but covered yourself with it and lived under it—what kind of conversation can we have about freedom? Remain bound to your tsar while your orthodox peasants are bound to you. On what grounds would landowners be free people?"

And the tsar would be correct.

Many among you wanted the emancipation of the serfs; Pestel and his friends placed this freedom as their first item of business. They argued at first whether emancipation should be given with or without land. Then they all saw the absurdity of emancipation into hunger and vagrancy, and the question became only the amount of land and the possibility of compensation for it.

In the provinces with the most estates—Penza, Tambov, Yaroslavl and Vladimir, Nizhny, and, finally, in Moscow, the question of emancipation found sympathy and never met that frenzy with which American landowners defended their rights over blacks.

The Tula nobility presented a plan, and in a dozen other provinces people deliberated and made proposals.

And then, suddenly, the nobility and the government had a falling out and all those wonderful initiatives fell from their trembling hands.

But there was nothing to fear; the flood of 1848 was too shallow to inundate our steppe.

Since that time everything has fallen asleep.

Where is that minority who made so much noise in Petersburg and Moscow drawing rooms about the emancipation of the serfs?...

What came of all those committees, meetings, projects, plans, and proposals?...

Our sleepy inactivity, our sluggish lack of staying power, and our passive compliance inspire sadness and despair. With this dissoluteness we have reached the point where the government doesn't persecute us but just gives us a scare, and if it weren't for the youthful story—full of valor and reckless-ness—of Petrashevsky and his friends, one might think that you had come to an understanding with Nicholas Pavlovich and lived with him in harmony.

Meanwhile things are getting awkward in the villages. The peasants are looking gloomy. House serfs are less obedient. All kinds of stories are mak-ing the rounds. A landowner and his family burned, another killed with chains and pitchforks, a steward strangled by women in a field, a Kammer-herr[2] flogged with a birch rod and forced to keep silent about it.

The peasants have clearly had enough of serfdom, only they do not know how to work together to accomplish something. For your part, you know that there can be no step forward without the emancipation of the serfs. Fortunately, it depends mostly on you.

Today it depends on you. We don't know what will happen tomorrow.

What are you really waiting for?

The government's permission? It gave you a sort of sly and ambiguous hint in 1842. You didn't make use of it.

What kind of permission is needed here? It is impossible to force some-one to possess others; that would be a completely new form of tyranny, a reverse confiscation.

Think carefully about our words, and understand them.

At this moment you have more than a right;[3] the fact of possession equals power. In either event, the key to the shackles is in your hands. It seems wiser and more *practical* to yield than to wait for an explosion. It's smarter to throw part of the cargo overboard than to allow the entire ship to sink.

We do not propose to you what Christ said to Nicodemus, to selflessly distribute your property; we have no paradise for you in exchange for such a sacrifice. We hate fine phrases and do not believe at all in mass generos-ity or in the unselfishness of entire social classes. On August 4, 1792, the French nobility acted in a way that was ten times wiser than it was selfless.[4]

Think carefully what is better for you—the emancipation of the serfs with land and with your assistance, or a struggle against emancipation with the assistance of the government? Starting with yourself, think carefully what is better—to begin a new, free Rus and amicably resolve a weighty is-sue with the peasants, or to begin a crusade against them with a weapon in one hand and a birch rod in the other? If Russia and the Slavic world are to have a future *the peasants must be free...*

Or there will be no Russia at all, and traces of her, marked by unnecessary blood and terrible victories, will little by little disappear, like the traces of the Tatars, like a second unsuccessful northern population after the Finns. A state unable to separate itself from such a great sin, so deeply embedded in its inner structure, has no right to either formation or development, or to a part in the business of history.

But neither you nor I believe in such a terrible future.

You and I know that the emancipation of the serfs is essential, incontrovertible, and inevitable.

If you are unable to do anything they will still be free by grace of the tsar and by grace of Pugachevism.[5]

In both instances you are lost, and with you is lost that education that you completed despite difficulties, humiliations, and great injustices.

It will be painful if emancipation comes from the Winter Palace; tsarist power will justify itself to the people, and, having crushed you, will strengthen its despotism more than ever before.

Pugachevism is also frightening, but let us be frank—if the emancipation of the serfs cannot be bought at any other price, then that will not be too dearly bought. Dreadful transgressions bring in their wake dreadful consequences.

It will be one of those terrible historical calamities which can be foreseen and avoided in time, but from which it will be difficult or impossible to save oneself at the moment of defeat.

You have read the story of the Pugachev uprising, and you have heard stories about old Russian rebellions.

Our heart bleeds at the thought of innocent victims, we weep for them in advance, but, bowing our head, we say: let this terrible destiny, which people were not able or willing to avert, come to pass.

If we thought that this cup could not be refused, we would not have appealed to you, because our words would then have been empty or would have seemed a mockery that was nasty and inappropriate.

Quite the contrary, we are certain that there is no fatal necessity demanding that every step forward for the people must be celebrated with piles of corpses. A baptism by blood is a great thing, but we do not share the savage belief that every act of liberation and every triumph must pass through this.

Must the terrible lessons of the past always remain unspoken? [. . .]

Study them while there is still time.

We still believe in you; you gave a pledge and our heart has not forgotten it, that is why we do not directly address our unfortunate brothers in order to tell them how strong they are, something they do not realize, show them remedies that they have not figured out, and explain to them your weakness, which they do not suspect, in order to say to them:

"Well, chaps, it's time for the axe. We won't be shut up in a fortress forever, or spend more time doing unpaid labor or as house serfs. Stand up for your sacred freedom; for too long the masters have had their fun with us, have defiled our daughters and broken sticks over the ribs of the old men... Well children, let's bring straw, straw to the master's house, and let the gents warm themselves for the last time!"

Instead of that speech we are telling you: prevent a great calamity while it is still in your power.

Save yourselves from serfdom and the serfs from the blood they will have to spill.

Have pity on your children and on the conscience of the poor Russian people.

But hurry—it is harvest time and there is not an hour to lose.

The feverish breath of a sick, weakened Europe is blowing revolution toward Rus. The tsar has fenced you off, but there are chinks in that government fence and the draft is stronger than the wind.

The coming upheaval is not so foreign to the Russian heart as it once was. Our people are still unfamiliar with the word *socialism* but its meaning is close to the soul of a Russian who has lived out his days in a rural commune or a workers' co-op.

In socialism Rus will meet up with the revolution.

Such an oceanic stream of water cannot be stopped by customs regulation and birch rods... If you do not want to be drowned, get out of the way or swim with the current.

...Maybe those of you who do not want the emancipation think that the tsar will help in case of a crushing defeat. They are accustomed to fierce military pacification, they are accustomed to the role of executioner, which the government so willingly takes on itself at the behest of the gentry. They are accustomed to the gentry's criminal deafness to the peasants' complaints and shameful pandering to illegal sales, extraordinary tax assessments, and the forcible settlement of peasants outside the village...

Maybe the tsar will help with such means as his *blessed* predecessor used to help introduce the military colonies, flogging to death every tenth or twentieth person... Maybe...

But if you make use of the tsar's protection, be sure to behave yourselves; forget about any kind of human dignity, about any sort of free speech, and about the dream of personal independence, for at that point you will be loyal subjects and only loyal subjects. [. . .]

Notes

Source: "Iur'ev den'! Iur'ev den'!", 1853; 12:80–86, 514–15.

1. Herzen lists four of the five Decembrists executed in 1826.

2. At first a court official in sixth place on the Table of Ranks, by 1850 it designated those in ranks three and four.

3. Herzen: "Every noble class in the West can refer to some sort of weak, transparent rights to own peasants; we don't even have that. The Russian nobility didn't acquire slaves by spilling its own blood, but through a series of police actions, base pandering by the tsars, tricks by the civil servants, and the shameless greed of their ancestors."

4. Herzen misstated the date; he meant August 4, 1789, when noble members of the Constituent Assembly renounced their feudal rights.

5. The Pugachev rebellion of 1773–75 was led by a Cossack adventurer, Emilyan Pugachev, who claimed to be Tsar Peter III, the latest in a series of pretenders to the Russian throne. His large band of followers, including escaped serfs, deserting soldiers, branded convicts, Old Believers, and Cossacks, achieved early success in the Volga and Ural regions and marched on Moscow until the rebellion was finally halted and Pugachev was executed. Alexander Pushkin wrote both a historical account based on archival research and a novel, *The Captain's Daughter,* concerning this historical episode. It was seen as a warning about the underlying violence in a repressed society.

⇢ 4 ⇠

Initially published as a separate sheet, the announcement of *The Polestar* was reprinted in its first issue, as well in the French newspaper *L'Homme,* where agents of the Foreign Ministry noticed it and sent it on to St. Petersburg (*Let* 2:238–41). Originally planned as a journal, the lack of fresh material from Russia in the early years led to its continuation as a series of eight almanacs (1855–59, 1861–62, and 1869), some consisting of several installments. Its contents included *Past and Thoughts,* banned poetry by Pushkin, Lermontov, Ryleev, and Ogaryov, and Decembrist memoirs. It was named in honor of the publication edited by Ryleev and A. Bestuzhev from 1823 to 1825, which was closed down by Nicholas; the cover of the revived *Polestar* bore an engraving by Charles Linton of the five executed Decembrists in profile. Herzen planned for the first issue to come out on the anniversary of their deaths, July 13 (O.S.), but it was delayed until the beginning of August 1855.

Herzen believed that readers would be moved by this title; a letter the exiled Decembrist I. Yakushkin wrote from Siberia (which Herzen evidently never received) said that *The Polestar* was read with joy and deep emotion; its appearance was a major event for the youth of the mid-1850s. Nikolay Dobrolyubov wrote in his diary for January 13, 1857: "At 10 I began reading the second volume of *The Polestar* and I didn't stop until five in the morning [. . .] And having closed the book I couldn't sleep for a while [. . .] A lot of heavy, melancholy, but proud thoughts coursed through my head" (Dobroliubov, *Polnoe sobranie sochinenii,* 6:451).

AN ANNOUNCEMENT ABOUT *THE POLESTAR*
[1855]

The Polar Star hid behind the clouds of the reign of Tsar Nicholas.

Nicholas has *passed on,* and *The Polestar* has appeared once more, on our Good Friday, the day when five gallows were erected for our five crucifixions.

A Russian periodic publication that appears without censorship and is exclusively dedicated to the question of Russian emancipation and spreading liberated thought throughout Russia, is taking this name to demonstrate the continuation of the legend and the work, the internal bond and the blood ties.

Russia has been severely shaken by recent events. No matter what, it cannot return to stagnation; thought will be more active, new questions will arise—must they really fade away and go silent? We do not think so. Official Russia has a voice and will find defenders even in London. And Young Russia, the Russia of the future and of hope, does not possess a single organ.

We offer it one.

Beginning on February 18 (March 2) Russia enters a new phase of its development. The death of Nicholas is more than the death of a person—it is the death of principles which were carried out with great strictness and which had reached their limit. While he was alive they could somehow stand firm, established by habit and resting on an iron will.

After his death it is impossible to continue his reign.

We do not fight the dead. From the moment that Dr. Mandt whispered to the heir: "The carotid artery beats no longer," the passion of our struggle changed to a cold analysis of the past reign.

Two principal thoughts, lacking any unity and interfering with each other, determine the character of Nicholaevan rule.

Continuing Peter's legend in external affairs.

Counteracting the Petrine line of internal development.

Expanding borders and influence in Europe and Asia, while constricting any kind of civil society in Russia.

Everything for the state, i.e., for the throne, and nothing for the people.

To return to the patriarchal-barbaric power of the Muscovite tsars, without losing any of the grandeur of the Petersburg emperor—that was the task Nicholas set himself.

The Muscovite tsar, that Byzantine despot, surrounded by priests and monks, dressed in some sort of gilded robe, restricted by exaggerated oriental ceremony and a bad government structure—is less than a soldier. The Petersburg emperor, as soon as he rejects the formative principles of Peter, is only a soldier.

From the first day of his accession, Nicholas declared war on every sort of education and every free aspiration. He roused a sluggish Orthodoxy, persecuted the Uniates, destroyed tolerance, forbade Russians to go abroad, imposed an outrageous tax on the right to travel, tormented Poland for its political development, displayed relics which Peter had forbidden, and boldly placed on his flag, as if to mock the great words on the banner of the French Revolution: *autocracy, orthodoxy, nationality!*

Autocracy as a goal. This is the naive philosophy of history of the Russian autocrat.

Everything went his way. Not because he had exceptional strength, but because the baseness of the world around him was exceptional.

The height of his grandeur was the moment when he read Paskevich's dispatch:[1] "Hungary lies at the feet of your highness!" [. . .]

Nicholas triumphed. But near the Winter Palace, i.e., near the Peter Paul Fortress, the Petrashevsky[2] society was founded. It seems that despite all efforts, revolutionary thought was not dead but was fermenting in minds and making hearts beat faster. The appearance of these noble, self-sacrificing, fine young men before the investigating commission was an ominous *memento mori* for Nicholas. It was not by chance that the ghost of the 14th of December appeared twenty-five years later, flourishing and youthful. What had been achieved by terrible oppression at home and universal baseness?

In addition, after the triumph there was a terrible emptiness. The futility of an autocracy with no goal but itself was fully apparent the day after the victory.

Not a single fruitful thought, not a single improvement, everything turned gray along with Nicholas, growing older and stiffer. There was one thing he could accomplish—to free the serfs, and he wanted to do it, but it is hard, terribly hard for an absolute monarch to give anyone freedom...

[. . .] Nicholaevan rule was lowered into the grave with him. Do not worry, it will not rise again; things may get worse, but they will not be the same.

We know almost nothing about his heir. But his wishes notwithstanding, the circumstances of his accession to the throne determine to some degree his situation.

What a difference!

In a shaky manner, Nicholas ascended the throne instead of his older brother. He was greeted by a rebellion that he defeated with grapeshot, but behind the fallen ranks of soldiers a colossal conspiracy came to light. All Russia was involved: the peasant was there as a soldier, the house of Rurik represented by princes, generals covered in glory, people covered with honor, literary figures, officers, civil servants in Petersburg, Moscow, and everywhere—all took part in the conspiracy. He was afraid to find out that his friend Adlerberg and Suvorov,[3] the grandson of the Italian prince, were implicated, and freed them from prosecution; the emperor Alexander was almost part of the conspiracy—Speransky and Karamzin wrote charters on his order.[4]

Two roads lay ahead of Nicholas—to become the head of the movement, get control of it, and move forward, or to go against the current, while he still had the strength. He chose the latter and until the present war had kept up his role. But the movement which dragged him into war is the best proof that he had neither stopped it nor gained control, and the man who began by disarming everything—mind and hand—finished by calling all Russia, even the serfs, to arms.

What is there in the 18th of February that resembles the 14th of December? The new emperor could not answer the bravery at Sevastopol with grapeshot; he could not forbid every kind of speech, when some people were coming to him to say that they would give their blood and others their money for the defense of Russia. Russia did not want this war, is ravaged by it, and obviously did not need it. But the subject here is not what used to be or what one desires, but the salvation and the integrity of the state; the people set off to correct the tsar's mistake with their blood—will the new tsar answer them with Siberia and new oppression? Enough!

In 1825 all Europe stood behind Nicholas, and in 1855 all Europe stands against Alexander. It is easy to disregard the people's groaning when there is no external enemy, but it is difficult to send people to their death with insults and abuse in parting. They have woken up to the extent that it has become a people's war. Once again the people have something in common with the tsar—that is why the tsar will depend on them.

The fourteenth of December was also born in a moment of animation, when the people for the first time after Pozharsky[5] walked hand in hand with the government. The thought of Russian liberation appeared on the earth that day, when a Russian soldier, tired after battles and long marches, rushed to finally rest in the Elysian Fields.

Can it be that after forty years a gigantic battle in the Tauride will take place with no effect?

Will the Sevastopol soldier, wounded and hard like granite, having tested his strength, present his back to the rod as before? Isn't an armed serf as apt to return peacefully to unpaid labor as a nomadic horseman from the Caspian shores—now guarding the Baltic border—is apt to go missing on his own steppe? Did Petersburg see the English fleet in vain? That is impossible. Everything is in motion, everything is shaken and strained... what would have to happen for a country that was so abruptly awoken to once again fall dead asleep?

It would be better that Russia perish!

But this will not happen. From far away another life is audible to us here, and a spring breeze wafts from Russia. We did not doubt the Russian people before, and everything written and said by us since 1849 testifies to that. The establishment of a printing-house is even more evidence. The question was about the best time, and it has been resolved in our favor.

Only let us not be mistaken about one matter; circumstances count for a great deal but they are not everything. Without personal participation, without willpower and without labor, nothing gets completed. This is what comprises the grandeur of man's action in history. He creates it, and the fulfillment of historical destiny depends on his supreme will. The more favorable the circumstances the more terrible the responsibility he bears to himself and to his descendants.

We summon you to work. It is not a lot, but it is physiologically important; we have made the first step, we have opened the gate—*to walk through it is your job!*

The first volume of *The Polestar* will appear on *the twenty-seventh of July* (August 7), and the second toward the New Year.

We don't want to start subscriptions before December; for subscriptions we need to know whether we will receive articles, and whether there will be support from Russia. Only then will we be able to determine whether we can publish *three* or *four volumes* a year.

Our plan is exceptionally simple. In each issue we would like to have one general article (philosophy of revolution, socialism), one historical or statistical article about Russia or the Slavic world, an analysis of some remarkable artistic work and one original literary article; after that, a mixture of letters, a chronicle, and so on.

The Polestar must be—and this is one of our most ardent desires—the refuge for all manuscripts drowning in the imperial censorship, all that have been mutilated by it. For the *third* time we are making a request to all literate people in Russia to obtain for us manuscript copies of Pushkin, Lermontov et al., which are being passed around and are well-known ("An Ode to Freedom," "The Dagger," "The Village," omitted parts of *Onegin* and "Demon," "The Gavriliad," "The Triumph of Death," "Polikrat Samossky"...).

The manuscripts will eventually perish—they must be preserved in print.

Our first volume is rich. A writer of unusual talent and a sharp dialectic as soon as he heard a rumor about *The Polestar* sent us a superb article under the title "What is a state?" We have read it ten times, amazed at the boldness and depth of the author's revolutionary logic.

Another anonymous writer sent us "The Correspondence Between Belinsky and Gogol." We knew about this correspondence before from Belinsky himself; it made some noise in 1847. In any case, there is no indelicacy in printing it since it has passed through so many hands, even those of the police, and we are printing something that is already well known. Belinsky and Gogol are no longer alive, Belinsky and Gogol belong to Russian history, and the polemic between them is too important a document to not publish out of faint-hearted delicacy.

We have already secured these two articles for our first volume. Besides these we will print excerpts from *Past and Thoughts,* an analysis of Michelet's *La Renaissance,* and tutti frutti—all and sundry.

Richmond (Surrey)
March 25 (April 6), 1855

Notes

Source: "Ob"iavlenie o 'Poliarnoi zvezde' 1855," 1855; 12:265–71, 536–38.

1. Prince Ivan F. Paskevich-Yerevansky (1782–1856), a general and field marshal who commanded the Russian army in campaign against Hungarian revolutionaries in 1848.

2. The Petrashevsky circle, organized by Mikhail V. Butashevich-Petrashevsky (1821–1866), read and discussed progressive literature, especially the French utopian socialists, and evidently included a secret inner core of proto-revolutionaries. Its members were arrested in 1849, in the wake of the European revolutionary activities, and a number of them, including Fyodor Dostoevsky, received sentences of prison and exile in Siberia.

3. Vladimir F. Adlerberg (1791–1859) was a general and minister at court, enjoying the special confidence of Nicholas I and Alexander II; Alexander A. Suvorov (1804–1882) was a grandson of the great general and close to Decembrist circles, as a result of which he was sent to the Caucasus, later serving as governor-general in the Baltic provinces.

4. Herzen has in mind work carried out for Alexander I by Mikhail Speransky. The relevant political essays by N. M. Karamzin were written on his own initiative.

5. Minin, a commoner, and Pozharsky, an aristocrat, are credited with leading the forces that liberated Russia in 1612.

→ 5 ←

The Polestar, Bk. I, 1855. Exiled to the Russian interior, Herzen met Alexander Nikolaevich Romanov when the heir to the throne traveled throughout the empire to get to know more about his future subjects. A few years later, still under the spell of this meeting, Herzen admitted that his idée fixe was to serve in the grand duke's suite, even if it were as a lowly librarian, preferring that to a much higher-ranking ministerial position (Gertsen, *Sobranie sochinenii,* 22:85). This is the first of Herzen's open letters to the new tsar. The verses come from Ryleev's poem "The Vision: An Ode on the Name-Day of His Imperial Highness Grand Duke Alexander Nikolaevich, August 30, 1823." Herzen refers to the fact that when Ryleev wrote this poem, it was believed that the next tsar would likely be Konstantin Pavlovich and not his younger brother Nicholas. As heir, Alexander II's tutor was the poet Vasily Zhukovsky. Herzen was mistaken about the easing of the conditions of the Decembrists' exile, which took place three years later, in 1837.

The liberals Kavelin and Chicherin found this letter more reasonable than many of Herzen's statements, and others went so far as to call it a noble deed (*podvig*), but the act of writing to the tsar was controversial across the political spectrum. Always willing to entertain other opinions, Herzen later published the objections he received to this document (Ulam, *Ideologies and Illusions*, 37). A member of the State Senate, K. N. Lebedev, wrote in his diary that the letter brought to mind the early stages of the French Revolution, when the National Assembly received impertinent letters from those who suddenly felt themselves equal in dignity to the government. Lebedev wondered whether the socialist Herzen knew what he really wanted, and whether he had active partners to help realize his agenda (*Let* 2:237, 268–73). Adam Ulam noted the "fantastic" quality of Russian politics in the late 1850s and early 1860s, when "the most radical people were never very far from petitioning or eulogizing the Tsar for this or that reform" (*Ideologies and Illusions*, 36).

Shortly after Herzen's death in 1870, an anonymous pamphlet ("A Few Words from a Russian to Other Russians"), possibly by V. A. Zaitsev, appeared abroad. Its author stressed the restraint and tact employed by Herzen in addressing those in whose hands lay the fate of the Russian people. "He did not disdain writing to the inhabitants of the Winter Palace, and there was a time when he was read even there—if only because it was the 'fashion'—and his words did not go to waste." But, the author laments, it was not yet an age when people like Herzen, Chernyshevsky, and Dobrolyubov could exercise a sustained influence. "In our North these are bright meteors, and the *Polestar*, which hid behind the clouds during the reign of Nicholas, reappeared only briefly, and with Herzen's death has vanished again for a long time" (Ivanova, *A. I. Gertsen*, 181).

A LETTER TO EMPEROR ALEXANDER THE SECOND
[1855]

> Perhaps, my lad, the crown
> Was designated for you by the creator.
> *Love the people*, respect the rule of law,
> Learn ahead of time to be a tsar,
> Love the voice of freedom's truth,
> Love this for your own good,
> And destroy the ignoble spirit of
> Slavery and injustice...
> —K. Ryleev, "Ode to the Grand Duke Alexander
> Nikolaevich," August 30, 1823

Sovereign!

Your reign is commencing under a very lucky star. There are no bloodstains on you, and you feel no pangs of conscience.

The news of your father's death was not brought to you by his assassins. You did not have to cross a square bathed in Russian blood to reach the throne; you did not have to proclaim to the people your accession by means of executions.

The chronicles of your dynasty hardly offer a single example of such an unsullied beginning.

And that is not all.

People expect from you mildness and a human heart.—You are exceptionally lucky!

Fate and chance have surrounded you with something that speaks in your favor. You alone of all your family were born in Moscow, and born at the time when it was awakening to a new life after the purifying fire. The cannons of Borodino and Tarutino[1] had scarcely returned from abroad and were still covered with Parisian dust when your birth was proclaimed from the Kremlin heights. I remember hearing it as a five-year-old boy.

Ryleev greeted you with advice—can you really withhold your respect for this powerful freedom fighter, this martyr to his convictions? Why was it that your cradle inspired in him this mild and peaceful verse? What prophetic voice told him that in time the crown would fall on your youthful head?

You were taught by a poet who loved Russia.[2]

On the day you came of age the fate of our martyrs was made easier.—Yes, you are very fortunate!

Then there was your journey around Russia. I witnessed it, and, what is more, I remember it very well; as a result of your appearance my fate underwent a geographical improvement and I was transferred from Vyatka to Vladimir; I have not forgotten that.

Exiled to a distant town beyond the Volga, I watched how the poor folk met you with a simple love, and I thought: "How will he repay that love?"

Here it is—payment time, and how easy you will find it! Give in to your heart. You truly love Russia and you can do so, so much for the Russian people.

I also love the Russian people, I have forsaken them out of love; I could not remain a witness—silent and with folded arms—to those terrible things that the landowners and bureaucrats were doing to them.

Being at a distance has not changed my feelings; in the midst of strangers, in the midst of passions called forth by the war, I have not rolled up my flag. Just the other day I publicly greeted the English people on behalf of the Russian people.[3]

Of course, my banner is not yours—I am an incorrigible socialist and you're an autocratic emperor; but there is one thing in common between your banner and mine—namely that love for the people about which we speak.

And in its name I am prepared to make a huge sacrifice. What could not be accomplished by long years of persecution, prison, exile, or tedious wandering from country to country—I am prepared to do out of love for the people.

I am prepared to wait, to step back a bit, to speak about something else, as long as I have a real hope that you will do something for Russia.

Your majesty, grant freedom to the Russian word. Our mind is constricted, our thought is poisoning our chest from a lack of space; it is groaning in the confinement of censorship. Give us free speech... We have something to say to the world and to our own people.

Give land to the peasants. It already belongs to them; wipe away from Russia the shameful stain of serfdom, heal the bruises on the backs of our brothers—those dreadful marks of disdain for human beings.

As he was dying, your father—do not be afraid, I know that I am speaking with his son—confessed that he was unable to do everything that he wished for *all* his subjects... Serfdom was gnawing at his conscience in the last moments.

He was *unable* during the course of thirty years to free the serfs!

Hurry! Save the serf from future crimes, save him from the blood that he will have to spill...

...I am ashamed at how little we are prepared to be satisfied with; we want things of whose justice you—and everyone else—have little doubt.

As a first step that will be sufficient for us...

It may be that on the height on which you stand, surrounded by a fog of flattery, you are amazed by my impertinence; maybe you even laugh at this lost grain of sand out of seventy million grains of sand that make up your granite pedestal.

But it is better not to laugh. I am saying only what is *kept silent* at home. For that purpose I have set up on free soil the first Russian printing press; like an electrometer, it will register the activity and pressure of suppressed force...

A few drops of water that cannot find a way out are sufficient to destroy a granite cliff.

Your majesty, if these lines reach you, read them without malice, alone, and then think about them. You do not often get to hear the sincere voice of a free Russian man.

10 March 1855

Notes

Source: "Pis'mo k Imperatoru Aleksandru Vtoromu," *Poliarnaia zvezda*, kn. 1, 1855; 12:272–74, 538–39.

1. In September 1812, Napoleon failed to defeat the Russians at Borodino; his forces were defeated the following month at Tarutino, south of Moscow, with an unusually large number of French guns falling into enemy hands.

2. Vasily Zhukovsky.

3. Herzen refers to "A Popular Assembly in Memory of the February Revolution," a speech that he gave in French at a London meeting on February 27, 1855, commemorating the events of 1848. The speech was published in English, French, and Russian.

⇥ 6 ⇤

The Polestar, Bk. I, 1855. Herzen published the infamous 1847 correspondence between Gogol and Belinsky, which was still banned in Russia, along with Gogol's reaction to Belinsky's article in *The Contemporary*. In *A Remarkable Decade*, Pavel Annenkov described Herzen's arrival at the hotel in Paris where a seriously ill Belinsky read his own letter in Herzen's presence. Although Herzen heard the letter in its original form in 1847, the copy he used for publication is faulty. His word for publicity—*glasnost'*—was widely employed during the first decade of Alexander II's reign, and, along with the word for restructuring—*perestroika*—was revived 130 years later by Mikhail Gorbachev.

———

A NOTE ON "THE CORRESPONDENCE BETWEEN
N. GOGOL AND BELINSKY" IN *THE POLESTAR*
[1855]

The circumstances which gave rise to this correspondence are well-known to our readers. In 1847, N. Gogol, who was living abroad, published his *Correspondence with Friends* in Russia. The book was a surprise to everyone. Its spirit completely contradicted his previous creations, which had so deeply shaken all Russian readers. Was it an internal, psychic reshaping, one of those painful stages of development by which a person reaches eventual maturity? Was it the result of a physical ailment, indignation, a long period spent abroad or simply dizziness? In any case, the publication of such a book by such a major talent had to stimulate a powerful polemic.

Admirers of Gogol, having accepted as truth the opinions which had shone through so brilliantly in his works, were insulted by his renunciation, his defense of the status quo, his *disparaging*, in the words of the neo-Slavs; they picked up the glove that he had thrown down, and, of course, there came to the forefront a fighter worthy of him—Belinsky.

He published a strong article against Gogol's new book in *The Contemporary*.

Hence the correspondence. In giving more publicity to these letters, we are far from any idea of condemnation and reprimand. It is time for us to look upon publicity with grown-up eyes. Publicity is a purgatory from which the memory of the departed passes on into history, the only life possible beyond the grave.

There is no need to hide anything; in publicity there is repentance, the last judgment and certain reconciliation, if there can be reconciliation. Moreover, nothing must be hidden; only that which is unimportant and empty is forgotten, lost without a trace.

The whole question is; do Gogol and Belinsky belong to us as public figures in the field of Russian thought? And if so—was there a correspondence between them?

As I have already said, Belinsky read me his letter and that of Gogol in Paris.

Notes

Source: "Primechanie k 'Perepiske N. Gogolia s Belinskim' v *Poliarnoi zvezde*," *Poliarnaia zvezda*, kn. 1, 1855; 12:275–76, 539–40.

→ 7 ←

The Polestar, Bk. II, 1856. "Forward! Forward!" is dated March 31, but the peace treaty ending the Crimean War was actually signed on March 30. This programmatic article identifies the commune (*obshchina*) as the cornerstone of Russian socialism and Russia's hope for the future. Herzen called upon advanced Russian society to become politically active now that Nicholas I was dead and the war had ended.

—

FORWARD! FORWARD!
[1856]

Keep moving now, do not stand in one place, it is difficult to say what will come and how, but there has been a real jolt and the ice has begun to break up. Move forward... You'll be amazed how easy it will be to go on after this.

This morning, Count Orlov threw the last clump of earth on the grave of Nicholas, having solemnly witnessed his death and along with it the beginning of a new era for Russia.

The war was costly for you and peace brought no glory, but the blood of the Sevastopol warriors did not flow in vain if you take advantage of that terrible lesson. Roads strewn with corpses, soldiers worn out before encountering the enemy, poor communications, confusion in the quarter-master service—all clearly demonstrated the incompatibility of a deadening autocracy not only with development and general welfare, but even with force and external order, with that mechanical supplying of the essentials that is despotism's ideal. To what purpose was the oppression of thought, the persecution of the word, eternal parades and instruction, to what purpose was police surveillance over the entire government, with hundreds of thousands of documents being received and issued?

The purpose was that *forty-two* years after the brilliant, young, liberal colonel M. F. Orlov signed on March 30, 1814 the capitulation of Paris in the name of those who defeated Napoleon, another Orlov, an old man, who was his brother and the chief of the gendarmes, bore the guilty head of Russia and accepted a peace given by another Napoleon, also from the ranks of the gendarmes.

"Do you really believe in the tremendous power of the tsar of which you speak?" I said in 1853 at a Polish meeting in London, and I repeat my words, because events have so sharply confirmed them. "Russia *is strong*, but *imperial power, as it is now constituted,* is unable to summon that strength. It has no roots in national consciousness; it is not Russian and not Slavic. It is a temporary dictatorship, a state of siege, introduced into the foundations of the government. Perhaps it was historically necessary, but it has outlived itself; it realized its destiny when Alexander I entered Paris as a liberator, surrounded by kings and crowned heads, whom he restrained from pillage and violence."

Alexander I knew this, and was somehow at a loss after the victory, feeling that it was impossible to continue on the path of absolute power, and he went sadly along with head bowed toward the 14th of December, lacking the strength to either gain control of events or to yield to them.

The same consciousness, on the other hand, was demonstrated by the tremendous conspiracy in which leading people from all active layers of Russian society took part. To remain any longer under the yoke of un-limited absolute power was so intolerable that a handful of heroic people proudly threw down a challenge to tsarist power "in the very jaws of the lion" as Michelet said. Strength won out over thought. With his cold and heavy arm Nicholas stopped the young life that pressed forward, stopped every kind of movement, and achieved what? In the *thirtieth* year of his reign a deadly quiet hung over his crushed, silent people; a restrained Poland was barely breathing, Russian literature had come to a halt, the 14th of December was defeated, and he—the representative and head of reaction in Europe—wanted at last to test his strength.

And this thirtieth year became for him a year of terrible atonement. With impotent wrath, with burning shame, Nicholas saw his troops, which he had taught so well to handle a rifle, beaten by the commissary; courts, boards, and councils were filled with thieves. Surrounded by informers and two or three different police forces, he knew about every liberal quatrain written by some student, every imprudent toast proposed by some young man, but he lacked the means to find out the facts and to reach the truth in every other matter.

Right next to him, alongside him, brazenly stood another power, elusive, omnipresent, stealing at one go the gold from his throne and the iron from the peasant's plow, with one hand not allowing the soldier's rations to reach them while stealing the peasant's piece of bread with the other hand.

Several months before his death (as the newspapers recount), Nicholas, angered by the theft of money for disabled soldiers, said that he knew of only one person in the service who did not steal, and it was *him*.

What a realization of weakness and what a punishment! Nicholas died beneath its weight.

Is it possible that Alexander and Konstantin, whose honesty we have no right to doubt, imagine that they are eradicating evil by handing over to the courts several rogues and publishing official circulars with critical remarks?

Evil fears the light, evil fears publicity, evil fears freedom—and yet absolute power fears all of this. This is the frightening mutual guarantee between the two powers. Theft was not a national problem in France, but ten years of the first empire was sufficient to turn French generals into robbers, and prefects into bribe-takers.

We *ourselves* have to fight evil, to raise our voice against it, to seek counsel and means, to display willpower and strength, if they were not in fact broken by the Nicholaevan yoke. If we do not, nothing will happen.

But he did not break them. The same year that was so merciless for the tsar showed us once again the inexhaustible, healthy might of the Russian people. How strange all this is and how full of deep significance! Rus came to life as he was passing away, and he was passing away because *he had no faith in his own people.* [. . .]

The air of 1612 and 1812 began to blow through Russia with the news of the enemy invasion, and not a single person mistook the Turkish crusade for "enlightenment and freedom."[1] We don't know how the war would have ended had it really turned into a popular uprising, but we are genuinely glad of the peace, all the more because it brings not splendor but *humility.* The iron of victorious swords can forge the strongest chains.

On the contrary, the modest peace obliges everyone to be thoughtful about our position. Everyone now sees that the former path will not do at all; however, we are sure that no one—neither the government nor you— has a definite idea, plan, or program. But to leave the future to the vagaries of fortune is a bad thing. People are not responsible for the way that events change ideas about the future, but the wish to master them and realize in them one's reason and will is integral to conscious human development.

We did not comprehend our actual situation because, attracted by superficial strength, we approached a historical task like forced labor. There are many reasons for this, and an exclusionary national identity is as much of a hindrance to understanding our original development as Western civilization. [. . .]

It is not only imperial power in its Petrine form that has outlived its time, but all of Petersburg Russia. What it was able to achieve has been achieved. We must free ourselves from the moral yoke of Europe, *that* Europe on which up to now our eyes have been directed. [. . .]

We are not petty bourgeois—we are peasants.

We are poor in cities and rich in villages. All efforts to create in our midst an urban bourgeoisie in the Western sense have resulted in empty and absurd consequences. Our only genuine city-dwellers are government workers; the merchants are closer to the peasants than to them. The gentry are naturally much more rural than urban dwellers. Thus—the city for us is really just the government, while the village is all Russia, the people's Russia.

Our peculiarity, our originality is the village with its communal self-governance, with the peasants' meeting, with delegates, with the absence of personal land ownership, with the division of fields according to the number of households. Our rural commune has survived the era of difficult state growth in which communes generally perished and has remained whole in double chains, preserved under the blows of the owner's stick and the bureaucrat's theft.

Naturally, a question arises at the very outset: should our commune be *formed* on the basis of an abstract notion of personal independence and a sovereign right to property, eradicating patriarchal communism and domestic mutual assistance, or, on the contrary, shouldn't we *develop* it on its popular and social principles, seeking to preserve and combine personal independence, without which there is no freedom, with a social inclination, with mutual assistance, without which freedom becomes a monopoly of the property owner. [. . .]

But in approaching this issue we are hindered not by the tsar but by the terrible crime of serfdom. Serfdom is Russia's guilty conscience, its right to slavery. The scars on the backs of the martyrs and suffering people of the field and the front hall are not in fact on their back but on our face, on Russia's face. The landowners are bound hand and foot by their absurd right.

Thus the first enemy with whom we must fight is right before our eyes.

There is, at first glance, something crazy in our inability to resolve this question. The younger gentry wanted this fifteen years ago in Moscow, Penza, Tambov, and I do not know where else; Alexander I dreamed about it; Nicholas wished it. The young members of the gentry have now become middle-aged landowners, and we have no reason to doubt that Alexander II opposes it. Who does not want this to happen? Who is the powerful figure who is stopping at the same time the people and the tsar, the educated part of the gentry and the suffering peasants?

Again it's the fantastic *boyards russes,* and once again the invented old Muscovite party. Well, the estates of these boyars are also mortgaged and the payments are overdue, so where is their power—no, it is not about them.

No, let us be frank, the question of emancipation has not been resolved because we did not know how to begin, and we did not know how to begin in part because it is not soluble from the point of view of the Petersburg government, which nurtured this evil and profited by it, nor from the point of view of that liberalism at the heart of which lies the religion of personal property, the unconditional and ineradicable admission that it is forever indestructible. [. . .]

How can we approach a solution to such a complex question? For that to happen we must discuss it, exchange ideas and check opinions. The censorship does not allow us to do this in print, and the police do not allow us to do this orally. Once again we have to run to those fruitless arguments between the adherents of an exclusive theory of nationality and the followers of cosmopolitan civilization...[2] Is it not a sin to waste one's strength on these sham debates, to wear down one's mind on this internecine strife, at the same time that one's heart and conscience ask for something else, and the same time that the melancholy peasant leaves his unsown field to do his compulsory labor, and the house-serf with clenched teeth awaits the birch rod?

At least we should ask the sovereign that all of us again be subject to corporal punishment, because it is totally repulsive that the protection of our gentry's backs gives us the right to be executioners...

...Isn't it clear that as a first instance our entire program comes down to the need for *open discussion* and that all banners disappear into one—the banner *of the emancipation of the serfs with land.*

Down with the ridiculous censorship and the ridiculous rights of landowners! Down with compulsory labor and quitrent. Free the house serfs!

We'll tackle other issues later on...

March 31, 1856

Notes

Source: "Vpered! Vpered! Pervaia stat'ia v *Poliarnoi zvezde," Poliarnaia zvezda,* kn. 2, 1856; 12:306–12, 546–47.

1. As was claimed by Napoleon III to justify the attack.
2. Herzen is referring to the arguments between the Slavophiles and liberal Westernizers.

⇥ 8 ⇤

The first edition of "Baptized Property" appeared in 1853. The head of the postal service, Adlerberg, informed the Third Department that the brochure was written in a way that was offensive and harmful to the government. While the tsar took great pains to prevent its penetration into Russia, the Russian ambassador in London purchased a copy for the Grand Duchesses Olga and Maria Nikolaevna (*Let* 2:158, 182–84). A few years later, the Crimean War and the death of Nicholas made additional comments necessary. The introduction to the second edition below was written in October 1856, and published in 1857 by the Free Russian Press. Herzen displayed his concern over government inaction, and yet he held out hope that the new tsar would free the serfs in due time.

Prince Yuri N. Golitsyn (1823–1872), to whom several lively pages of *Past and Thoughts* are devoted, wrote to Herzen on July 8 (20), 1858, from Dresden that he had sought out London publications in Russian "in order to find out abroad *what was going on at home.* [. . .] Among the ones I received and read with great delight was the brochure previously unknown to me: 'Baptized Property.' As a Tambov landowner familiar with peasant life, this article aroused in me the desire to share my thoughts with you." Golitsyn says that he does not mind having recently been criticized by a letter-writer in *The Bell*—his regard for the editor's importance to Russia overcame any hurt feelings Because of his foreign contacts and the discovery of a set of issues of *The Bell* that he had bound in revolutionary red and embossed with his family crest, Golitsyn was exiled to the provinces at the end of 1858. He spent two colorful years abroad in 1860–62, after which he returned to Russia and wound up composing patriotic music in gratitude when the tsar's life was spared in 1866 (Eidel'man, *Svobodnoe slovo Gertsena,* 365–68).

The Ukrainian poet Taras Shevchenko heard "Baptized Property" read aloud at a dinner in Nizhny-Novgorod and wrote in his diary about the powerful effect of sincere, truthful human words; the London exile was "our apostle" (*Let* 2:376). A number of Herzen's bolder articles were later reprinted and distributed by radicals in Russia; what made "Baptized Property" particularly dangerous was its being handed out several years later in rural areas following the Emancipation (*Let* 3:222–26, 476).

———

BAPTIZED PROPERTY

A Preface to the Second Edition

[1857]

Three years ago, while making my first attempts at Russian publishing in London, I printed a small piece on serfdom under the title "Baptized Property." I ascribe no great importance to that brochure; on the contrary, I find it highly inadequate, but the edition has sold out. Mr. Torzhevsky has expressed a desire to issue a new one and I saw no reason to deny him this right.

Many events have transpired in Russia during these three years, but *serfdom* remains as it was—a sore and a stain, the outrage of Russian life that humbles us and makes us—blushing and with a lowered head—confess that we are lower than all the peoples of Europe.

After the death of Nicholas, with what fervent hope and palpitations we awaited changes that were possible and common to all mankind and could be accomplished without tremendous upheaval, merely by a comprehension on the part of the government of its goal and purpose. From the distance of our exile we watched with hope and without the slightest ill will. At first the war got in the way... Then the war was over but nothing happened! Everything was put off until the coronation... The coronation took place— still nothing! And a new reign got into its daily routine. Up until now all the reforms have been limited to fine phrases and nothing has advanced beyond rhetoric.

And yet how easy it would have been to perform miracles; that is what is unforgivable, that is what we cannot bear. Our hearts bleed and vexation seethes in our breasts when we think of what Russia might have become with a departure from the gloomy reign of Nicholas; aroused by war, brought to consciousness, without the collar of slavery around our neck, how quickly, originally, and vigorously it could move forward.

There is not even the beginning of emancipation, that primer of civic development. Why were militias raised, why did the peasant bring his labor, his kopeck, and his blood to the defense of a soulless throne, that with some babbling about its gratitude returned him to the master's rod and hard labor in the fields?

They say that the present tsar is kind. Maybe the ferocious persecution that characterized the past reign is over; we would be the first to heartily welcome that.

But that is really very little, that is still a negative distinction. It is insufficient to not do evil while having so many resources to do good, which no other European monarchy possesses. But he does not know how to get started and what to do.

And there is no one to tell him. There it is—the result of enforced silence, that is what it means to rip out the people's tongue and place a lock on their lips. The Winter Palace is surrounded by a kingdom of the deaf, and within it only the Nicholaevan general adjutants speak. They, of course, will not be talking about the spirit of the times, and it is not from them that Alexander will hear the groans of the Russian people.

It order to hear this, in order to know about the evil and the means to eradicate it, it is not necessary now to pace, like Harun al Rashid, under the windows of his subjects.[1] One has only to lift the shameful chains of censorship, which soiled a word *before* it had been said. And the same Smirdin or Glazunov who supply books to mere mortals will bring to the tsar the voice of his people.[2]

But the servants of Nicholas, so steeped in slavery, do not want this.

They will ruin Alexander—and how one feels sorry for him! One feels sorry for his good heart, for the faith we had in him, for the tears that he shed on several occasions...

These people will drag him into the same routine, will lull him with lies, will frighten him with the impossibility, will drag him again into foreign affairs to distract him from the internal ones. All of this is happening already. [. . .]

At home the deceived peasant once more drags himself across the master's field and sends his son to the manor house—this is terrible! The government knows that they cannot avoid the task of freeing the peasants with land. The conscience, the moral consciousness of Russia demands that it be resolved. What do they gain by dragging it out and putting it off until tomorrow?

When we say that this is cowardice in the face of necessity and that this spineless sluggishness will result in the peasants solving the question with an axe, and we implored the government to save the peasant from future crimes, good people raised a cry of horror and accused us of a love for bloody measures.[3]

This is a lie and a deliberate refusal to understand. When a doctor warns a patient of the terrible consequences of the disease, does this mean that he loves and summons these consequences? What a childish point of view!

No, we have seen too much and too close at hand the terror of bloody revolutions and their perverted results to call them forth with savage joy.

We simply pointed out where these gentlemen are headed and where they will lead others. Let them know that if neither the government nor the landowners do anything—it will be done by the axe. And let the sovereign know that it is up to him whether the Russian peasant will take the axe from behind his sash!

Something has to be done—they cannot put off the question and ignore its consequences.

October 25, 1856, Putney

Notes

Source: "Kreshchennaia sobstvennost'. Predislovie k vtoromu izdaniiu," 1857; 12:94–96, 516–19.

1. Harun-al-Rashid (763–809), an Arabian caliph.

2. Alexander F. Smirdin (1795–1857), owner of a bookstore, library, and printing press in Petersburg. Ivan I. Glazunov (1826–1889), a bookseller and publisher, grandson of the founder of Russia's oldest book business.

3. This was the reaction to Herzen's article "St. George's Day! St. George's Day!"

→ 9 ←

The Polestar, Bk. III, 1857. The first separate issue of *The Bell* in July 1857 included this announcement with additional comments. During the dramatic trial scenes in *The Brothers Karamazov*, Dostoevsky had the defense lawyer Fetyukovich pull out all the stops, with quotations from the gospels and references to the well-known Schiller epigraph from *The Bell:* "As a man and a citizen I call out—*vivos voco!* [. . .] Not in vain is this tribune given us by a higher will—from here we can be heard by the whole of Russia."[1] Herzen did not have great faith in state-run trials either, but for fundamentally different reasons. Dostoevsky is more critical of the liberals and radicals who read *The Bell* than of its editor, who died a decade before the publication of *The Brothers Karamazov*.

————

THE BELL

A Supplement to The Polestar

[1857]

"Vivos voco!"

The Polestar comes out too rarely—we do not have the means to publish it more frequently. Aside from that, events in Russia are moving quickly, they must be caught on the fly and discussed right away. For this purpose we are undertaking a new periodical publication. Without fixing the exact times of its appearance, we will attempt to issue *one* sheet, sometimes *two*, every month under the title *The Bell*.

The success of *The Polestar* has far exceeded our expectations, and allows us to hope for a positive reception for its traveling companion.

Nothing needs to be said about its political tendency; it is the same as *The Polestar,* the same one that moves with constancy through our whole life. Everywhere, in all matters, to be on the side of freedom against coercion, the side of reason against prejudice, the side of science against fanaticism, and the side of advancing peoples against backward governments. These are our general doctrines.

In our attitude toward Russia, we passionately wish, with all the strength of our love, with all the force of our uttermost belief, that at last the old and unnecessary swaddling clothes that hinder her powerful development would fall away. For that purpose, now, as in 1855, we consider as the first necessary, unavoidable, and urgent step:

FREEDOM OF EXPRESSION FROM CENSORSHIP
FREEDOM OF THE SERFS FROM THE LANDOWNERS
FREEDOM FROM CORPORAL PUNISHMENT.

However, not limiting ourselves to these questions, *The Bell,* dedicated exclusively to Russian questions, will *ring out* from whatever touches it—absurd decrees or the foolish persecution of religious dissidents, theft by high officials or the senate's ignorance. The comical and the criminal, the evil and the ignorant—all of these come under *The Bell.*

For that reason we turn to our fellow countrymen, who share *our* love for Russia, and ask them not only to listen to our *Bell* but to take their own turn in ringing it.

The first issue will appear around the 1st of June.

London, April 13, 1857

It will be sold at Trubner and Co, 60, Paternoster Row, London (Price 6 pence)

Note

Source: "*Kolokol.* Pribavochnye listy k *Poliarnoi zvezde,*" *Poliarnaia zvezda,* kn. 3, 1857; 12:357–58, 557.

1. "I summon the living!" From the epigraph to Friedrich Schiller's 1798 "Song of the Bell" (for more on this quotation, see the introduction). The Dostoevsky quote is from the translation of the novel by Richard Pevear and Larissa Volokhonsky (New York: Farrar, Straus and Giroux, 1990), 744.

⇥ 10 ⇤

The Bell, No. 1, July 1, 1857. The epigraph was a poem by Nikolay Ogaryov about the years of enforced silence in Russia, which are coming to an end as all its bells sound forth. According to Herzen, Ogaryov convinced him to undertake this new project (Gertsen, *So-branie sochinenii*, 27:bk. 1, 265). This preface outlines the publication's direction, which Herzen hoped would be acceptable to the widest possible circles, including the new tsar, although he indicates some impatience with the slow pace of change during the two years since Alexander II ascended the throne. The political demands mentioned comprise the essential points of his program, and he frequently returned to this list in subsequent articles. Sections that appeared in the previous document are not repeated here.

A Preface to *The Bell*
[1857]

[. . .] The appearance of a new Russian organ which serves as a supplement to *The Polestar* is not a chance occurrence that depends on the whim of a single person, but the answer to a demand: *we must publish it.*

To explain this I must remind you of the short history of our printing press.

The Russian Press, founded in 1853 in London, was a form of inquiry. In founding it, I addressed our fellow countrymen with an appeal. [. . .][1]

[. . .] While awaiting what was to come, I began printing my own works and short pieces written by others. There was no response, or, worse, the only thing that reached me was censure, fearful babbling, and careful whispers telling me that publishing abroad would be dangerous, that it might be compromising and cause a great deal of harm; many people close to me shared that opinion. This frightened me.

The war came. At a time when Europe turned its greedy attention to everything Russian and bought up the entire press runs of my French brochures,[2] and the translation of my *Notes* into English and German quickly sold out—not even *ten* Russian books were sold. They lay in piles at the printer's or were given away at our expense, and, what is more, to no effect.

Propaganda was just beginning then to be an active force that could pay its own way; without that it is strained, unnatural, and can only serve a party function, but more often calls forth a quickly developed sympathy, which pales and withers as soon as the sounds of the words cease.

A minority realizes some portion of its ideal only when—apparently separating itself from the majority—it expresses the same thought, aspirations, and suffering. The majority is in general undeveloped and sluggish; feeling the burden of its contemporary situation, it does nothing; agitated by questions, it can remain without having resolved them. People appear who make these sufferings and aspirations their life's work; they act in word as propagandists and in deed as revolutionaries, but in both cases the real basis of one and the other is the majority and the degree of their sympathy for it.

Since 1849 all attempts by the London emigration to publish journals were unsuccessful; they were supported by donations, did not pay for themselves, and failed; this was clear proof that the emigration no longer expressed the thoughts of its people. They had come to a halt and were reminiscing, while the people had set off in another direction. And at the same time as the last broadsheet of the French democratic party in London faded away, four editions of Proudhon's book *A Manual of Speculation on the Stock Market* were snapped up in Paris.

Of course, the importation of forbidden books into Russia is made difficult by strict and ferocious measures. But hasn't simple contraband made its way despite all measures? Did the strictness of Nicholas stop theft by civil servants? There was courage enough for bribes, for robbing soldiers, and for contraband, but not for spreading free speech; it must mean there was no genuine demand for it. I was horrified to admit this. But inside there was *enduring faith* that caused me to hope despite my own conclusions; while waiting, I continued my work.

Suddenly the telegraphic dispatch about the death of Nicholas.

Now or never!

Under the influence of this great and beneficial news I wrote the program for *The Polestar*.[3]

[. . .] Twenty-nine years after the day our martyrs were executed the first *Polestar* appeared in London. With a strongly beating heart I awaited what would follow.

My faith began to be justified.

I soon started receiving letters full of youthful and ardent sympathy, notebooks of verse, and various articles. Sales began at first with difficulty and growing slowly; then, with the publication of the *second issue* (in April 1856), the number of requests increased to such an extent that some of our publications are completely sold out,[4] others have been republished, and of a third group only a few copies remain. From the second issue of *The Polestar* until the beginning of *The Bell* the sale of Russian books has covered *all the expenses of the printing house.*

There can be no stronger proof of the genuine demand for free speech in Russia, especially if one remembers the obstacles with customs.

Thus, our labor has not been in vain. Our speech, the free Russian word, is spreading throughout Russia, rousing some, frightening others, and threatening a third group with publicity.

The free Russian word will ring out in the Winter Palace, reminding them that steam under pressure can blow up a machine if one does not know how to manage it properly.

The word spreads among the younger generation to whom we will hand over our work. Let them, more fortunate than we, see in *action* what we have only talked about. We look at the new army, marching to replenish our numbers, without envy, and greet them amicably. For them, joyous holidays of liberation; for us, the ringing of bells with which *we summon the living* to the funeral of everything decrepit, outdated, ugly, slavish, and ignorant in Russia!

Notes

Source: "Predislovie k *Kolokolu*," *Kolokol*, l. 1, July 1, 1857; 13:7–12, 485–89.

1. Herzen proceeds to quote several paragraphs (concluding with the challenge that "if tranquility is dearer to you than free speech—keep silent") from his 1853 broadsheet announcing the beginning of the Free Russian Press. See Doc. 2.

2. Herzen: "*The Old World and Russia* was first placed in an English review and then in *L'Homme* and then printed on Jersey in a separate edition—and all sold down to the last copy."

3. Here Herzen includes sections from "An Announcement About *The Polestar*" (1855), which is translated in Doc. 4.

4. Herzen: "The press runs of *Interrupted Stories, Prison and Exile*, and the first and second issues of *The Polestar* are completely gone. *Baptized Property* came out in a second edition."

✦ 11 ✦

The Bell, No. 1, July 1, 1857. The French text of "Venerable Travelers" appeared in the London-based French newspaper *Le Courier de l'Europe* on June 27, 1857, with a sarcastic introduction by the editor, saying that it was a pity the Grand Duke Konstantin had not made it to London on his last European trip because he could have been shown something really interesting, the Russian printing house. Herzen still lacked regular access to Russian periodicals, but he made up for it with the skillful and highly satirical use of news from European papers. For *The Bell*, this piece appeared in a section called "Miscellany," under an epigraph from Gogol: "Through visible laughter to invisible tears!" (*Skvoz' vidimyi smekh—nevidimye slezy!*). In a letter to Shchepkin's son Nikolay, Herzen recommended his "touching" little article (Eidel'man, *Svobodnoe slovo Gertsena*, 199). "Venerable Travelers" was the first of what Herzen intended to be a series of sketches about the Russian royalty abroad; the second installment was to cover the journey of Grand Duke Konstantin Nikolaevich, but Turgenev and Ogarev convinced him to drop the plan, and the next part of the series was published only a decade later. (See Doc. 99.)

The Widowed Empress

[1857]

Since the death of Nicholas the embarrassing constraints on Russians' right to travel have been eliminated. Good deeds rarely happen without a reason; scarcely had Alexander II cut that rope binding us to his father when his own family made more use than anyone else of the newly granted right to movement. On all European roads—except English ones—grand dukes have appeared in their search for German brides, along with former German brides converted into Russians with patronymics. Once more the widowed empress has given Europe the spectacle of an Asian waste of money and truly barbarian luxury. Her loyal subjects could note with pride that every trip the venerable invalid makes and every holiday celebrated is the equal in Russia of a failed harvest, overflowing rivers, and a couple of fires. Once again all sorts of German princes—who have read Liebig and Moleschott about the non-nutritious Russian potato—hung about in Nice with their wives and children, sponging off Russian bread.[1]

Alexandra Fyodorovna, having been raised in the pious rules of evangelical-Potsdam absolutism and having flourished in the dogmas of Orthodox-Petersburg autocracy, could not immediately recover and was at a loss after the royal demise. It was painful for her to see the liberal tendency of the new emperor; she was bothered by the malicious idea of amnesties and the outrageous thought of the emancipation of the serfs. She saw with horror as the majestic supports on which the Nicholaevan dam rested (those German and Russian Kleinmikhels) grew unsteady. The specter that had haunted her for thirty years had risen once more from the moats of the Peter Paul Fortress, from beneath the Siberian snows, and it pointed an accusing finger at the Phrygian cap.[2] In fact, how could she not tremble when terrorists like Lanskoy and Sukhozanet were taking the helm of the ship that had been run aground by her dear departed and could not be refloated without Anglo-French assistance?[3] Foreseeing another 10th of August and 21st of January, mourning the loss of the Nicholaevan style of uniform and the comrades-in-arms of the "unforgettable one," the empress left the revolutionary palace and proceeded to Berlin.[4]

A new blow awaited her there from her nearest and dearest. Her brother the king, with a poor understanding of the roles of the sexes and befuddled by drink, suddenly awarded the empress—can you guess what?—*the rank of colonel of the dragoons.*[5] And in her old age she had to "take off her black attire" and dress up in a costume of which the Prussian newspaper said: "it was half unreal, half dragoonish!" Thus she presented herself—as a venerable androgyne and a widow-dragoon—to the officer corps, who were moved to tears, which one might have expected from Germans.

What would happen if the empress on her side had named him, her affectionate and crowned brother, the venerable headmistress of the Smolny Monastery? Would we see him appear at the assembly in décolleté with bare arms and riding breeches, or in the uniform of the former Kaiser-Nicolaus regiment, in a starched skirt with crinolines and... ornamental braid! Let him see for himself what it means to confuse the sexes.

This opened the eyes of the empress, and with every step in Europe she came more and more over to our side, and from an empress-colonel is becoming a citizen-empress. [. . .]

Having democratically spent some time with various Piedmontese officials and advisers to the authorities in Nice, our Orthodox Protestant went to see the pope. Pius IX recalled his youth, how he himself had served in the Guardia Nobile, so he put on his best cassock and, like a polite gentleman, assumed a dignified air and went off to visit her himself. No one knows anything about their pious tête-à-tête; maybe he asked the empress to convert Russia to Catholicism, and maybe he explained the benefit and advantage of his discovery of the immaculate conception![6]

We are most pleasantly surprised that in Rome, in this oldest of cities, the venerable invalid flutters about like a butterfly. We are, it is true, beginning to think that devotion and blind love dreamed up danger to the health of the imperial widow—after all, where is the proof? In Petersburg until the age of fifty she danced, got dressed, laced herself up, and had her hair curled. In Nice there were picnics, breakfast on yachts, music, pleasurable strolls—and I do not know what else. In Rome she went here and there, vanity of vanities: whether it was the same old illumination of St. Peter's or the lighting of fireworks, our Alexandra Fyodorovna was there. [. . .]

When Nicholas was in Rome, after leaving his comrade-in-arms and friend the Neapolitan king,[7] he inspected St. Peter's Basilica, found everything in order, and wrote on the cupola: "I was here on such-and-such a date and prayed for Mother Russia." Although it was not entirely appropriate and not at all good form for the head of the Eastern church to disturb God in someone else's quarters, evidently he prayed fervently, and not just about Mother Russia but also about the mother of his children, and God heard his royal prayer! [. . .]

Notes

Source: "Avgusteishie puteshestvenniki," *Kolokol,* l. 1, July 1, 1857; 13:13–18, 489–93.

1. Justus von Liebig was a German scientist interested in the soil, and Jacob Moleschott was a Dutch physiologist. The dowager empress Alexandra Fyodorovna spent the winter season of 1856–57 in Nice, renting three villas for her large entourage, which included many German nobles.

2. A symbol of liberty in ancient Rome, eighteenth- and nineteenth-century France, Ireland, and in the Americas.

3. Herzen is being ironic; S. S. Lanskoy quit a Decembrist group long before the uprising, and N. O. Sukhozanet was a member of the guards unit that mounted a defense against the Decembrists on Senate Square. The former was appointed minister of the interior in 1855 and the latter became minister of war the following year. The "Anglo-French assistance" was that by defeating the Russians in the Crimea, emancipation became a necessity for Alexander II.

4. On August 10, 1792, the French monarchy was overthrown, and on January 21, 1793, Louis XVI was executed. Alexander II ordered new uniforms for the military and dismissed several of his father's ministers. His mother left on a year-long trip to Europe in May 1856.

5. In place of the deceased Nicholas I.

6. In 1854, Pope Pius IX had announced the doctrine of Mary's immaculate conception.

7. The tsar visited Italy in 1845 and met with the king of the Two Sicilies, Ferdinand II.

⇥ 12 ⇤

The Bell, No. 2, August 1, 1857. A French translation of "Revolution in Russia" appeared in the Brussels newspaper *La Cloche* on October 1, 1862. As fundamental reform began to be discussed in his homeland, Herzen expressed a strong preference for a peaceful path forward over any kind of revolution, something he had already made clear in *From the Other Shore.* Nevertheless, he had no patience for reactionary forces, who threatened further delay and stagnation. Herzen knew relatively little about the new tsar, but was willing to place his hopes in anyone who was not Nicholas, as well as in the inevitable consequences for the country of the unsuccessfully fought Crimean War. For Russia, the time for change had come.

In the same issue, Herzen included the essay "Moscow and Petersburg" (1842), which he wrote in Novgorod during his second period of exile. Although his views had somewhat altered, he felt it would be wrong to censor himself. "I left the article as it was, through a sense of respect for the past." The satirical juxtaposition of the two capitals ends with feigned excitement over the railroad that is soon to join them. Herzen predicted that in the future, caviar would be cheaper in Petersburg, and Moscow would find out two days sooner which foreign periodicals had been banned (Gertsen, *Sobranie sochinenii,* 2:33–42).

REVOLUTION IN RUSSIA
[1857]

> Gentlemen, it is better that these changes
> came from above than from below.
> —Alexander II, a speech to the Moscow nobility

We are not only on the eve of great upheaval, we have already entered into it. Necessity and public opinion carried the government to a new phase of development, change, and progress. Society and the government came up against questions that suddenly acquired the rights of citizenship and became urgent. This excitation of thought, agitation, and renewed striving to solve the main tasks of governmental life, and to dismantle the historical forms through which it has functioned—is the essential soil of every fundamental period of upheaval.

But where are the signs that ordinarily precede revolutions? Everything in Russia is so quiet, and people look at the new government in such a beaten-down way and with such good nature, awaiting its assistance, that one is more likely to think that centuries will go by before Russia enters into a new life.

But what would be the purpose of these signs? In Russia everything has happened differently; it has only had one fundamental upheaval and that was achieved by one man—Peter I. Since 1789 we have been accustomed to see all upheavals proceeding by means of explosions and rebellions, every concession achieved by force, and every step forward come from battle—so that when there is talk of upheaval, we involuntarily look for the public square, barricades, blood, and the executioner's axe. Without doubt, an uprising and open struggle is one of the most powerful means of revolution, but it is hardly the only means.

[. . .] We are just people who are deeply convinced that the current governmental structures in Russia do not work, and we wholeheartedly prefer a path of peaceful human development to a bloody path, but with all that, we sincerely prefer the stormiest and most unbridled development to the stagnancy of a Nicholaevan status quo.

The sovereign wants changes and improvements; instead of a useless rebuff, he wishes to listen to the voice of reason in Russia, to people of progress and science, practical people who live with the common folk. They will not only be able to clearly understand and formulate what they want—better than the Nicholaevan burgraves—but, more than that, they will be able to understand for the people their desires and strivings. Instead of faint-heartedly cutting off their speech, the government itself should undertake the work of social reconstruction together with them, the development of new forms and new outlets for Russian life. We do not yet know what they are, nor does the government, but we are moving toward discovering them, and in that lies the remarkable interest that our future holds.

Peter I alone carried within himself that unforeseen, new Russia, which he brought about with harshness and threats against the will of the people, relying on autocratic power and personal strength. The current government does not have to resort to any kind of progressive terror. There is an entire milieu, mature in thought, ready to move with or against the government, in the name of the people and for their benefit. This circle may not be very large, but we absolutely do not accept that it is inferior in consciousness and development to any circle in the West. If it is unaccustomed to the consideration of social issues, then it is freer of everything traditional, and is newer, simpler, and more youthful than Western society. It has also lived through the suffering, failures, and trials of European life, but survived by means of its education, ideas, and heart, not having exhausted all its strength, but carrying in its memory the dreadful lesson of recent events. Like a youth who has been defeated by some great unhappiness that took place before his eyes, it quickly matures and gazes with a grown-up look at life through this sad example.

But for this common task the government has to step over the palisades and fences of the table of ranks that prevent it from seeing and heeding this grown-up speech, which is timidly and half surreptitiously expressed in literature and educated circles.

Can the thought of moving forward an entire part of the world to redeem three gloomy decades, to unite the two Russias between whom Peter's razor has passed[1]—a matter of purification, emancipation, and development, touching along the way fearful and colossal questions about landowner-ship, labor and its reward, the commune and the proletariat, before whom all European governments tremble—*is it possible* that this huge historic mission, coming of its own accord, will flatter Alexander II less than the empty and solitary height of absolute imperial power, limited by bribes, relying on bayonets, serfdom, liquor taxes, the secret police, ignorance, and beatings, ruling amidst general silence and suppressed groans?

We do not think so. And even if it were so, it is hardly possible to have a continuation of the Nicholaevan reign. We are certain that this merciless, backward-dragging despotism has run its course in Russia. The govern-ment itself senses this, but feels new and awkward in the world of reform, improvement, and the human word; it is shy and slow-moving, not believ-ing in its strength and confused by the difficulty and complexity of the task. This deadening notion of its own weakness, that we are not up to the task, exists among us, and, unfortunately, not just in the government but in us as well.

This is not modesty, but the beginning of despair and depression; for so long we were cowed and downtrodden, so accustomed to blush in the presence of other nations and to consider all the filth of Russian life to be irreparable—from bribes to birch rods—that we really almost lost faith in ourselves. This unfortunate feeling surely must pass. Goethe said quite correctly:

> To lose one's courage is to lose everything,
> It would be better not to have been born.[2]

Of course, the last three decades were hard, and our whole historical development followed a difficult and strange path, but didn't this time leave us pledges for the future? Did we really come to a stop, exhausted, did Rus split up into parts or fall under foreign dominion? No, we stand whole and unharmed, full of strength, unified in the face of a new path.

We are frightened by the backward and terrible condition of the people, its habit of lawlessness, and the poverty that is crushing it. All of this unarguably makes—and will make—development difficult, but, in contrast to Bürger's ballad,[3] we say: *the living stride fast,* and the pace of the popular masses, when they begin to move, will be very great. We do not need to lead them toward the new life, just to remove what is crushing their own traditional ways. [. . .]

For 150 years we have been living in the ruins of the old; nothing whole has remained and there is nothing to regret. We have an imperial dictatorship and rural life, and between them every sort of institution, attempt, initiative, and idea, coming more and more to life, not tied to any caste or to any existing order. Since Peter I we have been in a state of restructuring, looking for new forms, imitating, making copies, and a year later we try something newer. It is enough to change ministers for state serfs to suddenly become personal serfs of the imperial family or vice versa. What does not change is the foundation, the soil, i.e., there is still the village with its physiological character, its pre-governmental state and condition, a premise whose syllogism lies in the future rather than as a continuation of the Muscovite kingdom; it also existed at that time, that is all we can say. It would be very difficult to change it, and it is unnecessary; quite the contrary, on it will be built the Rus of the future!

Of course, it is not easy to go from military despotism and German bureaucracy to a simpler and more popular governmental structure. But where are the insurmountable obstacles? To be sure, it is difficult to see the truth if some are not permitted to speak it and others are interested in keeping it hidden. The sovereign sees nothing from behind the beams and posts of the chancellery and the bureaucracy and the dust raised by soldiers on maneuvers; that is why the government, as it enters into the era of reform, is feeling its way along, desiring it and not desiring it, and those who might give advice are floundering like a fish on ice, with no voice.

In order to continue Peter's work, the government must openly renounce the Petersburg period as Peter himself renounced Muscovy. These artificial contrivances of imperial administration have grown old. Having so much power and, on the one hand, leaning on the common folk, while, on the other, on all thinking and educated people in Russia, the current government could perform miracles without the slightest danger to itself.

No monarch in Europe has been in the position of Alexander II, but from him to whom much is given, much is demanded!...

June 15, 1857

Notes

Source: "Revoliutsiia v Rossii," *Kolokol*, l. 2, August 1, 1857; 13:21–29, 496–99.

The speech quoted in the opening epigraph was delivered on March 30 (April 11), 1856; it was not published but news of it spread quickly. In comparing the emancipation manifesto and the original address, Herzen later said that "the manifesto is unusually stupid, but the speech is unusually wise—they clearly scared themselves" (Gertsen, *Sobranie sochinenii*, 25:340).

1. Peter allowed the peasants and clergy to keep their beards, but insisted that the gentry shave. Old Believers had to pay a beard tax.

2. From the verse cycle "Maxims."

3. Herzen is referring to the ballad "Lenore" by Gottfried August Bürger (1748–1794).

☩ 13 ☩

The Bell, No. 6, December 1, 1857. The problem of corporal punishment was one that Herzen raised in a number of essays, and it was a central issue for many advocates of reform in Russia. (See Doc. 29.) In chapter 15 of *Past and Thoughts*, Herzen recalled what he learned in exile about the government's treatment of peasants who objected to absurd orders and corrupt behavior by officials sent from Petersburg. During the inquiry, everything was done in the usual Russian way. "The peasants were flogged during the examination, flogged as a punishment, flogged as an example, flogged to extort money, and a whole crowd of them sent to Siberia."

To Flog or Not to Flog the Peasant?
[1857]

To flog or not to flog the peasant? That is the question!—Of course one must flog him, and very painfully. Without a birch rod how can we convince a man that he must work for the master six days a week, with only the remaining time for himself? How can he be convinced that when the master takes it into his head, the peasant has to drag himself to the town with hay and firewood, and sometimes to hand over his son for the front hall and his daughter for the bedroom... Any doubts about the right to flog is by itself an infringement on gentry rights, on the inviolability of property as recognized by the law. And, in essence, why not flog the peasant if it is allowed, if the peasant tolerates it, the church blesses it, and the government takes the peasant by the collar and whips him?

Do we really have such heavenly souls if we think that an entire caste of people, who share with the executioner the right of corporal punishment, and, having the advantage of whipping according to their own desires and for their own profit—and people they know, not strangers—should such a caste for reasons of humanity and heartfelt emotion throw away the rod? Enough nonsense.

A few months back a ship's captain, on the journey from New York to England, flogged a boy, not a rare occasion, it seems, for us. When the ship reached England, the sailors complained. The captain was brought to court and then hung by the seashore. That is how to break the habit of misusing the rod!

A second instance. Three years ago some sort of officer quarreled in London with a cab driver; one word followed another and the officer struck the cabbie; the offended driver pulled out his whip and hit the officer across the face. The officer went to the police. The judge said: "For goodness sake, you are the one who should be punished, not the cabbie, you are guilty all around and yet you lodge a complaint. Go back to your quarters." That is how to break someone of the habit of misusing his fists.

This is how a person can be taught both one and the other lesson. Who does not know the story (blushing, we read various extracts in the *Times*) about an aide-de-camp (Elston-Sumarokov) who was sent to Nizhegorodskaia province for an investigation of indignant peasants? The matter is in itself remarkable. A certain landowner's serfs (I believe it was Rakhmanov) proposed paying for themselves; the owner took the money, i.e., stole it, and sold the peasants to someone else instead of giving them their freedom. The serfs of course refused to obey the new landowner. Is this a difficult matter to sort out? However, with us the courts count for nothing, and what are needed are a commission, aides-de-camp, aiguillettes, a military party, and birch rods. Elston-Sumarokov was sent with birch rods. The peasants fell to their knees (a rebellion on one's knees!). He asked them: "To whom do you belong?" The serfs mentioned the name of the former owner, while Sumarokov said the name of the new owner (Pashkov, it seems, or the other way around) and ordered that all the peasants should be flogged without distinction. The serfs gave in. Then the aide-de-camp got so worked up that he gave instructions to the provincial authorities that one section of the kneeling, rebellious peasants be sent to Siberia, another to punishment battalions, and the third group were to be flogged again. The provincial authorities would have been happy to fulfill this order but were not bold enough to take on such a clear violation of positive law and turned to the senate. In return for such an understanding of justice and such knowledge of the laws Elston-Sumarokov was made vice-director of one of the departments in the War Ministry.

And you are judging whether to flog or not to flog a peasant? Whip him, brothers, whip him in peace! And when you get tired, the tsar will send an aide-de-camp to help!!!

Some sort of *landowner* in the *Agricultural Newspaper* has rightly protested the impertinent objections to birch rods, and sensibly observed that "for insignificant misdeeds a punishment of *a few* blows of the rod (2, 20, 200, 2,000?) does not kill a man either morally or physically (sometimes, it is true, people die, but this is morally useful for an Orthodox believer, and the dead can feel no pain!). The landowner's power is that of a parent over his children, and according to our Orthodox beliefs children accept punishment from their parents without complaint. Punishment by the rod is not going to be replaced by any foreign notions, because *the birch rod* in the hands of a well-meaning and kind landowner is a genuine blessing for the serfs!" [. . .]

Notes

Source: "Sech' ili ne sech' muzhika?" *Kolokol,* l. 6, December 1, 1857; 13:105–7, 527–28.

⇘ 14 ⇙

The Bell, No. 8, February 1, 1858. This is Herzen's answer to a letter that—in the end—was never published, but which raised issues that Herzen felt obliged to address. It is one of Herzen's most significant statements on laughter, and on how he would treat, in his own manner, facts about the arbitrary behavior of Russian serf owners and bureaucrats, amidst concerns that he was turning liberal observations into radical propaganda.

Mikhail Bakhtin included some of Herzen's observations on laughter in *Rabelais and His World*.

———

A LETTER CRITICIZING *THE BELL*
[1858]

We recently received a letter severely criticizing *The Bell*.

This letter is full of such warm affection *for the cause* and a desire that our publications may help it, that we can only sincerely thank our anonymous critic and make use of that portion of his advice with which our conscience is in agreement.

We regret that the letter says that it must not be published, because we would have liked to acquaint our readers with it.

We will allow ourselves one observation. The author of this letter can see for himself how from the first issue of *The Bell* up to the most recent one we have fervently asked everyone sending us news to check it out carefully. What means of verification do we have? If on our pages, as in all periodicals, mistakes get past us, we are prepared to correct them—but we cannot always prevent them.

In the sixth issue it was said that Moscow chief of police *Bering* was still in place, but he has in fact retired. *Le Nord,* which carries semiofficial correspondence, in writing about the end of the student disturbances in Moscow, mentioned only the retirement of a policeman. After that we received a letter that directed our attention to the fact that "Zakrevsky had stood up for Bering." Then, days later, we saw that Bering had been replaced by Kropotkin.[1] We must confess our mistake, thank the sovereign, and advise Zakrevsky to surprise us in the same nice way.

As for humor, we are not entirely in agreement with our critic. Laughter is one of the most powerful weapons against something that is obsolete but is still propped up by God knows what, like an important ruin which prevents new growth and frightens the weak. I repeat what I said previously: "What a man cannot laugh about without falling into blasphemy or fearing the pangs of conscience is a fetish, and he is in its thrall, afraid to let it get mixed up with ordinary objects."[2]

Laughter is no joking matter, and we will not give it up. In the ancient world they laughed heartily on Olympus and on earth while listening to Aristophanes and his comedies, and they laughed out loud all the way up to Lucian. After the fourth century, humankind stopped laughing—they wept, and heavy chains fell on the mind amidst the groans and pangs of conscience. As soon as the fever of fanaticism began to abate, people again began to laugh. It would be extraordinarily interesting to write the history of laughter. No one laughs in church, at court, on parade, before the head of their department, a police officer, or a German boss. House serfs have no right to smile in the presence of their masters. Only equals can laugh amongst themselves.

If inferiors were permitted to laugh in front of their superiors and if they could not hold back their laughter then you can forget about respect for rank. To cause men to smile at the god Apis is to deprive him of his holy status and turn him into a common bull. Take the cassock off the monk, the uniform off the hussar, the ashes off the chimney sweep and they will no longer frighten children or adults. Laughter is a leveler, and people don't want that, afraid of being judged according to their individual merits. Aristocrats have always thought that way, and the wife of the *count's factotum* Figaro, complaining in *The Guilty Mother*[3] about the bitter results of the year 1789, says that now everyone has become *like everyone else,* like the whole world!

In general the Russian character shows an Asian tendency to a mannered servility on the one hand, and a haughty conceit on the other. [. . .]

And why are we so easily offended by a joke, but so strong when we are being scolded from above? Belinsky wondered about that fifteen years ago. Leaf through London's *Punch* and look at its political cartoons, in which the queen's consort is spared least of all. And what do Victoria and Albert do about this? They look at *Punch* and laugh with everyone else. That is the best proof of England's maturity. [. . .]

Notes

Source: "O pis'me, kritikuiushchem *Kolokol,*" *Kolokol,* l. 8, February 1, 1858; 13:189–91, 537–38.

1. Major-General Alexander Timashev-Bering was Moscow chief of police from 1854 to 1857. Count Arseny A. Zakrevsky was the governor-general of Moscow from 1848 to 1859. Prince Alexey I. Kropotkin was Moscow chief of police from 1858 to 1860.

2. Herzen provides the source: *Letters from France and Italy* by Iskander.

3. The third play in the Beaumarchais trilogy about Figaro.

> → 15 ←

The Bell, No. 9, February 15, 1858. Herzen's lead article for this issue was called "Three Years Later (February 18, 1858)," in which he recalls his 1855 letter to the new tsar (Doc. 5). The work of emancipation had begun, and nothing must stop its progress. State power (*vlast'*) and public opinion were now lined up against the opponents of freedom, so they labored in vain and would be punished by publicity. However, the openness was not without its limits; in 1858, the Russian government took measures to try to paralyze the work of the Free Russian Press, and the Kingdom of Poland was instructed to more effectively halt the transit of revolutionary Russian publications. After Russian agents in Berlin found many booksellers offering Herzen's works, the Prussian government was contacted about ending this practice, and authorities there issued an order forbidding the sale of *The Bell* in Prussia; in a letter Herzen referred to this as an "arrest of *The Bell*." Booksellers were also barred from placing other publications by the author on display in store windows. Foreign Minister Gorchakov ordered a Russian official to approach the government of Saxony, whose own foreign minister asked for translations of some of these works, after which the order forbidding their sale was issued.

Lackeys and Germans Refuse Permission
[1858]

[. . .] By an order issued January 29, *The Bell*, *The Polestar*, and *Voices from Russia* have been banned in Saxony. Prussia established a cordon sanitaire against us some time ago. They say that the Prince of Lippe-Valdek-Sundershausen and Meiningen[1] wishes to take active and energetic measures against us—if that is true, we are lost! [. . .]

They will not stop either the printing or the sale of Russian books with these measures, which serve as a free advertisement for us and give our publications international significance.

Let's explain this once and for all. For us, the cause of Russian propaganda is not a whim, a means of entertainment, or a source of income—it is our life's cause, our religion, a piece of our heart, and our service to the Russian people.

We labored without losing hope when there was no expectation of success. Now, when the Russian minister of foreign affairs and the German minister of the interior acknowledge our power and influence, could we possibly stop?

Be assured that we will not. With hand on heart we swear before all Russia to continue our work until the last heartbeat. It will not cease even with our death. We are not alone, and we will bequeath our printing press to the next generation who will take it up with new strength and new ideas.

The only thing that could stop us is the *elimination* of censorship in Russia, not the introduction of Russian censorship in German lands.

Do not think that these measures were taken *against* us; to an equal and much greater extent they were taken against the sovereign. The bureaucratic and military Masonic orders, having conquered the fourteen-step ladder that leads to the front hall of the palace, are trying to twist *The Bell*'s clapper with German obstacles so that its sound does not reach the Winter Palace.

The table of ranks is not angered at our theories since we are not professing any at present; we have taken as our motto:

Freedom for the serfs from landowners;

Freedom of the word from censorship;

Freedom for everyone from corporal punishment.

Is this really anarchy, sedition, robbery, rebellion, arson, Sodom and Gomorrah?

They are angry that we have begun to *point out individuals*. This prevents the conspirators from deceiving the sovereign and robbing the people.

Wishing to bring without fail information to the sovereign about measures that hide the truth from him, *for the first time* we are sending *The Bell* in a sealed package to him personally.

Will it reach him or not?... It's hard to make a bet on this! Is the sovereign under the watchful eye of the police or not? Do they open his mail or not?

We'll see!

Note

Source: "Lakei i nemtsy ne dopuskaiut," *Kolokol,* l. 9, February 15, 1858; 13:198–99, 541.

1. Herzen refers ironically to rulers of the tiny German principalities of Lippe, Valdek, Schwartzberg-Sundershausen, and Saksen-Meiningen.

⇥ 16 ⇤

The Bell, No. 12, April 1, 1858. Censorship drove Herzen abroad in 1847, and the rise and fall of restrictions on free speech and on freedom of the press in Russia were of enduring interest to him.

CENSORSHIP IS ON THE RISE
[1858]

Instead of abolishing the censorship, the censorship has been doubled and made more complex.[1] Formerly the censoring was done by censors, priests, and the secret police; now all departments will act as censors, and every ministry will appoint its own eunuch to the literary seraglio, this at a time when a relaxation of censorship was expected. Indeed, the new project was

presented to the committee of ministers, but Panin and, after him, everyone except Grand Prince Konstantin Nikolaevich unanimously, and with
noble indignation, rejected any change. In truth, we are beginning to think
that all this is being done for the benefit of *The Bell* and *The Polestar*. To
enforce silence after having permitted a small degree of conversation is
difficult and awkward. Russian literature will move to London. Along with
English freedom and our warm greeting, we are preparing the best paper
and excellent ink.

Note

Source: "Tsenzura usilivaetsia," *Kolokol*, l. 12, April 1, 1858; 13:255, 551–52.

1. A decree was issued January 25, 1858, supplementing the existing censorship with
officials from a number of ministries, including the imperial court, army, navy, interior, finance, justice, communications, and the general staff. This was in answer to the
proposal presented to the ministers by Prince P. A. Vyazemsky nine days earlier recom-
mending a new censorship statute, which was vigorously opposed by the ministers of
justice, finance, and communications (V. N. Panin, P. F. Brok, and K. V. Chevkin).

⇢ 17 ⇠

The Bell, No. 16, June 1, 1858. A continuation of the theme of the Russian government's
attempt, with the help of its conservative allies, to silence Herzen's publications.

———

LOGOPHOBIA
[1858]

The other day the *Kölnischer Zeitung* announced a new ban on *The Bell* in
Prussia. In Saxony all our periodicals are banned. In Naples the embassy
secretary is frightening the booksellers; commercial travelers of the Third
Department in the uniforms of adjutant generals, and councilors of state
who imagine themselves privy councilors, are floating all around the corrupted parts of Europe, nosing about the shops, making discoveries and
denunciations, using German ministers as police detectives and truffle
spotters and German princelings as bulldogs in pursuit of *The Polestar* and
The Bell. What is all this about? What is the source of this crude impatience?
It would be a pity if it comes from the sovereign: it is so unworthy of him.
It would be a pity if it comes from Gorchakov:[1] they tell us that he is a well-
intentioned person, and we were prepared to believe this!

Or are these the pranks of people in "supporting roles," volunteer zealots and Nicholaevan gendarmes who are left without anything to do?

Can it be that every power, even one that wishes to do good, is fated to have no other means of hearing the truth than when it is wrapped in completely servile phrases, and sweetened with vulgar flattery? The language of a free man grates upon ears grown soft with the rhetoric of Byzantine eunuchs in guards uniform, old stewards in the livery of their late master.[2] [. . .]

Notes

Source: "Slovoboiazn'," *Kolokol*, l. 16, June 1, 1858; 13:281–82, 563.

1. Prince Alexander Mikhailovich Gorchakov (1798–1883) was appointed minister of foreign affairs in 1856.

2. Herzen then quotes passages from "Lackeys and Germans Refuse Permission" about those who would prevent the sound of *The Bell* from reaching the Winter Palace.

⇥ 18 ⇤

The Bell, No. 18, July 1, 1858. Herzen increasingly doubts the expediency of appealing to the authorities, although he still hopes that the tsar will reach out to the people. The image of the fairy-tale hero at the crossroads, faced with difficult choices with serious repercussions, will reappear in *The Bell*, most notably in one of the final issues (Doc. 100). Natan Eidelman saw in this article Herzen's disillusionment with the government's program in a "concentrated" form; he also analyzes it for the reuse of phrases and arguments from letters to or from the author, evidently a common practice of Herzen in his journalism (Eidel'man, *Svobodnoe slovo*, 238). The *Bell* began to address a broader spectrum of readers than just the upper-class intelligentsia, who were the primary focus of early publications by the Free Russian Press. One of the final items in this issue was Herzen's announcement that the Holy Father had bowed to pressure from the Russian government and banned the sale of all Russian publications from London in his domain. Herzen was not surprised, since "inquisition is a papal activity," and he half expected to hear that anathema had been pronounced on *The Bell* and its pages consigned to the flames.

JULY 1, 1858
[1858]

A year ago the first issue of *The Bell* appeared. We stop for a moment and glance back at the path we have traveled... and feel sadness and heaviness in our hearts.

Meanwhile, in the course of this year one of our most ardent hopes has been realized; one of the greatest revolutions in Russia has begun, the one that we have predicted, craved, and called for since childhood—the liberation of the serfs has begun.

But we don't feel any better, and this year we almost took a step backward.

The reason is obvious, and we will state it directly and steadfastly: *Alexander II has not justified the hopes that Russia had at his coronation.* Last June he still stood, like the hero of our fairy tales, at the crossroads—whether he would turn to the right or to the left no one knew. It seemed that he would without fail follow the path of development, liberation, construction... taking one step, and then another—but suddenly he thought better of it and turned

From the left to the right.[1]

Maybe there is still time... but he is being hurried along by the palace coachmen, who are taking advantage of the fact that he does not know the road. And our *Bell* is ringing out to him that he has gone astray, ringing out Russia's distress and the danger that he faces.

But that is the problem—the powerful people of this world do not know how to either listen or remember. History lies before them, but it is not for them that it tells of the bitter experience of nations and of posterity's harsh judgment of tsars.

Not to make use of the remarkable position in which events in Europe and the previous reign left Alexander II is to such a degree absurd that it is difficult to find room in one's head for it.

Having the possibility of choosing one of two roles—Peter I or Pius IX— to choose Pius IX is the ultimate example of Christian meekness.

"But," they will tell us, "Peter I was a genius—geniuses aren't born every century, and not every tsar who wants to be Peter I can succeed." The thing is, to be Russia's Peter in our time one does not have to be a genius; it would be sufficient to love Russia, to respect and understand the human dignity in a Russian man, and to listen closely to his thoughts and his aspirations. A genius might do great harm, as Peter did; he would inject his own will instead of developing the new growth that has appeared, when one just has to avoid weeding it out, trampling it, or constraining it, removing any obstacles and allowing it to grow on its own. Peter I had to create and destroy—in one hand he had a spade, and in the other an axe. He made a clearing in the wilderness, and, of course, cut down the good along with the bad. But we have ceased to love terror, no matter what kind and for what purpose.

Terror is no more necessary in our time than genius. The active, thinking part of Russia is moving ahead rapidly, knowing what it wants and revealing it in the form of public opinion. At the end of the last reign, in spite of the danger and persecution, the thoughts fermenting in people's minds were so strong that they created an underground literature in manuscripts, which were passed from hand to hand. Subsequently, the same thought process led to expressions of delight with all the fine initiatives of the new government. Half of Peter's work—the most difficult half—is now being done by a chorus. Around Peter, everything was silent; waking earlier than everyone else, he had to rouse others, make guesses, and be inventive. Now many have woken up and gone ahead, waiting to be called to give advice. Except for a very few, everyone opposed Peter's reforms; now the entire nation, except for the decayed part of the gentry and old men who have lost their faculties, is ready to further the reforms of Alexander II. As for the sham service oligarchy, all the parvenus from the barracks and the inkwells, the mental hospitals and prison battalions of Nicholaevan students—they have no opinion. Today they beat the serfs who want to be free, and tomorrow they will shoot the gentry who do not want to free them.

However, it could be that the reforms that Alexander II has talked about in his speeches, manifestoes, decrees, orders, and official journals do not coincide with the wishes of thinking Russia, thoughts which have manifested themselves in literature and public opinion.

Not at all—they are exactly the same.

This is the boundless, heart-rending irony and tragicomedy of our situation. A government is never so powerful as when it is in agreement with public opinion. [. . .]

The tsar tries very hard to extend a hand to the people, and the people try very hard to take hold of it but they can't get past Panin and company.[2] It's like a scene out of Aristophanes! Just when the sovereign is completely ready, one of those gray-haired children—Orlov[3] or Zakrevsky—stands on tiptoe and touches his extended hand, shouting: "Your majesty, for God's sake! They will bite off your finger!"

Let them just try! The sovereign was in the Caucasus during the troubles there and he loves bear hunting.[4] What are Circassians and bears to him? Doesn't he daily face dangers from these pillars of the fatherland, who shield him from Russia and create around him a pleasant garland of old men, who, if needed, by moving slightly can form themselves into a noose?

And K. I. Arseniev[5] taught Alexander Nikolaevich the *criminal affair* that is Russian history from Peter I to Alexander I.

We have nothing to hide, as we are always saying. Let every reader, with hand on heart, say where in *The Bell* are to be found impossible demands, political utopias, or calls for rebellion?

The existence of *The Bell* marks a boundary and a turning point. With the promulgation of the rescript on the liberation of the serfs our path had to change, not in its essence but in its type of activity.[6] We sacrificed in part our polemics and restricted even more the scope of our questions. We came closer to the government because the government came closer to us. We are concerned with the form of government—we've seen them all in action and none of them will do if they are reactionary, and all of them are suitable if they are contemporary and progressive. We sincerely and frankly believed that Alexander II would replace the bloody era of revolution and would serve as a peaceful and mild transition from antiquated despotism to a humanely free state of Russia.

We may have been mistaken in this, but thinking as we did, for the six months while the rescript was in the works we consistently and almost exclusively occupied ourselves with its realization.[7]

What did we demand, and what did we write about?

We demanded that the gentry not snatch emancipation away from the serfs, and that the wish—expressed timidly and with an upper-class lisp by the government—concerning estates and land not be interpreted to the benefit of the landowners. Were we correct? The proof can be found in the eloquent words of Bezobrazov and Blank, in the central committee, in the increased censorship, gentry opposition, and the *forced resettlement* of serfs on poor land.[8]

Besides, we said that the emancipation of the serfs was not sufficient, that alongside the landowner was a second scourge of the Russian people— the government official, that is, the police and the courts. We said that until the Japanese-style table of ranks fell—while we still had an inquisitorial court behind closed doors along with official secrecy, and while the police admonish people with birch rods and lash them without *a trial*—until that time the liberation of the serfs would not bring genuine benefit.

It could be that the sovereign is frightened that the entire civil service— those fraudulent handlers of official papers—do not share this opinion, but if Panin affirmed or favorably received his proposal, then maybe we would have defenders for the accused and jurors, and the court would operate in the light of day.

The sovereign wished to make changes, but he is in the dark and does not know where to begin; everyone deceives him, from the lowest clerk to the chancellor, and the voices of people outside government do not reach him. The public status of those who are not in service or who have not served long enough is such that only the gentry might be allowed to dance in the tsar's presence at a ball, and the merchants might on some sad or happy occasion greet him with bread and salt on a golden platter.

This leads logically to our third demand—*openness.*

Isn't it absurd that they put up the dam themselves, bar access to it, and then are surprised there's no water? Lift the censor's floodgate and then you will find out what the people think, what is hurting, pressing, tormenting, and ruining them... maybe all sorts of rubbish will at first float to the surface—what does it matter as long as the water carries away all those half-dead Vladimir cats and Andreevsky hares.

With openness, there can be publicity about legal cases that will throw a terrifying light on the subterranean misdeeds of the police and the courts, like that of our articles about Sechinsky, the Kochubey trial, Vrede, Elston-Sumarokov, Governor Novosiltsev, and others.[9]

If one removes the censorship restrictions, then the *Third Department* can be closed down; writers will denounce themselves, and finally this nest of spies will be destroyed in Russia. [. . .]

Have we demanded anything else?

Whatever our theoretical opinions, however "incorrigible" we were about them, we did not express them, we expunged them willingly while the massive government coach plodded its way forward, but when it began to go backward, crushing legs under its heavy wheels, then we proceeded along a different path.

This is the third phase into which *The Bell* has entered.

We established a motto—I summon the living! Where are the live people in Russia? It seemed that there were live ones even at court and we addressed our words to them—we do not regret that. No matter what happens, the sovereign, having begun the process of liberating the serfs, has earned a great name in history and our gratitude is unchanged. But we have nothing to say to him. *The live ones* are those people of thought scattered all over Russia, good people of all castes, men and women, students and officers, who blush and weep when they think about serfdom, the arbitrariness in the courts, and the willfulness of the police; they are the people who ardently wish for openness and who read us with sympathy.

The Bell is their organ and their voice; on the barren, stony heights there is no one to listen to it, but in the valleys its pure sound rings out all the more powerfully.

Notes

Source: "1 iulia 1858," *Kolokol*, l. 18, July 1, 1858; 13:293–98, 569–70.

1. From a poem called "The Old Barrel Organ (Remembering the Unforgettable One)" ("Staraia Sharmanka. K vospominaniem o Nezabvennom"), probably by V. R. Zotov, which circulated in Petersburg and Moscow, and was published in *The Bell* on November 1, 1857. The "Unforgettable One" is the late tsar, Nicholas I.

2. Count Viktor N. Panin (1801–1874), minister of justice from 1841 to 1862.

3. Prince Alexey F. Orlov (1786–1861), head of the Third Department from 1844 to 1856, from 1856 chair of the State Council and Committee of Ministers, and from 1857 chair of the Secret and then Main Committee to examine the question of serfdom.

4. While still heir to the throne, Alexander II traveled to the Caucasus and visited military units actively engaged in combat, for which he was awarded the Order of St. George, fourth degree.

5. Konstantin I. Arseniev (1789–1865) was a statistician, historian, and geographer, who tutored the future tsar from 1828 to 1835.

6. In November 1857, the tsar instructed Vladimir I. Nazimov (governor of Vilna, Kovno, and Grodno) to allow local gentry to form committees to discuss how the serfs might be freed; copies of the rescript were sent to all the other governors and it was published. The "Secret Committee" Alexander set up in January 1857 to examine the emancipation question was renamed the Main Committee early the following year.

7. Herzen: "There are many who reproach *The Bell,* among them the Prussian *Kreuz-Zeitung,* with a disrespectful tone and familiar air toward people who, although they stand in the way of any improvement and are major scoundrels, still belong to the highest ranks. [. . .] In the ringing of our *Bell* there is a howl that arises from the jail cells, barracks, and stables, from the landowners' fields and the censor's slaughterhouse—*The Bell* definitely belongs to bad society, which is why it lacks the clerk's manners and the secretary's courtesy."

8. Grigory B. Blank (1811–1889), a Tambov landowner, strongly supported serfdom. Nikolay A. Bezobrazov (1816–1867), leader of the St. Petersburg gentry, wrote brochures about gentry rights.

9. Herzen refers to articles published in *The Bell* in 1857 and 1858, exposing crimes against serfs and others, and the absence of punishment for their tormenters.

⇥ 19 ⇤

The Bell, No. 27, November 1, 1858. While this public letter to the empress caused a stir, it was not without precedent. In 1826, poet Vasily Zhukovsky wrote to Maria Alexandrovna's mother-in-law, Empress Alexandra Fyodorovna, whom he had earlier tutored in Russian. Zhukovsky believed that then eight-year-old Alexander Nikolaevich should receive more than just a military education, because Russia needed enlightenment and new laws (Wortman, *Development of Russian Legal Consciousness,* 138–39). In his memoirs, Herzen claimed that Maria Alexandrovna wept when she read this open letter about the education of her children. Anna Tyutcheva, lady-in-waiting to the empress (and future wife of the Slavophile journalist Ivan Aksakov) wrote in her diary that the scoundrel Herzen was right, and not for the first time; Tyutcheva firmly believed that the empress understood better than anyone else the weaknesses in the education arranged for her sons (*Let* 2:455–56). The letter was well received by many close to the court for the intelligent and polite tone it adopted (*Let* 2:458), although at least one historian of Russia later found the entire idea of writing to the empress on such a subject "ridiculous" (Ulam, *Ideologies and Illusions,* 23). At the end of this issue of *The Bell,* Herzen invited the tsar to send him any royal speeches—like the one made to the Moscow nobility—that could not be published in Russia.

In *Scenarios of Power*, Richard Wortman described Nikolay Alexandrovich's tutor, August Theodore Grimm (1805–1878), as a man "whose pedagogy created a scandal that quickly went beyond the bounds of the court and brought the heir's education into debates on Russia's destiny." Wortman went on to say that "Herzen's letter reached its mark. Within a month it was circulating in the court." In 1859, Count Sergey Stroganov was chosen to supervise the heir; since the universities were undesirable centers of anti-monarchist politics, he invited respected scholars to read lectures at the palace (Wortman, *Scenarios of Power*, 2:95–99). Nikolay Alexandrovich, fifteen years old when the letter below was written, grew into a well-educated and promising young man, but tragically died from meningitis in 1865, which prompted Herzen to write another letter to the emperor (Doc. 68). The next in line, Alexander Alexandrovich, to whose education little attention had been paid, assumed the role of heir, and in 1881 succeeded his father as tsar.

A LETTER TO THE EMPRESS MARIA ALEXANDROVNA
[1858]

Your Highness,

We lack a present, and therefore it is not surprising that we are particularly concerned with the future of our country. The first dawns after a grim and prolonged winter have paled, having barely commenced... and we have grown poorer than we were before, without the hatred that we have lost and the indignation which has softened. We have given ourselves up to the spring breezes, and exposed our long-hardened hearts to feelings unknown since childhood... but we were not fated to see the fulfillment of these or other dreams... People and tsars in our transitional age are left with appeals and placards. To the next generation, *perhaps,* will belong action and drama.

We do not envy them. Our activity is coming to an end ... soon we will pass away, exhausted—but not defeated—by our thirty-year struggle. Let the new generation that comes to replenish our ranks find a better use for their strength. And you, Highness, can be in the forefront of this.

Unfortunately, the fate of autocratic monarchies depends to a great extent on the personality of the tsar. It was not for nothing that Peter I sacrificed dynastic interests and the life of his own son to his reforms.[1] Alexander I, who said of himself "Je ne suis qu'un heureux hazard," has passed into history.[2] It is in this game of chance that you can increase the possibility of winning in the near future, for the good of Russia.

Until now, the upbringing of the heir has been in your hands, but in a year or two it will slip out of them.

Think of this... when you are alone—when the noise of the court settles down, when all that unnecessary whirlwind of receptions, empty speeches, and empty responses abates, when all those Andreevsky and Vladimirsky stars *take a seat* and you—a woman and a mother—are left alone with your conscience... Think then about your great responsibility, and the great duty that lies with you.

It is said that you are intelligent, and that not for nothing has the current trend in ideas penetrated the double window-frames of the Winter Palace. It is said that you desire the liberation of the serfs. That means a great deal.

You love Russia—it could not be otherwise. How could you not love the country that, surrounding you with all possible blessings, has placed on you the imperial mantle? And that is not all; another link has been forged between you and the people. The crown which fell on your head during a gloomy year of war and internal desolation constituted for the people an exodus to a new life. With childlike faith they greeted the new reign. With the sovereign you shared those outbursts of popular delight that had not been heard in Russia since Alexander I, wearied by his triumph, returned in 1815 to a burnt-out Moscow. How could you not love Russia! In this country pulses beat strongly; in its very disorder and awkward movements one senses youthful strength, one senses that in this cradle and in these tightly bound swaddling-clothes our future history is straightening out its limbs. To take part in the growth and fate of such a people is a great and tremendous matter.

Your maternal heart long ago showed you what you can accomplish, and how you can show your gratitude to the people. You tried to save your son, the future tsar, from the worst kind of education for grand dukes, that is, a military education, surrounded by military discipline and German clientism. All Russia rejoiced upon hearing that you had summoned people with a higher *civilian* education. Many even thought that they would see your son on the benches of Moscow University, that Sevastopol of research and education, which religiously and at great sacrifice held its banner of truth and thought aloft during thirty years of persecution. And they would see him there without a group of general aides-de-camp, without an escort of both secret and regular police—as one sees the son of Queen Victoria in university halls. We blessed you from afar... But this could not have been pleasing to the *Black Cabinet*[3]—and what surprise can there be in that? Prior to this, weren't you acquainted with these people, who, like logs, hinder all progress, openness, court reform, and stand in the way of the liberation of the serfs? How could they look on with indifference as your son received a humane education? It was bad enough that La Harpe[4] nearly spoiled Alexander I. But why did you so quickly change your mind and hesitate on the very first step? Why, in a matter of such importance, did you allow behind-the-scenes intrigue in the torture chambers of the Third Department to force out of your son's classroom people upon whom Russia—and you yourself—looked with confidence, and allow in their place an undistinguished German pedant? [5][. . .]

Let us see what *von* Grimm is like. I am leafing through his *Wanderungen nad Südosten*.[6] This is what he said in the dedication to Konstantin Nikolaevich: "But such delightful memories are clouded by the very sad thought that the great man, under whose patronage and blessing we traveled, is no more amongst us—that great emperor whom you call father, in whom Russia found its pride and glory, and whom a Europe engulfed in strife saw as an unshakable polestar." [. . .]

Your poor son! If he were someone else, we would not care about him; we are aware that most of our aristocratic children are educated very badly. But the fate of Russia is bound up with his education, and that is why we are distressed to hear that a man who could write these lines has been appointed to look after him. What if your son actually believes that Nicholas was the greatest man of the nineteenth century and wants to be like him?

Or perhaps state wisdom and an understanding of Rus will be instilled in him by Zinoviev?[7] Where did he become a teacher and why is he more able than fifty... or even five hundred other battalion commanders and all sorts of generals who give orders in a hoarse voice and educate soldiers with a rod? We know of one virtue of his, a tender love for his brother, whom he removed as supervisor of an asylum and set up as a trustee of the Kharkov district, defending him against the right-wing students. But these family virtues, valued in Arcadia, are matched by crimes in government circles. Finally, even if Zinoviev were as educated as Zakrevsky, an orator like Panin, with a clear conscience like Rostovtsev, and chaste like Butkov,[8] wouldn't it be possible to find instead the kind of people pushed aside by him and the intrigue of the Black Cabinet—who are Russian, educated, love their country, and *do not wear epaulets?*

Epaulets are a grand thing, and a military uniform, like a monk's cassock, cuts a person off from other people; neither a monk nor a soldier are our equal and that is why they are set off from us. Both are incomplete people, people in an exceptional position. One has his arms always folded like a corpse, while the other has them always raised like a fighter. Neither death nor murder constitute life's best moments.

The title of Russian tsar is not a military rank. It is time to give up the barbaric thought of conquests, bloody trophies, cities taken by storm, ruined villages, trampled harvests—what kind of daydreams are Nimrod and Attila? The time has passed for scourges of mankind like Charles XII and

Napoleon. All that Russia needs is based on peace and is possible in peace-time. Russia thirsts for internal changes, it needs new civil and economic development, and, even without war, the military hinders both these goals. Troops mean destruction, violence, and oppression, and they are founded on silent discipline; that is why a soldier is harmful to the civic order, because he makes no judgments, and the sense of responsibility that distinguishes a man from an animal has been taken away from him.

Teach your son to wear a suit and enroll him in the civil service and you will be doing him a great favor. Occupy his mind with something nobler than an endless game of soldiers; the classroom of the heir to the throne should not resemble a *corps de garde*. This is a peculiarity of Prussian princes and other petty German princelings. The royal house of England seems to be no worse than others, so why does the Prince of Wales, instead of learning about the Horse Guards or the Royal Blues or the Coldstream Guards, sit with a microscope and study zoology?

With deep distress we hear stories of how a cadet is sent to the heir for them to play war in the halls of the Winter Palace... a game of Circassians and Russians... What shallowness, what poverty of interests, what monotony... and along with that, what moral harm! Did you ever think what that game means, what it represents... what is the reason for the rifle, bayonet, saber, why these bivouacs, for which the servant lights a spirit lamp on the floor instead of a campfire? This entire game represents the *misfortune* of battle, that is, wholesale killing and the triumph of brute strength... there's just one thing missing—blood up to the knees, the groans of the wounded, piles of corpses, and the savage cries of the victors. What kind of children's game is this, what kind of *dress rehearsal* for inhumanity or senseless behavior when it degenerates to the level of a corporal? [. . .]

Do not think that—carried away by sentimentalism—we wish to say that military science and military craft are useless for the heir to the throne. No! The sad necessity that in time of peace one must be ready to repel an enemy makes military organization necessary. In preparing to be head of state, the heir must know the military part of his responsibilities, but as one *part;* financial and civic questions, as well as judicial and social issues, have a greater right to be understood well by him.

Is it not sad to see the grand dukes learning the details of each regiment's uniform, all the secrets of handling a rifle, and how to command a platoon and a battalion, but not about civilian work, or the limits of various powers, or the economic state of the various parts of Russia, and they remain alien to Russian literature and those contemporary questions that shake the world and make the entire human race tremble. Ask any one of them and you will see whether or not we are correct. But why even ask?

Look at how barren their lives are, how useless is their wandering about for Russia... one travels to a stud farm, a second to look at the walls of some citadel, and the third to see the fifth or the fifteenth division...

It is terrible to think how hackneyed and empty our grand dukes' existence has become... A man lived and died in our midst; he may have been endowed by nature with a good heart, but his entire life was spent in unnecessary busyness and aimless bustle... What distinction did Mikhail Pavlovich[9] add to a life spent close to the throne? That he was head of artillery in the Russian army?

Mikhail Pavlovich did not know Russia, did not even know Petersburg; he knew the guards regiments, the artillery, cadets... and he died, having returned from a military exercise and having given Paskevich an imperial honor. [. . .]

Your Majesty, save your children from this kind of future!

I know very well that my words, if they reach you, will surprise you with their impertinence: the sharp words of a free man sound odd in the halls of the Winter Palace. But overcome your distaste and think about what my sad words express; maybe you will find in them the great sorrow that eats at my heart, and see my honest desire for the well-being of Russia more than any insult or impertinence.

You stand too high to take offense, and I am too independent to be impertinent.

In olden times, tsars sometimes took off their robes and, dressed like mere mortals, they walked around the markets and squares, listening to popular talk and gaining practical wisdom in the crowds. This practice has lapsed, and it really is not necessary—free speech has itself penetrated the cavalry guards at court. Do not push it aside—think about it, and, if it makes you happier, forget who wrote it, although he sincerely wishes you well.

November 1, 1858

Notes

Source: "Pis'mo k Imperatritse Marii Aleksandrovne," *Kolokol*, l. 27, November 1, 1858; 13:353–60, 586–87.

  1. Herzen is referring to the court decree of June 24, 1718, concerning the conspiracy which formed around Alexey Petrovich and was directed against Peter's transformation of the country. Alexey was condemned to death and Peter approved the sentence.

  2. "I am only the result of a stroke of luck."

  3. Herzen employs the term "Black Cabinet" to designate the most reactionary members of the Main Committee discussing the serf question: the police chief and head of the Third Department (V. A. Dolgorukov), the minister of government property (M. N. Muravyov), the chairman of the State Council (A. F. Orlov), the minister of justice (V. N. Panin), and an aide-de-camp (Ya. I. Rostovtsev). Herzen published an essay called "The

Black Cabinet" in the August 1, 1858, issue of *The Bell*. (See Gertsen, *Sobranie sochinenii*, 13:300–305, nn. 570–72.)

4. Frédéric-César de La Harpe (1754–1838), a Swiss government official who became tutor to Grand Duke Alexander Pavlovich, later Alexander I. Herzen refers ironically to the widespread opinion that La Harpe had a liberal influence on his pupil.

5. The person forced out was Moscow University law professor Konstantin D. Kavelin (1818–1885), who began tutoring Nicholas Alexandrovich in 1857, but had to step down the following year after his article on emancipation appeared in the April 1858 issue of *The Contemporary*. Grimm, tutor to the children of Nicholas I, succeeded him. The poet Fyodor Tyutchev, who served on the Foreign Censorship Committee, complained of another absurdity: while Grimm was being entrusted with the instruction of the heir, there was a proposal to ban his books from entering Russia (Choldin, *Fence Around the Empire*, 57–61).

6. Published in Berlin in 1858.

7. Nikolay V. Zinoviev (1801–1882), an aide-de-camp who from 1849 to 1860 taught the grand dukes Nikolay, Alexander, and Vladimir Alexandrovich.

8. Yakov I. Rostovtsev (1803–1860) directed the military academies, and served on the Secret and Main Committees for the serf question; Vladimir P. Butkov (1820–1881) was a state secretary from 1854 to 1865.

9. Mikhail Pavlovich (1798–1849) was the younger brother of Nicholas I.

⇥ **20** ⇤

The Bell, No. 27, November 1, 1858. In the years leading up to the emancipation a split developed between Herzen and two prominent liberals, the jurist and writer Boris N. Chicherin and Moscow law professor Konstantin D. Kavelin. They had already publicly disagreed with Herzen in the almanac *Voices from Russia*, and Chicherin continued to speak for what he said were the majority of enlightened, right-thinking Russians who did not respond positively to revolutionary propaganda. Chicherin visited London in the fall of 1858 to try to get Herzen to moderate his views; each recorded impressions of the meeting in their memoirs (Herzen, *My Past and Thoughts*, 2:624–29). Herzen's publication of an anonymous letter that called for emancipation from below, and "We Stand Accused," led to a strongly worded response from Chicherin, in which he envisioned Russian society moving in two different directions, one of which responded impatiently to conservative moves as the other sought a common language with autocracy. Despite the harsh tone he had adopted, Chicherin insisted that his personal respect for the editor of *The Bell* remained as strong as ever; the memory of Granovsky was sacred to them both (Zhelvakova, *Gertsen*, 435). Although Herzen felt that the attack was unnecessarily nasty, his belief in political dialogue led him to publish it, referring to himself and his antagonist as two officers who acknowledged each other's rank while fighting in opposing armies. Chicherin accepted this comparison, but still insisted that they agreed on the basics—freedom for the serfs with land and freedom of conscience—while disagreeing over tactics. If society was at this point not sufficiently unified to act responsibly, then it was too soon to demand action from the government (*Let* 2:451–57).

Chicherin claimed that Herzen's misuse of free speech would lead to greater repression back home. After this charge was made public, Herzen received many letters of support. Kavelin was particularly effusive in his expressions of respect and affection, reminding Herzen of the role that he, Belinsky, and Granovsky had played in Kavelin's life. "For me you are not an abstract idea, but a living person, and you have no advisors because you see so far into the future" (*Let* 3:67–69). Chicherin was sent a collective letter by Kavelin, Turgenev, Pavel Annenkov, and others, taking him to task for justifying persecution in Russia and for gladdening the government with this sign of serious disagreement among progressive forces. Even the conservative pedagogue and censor Nikitenko said that Chicherin's criticism of the London exile was harmful. Herzen gave a detailed answer to accusations made against him; this article and the one that follows led to a complete break in their relations, surprising and regrettable in a group of people who shared so many mentors and friends (*Let* 2:453).

WE STAND ACCUSED
[1858]

Liberal conservatives accuse us of attacking the government too much, expressing ourselves too sharply, and being too abusive.

The red democrats fiercely accuse us of making allowances for Alexander II, praising him when he does something good and believing that he desires the emancipation of the serfs.

The Slavophiles accuse us of a Western turn of mind.

The Westernizers accuse us of Slavophilism.

The strict doctrinaires accuse us of frivolousness and instability because in the winter we complain about the cold, and in the summer about the heat.

On this occasion, there will be just a few words about the final accusation.

It was provoked by two or three admissions on our part that we *were mistaken,* that we were *carried away by our enthusiasm;* we won't attempt to justify ourselves by saying that we were mistaken and carried away along with the rest of Russia, and we do not shirk the responsibility that we have voluntarily assumed. We must be consistent; *unity* is a necessary condition for all propaganda, and it is right to demand that of us. But while taking a measure of guilt upon ourselves, we wish to share it with other guilty parties.

It is easy to follow one line when you are dealing with a mature order of things and consistent types of activity. What's hard about taking a sharply defined position in relation to the English government or the French imperial house? Would it have been hard to be consistent under the last tsar?

But we do not find *unity* in Alexander II's actions; first he represents himself as the liberator of the serfs and a reformer, and then defends the

Nicholaevan harness and threatens to trample the shoots that have just emerged.

How can one reconcile the speech to the Moscow nobility with Governor-General Zakrevsky?[1]

How to reconcile the easing of censorship with the ban on writing about the liberation of the serfs with land?

How to reconcile the amnesty and the desire for open discussion with Rostovtsev's project and Panin's power?[2] [. . .]

The instability of the government is reflected in our articles. In following the government we lost our way, and did not hide the fact that we were annoyed at ourselves. In this there was a kind of link with our readers. We had not led, but had walked alongside them; we had not taught, but had served as an echo of thoughts and ideas suppressed at home. Swept up in the contemporary movement of Russia, we were carried rapidly along by the changing winds blowing from the Neva.

Of course, a person who silently awaits the outcome, stifling both hope and fear, will never make a mistake. History—that graveside oration—is better protected against blunders than any participant in ongoing events. [. . .]

While lacking an exclusive system or a party spirit that repels everything else, we do have an unshakable foundation and ardent feelings that have guided us from childhood to old age, and in them there is no *frivolity, hesitation,* or *compromise!* The rest seems secondary to us; there are many different ways to implement what is agreed upon... in this is the poetic capriciousness of history and it is impolite to meddle.

The emancipation of the serfs with land is one of the most important and substantial questions for Russia and for us. Whether this emancipation is "from above or below"—we will back it! If the liberating is done by peasant committees made up of the accursed enemies of emancipation—we will sincerely and wholeheartedly bless them. If the peasants liberate themselves first from the committees and then from those landowners who constitute the committees—we will be the first to congratulate them in a brotherly way and from the heart as well. Finally, if the tsar orders the removal of estates from subversive aristocrats and sends them somewhere beyond the Amur River to Muravyov—we will say equally from the heart: "Let it be as you command."[3]

It does not follow from this that we recommend these means, that there are no others, or that these are the best—not at all. Our readers know what we think on this subject.

However, since the most important matter is for the peasants to be freed with land, we will not argue over means.

In the absence of a binding doctrine, leaving it, so to speak, to nature itself to act as we cheer on every step that is consistent with our views, we may often make mistakes. We will always be glad for "our learned friends," sitting calmly in lodges on the shore, to shout out for us to keep "to the right or to the left"; but we hope that they do not forget that it is easier for them to observe the strength of the waves and the weakness of the swimmers than it is for us to swim... especially so far from shore. [. . .]

Notes

Source: "Nas uprekaiut," *Kolokol*, l. 27, November 1, 1858; 13:361–63, 587.

1. The speech on the need for the emancipation was delivered March 30 (April 11), 1856.

2. In the coronation manifesto issued by Alexander II on August 26, 1856, the surviving Decembrists and other political prisoners were granted amnesty. During the summer of 1858 there was discussion of Rostovtsev's proposal to set up temporary governor-generals in case of peasant agitation when the reforms were carried out. The project, supported by Alexander II, was opposed by Minister of the Interior Lanskoy. By taking this stance, Lanskoy risked dismissal, and foreign newspapers mentioned possible successors.

3. Count Nikolay N. Muravyov-Amursky (1809–1881) was governor-general of eastern Siberia from 1847 to 1861.

→ **21** ←

The Bell, No. 29, December 1, 1858. Konstantin Kavelin wrote to Chicherin early in 1859, criticizing the bureaucratic tone Chicherin took with Herzen and questioning his right to speak so condescendingly to a man who wanted the reforms to succeed without casualties. Chicherin forwarded Kavelin's letter and others written in a similar spirit to Herzen, who refused to publish them for fear of compromising the authors.

"A Bill of Indictment," which continues the open discussion with Chicherin, is one of several in which Herzen refers to irony as a distinctive characteristic of his writing and a deliberate choice in making his political message more effective. By March 1859 Herzen was ready to bring an end to this particular polemic. He continued to receive letters of support, including one from the Slavophile editor Alexander Koshelev (1806–1883), who described the "sobering" effect of uncensored free speech coming from London, and advised Herzen to pay no attention to the criticism of "doctrinaire liberals." In the May 1859 issue of *The Contemporary*, Chernyshevsky managed to weave support for Herzen into a review of Chicherin's writings (*Let* 3:15–16, 20, 38, 42, 46).

A Bill of Indictment
[1858]

I appear before our readers with a *bill of indictment* in my hands.

This time the accused is not Panin or Zakrevsky—the accused is *me*.

This accusation, expressed on behalf of "a significant number of thinking people in Russia," has great importance for me. Its final word is that all my activity, that is, my life's work, is bringing *harm to Russia.*

If I believed this, I would find the selflessness to hand over my work to others and disappear somewhere in the back of the beyond, lamenting how my entire life had been a mistake. But I am not the judge of my own case; there are too many maniacs who are sure that they are doing the right thing, and you cannot prove a case with ardent love, pure intentions, or your entire life. Therefore, I will turn over the accusation to the court of public opinion.

Until the time when the public speaks loudly on the side of the accuser, I will stubbornly follow the path along which I have been traveling.

Until the time when I receive dozens of ardent expressions of sympathy with the accusatory letter, I will persist.

While the number of readers continues to grow—as it is now growing—I will persist.

While Butenev in Constantinople, Kiselev in Rome, and I don't know who in Berlin, Vienna, and Dresden wear themselves out rushing about to viziers and pashas, to ministers' secretaries and cardinals' assistants, asking and begging for the suppression of *The Bell* and *The Polestar,* and until the *Allgemeine Zeitung* and Gerlach's *Kreuz-Zeitung* stop bewailing the fatal influence of *The Bell* on the nerves of Petersburg dignitaries, I will carry on.[1]

I stand before you in my "hopelessly incorrigible state," as Golitsyn junior characterized me in 1835, when I was being judged by a committee of inquiry.[2] Be as strict, cruel, and unjust as you wish, but I ask of you one thing: in the English manner, let us stick to business and leave personalities out of it.

I am prepared to print everything that is possible in terms of *quality* and *quantity.*

The "Accusatory Letter" which we have published today differs substantially from previous letters opposing *The Bell.* In those letters there was a friendly reproach and the kind of friendly indignation in which could be heard a familiar native sound.

There is nothing like that in this letter.

Those were written *from our side,* and in the very disagreement and reproach there was sympathy. This letter was written from a completely *op-*

posing point of view, that is, from the viewpoint of administrative progress and governmental inflexibility. We never accepted it and so there is no surprise in the fact that we did not follow that path. We never represented ourselves as government authorities or statesmen. We wanted to be Russia's protest, its cry of liberation and its cry of pain, we wanted to unmask villains who stand in the way of success and rob the people. We dragged them to the place of punishment and made them look ridiculous. We wanted to be not just Russia's revenge but its irony—and nothing more. What kind of Bludovs and Panins are we—we are the book publishers for *"a significant number of suffering people in Russia."*

And here I must add that we are not at all in the exclusive position that is often ascribed to us, and which is ascribed by the author of this letter, and against which I protest with all my strength. What kind of monopoly do we have on Russian publishing, as if we held the concession on Russian speech in foreign lands?

If we are, as the author of the letter says, *"the strength and power in Russia,"* then the reason is not that we are the only ones with an instrument.

Now that we have gotten the ball rolling, you can publish in Russian in Berlin, Leipzig, and in London itself.[3]

And if, in good conscience, we cannot recommend the Brussels periodical *Le Nord* as an outlet for Russian articles, what is to prevent placing them in *Russia Abroad?*[4]

To us belong the *honor of initiative and the honor of success,* but not a monopoly.

Notes

Source: "Obvinitel'nyi akt," *Kolokol,* l. 29, December 1, 1858; 13:404–6, 597–600.

1. Herzen complained about the campaign to suppress *The Bell* in earlier essays, including "Lackeys and Germans Refuse Permission" and "Logophobia" (Docs. 15 and 17). Apollinary P. Butenev (1787–1866) was Russia's representative to Constantinople from 1856 to 1858; Nikolay D. Kiselev (1802–1869) was the Russian ambassador to the papal court in Rome from 1856 to 1864. The *Kreuz-Zeitung,* so called because of the cross on the title page, was also called the *Neue Preussische Zeitung;* it was founded in 1848 in Berlin by the far-right leader Eduard Ludwig Gerlach, who proposed new periodicals to polemicize with *The Bell,* not only abroad, but within Russia itself.

2. Alexander F. Golitsyn (1796–1864) participated in a number of investigative commissions, including the one in 1834 that looked into the activities of Herzen, Ogaryov, and others. Herzen refers to him as "junior" to distinguish him from Prince Sergey M. Golitsyn (1774–1859), another commission member.

3. Herzen: "Besides our press, as the reader probably knows, there is another press in London run by Z. Swietoslawski."

4. The Russian government used *Le Nord* to try to influence public opinion in Europe. *Russkii zagranichnyi sbornik* was a liberal journal, edited in Paris and printed in Leipzig.

→ **22** ←

The Bell, No. 44, June 1, 1859. The title of the article below was written in capital letters and in English. This is the first detailed polemic against attempts made between 1857 and 1859 in The Contemporary and other Russian journals to discredit—in coded language—the journalism of exposure and denunciation, and to reevaluate the historical and socio-literary significance of the Nicholaevan era's "superfluous people," signaling that the time had come for action (Walicki, Slavophile Controversy, 452, 460). Herzen believed that the attacks on his journalism "served the interest of the most reactionary part of the tsarist bureaucracy, and that the young radicals might live to be decorated by the government" (Ulam, Ideologies and Illusions, 25). Natan Eidelman devoted many pages of analysis to this "family" quarrel, which pitched a more radical message inserted between the lines against a more moderate, but openly expressed, stance (Eidel'man, Svobodnoe slovo, 258–59, 271, 295, 308–15).

In several issues of The Contemporary, both before and after the appearance of "VERY DANGEROUS!!!" Dobrolyubov attacked pustozvonstvo ("idle talk," literally "empty ringing," a reference to The Bell), and claimed that unmasking particular abuses without criticizing the entire structure simply deflected attention from the main battle; he intimated that only the younger generation could effectively serve humanity (Gertsen, Sobranie sochinenii, 4:48–112). In answer to this article, "Last Year's Literary Trifles," and to criticism from conservative literary figures in The Library for Reading (where Herzen had read Pisemsky's A Thousand Souls) and Fatherland Notes (where he read Goncharov's Oblomov), Herzen boldly reaffirmed the power of his targeted laughter.

After Nekrasov heard in his St. Petersburg club of the attacks contained in "VERY DANGEROUS!!!" and its inference that The Contemporary had been "bought," he and Dobrolyubov considered traveling to London to demand that Herzen retract his remarks, and, in Nekrasov's case, to possibly challenge him to a duel (Let 3:48). In the end it was Chernyshevsky who made the trip, meeting with Herzen in late June–early July 1859. He commented afterward that while the trip was not made in vain, it would have been tedious to prolong the debate (Let 3:55). Letters and reminiscences from that period indicate that there was great curiosity about what the two men said to each other (Let 3:58). According to a prison memoir by S. G. Stakhevich, in 1869 Chernyshevsky claimed that his message to Herzen was that the accusations in The Bell helped the government better exercise control over local officials, while leaving the state structure intact. "But the essence of the matter is in the state structure, and not in the agents" (Evgen'ev-Maksimov, Sovremennik, 388–91; Woehrlin, Chernyshevskii, 254). In his 1860 article "The Superfluous and the Jaundiced" (included in the four-volume version of My Past and Thoughts), Herzen to some extent agreed with this criticism of expository journalism.

VERY DANGEROUS!!!
[1859]

Recently a pernicious current has begun to waft through our journalism, some kind of corrupted thinking which we do not accept as an expression of public opinion but as something inspired by the censorship's *ruling* and *edifying* triumvirate.[1]

Pure men of letters, people of sound and form, are tired of the civic direction in our literature; it has begun to offend them that so much is written about bribes and open discussion and there are so few *Oblomovs* and anthologized poems. If only the *Oblomov* that exists were not so completely boring one could forgive them their opinion. People are not to blame when they have no sympathy for the life around them that is breaking through and rushing ahead, and, realizing their frightening position, begin, let us say, to speak about it, however incoherently. In Germany we saw all sorts of Jean-Pauls, who, in light of the revolution and reaction, were overwhelmed, and composed lexicons or tales of the fantastic.[2]

Here, however, things have taken a further turn.

The journals that have built a pedestal of their noble indignation and almost a profession of their gloomy sympathy with those who suffer, split their sides laughing at *investigative* journalism and at unsuccessful attempts at *open discussion*. And this did not happen by accident; they set up a big booth to hiss at the first attempts of free speech in a literature whose hair has not yet grown back since its recent imprisonment. [. . .]

Laughter is convulsive, and if, during the first minute a man laughs at everything, during the second moment he blushes and despises his laughter and that which caused it. It took all of Heine's genius to make up for two or three repulsive jokes about the deceased writers Bërne and Platen and a lady who was still alive.[3] For a time the public shied away from him, and he made peace with them only through his extraordinary talent.

Without a doubt, laughter is one of the most powerful means of destruction; Voltaire's laughter struck and burned like lightning. From laughter idols fall, as do wreaths and frames, and a wonder-working icon turns into a dark and badly drawn picture. With its revolutionary leveling power, laughter is terribly popular and catchy; having begun in a modest study, it moves in widening circles to the limits of literacy. To use such a weapon not against the absurd Trinity of censors—in which Timashev plays the Holy listener—but as its trident, means to join it in the poisoning of thought.

We ourselves saw very well the blunders and mistakes of investigative literature and the awkwardness of the first open discussion; what is surprising in the fact that people who their whole lives were robbed by neighborhood police, judges, and governors now have a lot to say? And they have kept silent about even more!

When did our taste become so spoiled and refined? For ten years we put up with chatter about all the Petersburg camellias and courtesans, who, in the first place, are as alike as sisters the world over, and, second, have this in common with cutlets, that while one may from time to time enjoy them, there is simply nothing that need be said afterward.[4]

"But why are investigative writers such poor narrators, and why do their stories resemble court cases?" That comment may be relevant to individuals, but not to a movement. Someone who poorly and dully conveys the tears of the peasant, the brutality of the landowner, and the thievery of the police, you can be sure will do an even poorer job describing how a golden-haired girl spilled the water she had scooped up from a pool, and how a dark-eyed youth, seeing the swift-flowing liquid, regretted that it was not flowing over his heart.[5]

There were outstanding works in "investigative literature." Do you fancy that you can now noisily throw all the stories by Shchedrin and others into the water with *Oblomov*'s arms around their neck? Gentlemen, you are too extravagant!

You have no pity for these articles because the world about which they write is alien to you; it interests you only to the extent that one is forbidden to write about it. Plants native to the capital, you have sprung up between Gryaznaya Street and the Moyka Canal, and what lies beyond the city limits seems foreign to you. The coarse picture of a story like "Transport"—with carts stuck in the mud, and ruined peasants who gaze with despair at a ferry, waiting one day, and another, and a third—cannot interest you as much as the long odyssey of some half-wild, icy nature, which drags on, drifts off, and disintegrates into meaningless detail.[6] You are prepared to sit at a microscope and analyze this rot (not looking for pathologies, which are contrary to the purity of art; art must have no use and while it may at times be somewhat harmful, base utilitarianism will kill it)—doing so stimulates your nerves. We, quite to the contrary, cannot—without yawning and disgust—follow physiological descriptions of some sort of Neva wood lice who have outlived that heroic period in which their ancestors—and there were many—were Onegins and Pechorins.

And besides, the Onegins and Pechorins were completely authentic, and expressed the real grief and destructiveness of Russian life at that time. The sad fate of the superfluous person, a casualty only because he had developed into a *human being*, revealed itself then not only in narrative poems and novels, but on the streets and in drawing rooms, in villages and in cities. Our most recent literary recruits needle these delicate dreamers who were broken without a fight, idle people who could not find their way in the environment in which they lived. It's a shame they do not come to any conclusions—I happen to think that had Onegin and Pechorin been able—like many others—to make peace with the Nicholaevan era, Onegin would be Viktor Petrovich Panin, and Pechorin would not have perished on the way to Persia, but would, like Kleinmikhel, be running the transportation system and interfering with railway construction.[7]

The era of Onegins and Pechorins has passed. In Russia now there are no more *superfluous* people; now, to the contrary, there are not enough people for the work that is required. Anyone who cannot find something to do now has no one to blame—he is in fact an *empty* person, a piece of wood or a lazybones. And that is why Onegins and Pechorins naturally become Oblomovs.

Public opinion, pampering the Onegins and Pechorins because it sensed in them *its own suffering*, turns away from Oblomovs.

It is complete nonsense to say that we have no public opinion, as a learned commentator recently said, *thus demonstrating that we had no need of open discussion* because we had no public opinion, and we had no public opinion because we had no *bourgeoisie!*[8]

Public opinion has shown its tact, its sympathies, and its implacable severity, even during times of public silence. Where did all that uproar come from over Chaadaev's letter, over *The Inspector General* and *Dead Souls*, the *Tales of a Hunter*, Belinsky's articles, and Granovsky's lectures? And, on the other hand, how viciously it fell upon its idols for civic treachery or lack of firmness. Gogol died from its sentence, and Pushkin himself experienced what it means to strike a chord in praise of Nicholas.[9] Our men of letters were more likely than the public to forgive praises sung to an inhuman, barracks despot, as their conscience had been dulled by a refinement of the aesthetic palate!

The example of Senkovsky is even more striking. What did he do with all his wit, his Semitic languages, his seven literatures, his lively memory, and his sharp exposition?... At first the rockets, flashes, crackling, sparklers, whistles, noise, merry atmosphere, and free-and-easy laughter attracted everyone to his journal—they looked and looked and laughed and then, little by little, they went away to their homes. Senkovsky was forgotten, like St. Thomas week when they forget about some bespangled acrobat, who the previous week had interested the whole town, as people packed his booth and hung about him in crowds...[10]

What did he lack? It was the quality that Belinsky and Granovsky had in such abundance—that eternally troubling demon of love and indignation, visible in tears and laughter. He lacked the kind of conviction that would have been his life's *work*, a *map* on which everything would have been laid out with passion and pain. In the words that come from such conviction there remains a trace of the magnetic demonism under which the speaker worked, which explains why his speeches disturb, alarm, and awaken... becoming a force and a power that sometimes moves entire generations.

But we are far from judging Senkovsky unconditionally; he is vindicated by the leaden era in which he lived. He might have become a cold skeptic, an indifferent blasé, laughing at good and evil and believing in nothing— the same way that others shaved the top of their head, became Jesuit priests, and believe everything in the world...[11] It was all an escape from Nicholas— and how could one not try to escape at that time? The only people we do not forgive are those who ran to the Third Department.

What is there in common between that time, when Senkovsky clowned around under the name of Brambeus, and our time? Then it was *impossible* to do anything, even if you had the genius of Pestel and the mind of Muravyov—the ropes on which Nicholas hung people were stronger. It was only possible to martyr oneself, like Konarsky and Wollowicz.[12] Now everywhere there are calls for energetic people, everything is beginning, on the rise, and if nothing happens, then no one is to blame—not Alexander II, not his censorship trio, not the local policeman nor other powerful people—the fault will lie in your weakness, so blame yourself for the false direction you have taken, and have the strength to acknowledge yourselves a leaderless, transitional generation, the one of which Lermontov sang with such terrible truth!..[13]

That is why at such a time empty buffoonery is tedious and out of place; it becomes repulsive and nasty when it hangs donkey bells not on a troika called *Adlerberg, Timashev,* and Mukhanov[14] from the tsar's stables, but on one that—sweaty, exhausted, and occasionally falling back—is dragging our cart out of the mud!

Gentlemen, isn't it a hundred times better, instead of hissing at clumsy experiments while sticking to the beaten path, to lend a hand and demonstrate how to make use of open discussion? [. . .]

Notes

Source: "VERY DANGEROUS!!!" *Kolokol*, l. 44, June 1, 1859; 14:116–21, 492–99.

1. Herzen refers to an 1859–60 government committee whose goal was to exert a moral influence on journalism so that it would support official views; its members, which included Alexander V. Adlerberg (1819–1889, member of the Main Censorship Administration), Alexander Timashev (1818–1893, head of the secret police), and Pavel A. Mukhanov (1798–1871, member of the governing council for the Kingdom of Poland, in charge of internal and spiritual matters), were frequently criticized in *The Bell*.

2. Jean Paul Richter (1763–1825) was a German romantic writer with a taste for the humorous and grotesque.

3. Ludwig Bërne (1786–1837) was a German critic; August von Platen (1796–1835) was a German poet. The woman in question was a friend of Bërne.

4. Herzen has in mind "Petersburg Life," a series of feuilletons in *The Contemporary* by Ivan I. Panaev (1812–1862) describing the demimonde of the northern capital.

5. Herzen's remarks are a parody of common phrases from the poetry of Maykov and Fet, and have much in common with Dobrolyubov's criticism of "pure art" in *The Contemporary*.

6. "Transport" ("Perevoz"), by Ilya V. Selivanov (1810–1882), appeared in *The Contemporary* in the third issue published in 1857. The "long odyssey" is Goncharov's *Oblomov*, which appeared in the first four issues of *Fatherland Notes* for 1859. Herzen takes issue with Druzhinin's praise of the novel in *Readers' Library* and Dobrolyubov's strongly positive essay in *The Contemporary*, as well as Goncharov's role as a censor.

7. Panin was minister of justice. Count Peter A. Kleinmikhel (1793–1869) was director of transportation and public buildings from 1842 to 1855.

8. Herzen is challenging the basic argument of an article by Pollunsky in *Readers' Library*, 1859:3.

9. Nikolay Gogol was widely criticized for his 1847 book *Selected Passages from a Correspondence with Friends* (Doc. 6). On Pushkin, see Chapter V of Herzen's 1850 essay "On the Development of Revolutionary Ideas in Russia" (Doc. 1).

10. St. Thomas Sunday is the first Sunday after Easter, and begins a week (*fomina nedelia*) devoted to the apostle who only believed the miracle after he had seen the risen Christ.

11. In his 1859 article "Russia and Poland," Herzen mentioned the "Pecherins, Gagarins, and Golitsyns" who lived as Catholics in emigration, Vladimir Pecherin becoming a monk, and Prince Ivan Gagarin a Jesuit priest.

12. Konarsky and Wollowicz were Polish revolutionaries executed by the tsarist government.

13. Herzen has in mind Lermontov's poem "Thought" ("Duma").

14. The three super-censors whom Herzen has previously mentioned.

⇀ 23 ↽

The Bell, No. 49, August 1, 1859. Semi-public banquets, organized by progressive forces (on the model of France in 1848) were organized in Russia only after the death of Nicholas I. For instance, the Moscow intelligentsia gathered in November 1855, not long after Granovsky's passing, to celebrate the 50th anniversary of Mikhail Shchepkin's acting debut; anything honoring Shchepkin acquired extra resonance in pre-emancipation Russia because he was born a serf. Organized by Sergey Aksakov and Sergey Solovyov, the 200 guests included professors, literary figures, enlightened merchants, and members of the Moscow administration. Konstantin Aksakov gave a toast to "public opinion" (*obshchestvennoe mnenie*), which brought a standing ovation, this being the first time that phrase was used in public, and alarmed the Third Department agent deputized to attend (*Istoriia Moskvy*, 3:769–70; Christoff, *Nineteenth-Century Russian Slavophilism*, 3:164). Hearing about such events at a distance, Herzen was unable to gauge their effect, and fully aware that any praise of the living could only harm them. Herzen focused below on the hypocrisy of a dinner whose main purpose was to pay homage to those in power.

Political Dinners in Moscow
[1859]

I

We Russians have always liked to dine and to dine well, but recently we have learned to dine *politically,* and, while formerly we gathered for fish soup with sturgeon, now we gather for dinner *with a speech.* Even that consummate Nicholaevan Zakrevsky was given a dinner on April 24, 1859, with a speech by Kornilov; we cannot resist acquainting our readers with it.[1]

> Count Arseny Andreevich,
> Not long ago we celebrated the tenth anniversary of the governing of Moscow by your highness, and the same feelings of love and devotion to you have brought us together now. However, all that was then joyful in our feelings is now clouded by the genuine sadness of farewell. A severe blow has been sent to you from on high. It is not the first in your arduous, brilliant life; you had already traveled a difficult path.
> During 11 years of service under your thoughtful leadership, full of *good-humored* concern, we have grown used to seeing you always firm, always tireless, always indefatigable, strict toward yourself, and indulgent to others.
> That is how you behaved during the calamitous year when cholera devastated Moscow. Quickly, with sensible measures, having asked God's help, you *brought to an end* the calamity and lent a compassionate hand to the orphans and families of the epidemic's victims.
> Thus you behaved during the Crimean War, a terrible time for the Fatherland.[2] Vigilant under the weight of your responsibilities, you encouraged the inhabitants of Moscow and roused their patriotic feelings.
> We have seen the same in you during joyous times in our beloved fatherland.
> At this time of carrying out the magnanimous idea of our august Sovereign about the abolition of serf dependency[3] *you restrained the first premature impulses,* allowed the general opinion to form and mature and in your comments on the work of the Moscow committee you exceeded the *liberalism* of many who saw in your actions backward, late, and old-fashioned ideas and convictions.
> In private relations with us, you were not our chief, but our father. We boldly came to you with our joys and our sorrows. You refused no one advice, comfort, or help.

Everywhere and in everything you were always the model of lively, thoughtful, and prudent activity.

God grant that this courage and strength not fail you now when your peace of mind and your family have need of it.

And if the non-hypocritical love and devotion of your former subordinates can serve to comfort you, then, Count, we are all present, and our genuine tears tell you more eloquently than words how deeply we are feeling the misfortune that has struck you and everyone close to your tenderly affectionate heart.

May the one on high fortify you and heal your heart's wounds!

Gentlemen! To the health of our unforgettable and ever-dear Count Arseny Andreevich!

II

On May 10, there was a dinner for the Moscow head of government, Count Stroganov.[4] It was supposed to serve as an expression of the pleasure felt by Moscow residents that Zakrevsky had finally been replaced.[5] More than 400 people signed up for the dinner, *even those who had given the dinner for Zakrevsky.*

A quarter hour before the count's arrival a commandant arrived and asked in the count's name that there be no speeches.

Nevertheless, Voeykov[6] spoke and Stroganov responded, and then the dinner came to an end. After dinner, Professor Solovyov[7] caught up with Stroganov and said a few words to him. The remaining speeches were given *after the departure* of Stroganov. That's something new! [. . .]

Notes

Source: "Politicheskie obedy v Moskve," *Kolokol*, l. 49, August 1, 1859; 14:403–5, 618–19.

1. A farewell dinner was given for the governor-general of Moscow, on April 17, 1859. According to Petr Vyazemsky's memoirs, it was rumored that his dismissal had to do with his defense of gentry and landowner rights, and thousands of members of the gentry from Moscow and other regions gathered to show support. Alexey Kaznacheev, director of government property in Pskov, organized a dinner in his honor and composed a speech in which he described Zakrevsky's service to the fatherland, which was delivered by Fedor Kornilov, who headed the chancellery of the Moscow governor-general.

2. Herzen: "During the Crimean campaign, Zakrevsky supplied low-quality cloth, etc., from his factory for the militia, and his officials enriched themselves; but one ought not thank him for this!"

3. Herzen: "On the peasant question, Zakrevsky pressed the committee's minority, who were sincerely attempting to change the serfs' way of life, delaying their activities and threatening them, but, in the end, seeing that the wind from Petersburg on the mat-

ter of serfdom was blowing a bit more favorably for the minority, and wishing to please
his master, he presented the minority's project with his own additions."

4. Count Sergey G. Stroganov (1794–1882) was a member of the State Council,
trustee of the Moscow educational district, and military governor-general of Moscow in
1859–60; beginning in 1860 he was chief tutor for the grand dukes Nikolay, Alexander,
Vladimir, and Alexey.

5. Contemporary memoirs report that the more liberal members of Moscow society
openly greeted the news of Zakrevsky's dismissal with undisguised joy.

6. Voeykov was leader of the Moscow nobility from 1856 to 1861 and a member of the
Moscow committee to examine the peasant question.

7. Sergey M. Solovyov (1820–1879) was a historian and professor at Moscow University from 1847 to 1877.

⇾ 24 ⇽

The Bell, No. 55, November 1, 1859. In part 1 of Past and Thoughts, Herzen described his
part in a March 1831 student rebellion at Moscow University against Professor Malov of
the Politics Faculty. They succeeded in getting Malov dismissed, but Herzen and five
other students were held for several nights in the university prison. During the fall of
1859, students in the first year of Moscow University's medical school rebelled against
Professor of Comparative Anatomy and Physiology N. A. Varnek. One of the students
involved in this affair sent material to The Bell, which formed the basis of Herzen's article, information that was included in the case file by the Third Department.

———

The Supreme Council of Moscow University Pharisees
[1859]

Yet another shooting star…

It appears that Moscow University has lived through its age of glory. It is as
if the death of Granovsky drew a line. Was the weight of the Nicholaevan
press necessary to forge the teachers and students into a unified family?

Now things are too free, and that is why professors, at least the majority
of them, act like some kind of board of decency.

A year ago students stopped attending the lectures of some third-rate
professor named Varnek; the university authorities inflated the incident,
which ended with the expulsion of a dozen students, and it is through no
fault of the academic high council that the affair didn't take a Nicholaevan

turn. For some time we have known about this ugly story, but only recently did we obtain the details, which we will briefly convey to our readers.

The students chose as their deputy Zhokhov, who said to Varnek on their behalf: "Professor, we have not listened to your lecture, and in the future we will not cross the threshold of any auditorium where you are teaching. We ask you to allow us the possibility of having another professor."

The university authorities, whose academic-police dignity had been offended, resolved to break the will of the seditious students; they began their actions with *the expulsion of Zhokhov,* having announced that he was kicked out because of his ignoble verses *by order of the late emperor,* whose will had up to now not been carried out, because the trustee Nazimov had protected him, and another trustee, Kovalevsky, had somehow forgotten about him!..[1]

Second, they extracted from students a written obligation to attend Varnek's lectures. The tricks and ruses they resorted to are quite interesting. Thus, the inspector demanded that medical students, in small groups, appear before him from 11 to 12 at night, to avert the possibility of strikes. Also, not without ulterior motives, he began the signed statements with the scholarship students, who had to choose one of two things—to agree or to go off and be medical assistants. Finally, the necessary preparations had been made and on the 19th the dean posted an announcement that the following day at a certain hour Mr. Varnek would lecture in the anatomical theater. Long before the beginning of the lecture students crowded the corridor adjacent to the amphitheater. At 11:30 university officials began to appear. Finally, trustee Bakhmetev himself arrived.[2] He politely exchanged bows with the students and addressed them with the following words: "Gentlemen, we may now enter. It's time!" He pronounced this phrase in such a regular, affectionate voice, as if he knew nothing about the opposition that had formed. "We won't go!" shouted the crowd. "But gentlemen, remember that you gave your word of honor to the inspector." "Under the lash... they threatened us." "Then you absolutely don't want to go in?" "No! No!" "Then I ask you not to reproach me. I will act as *my conscience* demands. Rector, set up a commission to sort out this strange business. Whatever the decision, I will not hesitate to sign it, if it is *just.*" The trustee bowed politely to the students once again and left, without even having seen Varnek.

At 7 o'clock in the evening several first-year medical students were called to the governing body, where they found Alfonsky, Barshev, Leshkov, and Krylov; Armfeld had left, not waiting for the students to gather and, as the rumors suggested, having argued with the others over their too *honorable* intentions!..[3]

The accused were led into a room and there was another attempt to convince them. "Why have you refused to go to Varnek's lectures?" "Because he lectures badly." "Who told you that he lectures badly? How did you acquire so much information in just two months that you take it upon yourselves to judge a professor, a man of science? You are young and might easily be mistaken." "We are not the only ones who feel this way." "Who else?" "All the medical students." "Well, listen up, medical students," exclaimed Barshev, a professor of criminal law, "that means you have formed a conspiracy!" "The trustee," said the president, "out of sympathy for your youth, wants to bring this story to an end in-house. Agree to listen to Varnek and you will be left in peace and no one will be punished. Think it over—stubbornness is useless and even dangerous."

The students thought it over and repeated that they would not listen to Varnek. They were released. On the 23rd, first-year medical students were summoned to the mineralogical hall, where they were handed written questions and told that *no one could leave* until they had answered everything. The students, feeling that they were in the right, answered directly and sharply, without being in command of the full body of laws. That was sufficient; members jumped at the thoughtlessly severe phrases and, based on the degree of their sharpness, divided the accused into categories and handed the matter over for a final decision to the academic council. In this way the harshest punishment went to several people who had not taken part in the recent events, *solely on the basis of their liberal opinions!*

"But first," continues our correspondent, "before I say something about the decision of the university court, I will dwell for a moment on a curious episode which accurately characterizes the professors' *friendly* attitude toward the students. If I were to call them two enemy camps, I would not earn a scolding from my comrades for exaggeration..."

The student Klyauz, having spoiled the question sheet, asked the secretary for another one. "Don't give him one," said Barshev, "he was sent out to the corridor to see his friends, and they ordered him to give false information." "Professor, be careful with your accusations." "So," shouted Barshev, "you are still trying to vindicate yourself!" "I am not vindicating myself, but simply saying that you are lying." "Arrest him," ordered the enraged member to the inspector. "But he really didn't leave the room," said Ilinsky.[4] "In that case, pardon me, Mr. Klyauz," muttered the embarrassed professor.

The amusing anecdote ought to have finished with this, but, unfortunately, with us nothing has been done as one would have expected it for a long time. The next day *Klyauz was expelled.* On whose complaint and on whose command no one knows even now; Barshev didn't complain and the commission was not even thinking about punishing Klyauz! Isn't this act worthy of the defenders of openness in court proceedings, as our *men of science* present themselves?

On the 28th the academic council met, on the 29th Minister Kovalevsky presided, and on December 4 the decision of the famous mock trial was read in the auditoriums: "10 people are expelled *for bad behavior,* and about 100 with the right to return in a year."

Later, the second category were allowed to repent and given the form for an appeal: "I, the undersigned, promise to henceforth obey unconditionally all of the authorities' instructions." And out of 100 people only three refused this shameful appeal. That same day the minister strictly forbade students from gatherings *in crowds,* making speeches, etc., in the university garden and in the auditoriums.

What did the students in other divisions do? And, most of all, what about the young professors and associate professors... it would be interesting to have a record of these official opinions. [. . .][5]

In conclusion, we address ourselves in a friendly and brotherly manner to young Russians with advice and, to be more exact, a fervent plea.

We do not in the least share the military-judicial tendencies of the Moscow professors' high court. It would be shameful for you to doubt our sympathy. Our entire life and all the separate events in it can serve as a witness to the fact that even if fate put us in the place of the Barshevs and Krylovs we would still be true to our convictions; that is why—with a clear conscience and the candor of affection—we have decided to implore you *to be careful,* because you may ruin not only yourselves, but much more.

Russia requires this sacrifice of you. There are stages in an organism's resistance that demand stricter hygiene. And precisely now Russia finds itself in such a condition. The old has been uprooted and the new has not yet taken root. There is nothing on which to rely. Besides the sovereign's noble instincts, on the one hand, and part of society, on the other, besides the redoubled intellectual activity and that anxious expectation that anticipates a great future, *there is nothing* and nothing is guaranteed! Do not give any cause for the now-calm Andreevsky jackals and the secret executioners to be let loose on you. The memory of Novosiltsevs and Pelikans is not that old, and the five-year-old shoots are not so strong as to withstand a reaction.[6]

Right next to us there is an important example—look at the quiet ocean of the peasant world, awaiting in majestic peace the destruction of their shameful slavery. How happy the plantation owner-gentry would be if they could summon up a storm!

Your strength is Russia's strength, so preserve it, do not waste it in vain. Ahead of us there is so much to do, so many battles!

Notes

Source: "Sinkhedron Moskovskikh universitetskikh fariseev," *Kolokol*, l. 55, November 1, 1859; 14:191–97, 521–22.

The opening epigraph is a refrain from a song by the French poet Pierre Jean de Béranger (1780–1857).

1. Vladimir I. Nazimov (1802–1874) was a trustee of the Moscow educational district from 1849 to 1855, military governor of Vilna, and governor-general of Kovno, Minsk, and Grodno from 1855 to 1863. Evgraf P. Kovalevsky (1790–1867), also a trustee of the Moscow educational district from 1856 to 1858, was minister of education from 1858 to 1861.

2. Alexey N. Bakhmetev (1801–1861) was a trustee of the Moscow educational district in 1858–59.

3. Arkady A. Alfonsky (1796–1869) was a professor, a surgeon, and rector of Moscow University in 1842–48 and 1850–53; Sergey I. Barshev (1808–1882) was a professor of criminal law and rector from 1863 to 1870; Vasily N. Leshkov (1810–1881) was a lawyer and professor of police law at Moscow University; Nikita I. Krylov (1807–1879) taught Roman law, while Alexander O. Armfeld (1806–1868) taught forensic medicine.

4. Ilinsky was police inspector for the medical school at Moscow University from 1857 to 1860.

5. Here Herzen attaches an internal university council document about the case that outlines their deliberations in greater detail.

6. Count Nikolay N. Novosiltsev (1761–1836) held a number of senior government positions, including chairman of the Government Council and Committee of Ministers, and trustee of the St. Petersburg educational district. Ventseslav V. Pelikan (1790–1873) was professor of anatomy and surgery in Vilna, and chair of the military-medical academic council; he helped to judge participants in the 1831 Polish uprising. Herzen alludes to the approximately five years since Nicholas I died.

→ **25** ←

The Bell, No. 60, January 1, 1860. Herzen later said that this essay, with which he was very pleased, was his final effort to free the tsar from the influence of the gentry oligarchs, who were agitating for a greater role in governance in return for the imminent loss of their serfs. To his earlier requests for emancipation, an end to corporal punishment, and freedom of expression, he added a plea for openness in judicial proceedings. In November 1859, Herzen gained access to the records of fifty meetings of the Editorial Commission of the Main Committee on the peasant question, which rejected emancipation without land, proof of the influence of Nikolay Milyutin.[1] However, news of the illness of Yakov Rostovtsev, the Editorial Commission chair, led to concerns over a retreat from the progress that had already been made; conservative gentry opposition had increased and there was growing support for asking the tsar to convene an aristocratic assembly before emancipation plans were finalized. For the March 15, 1860, edition of *The Bell* (nos. 65–66), Herzen used a black border to highlight news of General Rostovtsev's death, and the appointment of Count Viktor Nikitich Panin to succeed him.

———

THE YEAR 1860
[1860]

I

Without exaggerated hope or despair we enter the *new decade* with the firm, even step of an old warrior who has known defeat, and who knows most of all difficult marches through the sandy, dusty, and joyless steppe. [. . .]

...No matter what, things cannot be worse than they were ten years ago. That was the honeymoon of reaction, and with a frozen tear in our eye and anger boiling up in our heart, we looked at the unsuccessful campaign and cursed the shameful age in which we had to live. [. . .]

The gloomy cloud of which we had a premonition from the sharp pain in our mind and heart, obscured more and more as it grew darker and darker, and everything became confused, twisted, and began to sink... heroes arose who served no purpose; words full of wisdom were spoken, but no one understood them. [. . .]

II

Later we felt relieved and could breathe again![2] Morning had come. Tamed by experience and memory, we greeted with tender emotion the brightly burning dawn of a new day in Russia. We rejoiced not because of *what* this did for us, but, like people recovering after the crisis in an illness, we rejoiced in the *right to hope*.

Wearied by everything that surrounded us, we gazed at this strip of light in our native sky without arrogant demands or youthful utopias. We limited ourselves to the desire that the coarse iron chains were removed from the poor Russian people, *making possible further development;* the rest, it seemed to us, would take care of itself, most likely after we were gone. It didn't matter, as long as we got to see for ourselves that there were no obstacles on the path.

Our thoughts and our speech went no further than:

The freedom of serfs from landowners,
The freedom of the word from censorship,
The freedom of the courtroom from the darkness of official secrecy,
The freedom of backs from the stick and lash.

While we thought and spoke about this, the famous rescript to the nobility of the three Polish provinces was issued.[3]

He who comprehends the depth of emotion and prayerfulness that filled Kant at the news of the proclamation of the French Republic, as he bared his head, and, lifting his eyes to heaven, repeated the words of Simeon, "Now let my soul depart in peace!"—he will understand what transpired in our soul when we heard the words softly proclaimed by the sovereign—but all the same proclaimed—*the emancipation of the serfs!*

We grew young again and believed in ourselves, and in the fact that our life had not been spent in vain... then the censorship was eased, along with an end to the shameful restrictions on traveling, the children's colonies and military settlements, and the introduction of projects concerning openness in the courts. We began to rest from our hatred.

Our program was being implemented, and it was easy for us to say: "You have conquered, Galilean!" (*The Bell*, no. 9).[4] We wanted to be defeated *in that fashion.*

An autocratic revolution could have led Russia to a major development of all its inexhaustible strengths and unknown possibilities, without having spilled a single drop of blood or having erected a single scaffold, and having turned the Siberian highway into a path of wealth and communication instead of a path of tears and the gnashing of teeth.

Yes, we were right to say to Alexander II at the time of his ascent to the throne: "You are exceptionally lucky!"[5]

Why are we entering a new decade without that radiant hope or firm expectation with which we greeted the epoch of Russia's renaissance?

Alexander II, like Faust, called forth a spirit stronger than himself and was frightened. A kind of exhausting indecisiveness, an unsteadiness in all his actions, and by the end, completely retrograde behavior. It is obvious that he wishes to do good—and fears it.

What happened? Was there a war? An insurrection? Is the government collapsing? Are the provinces seceding? Nothing of the sort! The financial situation is poor, but that is just normal Russian management—everything looks splendid and yet we have not a penny to our names! Besides, reactionary moves do not help the financial situation...

What frightened the sovereign? What are people afraid of in a cemetery?..

That is what human immaturity means, that people are afraid of nonsense and don't see the real danger, and that they lean against a rotten tree that is right next to a healthy one. Chasing fantasies, they let reality slip out of their hands; fearing ghosts in Jacobin caps, they pet jackals in a general's epaulets; fearing democratic pages in journals, they are unafraid of the oligarch's official document in a velvet cover.

You cannot travel two paths.

No matter what kind of Janus you are, it is impossible to go in two opposite directions at the same time, you can only move with one of your halves in reverse, getting in your own way and helplessly rocking in place.

You cannot desire open discussion and strengthen the censorship.

You cannot desire enlightenment and drive students away from the university gates.

You cannot respect your people as subjects and then not allow them to take their children abroad.

You cannot stand on the side of the people and call yourself "the first nobleman."[6]

You cannot desire open courts and keep as your thief of justice Panin.

You cannot desire the rule of law and have in your own chancellery an entire division of spies.

You cannot begin new construction and take your helpers from the workhouse of the past. [. . .]

This vacillation will make us lose patience and fall not into despair, but into deep sorrow, all the more because it is completely unnecessary and comes from taking decoration for the real thing, probably from a habit of seeing in a man first of all the kind of collar and buttons he is wearing.

If the sovereign would look carefully, he would notice that he is surrounded by an entire world of phantoms, and that Panin, for example, is not in fact the minister of justice, but a marionette, and made very poorly of sticks. Gorchakov[7] does not exist at all—there is just a uniform with a hole in the back in which the conjurer Mukhanov has thrust his fingers, as he pretends that the deceased is still alive, to the distress of the Polish people...

And with whom could you replace these experienced, venerable servants of the throne? *Experienced* in what? In the emancipation of serfs or the establishment of open courts?..

Here's another example: was Moscow really worse after Zakrevsky? Surely Tuchkov is ten times better than him... If Zakrevsky[8] had not read so many French novels and hadn't composed his own sentimental episode à la George Sand, he would still be oppressing Moscow, and the sovereign would believe that he was necessary to the tranquility of the ancient capital!

The cap of Monomakh is not only heavy, it is also large, and it can slip over one's eyes... If only it were possible for a moment to lift it up and show the sovereign—not in the manner of loyal subjects, but in a simple human way—all that is living and dead in Russia, all that will follow his lead if he himself does not abandon the path of development and liberation, and show everything that will oppose him... one would give a great deal for that to happen.

What strange times these are: *we have* no secrets, and we passionately want to show the sovereign all there is to know. But the Dolgorukovs and Timashevs,[9] his *professional* ears, keep many secrets from him and conceal everything except harmful gossip. And ever more carefully they conceal the fact that the highest layer of the Russian nobility is not only not the sole true support of the throne, but because of its sickly state is itself looking for something on which to lean. The era has passed in which the Petersburg government existed not only by the grace of God but with the help of boyar oligarchs and German generals. Back then there was *joint management* and a system of mutual guarantees: the government allowed the nobles to rob the people and beat them with a rod, and the nobility helped the government to gather up more lands and beat their inhabitants with a whip.

Since then everything has gradually changed. Since then the Russia of Biron and Osterman has grown old, and the Russia of Lomonosov has advanced.[10] Since then we have seen 1812 and December 14, 1825. The new milieu snuck in imperceptibly, like a wedge between the people and the grandees, and in this milieu you will find atoms from all the different social layers, but crystallized differently. There are the children of counts and princes and the son of a Voronezh cattle-dealer.[11] In this milieu you will find education, universities, all intellectual activity, books—and books now wield power.

Nothing is known about all this at court. [. . .] Nothing can reach the highest cells of the Winter Palace except people belonging to the first three ranks. It seems as if everything is proceeding as usual with the same uniforms sewn with gold thread, but what the uniform is filled with has rotted and shrunk, going out of its mind and out of its century, and has passed away, but has been magnificently embalmed. [. . .] Because of these bodies in gold-threaded uniforms on parade, the sovereign cannot see that the center of gravity and energy has changed, and that elements have entered the formula of Russian life that were unknown in the time of Peter I and barely heard of under Catherine II. He does not know that it is now *impossible* to forbid either science or literature, and that there are beliefs and convictions common to every educated person, except the majority of that higher nobility who in the oligarchs' books are depicted as the support of the throne.

[. . .] When has a Russian emperor had on his side—as is the case with the emancipation of the serfs and the introduction of open discussion—the Russian people and educated Russia, the common people and men of letters, the young clergy and all the Old Believers, and, finally, the opinion of the whole world from the greatest periodic outlets to the humble pages of *The Bell?*

It is only the throne's "sole support" that is *against* these changes; its slavish efforts extend no further than an easing of quitrent. [. . .]

But it is not the tsar who has been weakened by this opposition, but *them;* the earth is disappearing from beneath *their* feet. Supporting autocracy by its imperial shoulder, in essence they themselves leaned on it. Leave them to their own devices and in a quarter hour they will tumble from their "beautiful heights" and become "Comme tout le monde," as Susanna Figaro said. [. . .]

Can the sovereign really be afraid that these made-up counts, who remind one of Soulouque's aristocracy, these impoverished princes with archeological names, who with the help of the provincial Dobchinskys and local Bobchinskys, will force him—like Norman barons—to sign a *Magna Carta* of genuine liberties for the higher ranks of the civil service and the military or be led off to prison like Louis XVI?[12] [. . .]

All this is impossible because our Norman barons possess no power of their own or any from the people or from any contemporary idea—all their strength lies in the tsar's support.

There is only one thing they can do—spring from a corner and kill the tsar, because for this no strength is needed, you just have to be a villain. [. . .]

One could say to us that they are not the ones the sovereign fears. Then whom?

A popular uprising? It is difficult to imagine that the Russian peasant, who for centuries has put up with his disastrous state, would rebel because he was being liberated and begin to demand the return of serfdom!

Civil servants? People who take bribes will never rebel.

The merchants? What profit is in it for them? Tax-farmers would be the first to fall in battle for a paternalistic government...

You can look wherever you like in Russia—everywhere there are shoots and buds, everywhere grain is ripening, everywhere something is asking to come out into the light and develop, everything wishes to stretch its limbs after a long, long captivity, and nowhere is there any element of an uprising. One question that the people might raise concerns the liberation of the serfs with land, but that lies in the hands of the government.

[. . .] The government's harshest and most sadly despotic orders were directed against *literature* and now against *students.* That is what frightens them, that is where they see danger! It is strange, painful, and shameful, but that's how it is! The sovereign has been fussing over the censorship for, I think, three years—he curtails it, prolongs it, simplifies it, and then makes it more complex.

Cut off from any possibility of receiving journals in a timely fashion by the repulsive postal arrangements for book parcels in Russia, we thought for a long time that in Russia they were printing incendiary appeals, like the heretical books of Luther and the erotic works of Barkov.[13]

Not at all. When we received the March issues in November, and the February issues in December, we were able, little by little, to read through almost everything. The change from the Nicholaevan age is enormous. Thought that was repressed has revived, language has returned, and human thoughts and interests have found their reflection in the "Reviews." All journals without exception have energetically and enthusiastically supported this reign's most important idea—the liberation of the serfs with land. [. . .]

The problem, unfortunately, is that high above the ups and downs of everyday existence *a humane word is considered impertinent* and *thought is suspicious in and of itself.* Thinking and speaking (i.e., giving orders) should be done by the government; for a subject this is a luxury and leads only to gossiping about matters *that do not concern him,* for example, whether he can rightfully be confined to the Peter Paul Fortress without a trial, be sent hundreds of miles away without being told the reason, and so on. The ideal of government order and civilization for this ultra-first-class sphere is an eastern seraglio and a Prussian cavalry parade.[14] It is a seraglio in which people, renouncing their zoological dignity, got down on all fours in the sovereign's presence, and a military formation in which a man attached to a rifle butt is reduced to being a wax figure with four thousand legs rising at the same angle and descending at the same instant. [. . .]

In the most recent instructions to the Moscow censorship committee, it was stated that the government considers it *beneath its dignity* to turn its attention to facts uncovered by the press. During the past decade, replete with stupidities, I do not think that anything stupider than this has been said. It is wondrously stupid. As if there is only one noble means of uncovering the truth—*spying!*

It is the same in regard to the students. The civilizing government must have universities and students but it wishes the students to resemble soldiers in punishment battalions. [. . .]

What is it these gentlemen want from young people?

It's very simple—a *slavish* spirit, *slavish* discipline, and *slavish* silence! What can be meant by the order *from on high not to applaud* professors?.. And why is the sovereign taking up the role of school disciplinarian and inspector?.. How differently Pushkin understood the dignity of a tsar when he had Godunov tell his son that the word of the tsar, like the sound of church bells, should only ring out to tell of some great event or great misfortune!

One of the worst infringements on liberty in the previous reign was the persistent attempt to break the youthful spirit. The government lay in wait for the child during his first steps in life and corrupted the child cadet, the adolescent schoolboy, and the young student. Mercilessly and systematically it trampled the human embryos, breaking them of all human feelings other than submissiveness as if they were vices. [. . .]

Look at this generation—the portion that *survived* the spirit-killing government education—sickly, nervous, inwardly troubled, no longer believing in anything radiant or in itself.

And how many lay down their heads and died, never knowing a joyous day after entering the corps or the school? [. . .]

A silent nation, swallowing its tears, did not break discipline. [. . .]

III

These memories are oppressive! One would wish not to bring them into the new decade, but it is not we who have summoned the dark shades of the past.

Every blow of a government lash against youth and future Russia awakens in those aching hearts terrible images. [. . .]

Allow just one generation—you celebrated educators—to grow up in a humane way, able to look everything in the eye, to fearlessly speak their minds, to openly *applaud* and openly *gather*, just like what takes place in every school in England.

Can it be that an entrance hall where a dozen serfs keep silent in the master's presence and silently hate him is an educational model? Is the whispering of slaves more pleasing to you than the voices of awakening lives, their resonant laughter and even their occasionally arrogant words?

How backward are our educators! How far they are from a "human being" and how close to Arakcheev, how noticeable the smattering of barracks dirt and the *raznochinets*[15] petty official's ambition, which demands *not respect for the person,* but *subordination and fear of his rank!*

...We do not readily give in to the belief that it is so easy to stop them, and to the question of whether we think that all of these Nicholaevan rags can bring Russia to a halt and return it to the way it was before 1855 the answer is a decisive *no!*

But, on the other hand, we know that the path Russia is traveling can be twisted, covered with dirt, and sprinkled with broken glass; from a radiant, regular procession it can become a wearying march and continuous fight, in which the government—materially much stronger—would destroy a lot of people and create a lot of unhappiness without any need and without any purpose. That is why these reactionary moves, this return to a time which we need to forget, these shifts in the direction of the past do not plunge us into despair, but they do make us tremble with anger and vexation. That is why we are entering the new decade in a thoughtful mood and, as we cross the final boundary with the past, we are stopping once more to say to the sovereign:

Sovereign, awaken, the new year has rung in a new decade, which, perhaps, will carry your name. However, you really cannot use one and the same hand to brightly and joyously sign your name into history as the emancipator of the serfs and, at the same time, sign absurd injunctions against free speech and against young people. You are being deceived and you are deceiving yourself—it is Yuletide and everyone is in costume. Order them to take their masks off and take a good look at the ones who are friends of Russia and those who love only their own private advantage. It is doubly important for you that the friends of Russia *can still be* yours. Order them to take their masks off quickly. You will be surprised—this masquerade that surrounds you is not like the one that was organized two years ago for the grand dukes in the military academy. There, children pretended to be wolves and wild boars, while here, wild boars and wolves pretend to be senior officials and fathers of the fatherland!

Notes

Source: "1860 god," *Kolokol*, l. 60, January 1, 1860; 14:214–25, 526–30.

1. Along with his service on the Editorial Commission, Nikolay A Milyutin (1818–1872) was minister of the interior from 1859 to 1861 and state secretary for Polish Affairs from 1863 to 1866.

2. After the death of Nicholas I in 1855.

3. The Nazimov Rescript was issued in August 1857 and published in November of that year.

4. The dying words of Emperor Julian the Apostate, who had fought the rise of Christianity. Herzen had used this phrase at the beginning and end of his article "After Three Years," which appeared in the ninth issue of *The Bell* on Feb. 15, 1858.

5. From "A Letter to Emperor Alexander the Second," which appeared in *The Polestar* in 1855 (Doc. 5).

6. On September 4, 1859, in a speech to deputies from the provincial committees, the tsar stated that he had always and would always proudly consider himself the country's "first nobleman" (*pervyi dvorianin*).

7. Prince Mikhail D. Gorchakov (1793–1861) was governor-general of the Kingdom of Poland from 1856 to 1861, not to be confused with the better-known Prince Alexander M. Gorchakov, minister of foreign affairs.

8. Zakrevsky was relieved of his duties April 15, 1859, after granting written permission for his daughter, Countess Nesselrode, to enter into a second marriage without having ended the first one, and having threatened a priest with exile to Siberia if he did not perform the ceremony as ordered. Pavel A. Tuchkov (1803–1864) succeeded him as governor-general of Moscow from 1859 to 1864.

9. Prince Vasily A. Dolgorukov (1804–1868) was chief of gendarmes and head of the Third Department from 1856 to 1866.

10. The Baltic German Ernst Biron (1690–1772) was a favorite of the Empress Anna Ioannovna and regent in 1740; Count Andrey Osterman (1686–1747), born in Westphalia, entered Russian service in 1704 and occupied senior government posts until 1741; Mikhail Lomonosov (1711–1765), of humble birth, was a gifted scientist, writer, and the founder of Moscow University.

11. Poet Alexey V. Koltsov (see Doc. 1).

12. Faustin Soulouque (c. 1782–1876) fought in Haiti's war for independence and served as the country's president and emperor. Bobchinsky and Dobchinsky are characters in Gogol's play *The Inspector General*.

13. Ivan S. Barkov (1731–1768) was a poet, translator, and author of pornographic verse.

14. Under Paul I, a *Wachtparade* took place daily in the tsar's presence; under Alexander II, it was staged every Sunday.

15. Not of gentry birth.

⇢ 26 ⇠

The Bell, Nos. 68–69, April 15, 1860. This is one of the periodic attacks on Panin in Herzen's satirical style.

COUNT VIKTOR PANIN'S SPEECH TO THE DEPUTIES
[1860]

Gentlemen,
You recall the words of our sovereign emperor; I have deeply engraved them in my memory and I will act in conformity with them. You know that the plans of the Editorial Commission have not yet been confirmed, and for that reason I cannot say anything that will be *either reassuring or favorable* to you, and I hope that you will refrain from anything that might excite *major hopes or fears* among the gentry. Although I myself am a *wealthy* landowner, I will not forget the interests of landowners *of modest means*, and, recalling that peasants do not

have their own representatives here, I will keep in mind their benefit, all the more since I am completely convinced that there will be no way of avoiding sacrifices on the part of the gentry. Gentlemen, ours is a *private, family* matter, and it should not go outside this room, because there is no need *to disseminate information, and especially to write about it to those **abroad**.* And now, gentlemen, I have another request. I have heard that many of you gather at Count Shuvalov's, where members of the nobility are preparing for elections, and for that reason I ask you *to curtail your visits because people there might try to lobby you.*

My door is always open to you and to everyone, *but I request that you not visit me,* in order not to give credence to rumors that I am under the influence of one or another of you. Thus, gentlemen, I advise you to get to work. Gentlemen, in this regard I can offer my experience; there is no significant government business that cannot be concluded in fourteen days.

The nonsensical words of this count-bureaucrat have almost reconciled us to him, as we have begun to pity this lanky, sickly figure, whose brain had gone soft from the lofty heights (and, to be sure, it was not so firm before this). He is subject only to medical judgment; the court of public opinion is for those who placed him not in a madhouse but in the house of *liberation.*

Take note that every phrase is a *plus-minus—which equals zero.*

What can it mean that Panin has nothing to say that is *either reassuring or favorable?* What would he call reassuring? To leave things as they were? The rights to seize a dwelling, to receive one's quitrent in bed, to require six days labor... to the birch rod, to extortion? Why is the emancipation of the serfs a *private and family* matter, why must it be muted? This is a matter for an assembly of the land, it is historical, all-Russian, and not a family matter for *rich* landowners who feel the pain of the *poor ones.* And bragging about his own fortune is very nice! Imagine a judge who would say to a petitioner: "Despite the fact that I am rich and you are poor, I will defend you." For such a coarse bit of nonsense the minister of justice (if it weren't Panin) ought to have—through Topilsky—reprimanded him.[1]

The fear of *The Bell* is too flattering and we will stand on a chair and give him a kiss on the forehead for this. [. . .]

Note

Source: "Slovo grafa Viktora Panina k deputatam," *Kolokol,* l. 68–69, April 15, 1860; 14:254–55, 547–48.

1. Mikhail I. Topilsky (1811–1873) was a department director in the Ministry of Justice prior to 1862.

$$\rightarrow 27 \leftarrow$$

The Bell, Nos. 68–69, April 15, 1860. The comparisons, parallels, puns, and the parodic use of elevated language are typical of Herzen. Several of this article's themes are developed more fully in the introduction to the volume *After Five Years*.

LETTERS FROM RUSSIA
[1860]

"It is very, very sad! Shouldn't Russia tell Alexander Nikolaevich what Tatyana told Onegin: *But happiness was so possible, so close!*"

One of the many letters we have received during the past ten days ends with these poetic but endlessly melancholy lines.

The letters are remarkable in and of themselves: frightened and surprised people have found the need to announce their indignation, their cry of pain, after the unexpected resurrection of Nicholaevan times.

We will steadfastly get through this time of terrible ordeals, we will become kinder and will not lose faith in Russia's development just because a weak tsar, tripping over Panin, has fallen into the slush and mud of Luzhin's denunciations.[1] We are even sorrier that "after a five-year reign, which filled Roman hearts with hope, Caesar has changed for the worse!" This was said of Nero; we sincerely wish that these words of the Roman chronicler not be repeated by a future Karamzin.

One should not reproach us. We restrained ourselves up to the last instant, until there was open betrayal, until the criminal appointment of Panin, until the arbitrariness in the matter of *Unkovsky and Evropeus,* the *police* conspiracy as a result of which there were arrests of students, Professor *Kachenovsky,*[2] and we don't know who else.[3] We could draw back and yield when the mainstream was following the right channel, but now it is quite another matter!

Farewell, Alexander Nikolaevich, have a good journey! Bon voyage!.. Our path lies this way. [. . .]

We are grains of sand—physically cut off—of the awakening crowd, the Russian masses—we are strong only in our instinct, by which we guess how its heart beats, how it bleeds, what it wants to say but cannot.

We will return to that subject, but now we will look at the letters. We will relate only the factual parts and the rumors.

The myths and legends circulating about Panin's appointment are remarkable. One correspondent writes that "Muravyov and Panin were charged with sealing Rostovtsev's study. The sovereign himself appeared and found Panin alone; he waited one hour, and then another. 'Well, then I will name you the chair of the commission.'" Ben trovato![4] Absurdities ought to be based on dumb chance. When people play blind man's bluff the amusing part is that they do not know ahead of time *whom exactly* they will catch hold of. And if the sovereign had caught Muravyov, he would not have gotten a bad deal. It's annoying that only courtiers are invited to these *petit jeux*,[5] or maybe luck would have shone on the Parisian Kiselev—who understood the peasant collective even under Nicholas—or on the oldest fighter for peasant emancipation with land, N. I. Turgenev.[6] They would have managed this business better than the previous chair. But with the whole *embarrass du choix*[7]—between old Adlerberg and young Adlerberg,[8] between the tall Panin and the not-too-bright Dolgorukov—there is not much to choose. Diogenes with his lantern would not find anyone here except for Butkov.

There is another legend that is in no way inferior. Two correspondents write that the empress *helped bring about* Panin's appointment "as a result of her economic and religious ideas, which did not agree with the thought of *the emancipation of the peasants with land!*"

Indeed, neither pietism nor political economy will lead you to a land allotment. This is a purely German opinion, i.e., harmful, but *logisch conséquent.*[9] Christianity demands that we should all be poor and to some extent tramps; moreover, it teaches us to care more for our neighbor than for ourselves. For that reason it is no wonder that the empress, while herself remaining in worldly comfort, wished *first* to free the serfs from *temporary* land, making it easier for them to receive an eternal allotment—heavenly plowland—endless acres[10] which have been sown for ages and, what's more, with seeds not from any granary.

We do not blame the empress for simultaneously following the teachings of the apostle Paul and the apostle Malthus and for not knowing the Russian situation. But why should she interfere in such foreign matters as the emancipation of *our* Russian serfs and the allotment of *our* Russian land to them?

According to a third legend, it is said that, as he was dying, Rostovtsev nominated Panin to the sovereign. That is difficult to believe; could he really have wished to end his career as he began it, or did he die in a state of delirium?[11]

As for the hero of this novel, i.e., Viktor Nikitich [Panin], he immediately began to act like strychnine, inspiring a stupor and a stiffening in every living thing with his numbing formalism and the dead letter of the law. Here is what occupied this head on a pole, who had been summoned to trivialize the great business of emancipation: it ordered "members of the commission to appear in a civil service uniform or in tails, and ordered them to compile a *register* of all matters resolved and unresolved, those which can be taken up for discussion and those which cannot be discussed."

But the commissions themselves, through the sort of clairvoyance that comes to people just before death or a great calamity, went crazy, anticipating the strychnine-like action of the Ivan the Great of justice. "In the administrative branch Prince Cherkassky again raised the question of birch rods and the number of strokes (it is simply monomania on this man's part!). There was an objection that he had already renounced the birch rod in print, to which he answered that 'it was one thing in print but another in deed, adding in a Karamzinian-Ansillonian style:[12] 'Those who want popularity can speak against the rod (and against God and Novgorod the Great!), but those who *give it serious thought* cannot deny its necessity.' " [. . .] It is said that Solovyov[13] made a strong objection, and when a ballot was taken on Cherkassky's proposal the votes were divided evenly. A Hamlet-like question transposed in a Russian manner—*To beat or not to beat, and if to beat, then how many strokes?*—was sent to the general assembly, which produced the same split vote. The voice of the chairman Bulgakov (with whose rhetorical style we are familiar) should have tipped the balance.[14] The eloquent chair took pity on the fond-of-flogging prince, and he came down on the side of birch rods; they can serve as triumphant palm branches with which the members can appease the gods at the gates of the city of Jacob, when, from the Capernaum of justice, Panin enters, riding on the back of the modest Topilsky.

They say that liberal defenders of *birch rods* justify themselves by saying that only *twenty strokes* are permitted (what savage Tatars—let them add up on their abacus 20 + 20 + 20 + 20 = and what does that equal?). However, let the birch rods remain during this whole transitional period as a monument to the vile, disgraceful caste not of aristocrats, but of executioners and plantation owners. Honor and glory to those citizens *who do not seek popularity* and who upheld the ferocious and bloody appetites of the social class who, except for this, *might have been forgiven the past by the people!*[15]

Notes

Source: "Pis'ma iz Rossii," *Kolokol,* l. 68–69, April 15, 1860; 14:256–60, 548.

   1. Ivan D. Luzhin held various roles in the Russian government, as chief of police in Moscow, Kursk, and Kharkov, and as both a military and civilian governor.

2. Andrey M. Unkovsky (1828–1893) was the head of the Tver nobility from 1857 to 1859; Alexander I. Evropeus (1826–1885) was a member of the Petrashevtsy who, after serving his sentence, was, along with Unkovsky, a leader of the Tver gentry's liberal opposition, for which he was sent to Perm in 1860. Dmitry I. Kachenovsky (1827–1872) was a professor of international law at Kharkov University. Herzen, who knew and liked Kachenovsky, had announced his arrest in the previous issue of *The Bell*.

3. Herzen: "*The Times* on April 9 again mentions searches and arrests, and, by the way, the fact that papers were confiscated from Professor *Pavlov*."

4. Herzen: "Very clever!"

5. Herzen: "Parlor games."

6. Count Pavel D. Kiselev (1788–1873) was minister of government property from 1838 to 1856, and ambassador to Paris from 1856 to 1862; Nikolay I. Turgenev (1789–1871) was a Decembrist, and later an émigré and author of memoirs.

7. Herzen: "Difficulty in making a choice."

8. Father and son.

9. Herzen: "It follows logically."

10. The measure Herzen uses is the *desiatina*, which equals 2.7 acres.

11. Rostovtsev is known to have gained favor by betraying the forces of progress in December 1825.

12. Karamzin had an enormous influence on Russian linguistic style in the late eighteenth and early nineteenth centuries; Johann P. Ansillon (1767–1837) was a historian and theologian, and Prussian foreign minister from 1832 to 1837.

13. Yakov A. Solovyov (1820–1876), active in peasant reform, was a member of the Editorial Commission.

14. Petr A. Bulgakov (d. 1883) was a state secretary and, beginning in 1859, served as an expert member of the Editorial Commission on the issue of serfdom.

15. Herzen: "Two letters that we received disagree over one name. This is no joking matter. The people who voted for the birch rod in 1860 should be aware that their name will remain on a pillar of shame no matter what kind of bureaucrats, administrators, or colleagues they are. That is why we sincerely ask people to tell us whether this list on names is accurate:

Against flogging	For flogging
Girs	Pr. Cherkassky
Solovyov	*Samarin (?)*
Domentovich	*Milyutin*
Bunge	Galagan
Arapetov	Semyonov
Pr. Golitsin	Semyonov 2
Lyuboshchinsky	Bulgakov
Zablotsky	Tatarinov
Kulchin	Gradyanko
Kalachov	Zalessky
Bulygin	Zheleznov

Another letter says quite the opposite, that *Samarin* was completely against *Cherkasskian* flogging."

→ 28 ←

This was first published as the introduction to the anthology *Five Years Later*, and then separately in *The Bell*, No. 72, June 1, 1860. At this point, Herzen shifted his focus from the tsar as the primary agent of change to the progressive intelligentsia. The poet and journalist Alexey Pleshcheev (1825–1893) wrote to a friend that while he had not yet received a copy of the book, judging by recent issues of *The Bell*, it was likely to assume a hostile tone; however, since the powerful people of the world were unlikely to read it, the consequences would be minimal. Turgenev liked the introduction, but Tolstoy was critical of the scattershot effect and the incredible display of egoism, but he also acknowledged "the broad-mindedness, cunning, kindness, and elegance" as quintessentially Russian (*Let* 3:120–24, 135).

FIVE YEARS LATER
[1860]

> Farewell, Alexander Nikolaevich, have a good
> journey! Bon voyage!.. Our path lies this way!
> —*The Bell*, April 15, 1860

The publication of our political articles from the last five *years*, scattered in *The Polestar* and *The Bell*, by chance takes on a particular meaning on account of the gloomy events at the time of the collection's appearance.[1] Circumstances are turning it into a signpost. Once more we are entering some kind of new realm of chaos and twilight and again we must change our clothes and our language precisely because we remain unalterably true to our convictions. A certain depth is essential for navigation and the choice of channel depends not on us but on the stream; we will follow all of its twists and turns, provided that we are moving forward to our goal and not coming to a halt on a sandbank... while imagining that we are still in motion. *Five years* ago, for the first time after seven terrible years spent burying people, nations, hopes, and beliefs, we gazed a little more radiantly at the future and sighed, as people do when recovering from a serious illness.[2]

A flickering streak of pale light caught fire on the Russian horizon. We had a premonition, and made a prediction in the midst of the dark night, but did not expect it to happen that quickly—on it we focused all our remaining hopes and fragments of all our expectations. We were already so alien to the West that its fate was no longer a vital question for us. With deep interest, with a sympathetic melancholy, we followed its darkly developing tragedy, but, strengthened by what we had found out and, blessing the great past, we gathered ourselves together, like Fortinbras after Horatio's tale, to continue our journey.

We did not get very far—we were stopped by some sort of endless swamp which we had not expected and which threatened without any great noise to steal our last strength with its swampy, tedious filth, softening our despair with expectations and diluting our hatred with pity. [. . .]

Once again we were wrong *about the timing,* overjoyed by the pale dawn, not taking into consideration those uncontrolled, dark, insurmountable clouds over which light has no power, or with which entire generations must battle.

The fateful power of contemporary reaction in Russia—*senseless, unnecessary* reaction—is crushed with such difficulty because it relies on two strong points of the granite fortress, *the obtuseness of the government and the underdevelopment of the people.*

Slowness in understanding is a power, a force, and the greatest irony over reason and logic. Underdevelopment is not as stubborn, but it only yields to time, a very long period of time. This is what sends us into despair—we would sooner give up all things—our property, our freedom—rather than time. "Time is money," as the English say, and it is as expensive and as big a thing as possible: *time is us!*

But no matter how natural the annoyance that gnaws at a person when he sees that "happiness was so possible, so close," and is slipping away because of the clumsiness of his fingers, no matter how natural the horror that overcomes us when we cry out to our fellow traveler—who does not notice the abyss beneath our feet—and we feel that our voice is not reaching him, we must nevertheless submit to the truth. Instead of stubbornness and a waste of strength in defending paths that have been covered over by reactionaries, we must travel the path along which it is possible to get through. It is in this flexibility during a period of constant striving that all the creativity of nature consists, all the rich variety of its forms, notwithstanding a unity and simplicity of principles and goals.

We must get our bearings in the new situation. It is true that we are emerging poorer from these five years *of good hopes,* but, to make up for it, with less of a burden on our swampy journey.

We thought that the autocracy in Russia could still perform the noble deed *of freeing the serfs with land.* [. . .] But what did happen? Autocracy, which never gives anything careful thought, spilling blood and tears with the callousness of a locomotive encountering obstacles, shyly stopped as it pronounced the words "emancipation with land," and began to consult with generals and bureaucrats, with young scholars and old men "decrepit" in their ignorance. As if that were not enough, they summoned prominent people and ordered them *to keep their advice to themselves*. All of this taken together—the involuntary realization that the imperial house has no more faith in its moral power and in its blood ties with the people, leads both the government and the revolutionary to sense that they have the right to *act boldly!*

Our article from April 1, 1860, was the final effort to convince *ourselves* of the possibility of "the improvement of the imperial way of life" with its liberation from crude and ignorant nobles and the pernicious, numbing bureaucracy.

But already Alexander II, frightened by some kind of apparitions, held onto the endless tails of Panin's coat and said to him: "Do not deceive me!"

That is a kind of abdication.

Alexander II released his bow, and in this lies his historical significance; where the arrow lands is out of his control, and it does not even depend on whether Panin deceives him or not. Isn't this tsarist vacillation another kind of *vivos voco*?[3] Isn't it a bell reminding the minority of adults that it is time to do things themselves, that there has been enough of relying completely on the government? Let us leave administrative matters and diplomatic gossip to it. Let us withdraw from its place on the parade ground and take up our own affairs, and let it stand, like a Neva pyramid, like a mansion in which a dead person lives.

Be assured that there is nothing to expect from the government. Without an Achilles heel for reason, engaged in the preservation of old rituals and official uniforms, satisfied with magnificent robes and material power, it will sometimes, under the influence of the current flow of ideas, convulsively extend its hand to progress, and every time will take fright halfway there... This all may continue for a long time, at least until someone more daring peeps under the curtain and sees not that the emperor is dead but that the government had given the order: "long live the people!"

Who has not happened to see old citadels gloomily standing for centuries on end? Since the time when they poured death down on enemies, a new life has surrounded them with a garland of streets, gardens, palaces, stretching further and further into the fields and coming closer and closer to the embrasures with their rusty cannon, along which a watchman walks in businesslike idleness, while within, sparrows build their nests. Generations go by, and suddenly the question presents itself to everyone: what is the point of these walls, which are not defending us from anyone, why maintain a garrison, with an idle prankster with gray whiskers reporting every evening to the commandant? The city finds it ridiculous: the ancient fortress is reduced to rubble, and life quickly covers over the scars with its own little swellings and ditches.

Such a threatening fortress is our government. Everything is requisitioned by the commandant, everything, as is expected in a state of siege, willing or not, *does its duty*. Russia offers the fantastic spectacle of a state in which everything acknowledged to be a human being consists wholly *of officials,* military and civilian.

Only literature, the universities, and the peasant hut took no positive part in the establishment and maintenance of the autocratic official order, accepted as the government's goal. No attention was paid to the dispirited hut; only schismatic groups were being harassed by officials from time to time for violations of church *form*. Literature and the universities were roundly hated by Nicholas, an expert on these matters.

The entire people were under a guardianship, like some sort of adolescent. The late guardian had gone to the Herculean extent that he did not allow private individuals to build railroads with their *own money!*

After that, it remained for the people to finally conclude that they were adolescents, to assume a zoological form and quietly dwell in the company of residents of Khiva, beavers, Kirgiz, and lemurs. But it was precisely *here* that there proved to be some signs of life. A slave, constrained hand and foot, tied and bound to the "job," without a voice, tangled up in the bureaucracy's nets, sent to be a soldier and flogged, flinched at the incursion of a foreign enemy,[4] stretched his muscles, and on the edge of disgrace felt his own power. [. . .]

The tsar also flinched and he also opened his eyes... the silence of the steppe, theft nearby, theft far away, neither a friendly glance nor a human face nor devotion, all buttoned-up collars and properly sewn and fitted uniforms... while below are groans, armies perishing, the thunder of cannon, the fire's glow, ships sinking, blood flowing... a dispatch from Eupatoria fell from his hand and he died.[5]

Russia offered *five years of waiting* for a few kind words, for the desire to do good. And what happened? The very same proof of inability, of bankruptcy in doing good that after five years turned out to be *evil!*

And what follows from this? It is time to stop playing at garrisons. Let the *government govern* and let us take up our own affairs. For this we must go into retirement—the household is in disorder, the children need to be educated and landowner's sons need to be tamed.

We will weaken the government by our non-participation. Their business will suffer but the *office work* will not stop. Without us they still have enough assistants to fill all the official cracks—clerks, bureaucrat-Germans, and bureaucrat-doctrinaires. It has raised officialdom to a science and has lowered the government to the level of an office in charge of decorum. Out of gratitude they should remain with the government, like mice with a sinking ship...

But we will be off *on our own!*

April 25, 1860

Notes

Source: "Za piat' let," *Kolokol,* l. 72, June 1, 1860; 14:274–78, 555–56.

1. Herzen is referring to Panin's appointment, the exile of Unkovsky and Evropeus, and the harassment of students and professors at St. Petersburg University.

2. "Seven terrible years" refers to the reactionary period between the failed 1848 uprisings and the death of Nicholas I in 1855.

3. On *"vivos voco,"* see the introduction and Doc. 9.

4. French forces landed in the Crimea in 1854.

5. Russian forces were defeated near Eupatoria on February 5, 1855, news received by Nicholas I on February 14; his health took a serious turn for the worse within a few days and by February 18 he was dead. This rapid sequence of events led to rumors of suicide.

→ 29 ←

The Bell, No. 75, July 1, 1860. Earlier in 1860, Herzen responded to a letter from a Russian ship captain with an essay about the extraordinary importance of ending corporal punishment, a practice which offended both human dignity and natural empathy. "The great men of the 14th of December understand the importance of this so well, that members of the society undertook an obligation not to tolerate corporal punishment on their estates, and eliminated it from regiments they commanded" (Gertsen, *Sobranie sochinenii,* 27:bk. 1, 22).

The article below is one of Herzen's most direct and passionate public statements on the issue, one of the problems weighing on his mind when he established the Free Russian Press (Doc. 13). This became a cause dear to many in Russia's emerging civil society, but not one that soon led to new laws. Almost four decades later, at one of the lively and significant Pirogov medical congresses (April 21–28, 1896, in Kiev), the former serf D. N. Zhbankov made a plea for "removing the negative factors which retarded cultural development," including corporal punishment. Zhbankov wore a peasant blouse, even to the Pirogov Society dinners, in order to call attention to the peasants' situation (Frieden, *Russian Physicians,* 191).

Down with Birch Rods!
[1860]

We would like to make a very simple and possible proposal to the educated minority of the gentry—a proposal carrying with it neither responsibility nor danger. We propose that they set up

A UNION TO BAN CORPORAL PUNISHMENT

The degree of education of this minority, its conduct on the provincial committees, its maturity as expressed in a desire for self-governance—all this is incompatible with the savage beating and lashing of serfs. In times of backwardness and patriarchal brutality, the conscience of the person meting out the punishment was to a certain degree clear; he believed that this was not only his right but thought that it was his duty. No one believes that now, and now everyone knows that punishment without a trial—based on personal views—is a selfish application of the rights of the stronger person and is the same kind of torment as the lashing of a horse. Serfs in the field and the house are beaten exclusively and naturally for financial advantage and for petty convenience.

The government cannot and will not hinder such a *negative* union... The government does not impose on gentry the obligation *to lash their serfs*. It simply allows this and helps in a fatherly way. [. . .]

Let landowners think that flogging will not be around for long, and, following the awkwardness of the transitional state, one must, against one's will, part company with the rod... is it not better to give it up voluntarily? To cast off the rod like the French nobility threw their feudal charters into the fire on August 4th?[1]

It is noble to reject the right to flog in light of the Cherkassky party and Samarin and Milyutin who are united with Cherkassky.[2] And, really, what would the government take you for, thinking that you demand human rights for yourself and also want to flog without a trial, and this at a time when the government itself is beginning to limit beating in the military?

In every province let three or four landowners give each other *their solemn promise never* to resort to corporal punishment, never to allow themselves to beat anyone—that is enough of a beginning. Of course it is perfectly clear that the thing shouldn't be done halfway—it's little enough not to beat people yourself and not to send them to be flogged... it is necessary to forbid stewards, elders, and butlers, and to forbid it in such a way that the field and house serfs knew!

This is not the first time we have had to be embarrassed at the poverty of our demands... Yes, there is a great deal one must tame and keep silent in oneself in order to stretch out a hand as if asking for alms... for what?.. for recognizing human dignity in oneself and in those near to you!

If only our voice is not in vain, if only it reminded some and advised others that the time has come to leave off butchery; if only as a first instance it succeeded in sparing several peasants from torture and several landowners from a stain on their conscience.

We do not want to know what landowners did up till now. We close our eyes to the past, when much was done due to ignorance, habit, an awful upbringing, and the disgraceful example of the parental home... Amnesty and oblivion are also necessary here. But three years ago, the situation changed, and from the point when the question of emancipation was raised by the government, discussed in journals, sitting-rooms, and front halls, in the capital and the provinces—*since that time it has become impossible to be an honorable and educated person and beat one's people.* (Of course, we exclude theoretical fanatics of flogging, these are damaged people, and they can talk nonsense and still be the most honorable of people, like every madman.)

Let us give each other our word of honor not to flog our peasants and set up not just one union but hundreds of them in various provinces and various districts. Most of all, do not be afraid of your small numbers; two energetic people, firmly marching toward their goal, are more powerful than a whole crowd that lacks any goal. Didn't Wilberforce and Cobden begin with three or four people who came to agreement in a club or a tavern?[3] [. . .] Man is as weak as a *spark* and as strong as a *spark,* if he believes in his strength and comes upon a ready environment *in time.*

Throw away the despicable rod and join hands in the *Union to Ban Corporal Punishment!*

Notes

Source: "Rozgi doloi!" *Kolokol,* l. 75, July 1, 1860; 14:287–89, 561.

1. At a meeting of the Constituent Assembly in 1789.

2. Prince Vladimir A. Cherkassky (1824–1878) was an expert member on the Editorial Commission considering the issue of serfdom and emancipation; Yury F. Samarin (1819–1876) was a writer, public figure, member of the Editorial Commission, and a Slavophile.

3. William Wilberforce (1759–1833) was an English activist who successfully fought to end the slave trade in Britain; Richard Cobden (1804–1865) was an English political figure, opponent of the Corn Laws, advocate of free trade, and member of Parliament.

> → *30* ←

The Bell, No. 90, January 15, 1861. Herzen learned about Konstantin Aksakov's death through a letter from the deceased's brother, Ivan. Turgenev wrote to Herzen in February 1861 informing him that the article below made a deep impression on readers in Moscow and elsewhere in Russia, and that Turgenev himself appreciated the linking of his name with that of Belinsky and others in the essay "Provincial Universities" (that appeared in the subsequent issue) as much as he would a prestigious government award (*Let* 3:185). Ivan Aksakov later added that what Herzen wrote was much better than anything published in Russia about his brother or about Khomyakov (who died in September 1860). Despite differing on a number of issues, Herzen had deep respect for the Moscow Slavophiles, agreeing with Konstantin Aksakov on the need to emancipate the serfs with land, and on the hopelessness of the government in St. Petersburg. At this point he felt closer in some ways to the Slavophiles than to pro-government liberals or the increasingly intolerant progressive writers. The Ministry of Education banned a speech at St. Petersburg University about Aksakov by Professor Nikolay I. Kostomarov (1817–1885) because of Herzen's praise for the deceased in *The Bell*. Walicki notes that the Aksakov obituary was "lengthy and extraordinarily warm," reflecting an idealization of Slavophilism and a celebration of its utopia at a moment when Slavophiles were about to abandon this vision (Walicki, *Slavophile Controversy*, 592). Lengthy excerpts from this tribute were included in Herzen's memoir (*My Past and Thoughts*, 2:549–50).

In the same issue of *The Bell*, Herzen reported on the "arrest" of the papers of history professor Platon V. Pavlov (1823–1895) in St. Petersburg, in connection with a Kharkov student affair. Pavlov, who had previously taught in Kiev and Moscow, was exiled to Vetlyuga after an 1862 speech at a millennium celebration in St. Petersburg, later transformed and immortalized by Dostoevsky in the novel *Demons*.

KONSTANTIN SERGEEVICH AKSAKOV
[1861]

Following the powerful fighter for the Slavic cause in Russia, A. S. Khomyakov, one of his comrades-in-arms, *Konstantin Sergeevich Aksakov*, passed away last month.

Khomyakov died young, even younger than Aksakov; it is painful for the people who loved them to know that these noble, tireless activists, these *opponents*, who were closer to us than many of *our own*, are no more. One cannot argue with the absurd power of fate, which has neither ears nor eyes and cannot even be offended, and for that reason, with tears and a pious feeling we close the lid on their coffins and move on to that which lives after them.

The Kireevskys,[1] Khomyakov, and Aksakov *finished their work;* whether their lives were long or short, when closing their eyes they could with full consciousness say to themselves that they had accomplished what they wanted to accomplish; if they were unable to stop the courier's troika sent by Peter, in which Biron sits and thrashes the coachman to make him gallop along rows of grain and trample people, then they did bring a halt to mindlessly enthusiastic public opinion and caused all serious people to become thoughtful.

The turning point in Russian thought began with them. And when *we* say that, it would seem, we cannot be suspected of bias.

Yes, we were their opponents, but very strange ones. We had a *single* love, but not an *identical* one.

From our earliest years we and they were struck by a single, powerful, instinctive, physiological, passionate feeling, which they took as a recollection and we as prophecy—a feeling of boundless, all-embracing love for the Russian people, the Russian way of life, and the Russian way of thinking. And like Janus or a two-headed eagle, we gazed in different directions while *our heart beat as one.*

They transferred all their love and all their tenderness to the oppressed mother. For us, brought up away from home, that tie had weakened. A French governess had charge of us and we learned later on that our mother was not she, but a downtrodden peasant woman, which we ourselves had guessed from the resemblance in our features and because her songs were more native to us than vaudeville. We came to love her very much but her life was too cramped for us. It was very stuffy in her little room—all blackened faces looking out from the silver icon frames, priests and deacons—frightening the unhappy woman, who had been beaten by soldiers and clerks; even her eternal cry about lost happiness tore at our heart. We knew that she had no radiant memories, and we knew something else, that her happiness lay ahead, that beneath her heart beat that of an unborn child, our younger brother. [. . .]

Such was our family quarrel fifteen years ago.[2] A lot of water has flowed under the bridge since then; we have encountered *mountain air* that stopped our ascent, while they, instead of a world of relics, stumbled upon living Russian questions. To settle accounts seems strange to us because there is no patent on understanding; time, history, and experience brought us closer together not because they were drawn closer to us or we to them, but because we and they are closer to a true outlook than before, when we relentlessly tore each other to pieces in journal articles, although even then I do not recall that we doubted their ardent love for Russia or they ours.[3]

Based on this faith in each other and this common love even we have the right to bow to their graves and throw our handful of earth on their deceased with a sacred wish that on their graves and on ours young Russia will flourish powerfully and widely!

January 1/13, 1861

Notes

Source: "Konstantin Sergeevich Aksakov," *Kolokol,* l. 90, January 15, 1861; 15:9–11, 294–96.

1. Ivan V. Kireevsky (1806–1856), literary critic, editor of *The European,* and, along with his older brother Petr (1808–1856), one of the founders of the Slavophile movement.

2. Herzen refers to the years 1844–47.

3. Herzen: "Only once N. Yazykov insultingly 'lashed out' at Chaadaev, Granovsky, and me. K. Aksakov could not stand it and answered this poet in his own party with sharp verses in our defense. [. . .] Aksakov remained an eternally enthusiastic and infinitely noble youth. He got carried away, was distracted, but was always pure of heart. In 1844, when our quarrels had reached the point where neither we nor the Slavophiles wanted to have any further meetings, I was walking along the street as K. Aksakov went by in a sleigh. I bowed to him in a friendly way. He was about to pass me by when he suddenly stopped the coachman, got out of the sleigh and came up to me. 'It was too painful for me,' he said, 'to go past you without saying goodbye. You understand that after all that has passed between your friends and mine, I won't be coming to see you; it is such a pity but nothing can be done about it. I wanted to shake your hand and bid you farewell.' He rapidly walked back to his sleigh, but suddenly turned; I stood in the same spot because I was feeling sad; he ran toward me, embraced and kissed me. I had tears in my eyes. How I loved him at that moment of quarreling!"

↷ **31** ↶

The Bell, No. 93, March 1, 1861. In this article, Herzen is most likely taking into account information he received in a February 1861 letter from Ivan Turgenev, who said that the emancipation announcement would come soon, perhaps on the sixth anniversary of the death of Nicholas I (February 18). Turgenev believed that the main opponents of this act were Gagarin (either Ivan Vasilevich, Voronezh governor and author of an infamous project to defraud the serfs, or Prince Pavel Pavlovich, a member of the Main Committee on emancipation), Minister of State Properties Count Mikhail N. Muravyov, Minister of Finance Knyazhevich, and Minister of Foreign Affairs Prince Gorchakov. In the following issue of *The Bell,* Herzen urged Russian tourists to return home to witness this civilizational change, a message he also sent privately to Turgenev, saying that for men of the forties "this is our moment, our last moment—the epilogue" (Gertsen, *Sobranie sochinenii*, 27:bk. 1, 138–40).

ON THE EVE
[1861]

Holy Saturday has come and soon the bell will begin to ring for the morning service... and the soul feels frightened and oppressed. Why would we poison this festive moment? Like our poor peasants, we stand deep in thought, with incomplete faith, with a deep desire for love and with an insurmountable feeling of hate.

If only we could say once more: "You have conquered, Galilean!" how loudly and enthusiastically we would have said it, and let any one-sided doctrinaire and immobile front-line soldier of schoolboy science, while mocking us, produce proof that we do not continually repeat *one and the same thing*.

Russia did not have this much at stake either in 1612 or in 1812.

It is good that on the anniversary of the death of Nicholas they will lay to rest the Petrine era. We would like to say: "many thanks to it for a difficult lesson and for consigning to oblivion the evil caused by it!" But for this the evil must die, and it has not died out in the criminal, dishonest old men who do not repent of the money-grubbing and greed.

Foreign journals talk about the plantation owner opposition by the invalids. The grave will be an unquiet place for these gray-haired eunuchs if they succeed in disfiguring the Rus that is being born. This is not just about bribes and theft, this is a knife being driven into the future. Watch out, Muravyovs and Gagarins,[1] double traitors—of the people, whom you are pillaging, and of the tsar, whom you are robbing—if you manage to make your way to the swampy Petersburg cemeteries, your descendants will answer before the Russian people.

There are sacred, solemn moments in the life of people and nations during which wrongs are not forgiven!

Note

Source: "Nakanune," *Kolokol*, l. 93, March 1, 1861; 15:33–34, 310–11.

1. Ivan V. Gagarin was head of the nobility in the province of Voronezh from 1853 to 1859, a member of the province's committee on peasant issues, and author of a proposal to deprive serfs of any estate lands upon their emancipation and credit landowners with half the value of peasant dwellings.

→ *32* ←

This pamphlet was printed, but never distributed. Herzen awaited the imminent announcement about the serfs' fate with keen anticipation and regret that he could not be in Moscow himself (Gertsen, *Sobranie sochinenii*, 27:bk. 1, 139–40). This is the speech, dated March 24, that Herzen intended to give at an April 10, 1861, celebration of the emancipation in his London home, to which Russians in London and other sympathizers were invited. Part of the evening's festivities would be the premier performance of Prince Yury Golitsyn's "Fantasia on the Emancipation" (*Let* 3:198, 217). Herzen reminds his audience that reaching this milestone has been the primary focus of his life's work.

Herzen's speech was to be published immediately afterward in *The Bell,* with a French translation to be placed in Parisian newspapers, but it was never given. On the day of the celebration, he received news from a Polish colleague at the Russian printing house in London that Russian troops had once more attacked a peaceful demonstration in Warsaw. It was now unthinkable to offer a toast in honor of the tsar who permitted this attack (on March 27 [April 8]). During an evening that he later described as more "like a funeral" he did offer a brief toast to Russia's success, prosperity, and further development (*Let* 3:198). One memoir account says that prepared copies of the speech in Russian, Polish, English, and French were thrown into the fire instead of being distributed to guests, but Herzen's handwritten copy was preserved (*Literaturnoe Nasledtsvo*, 63:59–70).

FRIENDS AND COMRADES!
[1861]

Today we have stepped away from our printing press for the free Russian word in order to celebrate in a fraternal manner *the beginning of the emancipation of the serfs* in Russia. You know what this emancipation means for us. In the emancipation of the serfs *with land* lies the entire future of a Rus that is not autocratic, manor-house, aggressive, Moscow-Tatar, not Petersburg-German, but national, communal—and free!

The first word from our printing house was a word about *St. George's Day.*

The first booklet issued by it was about *baptized property.*

The Polestar and *The Bell* set as their motto: *the liberation of the serfs and of the word!*

And now its beginning has been declared—timidly, with equivocations—*but declared!*

Events have undergone major changes since we printed the first issues in 1853. Everything around us was gloomy and hopeless. An oppressive orgy of reaction reached the final stage, it was time to give up the struggle, but we began a strange kind of work, sowing, on the stony debris of foreign ruins, seeds meant for the far-off homeland from which we were cut off. What did we hope for? I don't know, and I will speak just for myself—whether it was because I was not then in Russia and did not experience the direct effect of arbitrary rule or for another reason—*but I believed in Russia at a time when everyone had doubts!*

Much water has flowed under the bridge since that time.

I turn to those who witnessed our beginning and ask you to think about anyone who had said in 1853 that in eight years we would be gathering at a friendly feast and that the hero of that feast would be the Russian tsar! You would have thought that such a person was crazy or worse... For my part I frankly confess that such a thing never entered my head.

Fortunately, gentlemen, none of us are guilty—there is only one guilty party, the man himself.

For giving him credit I will be scolded by revolutionary ascetics and rigorous thinkers—I have been scolded for many things I have said. But if I expressed my opinion when for that you could be imprisoned and exiled to Vyatka, if I was not afraid of irritating the haughty aristocratic spirit of a decrepit and self-satisfied civilization, then why would I stop at the opposite prejudices?

It is all the easier for me to acknowledge Alexander II's great deed because that acknowledgment is a guarantee of our sincerity, and we need people's confidence, as much confidence as possible!

The February 19 manifesto is a milestone; the whole road still lies ahead, and the mail is in the hands of the most savage Tatar coachmen and German riding-masters. They will do everything to overturn or to tie up the cart. But it is impossible to expose their machinations in Russia. The word has fallen behind—as before it is *firmly* censored at home—that is why publishing abroad is essential and we know our duty.

And let *them* not be anxious—their business affairs will not disappear: we will follow them with great fervor step by step, bribe after bribe, crime after crime, with the tireless attention coming from a hatred that senses its own rightness. We will lead them out to the place of punishment, we will bind them up in their own filth to the pillory—all these Muravyov-the-hangmen, prince-deacons, like Gagarin, and radiant gendarmes, like Dolgorukov; these soulless hoarders and embezzlers, rebels in the name of slavery, knights of the birch rod—not ashamed to steal from the people the first day of their celebration!

Our work really only begins now. Therefore, friends, let us go to the printing presses, to our service for the Russian people and for human freedom! But first let us drain our glasses for the health of our liberated brothers and in honor of Alexander Nikolaevich, their liberator!

For the Polish people, for their freedom and equality, for their complete
independence from Russia and for the friendly union of Russians and Poles!

A toast to the tsar

Notes
Source: Druz'ia i tovarishchi!.." April 10, 1861, 15:217–19, 419–21.

⇥ *33* ⇤

The Bell, No. 96, April 15, 1861. Kovalevsky is the minister of education who banned
the speech about the late Konstantin Aksakov at a St. Petersburg University assembly
on February 8, 1861. At the conclusion of the assembly, the students' loud demand
for a public reading of the speech caused the university authorities present to quickly
vanish. Several days later, Kostomarov gave the speech; it was received with great enthusiasm and students lifted the professor up in his chair and carried him out of the
auditorium.

THE BELL, KOVALEVSKY, KOSTOMAROV, A COPY, AND CANNIBALS
[1861]

In London, one is forbidden to hang indecent posters on walls; at Petersburg University there is so much freedom that some naughty fellow named
Pletnev posted the following announcement:

> By order of the minister of education and the trustee of the St. Pe-
> tersburg educational district, a proposal in my name, dated February
> 11, 1861, No. 782, directed that the following announcement be made
> throughout the university.
>
> *University Rector* Pletnev
>
>   (a copy)
> Every educated person is aware that lawful requests must be ad-
> dressed to the authorities in a prescribed way. On this basis, students
> of St. Petersburg University, as they have been told repeatedly, should
> declare every request of theirs to the authorities through their chosen
> colleagues.

Meanwhile, the incident at the university assembly on February 8, most unfortunately, showed that students did not follow the sole legal path for an explanation of their quandary.

This sad incident, which demeaned the dignity of the university, although carried out by a minority of the students, nevertheless brings infamy to the entire student body.

People *who consider themselves for the most part educated* gave a clear example of their lack of respect for the law and a crude indecency.

To prevent similar actions in the future, in addition to the announcement of December 18, 1858, forbidding any demonstration on penalty of the expulsion of the guilty parties from the university, *irrespective of their numbers,* by order of the highest authority it is announced that:

1) If disturbances of the type mentioned above are carried out by students as a group *at lectures* then students of that school and year, who, according to the schedule, were obliged to be at this lecture, will immediately be dismissed, with the exception of those who can offer absolute proof that they were not present at the university at that time.

2) If a similar disturbance is carried out by a group of students at an assembly or other public university gathering, then all students *as a whole* are subject to dismissal from the university unless they can offer the absolute evidence mentioned in point 1 that at the time of the incident in the assembly they were not present.

Certified true copy: *Council secretary* A. Savinsky

After a few days, the authorities ordered that this announcement—which we take as authentic on the counter-signature of the secretary Savinsky—be taken down.

If it were possible to take this as more than the *espièglerie*[1] of Pletnev and Kovalevsky,[2] then, based on the enlightened order of such a ministry, it follows that if all Russia organizes some kind of demonstration, they will *expel* all of Russia, with the exception of those Russians who can offer absolute proof that they live abroad.

All of this commotion ensued from Kostomarov's desire to give a speech about the work of the late K. Aksakov, but the fathers of the enlightenment along with the fathers of the Third Department found it impossible that in the university a professor publicly praised a man about whom *The Bell* had *written positively*. From this emerged the ban on the speech, from this came the displeasure of the students, from this the threat of expulsion of several hundred members of the audience who attended the university and the retention of those who could prove *that they did not attend it.*

It is remarkable that in all of this the loser was not Kovalevsky, Kostomarov, *The Bell*, the Copy, or the Cannibals, but Alexander Nikolaevich. Now the censorship will not allow a single word about him. We did him more justice than Aksakov, and even without that, we allowed no abuse of him.

So when is Pletnev's jubilee?

Notes

Source: "'Kolokol,' Kovalevskii, Kostomarov, kopiia, kannibaly," *Kolokol,* l. 96, April 15, 1861; 15:72–73, 336.

1. Mischief.

2. Petr A. Pletnev (1792–1865), critic, poet, professor, friend of Pushkin, editor of *The Contemporary* from 1838 to 1846, and rector of St. Petersburg University from 1840 to 1861.

→ **34** ←

The Bell, No. 96, April 15, 1861. Herzen reacts to the new fashion of celebrating the jubilees of reactionary officials. This essay displays the familiar use of puns and unexpected descriptive phrases.

———

The Abuse of a Fiftieth Anniversary
[1861]

For us every kind of public declaration of joy, grief, sympathy, and repugnance is still so new that like children, we do not know when to stop and we make the most innocent game offensive. After the imperial journey through Russia of Alexander Dumas and the election of Molinari into the company of genuinely secret great men[1]—we have flung ourselves into *fiftieth anniversaries.* Grech imitates the old men, Grech reads to the old men, with old lips Grech chews the jubilee victuals, and then describes the dishes and the old men in his own gray speeches.[2] The appearance of Grech at the table will soon inspire horror in a family, reminding them that someone is past seventy. We hardly had time to recover from the delightful feelings aroused in us by Grech's story of how, fifty years earlier, at the entry guardhouse to St. Petersburg, there arrived a young student from Kazan, poor in money but rich in *pure* mathematics, how he became a professor, despite the fact that he knew what his field was, that he—more an artist and poet—could not for long be satisfied with *pure* mathematics and entered the ministry of *impure* mathematics, and now has himself become minister and is now celebrating his jubilee, and all the same—the old Nestor of jubilees could have said—he is repelled by everything *pure* and because of that hindered the emancipation of the serfs.[3]

Thus we hardly had time to recover from the story of the young student from Kazan arriving fifty years ago at the entry guardhouse to St. Petersburg, when Grech presented a new old fellow, P. A. Vyazemsky, for a jubilee. What did he do fifty years ago with no Petersburg guardhouse? What is meant by *the beginning* of his literary activity fifty years ago?[4] But this question would have been unimportant, had he done anything sensible during these fifty years. His literary activity, as well as his service record, is known to everyone except the troubadour singing his praises in frightfully poor verse. What thought or thoughts did this anniversary prince give to the younger generation, what task did he accomplish in his half-century? To be "Karamzin's brother and Pushkin's friend" and the deputy Minister of Education does not give one the right to such recognition. We don't know what kind of brother or friend he was but he did a poor job as the deputy Minister of Education. Why all this agitation—the man barely had time to eat his dinner and listen to the singing poet, when he, the old man, was summoned to tea at Yelena Pavlovna's where the tsar drank to his health. Pogodin himself came from Moscow. What could be added for the fiftieth anniversary of Pushkin—would they really only add Grech's prose and Sollogub's verse?[5]

Notes

Source: "Zloupotreblenie piatidesiatiletiia," *Kolokol,* l. 96, April 15, 1861; 15:74–75, 336–39.

1. The elder Dumas traveled to Russia in 1858 and published a book of his impressions; the Third Department kept an account of honors bestowed on him by aristocrats and local officials. Gustave de Molinari, the Belgian editor of *Journal des Économistes,* contributed to the reactionary journalist Mikhail Katkov's publications; in 1860, he traveled to Moscow and was received with great honor by Katkov and his circle.

2. Nikolay I. Grech's own fiftieth jubilee was celebrated in 1854.

3. Herzen is referring to Minister of Finance Knyazhevich (1792–1870), whose anniversary was celebrated in the Petersburg assembly of the nobility on January 19, 1861. Grech's speech on the occasion was published in *The Northern Bee* two days later. Herzen made his own use of Grech's lofty rhetoric in a number of articles, and publicized Knyazhevich's minority stance against emancipation as a member of the Main Committee. Grech is compared to Nestor, a monk and chronicler from the Kiev Monastery of the Caves (late eleventh to early twelfth centuries).

4. Prince Peter A. Vyazemsky (1792–1878), a poet and critic and from 1855 to 1858 deputy minister of education, beginning in 1861 was a member of the Main Censorship Committee.

5. Grand Duchess Yelena Pavlovna (1806–1873), widow of Grand Duke Mikhail Pavlovich and the tsar's aunt, was famous for her salon, which was frequented by moderately liberal forces at court and in the government. Mikhail P. Pogodin (1800–1875) was a historian and journalist, and professor of history at Moscow University from 1826 to 1844. Count Vladimir A. Sollogub (1813–1882) was a writer.

→ **35** ←

The Bell, Nos. 98–99, May 15, 1861. Herzen was disturbed by violence against the Poles, Russian peasants, and students in Moscow and St. Petersburg, and wrote several essays on this topic. The first letter quoted in this article was sent to Herzen by Stepan S. Gromeka (1823–1877), a journalist and government official in Russia and Poland. The authors of the other two letters are not known.

RUSSIAN BLOOD IS FLOWING!
[1861]

Yes, Russian blood is flowing like a river!.. And there are vapid souls and timid minds who reproach us for our pained words of damnation and indignation!

The government could have prevented all of this, both the Polish blood and the Russian blood, but now—because of their unsteadiness, lack of understanding, and inability to carry anything through to the end—they are killing multitudes of our brothers.

The news coming from all quarters fills us with horror and tears. Those poor peasants! In Europe they do not even suspect what is meant in our country by pacification by soldiers, by adjutant-generals, and by aides-de-camp. Our only hope lies with soldiers and young officers. It is difficult to carry a weapon with the blood of your dear ones—fathers, mothers, and brothers—clotted on it.

We will stop; it is dark before our eyes, we are afraid to give voice to everything that groans within us, and we are afraid to express everything that is fermenting in our heart...

First we will present the facts.

Here are extracts from letters, without any alterations:

You are aware that the sovereign has sent his aides-de-camp and adjutant-generals to all the provinces.[1] The adjutants are carrying out their missions. In several provinces, birch rods and troops are in action and blood is flowing. I know for certain that the day before yesterday three new adjutant-generals (along with the ones already in action) were sent to the Kazan, Tambov—and in addition, it seems— to the Ryazan provinces. These new envoys are provided with the authority to hang and shoot people at their discretion. *In Kazan a Pretender has appeared* (in the Spassky district) claiming to be Alexander Nikolaevich, having been driven away by the gentry.[2] *Seventeen* villages have dug in and are joining battle with forces under the banner of that gentleman. It is not known who he is. But the clashes were terrible: 70 peasants have already fallen victim, and members of the forces taken prisoner by the peasants include a company commander, a local officer, and a few men of lower rank. No matter how much this resembles a fairy tale, it is a truth that will not be in the newspaper today or tomorrow. Efrimovich, a specialist on pacification, has raced there...

In one place, I don't know whether it is the Kazan or Tambov province, in the midst of a crowd into which the troops were firing, a peasant stood holding a manifesto above his head with his two hands—the rumor spread among the people that he was unharmed, although next to him was a pile of bodies.

From a second letter

The peasants almost everywhere are terribly dissatisfied with the new, temporarily obligatory "Law," and in many places they refuse to believe that the manifesto that has been announced is genuine; thus, for example, the aide-de-camp Count Olsufiev, who was sent to one of the western provinces,[3] met with a similar objection, and when— in order to persuade the peasants—referred to the fact that he was an aide to the sovereign, someone in the crowd began to say that they didn't know whether he was a real aide-de-camp or was in disguise. Olsufiev thought that the best argument against this was an order to his soldiers to beat the peasants with rifle butts and then whip them with birch rods.

In the Petersburg province, on General Olkhin's estate, military force was used against peasants generally believed to be in the right, and the unfortunate ones were treated roughly.

In the Chembarsky district of the Penza province there was a rebellion by peasants numbering in the thousands on the ancestral lands of Count Uvarov.[4] The military company that was sent to put them down was forced to retreat; the peasants were holding a representative of the local administration, the chief of police, a cadet, and several soldiers. Two battalions were sent to suppress it.

In the Spassky region of the Kazan province, a prophet who claimed to be the sovereign appeared in the midst of the schismatics; entire districts of up to 10,000 peasants, most of them belonging to the state, were up in arms; nothing came of the military forces that were sent and there was no battle. General Kozlyaninov and Apraksin, a general in the emperor's suite, set off with 12 companies. Apraksin ordered them *to shoot* as if on the battlefield: 70 bodies lay there, while the prophet remained at some distance from the peasants, kneeling and holding over his head a new "Law." Apraksin acted in this case on the basis of the authority to act in the sovereign's name in the case of disorder and to deal with the guilty according to the military field commander's criminal code, i.e., to shoot *and hang* at his own discretion.[5]

In the Perm province there have been powerful instances of dissatisfaction at factories.[6]

Ivan Gavrilovich Bibikov (the former military governor-general) was sent to Kazan to restore order. Efimovich, already well known for his many achievements in pacification, was sent to Penza. One should not have expected different results; that much was clear to sensible people who rebelled against this transitional era. The flowers and fruit would come when the "Law" was fully applied. It contained so much that was Jesuitical, so many loopholes for the swindling, robbing, and oppression of the peasants! Joint obligations were not mentioned in the section on bringing the "Law" into effect, where only two kinds of obligations were mentioned, quitrent and corvée; referring to that, peasants who had fulfilled joint obligations (i.e., the vast majority of those in the quitrent areas of the northern and central zones) considered themselves freed from everything except quitrent, but landowners referred to art. 70 of the "Law," quietly giving them the right to mixed obligations until the introduction of the statutory document. This alone would cost blood. And there were a lot of ambiguities like that. The wording of many articles was ambiguous, and for that reason Butkov had such power! He is in charge of the entire peasant question and is deceptive, pretending to be a liberal. According to the peasants, the manifesto is such that it will be *worse than before* for them and that in two years the landowners *will ruin them completely*. The right to complain far from satisfies them: "Their brother the landowner really likes to complain." In the words of the landowners, the valuation of the estates is terribly high.

From a third letter

In the Odessa district, 60 miles from the city of Odessa, on the estates of Kiryakov, Kuris, and Svechin (the district leader of the nobility), in the villages of Tashino, Novo-Kiryakovo, Malashevka, Tuzly, and Sakharovo, the peasants, through a misunderstanding, refused to work for the landowner, considering themselves completely free. Local authorities demanded military force to put down the *revolt*. Two companies of the Volynsk regiment were sent in carts from Odessa and another two from their location in the countryside. As soon as they arrived in the village of Tashino, by order of the district leader Svechin (who had by his side Khristiforovich, who had been attached by special assignment to Kherson's civilian governor), surrounded the peasants and began to read the manifesto. I continue with an extract from the official report presented by the company commander: "... having listened to the manifesto, the peasants flatly refused to work for the landowner and to be under his authority. The leader of the nobility made every effort to convince the peasants to obey the will of the sovereign emperor as it appeared in the manifesto, but all these efforts were in vain; then the leader of the nobility gave orders to the lower ranks to take those peasants who were the primary cause of the unrest to be beaten with rods, and, when one peasant was seized, all the peasants without exception fell to the ground and began to shout: 'Beat us all.' This force (of up to 140 people) drove back the lower ranks who held the peasant; when the peasant was once more seized, then again they fell to the earth and cried out the same thing: 'Beat us all.' Having freed the peasant from punishment a second time, they all rushed straight through the chain of soldiers, from time to time using their fists; the soldiers closed ranks in a rather tight square and were thus able to restrain the peasants. In this crush, when the soldiers restrained the peasants, the latter, in trying to break free, jostled the soldiers and scratched their weapons. When the peasants had been caught, there followed flogging *only of the chief* disturbers of peace and order, after which all the peasants submitted and were sent home..." With slight variations, the same thing happened in other villages. Sechin says he did not administer more than 30 strokes, but, according to the soldiers' stories, there were harsh punishments—from 300 to 400 strokes; the officers don't say this, but one cannot rely on them. In Tashina alone up to 80 people were punished.

Svechin was in charge, although he acted for his own goals like a landowner, forgetting, that before using the rod, according to the

"Law," there are fines and arrests; the rod can only be administered by the police and no more than 20 strokes.

They say that Stroganov, who has heard the rumors of Svechin's zeal, wants to carry out an investigation.[7]

Notes

Source: "Russkaia krov' l'etsia!" *Kolokol*, l. 98–99, May 15, 1861; 15:90–93, 350–52.

1. Alexander II issued this order at the beginning of February 1861 to prepare for possible disorders surrounding the emancipation announcement.

2. The Pretender was Anton Petrov, who claimed to be an emissary of Alexander II and was executed on April 19, 1861.

3. Vilna.

4. The Kandeevskoe uprising included twenty-six villages and spread to the neighboring Kerensky region.

5. Herzen will discuss Count Apraksin's role in what came to be known as the Bezdna massacre in Doc. 37: "April 12, 1861 (The Apraksin Murders)."

6. These factories were owned by the entrepreneurial Stroganov family.

7. Count Alexander G. Stroganov (1795–1891) held many high government positions before becoming the governor-general of Bessarabia and Novorossiisk in 1855.

→ **36** ←

The Bell, No. 100, June 1, 1861. Herzen frequently wrote on the subject of regulations governing such matters as beards and beardlessness, smoking in public, and the fanatical attention to buttons on uniforms, all of which bordered on the ludicrous at a time of momentous change and daunting problems.

———

THE SMELL OF CIGARS AND THE STENCH OF THE STATE COUNCIL
[1861]

The State Council, which displayed its cleverness in the emancipation of the serfs, is taking *ses revanches*. It is sufficient to have liberated the serfs—we will not liberate the smoking of cigars! These cripples decided that it is impossible to allow smoking on the streets, first of all, because it makes it more difficult for officers of lower rank to salute their superiors; second, there will be a nasty smell on the streets.

Pitiful orangutans of the first two ranks! What utter stupidity!

Notes

Source: "Dukh sigar i von' gosudarstvennogo soveta," *Kolokol*, l. 100, June 1, 1861; 15:106, 361–62.

⇢ *37* ⇠

The Bell, No. 101, June 15, 1861. This essay is devoted to the April 1861 massacre of peasants by government forces at Bezdna in the province of Kazan, already mentioned in "Russian Blood Is Flowing!" (Doc. 35). The Russian government hid information about this unrest from the public for a month, and only released an official announcement in the *St. Petersburg Gazette* after news began to appear elsewhere. Herzen and Ogaryov included "A Peasant Martyrology," in the June 1, 1861, *Bell*, and returned to the subject in 1862, when the peasants arrested in this incident were released from custody. Professor Afanasy Shchapov (1830–1876), mentioned by Herzen in a footnote, spoke sympathetically about the Bezdna victims at a memorial service attended by more than 400 students in Kazan's Kratinsky Cemetery four days after the tragic events (*Let* 3:204). What happened to Shchapov next demonstrates the government's confusion; the professor was sent by Kazan officials to Petersburg to offer an explanation, was arrested en route and turned over to the Third Department, then released to Minister of the Interior Valuev, who set him to work on matters concerning the Old Believers. Late in 1861 the Synod tried to have Shchapov exiled to Solovki, but public opinion in his favor prevented this. He wound up being tried in 1862 along with other accused followers of the "London propagandists," but managed to prove his innocence, although he had in fact sent Herzen articles and had received at least one very supportive letter in return, praising him as "a fresh voice, pure and powerful" who stood out amidst so many other writers who had become "jaded and hoarse" (Gertsen, *Sobranie sochinenii*, 15:370–71).

APRIL 12, 1861

(The Apraksin Murders)

[1861]

Our "Muette de Portici" has finally admitted to the spilling of peasant blood in Bezdna.[1] The official story is even viler and more repulsive than what was written to us.

The brain goes to pieces and blood freezes in the veins while reading the naive-ingenuous story of such villainy, the likes of which we have not seen since the days of Arakcheev.[2]

Where did these bloodthirsty aides-de-camp come from? Where were these impromptu butchers brought up? How were they schooled in such heartless villainy?

The government tolerates murders that are due to its inarticulateness, ignorance, and duplicity.[3] Didn't the new pedant Valuev[4] *clearly* distinguish serfdom's obligatory labor from obligatory labor *in anticipation* of emancipation? And because the people do not understand, and believe that the government is not deceiving them, five salvos are fired.

We do not recognize Russia... steaming blood, corpses all over the place! [. . .]

Fifty victims, according to the criminals themselves, and on this occasion the *genial* monarch was so used to this sort of thing that he did not ask Apraksin: "And how many soldiers were killed or wounded?"

The article states directly that the peasants' military actions consisted in the fact that some of them *went to get* wooden stakes.

And what was the rush in punishing Anton Petrov?[5] Who tried him? What was he tried for? Obviously the bloody traces should be hidden! What sort of instructions were given by the tender-hearted tsar?

Pugachev was tried in a court before Catherine and not quietly shot.

To hell with them—the bloody executioners!

And you, unfortunate brother schismatics, having greatly suffered but never having meddled with the Russia of landowners, executioners, and those who shoot the unarmed—preserve the day of new horrors, April 12, in your memory. The times of biblical persecutions are beginning; you know from the *Lives of Saints*[6] about the slaughter of Christians undertaken by the emperors, and you know who prevailed. But prevailing doesn't come without faith and without action. Be strong in spirit and remember the cry with which the peasants of Bezdna perished:

Freedom! Freedom!

Isk—r.[7]

We received three additional letters about details of the business in Kazan. The principal outlines of the events are the same and we will not repeat them, particularly after the *confession* in the *St. Petersburg Gazette*. But there are details too precious not to be preserved in *The Bell* for posterity and for our contemporaries.

From one of the letters. Apraksin did not approach the peasants, but dispatched someone to tell them to send eight people elected to carry out negotiations. They refused. Then a second time he sent the leader of the nobility Molostov[8] to try to convince them, and then a priest.

The priest asked them if they believed in God and in the Orthodox Church. They said that they did believe. Then the priest demanded that they *hand over the prophet,* but they refused to do this, and the priest and official witness returned; neither he nor the witnesses experienced the slightest show of violence.

After this, Apraksin decided to speak to the crowd; he got on his horse and, having ridden about 20 steps further away from his soldiers, who were 100 feet behind him, shouted: "Hand over the prophet, or you will be shot." At this time the prophet was calming them, saying that no more than three volleys would be fired and that the bullets would then turn back upon the soldiers. Then they rather calmly replied to Apraksin: "Shoot, little father, you won't be shedding our blood, but the tsar's." Apraksin shouted to the soldiers: "Fire." Two aides-de-camp of the governor—sent there to find out what was going on—rushed in vain to try and persuade him. In vain they told him that if these were insurgents, they would be armed with something and would have long ago surrounded them, and that, finally, nothing had prevented them from attacking the soldiers while the priest and official witnesses were returning, because it would have been impossible to fire at the priest.

To all of these objections Apraksin cried out: "Officers, stand at attention, fire!" Four salvos were given. Until the fourth salvo the crowd stood motionless, crossing themselves; several covered their faces with their work gloves. After the fourth salvo the crowd began to scatter; one group simply began to run, while another moved closer to the group around the prophet in order to find out why the bullets had not been turned back against the soldiers. Apraksin imagined that they were running to get wooden stakes and ordered five salvos one right after another. The rest is known: when the smoke cleared and the hero saw the heap of dead and wounded (these cannibals didn't even have a doctor with them!), Apraksin said: "Oh, there are a lot of them—well it will be possible to make it seem fewer, it's always done that way." But one local official pointed out to him that maybe that is what happens in wartime, but that here all the names would have to be written down.

The Kazan nobility wanted to give Apraksin a dinner, when he was up to his ears in peasant blood. Trubnikov, a member of the provincial administration, restrained these carnivorous freaks with the observation that "it is somewhat awkward to wash away blood with *champagne!*"

It's a shame that this was prevented; masks, away with masks, it is better
to see the animals' teeth and the wolves' snouts than feigned humaneness
and cheap liberalism.[9]

The names, the names—we implore you for the names of the officers
who took part in the handling of the bodies and the maggots who gathered
to feast on the corpses.

Notes

Source: "12 aprelia 1861 (Apraksinskie ubiistva)," *Kolokol*, l. 101, June 15, 1861; 15:107–9,
362–64.

1. "The Mute Girl of Portici," an 1828 opera by French composer Daniel Auber (1782–
1871). Herzen is ironically referring to the official government newspaper *St. Petersburg
Gazette*.

2. Count Alexey A. Arakcheev (1769–1834), artillery general, war minister from 1808
to 1810, who later organized the infamous military colonies. He is believed to have
brought out the worst side of Alexander I.

3. Herzen has in mind ambiguity in the emancipation law, which allowed differing
interpretations of several key points.

4. Herzen: "Valuev had already revealed himself in other ways. Maltsov (a plantation
owner) put eight peasants in shackles and sent them to Kaluga as insurgents. Governor Artsimovich released them and wanted to conduct an investigation. The plantation
owner [. . .] brought this matter all the way to Petersburg, and the new minister took the
side of the serf-owner. *Çela promet!* (That's very promising!)."

5. Anton Petrov was executed a week after the events at Bezdna.

6. Herzen refers to the *Cheti Minei,* a book of readings including lives of the saints
arranged by month and day, information about holy days, and teachings for Orthodox
believers.

7. Iskander is Herzen's most frequent pseudonym.

8. Herzen: "He received an amazing reward for his services. He was a retired staff-
captain, and was awarded the rank of retired *captain*. For Russian tsars time does not exist—the past is not the past, and it would be wonderful if for them there were no future."

9. Herzen: "The Kazan students behaved differently; they held a funeral service for
their dead brothers and the executed Anton Petrov. Professor *Shchapov* spoke, a gendarme denounced him (to each his own), the ministry dismissed him and the police
arrested him. As least some of the clean-shaven Russian people will not be considered
Germans and serf owners."

⇥ 38 ⇤

The Bell, No. 109, October 15, 1861. This issue opens with a message to the Russian
ambassador in London, revealing that Herzen and Ogaryov have received anonymous
letters which suggest that the Third Department would try to either kidnap or kill them.
Herzen warns the ambassador that if any harm comes to them, the Russian government

will be blamed. As regards the closing of the university, Herzen wrote to Turgenev that this was a sign that Alexander II was "going to the devil."

PETERSBURG UNIVERSITY IS SHUT DOWN!
[1861]

...The new administration has taken a sharp turn: students will be admitted to lectures by ticket, and non-students are forbidden to attend lectures, student assemblies are forbidden, they wanted to eliminate the library, and so on. Students gathered in the auditorium despite the fact that the doors were locked, invited the vice-rector Sreznevsky, and expressed their dissatisfaction.[1] On September 24 (October 6) it was announced that the university would be closed until further notice. The next day all the students (up to 1,500 people) gathered on Vladimirskaya street in front of Filipson's apartment and demanded that he appear, but suddenly Ignatev showed up with a platoon of guards.[2] Filipson emerged in full uniform and suggested to the students that they set off for the university, with him following on foot. A large crowd attached itself to them. Filipson, having gotten tired, rode ahead. When they arrived at the university, mounted gendarmes appeared, along with a fire brigade carrying axes, and the police. The students behaved with complete calm. An officer of the gendarmerie unsheathed his saber, and two gendarmes prepared to plunge into the crowd. Shuvalov and the brotherhood stopped them.[3] Student deputies approached them. At this moment Ignatiev showed up, saying: "Everything is ready, the operation may begin." Filipson answered that he knew from the Caucasus how with such means you can cause misfortune but you will not stop the young people. One of the students said: "There is no need for troops, I will be responsible for keeping order." Ignatiev insisted that Filipson had no right to negotiate with the students, but the latter took the responsibility on himself and promised that the library would open immediately, and that lectures would begin on October 2/14, and by that time new rules would be announced. The students promised to remain calm. The orderliness on the part of the students was remarkable, and the crowd showed them sympathy. There were a great number of officers and there was one person they wanted to arrest but they held back. One soldier in the guards unit shoved a student, who said: "Aren't you ashamed—you're armed and you shove someone who is unarmed?"...

the soldier blushed. One field officer violently shook a policeman's arm: "Hey you, did you come to do battle?"—"What can I do, your honor, they gave an order!" answered the policeman. One peasant said to another: "The blue caps are rebelling!" and heard in answer: "What should they do when their institution is shut down?" There were almost no military forces in the capital, and the soldiers were dispersed to their regular duties; they had been summoned by telegraph.

Thus, the university is closed! The government opposes enlightenment and freedom and *doesn't know enough to yield in good time*. We prophesied its *downfall* during the second part of this transitional era; it seems we were mistaken—*it will happen much earlier.*

Notes

Source: "Peterburgskii universitet zakryt!" *Kolokol,* l. 109, October 15, 1861; 15:164–65, 394.

1. Ismail I. Sreznevsky (1812–1880) was a philologist who taught in Kharkov, and, beginning in 1847, a professor at St. Petersburg University.

2. Grigory I. Filipson (1809–1883) was a lieutenant-general, senator, and in 1861–62, trustee of the Petersburg education district; Count Pavel N. Ignatiev (1797–1879), governor-general of Vitebsk, Mogilev, and Smolensk, and from 1854 to 1861, military governor-general of St. Petersburg.

3. Count Petr A. Shuvalov (1827–1889) was an adjutant-general who held high offices in the St. Petersburg police, the Ministry of the Interior, and in 1861 in the Third Department.

⤍ 39 ⤏

The Bell, No. 110, November 1, 1861. Herzen's call "To the people!" was answered a dozen years later, after the author's death, by the great populist pilgrimage of 1873–74. The tone of this essay differs from many others by Herzen; when speaking to Russia's young people, he dropped his characteristic irony and his enthusiasm bordered on euphoria. Since Alexander II was no longer Russia's hope, only Russia's youth could fulfill the promise of a brighter future. In the postscript, where he reacted to additional news from Petersburg, the irony returned. The "Great Russia" (Velikorus) affair concerns a radical pamphlet that circulated in Petersburg, terrifying the government and Russian conservatives. Critic Vladimir Stasov (1824–1906) recalled getting together with composer Mily Balakirev (1837–1910) to read this article, which is said to have inspired Balakirev's overture "1000 Years," especially its image of a wave rising up across the Russian expanse after years of calm (*Let* 3:623; Gurvich-Lishchiner, "Gertsen," 185).

A Giant Is Awakening!
[1861]

Yes, a sleeping "Northern Colossus"—"A giant, the tsar's obedient servant"—is awakening and he is not at all as obedient as in the time of Gavriil Romanovich Derzhavin.[1]

Good morning to you—it's time, it's time! You slept like a hero—now wake up like a hero! Stretch out to your full youthful length, breathe in the fresh morning air, and sneeze so that you can scare off the whole flock of owls, ravens, and vampires, the Putyatins, Muravyovs, Ignatievs and other bats. *You* are awakening and it is time for *them* to retire. It is filth in motion—all these cockroaches, wood lice, insects, deprived of their wings but not of their appetite, who are not compatible with the daylight. Sneeze, giant, and not a trace of them will remain, except for the spots of Polish and peasant blood that cannot be eradicated!

Lord, what a pitiful and ludicrous sight this terrible government makes! What happened to its cavalry officer aspect, its sergeant-major bearing, where is its husky army voice, which it used for thirty years to shout: "I will drive Demosthenes into his grave!" Well, soldier, it is clear that the times are different and so are the military forces, the uniform is too big for you, the helmet has been pushed down over your eyes... Go off, knight, to the hospital, or onto invalid status!

Well what happened, why was it struck dumb? Was there a revolution? Did Filaret incite Moscow to rebellion? Was Petr Oldenburgsky proclaimed emperor in the law school?[2] Guess! And then pick up *The Times* and read his superb correspondence.

The emperor is in Livadia. Petersburg is being governed by a committee of public salvation, consisting of Nikolay Nikolaevich and Mikhail Nikolaevich, and so that Gorchakov does not give them any sensible advice, that *intelligence-deflector* Ignatiev-Malkovsky has been installed by their side.[3] On the streets there are soldiers, gendarmes, Shuvalovs, and the Jacobin general Bistrom is angering the soldiers with a speech of the reddest sansculottism: "From these people," he said, pointing to the unarmed students, "will emerge petty officials, the petty officials who rob you, who rob the people—we will teach them a lesson!" Patkul[4] gallops to the right, then gallops to the left, one horse is worn out and another is fetched. Mikhail Nikolaevich asks Nikolay Nikolaevich: why is Patkul galloping about? Nikolay Nikolaevich, having risen with the first cock's crow due to his general love of chickens, tells Mikhail Nikolaevich that he does not know why Patkul is galloping about, but it must be that *this is an uprising*. One (or the other) says—ten regiments and he will pacify... Whom? Where are the enemy forces?

In the university courtyard.

The crude government, frightened by a Stroganov who had lost his mind, alongside petty persecutions and humiliations, began to insult the universities: with the appointment of Putyatin, with constraints on the schools, and with the heartless expulsion of the poor.[5] The students of St. Petersburg University selected deputies and instructed them to carry their protest to the authorities. The authorities treated them as savages on the Sandwich Islands behaved toward members of Parliament, and the same way that Peter *the large* behaved with Polubotok, and Nicholas *the long* with deputies of the soldiers from Staraya Russa, i.e., contrary to any understanding of honor and moral shame, they were seized.[6] The students resolved to ask that their comrades be freed, and that is why Bistrom-Santerre whipped up the soldiers, setting them against other social classes. Patkul wore out two horses, and Ignatiev-Malkovsky whispered to Filipson: "*Everything is ready. We can begin!*" Begin what? The slaughter of young people, carnage in the university courtyard?.. What can one add to that! [. . .]

In Russia the universities are closed down, and in Poland the churches closed themselves after being defiled by the police. There is neither the light of reason nor the light of religion! Where do they want to lead us in the dark? They have lost their minds—get them out of the driver's seat if you do not want to crash to the ground along with them!

But where can you go, young people, who have been barred from learning? Shall I tell you where?

Listen carefully, since the darkness does not prevent you from hearing: from all parts of our vast homeland, from the Don and the Urals, from the Volga and the Dnepr, there is increased moaning and a rising murmur—it is the initial roar of a wave which is boiling up, fraught with storms, after an awfully tiresome period of calm. To the people! To the people!—that is your place, exiles from learning. Show these Bistroms that you will not turn into *petty officials,* but warriors, not homeless mercenaries, but warriors of the Russian people!

Glory to you! You are initiating a new era; you have understood that the time of whispering, distant hints, and banned books is passing. You still *secretly* print books at home, but you *openly* protest. Praise to you, younger brothers, and our distant blessing! Oh, if only you knew how the heart beats, how tears were ready to flow, when we read *about the day of the students in Petersburg!*

ISKANDER.
October 22, 1861

P.S. This article was already written when we read in *The Times* (for October 22) about such vile, such base villainy, that despite all our limitless faith in the immorality of the Petersburg administration, we were almost in doubt. *The secret police* sent out fake invitations to the students to gather on the square in order to catch them all, but the students figured this out and did not show up. After this, can one be surprised at Bistrom's Jacobin speech and the fact that he is not on trial for this speech, and that the Third Department toyed with the thought of kidnapping me from England; can one just despise from afar the fact that when Mikhailov[7] was arrested, the gendarmes were busy with prostitutes (do not blush, Shuvalov, do not blush, Patkul, do not blush, Ignatiev, *the word* is not as shameful *as the deed*), women whom they had been instructed to search.

And these dregs of cheats, crooks, and whores we are obliged to accept as a government!

Notes

Source: "Ispolin prosypaetsia!" *Kolokol*, l. 110, November 1, 1861; 15:173–76, 398–99.

1. The quotation is from a poem written by Derzhavin on the occasion of the capture of the fortress of Izmail from the Ottoman Empire in late 1790–early 1791 by General Suvorov.

2. Filaret (1783–1867) was metropolitan of Moscow beginning in 1826. The imperial law school was founded in 1835 on the initiative of Prince Petr G. Oldenburgsky (1812–1881), who was its longtime trustee.

3. Alexander II was in the Crimea at the time of student unrest in St. Petersburg. Grand dukes Nikolay (1831–1891) and Mikhail (1832–1909) were the tsar's younger brothers. Herzen ironically refers to Governor-General Ignatiev as "Ignatiev-Malkovsky" because of his "heroic" and unjustified arrest of the merchant E. Malkov in 1858, which had been publicized in previous issues of *The Bell*.

4. Baron Rodrig G. Bistrom (1810–1886) was a general who took part in suppressing the Poles in 1830–31 and 1863; Herzen later calls him "Bistrom-Santerre" after a French revolutionary general, Antoine Santerre. Major-General Alexander V. Patkul (1817–1877) was head of the police in St. Petersburg and a member of the Military Council.

5. Count Sergey G. Stroganov was one of three members of a commission set up in 1861 to look at university regulations. Count Efim V. Putyatin (1803–1883), admiral and diplomat, was for a few months in 1861 the minister of education.

6. In 1723, hetman P. L. Polubotok was suspected of wanting to separate Ukraine from Russia; he was lured to St. Petersburg and imprisoned, dying the following year. In 1831 there was an uprising at military settlements in Staraya Russa; the soldiers were promised negotiations with Nicholas I, but instead were harshly punished.

7. Herzen: "*Mikhailov, Pertsov* and the officer *Kostomarov* were arrested in connection with the 'Great Russia' affair and the secret typography. *The Times* says that *Kraevsky*, Count *Kushelev-Bezborodko*, and *Gromeka* staged some sort of protest against the illegal detention of Mikhailov; we would very much like to know the details of this matter." Mikhail I. Mikhailov (1829–1865), revolutionary, poet, journalist, was arrested in 1861,

based on a denunciation by Vsevolod D. Kostomarov (whose brother Nikolay and the journalist Erast Pertsov were also arrested) and sentenced to hard labor for distributing a proclamation written by him and N. V. Shelgunov called "To the Younger Generation."

→ 40 ←

The Bell, No. 113, November 22, 1861. In October, Herzen received a letter from Bakunin after he had escaped from Siberia and had gotten as far as San Francisco. This information was passed on to Proudhon and to acquaintances in Russia. Bakunin arrived in London on December 27, 1861. Herzen wrote the first biography of the anarchist in 1851 for a French audience, and dedicated his book *On the Development of Revolutionary Ideas in Russia* to Bakunin. While this is a very brief notice, its importance would expand in the readers' minds and in discussion—the empire's borders were obviously not secure, and, based on Bakunin's previous exploits, it was a good bet that he would continue his revolutionary activities in the future. In the meantime, the *Echo de Bruxelles* published a rumor that Herzen had made a secret trip to Russia, where he had been arrested and sent to Siberia. Herzen had actually put off traveling outside of England, due to threats reaching him that he would be kidnapped or killed (*Let* 3:250–53, 266, 271).

BAKUNIN IS FREE
[1861]

MIKHAIL ALEXANDROVICH BAKUNIN is in San Francisco. *HE IS FREE!* Bakunin left Siberia by way of Japan and is on his way to England. We are spreading news of this with delight to all Bakunin's friends.

Notes

Source: "Bakunin svoboden," *Kolokol*, l. 113, November 22, 1861; 15:194, 408–9.

→ 41 ←

The Bell, No. 113, November 1, 1861. Herzen compiled information on the treatment of students which included letters from readers of *The Bell* and other information that came his way, framed by his own commentary. *The Bell* continued to publish materials the editors received on this topic in subsequent issues. Herzen's premonition about attacks on the tsar was later realized, beginning with Karakozov's attempt in 1866 and ending with the successful assassination of Alexander II in 1881, long after Herzen's own death. The image of Alexander II as a fairy-tale prince at a crossroads—offered three possibilities rather than the more familiar two choices in the West—has become a favorite of Russian political analysts (See Billington and Parthé, *Search for a New Russian National Identity*, 27–30, 92–3). In the original tale, Ilya Muromets sets out on a quest, only to find at the top of a mountain a sign pointing in three directions: the first way promised food for Ilya but not for his horse, taking the second meant that the horse would eat but not its rider, and the third warned that the champion would die. Strangely enough, Ilya "followed the third road, although the inscription said that on this road he would be slain; for he had confidence in himself" (Afanas'ev, *Russian Fairy Tales*, 571). According to Herzen, the new tsar is trying to travel all three at once, a path that is, literally, not viable. This motif recurs in the final issue of *The Bell*, in an excerpt from *Past and Thoughts*, but by this point, the knight at the crossroads is Herzen himself (Doc. 100).

———

Concerning the Assaults on Students
[1861]

One of the most difficult moments for a person investigating a criminal act is that moment when he enters a room where an evil deed has taken place: everything is quiet and peaceful... the drops of blood, the broken furniture, an overturned chair, broken glass... noise can be heard from outside where wheels are creaking, a barrel organ is playing, children laugh, and peddlers shout—while just a few hours earlier, here, in this place, muffled blows, a howl, swearing, moaning, and a heavy fall could be heard... and inside you experience a hysterical tremor... Meanwhile there is no choice, the investigation must be carried out while the tracks are fresh. If only one can find sufficient peace of mind to avoid heaping on the shoulders of the criminal even more guilt than he in fact ought to be carrying.

We are those investigators.

Before us sadly stand massive buildings that have lost their significance, cold, empty auditoriums, mute lecterns: a senseless force passed through here, blindly crushed young lives, then unrepentantly quieted down, and everything went back to its old routine, only there are no students and there is no learning.

Who is to blame? Where are the guilty parties? The good-humored emperor or the soulless Putyatin? Shuvalov or Stroganov? The Moscow police or those from the Preobrazhensky district?

Everyone is guilty, they all played the role of voluntary executioners, cruel executioners; but with that they enjoy the benefits connected with the title of masters of the rod: they are only responsible for carrying out the sentence. Let their conscience torment them, let society's contempt torment them. Finally, let them be punished on the same basis on which in England

beasts that cause a person's death are punished. To hell with them. Neither
their guilt nor their punishment explains the matter.

The university incident is not an accident, not a whim, but the beginning
of an inevitable battle. This battle must arise in one place or another, and it
arose on the most natural soil. The contradictions that lie at the basis of our
political life have moved so far apart that [. . .] either the established order in
Petersburg will perish or Russia will perish.

That feverish feeling of being *not quite right,* which has taken control of
all Russia—above, below, in the peasant hut and in the Winter Palace itself,
directly reveals how the organism works and by what means it seeks to get
rid of something dead, something poisonous and rotting.

The battle will come out one way or another, but eliminating the battle
is impossible. The inhuman efforts made by Nicholas delayed its discovery
for thirty years.

[. . .] For the Petrine empire, which survived, there remained *one living matter,* and with this matter it can redeem the past, heal the wounds
suffered by the people, and be revitalized—with this matter it tied a rope
around its neck... "You cannot force anyone to be saved," said Marshal
Bugeaud to Louis Philippe.[1]

First there was a loss of strength, and then of sense. The optical illusion of indestructibility dispersed along with the smoke of Sevastopol as
everyone saw that this was the scenery of power, but not power itself.[2] The
government was horrified by its own insignificance and its own absurdity;
that accounts for its frantic readiness to change everything, to do repairs
and restructuring, and, together with this, to desperately defend itself by
every possible means—the shooting of peasants, the bayoneting of wor-
shippers, the Preobrazhensky rifle butts, by gendarmes dressed like peasants, by the police use of public women... this is a sick person's internal
fear of death, the overwhelming realization that there is insufficient reason
for his existence. That is why they rush in one direction then another, that
is why there is this uneasy feeling... that is why the empress prays at night
before a Byzantine icon and reads the story of Marie Antoinette, that is why
they tremble for their dynasty when hundreds of young people do not want
to submit to wearing humiliating uniforms, that is why they hold onto their
Preobrazhensky troops and their gendarmes, like a loaded revolver under a
pillow. They know—and this is *the worst thing* that a person can know—*that
they are no longer needed!*

Eight or ten years ago I preached to a frightened Europe, which gazed at
the gloomy figure of an emperor in jackboots and the uniform of a cavalry
guards officer, who stood like some kind of snowy scarecrow on the other
side of the Baltic ice floes, and were horrified that *this snow was melting,* that

the Petersburg throne was not at all as strong as people thought, that it had
outlived its reason for being and had not had anything creative or construc-
tive going for it since the war of 1812, that Nicholas, from an instinct of self-
preservation, had gathered all his forces together for a single negative move
against the foundations of a new life that were arising.

No one believed me—it was before the Crimean War.

It's an old story, that people are convinced only by piles of corpses,
captured burial mounds, and burnt cities. MacMahon was more fortunate
than me.[3]

But it was not only Europe that saw the light due to the Crimean War;
Nicholas also saw the light and, when he looked about him and saw the
chaos and emptiness he had nurtured, his lungs ceased to breathe.

His entire reign was a mistake. A despot of limited abilities, uneducated,
he didn't know Europe and he didn't know Russia. More ferocious than
clever, he ruled with only the police, with only oppression. Frightened by
December 14th, he recoiled from the nobility, from the single milieu linked
in life and death to the Petersburg throne by the criminal mutual surety of
serf law. He wanted to crush those simple, necessary strivings toward civil
rights on which every Prussian and Austrian crown had yielded, at no loss
to themselves. But, while surreptitiously untying the imperial barge from
the landowners' raft, he did nothing for the people. He would have liked to
take away serfdom from the gentry in order to weaken that class without
giving freedom to the peasants. He saw them from an ordinary officer's
point of view and was not afraid of them, because the people didn't know
the word "constitution," did not demand rights, and considered only the
land that was due to them; in any case it was easy to control them and the
mute masses could be crushed noiselessly, without an echo.

The successor to Nicholas received a difficult inheritance: an unnecessary and inglorious war, shattered finances, widespread theft, grumbling,
mistrust, and expectation. Before him—as in our fairy tales—lay three
roads: to give genuine rights to the nobility and begin to resolve with them
the *lunar* freedom of representative government; to free the serfs with land
and begin a new era of popular and economic freedom; or, instead of one
or the other of these, to continue trampling every manifestation of life until
the muscles of the one who is trampling or the one who is being trampled
are exhausted. What road did our Ivan Tsarevich travel?[4]

All three...

This unsteadiness, this uncertainty of a man only half-awake is the distinguishing feature of the new reign. In it there is something weak-willed,
feeble, lisping, and—by virtue of that—compromising on everything, betraying everything. Literature, the nobility, the universities are all given some

privileges, but not real ones. The serfs are given freedom, but without land. Poland is given back its national identity, but without any autonomy. [. . .]

The story of the universities is a common occurrence, in which that same blundering, dissolute government thinking is expressed at full strength; they treated the young people the same way as the Poles, and the same way as the peasants, and the same way they will behave another ten times, if this foolish government is free to do its will.

Does experience really teach us nothing? Should we really wait for a fourth and fifth bloodletting?.. If we do nothing we will end up with terrible misfortunes: a single knife in the hands of a lunatic could cause terrible harm—what about five hundred thousand bayonets in the hands of a frightened and foolish government?.. The salvation of society, the salvation of the people, demands that the government must not be allowed to do its will, it demands that it be restrained.

Well—swing the lasso!

Notes

Source: "Po povodu studenskikh izbienii," *Kolokol*, l. 113, November 22, 1861; 15:195–99, 409–10.

1. This popular saying was used by Herzen in several articles; it was uttered when the enraged Marshal Bugeaud was refused permission by King Louis Philippe to bomb the Faubourg St. Antoine in 1848.

2. Tsarist Russia suffered an embarrassing defeat in the 1853–56 Crimean War.

3. French Marshal Patrice MacMahon (1808–1893) distinguished himself in the Crimean War with the taking of the Malakhov burial mound at the cost of many lives during the siege of Sevastopol. He served as president of the Third Republic from 1873 to 1879.

4. A frequent hero of Russian fairy tales is Ivan the Tsar's Son (Ivan Tsarevich).

⇥ 42 ⇤

The Bell, No. 121, February 1, 1862. Herzen revived an idea he raised most famously in *From the Other Shore*, that for theorists of all political stripes, the popular masses serve as inert, experimental material, sacrificial offerings on the altar of one or another abstract idea (Woehrlin, *Chernyshevskii*, 257). Isaiah Berlin discussed Herzen's views on this subject in a number of essays, emphasizing that Herzen developed this thesis early on and never altered his position. "No distant ends, no appeals to overriding principles or abstract nouns can justify the suppression of liberty, or fraud, violence and tyranny." Berlin calls this message "Herzen's ultimate sermon" (*Russian Thinkers*, 103, 197).

Herzen demands that theorists stop and listen to the people; by this he does not only mean revolutionaries like Chernyshevsky, who believe that the people are too backward to lead themselves. It is a sign of Herzen's evolution from the time when he saw a possibility for change in the efforts of the enlightened gentry and a well-intentioned tsar. The article below was influenced by Herzen's correspondence with the Slavophile Yuri F. Samarin in which Herzen rejected the charge that he saw revolution as a goal in itself, and he recalled his frequent printed statements in French, German, and Russian on this subject. "The Cannon Fodder of Liberation" is also a response to criticism in *Fatherland Notes* over Herzen's support for the revolutionary ideas of the younger generation.

THE CANNON FODDER OF LIBERATION
[1862]

[. . .] Many times we have heard the reproach: why, instead of a critique of the present, we have no program for the future; why, instead of disapproving of what exists, we do not lecture about what should happen. In a word, why do we tear down without building up... We have indirectly answered these attacks several times and were not at all prepared to speak about them now. But the reproaches have traveled abroad. [. . .][1]

We did not pay particular attention to this, not because we did not value opinion in the West, but because we were convinced that the journalists knew nothing about Russia and did not seriously want to know anything.[2] Besides, we have interests that are much closer and dearer to us than the desire to justify ourselves to them.

> When Paris, and Cologne, and the rustle of oaks
> Were still very new to us,[3]

and when public opinion rustled in printed sheets, imagining that our calling was to teach Russia, we did answer.

> Hélas, ce temps n'est plus,
> Il reviendra peut-être,
> En attendant...[4]

we will speak with and for our own people and for them we will begin our speech. The traveling reproach quickly returned home from Paris, having increased its strength tenfold. [. . .] In deflecting this ricochet effect we decided to say a few words.

First of all, this reproach is unjust: you have before you the two-volume work *After Five Years,* before you is *The Bell* for last year, and they do not contain legal dissertations or doctrinaire scholasticism, but you will find in them our opinion of what is needed by the people, the military, the landowners, and so forth.

"But that is not the same thing. Why didn't you *simply* propose a complete legal code, or, at the very least, the criminal statutes of a Code Pénal?"

"We would have loved to do that, but we know nothing about either of those things."

"Well, if you do not know, then do not criticize the existing ones; sixty million people cannot live without institutions, without a court, in expectation of future blessings."

[. . .] No, gentlemen, stop representing yourselves as throwers of thunderbolts and as Moses, calling down noise and lightning through the will of God, stop presenting yourselves as the wise shepherds of human herds! The methods of *enlightenment* and *liberation* thought up behind the backs of the people and constricting *their inalienable* rights and *their* well-being by means of the axe and the whip were already exhausted by Peter I and the French Terror.

Manna does not fall from heaven—that is a child's fairy tale—it grows in the soil; summon it, learn to listen to how grass grows, and do not lecture the *mature grain,* but help it develop, remove the obstacles in its way. That's all that a person can do, and that is evidently sufficient. One should be more modest, and stop trying to educate entire peoples, stop boasting about your *enlightened* mind and abstract understanding. Did France accomplish very much with its decrees on equality and liberty, and did Germany accomplish very much with its a priori structured state and doctrinaire legal dogmatism?

We have inherited a sad treasure, but still a treasure, of the bitter experience of others; we are rich in the painfully acquired wisdom of our elders. [. . .] The great, fundamental idea of revolution, despite its philosophical attributes and the Roman-Spartan ornaments of its decrees, quickly went too far toward the police, the inquisition, and terror; in wishing to *restore* freedom to the people and to recognize its coming of age, a desire for speed led to treating them like the material of well-being, like the *human flesh of liberation, chair au bonheur publique,*[5] like Napoleonic cannon-fodder.

But here, unfortunately, it turns out that the people had very little meat on their bones, to the point that to all reforms, revolutions, and declaration of rights it answered:

> We are hungry, wanderer, very hungry!
> We are cold, dear one, very cold![6]

And the lawgivers did not just break things, they also built them up, they not only unmasked, but also lectured, and more important than lecturing, they made people study, and maybe, the saddest thing of all in most cases, they were right...

Behind their own noise and their own speeches, the good neighborhood policemen of human rights and the Peter the Firsts of freedom, equality, and brotherhood for a long time did not hear what the *sovereign people* were saying; then they became angry over its rampant materialism... However, here as well they did not ask what was going on.

They were convinced that it was better to lecture the people than to learn from them, that it was better to build things up than to break them down, that it was better to work in the study on an account in the absence of the proprietor than to ask him about it... Sieyès and Speransky[7] weren't the only ones who wrote all sorts of pale constitutions, but the Germans, what did they write and elevate to a science!? And the abyss between them and the people not only did not shrink, but expanded, and this is the consequence of tragic, inevitable necessity. Every success, every step forward carries away the radiant shore; it moves more and more quickly and becomes more and more distant from the gloomy shore and the ignorant people.[8] With what can one fill the abyss, what doctrinaire scholasticism can be used to help, what dogmatic regulation and what kind of academic exercise can bridge it? An experiment was tried, it did not succeed, again because the socialists gave lectures before they knew what they were talking about, and organized phalansteries[9] without having found anywhere the type of person who would want to live in workers' hotels.

And from this very abyss there will emerge, there will come to the surface guillotines, red hats on pikes, Napoleons, armies, more armies, légitimists, Orléanists, a second republic, and, finally, *June days*[10]—days that created nothing, established nothing, days in which the best and unluckiest of peoples, driven by need and despair, went out into the street without a sound, without a plan, without a goal, out of despair and said to their guardians, lawmakers, and teachers: *"We do not know you!* We were hungry, and you gave us parliamentary chatter; we were naked, and you sent us across the border to kill other cold and naked people; we asked for advice, we asked you to teach us how to get out of our situation, and you taught us rhetoric. We are returning to the darkness of our damp cellars, a portion of us will fall in an unequal battle, but, before doing this, we are telling *you,* scribes of the revolution, loudly and clearly:

The people are not with you!"

Notes

Source: "Miaso osvobozhdeniia," *Kolokol,* l. 121, February 1, 1862; 16:25–29, 356–58.

1. Herzen then alludes to remarks made in such newspapers as the *Allgemeine Zeitung, Kölnische Zeitung,* and *Siècle.*

2. Herzen: "We are mostly speaking about journals whose inclination is pseudo-republican, administratively democratic, or Germanically Russophobic... In serious pe-

riodicals there are remarkable articles about Russia. As recently as the January 2 issue of *Revue des Deux Mondes* there was a very interesting article by Charles de Mazade, 'La Russie sous le règne d'Alexandre II.' [. . .]"

3. A quote from Pushkin's "Demon," which Herzen has altered.

4. Herzen: "Alas, that time has passed. It will, perhaps, return, and while we wait..."

5. Herzen: "The meat (or flesh) of social well-being."

6. From Nikolay Nekrasov's "Songs of the Poor Wanderer."

7. Abbé Emmanuel Joseph Sieyès (1748–1836) was an eloquent social and political theorist from the beginning of the French Revolution until Napoleon's coup d'état: his best-known pamphlet is *What Is the Third Estate?* (1789).

8. For both words, Herzen employs the adjective *temnyi* (lit. "dark") in different, but related, senses.

9. According to utopian socialist theories of Charles Fourier (1771–1837).

10. These references are all to France from the Revolution of 1789 to that of 1848. In June 23–25, 1848 (the June Days), there was an uprising caused by the closure of workshops set up by the Second Republic.

⇥ 43 ⇤

The Bell, No. 121, February 1, 1862. Herzen was dissatisfied with the September 1862 millennium ceremony staged in Novgorod, the city to which he had been exiled in 1841. He had requested Odessa, "the newest city in Russia, and they transferred me to Novgorod, the oldest city" (Gertsen, *Sobranie sochinenii*, 22:96). In an ill-tempered letter to friends, he had described "this city of worn inscriptions, reconstructed monasteries, Hanseatic memories, and Russian Orthodox liberalism" (Gertsen, *Sobranie sochinenii*, 22:97). Other than the ninth-century Varangian leader Rurik and the current governor, no one would go there willingly "since, like all provincial capitals, it is uninhabitable" (Gertsen, *Sobranie sochinenii*, 22:102).

Herzen particularly disliked the monument commissioned from the artist Mikeshin. That in the age of great reforms so much money and energy were wasted on jubilees was unfortunate, but what most offended Herzen were the heroes chosen for the very large and mute Novgorod bell, after he found out about the details for the design in a supplement to the official spiritual-cultural calendar (*mesiatseslov*) for 1862. Well aware of the mercurial nature of official favor in Russia, he suggested, tongue in cheek, that removable plaques should be made to celebrate "temporarily important people," and be changed every five years.

———

JUBILEE
[1862]

... The jubilee of Knyazhevich, the jubilee of Vyazemsky, the jubilee of Adlerberg, the jubilee of Sukhozanet,[1] and, finally, Russia's jubilee! How ridiculous in itself to mark the exact moment of the conception of a state, especially when it took place in such a remote location that people are still arguing about the identity of the father,[2] but we will not attack this, as it is an innocent affair. One could object that any sort of excess expense is now out of place, but, taking into consideration that the jubilee of any kind of useless, utterly insignificant person, whose total services consisted in, à la Maniloff,[3] a tender friendship with Nicholas, costs more than ten monuments, we are prepared to reconcile ourselves even to this expense. What offends us is the continuation of lies in the past, and we are offended by sculptural deceptions. There is something faint-hearted and obtuse in a deliberate distortion of history on the highest authority. Did Nicholas hide the participation of Ermolov and Tol[4] in the Battle of Borodino by omitting their names from a monument, did he hide from posterity the fact that Warsaw was captured by Tol and not Paskevich? Why have Rtishchev, Betskoy, Potemkin, Kochubey, Vorontsov, Paskevich, Lazarev, Kornikov, Nakhimov,[5] et al., et al. been elevated as *temporarily important people?*

We are not even talking about the crowd of every kind of high clergymen, these official *enlighteners,* whose carved faces appear in the list of historic celebrities. Among them are people of whom no one has heard, like Gury and Varsonofy, and there are those of whom we are accustomed to hearing about the negative side, like the schemer Feofan Prokopovich.[6]

If the deed is done and the carved likenesses have been commissioned, then we propose bas-reliefs for *temporarily important people* on removable plaques, so that they can be replaced as required by necessity and by the departure of new celebrities to join their forefathers.

Tikhon Zadonsky, keeper of fasts—with *Adlerberg*-the-elder.[7]

Mitrofan Voronezhky, the virgin—with *Baryatynsky.*[8]

The least talented of soldiers *Paskevich*—with the even less talented statesman *Panin.*

Gury and Varsonofy—with *Putyatin and Askochensky.*[9]

Rtishchev, who in 1648 organized a group to translate from the Greek—with *Pokhitonov,* who in 1858 organized a group to translate from all languages.

After five years these could also be discarded and new plaques installed... changed before opinions settle and legal measures for important people are established. Then the Russian people will in turn finally cry out:

The front or back of the head![10]

Notes

Source: "Iubilei," *Kolokol,* l. 121, February 1, 1862; 16:30–31, 358–59.

1. Vladimir F. Adlerberg (1790–1884) headed the Postal Department from 1842 to 1856, and then served as minister of the Imperial Court until 1872; Nikolay O. Sukhozanet (1794–1871) was an adjutant-general who took part in the suppression of the Poles in 1830–31 and later was war minister (1856–61).

2. Herzen: "Probably taking advantage of the fact that with us *la recherché de la pater-nité* (the clarification of fatherhood) is not forbidden, as it is in the French law code."

3. A character in Gogol's *Dead Souls*.

4. Alexey P. Yermolov was an artillery general, and in 1812 chief of staff for the western flank of the army; Count Karl F. Tol was adjutant general in 1812, and chief of staff during the suppression of the Polish uprising in 1831. Nicholas was believed to be jealous of these two generals due to the distinguished nature of their military service.

5. Rtishchev (1625–1673) was a government official interested in education in the time of Tsar Alexey; Betskoy (1704–1795) was president of the Academy of Arts and founder of what became the Smolny Institute; Potemkin (1739–1791) was a favorite of Catherine II; Kochubey (1768–1834) was a diplomat and minister under Alexander I; Vorontsov (1782–1856) headed civilian and military administrations in Bessarabia and the Caucasus; Lazarev (1788–1851) was an Antarctic explorer; Kornikov (1806–1854) and Nakhimov (1802–1855) were both admirals who took part in the defense of Sevastopol.

6. Gury was a sixteenth-century bishop who was canonized; Varsonofy was a sixteenth-century monastic leader, later canonized; Feofan Prokopovich (1681–1736) was a preacher, writer, vice-president of the Holy Synod, and the person Peter I most relied upon in spiritual matters.

7. Tikhon Zadonsky was an important eighteenth-century bishop canonized in 1861.

8. Mitrofan was a seventeenth-century bishop canonized in 1832; Prince Baryatinsky led Russian military operations in the Caucasus from 1856 to 1862.

9. Askochinsky was a reactionary journalist and editor of *Domestic Chats for Popular Reading* from 1858 to 1877.

10. Herzen: "The monument's form has really gratified us: a huge *bell*, placed so that it cannot ring. But all the same a bell! But—which one? The town council [*veche*] bell, or ours in London? It seems to us that it is neither one nor the other, but a bell that is very *sweet* [*sladkii*]; it was plastered over with all kinds of figures in immense quantities, among them one was plastered with wings and so ardently strains to get away that on its head is some sort of lamp. (See *The St. P. Calendar for 1862*.)"

❖ 44 ❖

The Bell, No. 125, March 15, 1862. *The Bell* gave extensive coverage to the student disturbances that flared up at Moscow University during September and October 1861 in connection with new rules set forth by Minister of Education Putyatin. Students asked that the rise in tuition costs be rescinded along with the ban on the student bank, and that they be allowed to send representatives to talk to university authorities. After several students were arrested, there was a march to the governor-general's home to ask for the students' release and to submit an address outlining their concerns to the tsar. There they were set upon by regular policemen, gendarmes in disguise, and shopkeepers who had been told that the students were opposed to the emancipation. Herzen was troubled by support for the government's repressive measures among university administrators and a number of once-liberal professors like Sergey Solovyov and Boris Chicherin. Understanding that this marked a further break with his former acquaintances in Moscow,

Herzen claimed that he wrote this article with tears in his eyes, but that some things were more sacred to him than any person. Kavelin sent a letter from Paris, saying that the article told the truth and that "for us, Moscow is a cemetery" (*Let* 3:290, 296).

———

ACADEMIC MOSCOW
[1862]

We have received three additional letters about Moscow University—dark, sad letters... Let them mock us for having a humane heart, but we will not hide the deep pain with which we read these letters. We do not slander ourselves with either feelings or a lack of feelings. The memory of Moscow University and our Moscow circle is very dear to us. We preserve a feeling of reverence for the friends of youth and for our Moscow alma mater. We spent the most sacred moments of youth in its auditoriums, and we endured all the insults of Nicholaevan despotism. [. . .] It is there that the idea of struggle to which we have remained faithful first formed and was strengthened. From there we dispersed to various places of exile and there we gathered a few years later around Granovsky's podium—*Granovsky*...[1] how hard it is to hear his name... It is now our turn to say of him what he said of Belinsky: "Blessed is he who dies in good time!" In 1849 the oppression was external; *over there*, where neither the ear of the gendarme nor the arm of the local police could reach, there things were *pure*... but now?..

And did friends, colleagues, and protégés of Granovsky really take part in these vile actions?

Who are they?.. Those who blush upon reading our words, those who feel that no matter how much you shout, you cannot drown out something troubling your conscience!

And if such people are not to be found?

Blessed is he who dies in good time!

The letters under discussion were seriously delayed. One of them sets out the complete history of the university business, and it will appear in the next issue; from the two remaining letters we will copy out a few small excerpts.

We hope that the writers are sure of the facts they are reporting to us. And once more we remind our correspondents that *each time they supply us with incorrect rumors, news taken from the street and exaggerated by party spirit* (as happened quite recently), *they do us much greater harm* than all the Shuvalovs with their various free and temporary agents.[2]

From the first letter.

...A few days ago I read an account by Moscow professors of matters relating to the students' address to the tsar. The thought expressed in it is the following: the government itself is guilty of the fact that such incidents, like the one with the address, are possible at the university, and it follows that at the very first signs of university agitation greater attention should be paid to the willfulness of the students and to seriously punishing the instigators.

From the second letter.

... Finally *The Bell* reached us that talks about university events. Not everything in the story you placed there is correct, and many details are missing. Your correspondent, for example, praised professor *Yeshovsky,* but on October 11, when students entered the professors' room for an explanation with the trustee, he barred their way, and talked about dissension between students and professors. When the students remarked that they had come not to see the professors but Isakov, he answered: "While Isakov is here, *we will not betray him!*"[3]

In general our professors have distinguished themselves. Lents and Nikitenko, the generals of St. Petersburg University, were struck by the zeal for order shown by *Solovyov* and *Babst,* who were called before a commission to examine the university statutes.[4]

You know about Chicherin's inaugural lecture—you probably know his philosophy of slavery, i.e., the obedience to evil laws, and how he offended the students who were under arrest. At first he got away with it. But when the students being held were released, they decided to hiss him on December 9th. Having found out about this, the section of those enrolled who sympathized with the scholarly professor sent *Solovyov's* students and *Sukhodolsky* to warn him. Chicherin showed up at the lecture along with *N. F. Pavlov* and *Korsh (one letter names the editor of* Moscow News *and another his brother).* When one group of students began to whistle, another group under the leadership of *Solovyov* shouted: "Whistlers get out!" This cry attracted even the distinguished guest, Mr. Korsh, who with complete selflessness shouted: "Whistlers get out!"[5]

At the following lecture, a group of about twenty-five students asked Chicherin to listen to a few words from them. The learned professor said that he could not stop during the lecture, but after the lecture *he would ask permission of the university inspector to speak with the students.* Evidently the inspector agreed because the learned professor returned to the auditorium. There began a long explanation, which ended with the professor fearlessly saying: "I stand for an unlimited monarchical form of government. I hold to those convictions which I consider to be true, and it is not my fault if they are not ones that appeal to you"... You can read what opinions appeal to the learned professor in *Our Times*.

To this not entirely favorable account *the second letter* adds more comforting news for the conservative professor and his friends:

> Mr. Chicherin's inaugural lecture met with loud approval in government circles. On October 30, Putyatin came in the tsar's name to thank the Moscow professors for conducting themselves so wisely while those in Petersburg were misbehaving, and he especially thanked Mr. Chicherin. After this, the censorship forbade any comments in writing against his lectures!

Notes

Source: "Akademicheskaia Moskva," *Kolokol*, l. 125, March 15, 1862; 16:80–82, 375–77.

1. Timofey N. Granovsky (1813–1855) was a charismatic professor of history at Moscow University and a key figure in Moscow intellectual circles from the 1830s until his death.

2. Working for the Third Department abroad.

3. Yeshovsky was a professor of general history in Kazan and from 1858 to 1865 in Moscow; Isakov was an official at court and a trustee of the Moscow educational district from 1859 to 1863.

4. Lents was a senior official in the Senate; Nikitenko, born into serfdom, was a literary historian, memoirist, professor, and censor; Babst was a political economist in Kazan and Moscow.

5. Sukhodolsky was a Moscow student; N. F. Pavlov was a writer and newspaper editor.

⇥ 45 ⇤

The Bell, No. 139, July 15, 1862. This is a polemic against positions taken by authors of the radical proclamation "Young Russia," which was generated by a group of Moscow University students and widely distributed in mid-May 1862 in Moscow, Petersburg, and provincial Russia. The pamphlet, written by Petr G. Zaichnevsky (1842–1896) while he was under arrest for anti-government propaganda, began with the declaration that Russia had entered the revolutionary phase of its development and that society had split into two enemy camps. It called for a seizure of power and the establishment of a minority dictatorship and a new social structure, with the agricultural commune as its foundation. It dismissed liberalism and declared itself in opposition to *The Bell*, accusing Herzen of having retreated from radical positions after the upheaval of 1848. "Young

Russia" shocked many progressive voices in Russia, and, coinciding with a higher in-
cidence of arson, gave the government ample reason to increase repressive measures.

Herzen wrote "in a mood of despairing sarcasm," as he witnessed—albeit from
afar—the suppression of journals, arrests, printing houses placed under Ministry of
Interior control, and all lectures and meetings subject to authorization by the Interior
Ministry and the Third Department (Lampert, *Sons Against Fathers*, 47). He was discour-
aged, but defiant, declaring that if Sunday literacy instruction for peasants was banned
"I will become the Sunday school" (Gertsen, *Sobranie sochinenii*, 27:bk. 1, 243–44).

In the same issue of *The Bell*, Herzen included news of an attempt on the life of
Grand Duke Konstantin Nikolaevich by an "ultra-Catholic." Although it was the Russian
government that brought people to this madness, Herzen said that he hated "any kind
of bloody retaliation," a point that he would make even more forcefully after Karakozov's
attempt on the tsar's life in 1866.

--◆--

Young and Old Russia
[1862]

In Petersburg there is terror, the most dangerous and senseless of all its
manifestations, the terror of dumbfounded cowardice, not leonine terror,
but calf-like terror,[1] terror in which a government—poisoned by fumes, not
knowing where the danger comes from, knowing neither its strength nor
its weaknesses and therefore prepared to fight to no purpose—gives aid to
society, to literature, to the people, to progress and regress...

The Day has been banned, *The Contemporary* and *The Russian Word* have
been banned, Sunday schools are closed, the chess club is closed,[2] reading
rooms are closed, money intended for needy students has been taken away,
printing presses are under extra surveillance, two ministers and the Third
Department must agree to the reading of public lectures. There are continual arrests, officers, aides-de-camp in prison cells, the inquisitor Golitsyn (called "junior" in an earlier time) is summoned to the Winter Palace
together with Liprandi ... who was pushed away with loathing by the same
Alexander II three years ago.[3]

[. . .] Evidently Nicholaevism was buried alive and is now rising up from
the damp earth in a shroud-uniform, all buttoned up—and the State Council, the archdeacon Panin, Annenkov-Tversky, Pavel Gagarin, and Filaret
with a birch rod are rushing round the corner to sing out: "Nicholas is
risen!"[4]

"Verily he is risen!"—even we say this to the undead corpse. It's a holiday on your street, only your street leads not from the grave but toward the
grave.

"Excuse me, excuse me—and who's guilty in this matter? On the one hand, the Shchukin yard is burning, and on the other hand, there is 'Young Russia'..."

"And when in Russia wasn't something or other burning? [. . .] Arson in our country is as infectious as the plague. [. . .]"

"Okay, fine, we know that arson has always been around, but 'Young Russia'?"

"What is this 'Young Russia'?" we asked with unease.[5]

"Oh, it is a terrible Russia! You know—the rejection of everything, where nothing is sacred, nothing at all: neither power, nor property, nor the family, nor any kind of authority. For them, 'Great Rus' hasn't gone much beyond *The Northern Bee,* and you are a backward commentator."

Finally, this document, which horrified the government and the literary realm, the progressives and the reactionaries, civilized supporters of a parliament, and civilizing bureaucrats, reached even us.

We read it once, twice, three times... with a great deal we are very much not in agreement (and we will talk about this in another article), but we must in good conscience confess that we do not understand the delirium tremens of the government, the whining of the conscientious journals, or the emotional confusion of the platonic lovers of progress.

[. . .] We address ourselves to genuinely honest, but weak, people and ask them: why were they frightened of "Young Russia"? Did they really believe that the Russian people would—just like that—grab an axe at the first cry of "All hail the Russian socialist and democratic republic!" No, they will answer in a chorus that this is impossible, that the people do not understand these words, and on the contrary, embittered by the arson, they would be prepared to tear to pieces those who pronounce these words. And yet every *honest* person feels obligated to abuse these young people, showering them with reproaches and curses, and feels obliged to be horrified, raising their eyes to the mountains.

Gentlemen, look more deeply at your feelings, and you will see with shame that what struck you was neither the danger, nor the lie, nor any damage, *but the audacity* of free speech. Your sense of *hierarchical discipline* has been offended—they are speaking way beyond their years and status...

If these young people (and we have no doubt that this flysheet was written by very young people) in their arrogance talked a lot of nonsense, then stop them, enter into argument with them, answer them, but do not call out for help, do not push them into prison cells because the Third Department *fara da se.*[6] And if they run out of spies there is auxiliary literature, which can be used to implicate them as incendiaries after a Russian-style, secret, torture-chamber investigation.

Thus this whole terrible affair, which has placed the Russian Empire and Nevsky Prospect on the brink of social cataclysm, having broken the last link between gradual and abrupt progress, is based on a youthful upsurge, incautious, unrestrained, but which did no harm *and could not have done any harm*. It is a shame that the young people issued this proclamation, but we will not blame them. [. . .]

Where is the criminality?

If the government were capable of understanding and did not retain the self-important seriousness of a commissionaire with a mace, what a big laugh they would have now, looking at the alarm of the brave liberals, the tough progressives, the courageous defenders of rights and of a free press, the intrepid denouncers of police chiefs and local supervisors—seeing how they, the dear ones, ran under the wings of those very same police, that very same government. [. . .]

"Young Russia" seems to us doubly mistaken. First, *it is not at all Russian,* but one of the variations on a theme of Western socialism, the metaphysics of the French Revolution, sociopolitical desiderata in the form of a call to arms. The second mistake is its inappropriateness: the accident of its coincidence with the fires intensified this.

It is clear that the young people who wrote this lived more in the world of comrades and books than in the world of facts, more in the algebra of ideas—with their easy and universal formulas and conclusions—than in a workshop, where friction, heat, bad casting, and internal flaws can alter the simplicity of a mechanical law and put the brakes on its rapid advance. That's how their speech appeared; in it there is none of that internal restraint that you get either from your own experience or *the structure of an organized party.*

But having said this, we will add that their fearless consistency is one of the most characteristic aspects of the Russian genius, *which is estranged from the people.* History has left us nothing cherished; we have none of those *esteemed objects of respect,* which hamper the Western man but which are dear to him. After the slavery in which we lived, the alienation from others like us, the break with the people, the inability to take action, we were left with a melancholy consolation, but a consolation nevertheless, in the starkness of the negation, in its logical relentlessness, and with some joy we pronounced those last *extreme* words, which our teachers, turning pale and glancing furtively around them, could barely pronounce. Yes, we pronounced them loudly, and it is as if it became easier in the expectation of the storm that they would provoke. We had nothing to lose.

Circumstances changed. The Russian land struggle began. Each struggle proceeds not according to the laws of abstract logic, but by a complex process of embryogeny. To help in our struggle we need the West's ideas and its experience. But to the same degree we do not need its revolutionary declamation, just like the French did not need the Roman-Spartan rhetoric with which it spoke at the end of the last century. To speak in someone else's images, to call something by a foreign name—that shows a lack of understanding of both the matter at hand and of the people, and a lack of respect for both as well. Is there a shadow of probability that the Russian people would rise up in the name of Blanqui's socialism, shouting out four words, among which three long ones are unfamiliar to them?[7]

You consider us backward, and we do not get angry; if we have lagged behind you in our opinions, we have not lagged behind in our heart, and the heart sets the pace. And don't you become angry when, in a friendly matter, we turn around your reprimand and say that your costume à la Karl Moor and Gracchus Babeuf[8] on the Russian square is not only old, but resembles masquerade dress. The French are a comical but deferential people; it was possible to confuse them with a Roman latiklave and the language of Seneca's heroes, while our people demanded the head of the unfortunate Obruchev.[9]

... And again a chorus can be heard—not underground, but from the second floor—a chorus of cowards, weak and hoping for only a slightly progressive movement.

"Yes, yes," they cry, "look what the celebrated people, that wild beast, is doing—this is what awaits us. Go explain to them that we are now not serf-owners but landowners, and that we do not demand the corvée, but a representative assembly, not quitrent, but the rights of citizens."

The people are a little slow to understand and cannot so quickly imagine that their age-old, bloody enemy who robbed them, disgraced their family, and wore them out with hunger and humiliated them, suddenly fell into such repentance—"my brother," he said, and that's all.

There are terrible historical misfortunes, the dark fruits of dark deeds; just before they occur, as before a storm, human wisdom falls silent and covers eyes full of bitter tears with its hands.

Our sacrificial victims, like Mikhailov and Obruchev, must endure a double martyrdom [. . .] the people will not know them—even worse, it will know them as members of the gentry, as enemies. They will not pity them and do not want their sacrifice.

This is where the split has led us. The people do not have faith in—and are prepared to stone—those who gave their lives for them. In the dark night in which they were raised they are prepared, like the giant in a fairy tale, to slaughter their children for wearing foreign clothing.

Our martyrs are bearing the terrible punishment of popular hate not for their own transgressions, but for those of others. These *others* rush to receive an amnesty; for their part, they were not so generous, and what did they really do—having lost the oyster, they decided to throw away the shell! Did the gentry Magdalenes in their own hearts really achieve repentance? Was the word *emancipation* really said by them—didn't they dig their heels in while they thought it was still possible to dig their heels in? Atonement is not achieved nor ancient scars forgiven so easily and with such a dissatisfied expression.

The scene on the Petersburg square was very sad, infinitely sad, but you, poor martyrs, should not give in to despair. Complete your noble act of devotion, fulfill your great sacrifice of love, and from the height of your Golgotha and from your underground mine pits forgive the people their unintentional sense of grievance, and say *to those others,* that the people *have the right to this mistake, and that you give them your blessing!*

Notes

Source: "Molodaia i staraia Rossiia," *Kolokol*, l. 139, July 15, 1862; 16:199–205, 410–15.

1. An adjective formed from the word *telënok,* "calf," which implies that the emotion is "foolish."

2. Sunday schools were a project of the intelligentsia to take advantage of the peasants' sole day off to spread literacy; in a number of cases, progressive political ideas were spread as well. The same was said of the popular reading rooms that had been set up. A chess club was organized in Petersburg in 1862 by writers in opposition to the government, including Chernyshevsky and Lavrov.

3. Prince A. F. Golitsyn (1796–1864) took part in the investigation of Herzen and Ogaryov in 1834–35, and in the Petrashevsky case in 1849. Liprandi's proposal to recruit spies among gymnasia students had been rejected by the tsar.

4. Herzen is mocking the Easter exclamation and response exchanged by Orthodox believers: "Christ is risen!" "Verily He is risen!" This is supposedly uttered by three high government officials and the Moscow metropolitan. Annenkov-Tversky was chief of the St. Petersburg police, and Prince Gagarin was a reactionary member of several state committees.

5. Herzen: "Unfortunately, we received it not before July 1st."

6. Will manage them itself.

7. Louis A. Blanqui (1805–1881), a French utopian revolutionary, participated in the 1830 and 1848 uprisings.

8. Karl Moor is the hero of Schiller's *The Robbers.* François-Noël Babeuf (1760–1797) was a French political activist and journalist whose nickname comes from his use of Roman democratic models and claim to be a true tribune of the people and enemy of the bourgeois; he was executed in 1797.

9. The latiklave was a broad purple band worn on a tunic by senators. Vladimir A. Obruchev (1836–1912) was arrested in 1861 for distributing the proclamation "Great Rus"; to make the greatest possible impression on the public, his civil execution (breaking a sword over the head before being sent to Siberia) took place right after the May 1862 fires in St. Petersburg.

⇾ 46 ⇽

The Bell, No. 141, August 15, 1862. Herzen develops ideas previously raised in "The Cannon Fodder of Liberation" (Doc. 42). He retains some faint hope that the tsarist regime can distance itself from the support of the elite and meet more of the people's needs, and that socialism can be achieved through a nonviolent process. Ivan Aksakov wrote a response to the ideas expressed in "Journalists and Terrorists," but its publication in *The Day* was blocked by the censorship (*Let* 3:436).

—

JOURNALISTS AND TERRORISTS
[1862]

[. . .] One of the oddest of all the oddities in the war being waged against us is that "Aging Russia" accuses us of a thirst for explosions, violent revolutions, terrorist impulses, and just about accuses us of arson, and, at the same time, "Young Russia" scolds us for having lost our revolutionary fervor and for having lost "all faith in violent revolutions."

Until unforeseen circumstances change, we will not answer "Aging Russia." What could you use to convince people who talk about *chair à canon*[1] after "the sacrificial offerings to liberation"? What can you say to people, who naively declare that if we were to scold *those people* and learn to love *these ones,* that everything would be fine? What can be done about the fact that an impertinent child who throws a stone at a street lamp is less repulsive to us than the self-satisfied lymphatic bedbug who *reprimands* him.

Why do we address "Young Russia"? They think that "we have lost all faith in violent revolutions."

We have not lost our faith in them, but our *love for them.* Violent revolutions can be unavoidable, and maybe that is how it will be with us; it is a desperate measure, the *ultima ratio*[2] of peoples and of tsars, and one must be ready for this, but to call for it at the beginning of the working day, not having made a single effort, not having exhausted any means, to settle on this seems to us as juvenile and immature as it is *improvident and harmful* to use it as a threat.

Those who are familiar with the maturing of ideas and expressions will recognize in the bloody words of "Young Russia" the age of the people saying them. Revolutionary terror with its threatening atmosphere and its scaffolds appeals to the young, the way that the terror in fairy tales with their sorcerers and monsters appeals to children.

Terror is easy and quick, much easier than labor [. . .] it liberates through despotism and convinces by means of the guillotine. Terror gives free rein to the passions, cleansing them by means of the common good and the absence of individual views. That's why it appeals to more people than does *self-restraint on behalf of the cause.* [. . .]

We long ago ceased to love either chalice full of blood, both the civil and the military, and in like manner do not wish to drink from the skull of our enemies in battle, nor see the head of the Duchess of Lamballe on a pike[3]... Whatever blood is flowing, tears are flowing somewhere, and if sometimes it is necessary to cross this threshold, then let it be done without blood-thirsty mockery, but with a melancholy, anxious feeling of a terrible duty and a tragic necessity.

Moreover, the May of death, like the May of life, flowers only once *und nicht wieder.*[4] The terror of the nineties will not be repeated; it had a kind of naive purity of ignorance, an unconditional faith in its innocence and success, which the terror that follows it will not have. [. . .]

The French Terror is possible least of all with us. The revolutionary elements in France flowed from other cities to Paris, and there they tripled in size in the clubs and the Convention, and marched with sword and axe in hand to preach philanthropic ideas and philosophical truths to every city rampart and every *urban dweller,* but rarely beyond that. Little bits reached the peasants, but by chance. The Revolution, like a swift stream, reached the edges of the fields and washed them away, but never lost its primarily municipal course.

Decentralization is the first condition of our revolution, which is coming from the rows of grain, from the fields, from the village, and not at all toward Petersburg, where until February 19, 1861 the people received nothing but troubles and humiliations. And not toward Moscow, where alongside holy relics dwell the living ones, who, like the righteous Simeon, are satisfied now that they have seen the newly born Rus.[5]

And the circumstances are completely different.

Revolutionary France wanted to renounce traditional daily life, which had grown stronger over the centuries, blessed by the powerful church and engraved with the sword of the victor on the heart of the defeated. The Revolution proclaimed a new, unprecedented right, the right of a human being, and on this basis it sought to establish a rational social union. Breaking with the past—whose representatives were very powerful—and up to its knees in blood, it hastened to proclaim to the world the news of earthly equality and brotherhood. It needed a republic gathered into one center, *une et indivisible,* it needed a Committee of Social Salvation, uniting in a single will all the rays of the Revolution and forging them into lightning.

These lightning bolts routed monarchical France, but they did not create a republic. A centralized police sat down on a throne that was covered with blood. As for the revolutionary idea—the people were not up to it.

We have no new doctrines, no new catechisms to proclaim. Our revolution must begin with a conscious return to the national way of life, to principles recognized by national ways of thinking and by age-old custom. By strengthening the right of each person to land, i.e., by declaring the land for what it is—*an inalienable element*—we are only affirming and generalizing the popular understanding of the relationship of a person to the land. Renouncing forms that are alien to the people, which began pressing in on them a century and a half ago, we continue our interrupted and deflected development, introducing to it a new power of thought and science.

The instinctive feeling that suggested to the government the idea of emancipation is vaguely fermenting in it, but, incorrigible in its routines and prejudices, it cannot decide on one road to travel, and instead swings like a pendulum, touching first one side, then another. It is impossible to remain for very long in this state of vacillation; with such questions as are being raised, the people cannot sit with folded hands while waiting for the foundations of Petersburg government, which are rotting from below and weathering from above, to collapse on their own. Rotted scaffolding can stand for a very long time and, for the most part, will stand until there is a storm. But before there is some sort of storm, has anyone attempted, with a strong sense of purpose or a strong voice, to point out the way?

Imperial power for us is *only power,* that is force, organization, *paraphernalia;* it has no content, it bears no responsibilities, it can turn into a Tatar khanate and a French Committee for Social Salvation—wasn't Pugachev the Emperor Peter III? What is there in common between Alexey Mikhailovich and Peter? Only limitless power, torture, and executions? By autocracy, Nicholas understood the combination of the powers of an Asian shah and a Prussian cavalry sergeant-major. The people under a tsar *of the land* are a kind of social republic covered with Monomakh's cap.

In the midst of the uncertainty and disorder of the present, when no one has said their final word, when everything is fermenting, everything is in a state of expectation—some for an assembly, others for land—when the people, no matter what the sovereign announces, no matter how the governors speechify in Russian and Ukrainian, stubbornly believe in *another kind of* freedom, you summon them to rise against the tsar and the nobility, i.e., against despised social groups *in which they include you,* and against state power in which they see their protector. Whether they are mistaken or not, it is all the same. They are sure that they are not mistaken, and for that reason they will not follow you and you will perish. No minority from among the educated can carry out an invincible revolution without state power and without the people—that is how the questions stand; as long as the country-side, the village, the steppe, the Volga and Ural regions are quiet, the only possible revolutions are those led by oligarchs and guards officers. [. . .]

Up until now the people have been deaf and dumb to all revolutionary aspirations, because they have not understood what the masters lacked. But in the current struggle the people are mixed in as a living force; the question of emancipation became a cross-border question for both Russias—the one at the summit and the one in the fields; the people and the gentry understood it that way. A clash was unavoidable. Until now it was not clear whether the people were prepared to yield on the land or whether the gentry were prepared to sell it cheaply. Both turned to the same mediator—the government. What did it do? Give the land? No. Take it away? No. There is a feeble impulse to do both one and the other. Let it try to take the land from under the peasants' feet, that is, to do what neither Peter I nor serf-dom was able to do. The people have already announced their passive veto. There's a good reason why they have not subscribed to either the statutory documents or moved from corvée to quitrent; they are waiting for the land.

While the land is *to all intents and purposes* theirs, the people will not rise up. It is difficult for the people to rise up; it is not the risk to themselves, or hard labor, or the executioners, but the complete ruin of their family, the unplowed field, hungry children, the descent of locusts. That is why the peasant is patient, is patient for a terribly long time, and only rarely, when the cup overflows, he turns up in some kind of gloomy despair and kills en masse not only his enemies but also his own children, so they will not be sent to military colonies.

A call to arms is possible only on the eve of battle. Any premature call is a hint, a piece of news given to the enemy, and an exposure of one's own weakness to them.

For that reason, leave off the revolutionary rhetoric and get to work. Unite more closely amongst yourselves, so that you are a force, so that you possess both unity and good organization; unite with the people, so that they forget your origins; do not preach Feuerbach and Babeuf to them, but the *religion of the land* that they understand... and be prepared. The fateful day will come; stand up, fall in battle, but do not call for it as *a longed-for day*. If the sun rises without bloody storm clouds, so much the better, and if it wears Monomakh's cap or a Phrygian one, it's all the same. Surely the French have shown that a translation from a feudal-monarchic language of gestures and ranks to a Roman-republican language is not worth the spilling of blood or even of ink. [. . .]

All that is now dissatisfied and noisy in our midst, from the *vieux boyards moscovites*[6] to the Russian Germans, from Nicholaevan generals to small-time plantation owners, will disappear, will be shaken off. How? Where? Where do mice and rats disappear with the first rays of the sun, where do crickets go during the day? [. . .]

In order for tsarist power to become popular power, it must understand that the wave that is washing away at its foundations and wishes to lift it up is in fact a wave from the sea, that it can neither be stopped nor sent to Siberia, that the rising tide has begun and that—a little earlier or a little later—it will have to choose between being at the helm of a popular state or in the silt at the bottom of the sea. [. . .]

Notes

Source: "Zhurnalisty i terroristy," *Kolokol*, l. 141, August 15, 1862; 16:220–26, 424–25.

1. Cannon fodder.

2. A final argument.

3. A reference to the murder of the Princess de Lamballe during the "September Days" of 1792. Her head was paraded through the streets in a celebration of the defeat of the counterrevolution.

4. And never again. Herzen is quoting Schiller's poem "Resignation."

5. Herzen compares Moscow liberals, who find the emancipation a source of new hope for Russia, with the righteous Simeon, called in Russian *bogopriimets* (the God-Receiver), of whom prophecy said that he would not die until he had seen the Christ child, which, according to Luke, is what indeed took place.

6. Old Russian boyars (member of the hereditary nobility, whose origins could be traced back to Kievan and Muscovite Russia).

⇥ 47 ⇤

The Bell, No. 141, August 15, 1862. The Tver arbitrators (*mirovye posredniki*) mentioned in the letter are thirteen members of the nobility who addressed the tsar in writing about the inadequacies of the emancipation and the need for peasants to receive an allotment of land along with their freedom. This address was published in *The Bell* on March 22, 1862. They also requested the convening of an assembly of representatives of all the Russian people. Alexander II's answer was to send General Nikolay Annenkov to Tver, where everyone who had signed the document was arrested. The Tver case was mentioned in another Herzen article, "To the Senators and Secret Advisors for Journalism," in the April 22, 1862, issue of *The Bell*. The prisoners were released, but were forbidden to enter government service or participate in any future elections.

A Chronicle of Terror
[1862]

We received a long letter from Petersburg. The terror is not abating; constant arrests, prizes for the informers, gratitude to men of letters who trample people in the dirt, the bribery of soldiers... all the ugliness of fear that
is not inhibited by anything—the fear of a young ignoramus and Nero put
together.

Here are excerpts from the letter:

> The zeal in searching out *incendiaries* is not slackening and the
> Third Department recently started a rumor that the government has
> in its possession the handwritten proclamations *of Russian publishers
> and arsonists living abroad.*[1]
>
> Every day one hears about new detentions. Every person return-
> ing from abroad is searched at the border, shoes and stockings
> are removed... On Saturday, July 7/19 Chernyshevsky and Serno-
> Solovyovich were arrested.[2] There are two active commissions in
> St. Petersburg: one concerning the arson, whose composition has
> been known for a while; the other concerning the distribution of
> the proclamation, under the chairmanship of *Prince Golitsyn.* Here
> the members are *Gedda,* a senior Senate official, aide-de-camp
> *Sleptsov,* and the former governor of Perm *Ogaryov,* a harmful
> and empty man.
>
> During the first days of July (between the 1st and the 8th), the
> case *of the Tver arbitrators* was decided. Their sentence was an-
> nounced and drawn up so absurdly, in such a repulsively foolish way,
> that one can't remember anything even vaguely approaching this
> level of stupidity for a very long time. The senators, for no reason at
> all, in a completely distorted way, doing the best they could, relied
> on article 319 of the "Sentencing Code." The Tver arbitrators were
> accused of *spreading works whose goal was to make unlawful judgments
> about the government;* they were sentenced to two and a half years con-
> finement, with some loss of class privileges. Suvorov[3] was struck by
> the absurdity of the senate's conclusions, and, it is said, has already
> asked the sovereign that this sentence not be carried out. [. . .]
>
> While in residence in Peterhof, the sovereign requested a list of all
> the residents of Peterhof; finding on it two students, he ordered that
> their parents be obliged, by signed statements, to remove these stu-
> dents from Peterhof. "This is a joke," said one *government* supporter,[4]

"could this really be possible?" Allow us to supply the names of the
students: *Meshchersky* and *Nabokov.* [. . .]

Notes

Source: "Khronika terrora," *Kolokol*, l. 141, August 15, 1862; 16:227–28, 425–26.

1. Herzen: "Is it really necessary to say that this is a despicable slander and a foul lie?"

2. Nikolay G. Chernyshevsky (1828–1889) was editor of *The Contemporary* and a well-known progressive journalist; after this arrest he spent his time in jail writing *What Is to Be Done?*, which, after being published through an oversight, became a bible of the Russian revolutionaries and Lenin's favorite literary work. Chernyshevsky spent the rest of his life in prison and exile. Nikolay A. Serno-Solovyovich worked for *The Contemporary* and helped organize "Land and Liberty."

3. Prince Alexander Suvorov was at this time the military governor-general of St. Petersburg.

4. Herzen's correspondent uses the word *potaplennik*, which relates to the first paragraph of this article, where there is a description of literary figures who criticize others to gain the authorities' favor as *potapstvuiushchie,* that is, people who trample others in the dirt.

→ 48 ←

The Bell, No. 141, August 15, 1862. Everyone on this list apparently visited Herzen in London during the spring and summer of 1862, and were observed by an agent of the Third Department, who kept watch on Herzen's house and was able to distinguish between those who came out of curiosity and a smaller group assumed to have a genuine interest in his "criminal affairs." Most of the latter were, in fact, subject to rigorous searches when they crossed the border into the Russian Empire. The list got to Herzen through one of his Polish correspondents. Herzen wrote to Vladimir Stasov, who was staying in London at the time, that his Sunday and Wednesday open houses would have to stop because "the spying has increased to the point of insolence" (*Let* 3:352). In a letter from 1858 on surveillance of his visitors, Herzen repeated a rumor that Alexander had responded to the earlier report with the words "leave them in peace" (*Let* 2:398).

———

A LIST OF PEOPLE SUBJECT TO ARREST BY THE GOVERNMENT
UPON THEIR RETURN FROM ABROAD
[1862]

We received from a Polish correspondent, whom we thank most sincerely, the names of people who are presently abroad, and whom our progressive

Petersburg government has ordered to be detained at the first Polish station on the railroad. Here is the list.

Stasov Vladimir	Pisemsky Alexander
Kalinovsky Balthazar	Betger Alexander
Albertini Nikolay	Zagoskin Pavel
Kovalevsky Petr	Sovetov Alexander
Kovalevsky Yulyan	Zhemchuzhnikov Nikolay
Kovalevsky Oskar	Rubinshtein Nikolay
Suzdaltsev Vladimir	Davydov Pavel
Plautin Fedor	Davydov Denis
Botkin Sergey	Dostoevsky Fyodor[1]
Korsh Valentin	

..."What a mix of garments and faces, tribes, dialects, and status!"[2] and what gigantic, colossal stupidity on the part of our government! [. . .]

Notes
Source: "Spisok lits, kotorykh pravitel'stvo velelo arestovat' po vozvrashchenii iz-za granitsy," *Kolokol*, l. 141, August 15, 1862; 16:229, 426–27.
    1. Aside from Dostoevsky, the other well-known names on this list include the writers Pisemsky (Alexey, not Alexander) and Zagoskin (Mikhail, not Pavel), the pianist Rubinshtein, the art and music critic Stasov, professor of medicine Botkin, and the liberal journalist Korsh.
    2. A line from Pushkin's poem "The Robber Brothers."

→ **49** ←

The Bell, No. 146, October 1, 1862. This is one of several articles by Herzen devoted to the tsarist regime's commemoration of the founding of Rus a thousand years earlier. While "Jubilee," from the February 1 issue (Doc. 43), focused on the Novgorod bell and the historical figures depicted on it, eight months later Herzen reported on the September ceremony itself. Alexander II expended considerable energy on the unveiling of the Millennium statue in Novgorod, which was intended to be a moment of national joy and well-being (Wortman, *Scenarios of Power*, 2:48–51, 86). Helping to set the tone, the historian Kostomarov arrived from the capital to give a public lecture to a packed house on the significance of Novgorod the Great in Russian history (Smirnov, *Gertsen v Nogorode*, 42). After the threat of non-participation in the dedication ceremony (local nobles were angry about the terms of the emancipation) had passed, the event came off as planned, with warm words from the tsar about how, after 1861, the various estates in Russia were even more closely bound together. Alexander II expressed a wish to the nobility that their descendants would continue to work with his descendants for the sake of the nation.

To emphasize the Russia-Romanov bond, the original suggestion by Minister of the Interior Lansky for a statue of the Varangian ruler Rurik was replaced by a sculptural ensemble on a much broader scale, covering the whole thousand years of Russian history; the list of heroic figures to be included was the result of many hours of heated discussion in St. Petersburg. The ceremony was held on the anniversary of the Kulikovo battle, which coincided with the heir Nikolay Alexandrovich's birthday; flexibility was possible since the chronicles mentioned only the year 862. Newly written prayers were read and the dinner included Alexander's toasts to Russia; the nobility answered with toasts at their ball (Wortman, *Scenarios of Power*, 2:86–87).

However much planning went into the Millennium celebration, it was criticized across the political spectrum. The poet Tyutchev found it lacking in a "religious feeling of the past" and thus untrue to Russia's history, and Fyodor Buslaev saw the bell-shaped monument as honoring only the Russian state. Ivan Aksakov labeled it an official occasion to which the Russian people were not invited. In any case, said Aksakov, the people experience their history differently, and "do not share the Western jubilee sentimentality," implying that this was a practice borrowed from Europe and, like many such borrowings, one that soon reached a hypertrophied state in Russia (Wortman, *Scenarios of Power*, 2:84, 87).

Herzen railed against the emptiness and bad taste of the entire jubilee enterprise. In the course of those September days, the government announced the latest recruiting goals, a cause of great misery in the countryside, and the tsar made a stern speech to representatives of the peasants about their unrealistic hopes (Tatishchev, *Imperator Aleksandr II*, 1:404–5). To add to the absurdity, Minister of the Interior Valuev made sure that news of his own sixtieth birthday got into the papers, leading Herzen to confess that the stupidity of all this left him almost speechless.

THE CELEBRATION OF THE MILLENNIUM
[1862]

The absurdity of the celebration in Novgorod has exceeded all expectations of even the fiercest admirers of the earthly tsar. What vulgarity and shallowness, what obstinacy and formalism, what awkwardness and lack of ability in all things, from the announcement of the recruitment misfortune—on the very day when good news had been expected—to the warning to Novgorod peasants not to expect a more genuine emancipation in the future!..[1] No, gentlemen of the Winter Palace, you have received no modern anointing, you don't know how to do anything right, no matter in what uniform you appear—as Sobakeviches or Manilovs[2]—you can't even organize a celebration. It's the prose, the pitiful prose of the Petrine era, which has retained its heavy Germanic style, but the thoughts have vanished! Perhaps

a very foolish-looking Rus will understand this lesson, and one can thank
Valuev[3] for that. He alone raised his voice in order—in his turn—to make
the millennium look ridiculous; he sent the following malicious gibe to all
the newspapers:

"The sixtieth birthday of the Minister of the Interior.
On the day of the dedication of the monument to the millennium
of Russia, September 8, the minister of the interior marked his sixtieth birthday." (St. P. September 10)

Since we cannot presume to come up with anything stupider and more
comical, this is a good place to stop.

Notes

Source: "Prazdnik tysiacheletiia," *Kolokol*, l. 146, October 1, 1862; 16:247–48, 440–41.

1. The recruitment targets for the first part of 1863 were published in a manifesto from
Alexander II on September 8. The tsar accepted the congratulations of Novgorod area
peasants on September 9; his scolding speech to the peasantry was published in Russia.

2. Sobakevich and Manilov are characters in Gogol's novel *Dead Souls*.

3. Petr A. Valuev was minister of the interior from 1861 to 1868.

✦ **50** ✦

The Bell, No. 157, March 1, 1863. Since 1861, Herzen and Ogaryov had been in communication with organizers of the secret circle that became the first Land and Liberty (Zemlia
i volia). While Ogaryov worked more closely with them, it was Herzen who suggested
the name, which was taken from his essay "What Do the People Need?" and this idea
was accepted in 1862. Herzen did not agree to closer ties with radical groups, but he was
still willing to help with producing and distributing propaganda and agitation materials.
By mid-1863, Herzen recognized the movement's weakness and the unlikelihood of its
program being realized, but he maintained his support until the group dissolved the following year. The essay below emphasizes the socialist essence of the peasant commune,
and the links between a free Poland and a free Russia.

LAND AND LIBERTY
[1863]

While the Petersburg eagle, having lowered one of its heads, tears apart the
bosom of the unfortunate Poland, clouds—its own, domestic ones—gather
around the other head... Let it wait and conduct a prayer service with its

Brandenburg hawk, which it summoned to the feast of the suppression of a great people.[1]

1863 is not 1831.

Europe may be the same, but Russia is not!

We know for certain that circles in the capitals and the provinces, united amongst themselves and together with officers' committees, have formed a single society.

This society has adopted the name *"LAND AND LIBERTY."*

And under this name they shall prevail!

Land and Liberty—are words that are very close to us, for with them we spoke out in the wintry Nicholaevan night, and with them we proclaimed the early dawn of the present day.[2] *Land and Liberty* were the basis of every one of our articles, *Land and Liberty* were on our foreign banner and on every page that issued forth from the London printing press.

Land and Liberty are two great testaments of two incomplete evolutions, two essential reinforcements of perennially dissolved hemispheres which join together, perhaps, the destiny of Russia. Russia has experienced the depths of what it means to have *land without liberty,* and it has seen enough of what it means to have *liberty without land...*

We greet you, brothers, on our common path! We will greedily follow your every step, with trepidation we will await news from you, with love we will pass it on, the unselfish love of people who rejoice at the evolution of their lifelong goals.

With your sacred banner it will be easy for you to serve the cause of the Russian people!

March 1, 1863

Notes

Source: "Zemlia i volia," *Kolokol,* l. 157, March 1, 1863; 17:56, 371–73.

1. The Brandenburg coat of arms, which also depicted a two-headed eagle, was adopted by the rulers of Prussia.

2. In Doc. 52, "1853–1863," Herzen reminds readers that he had kept these demands in mind from his earliest publications abroad up to the present.

✦ 51 ✦

The Bell, No. 158, March 8, 1863. Like other articles written by Herzen at the time of the Polish uprising, "A Lament" is a sharp expression of his love for Russia, a love which made him work for its liberation, but which was inseparable from the freedom of other nations under Russian control. He summons the Russian public to protest against the tsarist suppression of Poland, to feel shame for the behavior of their government, and his habitual irony is replaced by sarcasm and anger. In a letter to Ivan Turgenev, Herzen urgently requested the novelist's reaction, even if it was negative (Gertsen, *Sobranie sochinenii*, 27:bk. 1, 306–7). The historian Nikolay Karamzin's son, a state official with the Ministry of Justice, was so incensed by this article that he wrote to Katkov, deriding the man who compared the tsar to Stenka Razin and raised money for wounded Poles, and he suggested various humiliating punishments if Herzen were to fall into the government's hands (*Let* 3:489).

A LAMENT
[1863]

Brothers, brothers, what are these Germans doing to us? What are they doing to our soldiers, what are they doing to our fatherland?

Will you really cover this all with faint-hearted silence... after *the latest call-up for recruits?*

These are arsonists and highwaymen who do not recognize property rights, these are his imperial majesty's own communists! [. . .]

This is how Alexander Nikolaevich decided to become *the earthly tsar*—the tsar and Stenka Razin rolled into one![1]

An imperially approved Jacquerie![2] The beating—organized by the police and the military—of landowners and the confiscation of their homes! [. . .]

Well, if you are going to become Stenka Razins, then become Stenka Razins, but then it's no good to play at being a German general and the first nobleman of the land—a beard, a wide sash, an axe in hand, and *land and liberty* for the Russian people... that makes sense... But to represent at one go, for one's own advantage, Peter I, a serf, and a Moscow landowner—that's an old trick.[3]

You see that we were right when we said that *they* lack any moral compass; Nicholas, when he cynically placed *autocracy* on his banner, was just being naively candid.

A leftover from the history of the Merovingians, it is time either for them to perish, or for *Russia to perish*. Only the fall of this dynasty of German Tatars can wash away the soot from the fires, the innocent blood, and the guilt-ridden obedience.

For that reason, do not be silent. It will be terrible if you remain silent—one can be silent from fear, from indifference, or from obtuseness, without noticing that our Garrick[4] promises with one half of his face privileges and freedom, and with the other half he winks at his troops, a signal for them to burn, steal, and execute ...If no one pays for the Polish massacre, then, having at hand "the army in all its glory," steeped in blood and hardened by robbery and murder once again, the Romanovs will teach you a lesson!

There was a time when a high value was placed on a quiet tear in sympathy, a handshake, and a whispered word of concern during a tête-à-tête. This is no longer enough. [. . .]

A slave is silent when someone speaks. Speech belongs equally to me *and to him.* Speech belongs to everyone; speech is the basis of freedom. Speak out, speak because you must not remain silent. We await your orations! [. . .]

Notes

Source: "Plach," *Kolokol,* l. 158, March 8, 1863; 17:65–69, 377–78.

1. In 1670 the Cossack Stenka Razin mounted a rebellion in the south of Russia against the nobility and the imperial government; he was defeated and executed in 1671.

2. A general term for a bloody peasant revolt, which stems from an uprising in fourteenth-century France.

3. Alexander II used the phrase "the first nobleman" (*pervyi dvorianin*) in a September 4, 1859, speech to deputies from the provincial committees that were considering the serf question. In a November 28, 1862, speech to noble deputies from Moscow and adjoining regions, the tsar described the honor he felt at being "a Moscow landowner" (Gertsen, *Sobranie sochinenii,* 17:342, 345).

4. David Garrick (1717–1779), English, the best Shakespearean actor of his day.

→ **52** ←

This first appeared as a preface to the volume that marked the tenth anniversary of the Free Russian Press in London; an excerpt was later reprinted in the March 15, 1863, issue of *The Bell* (No. 159). Herzen traces the ideological journey made by the Free Press during its first decade, while emphasizing its "living tie" to progressive opinion in Russia.

— · —

1853–1863
[1863]

Ten years ago, at the end of February, an announcement was sent out about the opening of the *Free Russian Press* in London.[1] The first printed material came out in May, and since then the Russian printing press has never stopped working.[2]

That was a difficult time: it was as if Russia had died, and entire months went by without any word about it in the magazines. From time to time there appeared news of the death of some decrepit old official, or that one

or another grand duchess had successfully given birth... more rarely a suppressed groan reached as far as London, which made one's heart sink and
one's chest ache. There were almost no private letters, as fear caused all
contacts to cease...

In Europe it was different, but not better. It was the five-year period after
1848, and there was not even the slightest ray of light... it was shrouded on
all sides by a dark, cold night.

I became more and more distant from the milieu into which I had been
thrown.

An involuntary force pulled me homeward. There were moments when
I regretted having cut off any return trip, a *return* to that Siberia and to that
jail, in front of which marched for the twenty-eighth year a fierce sentry in
Hessian boots. [. . .] As a maelstrom and deep waters entice a man in the
dark of night toward unknown depths, I longed for Russia.

It seemed to me that so much strength could not be crushed so stupidly,
and get used up so absurdly... And, more and more vividly, I imagined the
people, sadly standing to the side and alien to everything that was happening, and the proud handful, full of valor and courage, the Decembrists, and
our enthusiastically youthful circle, and life in Moscow after exile. Familiar
images and views passed before me: meadows, forests, dark huts against
the white snow, faces, the sounds of songs, and ... and I believed in the near
future of Russia, I believed *when all others doubted,* and when there was no
justification for faith.

Maybe I believed because I was not in Russia at that time and did not experience for myself the insulting contact with the whip and with Nicholas,
and maybe it was something else, but I held firmly to my belief, feeling that
were I to let it out of my hands, I would have nothing left.

With the Russian printing press I returned home, and around it a Russian atmosphere was sure to form... could it possibly be that no one would
respond to that first *vivos voco?*[3]

However, the "living person" did not rush to respond.

The news that we would be printing in Russian from London frightened
people. The free word discomforted people and filled with horror not only
people from whom we were distant but also those who were close to us,
sounding so sharp to an ear that had grown used to whispering and silence.
Uncensored speech caused pain, and seemed like an act of carelessness,
almost a denunciation... Many advised us to stop and not publish anything;
one person close to us came to London for that purpose.[4] It was very difficult. I was not prepared for this.

"Well, if they do not respond, others will!" and I went my own way, without the slightest greeting or a single affectionate word, i.e., without an af-

fectionate word *from Russia;* in London there was a man who understood the idea of our printing press quite differently, one of the noblest representatives of the Polish exiles.

The prematurely aged and sickly Stanislav Worcell was roused by the news of a Russian printing house, and he helped me with the orders, counted the number of letters, and set up the press in the Polish printing house.[5] I remember how he picked up from my desk the first proof sheets, looked at them for a long time, and, deeply moved, said to me: "Oh my God! Oh my God! I've lived to see a free Russian printing press in London! How many terrible recollections from the recent past have been washed away from my soul by this scrap of paper, smeared with ash from the stove!"

As he faded away, the saintly old man saw the printing house's success and, before his death, blessed our work once more with his dying hand.

That first article that we were talking about was addressed to "the Russian nobility," and reminded them that it was time to free the serfs, and, moreover, with land, or there would be trouble.

The second article was about *Poland.*

The peasant issue and the Polish question were the very basis of Russian propaganda.

And since that time, dear Czarnecki, for ten years together with you we have printed without weariness or rest, and our press already has a considerable biography and a considerable pile of books.[6]

[. . .] Our beginning was slow and meager. For three years we were printing, not only without selling a single copy, but almost without the possibility of sending a single copy to Russia, except for the first leaflets, which were dispatched by Worcell and his friends to Warsaw. We still had everything we printed on our hands or in the basement storerooms of the pious Paternoster Row.[7]

We did not get depressed... and kept on printing and printing.

A bookseller on Berner Street once sent for ten copies of "Baptized Property" and I took that for success. I gave the young boy a shilling tip and with a certain bourgeois joy I found a special place for that *first* half sovereign earned by the Russian printing press.

Sales in the propaganda business are just as important as in any other. Even simple material labor is impossible to carry out with love knowing that it is done in vain. You can place the best actors in the world in an empty hall—they will perform very badly. The church authorities, whose rank requires them to know the subtleties of moral torture, sentence priests for theft, drunkenness, and other earthly weaknesses *to mill the wind.*[8]

But we did not mill the wind after all, my dear Czarnecki—our day finally came.

It began solemnly.

On the morning of March 4, I went as usual into my study at eight o'clock and opened *The Times*. I read, and read ten times more, and did not understand, did not dare to understand the grammatical meaning of the words placed at the head of the news received by telegraph: "The death of the emperor of Russia."

Beside myself, I rushed with *The Times* to the dining room, looking for the children and the servants, to announce this important news, and with tears of true joy in my eyes I handed them the paper... I felt years younger. It was impossible to remain at home. At that time Engelson[9] was living in Richmond, and I quickly dressed to go see him, but he had anticipated me and was already in the front hall. We heartily embraced each other and could not say anything except the words: "Finally, he is dead!"

As was his habit, Engelson pranced about, kissed everyone in the house, sang and danced. We had not had time to calm down when a carriage suddenly stopped at my front door and someone rang the bell in a frenzied manner; it was three Poles who, not waiting for the train, had galloped from London to Twickenham to congratulate me.

I ordered champagne to be served, and no one considered the fact that it was still only eleven in the morning, or even earlier. And then, for no reason at all, we went to London. On the streets, at the stock exchange, in the eating houses all talk was about the death of Nicholas, and I did not encounter a single person who did not breathe more easily knowing that this thorn had been removed from the flesh of humankind, and was not overjoyed that this oppressive tyrant in Hessian boots was a matter for the embalmers.

On Sunday, from the morning onwards, my house was full: French people, Polish refugees, Germans, Italians, and even English acquaintances came and went with radiant faces. The day was clear and warm and after dinner we went out into the garden.

Young boys were playing on the banks of the Thames; I called them to my gate and told them that we were celebrating the death of their enemy and ours. I tossed them a handful of silver coins to get beer and candy, and they cried out "Hurrah! Hurrah! Impernikel is dead! Impernikel is dead!" The guests also began to throw sixpences and three pence pieces; the boys brought ale, pies, and cakes, and a barrel organ, and began to play it and dance. After that, for as long as I lived in Twickenham, every time they saw me on the street, the boys would lift their caps and shout: "Impernikel is dead! Hurrah!"

The death of Nicholas increased our strength and our hopes tenfold. I immediately wrote a letter to the emperor Alexander—which was later printed—and I decided to publish *The Polestar*. [. . .]

The beginning of Alexander II's reign was a joyous period. All of Russia breathed more easily, raised up its head, and, were they able to, would have shouted wholeheartedly along with the Twickenham boys: "Impernikel is dead! Hurray!"

Under the influence of the spring thaw, people even took a more affectionate view of our printing press in London. Finally, we were noticed. There was demand for dozens of copies of *The Polestar* and in Russia it was being sold for the fabulous price of 15 to 20 silver rubles. The banner of *The Polestar,* the demands that it made, coincided with the desire of the entire Russian people, and that is why it began to gain sympathy. And, when I addressed the newly enthroned sovereign, I repeated to him: "Grant freedom to the Russian word, our minds are constricted by the fetters of censorship; grant *freedom* and *land* to the peasants and wipe away from us the shameful stain of serfdom; grant us an open court system and do away with the official secrecy about our fate!" When I added to this simple demand: "Hurry up so that you can save the people from bloodshed!" I felt and I knew that this was not at all my personal opinion, but an idea that was in the Russian air, exciting every mind and every heart—the mind and heart of the tsar and of the serf, of the young officer just out of military school and the student, no matter what university he attended. No matter how they understood the question and what side they took, they all saw that the Petrine autocracy had lived out its days, that it had reached a limit, after which the government had to either be regenerated or the people would perish. If there were exceptions, then they were only in the mercenary circles of rich scoundrels or on the sleepy summits of members of the gentry who had lost their minds.

Half of our program was carried out by the tsar himself. But—and this was the Russian in him—he stopped at *the very introduction* and came up with *a transition period,* the brakes of gradualness, and thought that everything had been accomplished.

With the same candor with which the Russian printing press in London addressed the sovereign in 1855, a few years later it addressed the people and said to its readers: "You see, the government *has acknowledged* the fairness of your demands, but it cannot *carry out* what it has acknowledged, it cannot break out of the rut of the barracks-like order and the bureaucratic uniforms. It has reached the end of its understanding and is moving backward. [. . .] It is losing its head, behaving cruelly, making mistakes, and is clearly afraid... Fear, combined with power, provokes a bitter rebuff—a rebuff without respect and without deliberation. From there it is one step to a rebellion. There is no point in waiting any longer for the government's *own recognition* of the rightness of what is being asked. [. . .]"

And in saying this we feel that this is not a personal opinion—the idea of an *Assembly of the Land* is in the Russian air. The Milyutins and Valuevs[10] exchange it for small provincial dumas; the assemblies of the nobility *keep silent* about it; but, even nameless, the Assembly of the Land, like Marie Antoinette in the matter of the necklace, is greatly implied.[11] The merchantry and the people speak about it, and the military *insist that it be summoned.*

No, the living tie between Russia and its small *vedeta*[12] in London has not been broken... and the very abuse of the greyhounds and the second-rate hunting dog journalists who work for the Third Department, which the dwarfs of enlightenment and roués of internal affairs use to hunt us down, convinces us even more that our printing press is not alienated from Russia.[13]

Let us return to it.

The demand for *The Polestar* hardly extended to the books we printed in the past. Only *Prison and Exile* somehow sold out, as well as some small brochures like "Baptized Property" and "Humor."

In May 1856 the second issue of *The Polestar* appeared and it sold out, taking with it all the rest. The entire mass of books moved out. At the beginning of 1857 there were no more books in the printing house and Trübner undertook at his own expense *second printings* of everything we had issued.[14]

There was so much work that our little press could not satisfy the demand, and in 1858 one of our fellow exiles, *Zeno Swentoslowski,* opened a Russian section in his own printing house and began printing Trübner's editions.

By the second half of 1857 the printing house's expenses began to be covered, and toward the end of 1858 there was a small profit, and about the same time two or three Russian presses opened in Germany.

Our press felt like a grandfather.

The time of trial and testing for our press was over, and the time of weak, fruitless efforts, and apathy on the Russian side had passed.

At the beginning of 1857 Ogaryov suggested publishing *The Bell.*

Its first issue appeared on July 1, 1857.

With the publication of *The Bell* began the period of growth of our printing press.

We will not speak about it here. The articles that came out in Czarnecki's *Anthology* relate to the first years of Russian publishing in London. The leaflets gathered there had been forgotten and scattered, becoming almost bibliographic rarities, and their republication seems very useful to us.

For us, these leaflets have the special character of an accounting, verification, and cleansing of the past. Much in them is immature, there is the imprint of another age, and the stern shadow of Nicholas casts a shadow on every page, obscuring every bright thought, irritating to the point of hatred every feeling, showing the dark lining of every hope. The major part of what has now become an incontestable event, was then only a premonition... As a result of these premonitions being fulfilled, we more and more have the right to conclude that we were not mistaken about the other ones.

> *Russia will have freedom,*
> *The peasants will have land.*
> *And Poland will have independence!*

Notes

Source: "1853–1863," *Desiatiletie Vol'noi Russkoi Tipografii v Londone*, 1863; 17:74–81, 380–84.

1. The announcement, written by Herzen on February 21, 1853, was lithographed by members of the Polish democratic movement and smuggled into Russia (see Doc. 2).

2. The first pamphlet after the announcement of the press was "St. George's Day! St. George's Day!" (Doc. 3).

3. "I summon the living," the phrase from Schiller that Herzen used as his motto for *The Bell* from the beginning.

4. At the request of mutual friends, the actor Mikhail Shchepkin visited Herzen during a trip to Europe in September 1853 (see Doc. 60).

5. Count Stanislav Worcell (1799–1857) took part in the Polish uprising of 1830–31 and was a leader of the Polish exiles.

6. Ludvik Czarnecki (1828–1872) was a Polish émigré who ran the Free Russian Press in London.

7. Sales of Free Russian Press publications were handled by the publisher and bookseller Trübner and Company, whose firm was located on Paternoster Row; Herzen plays on the street name's meaning of "Our Father."

8. The Russian phrase is *toloch' vodu*, "to beat water" in a mortar.

9. Vladimir A. Engelson (1821–1857) was a Russian journalist and revolutionary activist living abroad.

10. In 1863, Dmitry A. Milyutin was war minister and Nikolay A. Milyutin was the former minister of the interior; Petr A. Valuev was the latter's successor in the ministry and head of the special committee on the reform of local government.

11. In 1785, the French queen ordered a pearl necklace and then refused to pay for it, causing a scandal.

12. Sentry post (in Italian).

13. Herzen refers to the fact that Minister of the Enlightenment Golovin was very short.

14. Herzen: "N. Trübner in general was of great benefit to Russian propaganda, and his name ought not to be forgotten in the *Almanac of the Russian Printing House*. Aside from second editions of *The Polestar* and all our books, he undertook an entire series of editions in Russian: the poems of Ogaryov, the notes of Catherine II, the notes of Princess Dashkova, Lopukhina, Pr. Shcherbatov and Radishchev et al."

⇀ 53 ⇌

The Bell, No. 160, April 1, 1863. The *Allgemeine Zeitung* (No. 107) reported that Herzen had gone further than ever before by allying himself with a group whose goal was to replace Russia's thousand-year-old empire. However, in his correspondence with Oga-ryov, Herzen was already talking about loosening his ties to members of "Land and Liberty," who did not appear to be ready for the work they had undertaken. He declared the role of *The Bell* to be propaganda without compromise, "a deep, truthful *sermon*" (*Let* 3:486). Herzen intimated that he, too, would not reach the promised land of a liberated Russia.

The Proclamation "Land and Liberty"
[1863]

At last a word of active sympathy toward the Polish affair was proclaimed in Russia—it was proclaimed by means of *underground literature,* as one would expect in a country where journalists are held in detention for their opinions for more than half a year, and then are sent away for hard labor[1]— and it was proclaimed by "Land and Liberty." The proclamation, distributed on the 19th of February (March 3) in Moscow and Petersburg (*whose text we have not yet received*), concerned Poland. The authors extend the hand of young Russia to the Poles, and appeal to soldiers and officers to refrain from criminal acts.

This voice was essential, and with it begins the rehabilitation of Russia, and for that reason one is deeply grateful to those who made it possible.

The lackeys of the word, literary *oprichniki* and police *messengers,* both homegrown and those living abroad,[2] call both them and us betrayers of Russia, and say that we stand in the ranks of its worst enemies, etc.[3]

We will not answer them. They have gone beyond a moral boundary, beyond which there is neither insult nor offense. They enjoy special privi-leges, like people who have declared themselves bankrupt, like legal pros-titutes, and like their passive colleagues, who while not writing openly in favor of the government, do pay close attention to it for their own benefit.

It's no use to talk to them.

But perhaps among our friends there are people who are not completely free from the traditional prejudices, who do not clearly separate in their consciousness *one's native land and the state,* who mix up a love for their own people—and a willingness to suffer for them and contribute their labor and their lives—with a willingness to mindlessly follow every government. To them we wish to say a few words.

We are for Poland because we are for Russia. We are on the side of the Poles because we are Russians. We want independence for Poland because we want freedom for Russia. We are with the Poles, because we are chained by a single set of fetters. We are with them because we are firmly convinced that the absurdity of an empire that stretches from Sweden to the Pacific and from the White Sea to China cannot bring any blessings to the peoples who are kept on a leash by Petersburg. The vast monarchies of the Chingizes and Tamerlanes belong to the most elementary and wildest periods of development, to those times when the entire glory of a state consists of force and a great expanse. They are only possible when there is hopeless slavery below and unlimited tyranny above. Whether our imperial formation was necessary or not has nothing to do with us at this moment—it is a fact. But it has lived out its time and has one foot in the grave—that is also a fact. We are trying with all our heart to help it with the other leg.

Yes, we are against the empire because we are for the people!

Notes

Source: "Proklamatsiia 'Zemlia i voli,'" *Kolokol*, l. 160, April 1, 1863; 17:90–91, 388.

1. M. L. Mikhailov was arrested in 1861 as a cowriter (with N. V. Shchelgunov) of the proclamation "To the Young Generation," and was sentenced to six years, a sentence which was publicly announced on the 35th anniversary of the Decembrist uprising, and which he did not live to complete.

2. The Russian word *oprichniki*, which has come into usage in English, refers to special units set up by Ivan the Terrible after the worst of his crises; in the guise of rooting out treason, they terrorized their fellow Russians from 1565 to 1572. For Russian officials "abroad" Herzen uses the Latin phrase *in partibus*, which refers to Catholic bishops sent to predominantly non-Catholic lands.

3. Katkov lashed out against Russian supporters of Poland in the first issue of *The Russian Herald* (*Russkii vestnik*) for 1863, and similarly critical articles were placed by Russian authorities in *Le Nord*.

⇢ 54 ⇠

The Bell, No. 160, April 1, 1863 (Part I); No. 161, April 15, 1863 (Part II); No. 163, May 1, 1863 (Part III). Herzen wrote this article soon after receiving news of the distribution in Moscow and Petersburg of a proclamation called "Polish Blood Is Flowing, Polish Blood Is Flowing...." He saw the call for widespread sympathy with the Polish cause as historically significant, a turning point in the life of Russian society. While Herzen misjudged the long-term impact of this proclamation on Russian politics and society, his continued public defense of Poland—despite his private feeling that the Poles had acted in haste—diminished respect for Herzen's political journalism in Russia, with even liberals seeing his pro-Polish stance as unpatriotic. Along with its topical interest, this essay continues Herzen's exploration of skepticism and irony as appropriate responses to the political realities of Russia. His ironic tone is in full force in a brief note in issue No. 160 about a report that two peasants had snatched a beaver hat off the head of a pedestrian on Petersburg's Nevsky Prospect. The crime was reported to the tsar, who ordered that they be immediately conscripted and sent to serve far from the capitals. Herzen asks whether or not there are laws covering theft, which would make it unnecessary to inform the sovereign every time such an outrage occurred. One did not have to look hard to find absurdities in "reform-era" Russia.

1831–1863
[1863]

I

"Yet who would have thought the old man to have had so much blood in him..." said Macbeth.

"What, will this blood n'er be washed away! Water!.. give me water!.." said his wife.[1]

There are, in fact, old men who not only have a lot of blood in them, but whose blood is young... and so indelible that there is no possibility of washing it away.

Russia is experiencing all this... and God forbid there would be *a murdered man in the woods,* whose ghost would begin to appear at every feast.[2]

The Polish uprising has drawn a profound line. In future textbooks it will mark the end of one chapter of Russian history and the beginning of another. This is a turning point—it is possible to go on as before, but the break will be felt, and the line cannot be erased. The very same life on the other side of the line will *not be the same.* Russia will remember that the old man had a lot of blood in him, that this blood kept pouring down its arms... and that it did nothing to wipe it away.

"But was there really any less blood in Poland in 1831?"

"No, but Russia had less of a conscience, i.e., consciousness." History does not punish a half-conscious crime, a transgression done while half-asleep, it hands down an English verdict of "temporary insanity." The question is whether the Russia of 1863 has as much right to that verdict as the Russia of 1831?

We absolutely reject that.

The Polish uprising that followed five years after December 14th caught Russia off guard, dispirited and deep in thought. For almost the first time, Russians were then actually thinking about themselves. Nations come to a serious understanding rather late, the fruit of major ordeals, upheavals, and failures; the most developed nations can be in error for entire centuries under the influence of dreams and fantasies. For close to a century France believed itself to be liberal and even republican. Russia's thoughtful mood was completely appropriate. Boasting state significance and influence in European affairs, Petrine Russia imagined that it would be as easy to borrow political freedom from its neighbors as it was to borrow a military-police empire. Despotism increased tenfold, causing those who were not utterly crushed to fall into thought, and they began to doubt their path; their striving was sincere, but it was satisfied with ready solutions not appropriate to the phenomena of Russian life. The oppressive feeling of the lack of roots weighed as much upon what was being thought and what had been awakened as did the government's oppression. The way out of this was unclear and the weakness was obvious.

The Polish question was vaguely understood at that time. The leading people—people who were marching off to hard labor for their intention of curbing imperial despotism—were mistaken about it and came to a halt, without noticing it, at the narrowly official patriotic point of view of Karamzin. [. . .][3]

There was nothing to be said about the people; they were a sleeping lake, of whose currents flowing under the snow no one knew, and on whose frozen surface stood country estates, offices, and every sort of sentry box and barracks.

By that time Nicholas had somewhat recovered from the 14th of December and had calmed down. [. . .] Suddenly the news of the Paris revolution of 1830 came crashing down on him and he became flustered. Like a guards officer in a time of complete peace, he announced that soon it would be necessary to mount up, and ordered the army put on a wartime footing. He was rude to Louis Philippe without any call.[4] Perhaps only in 1848 did he surpass the year 1830 in his constraints on every declared thought and every word not in agreement with the foundations of an all-consuming absolutism. It was then that for the first time he hoisted his absurd banner of "autocracy, orthodoxy, nationality...";[5] since then, in contrast to what was going on in Europe, there began to form in his head that deification of the tsarist title in his person. [. . .]

But if no one believed in the divinity of imperial state power, everyone believed in its strength, those who loved it and those who hated it, Russians

and foreigners, the Duke of Wellington and Marshal Sebastiani, Metternich and Casimir Périer,[6] the orators who attacked Russia, and Pushkin,
who responded to them in verse.[7]

Thus, on the one side, a vague aspiration to throw off the despotic guardian who was paralyzed by the consciousness of alienation from the people.
On the other side, there was the repressive specter of the imperial state's
enormous power, against which it was possible to lay mines underground,
but impossible to even think of fighting face to face.

What sort of protest on behalf of Poland was possible in 1831? Hidden
sympathy—that existed, there were verses that burst forth with tears, there
was the enthusiastic reception of exiles, and the university youth (at least
in Moscow) were for Poland. The journals and literature had no political
significance under the censorship of that time. Society, which had fallen
into a serious decline, remained indifferent, although there was a minority
who had been raised under Western influence and hated Nicholas for the
cavalier nature of his despotism. [. . .]

After that followed years of the most prosaic epoch of the reign of Nicholas. The Poland that survived went abroad, telling other nations of savage
suppression [. . .] hatred toward Russia became the common sentiment of
women, children, aristocrats, and plebeians. The London rabble grumbled
aloud during the visit of Nicholas to England, and Lord Dudley Stuart sent
him a note in support of the Poles.[8] We had a drop of blood on us, and were
marked by our victory over the Poles.

At home, the dreary despotism continued. [. . .]

But thoughts that had arisen within reached maturity, and the word that
had been forcibly turned back ate away at the chest, undermined the prison
walls, and, while the stockade's façade remained the same, within it a great
deal had changed.

At first the pain, the loss of our dearest hopes, and the insults were too
fresh, and the humiliations irritated us too much. Many energetic, noble
natures were broken, and began to wither away physically or morally.
Pecherin sought salvation in Catholicism, and Polezhaev in merrymaking
and orgies.[9]

The question of a way out of this hell, out of this purgatory, became
such a tormenting question for a man of reason that, finding no solution,
some—as we just said—took flight or fell into a decline while others denied
the possibility of a way out, like Chaadaev.[10] *The poison* of profound thought
went deeper and deeper, as skepticism and irony were the literary signs of
an internally devouring flame. The Byronism of Pushkin and Lermontov
was not simply imitation; it was as timely and *national* for Petrine Russia as
Gogol's amazing laughter.

The level at which this work was going on was not accessible to the government—a whip doesn't cut that deeply. Nicholas was a completely uneducated and badly surrounded man; his secret police, compiled from card-sharps, broken-down officers, and petty thieves who had been caught stealing government money, floated on the surface. They were afraid of an impertinent word, a velvet beret à la Karl Sand, and cigars smoked outside; they sought classic conspirators with daggers, cloaks, and oaths, who make frightening sounds in the presence of highly strung women. They could not understand a huge, open conspiracy that had penetrated the soul without an oath and that walked the streets without a Calabrian hat; their fingers were too coarse.[11]

Everyone took part in this conspiracy, not only without having made any deals, but without even suspecting anything—that is how buds ripen, independently of each other and under the influence of the very same atmosphere, making up the general character of spring. Who was not its agent? The student who knew Ryleev's and Polezhaev's verse by heart, going off to be a temporary tutor in a manor house, a physician setting off to serve in a remote part of the country,[12] a seminary student coming back to his native village for the vacation, a teacher who read literature to military school students, and all universities, lycées, spiritual and military academies, theaters, corps, Westernizers and Slavophiles—Chaadaev and Polevoy, Belinsky and Gogol, Granovsky and Khomyakov.

Only native—not Petrine—Russia stood outside this movement. It did not know the Rus in which this movement was taking place, and it was not known there. Until this intellectual effort, until this inner protest, until these pangs of remorse, they had no business with it, and that is only natural. The people had not broken with their way of life in order to rise above it, it was not in their midst that there could or should arise doubts about their path; they *continued* their spontaneous way of life under the heavy yoke of their serf status, bureaucratic theft, and poverty. [. . .]

After the conquest of Poland, Russia settled in for five years of Nicholaevan ways in gloomy silence. Society declined more and more, literature remained silent or made distant allusions; only within university walls a living word was sometimes heard and an ardent heart was beating... yes, from time to time the mighty song of Pushkin, contradicting everything that was happening, seemed to prophesy that such a young and broad chest could shoulder a great deal.

People saved themselves individually—some with scholarship, some with art, some with imaginary activity. People individually turned away from everything that surrounded them and observed in the unattainable distance the movement of heavenly bodies in the west, but their inner pain and bewilderment could not quiet down, and they had to suffer through it until they reached the truth and found in themselves a means of expression. Chaadaev's letter represents the first tangible point at which two divergent interpretations branched off.

"Look around you. It's as if everything is on the move, as if we are all wanderers. No one has a fixed sphere of existence, there are no good customs, not only no rules but not even any family focus; there is nothing that would win over or awaken your sympathy or your aspirations; there is nothing constant or indispensable; everything passes and flows by without leaving a trace. It is as if we are billeted at home, like strangers in our families, like migrants in cities."

Genuine social development has not yet begun for the people if the conditions of its life have not been made right; our moral world is in chaotic ferment, in the type of cataclysms that preceded the actual formation of the planet."

Mea culpa, mea maxima culpa!

This negative consciousness could go no further—this *nihilism* is almost as tragic as the newer kind. What could be done after such an acknowledgment? Sigh, fold one's arms, and meekly bear the cross of one's native land. [. . .]

Chaadaev's gloomy confession met with a strong rebuff, the rebuff of a man who had been buried alive, the rebuff *instinctive* faith makes to one-sided doubt. The once-again departing Russian thought, like tsar Ivan Vasilevich, afflicted by illness and weak, listened behind the doors as Chaadaev read a prayer for the dying, and, quitting its deathbed, rushed to declare its right to live.

In the name of what? In the name of the people's way of life and *pre-Petrine Russia*, i.e., proceeding from the same aversion that their opponent had for *the empire.* "This is a temporary growth," they said, "foreign rags which have adhered to the body, but only to the skin, so they can be ripped off."

[. . .] The boundaries of the tournament were drawn.

Up until 1848 the pulse of a living heart was felt only in this *literary* battle.

II

We are not the ones who reduced this to a bookish battle—that's the way it really was. The entire intellectual life of Russia in the thirties and forties was reduced to literature and teaching. This quarrel occupied no more than

two or three hundred people, of whom half were very young. But this arith-
metic weakness—when the rest were not occupied with anything—meant
nothing. A minority, with excited thoughts, faith, and doubt, split off from
the drowsy and indifferent masses without having any precise direction, becoming by necessity a secular priesthood, i.e., beginning with propaganda
and preaching, they often finish with power and lead their flock along the
same path.

The circle of intellectual activity at that time was outside the government,
which was completely backward, and outside the people, who were silent
in their estrangement; it was located in the book and the lecture hall, in
theoretical argument and the scholar's study. And, actually, it was only in
literature and the universities that the government still had to keep things
in check; only there did life try to emerge from behind the cramped shores
of censorship and surveillance, and only there could resilience still be felt.
Literature and educational institutions were the only civically valiant, honest spheres of activity in the unyielding Russia of that time.

The Senate and the Synod, the civilian departments and the military authorities, the assemblies of the nobility and the beau monde feared not only
the opposition, but any originality; they feared that a suspicion of *having
opinions* might fall upon them. Respectable people watched with inner horror the courage of N. S. Mordvinov, who dared to not only have but to voice
opinions. Nicholas was barely able to contain his rage against the impertinent old man.[13]

Only literature, only the lecture halls, protested constantly, protested as
much as they could, with silence and absences when a word was not possible; *with forbidden* verses that passed from person to person, and hints that
slipped through the censor's fingers. The current corruption of literature
and educational institutions dates from the present reign. Paid-off journalists and police-professors, preaching a philosophy of slavery and writing
denunciations of entire conferences, are entirely new phenomena.[14] During
the entire Nicholaevan era, there was no lecture hall that would have listened with sympathy to the doctrine of blind obedience; conservative youth
and fans of the government did not exist at all then. For the development
of this kind of moral *rickets,* which is spreading far and wide, we are very
much obliged to the teaching and journalism of recent years.

Thus, we are not the ones who assigned historical importance to the
academic-literary quarrel of the thirties in the intellectual development of
Russia—that is the way it actually was. We will not enlarge on the quarrel
itself, so much has been written about it. We will only remind the reader
that one side sought to continue the Petrine coup in a *revolutionary* sense,

acquiring for Russia everything that had been worked out by other nations since 1789, bringing to our soil English institutions, French ideas, and German metaphysics. In rating Western forms of civic life more highly than the hatchet job of Peter and his successors, they were entirely correct, but in accepting them as the *sole life-saving* human forms, appropriate to every way of life, they fell into the eternal error of the French revolutionaries. Their opponents objected that the forms developed for Western life may have had a universal development, but, along with them, one must also preserve particular national elements. [. . .]

Neither one nor the other came to a clear understanding, but along the way many questions were raised; the February revolution arrived when this argument was in full swing. [. . .]

The persecution against the printed word and academia that began after the revolution of 1848 exceeded all limits of what was stupid and vile; it was nasty, ridiculous, and it reduced literature to a gloomy silence, *but it did not get it to speak in the tone of Nicholaevan conservatism.* The same thing happened in academia; stifled outwardly, it remained true within to its sacred mission of advocacy and humanization. And if professors in the capitals were at times constrained by the tiresome surveillance and denunciations, teaching went on as it had in provincial universities, gymnasia, seminaries, military schools, etc. This decentralization of education is extremely important [. . .] it infiltrated more deeply and disappeared at the very limits of literacy. The government's efforts came to nothing.

Pedagogy withstood what was in its own way a chef d'oeuvre—Rostovtsev's instructions to the teachers of military-training establishments.[15]

Who was able to do this?

This was done by a new formation of people, who had risen below and who introduced by degrees their new elements into the intellectual life of Russia. This group assumed more and more rights of citizenship during this time, as Nicholas knocked off the elite and with coarse strokes mutilated the nervously developed hothouse organizations.

The renegades of all social groups, these *new people*, these moral *razno-chintsy*, made up not a social class, *but a milieu*, in which in the foreground were teachers and literary men—working literary men, and not dilettantes—students who had graduated and those who had not finished their course of study, lower-level officials from the universities and from the seminaries, the lower gentry, the children of officers, officers who had graduated from military schools, et al. New people, humble people—they were not as noticeable but just as morally liberated as those who came before them, just as constrained in a material way. Poverty lends its own kind of circumspect strength and structure.

The Rus of gentry manor houses, in which, up till then, intellectual and literary development had been primarily concentrated, was, apart from persecution, in a false position. It could not advance a single idea without crossing over the barrier that protected its class privileges. Connected by its education to the forms of European life, it was connected by serfdom to the Petersburg regime; it had to renounce its exclusive rights or to unwittingly introduce a contradiction into every issue. For it, as a social group, there was only one future—to limit the supreme power of the tsar with an oligarchic Duma, but they did not have the material strength to do this. They lacked the moral strength to leave their class. This type of Anglophile and liberal gentry, stopped on their headlong path to parliamentary freedom by the emancipation of the serfs with land, will remain on the tombstone of Russia's noble gentry like gargoyles, which medieval architects used to decorate the tops of church pillars.

Aristocratic Russia retreated to a supporting role, and its voice began to grow weak; maybe, like Nicholas, it was embarrassed by the events of 1848. In order to remain popular in literature, it had to abandon urban life, take up a hunting rifle and slaughter, on the ground and on the wing, the wild-fowl of serfdom.[16]

Another force came to relieve them, another group took the place of the exhausted leaders and soldiers.

The sound of Chaadaev's funeral oration still sounded in people's ears; while stirring much in one's breast, it gave nothing but consolation *in the other world*, some kind of distant future [. . .] but already in hackneyed journalism, boring in Moscow and dissipated in Petersburg, features were being engraved of a real representative of young Russia, a genuine revolutionary in our literature.

Belinsky was an unusually free person, and nothing inhibited him: neither the prejudices of scholasticism nor the prejudices of his surroundings. He appeared, full of questions and in search of solutions, not playing around with conclusions and not fearing them. He openly made mistakes and sincerely looked for another solution; he had one truth in his sights and nothing except for that. Belinsky came on the stage without a crest, without a banner, without a diploma; he belonged to no church and no social class, he was bound by nothing and had sworn no one an oath. Nothing would be spared by him, but for that reason he could sympathize with everyone... The first moment when, bitten by the serpent of German philosophy, he was attracted by *the rationality of all that existed,* he fearlessly wrote his Borodino essay.[17] What frightening purity must you possess, what an original kind of independence and limitless freedom, to write something on the order of a justification for Nicholas at the beginning *of the forties*! [. . .]

In Belinsky we encountered that impressive aloofness from the latest ideas and authorities, which is the distinguishing feature and strength of Russian genius, something that Chaadaev vaguely foresaw, and about which we have said a great deal.

Maybe this aloofness, this inner freedom in the presence of outward slavery, deprived our life of many warm moments, many attachments, maybe it introduced an aching that manifested itself in the predominance of irony. But it gave us a terrible feeling of independence. Like children who knew neither father nor mother, we were poorer, but more free; our mother and our father were ideals, and therefore did not hinder us, and we infused them with our own purified image and likeness.

Belinsky's ideal, and our ideal, our church and parental home, in which our first thoughts and sympathies were nurtured, was *the Western world* with its scholarship and its revolution, with its respect for the individual, with its political freedom, with its artistic treasures and its unshakeable hope.

The ideal for Khomyakov[18] and his friends lay in the past of the Russian people, their everyday existence, transformed into an unbelievable purity. But its apotheosis, however exaggerated, was, in its principal features, true. *A saint's life* is required for every canonization, and in the ideal of the Slavs, who had preserved the everyday features of our people, there was a great prophecy that they saw as a memory.

Which of these ideals had to be overcome? Or on what point could they be reconciled and go forth arm in arm?

The revolution of 1848 and its consequences brought with it elements of a resolution of this question.

At the very least, since that time the argument about which we have been speaking has changed.

III

We have said a great deal about the revolution of 1848. Like the entire world, we were attracted to it. It even attracted its opponents; they also did not remain in place and move even further into their positions.

The attraction did not last long, but people had trouble going back to their old ways. [. . .]

And at the same time that revolution, beaten on all counts, gave up everything that had been achieved since 1789, the frightened autocracy in Russia, having crushed Hungary without need or sense, threw itself into the persecution of thought, scholarship, and every kind of civic endeavor.

It seemed that everything had abandoned the Russian development that had begun, it seemed that it would disappear like an unsuccessful experiment, and would plunge into a new millennium of serfdom, barbarity, and byzantinism.

The light from Europe that had entered through the cracks of our prison walls began to fade, and it was difficult to make anything out. In the West only dark clouds drifted by, jostling each other. [. . .] Russia grew silent. Having put up with it for a long time and seeing no way out, Granovsky, weary, worn out, blessed the fate of the deceased Belinsky and envied him his death!..[19] Then he who passionately loved Russia asked if some sort of position could be found for him in Belgium, because while he had the strength to die for Russia, he did not have the strength to live there any longer.

But life went on.

Russian life is tenacious—all the adversity, all the blows missed their mark. Why? Isn't it because they did not apply the blows in the places on which *the life and growth of this strange organism depended?*

At the very height of despotism and persecution in Russia and reaction in Europe, the dominant turn of mind in Moscow and Petersburg began to worry about other issues. Khomyakov, K. Aksakov, and their circle gave particular attention to the Russian *rural commune and the communal ownership of land.* The Petrashevsky circle in Petersburg made the study of *social-economic theory* their program of study.

In this way the Slavophiles abandoned archeology.

With the Petrashevsky circle, a retrospective movement began, which of necessity had gained control of minds after the 14th of December. A practical move, which had become bookish, rushed once more out of the book and into practical activity. The Petrashevsky circle formed a society, and the government took it to be a conspiracy. There was no conspiracy, but Liprandi, like a truffle hunter, sniffed it out.[20]

The Petrashevtsy were led out onto the square, the maneuvers for execution were performed, and they were led off in shackles to "houses of the dead," and hard labor; but their ideas fermented, and were expressed in private arguments and discussions.[21]

One thing horrified everyone—the force majeure of imperial power. All human aspirations struck uselessly against an impregnable, granite barrier...

Faith in the impregnable power of Nicholas himself saved Russia—it brought the fleet of Sir Charles Napier to the Gulf of Bothnia.

Nicholas went to take a look at it and returned with aged eyes and a sunken face.[22]

He understood the calamity... the magic disappeared.

With every salvo in the Crimea the echo shook Petersburg; the walls of the Winter Palace cracked. Everyone began to suspect that only the outside layer was granite, and that inside was filler. Given the historically bureaucratic construction of the Russian imperial state, as with all government construction, some quartermasters had indulged in theft.

Nicholas understood that it was impossible to cover this up; wandering sleeplessly like a specter through the halls of his palace and making the sentries kneel and pray for victory, he began to think about *betrayal, the betrayal* of all that he held sacred, for which he had trampled his own human heart and ruined two or three young generations.

He wanted to issue a call to the Slavs, to restore the hated Poland and to get Hungary, which he had recently crushed, back on its feet, if only to once again have the Winter Palace unshakeable and threatening, to have the granite covering once again taken for a solid cliff, to not see any more the oscillating masts of Sir Charles Napier, and to not hear the echo of the Sevastopol thunder... Let the peasants arm themselves; let military units choose their own officers!

This was the end of the dark Petersburg reign. [. . .]

The dismally suppressed dissatisfaction raised its head, and the whispering was replaced by a murmur: "What is this? After the blood, after the money, after being deprived of all human rights, they cannot defend the land from an enemy who lives at the other end of the world and sailed here on ships." This could not be printed—manuscript notebooks passed from person to person, were read aloud, because the former fear was gone. *He is dead*—what is there to fear? Everyone forgot that *another he* is alive. And through the burst dam rushed a cloudy foaming stream of liberal and conservative slops, carrying with it all kinds of things: shards of philosophical systems, the debris of social ideas, the corpses of drowned economic doctrines, the skeletons of constitutions, in a word, everything that had come up against the wall of censorship and had lain there for years rose to the surface in its old clothes, covered in slime and moss. This made respectable people angry because they wanted Russia to leave the embraces of Nicholas and emerge like Minerva, with an owl, a globe, and a compass. [. . .]

As soon as a person sees the possibility of taking part, of acting, action becomes a physiological necessity for him. It may be premature, not well thought out, even false, *but it cannot fail to take place.* No religion, no social theory can reach its full consciousness before the beginning of its implementation. [. . .]

The nonsense that rose to the surface floated away, but the movement of the waves remains. The habit of participating and declaring one's will and ideas—that will not pass away. [. . .]

Freeing ourselves surreptitiously from the idol worship of autocracy, without noticing it we came upon the path to another church, to another form of idol worship, but in it we did not find faith in ourselves. For every Western people the transition from a theological monarchy to a theologically liberal orthodoxy was easy. Our happiness and unhappiness lie in the fact that we are satisfied with less than they were, but demand much more. If you give us Protestantism, we will become spirit wrestlers.[23] If you touch serfdom, we will demand the land as well. Our senses tell us, who have lagged behind, who are slaves, that the social religion that has outstripped us *is not ours*. What is surprising about the fact that it was all expressed awkwardly, chaotically, with desperate nihilism and hopeless Orthodoxy? The idea made itself understood with all the extremes of going from an infantile state of instinct to the possibility of consciousness.

Whether or not the results were correct, whether there was in them more *maturity* than *seeds*, or the other way around, of one thing there can be no doubt: this was a new movement of life, a new splashing of a liberated wave; while remaining in the same fetters, under the same bolts, we became freer people.

In confirmation of this I introduce the following fact, to which little attention was paid. Alongside the corrupted literature, with journals on government contracts, and with the Third Department at university lecterns, there was an extraordinary rise in social morality. The courage of one's convictions, which was completely lost in the previous reign, appeared once again, unafraid of the consequences.

Along with the Decembrists, our *civic valor* disappeared. The heroic period of opposition ends with the struggle of these conquered—but not dethroned— titans. During Nicholas's entire reign the tone of political defendants was evasive and based on denial. Society's indifference killed off futile bravery.

That has changed recently.

Once more, a man who was persecuted for his opinions and his words stood proudly before the court; he sensed the sympathy of the choir on the other side of the wall, he knew that his words were listened to avidly, he knew that his example would be a mighty homily.

Sadly, but firmly, Mikhailov appeared before the Senate.[24] The almshouse of old men who judged him were stupefied and listened with their mouths open; during their long military and civilian service they had never heard anything like it. The zealous Buturlin demanded the death sentence because of the insolence of the accused.[25]

Calmly and steadfastly stood the three youths—*Arngoldt, Slivetsky, and Rostovsky*—before the military authorities, who had been ordered to sentence them to death.

"Did you write this unsigned letter to Liders?" Arngoldt was asked.

"I did," answered Arngoldt, "but I didn't have a chance to complete it," and he took a pen and signed his name.

And these are not isolated examples, not exceptions; they have become the norm. Other officers behaved this way, Obruchev, for example. [. . .][26]

"I am publishing my project under my own name; it is time for us to stop being afraid, and if we want them to stop treating us like children, we have to stop acting in a juvenile manner. A person who desires truth and justice must be able to fearlessly stand up for them."

When I read these lines in the brochure by Serno-Solovyovich, it seemed to me that I—that we—had grown up.[27] Such words, such expressions, did not exist in Nicholavean times; this was a milestone in our history by which one could measure how far we had traveled from that *unforgettable* stage. [. . .]

These words, these answers before a court of executioners, in sight of loaded rifles, in sight of hard labor—the younger generation can place these on scales. Better than anything else they justify *the children* against *the fathers,* if the fathers have in fact attacked them.[28] With this they can easily atone for the awkwardness of forms and the arrogant language.

This morally valiant attitude, which declared itself strongly in Russian society, not only did not allow it to choose between the tsar and Poland, *but between silence and speech.* The beaten-down, flustered man, who kept silent about everything, could remain silent and covered with innocent blood. But after Mikhailov and "Great Rus," and after the executed officers [. . .] when all of Russia sees the need for an Assembly of the Land in order to take charge of a government that was inept and evil as well, *we cannot remain silent* in the face of the murder of an entire nation, in the face of this murder, which is taking place with our hands, our money, our obedience. [. . .]

Make haste to speak out!

Make haste to untie your boat in time from the imperial barque and to raise your own private flag. Make haste to defend the Russian people. Make haste to protest against the despicable and corrupt state institutions compelling Russian soldiers to exterminate Poles, and let their dishonorable speech be drowned out by your cry of indignation.

We are awaiting you! *Land and Liberty* has set an example.

Notes

Source: "1831–1863," *Kolokol,* l. 160, April 1, 1863; 17:92–111, 388–92.

1. This is Herzen's version of lines from *Macbeth,* act 5, scene 1. These remarks are actually both made by Lady Macbeth.

2. A reference to Banquo in act 3, scene 4 of *Macbeth.*

3. In his discussions with Alexander I, the historian Nikolay M. Karamzin argued that the independence of Poland was incompatible with the greatness (*velichie*) and security of the Russian state.

4. After the revolution of July 1830 that overthrew the Bourbons and brought Louis Philippe to the throne as king of France, Nicholas declared him a usurper and moved to break diplomatic relations, but his failure to put together a coalition of like-minded rulers forced him to back off from this measure, and he confined himself to simply failing to observe the usual formalities and signs of respect between rulers in their subsequent correspondence.

5. In Russian: *samoderzhavie, pravoslavie, narodnost'*.

6. Wellington was British prime minister in 1830; Metternich was Austrian foreign minister; Sebastiani was the French foreign minister, and Périer was head of the French Palace of Deputies.

7. "To the Slanderers of Russia."

8. Stuart (1803–1854) was a British politician who strongly supported Polish independence.

9. Pecherin was a poet and professor of Greek philology at Moscow University; in 1836 he emigrated and converted to Catholicism. Alexander I. Polezhaev (1804–1838) was a poet whose tragic story was recounted by Herzen in *Past and Thoughts*.

10. Chaadaev, a political philosopher famous for one published and other circulated manuscripts, was subjected to a yearlong house arrest by Nicholas I. Herzen describes Chaadaev's impact on Russia in his memoirs.

11. Karl Sand (1795–1820) was a radical Prussian student executed for his murder of the conservative writer Kotzebue. The Italian province of Calabria was very poor and full of bandits.

12. Herzen: "In 1835, during my exile to the province of Vyatka, I found in the town of Sarapul a wonderfully organized library, which received all the new books and journals in Russian. Members could take books home and there was a reading room. All this was set up with incredible effort, sacrifices, and great persistence by the district physician, who had graduated from Moscow University. His name, I think, was Chudnovsky."

13. Admiral Nikolay S. Mordvinov (1754–1845) served as a senator, member of the State Council, and, from 1823 to 1840, as head of the Free Economic Society. Mordvinov submitted his opinions and proposals to the State Council under Alexander I and Nicholas I, and they also circulated widely in society. He believed that the economic development of Russia depended on a strengthening of the rule of law and the educational system.

14. This is a criticism of Moscow University professor B. N. Chicherin, among others.

15. General Rostovtsev (1803–1860) was put in charge of all military schools in 1835. In an 1849 letter to Herzen, Granovsky described the new instructions as something that Jesuits would envy.

16. A reference to Ivan Turgenev's collection of stories called *Notes of a Hunter* (*Zapiski okhotnika*, 1852).

17. The article "The Anniversary of Borodino" appeared in *Fatherland Notes* (*Otechestvennye zapiski*) in October 1839, while Belinsky was under the influence of Hegel. The idea of reconciliation with reality was advanced in this and other Belinsky articles in 1839 and 1840.

18. Alexey Khomyakov (1804–1860) was an influential Slavophile essayist.

19. In June 1849, Granovsky wrote to Herzen that the situation was getting worse daily, with any attraction to the West stifled, and denunciations multiplying rapidly. There was every reason to go mad, and Belinsky had picked the right time to die.

20. Major-General Ivan P. Liprandi (1790–1880) led the Interior Ministry's yearlong surveillance of the Petrashevtsy and compiled a list of everyone who could be linked to the group.

21. A reference to Dostoevsky's prison memoir *Notes from the House of the Dead* (*Zapiski iz mertvogo doma*, 1860–62).

22. Admiral Charles Napier (1786–1860) commanded the British fleet in the Baltic during the Crimean War. On July 25, 1854, Nicholas visited Kronshtadt.

23. Spirit wrestlers (*dukhobortsy* or *dukhobory*) are one of the many sects that arose in Russia in the eighteenth century; three decades after this essay was written, Leo Tolstoy helped the Dukhobors to immigrate to Canada in order to avoid further persecution by the tsarist government.

24. Mikhailov took responsibility for the pamphlet and its distribution upon himself and was sentenced to hard labor. In the May 1, 1862, issue of *The Bell*, Herzen described "Milhailov's Answers" to the Senate.

25. General Alexey P. Buturlin (1802–1863) helped to suppress the Polish uprising in 1831 and peasant disorders in 1841, and served as a governor for fifteen years; he became a senator in 1861.

26. Arngoldt, Slivetsky, and Rostovsky were officers serving with the Russian army in Poland who were shot in June 1862 for spreading revolutionary pamphlets and harmful ideas among the Russian forces. General Liders was the tsar's deputy in Poland. Obruchev was a retired military officer who worked at *The Contemporary*, was arrested in 1861, and sentenced to hard labor for distributing the "Velikorus" proclamation.

27. Nikolay Serno-Solovyovich (1834–1866) was one of the organizers of "Land and Liberty" in 1861 (not to be confused with a second, more radical, movement of the same name in the 1870s), met with Herzen in London, was arrested in July 1862, and sentenced to hard labor. His brochure, "The Final Resolution of the Peasant Question," came out in Berlin in 1861.

28. Ivan Turgenev's novel *Fathers and Sons*, which had appeared in 1862, stimulated a vigorous debate over the political portrayal of the generations.

> 55 <

The Bell, No. 163, May 15, 1863. This polemic against Katkov and *The Moscow Gazette* (*Moskovskie vedomosti*) displays the familiar ironic style of Herzen's journalism, especially with its abundance of rhetorical questions and punning.

What Kind of Government Does Russia Have?
[1863]

The Morning Post suddenly, without warning, reveals that the government in Russia is *despotic*.[1]

Do you hear that? In Russia the government is *despotic?* What kind of lunacy is this!

So Paul I was a despot?

So Nicholas I was a despot?

So even Alexander II is a despot? It is true that since we have begun to forget the unforgettable one, the form of government has not changed.

No, these Jacobins do not understand the Russian government. [. . .]

If Poland rebelled, that is because the Russian autocracy had little freedom to operate, being very much constrained by free institutions. If officers were shot, this is no despotism but Liders's doing.[2] If people are held in jails and exiled for their words, without a trial, well, it's all legal and according to the code of laws... chapter and verse, and not despotism. It was clear that *The Moscow Gazette* could not tolerate such an *affront,* despite the fact that it was written in the English alphabet, on English paper, in England. The head of *The Moscow Gazette* quite rightly says that he cannot *say* "just how painful it is for a Russian person to hear that a serious organ of public opinion in Europe feels it has the right to call our form of government despotic."[3]

Surely if Palmerston's paper had been more thoughtful, they would not have made this mistake and it would not be "painful for a Russian person."[4] The head of *The Moscow Gazette* "had distinguished himself" by preaching with a schoolboy's bitterness—following Gneist[5] and other Germans—the English constitution, the English court, a bicameral legislature, the power of wealth, equality in the face of hunger—in a word, everything up to and including English medical plasters and English salt, and now, with even greater bitterness, defends the government which has entrusted him with such an important job. From that he concludes that the government he defends is parliamentary, free, and not despotic. [. . .]

Notes

Source: "Kakoe upravlenie v Rossii?" *Kolokol,* l. 163, May 15, 1863; 17:145–46, 413–14.

1. An editorial to this effect was published on April 9, 1863.

2. The commander of the army in Poland was adjutant-general Count A. N. Liders (1790–1874), who had helped suppress the earlier rebellion in 1831 and the Hungarian revolution in 1849. Herzen mentioned the execution of the three officers—Arngoldt, Slivitsky, and Rostovsky—on June 16, 1862, in several articles (see Docs. 54 and 72).

3. This is from a response published in *The Moscow Gazette* on April 5, 1863.

4. The Liberal Palmerston was at that time prime minister.

5. Rudolf von Gneist (1816–1895) was a jurist, legal reformer, and political theorist.

→ 56 ←

The Bell, No. 166, June 20, 1863. Herzen was well informed on activities in the Russian provinces; he saw the hand of some organization other than Land and Liberty in the appearance of a fake proclamation from the tsar to the serfs, and he felt a duty to criticize the ideological position and tactics of any group who, supposedly in Alexander II's name, summoned peasants to confiscate private and government-held lands. This kind of deception became an even more widespread tactic by the end of the 1860s. Despite Herzen's stand, Valuev believed that the manifesto was the work of "Herzen and Company" (*Let* 3:503).

THE VOLGA MANIFESTO AND RUSSIA IN A STATE OF SIEGE
[1863]

Here is the text of a manifesto that was distributed in villages along the banks of the Volga.[1] We are taking it from a printed copy.

By the grace of God,
We, Alexander the Second, etc.

In Our unceasing concern for the well-being of all Our subjects, We, by an edict of the 19th of February 1861, acknowledged the desirability of removing the bonds of serfdom from the rural population of the Russia that has been entrusted to Us by God.

Yielding to the entreaties of the landowners, We, however heavily it weighed on our royal heart, ordered all serfs to remain in complete subservience to their former owners for a period of two years, that is, until the 19th of February of the current year, 1863.

Now, having called upon the Almighty for aid, We declare in this manifesto the complete freedom of all of Our subjects, no matter to which rank or status they belonged. Henceforth freedom to believe and practice one's faith will be the right of every person.

To all former serfs, both private and state, We give a fixed amount of land without any payment for it either to the landowners or to the state, for their full, inalienable, hereditary use.

Relying on the loyalty of our people and recognizing the benefit to the country of abolishing Our army, We, from this day forward and forever, free Our beloved subjects from every kind of recruiting and military obligations; for that reason, We are ordering the soldiers in Our army to return to their native regions.

The payment of poll tax for the purpose of maintaining such a vast army, from the day this Manifesto is published onward, is abolished. We command that all soldiers returning from service, as well as all house serfs, factory workers, and urban dwellers be given without any charge an allotment of land from the public holdings of our vast empire.

In every region,[2] as in every town, the people will choose four people who enjoy their confidence, who, after meeting in a district center, will choose in common the district representative and other district authorities, four from each district; in the provincial capital, they will choose a provincial representative and other provincial authorities. Deputies from every province, summoned to Moscow, will compose the State Council, which, with Our assistance, will govern the entire Russian land.

That is Our royal will.

Anyone who declares the contrary and does not fulfill this Our royal will is Our enemy. We trust that the devotion of the people will protect Our throne from the attacks of ill-intentioned people who do not justify Our royal trust.

We command all Our subjects to believe only Our royal words. If troops, deceived by their commanders, if generals, governors, and intermediaries dare to oppose with force this manifesto, then each person should rise up to defend the freedom given by Me, and, not sparing your life, enter into battle with all who dare to oppose this Our will.

May the Almighty Lord bless our undertakings!

God is with us! Come to your senses, heathens, and submit, for God is with us!

Issued in Moscow, on the thirty-first day of March, in the one thousand eight hundred and sixty-third year since the birth of Christ, and the ninth year of Our reign.

In the original copy signed by HRH[3]

Alexander

Printed in St. Petersburg under the auspices of the senate.

The authors of such an appeal take a great responsibility upon themselves. This is a dangerous path: the people will stop believing in the printed word.

We are confident that the *Land and Liberty* group, who as a rule dismiss such isolated actions, have nothing to do with the composition of this manifesto.[4] We do not doubt that this appeal was made by people who are decent, but who, meanwhile, do not understand that it maintains the old, unfortunate notion that the tsar wishes to bestow genuine liberty, but is always being prevented from doing so, while it is clear that not only are others hindering the tsar but he is hindering himself, because he himself does not wish to bestow genuine liberty.

If this manifesto was published by a particular circle, then they and others must be advised to join together with the main society and then act with a unified plan.

It is very nice for the government, who for the distribution of some kind of leaflet *that involves no action of any kind,* to have given all Russia and all Russians over to the caprice of provincial authorities, i.e., terrible governors like Perm's Lashkarev.[5] "Such crimes cannot remain unpunished, even if the goal toward which they were directed was unattainable. Provincial officials have been given the duty on the highest authority to subject the distributors of the false manifesto and *other* provocative appeals to the military courts *on the same principle*[6] on which in the previous year military courts were ordered in the matter of the arsonists."

Notes

Source: "Volzhskii manifest i Rossiia v osadnom polozhenii," *Kolokol*, l. 166, June 20, 1863; 17:198–200, 433–35.

1. In April 1863, members of a pro-Polish group and students linked to the Kazan branch of Land and Liberty made attempts to distribute the manifesto in the Kazan, Nizhegorodsky, Tambov, and Vyatsk districts.

2. *Volost'*, the smallest administrative division in tsarist Russia.

3. The Russian is "v. i v." (*velikoe imperatorskoe velichestvo*).

4. Herzen was correct in believing that the document was not the work of the Land and Liberty leadership. It was initiated by a Polish committee whose members decided to make use of strong feelings about land allotments for their own purposes, and composed in Moscow by member of Land and Liberty without the leaders' knowledge, then printed in Vilna (Venturi, *Roots of Revolution*, 310, mentions another theory about it being printed in Norway and spirited into the empire through Finland), and given to the provincial Polish group for distribution in the volatile Volga region. When the Land and Liberty central committee learned of the false manifesto's imminent appearance, they rushed to issue their own proclamation to neutralize its effects.

5. Major-General Alexander G. Lashkarevich (1823–1898) was governor of Perm from 1861 to 1865. The quotation that follows is from an order given by Alexander II and published in the *Northern Post* newspaper on May 18, 1863.

6. Herzen notes here that this means to shoot without justification, as had occurred with an unfortunate Jew in Odessa convicted of arson two years earlier. In the case of the Kazan group linked to the false manifesto, arrests were made in April and May 1863 and the accused were handed over to a military court; four ringleaders were executed in 1864, one more in 1865, while other participants were sentenced to hard labor.

⇥ 57 ⇤

The Bell, No. 169, August 15, 1863. Ivan I. Kelsiev (1841–1864) was an auditor at Moscow University and an active participant in the student demonstrations of October 1861 that included a march to the home of Governor-General Tuchkov. As one of a three-student delegation hoping to negotiate with Tuchkov, Kelsiev was arrested, exiled to Perm, then arrested once more on suspicion of involvement in revolutionary propaganda, including articles intended for publication in *The Bell.* Held in a private dwelling in Moscow while awaiting sentencing, Kelsiev escaped to Constantinople with the help of Land and Liberty, only to die the following year. Nikolay I. Utin (1841–1883), leader of the student movement at St. Petersburg University, was arrested in fall 1861 and held for several months. After his father successfully lobbied for his release, Utin joined Land and Liberty in 1862, but escaped to London when he learned that the police planned to arrest him again; after a search of his apartment, he was tried and sentenced to death in absentia. He later served as secretary for the Russian section of the First International. In this article, Herzen frequently employs puns in referring to jails and to Russia as a whole.

I. Kelsiev and N. Utin
[1863]

Two energetic representatives of university youth—from two very different sides—have been saved from the St. Petersburg government's persecution.

I. Kelsiev, the brother of the publisher of Old Believer anthologies, was arrested in connection with the Moscow student affair and sent to Verkhoture. From there he was sent for questioning in the matter of Argiropulo and Zaichnevsky.[1] Argiropulo died in prison, and Zaichnevsky was sentenced to hard labor. Kelsiev was sentenced to six months of incarceration, after which he was to continue his exile in Verkhoture. [. . .] He preferred—and very wisely—to leave the private dwelling in which he was held, and then the common prison in which the whole of Russia is confined. He is now abroad.

N. Utin was at St. Petersburg University, and his name, like that of Kelsiev, is well known to our readers. He was among the *instigators* of the

Petersburg University demonstrations, was held in the Peter Paul Fortress and, when faced with a new arrest, decided to leave Russia.

We enthusiastically welcome them to Europe.

Note

Source: "I. Kel'siev i N. Utin," *Kolokol*, l. 169, August 15, 1863; 17:234, 446–47.

1. Perakl E. Argiropulo and Petr G. Zaichnevsky were student leaders in Moscow, arrested in 1861 along with other students, on suspicion of illegally printing forbidden texts and revolutionary decrees. Argiropulo died in a prison hospital in 1862; Zaichnevsky was sent to hard labor for a year, and then into Siberian exile.

⤞ 58 ⤝

The Bell, No. 169, August 15, 1863. Herzen cannot rest while journalism in Russia is supporting the bloody work of the state. He wrote to Bakunin that "however vile the government was, journalism and society were even more vile" with dinners and toasts for the worst of the lot, Muravyov and Katkov (*Let* 3:532).

———

GALLOWS AND JOURNALS
[1863]

We will no longer take note of political killings carried out by the Russian government, nor provide excerpts from Russian newspapers. Executions have become part of the daily routine in our country. Since Peter I practiced doing this with his own hands, there has been nothing like it in Russia, even in the time of Biron[1] or Paul I. We turn away in shame and sorrow from the gallows and their daily lists.

The year 1863 will remain noteworthy in the history of Russian journalism and in the history of our development as a whole. The heroic era of our literature[2] has ended. Since the university events and the Petersburg fire, it has taken a new turn: it has become official and officious,[3] denunciations have appeared along with demands for *unheard of* punishments, etc. The government, while winning over and encouraging favorable journals by all available means, has, in the French manner, banned all independent organs. Police literature took advantage of this and expressed itself without restraint, since no one in Russia could object. Of the independent journals with a political direction only *The Day* has held on; its Great Russian patriotism has placed it in a special position. We know the direction of *The Day*, but, speaking frankly, if anyone had said a year ago that *The Day* would call honest adversaries who are fighting for the independence of their homeland *bandits*, and the Polish authorities—who organized the uprising and are steering their entire nation between life and death—a *den of thieves and hangmen*, we would not have believed it, just as we would not have believed that to the question of what to do with insurgents in the provinces, that same journal would have answered: of course, *execute them*, and this without any need since they would have been executed anyway, but just to show sympathy and approval.

This patriotic frenzy brought to the surface everything of the Tartar, landowner, and sergeant that in a sleepy and half-forgotten way was fermenting in us; we now know how much Arakcheev[4] there is in our veins and how much Nicholas in our brain. This will cause many to think carefully and many to submit. Evidently educated Russia had not run that far away when faced with the government. Neither the French language in days of old, nor philosophy from Berlin, nor England according to Gneist did much of anything. While speaking in a pure Parisian dialect we beat our serfs in the house and field; while discussing Gneist, we demand confiscations by military authorities and executions by secret courts. The Slavophiles have much over which to rejoice: the national, pre-Petrine foundation[5] has not changed, at least in our savage exceptionalism, in hatred toward anything foreign, and in the indiscriminate use of courts and harsh punishments. [. . .]

What kind of excerpts and arguments can one have in this case? Having sadly escorted an old acquaintance to the madhouse, we will await his recovery, visiting now and then, and having faith in a healthy organism that can endure anything. The patriotic fury is too fierce to prevail for very long.

Those who have defiled our language will pay for it. Conscience will be awakened—if not theirs, then that of the younger generation, not those noticed by Moscow professors or by the court in Petersburg; they will recoil with horror from those who sings psalms to the hangmen, from the fawning admirers of Muravyov, from all these Kotzebues[6] and journalistic Arakcheevs. We do not doubt this and for that reason we will leave them to rage on and finish their unhealthy intellectual ferment.

August 5, 1863

Notes

Source: "Viselitsy i zhurnaly," *Kolokol*, l. 169, August 15, 1863; 17:235–37, 447–48.

1. Ernst Biron (1690–1772) was close to Empress Anna and the de facto ruler of Russia from 1730 to 1740, a gloomy era that was later referred to as the *bironovshchina*.

2. By literature, Herzen clearly means journalism as well as other more artistic writing.

3. The word *ofitsioznyi* refers to a morally reprehensible degree of support for government activities, with an eye to currying favor.

4. Count Alexey A. Arakcheev (1769–1834), a general who served the governments of both Alexander I and Nicholas I, was tasked with organizing military colonies; his influence on the governance of Russia is marked by the use of the word *arakcheevshchina* to refer to the years during which he was most influential.

5. Herzen used the French word *fond*.

6. General Pavel E. Kotzebue (1801–1884), head of the army general staff until 1862, then governor-general of Novorossiisk and Bessarabia from 1862 to 1874.

⇢ 59 ⇠

The Bell, No. 170, September 1, 1863. This essay continues Herzen's polemic with reform-era liberals, especially those like M. N. Katkov, N. F. Pavlov, and B. N. Chicherin who had begun to craft a kind of liberal conservatism, which included strong nationalist sentiments. Herzen saw this as a new stage in Russia's ideological development, which manifested itself in a number of ways, including increased attacks on him, a declining interest in his London publications, and greater difficulty in successfully sending them to Russia. "Literature" for Herzen includes journalism.

AT THIS STAGE
[1863]

They are kicking us... by the weakness and shape of the hooves it is not difficult to guess what kind of beast is rushing to keep up with police horses of the same color and water-carrying patriotic nags who are frankly convinced that the peasant world will stop eating oats and will lose all the virtues of a stable if they were to remove the fatherland's yoke.[1] Their zeal and their enterprising and cavalier spirit demonstrate clearly that we are *out of favor* not only with the Winter Palace, but with the majority of the readers in Russia.

We have become accustomed to disfavor, we were always in the minority, otherwise, we would not have wound up in London. Up till this point it was state power that persecuted us, but now a chorus has joined them.

The alliance against us of police and ideologues, Westernizers and Slavophiles is a kind of negative affirmation of our "moral citizenship" in Russia. Behind the genuine neighborhood policeman and the fake homespun coat, all that is weak and unsteady, neither one thing nor the other, has pushed away from us—those poor in spirit and weakened in body, hangers-on from literary circles, patients living off crumbs at the tables of ideologues—they have all gone over to the other side and transferred over there the optical illusion of their existence. They represent a false strength: you think those are muscles, but it is really a tumor; that is dangerous during a struggle, which is why they did a good thing by leaving. We candidly admit that we absolutely do not fear being left in the minority, not even in a completely empty room.

Fifteen years ago we were in the same position with European reactionaries; we did not yield an iota, and, having said all that we thought, we withdrew, conscious that *truth* is on our side.[2]

This time we will not withdraw and will not keep silent—in the Russian case the realization that we are right is not enough, we want to participate. It is developing in a misshapen, crazy, criminal fashion, *but it is taking its course.*

We do not know whether or not Western man will free himself. The process drags on and is far from being finished. In any case the task is a difficult one; the threads are strong, the knots are tangled, and all of it has not only entered the body but has grown into it.

We are not at all in that position; our life has not taken on a definitive form. There is a great deal that is bad in its instability and contradictions, but that is not the point. The point is that we have not joined the *conservative era* of our existence—for us conservatism is either police resistance, or ideological imitation of the West. [. . .]

The uncertainty and disorder of Russian life, leading it, on the one hand, to ugly extremes and contradictions, to an anxious tracking down of principles and a foolish grasping at everything in the world, and, on the other hand, our national life's elementary strength and endurance, its indifference to experimental reforms and improvements—all this demonstrates clearly that our life has not taken on a definitive form, has not run across forms that are appropriate to it, and has not developed them from its own existence. It cannot find itself in other people's homes; it cannot settle down, and lives like a nomad.

The first time that the two ways of life, the two Russias, met in this borderland, the first time that the question occupying them was not resolved with a whip, it was resolved *not in a Western manner.* It is impossible to even *pose* this question in a Western manner. Since the day when the government indirectly admitted the peasant's right to land, when literature began to discuss whether the serfs should be freed with or without land, and if with land, then how to own it, collectively or individually, the first serious compromise began between the Russian national way of life and the ideal of Western civilization. That is why the peasant, silent for centuries, began to talk, and began to talk sense.

Now, after this first and maybe most important step, now we need a great deal of coming together, freedom of thought, border posts open on all sides and, most of all, with the beams removed, discarded models whose originals had turned out to be unsuited for the West. And now, at the right time, "traitors" have turned up, who preach a west-east conservatism of Petersburg puppet shows.[3]

That which a civilizing empire did not accomplish is being attempted by doctrinaire civilizers.

The cords with which the government entangled us are easy to sever; it is a matter of muscles, *and not conscience,* as in the West. The literary Muravyovs want to tighten the noose, while still assuring us that it is all for our good; they want not only to overwhelm us with their power and corrupt us with their conviction. Now, at a time when we must lay out our plan and erect signposts, they want to narrow our thinking. [. . .] cultivate in us the conservative senility of Europe and wind up just cultivating its chronic diseases. [. . .] They themselves can easily do without free institutions, without freedom to publish, and congratulate themselves with their victory over the *revolution* of 1862 in Petersburg, of which none of us has heard.

This unnecessary, boring page from our textbook must be torn out. We were drilled sufficiently during the Petrine era, and there is no need, while abolishing corporal punishments, to introduce ones that are spiritual.

For our part, however, much strength remains [. . .] we will keep the mandarin-spiders from weaving us into this web, we will oppose this second and superfluous German invasion. The fact that they will try to stop us with the hindquarters of their police horses, to the accompaniment of the approving neighs and brotherly help of their imitators, will not stop us. It is a shame, though, that prior to kicking they did not wipe off their hooves because there is already a lot of mud, but *à la guerre comme à la guerre.*

August 20, 1863

POST SCRIPTUM

It is impossible to go any further, without glancing at the path we have traveled since the previous stage.

While we trudged along, laying down a modest road to our printing press, events moved on and came to some kind of turning point; the shadows obviously are falling in a different direction.

Ten years ago Russia was silent, and we faced a single enemy—the government. It did not have defenders in literature and fierce partisans in society. Literature kept silent about it and society feared it. Literature—with the exception of police organs that were despised by everyone—was in opposition. Society was not in opposition: indifferent and sleepy, it had no opinion, and *amused itself* under the shelter of autocracy.

Then society split: one part hated the government for the emancipation of the serfs, while the other loved it for the same reason. On this issue, all literature stood with the government, and, once that had happened, backed the government on a few other issues. Men of letters for the first time saw the possibility and pleasure of keeping all the advantages of liberalism without any of the disadvantages of being in opposition. In that way, by degrees there began a system of *hopes and expectations* on the part of literature and a system of *a little bit of good at a time (gradualness with the chronic delay of progress)* on the part of the government. Russia lived in a kind of optical illusion: the government did not yield a bit, while literature and a portion of society were convinced that they were getting everything. Even those trifles that the government allowed were not made law and could always be taken back. Literature, enjoying some openness and temporarily relaxed censorship, imagined that we were on the eve of radical change, that a constitution was being written, that freedom of the press *est garantie,* that only a few formalities remained, but the main business was already taken care of. The journals which had come to believe this immediately took on an extraordinarily European character a bit conservative, but not at all against progress; they began to speak about political parties, opposition pamphlets—democratic, federal, socialist—forgetting that we have a great many policemen and very few rights, that censorship *really existed,* and the court system existed *only in a formal sense,* making significantly easier, in that way, the work of the Third Department.

Journalism and the government during this honeymoon of government-sponsored liberalism behaved on terms of the most delicate civility. The journals displayed the greatest faith in a reforming government, while the government said how badly it felt that it could not improve and correct all institutions as fast as it would like, and it spoke of its love for open discussion and its hatred for monopolies.

They resembled two honorable people, competing with each other in politeness—one, in demanding a debt, said that he fully appreciates that his debtor intends to pay; the other puts it off, assuring him that he is making a sacrifice in postponing the delight of payment.

This has become annoying, and not without reason, especially to the government. No matter what crack it is that the light shines through, it lights up something indecent, in no matter how distorted a form freedom of expression is given, it gets to the point. The government frowned, and awaited some kind of disturbances in order to have a pretext; there were no disturbances, so it was necessary to take decisive measures. They came up with student lists and Putyatin, packed the Peter Paul Fortress with students, lured the students themselves onto Tverskaya Square in Moscow, but it did not work. The public opinion that had begun to develop was not in favor of such persecution, and journalism, still holding on to some sense of shame, displayed neither love for the students, nor tenderness toward Putyatin, nor approval of street battles with unarmed people, and young ladies had no wish to dance with the conquering Preobrazhensky victors. The persecutions did not succeed; the government, in order to cover up its mistake, got rid of Putyatin and Ignatiev. *Revolution* in Petersburg (according to *The Moscow Gazette*) continued, the terror continued, the government did not know what to fabricate next, what new lists of students... fortunately the fires came to their aid. There's a reason the Russian people love arson.

In 1812 Moscow saved the nation from foreign captivity with a fire, and fifty years later Petersburg with the same means freed imperial power of the yoke of liberalism and many commentators of the constraints of pretending to be honorable people.

The revolution and terror were defeated. The storm clouds hanging over their heads went away, and the stone lying on their chests was transformed into an order of Stanislav of the first degree... Frightened public opinion drew closer to the government and journalism supported it. At that time the first attempts at denunciations appeared in print, the first demands for *energetic* measures, i.e., executions. The government, seeing this mood, made use of it.

What would our unforgettable Chichikov[4] say if he were to see how—on the ruins of make-believe barricades and on the ashes of the flea market—Golovnin and Valuev[5] set up open markets at which "dead souls" *of the literary world* were bought up? Remount officers were sent to Moscow, where there had not been a living soul since the death of Granovsky, and, consequently, countless multitudes of dead souls. [. . .]

A confused society did not know where to turn; the fires had frightened them, but they weren't there and the government refrained from any explanation of this matter and began to explore the possibility of death sentences, and hard labor... Once again the grumbling began, but luckily for the government Poland rebelled. The gentry, which had shied away from the government because of the emancipation of the serfs, passionately dashed toward it at the first news of the enslavement of Poland and announced its readiness to take part in this.

And now there are before us, instead of a single Nicholas, three enemies: the government, journalists, and the gentry—the sovereign, Katkov, and Sobakevich.[6]

Notes

Source: "V etape," *Kolokol*, l. 170, September 1, 1863; 17:244–51, 449–52.

1. The word used here is *duga*, or "shaft-bow," a wooden bar arching above an animal's neck as it holds together two shafts and the harness.

2. Herzen is referring to *From the Other Shore*.

3. The Russian word used here is *balagan*, a temporary fair booth with room for a stage and benches for spectators, erected for performances during Shrovetide and other holiday seasons.

4. Chichikov is the picaresque hero of Nikolay Gogol's novel *Dead Souls* (1842).

5. Alexander V. Golovnin (1821–1886) was minister of education from 1861 to 1866.

6. Katkov edited *The Moscow Gazette;* Sobakevich is a character in Gogol's *Dead Souls*.

⇥ 60 ⇤

The Bell, No. 171, October 1, 1863. Herzen composed this tribute after hearing about the death of Shchepkin in August 1863. Born into serfdom, Mikhail Shchepkin became one of the most famous Russian actors of his day, and a prominent figure in Russian society. Because of his humble background, his successes took on a political resonance as Russia moved toward emancipation. The celebration of his fiftieth anniversary on the stage in 1855, and his election to the English Club in Moscow in 1857, the first actor and the first ex-serf allowed to join, were events of more than personal significance, a fact duly noted by the Third Department. Shchepkin was friendly with both Slavophile and Westernizer circles, including the Moscow circle that gathered around Timofey Granovsky, and was a much-loved and much-respected figure in an age of strong friendships and even stronger antipathies. Herzen evaluates Shchepkin's gifts against the background of the Russian theater—where his chief rival for several decades was Pavel Mochalov (1800–1848)—and the European stage, with which Herzen was familiar. This article recounts the actor's visit to London in 1853, the first visit to Herzen by one of his old Russian circle after the series of family tragedies he had suffered. That Shchepkin turned out to be an emissary from his Moscow acquaintances was an early warning to Herzen that even the liberals of his generation were turning conservative.

MIKHAIL SEMYONOVICH SHCHEPKIN
[1863]

Moscow grows empty... and the patriarchal face of Shchepkin has disappeared.... And it was firmly intertwined with all the memories of our Moscow circle. A quarter-century our senior, he was on very good terms with us, more like an uncle or an older brother. Everyone loved him madly: ladies and students, elderly people and young girls. His appearance introduced calm, his good-natured reproach brought nasty quarrels to an end, his meek smile of an affectionate old man caused others to smile, and his limitless ability to forgive another person, to find extenuating reasons, was a school for humane behavior.

And with that he was a great performer, a performer by vocation and by his labor. He created *moral truth*[1] on the Russian stage, and he was the first to become *untheatrical* in the theater. His performances lacked false phrases, affectations, and caricatures; the characters he created were like figures from the paintings of Teniers and Ostade.[2]

Shchepkin and Mochalov, are, without doubt, the two greatest actors of all I have seen during the course of thirty-five years and across the expanse of Europe. They are both *hints* of the inner strength and potential of the Russian nature, which make our faith in Russia's future unshakeable.

We will not go into an analysis of Shchepkin's talent and significance on the stage; we will merely note that he did not at all resemble Mochalov. Mochalov was a man of impulse and of an inspiration that was not made obedient or structured; his gifts did not obey him, rather, he obeyed them. Mochalov did not work; he knew that at some point he would be visited by a spirit that would turn him into Hamlet, Lear, or Karl Moor, and he waited for that... and if the spirit did not come, he remained an actor who knew his role poorly. Endowed with unusual sensitivity and a keen understanding of all the shades of a role, Shchepkin, in contrast, worked terribly hard and never left anything to the arbitrary nature of a moment's inspiration. But his role was not the result of study alone. [. . .] Shchepkin's style from cover to cover was suffused with warmth, naïveté, and his study of the part did not inhibit a single sound or gesture, but gave them firm support and a firm foundation.

However, it is likely that much will be written in Russia about his talent and his significance. I would like to write about my last meeting with him.

In Autumn 1853 I received a letter from M. K. in Paris, saying that on a certain date Shchepkin would be arriving in London from Boulogne. The joy I felt frightened me... In the image of that radiant old man my early years looked out from behind the graves, the entire Moscow period... and at such a time... I have spoken about the terrible years between 1850 and 1855, about that five-year-long bleak ordeal in a populous wilderness. I was completely alone in a crowd of strangers and slight acquaintances... At that time Russians did less traveling abroad and were all the more afraid of me. The heightened terror that continued until the end of the Hungarian War[3] turned into a uniform oppression, which plunged everyone into a hopeless despair. And the first Russian traveling to London who was not afraid to shake my hand was Mikhail Shchepkin.

I couldn't wait and the morning of his arrival I took an express train to Folkstone.

"What will he tell me, what news will he bring, whose greetings will he relay, what details, whose jokes... or speeches?" *At that time* there were still many people whom I loved in Moscow.

When the steamer docked, I could make out the plump figure of Shchepkin with a gray hat and a stout walking stick; I waved a handkerchief and rushed down. A policeman did not let me through but I pushed him aside, seeing with amusement that Shchepkin looked on merrily and nodded his head, and I ran onto the deck and threw my arms around the old man. He was the very same as when I left him: with the same good-natured appearance, his vest and the lapels of his coat covered with spots, as if he had just left the Troitsky restaurant on his way to Sergey Timofeevich Aksakov's place.[4] "What got into you to come such a distance to meet me!" he said to me through his tears.

We traveled together to London; I quizzed him about all the details, all the trifles about our friends, trifles without which people cease to be alive and remain in our memories in broad outlines, in profile. He talked of nonsensical things and we laughed with tears in our voices.

When my nerves had settled, little by little I noticed something sad, as if some sort of hidden thought was tormenting the honest expression on his face. And, in fact, the next day little by little the conversation turned to the press; Shchepkin began to talk about the troubled feelings with which Moscow accepted my emigration, then the brochure "Du développement des idées révolutionnaires..." and, finally, the London printing-house. "What use can come of your publishing? With the one or two leaflets that get through, you will accomplish nothing, but the Third Department will read them and make a note of it, and you will destroy a huge number of people, you will destroy your friends..."

"But, M. S., up till now God has spared us, and no one has been caught because of me."

"Do you know that after your praise for Belinsky, it is forbidden to mention his name in print?"

"Along with everything else. However, I have doubts about my part in this. You know what role Belinsky's letter to Gogol played in the Petrashevsky case.[5] Death spared Belinsky—I was not afraid of compromising the dead."

"But Kavelin, it seems, is not dead?"

"What happened to him?"

"Well, after the publication of your book where you talk about his article on the ancestral principle and the quarrel with Samarin, he was summoned to Rostovtsev."[6]

"Well!"

"What do you want? Rostovtsev told him *to be more careful in the future.*"

"Mikhail Semyonovich, do you really consider that a martyrdom—to suffer the tetrarch Yakov[7] to advise him to be more careful?"

The conversation continued in this manner, and I could see that this was *not only* Shchepkin's personal opinion; if that were the case, his words would not have taken such an imperative tone.

This conversation was noteworthy for me, because in it were the first sounds *of Moscow conservatism*, not in the circles of Prince Sergey Mikhailovich Golitsyn,[8] of frivolous landowners, or frivolous officials, but in a circle of educated people, men of letters, actors, and professors. For the first time I heard this opinion expressed in such a clear manner; it struck me, although at the time I was at too great a distance to understand that from it would develop that stubbornly conservative direction that turned Moscow into Kitay-gorod.[9]

At this time it was still just *weariness, a broken spirit*, the consciousness of one's own powerlessness and a maternal fear for one's children. Now Moscow insolently and bravely drinks the health of Muravyov...[10]

"A. I.," said Shchepkin, as he stood up and paced back and forth uneasily, "you know how much I love you and how all of our group loves you... In my old age, not speaking a word of English, I came to see you in London. I would get down on my aged knees before you to ask you to stop while there is still time."

"Mikhail Semyonovich, what is it that you and your friends want from me?"

"I speak only for myself and I will say directly: in my opinion, go to America, write nothing, let them forget about you, and then in a year or two or three we can begin to work on getting you permission to return to Russia."

I was extremely sad; I tried to hide the pain that these words caused me out of pity for the old man, who had tears in his eyes. He continued to develop this alluring picture of happiness—to live once again under the merciful scepter of Nicholas. However, seeing that I did not answer, he asked: "Isn't it possible, A. I.?"

"No it is not, Mikhail Semyonovich. I know that you love me and wish me the best. It is painful for me to upset you, but I cannot deceive you: let our friends say what they will, but *I will not shut down the printing press*. The time will come when they will look differently on the mechanism I have set up on English soil. I will continue to print, and will print without stopping... If our friends do not value my activities, it will cause me great pain, but it will not stop me; others will value it, the younger generation, the next generation."

"So neither the love of friends nor the fate of your children matter?"

I took him by the hand and said:

"Mikhail Semyonovich, why do you wish to spoil for me the festive occasion of our meeting—I am not going to America, and under the present state of affairs I am not going to Russia either; I will be printing because it is the only way of doing something for Russia, the only means of maintaining a living connection with it. If what I print is bad, then tell our friends to send manuscripts—they must feel the lack of free speech."

"No one will send anything," said the already irritated old man; my words had really upset him, he felt a rush of blood to his head and wanted to send for a doctor and leeches.

We did not return to this conversation. Only just before his departure he said sadly, shaking his head:

"You have taken so much joy from me with your stubbornness."

"M. S., let us each follow our own path, and maybe one of them will lead somewhere."

He left, but his unsuccessful mission still fermented inside him, and he, who loved powerfully also angered powerfully, and as he left Paris he sent me a stern letter.[11] I read it with the same degree of love with which I threw my arms around him in Folkstone, and *followed my own path*.

Five years had passed since my meeting with Shchepkin when the Russian press in London again crossed his path. The management of the Moscow theaters withheld money from the budget that was due to the actors. That was an age of *making claims*, and the actors chose Shchepkin as their intercessor in Petersburg. The director at that time was the well-known Gedeonov. Gedeonov began by flatly refusing to issue the past payments, saying that the books had been checked and it was impossible to alter previously made arrangements.

The conversation became more insistent on Shchepkin's part, and, of course, bolder on the side of the director.

"I will have to see the minister," said the actor.

"It's good that you told me. I will report to him about this matter and you will be refused."

"In that case I will submit an appeal to the sovereign."

"You dare take such garbage and push your way to his imperial highness? As your superior, I forbid you."

"Your excellency," Shchepkin said, bowing, "you agree that the money belongs to the poor actors. They entrusted me with obtaining it; you have refused and promised a refusal from the minister. I wish to ask the sovereign, and, as my superior, you have forbidden me... I have only one means left—I will relate the entire matter to *The Bell*."

"You have lost your mind," shouted Gedeonov. "I wonder whether you understand what you are saying—I will order your arrest. Listen, I will excuse you only because you said this in the heat of the moment. You should be ashamed of making such a commotion over these trifles. Come to the office tomorrow and I will see what can be done."

The following day the money was allocated for the actors, and Shchepkin went home.[12] [. . .]

September 10, 1863

Notes

Source: "Mikhail Semenovich Shchepkin," *Kolokol*, l. 171, October 1, 1863; 17:268–74, 458–61.

1. Herzen uses the word *pravda*.

2. Seventeenth-century Flemish painters.

3. The Russian army intervened in Hungary in 1849 and helped to crush the revolutionary movement.

4. Shchepkin was in the party that accompanied Herzen and his family on the first stage of their journey out of Moscow in 1847. Sergey T. Aksakov (1791–1859) was a writer, theater critic, and the father of two prominent Slavophiles, Konstantin and Ivan, and was deeply respected by Herzen. It was safe to mention the father's name in *The Bell* since he had also passed away.

5. A reference to the arrest (April 1849) and trial of a progressive Petersburg circle in the wake of the 1848 upheavals in Europe that so frightened Nicholas I; Dostoevsky was accused of having read Belinsky's letter to others in the group. The letter the critic had written to Gogol criticized what Belinsky saw as fawning praise for a repressive regime in *Selected Passages from Correspondence with Friends* (1847).

6. Konstantin D. Kavelin (1818–1885) was a law professor and writer, and, briefly, tutor to Grand Duke Nikolay Alexandrovich. In 1847 his article on legal practices in pre-Petrine Russia appeared in *The Contemporary*, stimulating the Slavophile Yury Samarin to write a response. Without mentioning names, Herzen described this polemic in his book. Kavelin, who in 1850–53 served in the administration of the military academies, was subsequently summoned by its director, General Rostovtsev.

7. Herzen ironically compares Yakov Rostovtsev to the Tetrarch Herod in the gospel according to Matthew (chap. 14).

8. Sergey Golitsyn (1774–1859) served as trustee of the Moscow educational district from 1830 to 1835.

9. Kitay-gorod is one of the oldest areas of Moscow, located not far from the Kremlin.

10. General Mikhail N. Muravyov (1796–1866) was known as "the hangman" for his harsh suppression of the Polish rebellions of 1830 and 1863.

11. In the letter, Shchepkin advised Herzen to let the world develop according to its natural laws and to confine himself to assisting in humanity's moral development, to spread ideas but not violence. Herzen considered Shchepkin to have been worn down by the age in which he lived.

12. Herzen: "This anecdote, which we heard at the time from a direct source, we did not print for obvious reasons." One source was Turgenev, who wrote to Herzen soon after the incident (*Let* 2:390).

⇥ 61 ⇤

The Bell, No. 177, January 15, 1864. This article is related to ongoing commentary in *The Bell* about the behavior of Russian liberals. It criticizes the fashion for repentance, especially by a gray-haired "Magdalene" (Ivan Turgenev), who submitted to questioning by the Russian government at the Paris Embassy in March 1863. Turgenev reportedly explained at some length his political differences with Herzen, Ogaryov, and Bakunin. The writer was summoned back to St. Petersburg to testify before the State Senate in January 1864; soon after that he was allowed to return to France. Herzen was also critical of Turgenev's behavior in connection with the "Trial of the 32" (discussed in Doc. 70). Turgenev wrote to Herzen on April 2, 1864, about these remarks, saying that he expected as much from Bakunin but not from such an old friend as Herzen.

SCANDAL, SOOT, A CANDLE SNUFFER, ETC.
[1864]

After the New Year, we received several letters from Russia and from Russians abroad. The general impression was awful, although the signs of a turning point are not only continuing, but are clearly intensifying. Far-sighted cowards are beginning to abandon the camp of the *reds* (i.e., of the butchers, as the word "reds" is used in one of their letters). We are asked not to print the details so as not to threaten the purity of the sinners who have repented...

But then repentance of all kinds is the fashion—evidently, the end of times is upon us. Not only are *reds* repenting, but the blues, the skewbald, and those of no color whatsoever are repenting of everything that was in their thoughts and dreams, things in the distant past and those that have not yet happened, all sorts of different sins, even those that neither have nor ever could have anything to do with them.

Our correspondent tells of a certain gray-haired Magdalene (of the male sex), who wrote to the tsar of losing sleep and appetite, peace of mind, white hair and teeth, tormented that the tsar still does not understand the heart-felt repentance, as a result of which *"all ties have been broken with youthful friends."*

[. . .] The terror cannot be appeased—otherwise it would not be terror—and one cannot stop halfway. One will not be saved by lyrical exclamations about the might and great expanse of Russia, in the manner of Gogol,[1] or by constantly berating the Poles; it is necessary to offer denunciations, and to dishonor oneself. Rhetorical spasms of love for the people are not needed; rather, one must despise the people in the name of a strong state, and demand executions for the glory and strength of the Petersburg administration...

Note

Source: "Spletni, kopot', nagar i pr.," *Kolokol*, l. 177, January 15, 1864; 18:35–36, 543–45.
  1. Herzen has in mind the final pages of Gogol's *Dead Souls*.

<h1 style="text-align:center">⇥ 62 ⇤</h1>

The Bell, No. 177, January 15, 1864. Herzen introduces the image of the three winged goddesses of classical mythology, who pursued sinners with a vengeance.

———

<h2 style="text-align:center">THE FURIES
[1864]</h2>

The January 10 issue of *Le Siècle*,[1] speaking about a charming address to Muravyov by Petersburg ladies, asks with astonishment: "Don't these mothers, wives, and sisters have sons, husbands, and brothers?" etc. O naive *Siècle*! Don't they know what kind of beast is the *female Russian landowner* from Saltychikha[2]—jailed in chains by Catherine II—up to... here's one, for example: an Englishman, *very well known and much respected*, told the story in London that he was recently at a grand dinner in Moscow and sat next to an old maid (he said her name, which is from a minor princely family), who, displeased with the Polish uprising, said *to him, an Englishman:* "With all my heart and soul I wish they would string up every single Pole!"

It goes without saying that there are many exceptions, but the general type of the charming sex from our *democratic* nobility, the Russian lady landowner, is a kind of she-wolf who gobbles up ten or twenty chambermaids and servants without the slightest regret, tirelessly, and without rest.

There is no way these Furies would have changed in the space of two years. The only thing new in the old maid's remark is cynicism. In the past they duped foreigners with humane sentiments, but now boast in their presence of energetic measures and homespun patriotism.

Here is a job for all the Old Maids and Baba-Yagas[3] of our beau monde—to greet in Moscow and Petersburg, with garlands and bouquets, Muravyov, who, it is said, is coming to preside over a new commission *for the extinction and destruction* of Poland[4]. [. . .]

Notes

Source: "Furii," *Kolokol*, l. 177, January 15, 1864; 18:37, 545.

1. *Le Siècle* was a politically liberal Parisian daily.

2. Darya N. Saltykova (1730–1801), known by her nickname "Saltychikha," was a famously cruel serf owner, whose 1768 sentence included an hour in the pillory, after which she spent the rest of her life confined to a convent.

3. Baba Yaga is a well-known and fearsome character in Russian fairy tales.

4. At the beginning of January 1864, a committee of five was formed, under the chairmanship of Alexander II, to prepare a land reform plan for Poland.

⇥ 63 ⇤

The Bell, No. 179, February 15, 1864. Herzen carried on an emotional polemic with Ivan Aksakov's *The Day*, revealing a much harsher opinion of him than did Ogaryov.

———

THEY'VE GONE COMPLETELY OUT OF THEIR MINDS
[1864]

In several Russian newspapers (*The Siberian Gazette, The Northern Bee*) there is a description of an execution that took place on January 5 in the town of Ostrov. *Felix Ambrozhinsky* was accused of being a gendarme in the Polish service, executing *someone* (no name was given), and "providing food supplies to the rebels." None of this is surprising any more. But listen further: "Along with the troops, Ambrozhinsky's accomplices were present, gendarmes like him (*whose crimes had not yet been investigated*), *who had to play the role of executioners*. After the reading of the sentence, the criminal kneeled, kissed a cross that was held by the priest, said: 'Forgive me,' and stood up. The men—*accomplices of the criminal*—led him to the scaffold [. . .] and performed *a task probably familiar to them* with the noose."

We address all honest people... We address, yes, we address, for example, you, Mr. Aksakov, publisher of *The Day* [. . .] yes, we turn to you—you bear a pure and honest name, a name that we are accustomed to respect in your father and to love in your brother—take care with whom you stand and *what kind of* energetic actions you praise. People *whose crimes had not yet been uncovered,* were forced *to kill their* comrade! [. . .]

Words fail, for language cannot supply sufficient reprimands and swear-words for this evil deed. Take care, Mr. Aksakov, that in supporting, for your own important political reasons, this unleashing of blood and brutal measures of such refined artistry, you have accumulated, instead of aid for the Bosnyaks, Croats, and Dalmatians, terrible remorse. You felt badly for us in *The Day*[1] and we feel badly for you in *The Bell*.

Note

Source: "Oni sovsem soshli s uma," *Kolokol*, l. 179, February 15, 1864; 18:49–50, 548–49.

  1. Ivan Aksakov said that he regretted that Herzen was friends with Bakunin, who had betrayed the Russian people through his support for the 1863 Polish uprising. While he had never respected Bakunin, from Herzen he still hoped for repentance.

→ **64** ←

The Bell, No. 186, June 15, 1864. This essay, full of respect and concern for a famous prisoner of the tsar, was reprinted in French soon after it appeared in *The Bell*. Ironically, during his trial Chernyshevsky had used the fact of Herzen's previous attacks on him in "VERY DANGEROUS!!!" (Doc. 22) and other essays as proof of the distance and mutual dislike between the two men (*Let* 3:283). The sentence handed down by the State Senate was published on May 9, 1864, in *The St. Petersburg Gazette*, and on May 18 *The Stock Market Gazette* announced that the "civil execution" would take place the following day on Mytinskaya Square. Herzen had previously commented on the Chernyshevsky case; here he includes eyewitness accounts of the public spectacle favored by the Russian government. The lack of support shown Chernyshevsky by Russian liberals was a particular irritant. K. D. Kavelin had written Herzen on August 6, 1862, that he was not especially upset by the wave of arrests. "This is war, and one of them will win out over the other" (*Eto voina: kto kogo odoleet*). Kavelin saw each side as permitting itself any and all means to achieve its end. Chernyshevsky's propaganda had drawn a line between "young Russia" and a Russia that was "a little liberal, slightly bureaucratic, with a whiff of the serf owner" (Ivanova, *A. I. Gertsen*, 188), and that distinction became clearer as the 1860s progressed.

N. G. CHERNYSHEVSKY
[1864]

Chernyshevsky has been sentenced to *seven years of hard labor* and permanent exile.[1] May this boundless villainy fall like a curse upon the government, upon society, and upon the despicable, corrupt journalism that called for this persecution, and exaggerated the case for personal reasons. They schooled the government in the murder of prisoners of war in Poland, and the affirmation of sentences in Russia by preposterous ignoramuses in the Senate and the gray-haired villains of the State Council. [. . .]

The Invalid recently asked where was the *new Russia* to which Garibaldi had offered a toast.[2] Evidently, it is not entirely "beyond the Dnepr" as one victim falls after another... How can one reconcile the government's terrible executions, the terrible acts of retribution, and confidence in the restful serenity of its hack writers? What does the editor of *The Invalid* think about a government that, without any real danger, without any reason, shoots young officers, exiles Mikhailov, Obruchev, Martyanov, Krasovsky, Truvelier,[3] and twenty others, and finally condemns Chernyshevsky to hard labor.

And this is the reign that we greeted ten years ago!

Isk—r.

P.S. These lines had already been written when we read the following in a letter from an eyewitness to the civil execution: "Chernyshevsky had greatly changed, his pale face was swollen and bore the signs of scurvy. They made him kneel, broke the sword, *and displayed him for a quarter hour at the pillory.* A young woman threw a wreath into Chernyshevsky's carriage—and they arrested her. The well-known man of letters P. Yakushin shouted out to him 'Farewell!' and they arrested him. When Mikhailov and Obruchev were exiled, *they* were taken out at 4 in the morning, but now it is done in broad daylight!..."

We congratulate all the various Katkovs—they have triumphed over this enemy! Well, do they feel good about it?

You placed Chernyshevsky at the pillory for a quarter-hour[4]—how long will you, Russia, remain tied to it?

Damnation to you, damnation—and, if possible, vengeance!

Notes

Source: "N. G. Chernyshevskii," *Kolokol*, l. 186, June 15, 1864; 18:221–22, 578–79.

1. Chernyshevsky was first sentenced by the Senate to fourteen years of hard labor, which was confirmed by the State Council but cut in half by the tsar.

2. During a visit by Garibaldi and Mazzini to Herzen in London on April 17, 1864, the latter toasted a new, democratic Russia. The reactionary newspaper *The Russian Invalid* made fun of this new Russia that had been educated by Herzen, whom they characterized as "our émigré from beyond the Dnepr" (579).

3. These men were arrested for distributing radical literature and were sentenced to varying terms of hard labor and exile.

4. Herzen: "Will none of our Russian artists paint a picture of Chernyshevsky at the pillory? This denunciatory canvas will be an icon for future generations and will increase the exposure of the dim-witted scoundrels who have bound human thought to the criminals' pillory, making him a companion on the cross."

> ⟿ 65 ⟸

The Bell, No. 187, July 15, 1864. Herzen summarizes the evolution of the Russian liberal gentry. The radical émigré Nikolay Utin (1841–1883), a member of the first Land and Liberty group who continued his radical work abroad, wrote to Ogaryov that this was the kind of categorical statement that Herzen should continue to write after the move to Geneva and the transfer of other work to younger revolutionaries (*Let* 4:23).

———

VII Years
[1864]

Seven years ago, in July 1857, the first issue of *The Bell* appeared. Since that time we have often stopped to check our path against events, and have asked ourselves whether we are moving in the right direction and in the right way. Our goal, our fundamental beliefs were unaltered; our problem remained the same, but the means of solving it had to change. Whether a stream is small or large, its path depends not on itself, but on the general slopes and inclines of the land.

However, approaching the seventh anniversary, we were occupied with another question, namely, ought we in general *continue* or *to come to a halt* and await outbursts from the absurd forces of reaction?

Russia has clearly left the path on which it landed in 1855, and for the third year is rushing along with a series of crimes and absurdities toward a series of disasters, which may exhaust it, but for which, at any rate, it will pay.

The howl, the wail, the hissing sound of the person being executed—and of fierce patriotism—drown out all human speech. Educated Russia turned out to be much more barbarian than peasant Russia. Because of this barbarity, terrible deeds and terrible words became possible: executions in Poland, penal servitude in Russia [. . .] Chernyshevsky, placed in the pillory in broad daylight, and all the other savage acts of the government and society.

While this "addiction" to drinking blood continues, what is the point of our speech? Who is there for us to talk to, for whom would we write and publish?

If it were not so painful to be silent, we would have done it... To be silent means to turn away, to forget for a while, and that is beyond our strength. [. . .]

The past places obligations on us. We had sufficient opinions and daring to begin to speak... we continued amidst applause from above and below—

we had to have the courage to continue speaking while the drunks sobered up. We had to continue so that the last word of protest did not fall silent, so the pangs of conscience did not subside, so that it would not be doubly shameful afterward. [. . .]

And so our ringing will, as before, *summon the living* until they come or until we convince ourselves that they no longer exist.

When we began our propaganda we never expected that such a terrible time would come that we would have to say something like this—but did anyone expect it?

In 1855 and 1857 an awakening Russia lay before us. Its tombstone was removed and carried to the Peter Paul Fortress.[1] There were signs of the new age everywhere—in the government, in literature, in society, and in the people. Much of it was awkward, insincere, and vague, but everyone sensed that we had made a start, we had set off and would continue moving along. A mute nation became accustomed to speech, a nation of official secrecy got used to openness, a nation of serf slavery—to grumble about their chains. [. . .] The party of fools and the party of old men were in despair as serf owners pretended to be constitutional liberals...

In the second half of 1862, the wind shifted direction. The incomplete emancipation of the serfs had exhausted the strength of the government and society, and the machine put the brakes on and began moving backward.

We ask every public figure who appeared after the death of Nicholas [. . .] let them put hand on heart and say whether any of them foresaw the bloody filth into which Russia has been mired thanks to a coachman like Muravyov, and lackeys who urge him on, like Katkov?

Did they foresee that the death penalty would become for us an ordinary, everyday matter, that prisoners of war would be shot, that the wounded would be hung, and that on a single day as many as six people would be executed on the orders of a worthless general?

That for a secretly printed leaflet,[2] full of youthful dreams and theoretical utopias, honest, pure young people would be sent away for *hard labor* and permanent exile, irrespective of their talent and good name? [. . .]

That among us a literature of denunciations would develop, and that it would become the literature of the day, that the language of journalists would descend to the language of quarreling policemen, and that, when opening the newspaper, we would enter the lobby of the Third Department and the office of a police station? [. . .]

No one could have foreseen this. Horrors that made your heart bleed and took your breath away happened all the time under Nicholas. A downtrodden and cowardly society was silent, displayed no concern, lied to themselves about empathizing, but they did not applaud. Self-interested officials became cold executioners. Now, society applauds, and the executioners punish with enthusiasm, becoming virtuosos as they exceed their orders.

We cannot accustom ourselves to this terrible, bloody, disgraceful, inhuman, insolent Russia, to a literature of informers, to butchers in generals' epaulets, to policemen at university lecterns. [. . .]

...Why, Russia, why must your history, having already gone through terrible misfortunes and the dead of night, continue to travel along the drainpipes? Why didn't you, on the day after the emancipation, when, for the first time since your birth, you could have shown to the world, with a joyously raised head, what a golden fleece you had preserved while poor, while under the landowner's rod, the policeman's stick, and the tsarist whip— why did you allow yourself to be dragged into this ditch, into this cesspool? Be patient now, Russian people. [. . .] You alone will emerge from this in a pure state. Lacking the leisure time for thought, you are not guilty of the path chosen by them; you were forced to shave your heads, forced to take up a rifle, and you set off, obeying unthinkingly, to kill and steal out of hunger. Just do not boast about it—on the same basis, the sea is right in having drowned a ship and the wolf in having killed a traveler...

But you *non-people,* who support the current order of things, sons of the fatherland, the intelligentsia, civilization, sound interests, the *democratic* gentry, commanders and teachers... you do not deserve the fate of the prisoner, you really cannot manage anything and will remain as you are. [. . .]

What have you achieved after a century and a half of training, paid for with the sweat, hunger, and cold of an entire people, with the scars on their backs?.. And wasn't even that taught to you by Germans, academies, military schools, lycées, institutes, Smolny Monasteries, tutors, and governesses? Isn't it clear that the stable in your parents' home was a more eloquent teacher, and that the nature of a lackey-slaveholder is not so easily tucked behind a sash of French grammar? I offer my congratulations—your day has come, only it will be a very short one. You do not even understand that you went toward one room but wound up in another.[3] You don't know to whom you have given your hand—you never were very discriminating, just arrogant. [. . .] You will perish in the abyss that you are digging together with the police. [. . .]

And as for you, for goodness sake do not think that we pity you. Please, it is time for you to leave the stage, you have done what you were going to do. You did it reluctantly and for that you deserve no respect; you did it thinking only of yourself and for that deserve no thanks. You were that frivolous milieu, that transparent conduit, by means of which the light of Western science illuminated our ignorant life—the deed is done and life will advance without you. [. . .]

Why should you be pitied? Because Ivan the Terrible tortured you and you sang psalms to him? [. . .] Because your grandfathers in the time of Nicholas danced at his coronation, while their sons, in shackles, went on their way to penal servitude? *Because of those sons?*

For them, for our great guides, one could indeed forgive their predecessors a great deal.

But what can one say about their sons?

They had no real sons, but they did have adopted children, to whom they left a legacy. They bequeathed them the milieu in which would emerge and grow toward the light a *New Russia,* well fitted-out for the difficult journey, tempered by need, grief, and degradation, its life firmly bound to the people, to learning, and to science. It received only insults from above and mistrust from below. It inherited the great task of developing national life from its badly organized elements—with a mature way of thinking and the experience of foreigners. It had to save the Russian people from the emperor's autocracy and *from itself.* It possessed neither ancestral property nor ancestral memory, had little capital, and virtually no attachment to what currently exists. It is free of obligations and the chains of history. [. . .]

A milieu that is diverse and chaotic, a milieu for intellectual ferment and personal development, it is composed of everything on earth—of *raznochintsy,* and the children of priests, of gentry-proletarians, of urban and rural priests, of military-school cadets, students, teachers, and artists; infantrymen and the occasional child of a military family, clerks, young merchants, and stewards... in it there were examples and fragments of everything in Russia that was floating above the popular mixture. [. . .]

Blow after blow struck this milieu, and its head was smashed, but *its cause* was not damaged, it was less damaged than on December 14, and the plow went further and deeper. [. . .]

We want to write for this new milieu and add the words of distant pilgrims to what is taught them by Chernyshevsky from the heights of the tsarist pillory, to what underground voices from the imperial *storerooms* tell them, to what the tsarist fortress preaches day and night—our sacred dwelling place, our melancholy Peter and Paul Monastery on the Neva.

In the midst of the horrors that surround us, in the midst of the pain and degradation, we want to repeat again and again that *we are on their side,* that our spirit lives... and we no longer desire to correct the incorrigible, or cure the incurable, but to work with them on searching for the paths of Russian development, and the explanation of Russian questions.

June 1, 1864

Notes

Source: "VII let," *Kolokol*, l. 187, July 15, 1864; 18:238–45, 584–86.

1. In referring to the death of Nicholas I, who was buried in the cathedral in the fortress, Herzen uses an image from Matthew 28 of the stone removed from the tomb of Christ as a sign of the resurrection.

2. "To the Young Generation," by N. V. Shchelgunov and M. L. Mikhailov.

3. A paraphrase of a remark made by Sofya in act 1, scene 4 of Griboedov's *Woe from Wit*.

⇒ 66 ⇐

The Bell, No. 190, October 15, 1864. Herzen exposes the manipulations of both government officials and the writers who backed them with his satirical, punning subtitles. Katkov attacked Herzen in almost every issue of *The Moscow Gazette* for seeking the destruction of Russia. After completing this article, Herzen hoped to go to Nice to see the monument he had ordered for his wife's grave, but was prevented from doing so by the arrival there of the empress, Alexandra Fyodorovna (*Let* 4:40–41).

GOVERNMENT AGITATION AND JOURNALISTIC POLICE
[1864]

HERR KATOFF——LE GRAND

Had Katkov not been spattered with Muravyov and with blood, had poison from his ink not fallen on sentences for penal servitude, he would have been the most amusing fool of our times. His foolish side is completely serious, completely naive, and for that reason has such an irresistible effect on one's nerves.

A terrible professor, he abandoned the lectern, taking from his scholastic activity a teacher's tone, an oppressive pedantry, a pompous arrogance, and, with all this, set off to preach constitutional liberalism.[1] After the death of Nicholas, this was a novelty in the Russian press, and people began to read him. As soon as he realized this, he ceased writing, and began in a paternal way *to suggest* or in an imperious manner *to upbraid*. It was easy to guess that if some daring fellow did not take heed, the teacher would go to the authorities, i.e., with a denunciation, which is exactly what he did after the Petersburg fires.

That fire was the happiest day in Katkov's life. This is where his government career began. The government and society needed someone to blame for these fires, and Katkov accused his literary enemies. Such a brave man was a real treasure for the government.

The liberal publicist, promoted from the third or fourth rows to the very stage, began by throwing his liberalism, constitutionalism, worship of Europe, etc. overboard, and suddenly felt himself to be a frenzied patriot, a frenzied support of autocracy, and a terrorist, and started to preach Muravyov, Russification, and confiscation...

[. . .] And with this came the crude flattery of the former serf owners. [. . .] Katkov, a demagogue in his criticism of the Polish gentry, felt himself to be a hereditary grandee and became a defender of the Russian landowners against the rabble.

All of this taken together drove him mad. He began [. . .] to use "we" when speaking of the empire and posed as Godunov, having relinquished the throne. [. . .]

But fame has its drawbacks. Katkov's fame resounded throughout the world, everyone looked at him, everyone asked who was higher than the pyramids, eclipsing Alexander and illuminating Mikhail?[2] The Germans wrote brochures about him, Belgium published books about him ... his modesty suffered and our journalistic Saul took up his pen in a fury and wrote in issue No. 195 of *The Moscow Gazette*:

> We must at last inform our readers about a very interesting phenomenon that has arisen on the political landscape of Europe—that phenomenon is *us*. For a while we have been a subject of attention, study, and agitation, open and secret, a subject of correspondence and editorials in the foreign press, and finally, the subject of books. Remarkable legends have appeared about us in serious foreign journals; the European public has been informed, for example, that in far-off, frozen Russia a dragon has been born, whose name is Herr Katkoff, and that he sits in Moscow and from there devises his devastating raids, that an entire nation languishes under his iron yoke and tearfully prays for deliverance from this constriction and let a Saint George appear from beyond the seas to strike down this monster for the pleasure and exultation of the Russian people. Readers might think that we are joking; we solemnly assure them that such legends have appeared in foreign journals. [. . .]

Brilliant... Why didn't he send this inspired article to *The Bell*? No one has written anything more vicious about him than this and no one ever will.

Notes

Source: "Pravitel'stvennaia agitatsiia i zhurnal'naia politsiia," *Kolokol*, l. 190, October 15, 1864; 18:269–73, 598–99.

1. From 1845 to 1851 Mikhail Katkov was an adjunct professor of philosophy at Moscow University. In January 1856, Katkov began to publish *Russkii vestnik* (*The Russian Herald*), in which he printed a series of articles calling for the kind of broad self-government that existed in England.

2. The pyramid metaphor comes from Horace's poem "A Monument." Mikhail Nikolaevich was the tsar's brother and a prominent general.

⇥ 67 ⇤

The Bell, No. 193, January 1, 1865. Herzen wrote this on the eve of a gathering of younger émigrés in Geneva, as a public answer to their proposal to turn *The Bell* into an outlet for the radical Russian émigrés, which would fundamentally alter a role that Herzen had defined as "words, advice, analysis, denunciation of evil [*oblichenie*], and theory" (*Let* 4:68). Nikolay Utin had written to Herzen in July 1864, urging him to provide this crucial center for all the forces of change, which would prepare "missionaries" to carry out agitation amongst the people. For this to be effective, the publishing enterprise would have to move to Switzerland, where the majority of young revolutionaries were now located. Herzen had long been in favor of such a move, but did not agree with other suggestions in Utin's correspondence; a meeting was organized in Geneva to discuss these issues in late 1864. Even before Herzen's arrival, a platform had been drawn up which insisted that the program of *The Bell* must be clearly defined, and that it must no longer consist of a random assortment of articles, arranged according to the tastes of Herzen and Ogaryov. Herzen offered to transfer the press to Switzerland, to include work by younger expatriates in *The Bell*, and to provide them some financial support, but he insisted that the main work of propaganda could take place only in Russia itself. In addition, he was loathe to turn over what had been a very literary journal to people who did not read literature. In a January 4, 1865, letter to Ogaryov, Herzen said that he was terribly bored in this company where "no one is learning anything or reading anything" (Gertsen, *Sobranie sochinenii*, 28:9). While Ogaryov generally was more supportive of this group, he co-signed the article "1865" in solidarity with Herzen.

———

1865
[1865]

In view of the difficult events of the past two years, we have had to express our opinions on more than one occasion, and, as we embark on a new year, we consider it unnecessary to repeat our creed and our protest.[1]

We are continuing our path, and not embarking on another.

The Bell will remain what it has been—*an organ for the social development of Russia*. As before, it will be against everything that hinders that development, and for everything that furthers it.

It is hindered by: military-bureaucratic governance, class-based laws, the ruling clergy, the ignorance of educated people, contradictory ideas, and idolatry of the government to whom everything is sacrificed—the welfare of individuals and the masses, and one's mind and heart. All of this taken together does not smash those foundations, deeply embedded in the life of the people, on which our hope is based. They were not smashed by Tatars, by Germans, by Moscow, or by Petersburg, no matter how much development was hindered, no matter how much it was distorted, sullying the people with unnecessary blood and undeserved filth.

Against these dark forces, which rely on the ignorance of some and the self-interest of others, we will fight as we did before, and, even more than before, we will issue a call for assistance.

It is time to concentrate our thought and our strength, to clarify our goals and take stock of our means.

It is clear that propaganda is splitting in two. On the one hand, there are words, advice, analysis, denunciation, and theory; on the other hand, there is the formation of circles, the organization of communications, and internal and external relations. We will dedicate all our activity, and all our devotion to the first of these. The second cannot take place abroad. It is something we await in the *very near* future.

Note

Source: "1865," *Kolokol,* l. 193, January 1, 1865; 18:313, 607–9.

1. For "creed" Herzen uses the ecclesiastical term *simvol very*.

⇢ 68 ⇠

The Bell, No. 197, May 25, 1865, was the first issue published in Geneva, where the Free Press had moved from London. The letter below was written after the death in April of the heir to the throne, Nikolay Alexandrovich. By the time the presses were set up in Switzerland, the shocking news of Lincoln's assassination had also reached Herzen. The more radical Russian émigrés disapproved of any conciliatory gesture towards the imperial family, even though Ogaryov assured them it was not in any way an endorsement of the tsar and his current policies. The radicals were adamant about any future changes coming from below, making any direct address to the sovereign irrelevant. In his private correspondence, Herzen characterized the Romanov dynasty as having "come to nothing" (*Let* 4:121–22, 133–34). Alexander Nikitenko said in his diary that Herzen was

in a bad mood because he had not been able to rouse the people with his *Bell*, and that
the public letter was "the height of indecency" and not even very clever (*Let* 4:187).

————

A Letter to Emperor Alexander II
[1865]

Sovereign, fate has touched you inexorably, dreadfully. It has reminded you
in a formidable way that, despite the anointing, neither you nor your family
are exempt from the general law, but are subject to it. Twice it has taken
note of your family, once with the cutting edge of the scythe and once more
with its dull side—the death of your son and the strange rumors concerning his brother.[1]

To the limitless number of Polish families who have been subjected to
the deepest grief, having lost their sons, can be added one more family
in mourning—your family, Sovereign. Your family is more fortunate than
theirs, since no one will insult your grief. Among those of us who oppose
your power, not one heartless scoundrel can be found who would accompany your son's casket with insults, who would wish to rip the mourning
veils from his mother or sister, or who would remove the body and the
tombstone in the presence of the tearful parents... all things that Muravyov
has done and is still doing in Poland.

In the life of man there are moments of terrible solemnity, in which a
person awakens from his daily cares, stands at full height, shakes off the
dust, and is renewed. A believer does this with prayer, and a non-believer
with thought. These moments are rare and irretrievable. Woe to the person who lets them go absentmindedly and without a trace! You are living
in such a moment, Sovereign—seize it. Stop under the full weight of this
blow, with the fresh wound on your chest, and think—without the Senate
and the Synod, without ministers and the General Staff—think about what
has happened, and where you are heading.

If the death of your son cannot rouse you and wrench you from the spec-
tral environment in which your birth placed you, then what could possibly
arouse you? Only being deprived of the throne, i.e., with the emptiness and
melancholy leisure that inevitably accompanies a loss of this kind. However, such a late awakening might be good for you, but would be of no use *for
others*. And these others, when one is speaking of you, are *the entire Russian
people*. This is what compelled me to persist in writing to you once more.

My first letter to you was not written in vain.[2] An involuntary shout of
joy, torn from the depths of voluntary exile, had an effect on you. For a moment you forgot that by rank I had no right to speak with you.

The language of a free man was something new for you. In its sharp words you understood its sincerity and love for Russia—at that point you had not sent utopias off to hard labor, and were not tying human thought to a pillory. This was the honeymoon of your reign, and it concluded with the greatest act of your entire dynasty—*the emancipation of the serfs.*

The conquering Galilean, you were unable to make use of your victory. You didn't know how to stand firm on that height, on which the manifesto of February 19 had placed you. Your hesitancy was noticed, bad people surrounded you, and you were distracted... and you left your pedestal by the light of some sort of burning marketplace, placing your reliance on the secret police and an obviously corrupted journalism.[3] Believing the absurd slander, you took fright, not suspecting that this was just slander, even when your inquisition and inquisitors, working up a sweat for an entire year, with a breadth of resources and the irresponsibility enjoyed by the Russian police, did not come up with even one guilty person.

You were frightened by a couple of printed leaflets in which the unfettered word, after a silence of thirty years, evaded the censorship.[4] [. . .] You began a struggle with the younger generation—a struggle of brute power, bayonets, and prisons—against enthusiastic ideas and inspired words. Your predecessor fought children in Poland, and you will do battle in Russia with young people and adolescents, who have tried to convince you and your government that a new era has begun in Russia.

With the dying glow of this unfortunate fire even you turned pale, you became flustered, and you retreated to the background, and in your place a system familiar to us was set up—of repulsion and oppression, the arbitrary behavior of individuals and the unlawfulness of the courts—your father's system with the addition of rhetoric and blood.

Russian blood, first of all.

What a black day it was for Russia and what a great sin you took upon your soul when, under the influence of panicky fear and the slander of your minions, you allowed there to be *blood,* and, even worse, you vested your generals with the authority to shed it, as if you didn't know what kind of people they were.

Is it possible that you slept peacefully when first Anton Petrov, then Arngoldt, Slivitsky, et al., were felled by bullets. Is it possible that you didn't freeze in horror when they shot people in Nizhny on mere suspicion, and in Kiev for fighting and rude responses?[5] [. . .]

You cannot bring back the dead. Atone for your sin before the living, and, standing at your son's grave, renounce bloody reprisals. Give us back our pride in the fact that, in spite of our underdeveloped legal system, there was no death penalty, and an executioner ascended a scaffold, frightening everyone with his *unlawful* appearance, once or twice a century.

... Just think, how your situation has changed since you first sat on the throne. Then you had only to freely make a move, to lead, and you emancipated the serfs. Everyone expected something good, something fine from you—at that time you buried the past.... Now it is gloomy all around you, matters have gotten bogged down, there's no money, an entire region is getting beaten up, young people are being sent off to hard labor, the people's teachers are being sent off to hard labor, on fortress embankments they are hanging and shooting people, and you are burying your *future*.

Sovereign, the moment has come when you must decide on which path you will continue... Your son's gravestone stands as a road sign and a terrible reminder.

Decide now, do not await a second blow—by then it may be too late, and the blow may be too strong.

You can see clearly—and it would be difficult to hide—that the rusty and creaking old mechanism constructed by Peter in the German manner, and adjusted by the Germans for Russia, is no longer suitable. You can see that it is no longer possible to direct a population of seventy million as if it were a military division. The front will no longer remain "at attention." People are talking, thinking, dissatisfied, having guessed in the Crimea that the command structure is poor. [. . .] You lived through and endured all this—do you think that by replacing tax farming with excise duties, and the Assembly of the Land with district councils, you have met Russia's needs?

If you think this, it is because you do not know what Russia suffers from nor what it desires. And how would you know? The press is not free, and you do not read very much anyway. You see only servants who depend on you and tell lies in your presence! You punish free people who raise their voices. [. . .] There was a peasant who believed in you, seeing in you his "earthly tsar," an enraptured fanatic; he openly and passionately wrote you a letter in which he spoke of the people's needs. He wrote you from London and put himself into your hands, and you sent him to the mines.[6] With unparalleled ferocity you convicted the only remarkable publicist to have appeared in your time. Do you even know what Chernyshevsky wrote? What his point of view was? What was the danger, what was his crime? Can you answer this question on your own? You would not be able to understand anything from the absurd Senate records.

It is clear that louder and more powerful voices are needed to shout down the trumpets and drums that surround you, so that the words would reach beyond the horse-guards and the *"oprichniki,"* as they were recently called...[7] Why are you pushing away the truth, why are you deceiving yourself that you—against popular advice and free speech—can take Peter's little wooden boat from the rocks back out to a deep channel?

Do as you wish, shoot people or give them a medal, send them to hard labor or to a lucrative post, take the side of Muravyov and his Russian executioners, or the side of the Germans and their Baltic civilizers—you won't be able to preserve or revive autocracy in its Nicholaevan innocence and purity.

You are stronger than your predecessors, but you are stronger by virtue of the *emancipation*. Your union with the people should not distract you. In the wreaths woven of grain and rural flowers that village elders have brought you there are thorns and the seeds of plants that are dangerous to those in power. You drew close to them not in the name of a conservative idea, but in the name of a *revolutionary principle,* in the name of a democratic leveling of the gentry and the acknowledgment of the agrarian principle in the land allotment. The decrepit Petrine robes were strengthened with a lining made from Pugachev's kaftan.

Take a clear and simple look from the Mont Blanc on which fate has placed you, chasing away the flocks of jackdaws and ravens who have access to the court, and you will see that you won't go far by maneuvering between official government-issue progress and reactionary police. [. . .]

Wouldn't it be better and more valorous to resolve common issues with common strength and summon from all corners of Russia, from all levels of society, chosen people? Among them you will hear severe judgments and free speech, but it will be less dangerous than it was for your grandfather, surrounded by moats, walls, and the lances of the horse-guards in the servile silence of the Mikhailovsky Palace?[8]

Fate, in extending the cold hand of death to your family, has restrained you—take advantage of that. You intended to continue on the terrible path you have followed since the second half of 1862. From the funeral of your son, turn back to your previous path. Repentance is never easier and cleansing more complete than at the foot of a coffin of one dear to us. It is essential in order to prepare for great earthly tasks.

... But first of all stop the hand of the executioner, bring back the exiles and banish the illegal judges, to whom you entrusted the tsar's vengeance and illegal persecution.

Forgiveness is not needed for your innocent victims or the suffering martyrs. *It is necessary for you.* You cannot go forward in a humane way without an amnesty from them.

Sovereign, be worthy of it!

Iskander

Geneva, Boissière, May 2/April 20, 1865

Notes

Source: "Pis'mo k Imperatoru Aleksandru II," *Kolokol*, l. 197, May 25, 1865; 18:337–41, 622–23.

1. Nikolay Alexandrovich died on April 12, 1865, in Nice at age twenty-two from meningitis. His brother Alexander, who succeeded him as heir, was rumored to be of limited intelligence.

2. Dated March 10, 1855, on the occasion of Alexander II's ascension to the throne, and calling for a free press, and land and freedom for the Russian peasants. See Doc. 5.

3. A fire broke out in St. Petersburg's Apraksin Dvor on May 28, 1862, destroying hundreds of stalls in the flea market. This and other fires in 1862 were blamed on revolutionary youth.

4. A number of revolutionary pamphlets, including "Young Russia," were secretly printed and distributed in St. Petersburg between 1861 and 1863. (See Doc. 45)

5. Anton Petrov was shot in April 1861 for spreading word of a different emancipation document among peasants and leading an uprising in Bezdna; Arngoldt, Slivitsky, and Rostkovsky were executed in June 1862 for propaganda among soldiers; in August 1863 a military court in Nizhny condemned a man on suspicion of robbery; in Kiev a Jewish soldier was killed for ripping off an officer's shoulder straps in a fight, and for muttering curses instead of giving answers at his trial.

6. Petr Alexeevich Martyanov (1834–1865), the freed son of a serf, made Herzen's acquaintance in London while there on business matters; he expressed his utopian ideas to the tsar in 1862, a letter which was published in *The Bell*, and was arrested upon his return the following year and sentenced to hard labor and perpetual exile. Martyanov had also expounded on his theories in a pamphlet, "The People and the Government," which was published by the Free Russian Press. Herzen wrote about Martyanov in the January 1, 1864, issue (No. 176) of *The Bell*.

7. *Oprichniki*, a term that has come into English usage, referred originally to a special administrative elite set up by Ivan the Terrible and responsible for a reign of terror in sixteenth-century Russia. D. D. Golokhvastov, in a speech to the Moscow Noble Assembly in January 1865, used the word *oprichniki* to characterize the highest levels of Russian government officials.

8. Paul I was killed in his new palace on the night of March 12, 1801.

> ⇥ **69** ⇤

The Bell, No. 197, May 25, 1865. After the great success of *The Bell* between the years 1859 and 1862, increased police activity made it more difficult to send correspondence to London and to distribute the publication in Russia. Switzerland was a stopping-off point for Russians going to and from Italy and France and the residence of a growing number of expatriates. When the great reforms proved to be narrow and incomplete, Herzen turned his attention to finding ways to help the Russian masses voice their concerns. This issue also contained one of Herzen's occasional theoretical articles in the form of a "letter to a traveler." The addressee may have been Vasily

Bodisko (1826–1873), a cousin of Granovsky, who had worked in the Russian embassy in Washington.

———

To Our Readers
[1865]

We have moved our printing press to Switzerland, and from May 25 on, *The Bell* will be published in Geneva. Our move will not bring any internal changes to our publication. We stand on the same ground, more firmly than ever. We see no need in defining it and expressing our *profession de foi* on the occasion of this geographical move. The basis of our outlook has been known to you since the foundation of the first Russian free press in London. You knew them even before that, but know them even better from *The Bell*. For eight years it has been tolling one and the same thing; *the tasks* to which it summons you have changed, but the *religion and the spirit* have remained the same.

Now it is time to call people to a Council, an egalitarian assembly of the land. Our ringing will reach someone's ears and set people thinking about it. If we believed that it was fruitless, we would have just folded our arms.

Many of our ardent, secret wishes were made flesh and came true—and if it happened awkwardly and incompletely, it still happened.

Ten years ago serfdom stood firm, jealously guarded as the foundation of the empire. From Avacha[1] to Odessa the Russian people were beaten with a court and without one, in barracks and front hallways, in private homes and in barns. The slightest murmur, a word of indignation, or a sign of the cross made with two fingers, was punished more severely than theft or robbery... and we said to the heir of Nicholas when he ascended the throne: "Do away with serfdom, give land to the Russian peasant, free the word from censorship, the Russian's back from the stick, open the courtroom doors, and grant freedom of conscience."[2]

...We spoke these words and repeated them in various ways for years on end. And everything that we touched began to sway.

Serfdom collapsed and barely hung onto the land.

Corporal punishment was eliminated for those *judged guilty by a court,* and one would think that soon they will stop beating and whipping *the innocent.*[3]

The closed doors of the courts are opening, and judicial reform—of some sort—is a direct acknowledgment on the part of the government of the unsuitability of the previous harsh punishments.[4]

The censorship cracked and has remained as more of a permitted evil than a defensible necessity.[5]

The two-fingered sign of the cross is no longer punished as if it were murder, and the government has placed the Old Believers in a comparable position to prostitutes—they are not so much permitted as tolerated.[6]

We are not saying that our bell summoned these *initiatives*, but they were carried out *not without it*—it anticipated them, it called for them, and it was the first to loudly and repeatedly discuss them. What the bell's share was in the actual substance of events, how it was changed by them and how it also effected change—who can capture that, who can retrace and measure it, and to what purpose?

[. . .] The reforms carried out by the government are unsatisfactory. They are all unfinished, lack openness, are oblique, and all have the quality of a temporary deal, something *for the time being,* done offhandedly, faute de mieux.[7] Their real importance is as an *initiative* and an involuntary rejection of the existing state of affairs. But in all this, only the government spoke and acted while we listened and accepted it mutely, without even having the right to refuse. That the time has come for us to say our piece is so obvious, that the government itself constantly stops and listens (like the notorious police chief of Moscow)[8] *to the silence...* and if anyone takes it into his head to say something that rubs them the wrong way, he gets sentenced to a prison cell or hard labor. Such a doubly absurd situation must end, and the voice of the people must receive the rights of citizenship. For that reason an *Assembly of the Land* is Russia's most immediate and pressing need.

Along with this, there is a growing necessity for an explanation of the social, economic, civic, and judicial issues which are pressing their way forward in the contemporary movement of Russian thought and Russian life.

The assembly must not catch us off guard.

We would also like, as far as possible, to take part in this explanation of issues, and—while sticking to our previous critique of official plans and our exposé of official planners—to put forward the principles of a possible new system. This compels us to broaden the scope of our publication.

We no longer exclude either purely theoretical articles or historical monographs, as long as they have a direct correlation to our Russian social and civic development. If there are a lot of them, or they are too long for *The Bell,* we will once again start up *The Polestar.* Send us articles that you cannot publish in Russia even under the current situation of freedom of the press *with censorship.*[9]

And since we have already asked you for articles, we will mention in conclusion another requirement of ours. Despite all our efforts, despite all our editorials, we cannot make *The Bell* a living Russian organ *without cor-*

respondence from the regions. During there past two years there has been very little of this. We *are announcing this to you.* We do not have to plead for correspondence; open discussion abroad is your business as much as ours, and your conscience should decide for itself what must be done. There are no serious problems in delivering letters to us.

The next issue of *The Bell,* No. 198, will appear on June 15.

The price is *fifty centimes.* Booksellers outside of Russia have no right *to raise the price.*[10]

Notes

Source: "Nashim chitateliam," *Kolokol,* l. 197, May 25, 1865; 18:386–89, 637–40.

1. A river on the Kamchatka Peninsula in the Russian Far East.

2. This quote is a paraphrase of what Herzen wrote publicly to the tsar in 1855; see Doc. 5 in this collection.

3. Alexander II signed an order ending corporal punishment on April 17, 1863, but significant exceptions were made for peasants condemned by their local courts, for soldiers in disciplinary battalions, and repeat offenders in exile and at hard labor.

4. On November 20, 1864, the new judicial system was signed into law by Alexander II after two years of discussion.

5. "Temporary Rules on the Press" were published April 6, 1865, which were in effect until the Revolution of 1905. Preliminary censorship was waived for certain publications not intended for a mass readership, but since the penalties for anticipating incorrectly the reaction of the authorities were high, Herzen saw this as yet another unsatisfying reform.

6. Alexander lifted some restrictions in 1855, and in August 1864 an order was issued which allowed freedom in matters of faith for the "less harmful sects," setting up a commission, which worked very slowly. Herzen and Ogaryov cultivated the Old Believers as a source of anti-government sentiment, but were for the most part disappointed in the response.

7. For lack of a better alternative.

8. General Alexander L. Potapov (1818–1876), police chief of Moscow and then director of the Third Department.

9. Herzen: "Such works demand a lot of time and reference works, and not everyone can work for free. We invite those who wish to be paid for articles placed in *The Bell* or *The Polestar* to write to us on this subject."

10. Herzen lists the names and addresses of booksellers in fifteen European cities where issues of *The Bell* will be available.

÷ 70 ÷

The Bell, No. 200, July 15, 1865. Nikolay A. Serno-Solovyovich was one of the founders, along with his brother Alexander, of the first "Land and Liberty" group (1861–62), which "had sprung up so casually from the first network of correspondents and readers of *Kolokol* or the ideas preached by the *Sovremennik*" (Venturi, *Roots of Revolution,* 268, 278). He was arrested on July 7, 1862, the same day as Chernyshevsky. An agent of the Third Department had sent word from London that someone would be crossing the Russian border in July 1862 with letters from Herzen, Bakunin, and others; once the courier was seized, the police were able to arrest thirty-two people, fundamentally weakening Land and Liberty (Venturi, *Roots of Revolution,* 263). Herzen reacted painfully to the arrest, calling it a "wound on the heart" (Gertsen, *Sobranie sochinenii,* 18:644). Serno-Solovyovich was a key figure in the "Trial of the 32," and was admired for the dignified way he conducted himself. He said that while he loved his country, he would never be forced to act against his conscience, and saw no obligation to inform the government about his conversations abroad in 1860 with Herzen and others. Although his sentence was reduced from hard labor to exile, his health rapidly declined and he died in 1866. Alexander Serno-Solovyovich lived in exile abroad and wrote critical articles on the evolution of *The Bell*'s politics, and quoted another Russia radical to the effect that "Herzen's only use now would be to get himself killed on the barricades, but in any case he will never go near them" (Venturi, *Roots of Revolution,* 279).

THE SERNO-SOLOVYOVICH CASE
[1865]

One of the most noble and pure people in Russia, N. A. Serno-Solevyovich has been sent into permanent exile. "A wise government," said one member of the State Council, "would be better off trying to get such people on its side"—yes!.. *a wise government!*

We implore our friends to send us in extenso the Senate record for this case.[1] This sentence, with its colossal absurdity, its absence of any unity, and so carelessly done (there was no time to rewrite it properly!) abandons the judicial masks with which tsarist vengeance had covered itself. For almost *three years* people were held in prison cells, and at rare intervals there were rumors of the significance of the case. The herd in the Senate sentenced them to hard labor, then, seeing that they had exceeded all limits, stepped back.[2] What is the case about? It's about the fact that *there is no case.* [. . .] Serno-Solovyovich was acquainted with *the London propagandists,* read their publications, gave them to others to read, and met with *a judicial rarity of the first magnitude* (who did not become acquainted with them?)—the *unconvicted state criminal* Kelsiev, who is portrayed from afar as some sort of Tamerlane,[3] who shook up the Russian Empire...

[. . .] The guilt of Vetoshnikov, Vladimirov, and others who received lesser sentences is, obviously, less significant.[4] Here the sentence is distinguished by a remarkable casuistry. Serno-Solovyovich is being punished for the distribution *of foreign works their criminal content* (there isn't even the correct punctuation), while Vetoshnikov and Vladimirov only *for the distribution of criminal works* (without content?). This is followed by one bit of nonsense after another: Lyalin was sentenced for *suspicion* of correspondence with Bakunin. The English citizen *Arthur Bennie* was convicted of *not informing* the government of Kelsiev's arrival *in Petersburg*. [. . .] We do not know which treaty obliges English citizens to do such a favor for the Russian police, and we ask the Foreign Office to look into this question. The young lady *Marya Chelishchev* was accused of having in her possession forbidden publications and illustrations, and was kept *under arrest* for ten days. In the worst days of the fury of our unforgettable Saul,[5] there was nothing fouler than this. The failure to denounce—a criminal offense![6]

[. . .] The fate of Serno-Solovyovich and his comrades has been mitigated. The sentence was *deliberately* published following the burial of the heir, with whom he has so little in common. [. . .] They wanted the Sovereign in his distress to suspect that he had eased the lot of the condemned . [. . .] But in the lessening of the sentence of Serno-Solovyovich and the others *he took no part.* They were defended by one member of the State Council[7] who had been struck by the nobility, frankness, and strength of Serno-Solovyovich's responses; he looked into the case, and, surprised by its inquisitorial and, along with that, obtuse police characteristics, defended Serno-Solovyovich as best he could. [. . .]

There is nothing surprising in the fact that Serno-Solovyovich's responses impressed a decent man. Serno-Solovyovich belonged to those vessels who are chosen to provide a great example, those faces which are anointed ahead of time for martyrdom, who peacefully travel their path and clearly look enraged judges in the eye. Before such people power fails and that is why it is reluctant to raise its hand to them. Unlike the instructive example of Tiberius, one cannot defile them in prison in order to render them worthy of punishment. Such a person was Granovsky, and Nicholas left him alone. The merciful Alexander II, and Prince Orlov—who kissed Serno-Solovyovich on the lips[8]—are unable to make such distinctions.

Notes

Source: "Delo Serno-Solov'evicha," *Kolokol*, l. 200, July 15, 1865; 18:395–97, 644–47.

1. This statement is attributed to Prince Alexander A. Suvorov (1804–1882), who was close to the Decembrists in his youth. From 1861 to 1866 he was governor-general of St. Petersburg and a member of the State Council. Suvorov had met N. Serno-Solovyovich and was impressed by his charm and education.

2. The State Council followed the Senate's lead in softening the harsh sentence, although the civil execution was still carried out.

3. Tamerlane (1336–1405) was a Central Asian military leader who sought to restore the empire of Genghis Khan. Vasily I. Kelsiev (1835–1872), who emigrated in 1859, re-

turned to Russia illegally in March 1862 with Turkish citizenship papers and the goal of establishing links with Old Believers and distributing publications of the Free Russian Press. Expelled from Russia, he returned in 1867, saying that he repented of past acts.

4. Pavel A. Vetoshnikov was employed by a trading company and Nikolay M. Vladimirov worked for a Petersburg export firm; both were accused of transporting forbidden publications back to Russia and were exiled to Siberia.

5. Nicholas I.

6. In Stalinist Russia, beginning in the 1930s, this crime (*nedonositel'stvo*) was enshrined in law.

7. Nazimov, former governor of the Vilna, Grodno, Minsk, and Kovno provinces was removed for using insufficient force in putting down the Poles.

8. In 1858, Serno-Solovyovich, while serving as a clerk for the Main Committee on emancipation, approached the tsar with a letter revealing the deceit and red tape that was harming the preparations for the peasant reforms, and the alarming situation in the country. Alexander sent the note to Prince Orlov, chairman of the State Council, saying that Orlov should summon the young man, inform him that the tsar was not angry at his boldness, but thankful for his information. Orlov is said to have kissed the young man in the tsar's name.

⇁ 71 ⇼

The Bell, No. 200, July 15, 1865. This unsigned piece is attributed to Herzen because of the subject matter, in which he was deeply interested, and the style.

————

Russia Is Still Burning
[1865]

There are fires in twenty provinces! And all of them arson, according to *The Moscow Gazette*. But who is committing this arson? Is it possible that not once have the police ever gotten their hands on a *genuinely* guilty person, except for some holy fools and juveniles, from whom you could not get a sensible word? Isn't it time to sack such a police force, with all its special and general officers, and the civilian and military governors and governor-generals? If there are no arsonists or if they are a great rarity, then isn't it time to get rid of all the worthless journalistic alarmists, all those *moral poisoners* of public opinion?

Notes

Source: "Vse eshche gorit Rossiia," *Kolokol,* l. 200, July 15, 1865; 18:398, 647.

→ 72 ←

The Bell, No. 209, December 1, 1865 (Part I); No. 210, December 15, 1865 (Part II). Herzen wrote this essay in answer to criticism from radical democratic (young émigrés and Bakunin), "court liberal" (Chicherin), and conservative (M. P. Pogodin) circles. It covers not just 1865, but the line taken by *The Bell* during the past few years. To those on his left and right, Herzen declares his unchanged views on Russia's path toward liberation. He saw the period that began in 1862 as one of harsh reprisals, the corruption of Russian journalism, and the movement of a confused society to the right. Herzen defends his complex attitude toward Alexander II, and affirms his faith in the powerful legacy of the peasant commune. Bakunin was not satisfied with the tone of this document, noting that Herzen still felt sad about the decline of Russian liberalism and his disappointed hopes in the tsar. According to Bakunin, what was needed was an end to the commune and a popular uprising (*Let* 4:283).

———

As the Year Comes to an End
[1865]

I

We are surviving the year 1865, as we survived 1863 and 1864.

After delirium tremens lasting two years, the tedious period of recovery has come—slow, concealed, with continuing flashes of heat and the return of delirious episodes. A clear turning point, in which the old doctors believed, did not happen, but the attacks of rage have apparently weakened, and, taking everything into account, things are not getting worse.

For us, it's even demonstrably better.

Since last spring our ringing has again begun to reach Russia, has again begun to rouse some people and upset others. We are being scolded more often, more people are writing to us, and we have more and more correspondence and readers... And we are traveling along *our very same path* and have no intention at all of changing it, that is, the path itself—we do not answer for the tone and the coverage, because they depend on events and not on us, and we have said this many times.[1]

To travel one's own path under the circumstances under which we traveled for the past three years was difficult, and we would never say—given the prevailing confusion of ideas and passions, and the streams rushing in opposite directions—that *we were not from time to time carried to one side,* but we were not dislodged from the main line either by the frenzied abuse of independent or government-supported enemies, or by the advice of stubborn friends.

The Bell has remained what it was, has remained *itself;* it represented the same line of thought and did not represent any coterie. Abandoned by almost everyone, it did not rush either into the patriotic camp or toward the democratic alarmists. [. . .]

We know and see that our enemies followed a different road and took nine-tenths of our friends with them. What we do not know or see is whether the Russian reading public, the only people for whom we write, will follow them for very long. We were unable to follow our enemies along the path of bloody and crude patriotism; to the extent that this will cool down and resistance grow to *The Moscow Gazette* and Muravyov's actions, to that extent readers will return to us.

That personally strong people and lively talents, full of youthful freshness, not only can but should overtake us—we not only know this but rejoice in it, like any person who has cleared a path and takes pleasure when people walk further along it.[2] However, we do not know and seriously doubt that public opinion in Russia has outstripped our propaganda. [. . .]

Neither abstract thought, nor far-off ideals, nor logical severity, nor a sharp consistency, in and of themselves, will help the work of everyday propaganda, if they are unable to grasp close-range ideals, today's strivings, and the doubts of the masses. The town square and the club, the auditoriums and every sort of gathering differ from the closed circle of school friends, in that the former pay attention while the latter were engaged in study, or were supposed to be studying.

It wasn't easy to follow from afar the changing stream of opinions, especially from a public so young, unbridled, and only partly free. We trusted our instinct, and steered as best we could through the dark and stormy night between opposing beacons, even losing our ballast.

However, we do not blame ourselves for that. There is only so much coordination with the direction of society possible; any further and it becomes a *betrayal*. The sounds of *The Bell* were lost, and caused rage and indignation to the degree that the popularity of Muravyov and *The Moscow Gazette* grew. Muravyov *was cast aside, The Moscow Gazette* passed its apogee *and will likely begin to fade*, we have survived the worst period, and soon our prodigal children, with gray hair or without any hair at all, will once again appear when we ring out, back from the patriotic herd where they did not graze but were tended. [. . .]

We return now to our difficult path with precipices on either side. No ascetic monk in the wilderness was so persecuted, so tempted from the right and from the left sides.

This did not begin just yesterday. When CH attacked us in 1858 with his doctrinaire-administrative indictment, we already possessed several purple-red letters,[3] accusing us of moderation,[4] and there was a lot of abuse for socialism, Jacobinism, various kinds of disrespect, impertinence, etc.

Since that time, some people have consistently regarded us as anarchists, others—as pro-bureaucracy, [. . .]
some—as bloodthirsty terrorists,
others—as gradualist progressives,
some have said in horror: "They summon people to use axes and write appeals!"
others say while gnashing their teeth: "They do not call people to use axes and write not only to the emperor but to the empress as well."

We received two letters recently, one from an old friend and the other from an old enemy.[5] "You're exhausted," writes the friend, "you are perishing, you have run aground because you lack the courage to go full sail; you think that development should follow a peaceful path, but it will not follow a peaceful path; in this unhappy eleventh hour you still place your hopes in the government, but it can only do harm; you have stumbled on the Russian hut, which itself has stumbled and has stood for centuries in oriental immobility, with its insistence on the right to land; summon people, gather them together, issue a call, a great time is approaching, it is near..."

"You are drowning," writes the enemy, "in some kind of mud, and I pity you. At times a Promethean howl bursts forth from you, but all the same you sink further and further into your abyss. You should change the atmosphere and forget the past, revive and restore yourself, and acquire a different language. At present it is difficult for us Russians to read your speech, because *we do not hear a single kind word from you.* You do not encounter in our homeland *even the slightest positive trait,* as if Russians are some kind of nation of outcasts... Twenty-five million private serfs and twenty million owned by the government are receiving freedom and land. Members of the landowning class are enduring their privation with patience and calm, while free voices are heard in the councils, the landed assemblies, and in the press. The troops are unrecognizable. The clergy is undergoing a renewal... does none of this *find any response in the soul of one who truly loves* the fatherland? No, your *Bell* has cracked, you cannot spread good news, and it is a crime to spread bad tidings... Ring out the De Profundis and write an epilogue..."

In reading this, you so much want to sprinkle ash on your head and go off to the Solovetsky Monastery, and then hand yourself over to the worldly authorities. [. . .]

We were tormented by the knowledge that *a great transformation* was "so close, so possible,"[6] and was for no reason slipping out of our hands. We pursued the emperor, we grabbed at his coat, we stood in his path with *The Bell* hidden in our jacket (at that point he was still reading us), and pointed out to him briefly and boldly, pleading and growing irritated, that he was turning off the path. [. . .]

We felt sorry for him. We did not represent any systematic opposition, nor a demagogic, forced hatred; we were the first to greet him with a free Russian word when he ascended the throne, and, together with the old world's exiles and the leaders of European revolution, we wanted to drink to the liberator of the serfs, and we would certainly have done that, if the terrible news of April 10, 1861, from Warsaw had not filled our glasses and vessels with Polish blood.

We grew thoughtful over this blood and sadly asked ourselves: "In the end, who is he and where is he going?" Of course, the Polish question had become urgent, and they feared Poland. All the same, to tease them with promises and then shoot unarmed people... that is too much!

Suddenly there was a shot from a different direction—Anton Petrov fell, executed, on a pile of dead peasants...

Could a mistake or fear really lead to this?.. He was deceived—this was the slander of serf owners, their revenge.

There was another flash of lightning—Arngoldt, Slivitsky, Rostovsky... This was no longer a mistake, but a crime...

And so it went, one incident after another... the case of Mikhailov, Obruchev,[7] the students, the persecution of journals, the support for corrupt literature... No, none of this was a mistake, but some kind of absurd and immoral conspiracy.

"Yes, but what about 1862!"

"What really happened during that notorious 1793 on the Neva?[8] Four years have passed since then, and it is time for people who closed their eyes in fear to open them and blush. One would need all the nasty spite of a pedant laughed at by young people, all the vindictiveness of puffed-up mediocrity, raised by unfortunate events to the level of the police and the out-of-control prosecutor, to persuade anyone that the government and society were treading on an underground constructed by "Young Russia," and that two more days and a handful of students along with a couple of officers would proclaim—on Admiralty Square—a republic circumscribed by nihilism and Pugachevism.[9]

The government put on a frightened face—it wanted to be frightened. It had begun to be disturbed by free speech, it had toyed with liberalism but the joke had begun to wear off, and, seizing upon the fire, which had nothing to do with the secretly printed leaflet, organized a general investigation.

[. . .] No matter how closely we looked and scrutinized the situation, we did not see in the Russia of 1862 a single element that was sufficiently strong and mature, nor a single topic sufficiently elaborated and of general importance, that one could—in its name—amass power, and sufficient power, to throw down the gauntlet to the government. [. . .]

Of all the problems that had been raised, not a single one was elaborated or generalized or clarified in a way that would allow it to serve as a banner. A purely political question was not of interest. The question of peasant land allotment and the commune did not coincide with the exotic socialism in literature or with gentry liberalism—it went against both one and the other. The government was imperceptibly shaky, in the absence of any kind of firm attributes. [. . .] It attacked the younger generation and would have collapsed if not for the help of its most vicious, most legitimate, and ancient enemy—*a Polish insurrection.*

A Polish insurrection, relying on Europe, halted in an instant the intellectual ferment and the growth of forces eating away at the dilapidated organism of the Russian imperial government, and gave the government a rallying point and a justification.

The opinion of *The Bell* about Poland and the Polish question had been expressed in a series of letters (1859–1860), and we never changed it one iota: Poland is fully entitled to an independent state, and no person of good conscience can have any doubt of that. They can trample Poland, kill it, transport it to Siberia, and force it in to Europe—all that depends on force. [. . .]

But in recognizing Poland's right, the question remains whether the claim was made at the best time. We think and we thought that they could not have picked a worse moment. [. . .]

We knew the kind of beast that had roused and teased the Poles with its demonstrations and gunshots, and we trembled for them and for Russia and pleaded to the very end with them to stop. We told them that in Russia everything was in preparation and yet *nothing was prepared.* That the movement that they observed was sincere and deep, but far from being the "organization" they dreamed about, and we repeated a hundred times that Europe would not lift a finger to save them, and that all the sympathy and big talk was just an "exercise in style." We said that the participation by Russian officers was *negative* more than anything else—they didn't want to be executioners... We knew this and together with them we implored the government and Konstantin Nikolaevich to spare Russian blood and Russian honor, and not tempt officers to go against duty and conscience. That was what we said on the eve of the Belopolsky conference, and by the next day blood was flowing in the Kingdom of Poland. [. . .]

The trouble erupted at full strength... villages and small towns burned, soldiers looted and killed, their superiors looted and executed, the Poles began to seek revenge, the Russian people were roused with rumors of another 1812. Muravyov—hated by all Russia—went to Vilnius and society applauded his appointment. [. . .]

We protested, that is, we did everything that one person can do in the face of savage force, we added our voice so that in the future it would bear witness to the fact that such a perversion of public opinion and civic speech could not happen without resistance, without a weak, isolated, lost, but indelible veto.

There were moments when we wished to be silent, but neither the slander nor the constant repetition of these terrible crimes left us in peace. The insolence grew, and to submit to it was beyond our strength. [. . .]

And with all this it was absolutely impossible to keep silent. Along with the despair, another powerful voice stated loudly that our future would find its way out of this filth and blood.

II

[. . .] The vestiges of our servitude are shameful and striking, like the marks left by a birch rod, and like those marks, remain on the surface.

Neither the government, nor the gentry, nor the serfs, nor the clergy, nor the senate, nor the synod—no one in essence believes in the truth of their power or powerlessness. That is why everyone is afraid of everything. [. . .] And for all that, a printed leaflet from a secret press, a warehouse that unexpectedly goes up in flames horrifies them, and every young person who looks forward like a free human being, causes trepidations. They're afraid of Mikhailov, they're afraid of Chernyshevsky. Orlov-Davydov requests a constitution to ward off Buckle and Buntzen, while Bezobrazov publicly thanks Katkov for saving the fatherland and for trampling *The Bell*.[10]

The government, as if rejoicing at the Polish rebellion and the fires, from the end of 1862 on began to lay siege on all fronts and all issues... Since that time it continuously fusses, crushes, shouts, erects barriers, fights, kills, forces the people back with its chest and a horse's rear end, i.e., the secret police and *The Moscow Gazette*. Obviously no one gets in its way and nothing moves *backward*—it just keeps vacillating, going first to the right and then to the left.

If each step in this chaos were not covered in blood, accompanied by executions, prison, hard labor, then the spectacle that Russia now presents would have been performed with comedy and irony on a world-historical scale, which not a single divine or demonic comedy had ever achieved. It is a kind of Babylonian chaos, an orgy, a geological cataclysm applied to the strata of civic life. Everything is strange, massive, and confused. The government is violently wringing its hands, the liberal gentry is becoming a painful *obstruction* to any solution, and the only conservative element is agrarian communism—all of this mixture is under the observation of the police, who do not interfere in anything, but ask "who should be beaten?" and then beat them.

It's a terrible muddle.

Yes, gentlemen, and long may it live! Let us give thanks for the blind man's bluff that we are playing. In this chaos, in this ferment, in this lime pit, new forms will solidify, different foundations will crystallize, those which are close to our heart and which would have greater difficulty breaking through with fixed conceptions, established procedures, and the belief that a soldier by rights draws a line in the sand.

In the West, reactionaries have unity and meaning.

[. . .] It is clear that we cannot have any proper kind of reactionary movement, because there is no actual *necessity* for it... And as soon as reactionary activity is meaningless, then it must carry that meaningless character that it has among us. Accidental causes, accidental measures, whims, incomprehension, state power unrestrained by reason and not fearing accountability, Asian customs and a barracks upbringing, with no kind of plan and no kind of system. The main resistance always concentrated on the external, the word and not the deed. In half of the cases of persecution, the cowardice of an uneasy conscience and government touchiness are mixed in. The model of Petersburg measures remains the shaving of beards, the cutting off of hair, the return of an official document from an office because *it was not signed according to regulations.* Nicholas himself, who for thirty years defended Russia from any progress and any revolution, limited himself to the system's *façade,* not order, but *the appearance of order.* In exiling Polezhaev and Sokolovsky[11] for their bold verses, removing the words "liberty" and "civic spirit" from print, he let Belinsky, Granovsky, and Gogol slip through his fingers, putting the censor in jail for empty hints, not having noticed that literature from two directions rapidly drifted toward *socialism.*

Embarking once again on the path of resistance and reaction, the government of "emancipation and reform" demonstrated that it had not gotten any wiser.

It ruined a huge number of people, which would have horrified any Benkendorf or Dubelt[12]—that's that. The movement was not stopped, it was not even driven underground, like it was under Nicholas.

Meanwhile, the government had never been more powerful. Everything served its purpose—the good and the bad, Sevastopol and the Peace of Paris, the emancipation of the serfs and the Polish insurrection, Europe's empty threats and the long-awaited reforms. Literature had changed and the journals turned into observation towers for the Third Department, while university departments turned into sentry booths for the police, the gentry paralyzed themselves with nostalgia for serfdom, and the peasants continued to expect genuine freedom from the tsar.

The government, in the way that it was set up, could have produced *positive and negative miracles*. What did it actually do?

Constantly frightened and on its guard, it punished and continues to punish on the right and on the left, which governments never do when they feel the earth firmly beneath their feet. They executed Poles, having already defeated them with weapons. They executed arsonists, later announcing that the arson about which their literary spies had written so extensively didn't exist at all; they alluded to appeals, to letters that had been intercepted, to the reading of *The Bell*, and beat indiscriminately every person who stood out not according to the wishes of the authorities and *not in an acceptable way*. The peasant Martyanov returned from abroad with a poetic faith in the earthly tsar, and with trust that would have moved not just an anointed ruler but a painted African king—and Martyanov is grabbed, hit in the head with a club, and sent off to hard labor.

And at the same time other forces were growing alongside it, both far away and close by, and were outstripping the *official* power that lived in the Winter Palace. Even those forces that the Winter Palace had itself summoned, bought, trained, and rewarded, turned out to be serpents who had warmed themselves on its breast.

The government unleashed crude declarations of patriotism, stirred up popular hatred and religious intolerance with the libel in its journals, which summons the people to act as judges. Like 1812, before the occupation of Moscow by the French, when Count Rostopchin led Vereshchagin[13] out into the square and handed him over to the savage crowd, our *open*[14] government has been handing over its opponents to a pack of dirty hack writers, applying censorship to every justification and every defense. The popular assemblies, the open discussion of the land question, the declaration of their support for government officials and measures, the political banquets, demagogic toasts, and terrorist icons—everything was permitted. The wise statesmen rubbed their hands together and could not get over how they had "splendidly lit up" public opinion and how nasty were the bloodthirsty agents of the literary-police gang that they had unleashed. These profound psychologists with portfolios imagined that, having become accustomed to the groans of human beings and human blood, their creatures, like Krylov's mongrels, would howl and then quiet down, as soon as their masters whistled—but that did not happen.

Two and a half years had not gone by before the government—which had changed in a real sense—wanted to lasso its pack of hounds, but could not do it. One minister was badly bitten, and others found their undergarments in shreds. And not just the ministers, especially the *civilians!* Konstantin Nikolaevich himself was not spared. *The Moscow Gazette* even pestered him.[15] [. . .]

The government, dumbfounded, to this very day sees before it an unfamiliar power, which it wishes—because of changed circumstances—to banish, but which is not going anywhere... Why did it have to get mixed up in a family concert of unauthorized musicians?

The comic single combat of the minister of enlightenment with an official leaflet—published in opposition to him by one of the institutions under his jurisdiction—will pass away.[16] The vile state of public opinion—on which a vile newspaper relies—will also pass away, but *the realization of what a journal may do when public opinion is on its side, will remain.*

We see the same thing in another sphere, which is closer to the matter at hand.

The patriotic banquets have ceased, no one is singing to Muravyov any more either in person or by telegraph, no one is sending affectionate addresses to the sovereign, and the day when one will blush in recalling this excess of servility is not far off. But the custom of gatherings, with collective discussion and abasement, continues. The address by the Moscow nobility, in which they desire not only to *love* the sovereign, but to speak with him without witnesses, without guardians, and to speak precisely about the disgraceful behavior of bureaucrats, will become the foundation stone of constitutional agitation, which will engulf all Russia and in its turn will stir up another kind of agitation than that dreamed of by the Bezobrazovs and Davydov-Orlovs. If Alexander II, governed by the example of his father, had not silently crushed the Poles and silently sent off to hard labor his own people, the question would not have been raised so soon of establishing some control over the autocracy...

Ne réveillez pas le chat qui dort!..[17] Only unfortunately, to wake the cat or not does not depend on personal will as much as it might seem. And there is no fatalism in this, but simply embryogenesis, certain phases of organic development. Yesterday, the fruit was not ripe and the cat slept soundly, today it is riper... and the cat sleeps innocently, but to make things worse everyone keeps trying to wake it.

The thing is, *our pear is ripening* rapidly, and for that reason everyone is trying to rouse us—the emperor Alexander and "Young Russia," the Moscow nobility and the Petersburg nihilists, privileges and hard labor, fair weather and foul. It is time for us to be convinced of this and act according to our convictions.

We will certainly reach the place toward which we are traveling without compass or sextant, if our strength—new and unexpected—does not fail us; consciousness will light the way and prevent aimless wandering from one side to the other, steps taken backward in confusion, and crude errors. [. . .]

Notes

Source: "K kontsu goda," *Kolokol*, l. 209, December 1, 1865; 18:451–69, 673–76.

1. Herzen: "Whether a stream is small or large, its path depends not on itself, but on the general slopes and inclines of the land" (*The Bell*, 1864).

2. Herzen most likely has in mind the young revolutionary democrats, followers of Chernyshevsky.

3. Herzen uses the word *Cherv*, the Old Slavic name for the letter that begins the name of his frequent adversary, Boris N. Chicherin (1828–1904), a proponent of what Herzen called "administrative progress." *Cherv* also means "worm," and the word for "purple-red" is the similar-sounding *chervonnyi*.

4. *Modérantisme* is a term for the party program of moderate republicans during the French Revolution.

5. The friend is M. A. Bakunin; the enemy is M. P. Pogodin.

6. A paraphrase from *Eugene Onegin*, chap. 8.

7. Vladimir Obruchev (1836–1912), on the staff of *The Contemporary*, was arrested in 1861 for the distribution of the "Velikoruss" proclamation and sentenced to hard labor and Siberian exile. The other names mentioned here have appeared in previous documents in this collection.

8. Herzen compares the revolutionary dictatorship's terror of 1793 with the tsarist regime's repression of 1862.

9. The 1862 proclamation "Young Russia," with its calls for violence against the existing order, was seen by liberals and even some to the left of them as having gone too far by provoking a strong reaction by the government (Doc. 45).

10. Vladimir P. Orlov-Davydov (1809–1882) and Nikolay A. Bezobrazov (1816–1867) were leaders of the nobility in the Petersburg region. The work of Henry Buckle, the English historian, had been translated into Russian; Christian Buntzen was a Prussian official and the author of theological works. Bezobrazov, who advocated a noble assembly, praised Katkov more for his attacks on *The Bell* than for other services to Russia, a fact which convinced Herzen that *The Bell* was a force to be considered, and that the sound of *The Bell* would outlast that of Katkov's *Moscow Gazette*. Orlov-Davydov and Bezobrazov are discussed in "Corrections and Additions" ("Popravki i dopolneniia"), *The Bell*, No. 196, April 1, 1865 (Gertsen, *Sobranie sochinenii*, 18:327–31).

11. Polezhaev was arrested in 1826 for his student lampoons. The poet Vladimir I. Sokolovsky (1808–1839) was arrested in 1834 for his part in a group that sang "libelous" verses. Both were sent to the Caucasus. Herzen was also implicated in the Sokolovsky

case and imprisoned for the first time. Polezhaev and Sokolovsky are discussed in Herzen's memoirs.

12. Count Alexander Khr. Benkendorf (1783–1844) became head of the political police and the Third Department in 1826; Leonty V. Dubelt (1792–1862) was the head of the Third Department from 1839 to 1856.

13. Count Fyodor V. Rostopchin (1763–1826) was the governor-general in charge of Moscow in 1812; Mikhail N. Vereshchagin (1789–1812), a merchant's son and translator, was accused of treason and killed by a mob at the instigation of Rostopchin.

14. At the beginning of his reign, Alexander II had embraced the policy of *glasnost'* (openness), to which Herzen makes a sarcastic reference.

15. Grand Duke Konstantin Nikolaevich (1827–1892) was chair of the State Council from 1865 to 1881; Katkov spoke out against his liberalism.

16. Katkov's *Moscow Gazette* was published by Moscow University. Alexander Nikitenko recalls this episode in his memoirs.

17. Don't wake a sleeping cat!

→ 73 ←

OUR FUTURE PEERS AND OUR FORMER ANGLOMANIACS
[1865]

Le Nord[1] relates how a deputation from the English Club (we await with impatience to learn whether there will be a deputation from the Troitsky inn and the Krasny tavern) asked the governor-general of Moscow *to ban* Potekhin's play *A Cut-off Piece*, because it comes down hard on serf owners.[2] The governor-general refused, and rightly so, but the "imperial theater and the imperial actors got a dressing-down" from the ex-Anglomaniacs, who have paid for rights to *The Moscow Gazette*.[3]

It's just as well that Fonvizin[4] was able in good time to get his barnyard of wild landowners on the stage, and Gogol was able to publish his graveyard of *Dead Souls*... It is also fortunate that Turgenev, without going over to the *fathers*, narrated how when he was still a *son*, he used to go hunting. [. . .]

Notes

Source: "Nashi budushchie pery i nashi proshedshie anglomany," *Kolokol*, l. 209, December 1, 1865; 18:471, 677–78.

1. *Le Nord* was a political newspaper, published first in Brussels (1855–62, 1865–92) and Paris (1863–64, 1894–1907), and subsidized by the Russian government.

2. Alexey Potekhin's comedy was published in the October 1865 issue of *The Contemporary*. Nominated for the Uvarov literary prize, it was declared by Nikitenko to be subversive.

3. Mikhail Katkov and classics professor Pavel M. Leontiev (1822–1874) paid Moscow University for the right to run *The Moscow Gazette*. Katkov and Leontiev also edited *The Russian Herald* (*Russkii vestnik*), a monthly, that over its fifty-year run (1856–1906), moved between liberal, conservative, and reactionary profiles.

4. The plays of Denis I. Fonvizin (1745–1792) include *The Brigadier* and *The Minor*.

→ 74 ←

Nicholas the Orator
[1865]

In the August issue of *The Russian Herald* there is an article about "Events in the Province of Novgorod During the First Cholera Epidemic."[1] After a description of the unbelievably stupid and awkward measures taken by authorities in Novgorod province during the cholera epidemic of 1830, and several episodes from the sad account of old Russian *revenge* by military settlers in 1831,[2] the author, a witness to these events, includes *a short, but eloquent* speech given by Nicholas to the assembled settlers. The speech was such a chef d'oeuvre that we cannot refuse ourselves the pleasure of relating it in full. This is the real Nicholas, sincere, naive, natural, just as his mother bore him and the riding school raised him. "What are you doing, you fools? Where did you get the idea that you were being poisoned? This is God's punishment. On your knees, blockheads! Pray to God! *I'll show you!*" What sort of matchless line from Corneille is this "*I'll show you!*"

The artless eyewitness adds: "The military settlers were tried by a military court and all received worthy retribution for their deeds," however, he forgets that before the retribution they had received the tsar's forgiveness, *but after their amnesty* the guilty were forced to run the gauntlet.

We did not think that the *Russian Herald* would be the one to throw this heavy stone at the grave of Nicholas... *On n'est trahi que par les siens!*[3]

Notes

Source: "Nikolai kak orator," *Kolokol*, l. 209, December 1, 1865; 18:472, 678.

1. The reference is to an article by staff writer G. F. Sokolov, who identifies himself as an eyewitness. Herzen's version of the title is essentially, if not completely, correct.

2. Military settlements existed in Russia between 1810 and 1857. They brought married soldiers and their families together with state peasants in newly constructed villages, so that the soldiers, when free, could help with farm work and the peasants could

help relieve the government of costs associated with the military. The misuse of power by officers and commanders and the difficulty of fulfilling both military and agricultural needs led to uprisings, low military readiness, and high costs.

3. One is only betrayed by one's friends.

⇥ 75 ⇤

The Bell, No. 210, December 15, 1865. This is Herzen's response to the government's repression of literature and journalism in November 1865, only two months after the introduction of new regulations on periodicals, which freed them from pre-publication censorship. The main target of the government's actions was *The Contemporary*.

———

THE FIRST BAN, THE FIRST WARNING, THE FIRST TRIAL! [1865]

I. The Ban on Potekhin's Play

A Cut-off Piece has been banned all the same! Long live the *English Club*![1] What a thoroughly dissolute government—there is neither self-control nor unity. It is like the drunken sailor whom Suvorov made to walk "the plank," but who, in his zeal, *walked two of them.*

II. The First Warning

Instructions from the Minister of the Interior, November 10, 1865.

Taking into consideration:

that in the article "Modern Times," placed in the August issue of *The Contemporary*, especially on pp. 376, 383–4, *the principle of the marital union* is offended;[2]

that in the article "Notes of a Contemporary," appearing in the same issue, especially on pp. 308–21, there is an indirect negation of the principle of private property as applied to capitalists, who supposedly unfairly appropriate for themselves the savings of the working class;

that in an article of the same name in the September issue of the same journal, in the section entitled "How Can One Measure the Approximate Debt of the Civilized Classes to the People?", especially on pp. 93–5, the principle of private property is directly subjected to dispute and negation, and

that in the same article, especially on pp. 97, 98, 103–12, there is a stirring-up of enmity toward the upper classes, particularly property owners, who, by the very principle of their existence, are immoral and harmful to the popular well-being,

the minister of the interior, on the basis of articles 29, 31, and 33, approved of at the highest level on the 6th of April of the current year by the State Council, and in accordance with the conclusion of the Council of the main department on publishing issues has determined: to announce a *first* warning to the journal *The Contemporary*, in the person of its publisher-editor Nikolai Nekrasov, and member of the landowning class, and its editor Alexander Pypin, who holds a civil rank in the VII class.[3]

Finally we can see with our own eyes the game of "warnings," this *French disease* of an unfree *freedom* of the press. [. . .]

The Contemporary has been doomed for a long time. Two more of Valuev's "warnings" and the chronicle will be finished.[4] We can neither harm nor help him; the edge of his clothing didn't get tangled up in the wheel of the Petersburg machinery just now, and this is not the case of Potiphar's wife—you can't escape her with a piece of your robe.[5] On the day when Chernyshevsky was taken without any judicial basis, having been freed by the Senate from accusations made by the State Council, when he, completely innocent, was placed in the stocks and then sent into exile—without the government considering it necessary or even possible to tell its loyal subject what the case was about—on that day the fate of *The Contemporary* was decided. Valuev wanted to amuse himself with "warnings." It was a new toy, and a Parisian one at that, something liberal, legal, literal—but the end will be the same: *they* will decide the fate of *The Contemporary* without a trial.[6]

The cause for which the warning was issued is also quite remarkable.

The Russian minister of the interior is turning into the minister for a moribund civilization—that is the way the liberal *Kölnishche Zeitung* understood it. [. . .]

One can apply the *considérants*[7] for Valuev's warning not just to *The Contemporary* but to just about all of contemporary Russia. Many people avoided a ministerial dressing-down only because they published their article before the lifting of censorship.

If we had *freedom* of the press in 1861,[8] we would have undoubtedly read that the "minister of the interior,

Taking into consideration:

that in the 'Statutes,' printed separately and in the publication of the Editing Commission, there is an insult to the principles of the *serf agreement*, there is an indirect negation of private property as applied to landowners, as if they had unjustly appropriated the labor of serfs and peasants;

that in the same 'Statutes' the principle of land ownership is directly contested, and a careless distinction is made between *property and its utilization*—a distinction inevitably leading to enmity between property owners and users—

the minister of the interior, on the basis of article 29 et cetera, has decided to announce *the first* warning to the Editing Commission and the publisher of the 'Statutes' in the august person of our currently reigning sovereign, the emperor Alexander Nikolaevich." [. . .]

III. The First Trial[9]

On November 19 (December 1) in the St. Petersburg criminal court several cases were heard *publicly* "concerning crimes against the press laws. At first there was a report given *behind closed doors* about Blyummer,[10] who was handed over to the court for the publication abroad of the journals *Free Speech* and *The European*. Blyummer was under arrest and from the chambers was taken back to prison."

Following this gloomy and mysterious incident *behind closed doors, the doors opened,* but it was not the beneficiary *Bibikov,* "called to account for the publication of the book *Critical Studies,*" who walked through them. Despite the fact the Bibikov did not appear, the court took up a discussion of John Stuart Mill, Darwin, Fourier, and the rest.[11] "Two salient points" were discovered in Bibikov's book (according to *The St. P. Gazette*): first, that he sympathizes with Fourier's desire to equalize the rights of women and men; second, he does not sympathize with the petty bourgeois Krasnov, who kills (fortunately in Ostrovsky's comedy, and not in real life) his wife—the "report" would like to see in Bibikov particular sympathy for the murderous philistine. The "Report" sees in this Bibikov's desire to undermine the strength of the marital union, not realizing that the murder of a wife to a certain degree in fact does undermine that union's strength.

The family affairs of the Krasnovs caused the compilers of the "Report" to have doubts about Bibikov's conduct, and here we see a very successful and *purely Russian* addition to European laws on the press: instead of judging the book, the speakers went off to gossip with and interrogate Bibikov's friends, and even under oath to ask about his conduct. It turned out that Bibikov behaved like a "good citizen." And, in addition, *"during a search of Bibikov's apartment, nothing suspicious was found."* Excellent!

What was also wonderful was the reference to article 1356 in the Law Code, which begins with the words: *"If anyone in secret from the censorship or in some other fashion publishes something"*... but censorship has been lifted! "Whether there has been a decision or whether it has been put off until another session—*is unknown.*"[12]

Notes

Source: "Pervoe zapreshchenie, pervoe predosterezhenie, pervyi sud!" *Kolokol*, l. 210, December 15, 1865; 18:473–77, 678–80.

1. News of the ban was announced in *The St. Petersburg Gazette* on November 11, 1865, and the document below was published there the following day.

2. This was the translation of an article by M. Conway that originally appeared in the *Fortnightly Review* about social reform advocated and practiced by a community in New York.

3. Alexander N. Pypin (1833–1904), a cousin of Chernyshevsky, was coeditor with Nekrasov of *The Contemporary* from 1865 to 1866. After that he contributed to *The Herald of Europe* (*Vestnik Evropy*), and became a well-known literary historian and ethnographer, and a member of the St. Petersburg Academy of Sciences.

4. Herzen paraphrases a comment by the monk Pimen from the drama *Boris Godunov*.

5. This is a somewhat incorrect reference to the biblical story (in Genesis) of Joseph's escape from the advances of Potiphar's wife; the fact that his cloak was left behind is what condemned him to prison.

6. On December 4, 1865, a second warning was issued to the journal and punitive measures against it—closure—were already being discussed.

7. The motivation.

8. Herzen fantasizes about how the current post-publication censorship might have been applied to the manifesto announcing the emancipation of the serfs.

9. Description of the official investigation of Petr A. Bibikov's book *Critical Studies* appeared in *The St. Petersburg Gazette* on November 20, 1865. Using this material, Herzen offers his own ironic account. Bibikov (1832–1875) was a commentator on current affairs (*publitsist*) and a translator.

10. Leonid P. Blyummer (1840–1888), identified in the article as having a graduate degree, was a journalist who worked in Berlin, Brussels, and Dresden between 1861 and 1865.

11. Of the seven essays in Bibikov's book, three were deemed subject to prosecution: the essay on Fourier's teaching, on Mill's logic, and on Darwin's theory.

12. Bibikov was sentenced to seven days in the guardhouse.

→ 76 ←

The Bell, No. 211, January 1, 1866. The behavior of unrepentant serf owners serves as a continuing source of material for Herzen.

—•—

SERF OWNERS
[1866]

Wake up, sleeping beauty![1]

We do not know whether Russia will enter the New Year on its right or left leg; we think it is more likely to be on its *left* leg, but whatever happens, every step will be exceptionally interesting.

The dead, half-decayed, will leave their graves, not wishing to remain in the earth if it is to be turned over to the peasants.

The government foolishly lashes out at social theories, while serf owners stroll about with unfurled banners.

We have heard that just before death, scars from the whip show up on the prisoner, but we have never heard that they showed up on the executioners.

A year ago, Katkov himself, soiled with every kind of filth, having insolently smiled when he was called an "informer," rejected the accusation of serf ownership.

Now, completely to the contrary, an entire band of former slave owners openly weep over their lost serf rights. The 19th of February 1861 is remembered as a day of great misfortune, the way the French republicans remember the 2nd of December.[2] We do not doubt that they always had these feelings, but they were hiding them. What has untied their tongues?

Two years of terror, of tsarist demagogy, awash in blood and violence, two years of paid-for slander and official journalism.

This is the first fruit of that corruption of public opinion—so masterfully carried out by the government—of that bloodthirsty mood which the government's defenders had stirred up since the year 1862. These are the first laurels from the Polish victories, from the pillories in St. Petersburg, from the exiles, executions, torture...

The lack of ceremony with which serf owner reaction has appeared in our midst is rarely met with in history. Those who weep for the past ordinarily give it the appearance of a revered relic, a moral sense, and throw a cover over its disgraceful wounds and filthy nakedness. Nothing of the kind happened with our neo-serf owners: they regret their rights to the labor of others, and are angry at the obstacles in their way, as thieves are angry at the arm of the law that prevents them from stealing. In our time only one country achieved these Hercules columns of depravity of thought and word—these are the American southerners, who appeared in churches and journals to defend slavery. Birds of a feather flock together.

What calamities await Russia, if it can produce such poison and is not able to get rid of it? The rotten emaciation we inherited from entire generations who were born into the depravity of slaveholding ferments in our veins, deadening our heart, clouding our mind, and bringing sorrow for the loss of unjust gain to the point of a daring protest—as if mere passion for unearned profit could lead us out of our apathetic drowsiness and passive obedience.

The jubilee of the *Free* Economic Society afforded an occasion for our neo-serf owners. Everyone knows what this *Free* society really is, and anyone who does not know should read the account by V. Bezobrazov.[3] This is one of those unskillful bits of window dressing with which Catherine II deceived Europe, like the cardboard villages with which Potemkin deceived her. Empty, frivolous, and lifeless, it lasted a hundred years with the same usefulness as parrots and ravens that live as long. Knowing with whom they were dealing, the government allowed the hundred-year-old *free* society to gather from all corners of Russia rural proprietors,[4] to consult with them, and, if necessary, to make statements, i.e., the government gave them the right to organize a congress on the most important issue of national life and gave them the right of petition, which they had denied to the Moscow nobility.[5]

This conclave, this convention of rural masters, wanted to demonstrate that it was an active force, and it decided... what do you think?.. Guess!

Our dear drones, disguised as bees, decided to disturb the government. *On the passing of legal measures promoting the collapse of the rural commune.* The chairman of this division was himself ashamed, and he remarked to these utter slaves that these matters may be judged and debated, but that one does not request such arrangements from the government.[6]

Fortunately, there was a man in the auditorium who could not stand it and defended the commune. Mr. Panaev[7] concluded his speech (which the Petersburg newspapers were careless enough to relate briefly) by saying that it would be unjust to decide the question about finding ways to destroy the commune at a meeting of representatives of capital without any representations of labor present. "Mr. Panaev himself sees the commune as the best resolution to the question of the relationship of capital and labor— a great principle, found only in our midst. This principle is *the right of a*

person to land. 'The right to land is the same as the infamous *right to work!'*
noted Mr. Bushen."[8]

With this *hint* the matter was not concluded, but only begun, a bouquet
having been prepared by Mr. Skaryatin,[9] the editor of *The News:* "Boldly,
clearly and smugly he gave a long speech... in defense of serfdom. [. . .]
Serfdom was a great productive force, said Mr. Skaryatin, enumerating the
blessings of serfdom, which consist of the fact that the landowner kept an
eye on the peasant's work and helped him, encouraging the hard-working
peasants and reforming the careless ones. He concluded by saying that:
*'Everyone benefited from this order of things, and this entire order collapsed on
February 19, 1861.'* The commune could not take its place, and therefore—
given the proliferation of farm laborers—it made sense to dissolve it."

[. . .] What has happened to all the zealous, experienced friends and the
defenders of their younger brothers, of the commune, and of communal
landholding?..

Where is Ivan Aksakov?

Where is Yury Samarin?

Wouldn't it be better that in place of the *spiritual "Day"* to publish a
worldly "Day" and to do battle over our *right to the land* than to spend un-
bearably dull pages answering some sort of Father Martynov,[10] whose letters no one has or will read?

Wake up, Brutus! While you celebrated victory over the Poles and occupied yourself with the destruction of the Jesuits, look how the class of
Orthodox landowners has raised its ugly head.

Notes

Source: "Krepostniki," *Kolokol,* l. 211, January 1, 1866; 19:7–12, 365–67.

1. "Tu te réveilles, belle endormie!" This is the first line of a song by Charles Dufresny,
which Pushkin quotes in the fifth chapter of *Eugene Onegin.*

2. On the night of December 2, 1851, Louis Bonaparte, president of the French Republic, dissolved the Parliament and the State Council and arrested leaders of all opposition
parties.

3. The Free Economic Society was created in 1765, with the approval of Catherine II,
and lasted, except for a brief closure in 1900, until 1919, when the Bolsheviks finally
abolished it. Despite Herzen's disapproval, it is considered to have been a fairly liberal
group, interested in acquiring the best machinery from abroad for the improvement
of agriculture, and in stimulating new ideas about farm management and the peasantry through numerous essay contests on subjects of vital national interest. In the
months after the emancipation, the Free Economic Society organized a literacy committee. A survey of the society's first century of activity was prepared by A. I. Khodnev (not
Bezobrazov, as Herzen believed), and was published in *The Northern Post* in 1865 (nos.
237–239). For more on the Free Economic Society, see Bradley, *Voluntary Associations
in Tsarist Russia.*

4. The meeting dedicated to the centenary of the Free Economic Society was ceremonially opened on October 31, 1865, and went on for six days in the hall of the Petersburg Assembly of the Nobility.

5. On January 11, 1865, the Moscow nobility presented an "address" to Alexander II in which they asked permission to summon "a general assembly of chosen people from the Russian land to judge the needs common to the entire state." The text of this address and a report on meetings of the noble assembly was published in *The News* (*Vest'*) on January 14, which led to the newspaper being closed down for eight months, while its editor was taken to court.

6. Herzen makes use of an account of the fourth meeting day, which was published in the November 7, 1865, issue of *The St. Petersburg Gazette*. At this meeting the resolution by some members to get the authorities to weaken the peasant communes was proposed by a government statistician and editor, Artur B. Bushen, and opposed by professor of economics Ivan V. Vernadsky (the chair mentioned by Herzen). *The Bell* goes on to discuss speeches by others present that day.

7. Valerian A. Panaev (1824–1899) was a railway engineer, a commentator, and the author of a plan to free the serfs that was published in the 1858 collection *Voices from Russia*.

8. Herzen notes that he is citing *The St. Petersburg Gazette*.

9. Vladimir D. Skaryatin was an arch-conservative nobleman, one of whose family members had participated in the assassination of Paul I.

10. Ivan M. Martynov was a Russian emigrant and Jesuit whose letter published in the March 4, 1864, issue of *The Day* was an answer to an article criticizing the Jesuits. The answer by the prominent Slavophile writer Yury Samarin, as abstract as Martynov's, was spread over four issues and also published separately. Herzen's own published political criticisms of material in *The Day* remained unanswered.

> 77 <

The Bell, No. 212, January 15, 1866. Herzen's interest in the Decembrists dates back to 1825; the uprising was without doubt one of the most decisive influences in his life. He used the Free Russian Press to publish materials by and about the Decembrists, and the title *Polestar* was a tribute to the five martyrs. For all these reasons, to speak with a survivor was an exciting and deeply moving experience. After being released from exile in 1856, the Decembrist Sergey Volkonsky traveled abroad for his health, meeting with Herzen in Paris in late June–early July 1861. The two got along very well and met on several occasions, allowing Herzen to learn a great deal more about the Decembrists. He found Volkonsky an admirable and fascinating figure, an example of righteousness and resilience in a progressive cause; one witness to their meetings said that Herzen's affection for Volkonsky was that of a son (*Let* 3:224–26). Friends and family members of the last prince were not entirely happy with the tribute below, which they claimed was a "distorted view" of the old prince, who was highly unlikely to have revealed so much information in the presence of strangers. The Decembrist legacy was problematic for the prince's son, M. S. Volkonsky, a rising figure in government service in the 1860s, and for grandson S. M. Volkonsky, who in spring 1917 was horrified by the thought that Decembrist memoirs might wind up in a museum of the revolution (Eidel'man, *Svobodnoe slovo*, 390–91).

In *Natasha's Dance: A Cultural History of Russia*, Orlando Figes adds substantially (72–146) to the biographical details presented in the document below. Volkonsky's ancestors include the fourteenth-century prince Mikhail Chernigorsky, whose service to Muscovy against the Mongols led to his canonization. By Alexander I's reign, this ancient family was closer than any other to the tsar, with more than a few Volkonskys serving at court, including the young Sergey Grigorevich, who was awarded the right to enter the emperor's private apartments unannounced. He even spent time with the much younger Nikolay Pavlovich—the future Nicholas I—playing with toy soldiers. After more than fifty real-life battles, including Borodino, and the triumphal march to Paris and Vienna, Sergey Volkonsky returned to Russia convinced of two things: Russia could not realize its potential without civil rights, and the serfs had shown beyond any doubt the depth of their patriotism. As a member of the Union of Welfare, Volkonsky was asked to recruit Pushkin, a close friend of his wife's family, but refrained from doing so. Once he was convicted, his mother's influence at court spared him a death sentence, but he lost his title, rank, and battlefield medals, and was sent to hard labor and exile by the tsar he had entertained, and by chief of police Benkendorf, an old friend from school and service.

During three decades in Siberia, Volkonsky rejected aristocratic ways and embraced peasant life, including the commune, although it is said that he retained his impressive conversational skills in French. Released by Alexander II, Volkonsky found in European Russia servility, hypocrisy, and a lack of dignity, which he deplored in his memoirs. The tsar finally returned the general's war medals in 1864, and in 1903 his portrait found its place again among the Hermitage's heroes of 1812 at the request of his nephew, who was at that time the gallery's director. In Volkonsky, Herzen found a perfect hero.

Prince Sergey Grigorevich Volkonsky
[1866]

The great martyrs of the Nicholaevan era, our fathers in spirit and in freedom, the heroes of Russia's first awakening, participants in the great war of 1812 and the great protest of 1825, are going to their graves...

It is becoming empty...and petty without them...

Prince Sergey Grigorevich Volkonsky died the 28th of November (the 10th of December).

With pride and tender emotion we remember our meeting with the venerable old man in 1861. Speaking about it in *The Bell* (No. 186, 1864), we were afraid to name him.[1]

"... The venerable old man, the stately old man, eighty years old, with a long silver beard and white hair that fell to his shoulders, told me about those times, about *his people,* about Pestel, the solitary prison cell, hard labor, to which he was sent as a brilliant young man and from which he returned gray, old, still more brilliant, but from another world.

"I listened and listened to him, and when he had finished, I wanted to ask his blessing for life's journey, forgetting that it had already passed. [. . .] Between the gallows on the Kronverk rampart and the gallows in Poland and Lithuania, these milestones of the imperial highway, *three columns* had passed, relieving each other in the cold, dark twilight...soon their outlines fade and are lost in the distant blue sky." [. . .]

A remarkable group of people... Where did the 18th century get the creative force to bring forth giants everywhere and in everything, from the Niagara and Amazon rivers to the Volga and Don?.. What remarkable fighters they were, what personalities, what *people!*

We hasten to pass on to our readers the obituary of S. G. Volkonsky, sent to us by Prince P. V. Dolgorukov.[2]

AN OBITUARY

Prince Sergey Grigorevich Volkonsky was remarkable for the firmness of his convictions and the selflessness of his character. He was born in 1787, and everything smiled upon him from birth: wealth, nobility, connections—fate gave him everything: he was the son of a holder of the St. Andrew's cross and a lady-in-waiting; he was the grandson of Field Marshal Repnin, in whose house he was raised until the age of 14, i.e., until the death of his grandfather; at 24 he was a colonel and an aide-de-camp; at 26 he was promoted to major general and a few weeks later, in recognition of the Battle of Leipzig, he was awarded a ribbon of the Order of Anna... He sacrificed all of this to his convictions, to his burning desire to see his homeland free, and at the age of thirty-nine he set off for hard labor in the Nerchinsk mines... just when Volkonsky had intended to quit the service completely and travel, he was accepted into the secret society by Mik. Al. fon Vizin in the house of Count Kiselev, where Pestel read excerpts from his "Russian Justice." Pestel and other members of the society demanded that Volkonsky continue serving without fail, because there was the possibility that, due to his rank, he would receive a brigade and maybe even a division, and he could be useful to the society in case of an uprising.

The Emperor Alexander knew that Volkonsky was taking part in the schemes of the better part of contemporary youth; he commanded the first brigade of the 19th Infantry Division, and when the commander-in-chief, Prince Wittgenstein, asked the sovereign in 1823 about naming him a division commander, saying that Volkonsky had excellent preparation for the service, Alexander answered: "If only he confined his activities to the service he would long ago have commanded a division!" One day, on maneuvers, Alexander, having summoned Volkonsky to congratulate him on the excellent condition of the Azovsky and Dneprovsky regiments, said: "Prince, I advise you to occupy yourself with your brigade and not with government affairs; it will be more useful for the service and for you."[3]

When Alexander died and Maiborod's denunciation was found among his papers, Chernyshev was sent from Taganrog to Tulchin [Tulcea], where Wittgenstein's headquarters were located, to arrest Pestel and the others. Passing through Uman, where Volkonsky was located, Chernyshev met with him, and, from his words and several questions, guessed that things were in a bad state... He himself went to Tulchin and found that Pestel had already been arrested and taken from his regimental quarters to Tulchin. Kind Wittgenstein, having known Volkonsky since childhood, warned him of the fate that awaited him. "Be careful," said Wittgenstein, "don't get caught: Pestel is already under arrest and tomorrow we will send him to Petersburg; be careful that you don't get in trouble as well!" Countess Kiseleva, née Pototskaya, advised Volkonsky to flee abroad; she offered as a guide a Jew who was devoted to the Pototsky family, and who would undertake to accompany Volkonsky to Turkey, from where it would be easy for him to seek asylum in England. Volkonsky refused to flee, saying that he did not wish to abandon his comrades in time of danger. After dining with Wittgenstein, he went to the general on duty with the 2nd Army, Iv. Iv. Baikov, where Pestel was being held, and found Baikov and Pestel having tea. Taking advantage of a minute when Baikov had to go to the window in order to speak with a courier from Taganrog, Pestel hastened to tell Volkonsky that "even if they torture me, they will learn nothing; the only thing that could destroy us is my 'Russian Justice.' Yushnevsky knows where it is; save it, for God's sake!"[4]

Returning to Uman, Volkonsky took his wife, who was near her time, to her father, Nik. Nik. Raevsky, in the countryside, where she gave birth on January 2, 1826, to a son, Nikolay. On January 7 he left his wife with the Raevskys, having told her that he was instructed to go around to all the regiments; he ignored the advice of old Raevsky, who tried to convince him to flee abroad, and set off for Uman. On

the way, he encountered a faithful servant with the news that a special courier had arrived from Petersburg, that the prince's study had
been sealed up, and a guard placed at his house. Volkonsky continued his journey, arriving at his quarters in Uman late in the evening,
and the following morning was arrested by his division commander
Kornilov, the same person who, three weeks earlier, upon returning
from Petersburg, had said to him: "Ah! Sergey Grigorevich, I saw
the ministers and other such people there who are governing Russia:
what a country! one ass sits on top of another and urges on the other
asses!"

Taken by the courier to Petersburg, directly to the Winter Palace,
brought to the study of Nikolay Pavlovich, he had *extremely vulgar*
abuse and swearwords heaped on him by the most exalted mouth! He
was then taken to the Peter and Paul Fortress and imprisoned in the
Alekseevsky ravelin. Upon entering the building, on the left were the
rooms of the steward Lilienleker, a terrible bribe-taker, who fed those
incarcerated miserably; to the right the solitary cells began, of which
there were seventeen that round the entire ravelin, in the middle of
which was a small courtyard with stunted greenery, and here was
buried the false Tarakanova[5] (she died after giving birth in December
1775, and a made-up story was spread that she had drowned in a flood
that took place two years later). In the first cell on the right sat Ryleev;
next to him was Prince Yevgeny Obolensky; in the third corner cell
was a Greek named Sevenis, who had stolen a pearl from another
Greek, Zoya Pavlovich; Volkonsky was placed in the fourth cell;
next to him was Ivan Pushchin; further along—although Volkonsky couldn't recall the exact order—were Prince Trubetskoy, Pestel,
Sergey and Matvey Ivanovich Muravyov, Prince Odoevsky, Vilhelm
Kukhelbeker, Lunin, Prince Shchepin, Nikolay and Mikhail Alexandrovich Bestuzhevy, Panov, and Arbuzov.

At the interrogations Volkonsky behaved with great dignity.
Dibich, who, because of his passionate character was called the
"samovar-pasha," at one session had the indecency to call him a
traitor; the prince answered: "I was never a traitor to my fatherland,
which I wish only good, which I served not for financial considerations, not for rank, but from the duty owed by a citizen!" Volkonsky,
as we have said, commanded a brigade made up of the Azov and
Dnepr regiments; of the nine officers of the Azov Regiment and the
eight from the Dnepr who were brought into the plot by Volkonsky,
only one staff-captain from the Azov Regiment, Ivan Fedorovich
Fokht, was arrested and tried, and that as a result of his own care-

lessness; the remaining sixteen completely escaped the government investigation thanks to the firm self-control of Volkonsky at the interrogations.

One day, during a confrontation between Volkonsky and Pestel, Pavel Vasilevich Golenishchev-Kutuzov, who in his youth was among the assassins of Paul I, said to him: "I am amazed, gentlemen, that you could decide on such a terrible business as regicide?" Pestel answered: "I am amazed at the amazement of your excellency; you should know better than us that this wouldn't be the first time!" Kutuzov not only turned pale, but turned green as well, while Pestel, turning to the other members of the commission, said with a smile: "It has happened in Russia that people were awarded Andreevsky ribbons for this!"

Of the numerous members of the supreme criminal court only four were against capital punishment; Admiral Mordvinov, Infantry General Count Tolstoy, Lieutenant General Emmanuel, and Senator Kushnikov. As for Speransky, having taken part in the conspiracy, he agreed to everything and did not oppose capital punishment.[6]

Volkonsky was sent to the Nerchinsk mines, and you can read about the sojourn in this horrible place in the *Notes* of Pr. Yevgeny Obolensky. You can imagine what he endured at hard labor, where the officer in charge, Timofey Stepanovich Burnashov, once threatened to beat him and Prince Trubetskoy with a lash. He was joined by his wife, Princess Maria Nikolaevna, whom he had married at the beginning of 1825. The 17-year-old beauty did not want to marry a 38-year-old man; she yielded only to the advice and urging of her parents, but, once having married, throughout her entire life she behaved like a true heroine, earning the admiration of her contemporaries and posterity. Her parents did not want to let her go to Siberia; she went, having escaped their watchfulness, and left behind her baby son (who died soon after). Arriving in Irkutsk, she was overtaken by a courier bringing her a letter from Benkendorf, who, in the name of the sovereign, tried to convince her to return, which she refused to do. The Irkutsk authorities presented her with the regulations concerning wives of convicts, where it was said that the factory authority could use them for private jobs, and might force them to wash floors. She announced that she was ready for anything—she had come to be with her husband and never to part from him again. In August 1827, Volkonsky and his comrades were transferred from the Nerchinsk mines to a fortress especially built for them at the confluence of the Chita and Ingoda rivers (and where the city of Chita is now located), and where they found many Decembrists who had been brought from the Petersburg fortress. There were 75 people in all at Chita. They organized their household in common; it was decided that each one would contribute five hundred paper rubles annually; but, in order to relieve the burden of payment on poor comrades, Volkonsky, Trubetskoy, fon Vizin, and Nikita Muravyov each gave up to three thousand a year; Vadkovsky, Ivashev, Lunin, Svistunov, and several others also gave more than the assigned amount; the affluent ones pooled their resources together for books and journals for common use. In August 1830 they were all taken to the Petrovsky factory settlement, 400 versts[7] from Chita, and afterward, little by little, scattered about Siberia. In December 1834, Volkonsky's mother died, and on her deathbed she asked the sovereign to lighten her son's fate; he was allowed to live at Petrovsky as a settler and not a convict, i.e., live not in the fortress, but in his wife's house. In 1836 he was transferred to the settlement of Urikovskoe, 19 versts from Irkutsk. Several years later he was allowed to live in Irkutsk itself as a Urikovskoe settler, and he remained there until 1856. The Russian government, which knows how to execute, exile, and punish fiercely and incoherently, did not know how to forgive; they would not allow Volkonsky to live in Petersburg, and they only allowed him to spend time in Moscow because of the serious illness suffered by his in-law Molchanov. The years had taken their toll; Sergey Grigorevich had aged and he suffered from gout, but he was still in good spirits and took a lively part in everything happening around him; everything noble found an echo in him, and the years-long suffering did not diminish the limitless goodness in his heart, the distinctive feature of this attractive man, who in his venerable old age had preserved all the warmth of his exalted youthful feelings. In August 1863 he lost his wife, and this blow struck him inexpressibly. Since that time his health began to fail, he lost a leg, and, on November 28, 1865, at the age of 78, he quietly died in his daughter's arms in the village of Voronki, in Kozeletsk region of the Chernigov province.

Every true Russian, to whom the Winter Palace kind of servility is alien, will remember with tender emotion this man, who sacrificed all his earthly blessings to his convictions, and his desire to see his homeland free: wealth, reputation, even his own freedom! May he rest in peace, this noble, venerable victim of a vile autocracy, who out of love for his fatherland exchanged a general's epaulets for a convict's shackles...

Prince Petr Dolgorukov

Notes

Source: "Kniaz' Sergei Grigor'evich Volkonskii," *Kolokol,* l. 212, January 15, 1866; 19:16–21, 369–70.

1. What follows is an excerpt from a long series of "Letters to a Future Friend," four of which appeared in *The Bell* in 1864, and a fifth in 1866, and which marked a deepening rift between Herzen and the liberals.

2. Prince Petr V. Dolgorukov (1816–1868), a historian and commentator, emigrated in 1859, and from 1860 to 1864 published newspapers and journals in Leipzig, Paris, Brussels, and London.

3. Herzen mentions in a footnote that Volkonsky related much of this story to him as well, but asked that any published work attributed to him be delayed until after his death. Volkonsky's account of the three traitors—Boshnyak, Maiborod, and Shervood—was published earlier in the ninth issue of Herzen's journal *Listok* but as the notes of "a *deceased* Decembrist."

4. Herzen adds that Yushnevsky had given the document to two others, Kryukov and Zaykin, who shared quarters in Tulchin. Hearing of Pestel's arrest, they buried it in the ground in a neighboring village. During the investigation, Zaykin was tortured into a confession, and was taken from Petersburg to the site to retrieve it.

5. The liaison and possibly secret marriage between Empress Elizabeth and the Cossack turned count Alexey Razumovsky gave rise to legends about offspring. The first false Princess Tarakanova retired to a convent; the woman mentioned here is the second pretender, who was brought from Italy in 1775 by Count Orlov on orders of Catherine II and was imprisoned, dying soon afterward.

6. Speransky wrote a very liberal reform plan—a constitutional government based on a series of ascending dumas—for Alexander I in 1809, was dismissed on the eve of the 1812 campaign, made governor-general of Siberia in 1816, and asked by Nicholas I to codify all existing Russian laws. His role in 1826 was a loyalty test set by the new tsar, which he passed.

7. A *verst* is slightly longer than a kilometer.

→ 78 ←

The Bell, No. 214, February 15, 1866. The theme—harassment of progressive journalists—and the ironic tone are familiar, as are the government's misgivings about the zemstvos (institutions of local self-government), which were the products of its own reform program.

———

FROM PETERSBURG
[1866]

There was a speech in the committee of ministers about closing the zemstvos, in light of the fact that the zemstvo assemblies are seeking more and more to become independent of the administration, taking up issues that do not directly concern their mandate. Speeches are given that agitate people, and the development of these institutions is leading to a limitation of autocratic power.[1] The proposal to take repressive measures against the zemstvos came from Warsaw-Milyutin, as he is called, and the majority of ministers were on his side. Only Valuev defended the zemstvo institutions, and the matter ended in some sort of compromise.[2]

The bureaucrats were frightened by the first signs of a lively spirit in the zemstvo assemblies, and are conspiring in their departments against the zemstvos. They tremble over the financial support, the extraordinary sums, and the government quarters. They are frightened by the thought that maybe, one day, they will have to give an account of their actions not to the authorities, but to representatives of the people. With all their limitations, they understand that the present order of things will not remain forever and ever in Russia, that it will not always be in the grip of the limitless power of a spendthrift government and its thieving officials.

The bureaucrats will likely draw the government toward repressive measures, and in that case they will themselves call forth and prepare the soil for a violent revolution.

The publisher of *The Contemporary*, after two warnings, asked Valuev to place *The Contemporary* under censorship control once more.[3] Valuev refused, referring to the fact that to transfer *The Contemporary*, "that freedom-loving journal," back to the censorship would amount to directly admitting that the new, censorship-free situation for Russian journalism was worse than under the previous censorship. However, without fulfilling Nekrasov's request, Valuev reassured *The Contemporary* with the following advice: "Carry on your publication under the same conditions, and I *give my word* that I will not administer a third warning and will not close down the journal... as long as the editors of *The Contemporary* agree to present me with articles *for my preliminary examination*..."

The People's Chronicle will not be published.[4] At first, there was permission to launch this newspaper but its program was forbidden, and then Valuev asked for an approximate list of the contributors. The names of Antonovich, Eliseev, Zhukovsky,[5] and others were pointed out to him, after which Valuev politely answered that this was all fine, but upon the publication of the first issue of the newspaper it would receive its first warning, the second issue would bring a second warning, and so forth. "While I am minister," he added, "I will not help any *nihilistic dough* to rise" (Antonovich, Eliseev, Zhukovsky—nihilists!!!).

In *The Russian Gazette* someone writes from Korsun: "As a consequence of all the difficulties in cultivating grain with hired labor and a minimal profit—or none at all—the landowners each year have reduced the amount of tillage, and, obviously, receiving from it even less income, have sold for a pittance their redemption certificates, have gone through the money they received from that and as a result have reached such a state that they are left like fish on a sandbar. Finding themselves in such a hopeless position, many of the landowners have decided with their last kopeck to set up in business, primarily the sale of liquor. After a brief period, very little promise has come of these ventures; hardworking people, looking after themselves, and, most importantly, leaving behind their gentry ways, have succeeded; those who are used to looking at business condescendingly and to use others to pull their chestnuts out of the fire, have been utterly ruined. The same has happened to the small landowners. They went through their redemption money, there was no further income, and it became necessary to sell the final bits of land for a pittance and with their last kopeck to set up a tavern. Lots of these establishments have sprung up in our province, up to almost five thousand. Careful people who didn't knock the price down too much, didn't get mixed up in vodka, and conducted their affairs in an orderly way, were able to earn enough on which to live. But the majority of these petty merchants went down another path."

Aksakov's *The Day* will not be published. What does that mean? One wonders whether private circumstances could have caused the publisher to curtail the journal, which he advertised a month ago. Our Valuev is up to something. [. . .]

Wouldn't it be simpler to instruct Katkov to publish five or six journals in both capitals with different names and a single direction? [. . .]

Notes

Source: "Iz Peterburga," *Kolokol*, l. 214, February 15, 1866; 19:31–33, 374–76.

1. The new provisions for local government were announced January 1, 1864, and went into effect the following year. While the zemstvos had responsibilities on the local level—in such areas as schools, health care, and road maintenance—without any meaningful power, the provincial administrations were uncomfortable with even a limited amount of autonomy. The zemstvos lasted until 1917, when the Bolsheviks abolished them.

2. Minister of the Interior Valuev took part in the planning for the zemstvos from 1861 to 1863, which explains his position in 1866.

3. Rather than risk a third post-publication warning, which would shut them down.

4. In April 1865 *The People's Chronicle* was ordered to cease publication for five months, but when the time was up it was not allowed to begin again.

5. Maxim A. Antonovich (1835–1918), Grigory Z. Eliseev (1821–1891), and Yuli G. Zhukovsky (1822–1907) worked for several progressive journals.

→ **79** ←

The Bell, No. 217, April 1, 1866. A correspondent from Switzerland (V. D. Skaryatin) wrote in *The News* (*Vest'*) that, while remaining revolutionary, *The Bell* had adopted a more moderate tone. In reference to the article below, the same correspondent noted that the "family quarrel" between state and nobility was a source of great joy for the revolutionaries (*Let* 4:257).

1789
[1866]

Yet another step and we will see the Etats Généraux on the Neva.[1] We are moving directly toward 1789. We are not surprised—we talked about this from the very first issue of *The Bell*. For a long time we have assessed and understood the depth, the force, irresistibility of *the movement,* which arose after the Crimean War and the death of Nicholas. Sometimes this type of movement loses its way, sometimes it gets stuck in the mud, but it does not come to a stop, and it is certainly not stopped by police measures, acts of cruelty, and senseless banishment.

Petersburg despotism can only last by not noticing its own decrepitude, in the mute silence of slavery and the stagnation of all living forces. At the first oscillation, the Archimedes point slipped out of the government's hands, and they were left with only worn-out reins and a rusted brake... with every step the slope grows steeper and steeper... We do not know where we are headed, *but it cannot be stopped!*

...It seemed that the "heartfelt agreement" between the government and public opinion on the Polish question would swallow up *the movement*—not at all! *The movement* grew more powerful, and became convinced of the government's weakness and its own strength, it saw the government confused at the moment of danger and bloodthirsty from fear in the presence of people shouting. It saw the Winter Palace dependent on the two English clubs and ceased to respect it, and it saw the sovereign talking nonsense, weeping, wishing to stop, carried along against his will—and ceased to fear him. The man, who in the first moment of danger, called forth declarations of devotion, must accept another kind of declarations, as Prince Shcherbatov rightly noted in his speech.

The incident in the Petersburg noble assembly carries the significance of a historical event—a revolutionary, oppositional event, with the full flavor of '89 along with several original touches, as one might expect, with Suvorov, for example, who (according to *Le Nord*) with deep regret relayed the veto by "the executive branch," rushing to such a degree that he answered before the question had been officially asked, probably as a result of informing carried out by some sort of spy.[2]

Readers know the details better than we do; thanks to the modesty of the *free* Russian newspapers we haven't even read the four points proposed by Shcherbatov.[3] We await further correspondence. [. . .]

However, we do not consider it out of place to express our opinion of the new phase of the revolutionary movement.

We are not on the side of the nobility as a social class.

We are not on the side of the government in its Petrine form.

The government and the nobility have their own accounts to settle. Why did the former at the beginning try to win them over, giving them land and people? Why did it first make them a terror squad and courtiers, and then begin to take back from the children what had been illegally given to the fathers?

Why was the gentry so thick-headed when the government handed over the people to rob and beat, and became impatiently, feverishly liberal when *a portion of their gain began to be taken away?*

We will not involve ourselves in their family quarrel.

However, if we are not on the side of the nobility and not on the side of the government, then we are absolutely on the side of *the movement.*

Everything that can undermine and wash away the barracks and the government offices, everything that can carry into the general flow—and there dissolve—the bureaucracy and class monopolies, the military administration of civic affairs, the clerks who rob the treasury, the treasury which robs the people—all this we will accept with joy and delight, *no matter by whose hands it is accomplished.* Smash things, gentlemen, and smash each other most of all. With this smashing your lives and ours will disappear... Later on our children will settle accounts. Revolutions in general do not hand down an inheritance intact, but half-achieved ideals and newly opened horizons.

It's an odd thing—two fighters went at it, and victory depends on *a third:* with whomever he makes an alliance, that one will prevail, and this third fighter is the wordless people, the silent majority. It *still remains silent* and holds onto the land.

Only by bringing them into the movement, making their affair into a common affair, a popular affair for a landed assembly, rejecting monopolies, can the nobility have a serious talk with the government.

And the government can only undermine the oligarchic claims by confronting them with the popular majority, with the popular will, which insists and will insist on its right to land.

Notes

Source: "1789," *Kolokol*, l. 217, April 1, 1866; 19:46–48, 379–80.

1. The Etats Généraux were summoned May 5, 1789, on the eve of the French Revolution, to resolve the financial crisis which had arisen during the reign of Louis XVI, and became the National Assembly. Herzen ironically compared this to the meeting of the Petersburg Noble Assembly from February 27 to March 4, 1866. At the March 1 session, Grigory A. Shcherbatov (1819–1881), the leader of the nobility, spoke in favor of expanding the rights of the zemstvos and of permitting the zemstvo assemblies the right of petition. Shcherbatov's proposal passed by an overwhelming majority. On March 3, however, several members in the minority resolved to submit their own opinion, but the assembly turned them down, and the majority view was sent to the government. Five days later, it was reported in *The St. Petersburg Gazette* that the proposal had been rejected as incompatible with the zemstvo law.

2. Count Suvorov was the military governor-general of St. Petersburg from 1861 to 1866.

3. Shcherbatov's speech was not published and was only briefly mentioned in the newspapers.

⇥ **80** ⇤

The Bell, No. 219, May 1, 1866. Herzen reacts here to the first assassination attempt against Alexander II, as a member of the younger generation "answered accusations of 'nihilism' with a shot. [. . .] and *action* overtook *words*" (Ivanova, *A. I. Gertsen*, 189). Herzen states his objection to individual acts of terror and "surprises" as a way of changing history, which brings to mind the Marquis de Custine's comment on the suppressed history of palace coups: "The Russian government is an absolute monarchy moderated by assassination" (de Custine, *Letters from Russia*, 126). Herzen himself had once characterized Russian history since Peter the Great as a "criminal affair" (Doc. 18).

The labeling of Karakozov as a "fanatic" angered the younger generation of Russian radicals (Verhoeven, *The Odd Man Karakozov*). Herzen received anonymous letters from Polish émigrés with threats to publicly label Herzen a traitor for his negative attitude, while Mikhail Bakunin mourned the loss of *The Bell*'s influence and urged his old comrade in arms to change direction and show the nihilists "where to go and where to lead the people" (*Let* 4:264–65, 283). "Irkutsk and Petersburg" takes note of the absurd honors shown the declared "savior" of the tsar, the peasant Komissarov, who was fêted at banquets, and whose name and image appeared on everything from beer to candy and cigarettes, while the hero's wife used this instant fame to get discounts on her purchases (*Let* 4:66–84).

IRKUTSK AND PETERSBURG

(March 5 and April 4, 1866)

[1866]

We have no opportunity to even indirectly say something in favor of the ruling powers. The shot on April 4 was not to our liking. We expected from it calamity, and we were troubled by the responsibility that some fanatic took upon himself. In general we cannot stand surprises, whether at birthday celebrations or in the public square: the first kind never succeed, and the second kind are almost always harmful. It is only among wild and decrepit peoples that history changes through murders. Murders are useful only to those who gain by the dynastic change. Petersburg got used to the regular removal of anointed rulers, and forgot neither Ropscha nor the Mikhailov Palace.[1]

We do not require bullets... we are moving at full strength along the high road; there are many traps and a great deal of mud, but our hopes are even greater; on our legs are heavy stocks, but in our heart there are colossal claims that cannot be removed. It is impossible to stop us—we can only be turned off the high road onto another, from the path of orderly development to the path of a general uprising.

While we prepared to express this in other words, our speech gave way to the terrible news from Irkutsk: *Serno-Solovyovich* died March 5...

...*These* murderers do not miss their mark!

The most noble, pure, and honest Serno-Solovyovich—and they killed him...

The reproachful shade of Serno-Solovyovich passed before us in melancholy protest, the same kind of reminder as the news of the Warsaw killings of April 10, 1861, rushed by like a terrible memento and covered with mourning our celebration of the emancipation.

The last Marquis Poza,[2] he believed with his innocent young heart that *they* could be brought around, and he spoke to the sovereign in ordinary language, and he moved him—and then he died in Irkutsk, exhausted by torture and three years in solitary. For what? Read the senate minutes and you will throw up your hands.

Our enemies, sworn conservatives and members of the State Council, were struck by the valor, simplicity, and heroism of Serno-Solovyovich. He was so unsullied that *The Moscow Gazette* did not berate him or denounce him during the investigation, and made no insinuations that he was either an arsonist or a thief... This was one of the best, most youthful proclaimers of a new age in Russia... And he has been killed... "But they did not desire his death." What nonsense! Mikhailov died, Serno-Solovyovich died, Chernyshevsky is sick... What are the conditions in which they place robust young people, so that they cannot last five years? In this method of torturing one's enemies a little bit at a time, without any direct responsibility, there is such a depth of lies, cowardice, hypocrisy, or such criminal negligence, which any upright tyranny feels itself above, as a brigand feels superior to a simple thief.

Are the lives of these people *really not as* sacred for Russia, *really not as* protected as the life of the emperor, are they really not among *those,* who together with him took part in the awakening of Russia, in the peasant question, in hopes for the future?..

No, our voice is not needed in the cathedral choir of exultation, indignation, protestation, and demonstration. Let those awaiting a reward rejoice at the *hints* and weep over the *denunciations,* let the servile hypocrisy that is corrupting youth to the extent of sham idolatry, to the extent that engineering students order an icon, and Moscow students are herded to the Iberian Mother of God to attend a public prayer service[3]—let them take part in the concert. The sound of our voice will not be in harmony with them.

We cannot understand each other.

Here's an example.

An insane fanatic or an embittered person *from the nobility* takes a shot at the sovereign; the unusual presence of mind of a young peasant, his quick calculation and dexterity save the sovereign. And how do they reward him? *With elevation to the noble rank!* To equal the social position of the shooter? [. . .] put a ribbon across his shoulder, but over a peasant coat, give him a medal on a diamond chain, give him the largest diamond from the crown on a chain full of medals, give him a million rubles (metal, not paper, by the way), only let him remain *a peasant,* do not turn him into von-Komissarov.

Taking Komissarov out of his environment is an insult to the peasantry; putting a noble uniform on him makes him ridiculous and vulgar. What understanding does the sovereign have of the peasantry, if he thinks that a man who performs an act of heroism should be wrenched out of that swamp? [. . .]

We have no doubt that the April 4 assassination attempt has once again—along with sincere concern—stirred up all the servility of Russian society, all the police mania of self-proclaimed spies, journalist-informers, literary executioners, all the clumsy baseness of the half-educated horde, and all the ungovernable behavior of the bureaucrats as they try to gain favor by humbling themselves. And yet we cannot read without blushing at the shamelessness of their actions and expressions. [. . .]

We are absolutely convinced that this mania for police is one of the most severe forms of insanity and that psychiatrists pay too little attention to it. It stands to reason that this sickness develops not in normal people, but in specially prepared and capable organisms, consumed by envy, pride, self-absorption, a desire for power, awards, an important place, and revenge. All that is true, and once having destroyed everything human in a subject, there is no holding back the sickness. Suspiciousness, denunciation, slander become a necessity, a hunger, a thirst... When there is no one to denounce, the patient becomes sad, and he invents a Young Georgia, and a Young Armenia[4]... And suddenly *we are shot at*. Katkov cannot separate himself from a unified Russia, or from the sovereign—he is at once the sovereign and Komissarov. Saving Russia is a familiar matter for him. On the eve of the assassination attempt (April 3) he revealed that he bore the oil of the tsar's anointing, declaring that he did not intend to obey ministerial directives, that he would submit to no one but the sovereign, that he knew his Alexander Nikolaevich, and had no wish to know anyone else. The humble ministers put up with this, and wisely so... or else things wouldn't be so different than they were with Konstantin Nikolaevich and Skedo-Ferronti... who were really catching it with the assistance of Muravyov.[5] Having heard the bullet's whistle and having pushed aside the hand of the murderer, Katkov, still unshaven, rushes about on a short leash like a bulldog who isn't allowed to run free—he jumps about, yelps, and barks, trying to bite everyone.

Having received a telegram from Petersburg, here is what he writes: "Today at half past 4 in the afternoon, there was a shot... It is thought that this was a revolutionary emissary *in plain clothes*," and then "Not long ago the glow of fires illuminated the entire expanse of Russia; now there has been an attempt on the life of its sovereign. Will we now really be unable to find *the means to penetrate* the secret of this evil act and get to its roots?"

Who came up with this? And what is meant by an emissary *in plain clothes*? Do revolutionary emissaries really have their own uniforms, with braid and tabs, like the gendarmes? [. . .]

It would be impossible to confer an award more awkwardly than the sovereign has done with Komissarov. But even here his loyal subjects tried to compete and not without success. The oppositional Shcherbatov found that saving the tsar demonstrated serious economic ability, particularly in the area of "agriculture," and proposed him as a *member* of the Economic Soci-

ety.[6] With this they went on to make Komissarov a member of clubs, scholarly societies, assemblies, museums, lycées, and so on. Before you know it
the corporation of privileged Moscow midwives will elect him an honorary
mid-grandpa, and the society of spas will include him among the honorary
sick and force him to drink free Ems mineral water and every other type,
both sour and bitter... Why do you make such fools of yourselves? Have
some pity on the man who saved the sovereign's life.

Notes

Source: "Irkutsk i Peterburg," *Kolokol*, l. 219, May 1, 1866; 19:58–65, 381–84.

1. Peter III was killed in Ropscha, near Peterhof, in 1762; Paul I was assassinated in
the newly built Mikhailov Castle (*zamok*, not *dvorets*, as Herzen mistakenly calls it) in
1801. He also misstates the date of Serno-Solovyovich's death, which was February 14,
not March 5, 1866.

2. A character in Schiller's historical drama *Don Carlos* (1787).

3. Officers in the engineering corps asked the authorities if they could show their
gratitude for the tsar's safety by funding an "April 4, 1866" engineering scholarship,
and, along with engineering students, commissioning icons of the Savior and those
saints whose holy day falls on April 4.

4. A reference to the radical pamphlet "Young Russia," which circulated in 1862.

5. With the support of Muravyov the "Hangman," head of the investigative commission, Katkov increased the attacks in *The Moscow Gazette* against not just revolutionaries
but also Grand Duke Konstantin Nikolaevich and his liberal circle, and Skedo-Ferroti
(pseudonym of Baron Fedor I. Firks, 1812–1872) for his brochure about Poland.

6. Grigory A. Shcherbatov (1819–1881) was a leader of the Petersburg nobility from
1861 to 1864, and after that served as a representative of the Petersburg assembly of
rural landowners.

→ 81 ←

GENTRY BENEFACTORS

(Countess Orlova-Denisova, Baron Ikskul, Count Sheremetev)

[1866]

People have written to us from Russia about the following beneficial and
patriotic measures taken by various landowners to increase the well-being
of the peasants. In relating these facts, we leave their trustworthiness to the
conscience of our correspondent.

Countess Orlova-Denisova, at the time of apportioning the arable land with the peasants, took the best land for herself, and for her peasants in Kolomyagi (in which province?) assigned land consisting of moss and quagmire. In order to smooth this over, she won over several peasants, and, to the most important of them, who had influence on the others, she gave permission to open a shop.

Baron Ikskul has been trying for a long time to take away the homes of his former serfs in Gatobari, claiming that these houses belong to the manor: he owns a factory here. The residents had to literally move to a swamp. At first the case went in favor of the peasants, but then he managed the business very cleverly, and it went Ikskul's way. Now the case is being examined at the highest level.

Count Sheremetev had a very large number of house serfs.[1] Several of the house serfs had received land as a reward for their service. When the February 19 manifesto went into effect, the count began to take back the land that he had given to the house serfs on the basis that according to the manifesto land was not assigned to house serfs. Several families of house serfs from the famous Ostankino estate began a lawsuit; it has dragged on until now with doubtful prospects of success for the house serfs, since they have no documents verifying the gift. Several peasants of that same Sheremetev acquired land under serfdom in the name of the radiant landowner. When the emancipation's provisions went into effect, these lands were considered as part of the landowner's portion. That last operation has already been reported on in *The St. Petersburg Gazette.*

Note

Source: "Blagodetel'nye pomeshchiki," *Kolokol,* l. 219, May 1, 1866; 19:66–67, 384.

1. This case would seem especially egregious since the Sheremetevs were known to be one of the greatest landowning families in Russia.

→ 82 ←

The Bell, No. 220, May 15, 1866. Herzen offers additional comments on the attempted assassination. In his massive historical series *The Red Wheel,* Alexander Solzhenitsyn said of the abdication of March 1917 that it "happened almost instantaneously, but had been played out for 50 years, beginning with Karakozov's shot" (*Publitsistika* 1995, 481).

The News From Russia
[1866]

The news from Russia is endlessly sad.

The April 4 shot grows not by the day but by the hour, and by the hour into a *general calamity* which threatens to grow into more terrible and undeserved misfortunes for Russia.

The police fury has reached monstrous dimensions. Like a bone tossed to a savage pack of hounds, the shot once again stirred up the combatants and blew off the faint ash which was beginning to cover the smoldering fire; the dark forces raised their heads yet higher, and the frightened helmsman is steering Russia at full speed to such a terrible harbor that at the thought of it one's blood turns cold and the head grows dizzy.

The shot was insane, but what is the moral condition of a state when its fate can be altered by chance actions, which cannot be foreseen or prevented exactly because they are insane? We absolutely do not believe in a serious or vast conspiracy. [. . .] That kind of action could be the revenge of that which is passing away, or an act of personal despair, but it cannot be the establishment of something new... To whom would its success be useful? Perhaps to conservative landowners.

The shot was understood perfectly among the people. They turned it into a celebration. What kind of ovation, coronation, or anointing with holy oil could have done more to shore up the throne, to strengthen the sovereign's personal power than this shot, with the peasant's saving arm, with all the circumstances? If there and then the sovereign would have risen to his full height, in the fullness of his magnanimity... and would have turned the shooter over to an ordinary court, but an open one. He did not do that and could not do that—he is surrounded by a different kind of conspiracy, he is surrounded by a *secret Russian cabal*. A dark intrigue has turned this shot into a banner of destruction, the kind of banner that in ancient German illustrations we see in death's hand together with a scythe... Yes, this cabal will strike to the right and to the left, strike first of all its enemies, strike those who are freeing the word, strike independent thought, strike heads that proudly gaze forward, strike the people which it now flatters, and all this in the shadow of the banner proclaiming that *they* are saving the tsar, that *they* are avenging him. Woe to Russia if the tsar believes *completely* that this secret force is saving him. We will experience the most terrible Biron-Arakcheev era, we will experience the torture chamber sanctimony of new Magnitskys,[1] we will experience all the terrors of the secular inquisition of the Nicholaevan era but with all the improvements introduced with fake openness and a foul-mouthed police literature.

Under Nicholas they tormented and tortured people, threw them into solitary and sent them into exile silently. *There was no insult.* Now there is no punishment, no hard labor that can protect a person from the abuse and slander of the official howling dogs. Shameless, nasty, and base, they beat people lying on the ground, they insult corpses... for them there are no limits... once again it is our "riff-raff" put to the use of the police... From people they move on to ideas and institutions... and nothing can stand up to these *nihilists of conservatism*... Haven't we heard the cry raised against the education of the poor, against a too easy access to higher learning?.. Haven't we read the denunciations over the graves where the dead are buried, and over graves where they have buried the living?.. [2] Don't they lead shadows in chains from hard labor and the mines?.. They wish to judge history and tie it to the pillory, like they tied Chernyshevsky...

Notes

Source: "Novosti iz Rossii," *Kolokol*, l. 220, May 15, 1866; 19:69–70, 386–87.

1. Mikhail Magnitsky served under Alexander I.

2. This is a reference to a criticism of authorities in Tobolsk for a slackening of their vigilance toward Mikhailov, who was already dead by the time the accusatory materials were released by the Senate.

→ **83** ←

The Bell, No. 220, May 15, 1866. *The Moscow Gazette* was issued a warning on March 26, 1866, and Katkov paid a fine, but he preferred to cease publication rather than publish the warning as instructed, as a result of which a second warning was proposed. This decision was overturned by Minister of the Interior Valuev, who saw a need for the newspaper in the wake of Karakozov's act. However, once Katkov began to vigorously attack the committee on the press, Valuev agreed to second and third warnings, followed by suspension of the paper for two months. Before the assassin's identity was released, Katkov insisted that it had to be a Pole. Even after the name became public, the press insisted that "Karakozov" was not from a Russian family registered with the Saratov nobility, but a Tatar agent of exiled Russian revolutionaries, acting in concert with Poles. Some Petersburg newspapers muted their comments, fearing the final triumph of reactionary forces in Russia, which led Katkov to ask "Since when does liberal politics mean allowing the *terrorization* of society by evildoers aiming at the destruction of the state?" (Verhoeven, *The Odd Man Karakozov*, 45–47).

A Second Warning and a Second Godunov
[1866]

The chief directorate for press affairs has received a *second* warning from Katkov. With its head hanging down it awaits a third warning and then a dismissal. The thoroughly frightened Valuev, who became so eloquent that the "halls of the noble assembly" call him *"le prince de la parole,"*[1] hurried to propitiate the ruling editor with humility and disparagement—and with a praiseworthy meekness. But that is insufficient for their agent, and, if the repentant administration fails to strike itself in the chest and on the cheek because of its warning, he threatens to give up his regency. We foresee a great light, which will eclipse Komissarov. Noblemen, self-selected, will come from all corners of Russia on long-distance carriages and post-chaises to pay obeisance to the father-editor and autocrat... local police and gendarmes, agents of the secret police, priests, and opponents of reform will send telegrams... Russia will emerge exhausted by such addresses, as it was exhausted a few years back by jubilees. Katkov will refuse, like Boris Godunov, like Ioann in Alexandrovsk, and the nobility will pay his fine and bring him another inkwell[2]... The sovereign will be forgotten and Karakozov (a Tatar) will be executed[3]... Muravyov will soothe the heart of the editor-regent.

And it will be soothed, but on what conditions? They shouldn't stint on paying him for the second salvation of Russia: Konstantin Nikolaevich in retirement, all those connected to the warning in Siberia, the destruction of the entire Korsh family, Kraevsky to the gold mines in Kamchatka, *Skedo-Ferroti* to hard labor, the death penalty for three Poles of his choosing; finally, he should be mentioned during Orthodox services: "Let us pray for the savior of Russia's unity, the warrior-journalist and arch-strategist of Moscow and all Russia, the boyar Mikhail and his spouse."

If he holds out he will get it all... Fear is very gracious and generous.

And as a matter of fact, if he left *The Gazette*, what would happen to Russia, to whom would the tsar be abandoned, to Muravyov *alone?* Anyone would be terrified to be left in a room *alone with him*.

Notes

Source: "Vtoroe predosterezhenie i vtoroi Godunov," *Kolokol*, l. 220, May 15, 1866; 19:76–77, 389–90.

1. Herzen read an account of Valuev's speech at the April 10, 1866, gathering of the St. Petersburg Noble Assembly in the April 13 issue of *The News*. He comments that while the minister's speech was empty, unclear, and full of clichés, Valuev knew how to flatter the audience by speaking in a style familiar and dear to them from their nannies and servants.

2. "Ioann" refers to Ivan the Terrible, who removed his family to Alexandrovsk in 1564 to await a delegation of Muscovites begging him to return to Moscow and rule and punish treason as he saw fit. Katkov was presented with an inkwell by the Moscow Noble Assembly.

3. Herzen has noted before the absurdity of referring to Karakozov as a non-Russian, because his surname, like that of many prominent families, was of Tatar origin.

⇥ 84 ⇤

The Bell, No. 221, June 1, 1866. Over the years Herzen had written and published several letters to the tsar (in 1855, on the ascension to the throne; in 1857, in connection with a publication about the Decembrists; and 1865, on the death of the heir), as well as one to the empress in 1858, about the education of the future tsar. Here he includes quotations from the three previous letters. Herzen assumes that this will be his final letter to Alexander II, as the expectation of serious political reform from above had faded. He wrote to his son as the issue was going to press that the letter "will create a lot of noise in both camps," and mentioned that he had mailed this issue of *The Bell* directly to the tsar (*Let* 4:267). Bakunin objected to the inference that anything beneficial to the people could come from the government, and his misgivings were echoed by other radicals who believed that *The Bell* was too personal an enterprise and its political orientation determined too much by chance (*Let* 4:282, 356–57).

————

A LETTER TO EMPEROR ALEXANDER II
[1866]

Sovereign,

There was a time when you read *The Bell*—now you do not read it. Which of the eras was better, the era of liberation and light, or the one of confinement and darkness? Your conscience will tell you. But whether or not you read us, *you must read* this sheet.

You are surrounded by deceit, and there is no honest person who would dare to tell you the truth. Torture is being carried out near you, despite your order, and you do not know this. You are assured that the unfortunate fellow who shot at you was the instrument of a vast conspiracy, but *there was no conspiracy at all*, large or small; what they call a conspiracy is the aroused thought and untied tongue of Russia, its intellectual movement, your good name along with the emancipation of the serfs. You are led from one injustice to another, you will be led to destruction, if not in this life then in the future light of history. You will, in fact, be led to destruction by conspirators—the ones who surround you—not because that is what they wished, but because it is advantageous to them. They will sacrifice you the same way that they now sacrifice hundreds of innocent people of whose innocence they are aware, the way they sacrifice the honor of families, handing out prostitute tickets to honest women...[1]

That this cannot please you I am certain, and that is why I resolved to write to you. But this is not enough. Find out the truth *for yourself,* and carry out *your will,* as you did at the time of the emancipation.

For the fourth time I have set out along the path that you are traveling, and have stopped on it, in order to turn your attention not to myself but to you.

"People expect from you mildness and a human heart," I wrote when you ascended the throne. "You are exceptionally lucky!" "And they are still waiting—faith in you has been maintained," I added two and a half years later.

Seven years went by, and how much happened during those seven years! I was in the south of France when your son expired. The first news that I heard in Geneva was news of his death. I did not hold back, and, although cursed by many, picked up my pen and wrote you a third letter, in which I said: "Fate has touched you inexorably, dreadfully; in human life there are moments of terrible solemnity. You are at such a moment, so seize it. Stop under the full weight of this blow and think, only without the Senate and the Synod, without ministers and the General Staff, think about what has happened and where you are heading. Decide now, do not await a second blow."

You did not make up your mind. Fate touched you a second time—let them call me crazy and weak, but I am writing to you because it is so difficult for me to abandon the idea that you have been drawn by others to this historical sin, to this terrible injustice that is going on around you.

You cannot wish evil for Russia in return for its love for you. That would be unnatural. Stand up for it at full height, it is exhausted under the weight of slander and frightened by the secret court of law and by obvious arbitrariness.

In all likelihood this is my last letter to you, Sovereign. Read it. Only endless and agonizing grief about the destruction of youthful, fresh strength under the impure feet of profane old men, having grown mean with their bribes, dirty tricks, and intrigues—only this pain could make me stop you once more on the road and once more raise my voice.

Pay attention, Sovereign, pay attention to matters at hand. Russia has the right to ask that of you.

ISKANDER

Geneva, May 31, 1866

Note

Source: "Pis'mo k Imperatoru Aleksandru II," *Kolokol,* l. 221, June 1, 1866; 19:81–82, 392–93.

1. Muravyov did this to discourage radical young women from continuing to display distinctive hair styles and wear unconventional clothes (Verhoeven, *The Odd Man Karakozov,* 114–17).

→ **85** ←

The Bell, No. 221, June 1, 1866. The previous month Herzen had written an article on the atmosphere in Russia; however, as indicated below, he destroyed it when a letter full of fresh information arrived. He sent a French version of the article "From Petersburg" to his son for placement in other periodicals, so that the fact that Karakozov was not part of a conspiracy would become better known in Europe (*Let* 4:265). The case records were only made partially available to the public at the time, and some of the information from Herzen's correspondent appears to have been incorrect; Karakozov had received electro-therapy once in Botkin's St. Petersburg clinic in March 1866, but having experienced great discomfort, he chose not to undergo further treatment (Verhoeven, *The Odd Man Karakozov,* 141).

FROM PETERSBURG
[1866]

Finally, a letter from Petersburg. I relate its most important section:

> The most outrageous and groundless arrests continue. No matter what the cost, they wish to frighten the sovereign and convince him that his meekness and placid nature have allowed a plot to mature that now encompasses all Russia, and that decisive measures are required. The evil caused by the denunciatory journals is boundless. At first the whole of society was ready to believe that if not today then tomorrow an immense conspiracy will be revealed; everyone was ready to aid the police, and at the forefront were the *Guards officers.* The secrecy with which the case is being handled, after Muravyov's promise of openness, dampened the ardor of many, and they began to suspect some intrigue. But the deed is done and the push has been given... Trepov[1] expels everyone from the police who, according to his understanding, is incapable of maliciously persecuting all that is young and lively, and teachers are being expelled from schools if their

students behave in an unduly familiar manner during lessons. There are a huge number of spies here, many have been sent to Moscow and to the provinces and abroad, especially to Switzerland (*welcome!*). Muravyov has doubled their salaries.

Karakozov does not acknowledge himself to be Karakozov and does not recognize his cousin who acknowledged him. Muravyov demanded that Chernyshevsky be brought back from Siberia, *to which the tsar did not agree.* Among well-known people who have been arrested: *Blagosvetlov, Eliseev, Evropeus* with his wife and brother, *Kovalevsky, Sleptsov;* many young ladies and women have been arrested (nihilists). Among the latter several have been released and given *a yellow ticket, which is given to prostitutes.*

"Have signs of any society been uncovered?" Muravyov was asked by an acquaintance. There is no society, but there will be if the harmful tendencies are not destroyed. Muravyov searches for these tendencies everywhere, even abroad. He wishes to drag into the business of April 4/16 not only the unmaskers, negators, and nihilists found here, but also those who are abroad. It is said that an auditor at the medical academy, *Belsky* (or *Belgin*), a healthy, handsome young man, while under arrest became ill, and was sent to a secret section of the military hospital. Last Saturday, April 30 (May 12), at 9 in the morning, he hung himself in his cell. On the wall he had written: "On Muravyov's orders I was flogged."

They say that Karakozov has been tortured in many innovative ways. He answered firmly at the first session. At night the questioning began again and went on without a break for three days. They do not dare torture him by surgical means; *they claim that the sovereign had not ordered it,* and therefore they have resorted to new means *that do not leave a trace* and to science. At first they placed him in some kind of case, but Doctor *Edenkauer* said that he would either die or go completely out of his mind, and therefore the learned doctor advised them to replace the case with an electrical shock. (Edenkauer was elevated on April 16/28 to the rank of *privy* councillor!) The unfortunate patient became ill, stopped eating, and they say he is close to death. Many insist that he died May 2/14 (?). (What will Muravyov do, find a fresh Karakozov?)...

On the day the shot was fired, Countess Ridiger said to the empress that she had been hearing for some time there would be an attempt, that she had heard this from Pototsky and had told Annenkov, who did not believe it. Pototsky has been imprisoned and went out of his mind (this fact we read in *The Times*). Muravyov's party and *The*

Moscow Gazette are trying on the sly to cast suspicion on Konstantin Nikolaevich... Muravyov has already quarreled with Shuvalov.

P.S. The Kurochkins have been released.

In the presence of this letter we stopped in a kind of endless, burning pain... Here is where this reign of *liberation* has arrived, and it is not the tsar's fault (from the letter it is clear how he is struggling in the darkness which has been created around him), but *society*, which has turned into the police, and the immoral *press*, which has been society's informer and accuser under Muravyov.

It is an unfortunate nation, in which such an insolent and distorted environment could arise and mature, teaching, applauding, and stirring up the executioners with impunity!

"We have yet to mature," said someone in Petersburg, and everyone was angry with him. "*But have already decayed,*" we added, "*decayed terribly...*"

Our article was finished, but having read the letter, we tore it up—it was weak and poor, words failed us, and we felt it deeply!

But one cannot simply fold one's arms in idle bitterness, and one cannot simply remain silent with a curse on the lips! No, that would be a betrayal of our entire life, and there isn't much left of it. We will use what remains of it to expose to the world the historic crime taking place in Russia, and to sustain and comfort the unhappy younger generation, being martyred for its sacred love for truth and its youthful faith in Russia. We, the old men, stand at the bedside of those being persecuted, wiping away the stains of slander and blessing the lost prophets of a *future Russia*.

They will not torture it away, and Edenkauer will not cure it with his electric shock.

...But it is good that electricity was used. Science and the press, fulfilling the function of executioner and instrument of torture... Humanity cannot decline much further than this.

What, then, can one add? Perhaps the *yellow tickets* that were given to young ladies and women because they cut their hair and dreamed that it was better to live by their own labor than on someone else's account, and the journal that threw mud at them...

We were recently criticized that we laugh as we speak about the vileness and brutality now taking place in Russia.

Our laughter has not been understood.

Never mind; we will speak seriously, and, first, will pose a question about the origin of the vastly increased impatience in society that circles, like a wreath, the investigative factory, in which Muravyov weaves a nonexistent conspiracy? Whence this new frenzy against *nihilism*, by which is now meant every kind of free, independent thought, every kind of learning that does not resemble the preaching of the neo-serf owners?

Can it simply be out of love for Alexander Nikolaevich, who freed the majority of the most furious unmaskers from half their income?[2] They are not that sentimental: here the roots go much deeper.

...Two years ago, for the first time at the summit of the nobility in Russia, a demand appeared for mature institutions, and a wish was expressed for civic freedom and private control of one's affairs. That took place in Moscow—what could be better?

But here's what is not so good. The *first* word spoken by the Moscow assembly of the nobility was hostile to the independent press, and, following the expression of gratitude to the journalist-denouncer there was the feeble speech of Orlov-Davydov,[3] who demanded limitations to autocracy and to *book-publishing* (among us!), cursing the arbitrariness of bureaucrats and the translation of Buckle...

An environment that cannot bear free speech has chemically combined with inquisitors and executioners. As for Karakozov—or whatever he is called, the matter is not about him and he was immediately pushed into the background—with denunciations in their journals and blame for the assassination attempt placed on all *freethinking people in Russia,* dating from the nihilists to Chernyshevsky, and from Chernyshevsky to Petrashevsky, reaching Belinsky, and so on. Whether Karakozov lives or dies is all the same to them: that is the reason for such *secrecy* with the public and even doubly so with the sovereign, who must at all costs believe *in a universal conspiracy.*

What kind of *freedom* was necessary to these Asiatic slaves with their fear of freedom of thought and speech? What use is it to them? They are permitted to weep for serfdom—they themselves do not know how to go on without livery: they grew used to it and it will be awful and cold for them in the open air... It's the same old landowners and the same old bureaucrats in a different form. Their weapons were taken from the jails and the criminal courts, and their literature is the investigative file; neither they nor their journals are interested in a serious debate. In a serious debate we were the first who were prepared to throw down the gauntlet; other locations could have been found if their objections did not carry a whiff of the Peter and Paul Fortress. They do not argue, but complain about the administration; they address themselves not to their adversaries, but denounce the disorders; they provoke not objections but executions, and wish not to convince but to *suppress.*

While the conservative-liberal gentry was united with its literary majordomos in weak-nerved opposition, it was ludicrous. Now that it is in unison with Russia's fears, with Muravyov, with three police forces, the army, and electric shocks—even Valuev consenting to be on their side—it is no laughing matter.

Together they represent that dark force which leads the weak sovereign from one crime to another and pushes Russia toward its former chaos.

...Why does the sovereign lack the energy to break free of these constraints? Why can he not do what Napoleon I and Sully managed, and question Karakozov himself, in order to learn the truth not only about the shot but with that the truth about how investigations are carried out in Russia in the second half of the XIX century?

Why?..

Notes

Source: "Iz Peterburga," *Kolokol,* l. 221, June 1, 1866; 19:84–88, 393.

1. Fyodor F. Trepov (1812–1889) became chief of police in St. Petersburg in April 1866.

2. Journals that received warnings, like *The Contemporary* and *The Russian Word,* saw their subscriptions decline.

3. Orlov-Davydov spoke at the January 9, 1865, meeting of the Moscow Assembly of the Nobility.

→ **86** ←

The Bell, No. 222, June 15, 1866. Herzen predicted that this article would delight everyone, and Ogaryov judged it one of the best that had appeared in *The Bell.* In a June 13, 1866, letter to Natalya Tuchkova-Ogaryova, Herzen said that he himself sensed *"two flames coursing through it: irony* and *faith* together..." (Gertsen, *Sobranie sochinenii,* 19:397). In contrast to this juxtaposition, Andrey Sinyavsky (writing as Abram Tertz) observed almost a century later that such "flames" were incompatible: "Irony is the faithful companion of unbelief and doubt; it vanishes as soon as there appears a faith that does not tolerate sacrilege" (Tertz, *On Socialist Realism,* 199). Herzen reproduces here, with slight changes, the rescript issued after Karakozov's attempt that was published in *The Northern Post* for April 14, 1866; he follows this with his own comments. As expected, not everyone was delighted, and the editor of *The News,* while crediting Herzen with a "brilliantly witty pen," declared that comparing the persecution of early Christians and present-day socialists was a sign of mental derangement. Herzen was well advised, the editor continued, to rethink his position and turn away from socialism before it destroyed more young people (*Let* 4:280).

From the Sovereign to P. P. Gagarin
[1866]

Prince Pavel Pavlovich,

The unanimous expression of loyal devotion by the people whose
rule was entrusted to me by divine plan is a pledge of the sentiments
in which I find the greatest reward for my efforts toward the good of
Russia.

The more comforting is this realization for me, the more I fulfill
my obligation to preserve the Russian people from those *kernels* of
false teaching, which in time could shake the smooth functioning of
society, if no obstacle was made to their development.

The event that summoned from all corners of Russia declarations
of loyalty also served as an occasion for a more precise examination of those paths by which these pernicious false teachings were
promoted and spread. The investigation being carried out by the
special commission I have ordered is already pointing to the *root* of
the evil. In that way Providence was pleased to open the eyes of Russia to the consequences that one can expect from the aspirations and
philosophizing of those who would brazenly encroach on all that has
been sacred to it from time immemorial, on religious beliefs, on the
principles of family life, on property rights, on obedience to the law,
and on respect for the powers that be.

My attention is *already* directed to the upbringing of young people.
I have given instructions to the effect that it be organized in the spirit
of religious truths, respect for property rights, and observance of the
fundamental principles of the social order, and that in educational
institutions of all types no overt or clandestine preaching will be
allowed of those destructive concepts which are equally harmful to
all aspects of the moral and material well-being of the people. But
instruction which meets the true needs of youth would not bring the
benefit expected from it if in private family life there was teaching not
in accord with the rules of Christian piety and the obligations of loyalty. For this reason I have the firm hope that my views on this subject will be fervently acted upon in the sphere of domestic education.

No less important for the true benefit of the state in its totality and
for every one of my subjects is the complete inviolability of the right
to property in all its aspects, as determined by the general laws and
by the Statutes of February 19, 1861. Independent of the legality of
this right, one of the most fundamental principles of well-functioning
civil societies, it is indissolubly tied to the development of private and

national wealth, which are tightly linked to one another. Any doubts
about these relationships could only be raised by enemies of the
social order.

The affirmation and preservation of these principles should be the
aspiration of all those invested with the rights and responsibilities
of government service. In a proper state system the first duty of all
those called to serve me and the fatherland consists of precise and
active fulfillment of their responsibilities without any deviation in any
branch of government. The authorities' excessive behavior and their
lack of action are equally harmful. Only with the steadfast fulfillment
of these responsibilities can the unity of government actions, which
is necessary for the realization of its views and the achievement of its
goals, be guaranteed.

I am aware that *some people in government service* have participated
in the disclosure of harmful rumors or judgments about the actions
or intentions of the state and even in the dissemination of those
teachings, contrary to social order, whose development should not
be permitted. The very rank of civil servant renders, in such cases,
greater weight to their words and in the same way facilitates the
distortion of the state's views. This type of confusion cannot be tolerated. All those in management positions *must keep track of the actions
of their subordinates* and require of them the direct, exact, and unswerving fulfillment of their assigned responsibilities, without which
harmonious governance is impossible, and by which they themselves
must set an example of respect for authority.

Finally, for the decisive success of the measures being taken
against the ruinous teachings which have developed in the social
sphere and which seek to shake the most fundamental bases of faith,
morality, and social order, all heads of the separate branches of government are required *to keep in mind those other healthy, conservative,
and reliable forces* with which Russia has always been richly endowed,
and which, to this day, thanks be to God, it has in abundance. These
forces consist of all the classes in which property rights are valued,
the right to landownership, guaranteed and defended in law, social
rights founded in and determined by law, principles of social order
and social security, principles of state unity and sound organization,
the principles of morality and the sacred truths of our faith. In view
of their important properties these strengths must be utilized and
preserved when officials are appointed in all branches of government. In that way we will be saved from ill-intentioned reprimands
in all levels of society concerning their confidence in the governing

authorities. Toward this goal, in accordance with my customary
wishes and my frequently expressed desire, it behooves all branches
of government to pay complete attention to the preservation of the
rights of property and *entreaty, in relation to its use and need* (the right
of petition!) by various districts and various sections of the population. *It is important to curtail* the repeated attempts to stir up enmity
between various classes *and particularly the stirring up of enmity
against the nobility and against landowners in general,* in which enemies
of social order naturally see their immediate opponents. A firm and
unswerving observance of *these general* principles will place a limit on
those criminal aspirations, which have now been uncovered with sufficient clarity and must be subject to the just retribution of the law. I
direct you to announce my rescript to the appropriate leadership, to
all ministers and all heads of all the divisions.

I remain, etc.

ALEXANDER

In Tsarskoe Selo, May 13/25, 1866

...There we have it, the final echo of the shot!

Fear in the face of something indeterminate, pious—but hardly new—
thoughts, a poor style, nameless hints, a lesson learned by heart and a
moral coup d'etat...

We decided to reprint in its entirety this gloomily thought-out and
gloomily written dissertation,[1] because in it we see a kind of historic border
post, a poorly made, poorly painted, clumsy boundary marker, but all the
same a marker.

If this were a rhetorical exercise about the corruption of minds and
hearts, about false teachings and theories of property [. . .] we would not pay
it the slightest attention. We have read such marvels in the journals that
stand in the way of Russian development. But a royal diatribe, cast down
from the heights upon which the throne stands, is a completely different
matter. No matter how little genuine substance there is, it must fly down
to our low-lying fields like a cannonball and either smash something or get
smashed itself.

Looking closely at this royal document, which reminds us—with its
worldly philosophy—of the spiritual icon painting with which Metropolitan Filaret adorned the emancipation manifesto,[2] we are struck most of all
by *three things.*

First, it is as clear as day that that *there was no* conspiracy linked to the
shot on April 4/16 (as we have stated and repeated), *to the extent that* they
could not draw one out no matter the shadows in which the investigation

was carried out, nor the choice of an investigator, nor the methods which he employed. A conspiracy and Poles, the participation of nihilists and international revolution—all of this is intrigue, lies, and slander. They did not dare put this in the mouth of the sovereign. What remained was to exploit *moral participation,* i.e., immoral *complicité morale,* having intercepted correspondence between friends and family and having made note of certain thoughts, then confused them with all thinking people in the younger generation, all those who awoke to intellectual life and breathed freely after the death of Nicholas. It is impossible to make out to what guilty people the letter refers. In the Karakozov case, the only guilty ones are *those who participated with him,* and not all those people who think that the Russian government is not the ideal of all forms of governance and who debate property rights. [. . .]

A *single* adversary was pointed out and identified, not by name, but as a living force, a rival with whom it is necessary to contend, which is growing and will continue to grow unless it is suppressed now. [. . .] The giant in the cradle, which the government fears and in which it senses its future successor, is *social thought,* the ideas of a few inconsequential writers, young people, nihilists, and, I am ashamed to say, us. The character of this movement, which seeks to break down the old forms of Russian life that prevent its new forces from taking shape, is instinctively recognized as *social*[3]... and for that reason the government stands on the eternal peaks of conservatism and reaction, in favor of landed property; it wishes to defend it and be defended by it... to its aid it summons the catechism, domestic education, spying by department heads, and all of its forces, i.e., all its police.

This tsarist adornment we see as *a second victory.*

The third victory—"not unto us, not unto us," but also not unto *the Russian people.*[4] Apropos of the people: one of the most remarkable facts about the letter to Gagarin is the utter absence of *the people,* who were so recently being flattered... not one tender word, not one greeting, not even a thank you for saving his life! They are tired of the *paysans.* [. . .] The third victory goes to the tsar's old childhood friend—*the gentry landowner.* Like a weak little chick, the two-headed eagle takes it under both wings, and the government, like Mitrofanushka's mama,[5] is prepared to scratch out anyone's eyes for the sake of the perpetual young oaf. The letter *puts an end to* any open discussion of the great process involving landowners and peasants.

That's all.

Then the sovereign, through Gagarin, tells the people that he wants to lead Russia along *a different* path. *Which one?* It seems that he himself does not thoroughly understand but it is clear that it will be a nasty one. From this letter the irritation is obvious, the desire to govern more severely, to tighten the reins, to press harder, to trample more firmly... With this goal, Prince Gagarin's sovereign correspondent proposes turning all department heads into spies over their subordinates, and then *instructs* them to "keep in mind *those other* healthy, conservative and reliable forces with which Russia is richly endowed." [. . .]

...We imagine how the sovereign, bored by this lengthy missive from Gagarin to Gagarin, wiped the sweat from his powerful face and, throwing down the pen with which he had signed it, said: Well, thank God, the throne, altar, nobility, property, morality, and order have been saved. [. . .]

The sovereign lets out a sigh.

And the nobility, who since the year 1860 have been trembling with fear and anger, also let out a sigh. [. . .]

Sleep, brothers, rest yourselves!..

And you, poor exiles, held in captivity, surviving in chains, toiling in the mines, persecuted friends—take heart. Together we lived to see a great age. You do not suffer in vain, and we have not worked a lifetime in vain. *This is the dawn of the harvest, a day which we have long awaited.*

...When the Emperor Trajan sent Pliny to investigate the false teaching of the Nazarines, when the Roman senate pondered the spread of the absurd and immoral sect of the executed Judean, while Tertullian defended it from the vile accusation of *murders,* when earlier Nero had heaped blame upon them as *arsonists* for a fire, and other caesars tormented them *openly and publicly,* like naive Muravyovs let out of a menagerie—the case of the Christians was won.

And we march forward holding caesar's most recent missive. The tsar's countersignature is there and we will not forget May 13/25, 1866.

It is the beginning of the battle... it is the beginning of the war.

We shall not see its end... it is unlikely that even the very youngest will see it. History develops slowly, and what is passing away defends itself stubbornly, and what is establishing itself comes into being slowly and dimly... but the process itself, the very drama of historical gestation, is full of poetry. Every generation has its own experience, and we do not grumble over our share, we have lived not only to see a red patch of light in the east, but also long enough for our enemy to see it. What more can one expect from life, especially when a man, with his hand on his heart, can say with a clear conscience: "And I took part in this massive struggle, and I did my bit..."

...And you, Pavel Pavlovich, write another letter to yourself, some sort of commentary on the Tsarskoe Selo missive, or like Pliny the Younger, write to Caesar himself about bringing down the new Christians, about their insignificance, about your contempt for them... just keep writing!

Notes

Source: "Ot gosudaria Kniaziu P. P. Gagarinu," *Kolokol*, l. 222, June 15, 1866; 19:95–101, 396–98.

Prince Pavel P. Gagarin (1789–1872), a senator, served on the commission investigating the Petrashevsky circle, the emancipation committee, and was chairman of the court that tried Karakozov.

1. Herzen: "In all probability, Gagarin wrote this letter 'to himself.' This is all a continuation of the system set up after the infamous fire in Petersburg, the system of intimidation of the sovereign. He is assured and frightened, and he assures and frightens himself, and signs, like a future constitutional monarch, not knowing what it is—*il règne, mais ne gouverne pas.*"

2. The initial draft of the manifesto by Yu. Samarin and N. Milyutin was profoundly altered by the Moscow metropolitan Filaret.

3. Herzen: "It stands to reason that not a single serious social teaching has ever attacked property rights from the viewpoint of theft." Herzen goes on to call Gagarin's view that serfs should not receive any post-emancipation allotment as an endorsement of theft as the foundation of landowners' rights.

4. This quote from Psalm 113 (115 in the King James version) appeared on Russian coins under Paul I and later on 1812 war medals.

5. In Denis Fonvizin's 1782 play *The Minor*.

⇥ 87 ⇤

The Bell, No. 225, Aug. 1, 1866. This article focuses its sarcasm on the most prominent pro-government journalist.

KATKOV AND THE SOVEREIGN
[1866]

The sovereign could not manage without Katkov and once again appointed him to look after the floodgates of the Moscow sewer, from which filth and sewage have flowed for the past four years, contaminating all Russia. After two weeks, the sovereign could wait no longer and, like a physiologist, decided that a six-week-long cleansing was sufficient for Katkov.[1] For his part, Katkov did not reconcile with the sovereign for free: *he set conditions, and they were accepted.* He won for himself the right to leave Russia to the whims of fate and separatism after the *first* subsequent warning. With this threat in the air let *any sort of Valuev* interfere with his committees and issue a warning...

[. . .] Now the Karakozov case will proceed very smoothly. Nekrasov will be satisfied:[2] *they will get to the roots of the matter,* and if there are none, they will grow some in *The Moscow Gazette*. Now a universal conspiracy will come to light, from London, Paris, Switzerland, and Sweden to Tulcea, Jassy, Bukhara, and Samarkand... "Evildoers of the world, tremble!"

They definitely needed Katkov on the eve of the execution... in order to whip up people's minds, in order for the government itself to believe that it had to feel rage. Without him, Muravyov was incomplete, unfinished—wasn't that the reason that he failed to discover a conspiracy, because he was deprived of the leadership of *The Moscow Gazette?*

But nothing was lost. Katkov, having rested in the summer sun, concentrated his best poison on humiliation and malice, and issued one of his most priceless drops of it when he started up again with an article in issue No. 134 of *The Moscow Gazette.*

[. . .] He speaks of a certain *nihilist* who influenced Karakozov and brought back with him from abroad "a newly arisen doctrine in world-revolutionary circles about the need to exterminate all the crowned heads of Europe."[3] What next? Judges will calmly sign off on sentences for every nihilist who has traveled abroad.

"World revolution"[4] and a nihilist returning from abroad present a great opportunity for the restored detective to tie everything in the world to the Karakozov case, and, to do him justice, he did not forget anyone—not Bakunin, *The Bell,* our powerful agency in Tulcea, the Poles, or the fires... All this nonsense, mired in the filth of police reports and in the even greater filth of his own imagination, at another time would not have merited any attention, but at the present time, when it pushes people toward the gallows and hard labor, one cannot remain silent.

Where will our degradation end? Where will we touch bottom, the limit of our baseness and heartlessness? We go on sinking lower and lower... Recall the howl of indignation that greeted the doctrine of blind obedience, when it was expressed by a Moscow professor,[5] but *now*—now what is being preached is not the philosophy, but *the poetry of slavery, the madness of slavery.* Have you read anything in the basest excesses of Byzantine servility and Eastern self-abnegation that matches the following lines from the June 3/15 issue of *The Moscow Gazette:*[6]

> For us, the state and the dynasty are not a matter of party, and the sovereign for us is not the leader of an armed force, but is designated by birth to lead his entire people, in the calm and indisputable possession of supreme rights. For that reason not only officials, who have been placed in various positions in accordance with executive authority, but every honest citizen must, in good conscience, see

himself as a servant of the sovereign, and concern himself, as our ancestors would say, with his sovereign's affairs, which for every person
ought to be a vital matter to him as well.

... If you are eating, you are eating for the sovereign; if you have cholera,
the sovereign is sick; if you marry, then the sovereign has married; if you
take medicine, then you are treating his majesty!

Notes

Source: "Katkov i Gosudar'," *Kolokol*, l. 225, August 1, 1866; 19:117–20, 406–8.

1. Katkov was allowed to resume publication of *The Moscow Gazette* two weeks before
the end of the official suspension.

2. A reference to Nikolay Nekrasov's appearance at the English Club in St. Petersburg
on April 16, 1866, where he read a poem he had written in honor of Count Mikhail
Muravyov—who was at the time presiding over the Karakozov investigation—in an attempt to save *The Contemporary* from being permanently shut down (Gertsen, *Sobranie
sochinenii*, 19:388–89).

3. Herzen is partly quoting, partly paraphrasing the article "Nihilist" that appeared in
issue no. 134 of *The Moscow Gazette* on June 28, 1866. Katkov had in mind the folklor-
ist and revolutionary Ivan A. Khudyakov (1842–1876), who was arrested in connection
with the Karakozov case and sentenced to perpetual exile in Verkhoyansk. Khudyakov
had traveled to Geneva in 1865 to establish ties with Herzen, Ogaryov, and Bakunin,
and when he returned to Russia at the end of the year he joined several radical circles
in Moscow. Katkov was making use of information from the closed trial proceedings,
which he saw before it was released publicly.

4. Herzen: "In the same issue of *The Moscow Gazette* Katkov himself says that world
revolution is a fantasy." Katkov goes on to say that the danger comes from the Poles and
their supporters, especially at *The Bell*, who curse Russian patriotism (*Let* 4:280).

5. In his October 28, 1861, inaugural lecture in a course on state law, Boris Chicherin
set forth this theory.

6. What follows is a quote from the lead article in issue no. 138 of *The Moscow Gazette*,
in which Katkov expresses his delight at Alexander's May 13 rescript (see Doc. 86).

⇥ 88 ⇤

A FRENZY OF DENUNCIATIONS

(Kraevsky's First Warning)

[1866]

We are overcome by the raging of denunciation—the wall separating the
secret police from literature has fallen, and spies, informers, journalists,

professors, and detectives have been merged into one family. The English Club has turned into an auxiliary chamber of the Third Department, the sovereign writes editorials in Gagarin's name, and Gagarin places them in the journal of the "committee of ministers." This is all fine, but our informers have begun to reach into the area of private life... in six months we will become accustomed to this, but at first it was startling. Two weeks ago in a feuilleton in *The Voice,* which Orthodoxy has sorely missed *since the time of the missionary* Count Tolstoy,[1] there were several stories about a certain noblewoman–Old Believer who has a male friend, and about a certain male Old Believer who has a French lady. Various details were added, street names and so forth. We believe that like Heine, our brother in Christ Andrey has begun in his old age to fear death and his past sins, and, as a clever man, has begun to be zealous for the ministerial church, and not about any other. How else to explain that he has at once—like the petty Katkov— gone in for petty denunciations? Of course Kraevsky does not write them himself—even his enemies will not accuse him of excessive literacy—but if he has chosen for himself the place of honor as caretaker of two *occasional* journals,[2] then keep a watch out that there is no debauchery in them, and that everything proceeds in an orderly and proper manner.

As you grow older, Andrey, you should take more care!

It is *the detention* of Katkov that has caused all the trouble. The small-fry rag-and-bone dealers got going during the absence of *the father of denunciations,* with all sorts of gossip and hints... while "We, Katkov, will have a 'rendezvous' with the sovereign and with our inkwell and golden quill."

Notes

Source: "Beshenstvo donosov," *Kolokol,* l. 225, August 1, 1866; 19:122, 409.

1. Count Dmitry A. Tolstoy (1823–1889), the head of the Holy Synod (1865–80), was also appointed minister of enlightenment (1866–80).

2. Andrey A. Kraevsky (1810–1889) was at this time editor of both *The Voice* (*Golos*) and *Fatherland Notes.*

⇥ 89 ⇤

The Bell, No. 227, September 1, 1866. This essay offers additional commentary on the Karakozov trial and on Katkov's shift from pro-constitutional liberal to darling of the reactionary camp.

A QUARREL AMONG ENEMIES

Separatism at The Moscow Gazette

[1866]

Within the darkness of the government, at the very focal point of the political cancer that is eating away at Russia, a remarkable split has been revealed. *The Moscow Gazette* is turning into an organ of separatism, of the old enmity between Moscow and Petersburg. The publisher of *The Moscow Gazette,* having been forgiven by the sovereign, has not forgiven Valuev or an article on the Karakozov case printed in the official journal of the ministry of internal affairs, which Valuev must have read ten or twenty times, and which sounded like it was written by a Pole, Konstantin Nikolaevich, or Golovin.[1]

The thing is, *The Moscow Gazette* is not happy that the secret socialist groups about which the article speaks were organized in Moscow. They would like at all costs to ascribe them to poor, plague-infected Petersburg. They forget that, according to their doctrine, Petersburg possesses the alpha and omega of all Russia, its object of worship, the emperor—all power be to him—the law and the court system, the source of reason, truth, warmth, and light. We do not know by what right Moscow opposes itself to the city of the emperors. We do not understand why Moscow stands out from the monotony of the orthodox and faceless flock for whom the Petersburg tsar thinks and knows, freezes and sweats. Moscow's independent stand disturbs the impersonal unity of the sovereign's herd. Can the state move along one path, when the city of the Winter Palace pulls in one direction, while the city of the Palace of Facets pulls in another, when the Peter Paul Fortress goes this way, and the Kremlin goes that way? Won't this enormous empire—whose peripheries are held together by lead and blood, while in its heart hatred and the jealousy of one half toward the other take root—crack at its very center?

In order to shield Moscow, Katkov is sacrificing some of his false denunciations and some of the slander that he placed at the base of the torture rack upon which his journal is published. In order to demonstrate that Karakozov has as his origin Petersburg ideas and world revolution, he mocks the importance given to Moscow high school and college students and the ideas ascribed to them:

Listen:

> The author of the article in *The Northern Post* speaks about Moscow circles consisting of several high school and college students as if

this were a serious secret society of long standing, or a revolutionary organization extending over almost all Russia. But the investigative commission, which, of course, studied everything concerning these people down to the smallest detail, found no traces of participation by these revolutionary activists in the arson of 1864 and 1865. If these circles possessed even a hundredth part of the significance given them by the author of this article, then could it have happened that they stood idly by at the time of this arson, which destroyed so many cities and villages? It is obvious that other revolutionary elements were active then who bear no resemblance to the Moscow socialists, who are no more than the victims of these more secretive and serious enemy forces.

We do not know what conclusions the investigative commission came to concerning these more secretive sources of evil in the Karakozov case. But one must think that in their further inquiries the investigative commission does not limit itself to the examination of teachings comprising the philosophy of nihilism, but has or will make use of all steps that could lead it to other areas. It is obvious that the tracks left by Karakozov and his comrades will not lead to the original source for the plan that was carried out in the assassination attempt on the 4th of April.

This is Katkov? Leontiev himself wouldn't recognize him in this new attire. Isn't he the one who since 1862 has talked of nothing but the fact that young people are all socialists, arsonists, and hasn't it been *The Bell* that has constantly said: "The investigation has revealed nothing"?

...Well done! He has distanced himself from the fires as he did from the theories of Gneist; now place your hopes in the Muravyovs and the tsars.

And what sort of irony is this on the analysis of the philosophy of nihilism? Who can fail to see that we were right in pointing out all the absurdity of bringing socialism, nihilism, positivism, realism, materialism, journal articles, student dissertations, etc., into the Karakozov case?

The truth is beginning to be uncovered ahead of the gallows.

Apropos of the gallows: Katkov is also dragging one of the accused[2] toward it. Did the gentleman write something against him or shoot his mouth off?

In the end, as one expects, there is an *elusive* hint. About whom, it is difficult to say; that's where the secret lies, and as the Germans say, Pass. One might think that he has in mind Suvorov, the Grand Duke, and la bête noire Golovin.[3]

Notes

Source: "Ssora mezhdu vragami, Separatizm 'Mosk. Vedomostei,'" *Kolokol*, l. 227, September 1, 1866; 19:133–35, 414–15.

1. In the August 11, 1866, issue of *The Moscow Gazette*, Katkov responded to an article that had appeared in no. 167 of *The Northern Post* (*Severnaia pochta*).

2. In Doc. 87, Herzen mentioned Katkov's references to Ivan Khudyakov, a young revolutionary who had met with Russian radical circles in Europe, was arrested back in Russia, and sent into perpetual exile.

3. Suvorov's retirement as minister of enlightenment was seen as a sign of the increased strength of reactionary forces after Karakozov's attempt on the tsar's life.

⤖ 90 ⬿

The Bell, No. 228, October 1, 1866. A year after this essay appeared, U.S. Secretary of State William Seward finalized the purchase of Alaska from Russia. In the early 1850s, Herzen had rejected a suggestion from his Moscow friends that he move to America until there was a new tsar, but he took a lively interest in America's affairs and in how it compared to Russia.

AMERICA AND RUSSIA
[1866]

The Pacific Ocean is the Mediterranean of the future.

All the Russian and non-Russian papers are full of news about rapprochement in the North American alliance with Russia.[1] Western commentators are angry and frowning (for good reason). The Russians are reprinting in ten different ways, with a number of variations, what we said somewhat earlier, namely *eight years* ago. This is what was published in our lead article in *The Bell* for December 1, 1858:[2]

> We have not been spoiled by an excess of sympathy from other peoples, and have not been spoiled by their *understanding* either. There were a lot of reasons for this, most of all Petersburg policy since the year 1825. But Russia is emerging from this period—why is it America alone that guessed this and is the first to welcome it?
>
> Because Russia and America are meeting *on the other side*. Because between them lies an entire saltwater ocean, but not an entire world

of outdated prejudices and concepts, envious precedence, and civilizations that have ground to a halt.

It will soon be *ten* years since we expressed our thoughts about the mutual relations of these *futures* on the road of contemporary history. We said that in the future Russia has one comrade, one fellow traveler—the Northern States; we have repeated this many times, and just a few months ago we had the opportunity to say: only empty, irritated diplomatic pride—what's more, Germanic—causes Russia to get involved in all Western issues. In the forthcoming battle, toward which Europe is unwillingly being drawn, there is no need for Russia to take an active part. We have no legacy there, and we equally are not bound by memories or expectations with the fate of that world. If Russia *will liberate itself* from the *Petersburg* tradition, it has one ally only—*the North American States.*

Everything that we witnessed, raising the issue at our own risk in a hostile West, everything that we predicted—from the secretly roving forces, from the inevitable emancipation of the serfs with land to the electoral similarity with the North American States—all this is happening before our eyes.

This chronological *privilege* is too precious for us to yield, especially at a time when a page of history is turning, and, with a new page, those laborers who came to work, having anticipated the new morning, will be forgotten.

However, no special gifts of prophecy were required in order to say what we said; it was only necessary to free oneself from domestic and other prejudices, from the leaden Petersburg atmosphere, and from forgotten concepts of an old civilization. It was sufficient to take an independent look at the world. It was clear that America and Russia *were next in turn.* Both countries have an abundance of strength, flexibility, an organizational spirit, persistence that knows no obstacle; both have a meager past, both begin with a complete break with tradition, both spread over endless valleys, seeking their borders, both—from different directions—reach across terrible expanses, everywhere marking their path with cities, villages, and colonies, reaching the Pacific Ocean, this *"Mediterranean Sea of the future"* (as we once named it and then saw with joy that American journals repeated this many times).

The contrast between the Petersburg military dictatorship—which destroys all people in the person of the autocrat, and the American autocracy of each person—is enormous. And that's not all—isn't the most fateful contradiction, with which the history of the West is coming to an end, once again the way America breaks down into individuals, on the one hand, and Russia into communal fusion, on the other?

Notes

Source: "Amerika i Rossiia," *Kolokol*, l. 228, October 1, 1866; 19:139–40, 416.

Herzen first used this phrase in the opening epigraph in 1853 in his essay "Baptized Property" (Doc. 8) and reused it in *Past and Thoughts* and other writings.

1. An American diplomatic mission visited Russia from the end of July to the beginning of September 1866.

2. The rest of this document is a citation, with slight changes, from "America and Siberia."

⇢ 91 ⇠

The Bell, No. 229, November 1, 1866. In "The Gallows and Muravyov," which was written soon after Karakozov's execution and appeared in no. 228, Herzen reacted to the chaos that ensued from having "an absolute monarch who rules over nothing" (Gertsen, *Sobranie sochinenii*, 19:137–38). He wondered whether a historian with the combined abilities of Tacitus and Dante could be found to capture this historical moment. Here, Herzen continues to explore different aspects of the Karakozov theme, which dominated his lead articles for much of 1866. At the top of the first page of issue no. 229, Herzen made his views clear with the words "THERE IS NO PLOT!" (ZAGOVORA NE BYLO!) in large capital letters. In chapter 12 of *Past and Thoughts*, Herzen told the story of another conspiracy, the one that was manufactured about an 1834 gathering that he did not attend, but which nevertheless resulted for him in jail and years of exile.

THE QUESTION OF A PLOT
[1866]

The conspiracy that many suspected after Karakozov's shot is revealing itself more and more. Over and above the individual rumors, *L'Indépendance* and the *Kölnishche Zeitung* have dropped two or three remarkable hints. It is clear that Muravyov stood at the head of the plot consisting of advocates of serfdom, old fools, and the reactionaries in general. The *Kölnishche Zeitung* says that he retired because the sovereign was displeased with police pranks and began to suspect the reason for the excessive zeal. A few days before the commission shut down, Muravyov left for the countryside, "where he was sent documents," say the Russian newspapers.[1] But how could he have dared to leave, not having completed a matter of such importance? To bless

a church is hardly an urgent matter. He left in disfavor. One of his chief accomplices was the first to untie his cart from the drowned beast... *The Moscow
Gazette* was very modest in its laments over the grave of the new Pozharsky[2]
(not even having become a prince, which Muravyov really wanted).

In this matter the sovereign behaved in as unsteady and foolish a way
as in all other matters. Instead of naming another commission over Muravyov's and following along fresh tracks all the tricks of the black Russian
gang, he did not even order the publication of Muravyov's papers, and limited himself to freeing the Perm infantry of the executioner's name. Now,
of course, it is a bit late to learn about the entire intrigue, *although it is still
possible.*

Notes

Source: "Po delu zagovora," *Kolokol*, l. 229, November 1, 1866; 19:160, 423–24.

1. Muravyov had gone to his estate near Petersburg for the dedication of a new church,
and died there the night of August 28, 1866. His intention had been to declare the commission closed on the August 31.

2. Prince Dmitry M. Pozharsky (1578–c. 1641), together with Minin, headed a force
that liberated Muscovy in 1611–12 from Swedish and Polish invaders.

⇥ 92 ⇤

The Bell, No. 230, December 1, 1866 (Part I); Nos. 231–32, January 1, 1867 (Part II); and
No. 233–34, February 1, 1867 (Part III). Herzen's notes indicate that he intended to continue this essay in subsequent issues. The first part is devoted to Europe, and Herzen
reveals a greater optimism about social and political change than he had expressed in
the aftermath of 1848, with its return to reactionary regimes and popular lethargy. The
article below was written in October 1866, under the influence of the founding congress
of the First International held in Geneva, and the thoughts it stimulated in Herzen (*Let*
4:297). Part II is a transition from the situation in Europe and the ideas of the utopian
socialist Blanqui to Russia, where the promise of Alexander II had gradually dissipated
and any influence *The Bell* might have had on him had been greatly reduced. Part III
continues the theme of Russia, ending with an embrace of the 1862 Land and Liberty
banner. Radicals objected to Herzen's characterization of St. Petersburg activists, and
Serno-Solovyovich's brother Alexander answered "Order Triumphs!" with a brochure
that called Herzen "a poet, artist, performer, storyteller, novelist, anything you want,
only not a political activist and even less a theoretician and founder of a school" (*Let*
4:357, 392–93).

ORDER TRIUMPHS!
[1866–1867]

L'ordre règne a Varsovie!
—Sebastiani, 1831

I

If Sodom and Gomorrah perished in as interesting a manner as the *old order* in Europe is perishing, then I am not at all surprised that Lot's wife did not turn back in time, knowing that she would be punished.

Having just come to the end of the year 1866, we are drawn to glance backward.

What a year!.. *Both abroad and at home*—it was a fine one, and it cannot be said that it was lacking in events...

We almost never speak about the West. [. . .] There was a time, incidentally, when we expressed our opinion in great detail. But developments are so substantial and abrupt, and are flowing by so rapidly, that by necessity you stop before them to verify what you have thought, alongside what is taking place. [. . .]

The decay of the *old* world is not an empty phrase, and it is difficult to doubt it now. The character of organic decay is that elements, entering into a given relationship with each other, do not do what they are supposed to do and what they wish to do, and that is what we are seeing in Europe. [. . .]

There was a sick man in Europe, and Nikolay Pavlovich, himself not very well, tried to obtain it;[1] now, all Europe is a hospital, a sick bay, and, most of all, a madhouse. It absolutely cannot digest the contradictions that it has lived to see. It cannot cope with the fractured revolution within, with its two-part civilization, one in science, one in religion, one almost of the twentieth century, and the other barely in the fifteenth. Is it so easy to fuse into a single organic development bourgeois freedom and monarchical arbitrariness, socialism and Catholicism, the right of thought and the right of force, criminal statistics that explain a case, and a criminal case that cuts off the head[2] so that it understands. [. . .]

In 1848, reaction revealed itself as *reaction*, and promised order, i.e., police, and it established a *police* order. But ten years or so of an asylum with no amusements has gotten tedious and futile, and the negative banner of police action and a well-run state has worn out. And, little by little, a new banner has begun to appear, amphibious, if you can call it that; it has been hoisted between reaction and revolution, so that, like Caussidière,[3] it be-

longs both to one and the other, both to order and disorder. The liberation
of nationalities from a foreign yoke, *but not at all from their own,* has created
a common thoroughfare of opposing principles. [. . .]

It is a fine mess to which the saving *reaction* of our Western elders has
brought us:

> *Revolution—is defeated,*
> *The reds—are defeated,*
> *Socialism—is defeated,*
> *Order—triumphs,*
> *The throne—is strengthened,*
> *The police—make arrests,*
> *The court—puts to death,*
> *The church—gives its blessing...*

Rejoice and give your blessing in turn!

... After all, it's become so simple—don't you just stick your head in your
feathers and wait for trouble to break out?

And trouble will break out, there's no doubt of that, but there is no need
to hide your head. Better to raise it selflessly, look directly at events and, by
the way, look at your own conscience.

Events are as much created by people as people are created by events;
this is not fatalism, but the interaction of elements in an ongoing process,
the unconscious aspect of which can change one's consciousness. The business of history is only the business of the living *understanding* of existence.
If ten people understand clearly what thousands vaguely wish for, then
thousands will follow them. It doesn't follow that these ten will lead them
toward something good. That is where the question of conscience enters in.

On what bases did Napoleon and Bismarck lead Europe? What *did they
understand?*

Napoleon understood that France had betrayed the revolution, that it had
come to a halt and had taken fright; he understood its *miserliness,* and that
everything else must be subject to it. He understood that the old, established society in which the active forces of the country were concentrated,
all the material and immaterial wealth, does not desire freedom, but its
imposing scenery, with complete rights *d'user et d'abuser.* He understood
that the new society, marching directly toward a socialist revolution, hated
everything that is old, but impotently. He understood that the mass knows
neither one thing nor the other, and that, outside of Paris and two or three
other centers, they live with Gothic fantasies and childhood legends. He
understood all of this, amidst the noise and exclamations of the republic
that was coming to an end in 1848, amidst the arrogant claims of various

parties and the indefatigable opposition; that is why he remained silent and waited for "the pear to ripen."

For his part, Bismarck, no less than Napoleon, knew the value of his philistines; on the benches of the Frankfurt parliament, he could assess them at his leisure. He understood that Germans needed as much freedom in politics as the Reformation had given them in religion, and that this freedom was necessary *der Theorie nach,* that they had become accustomed to obey authority, and had not become accustomed to a strict English self-governance. This would have been sufficient, but he understood more: he understood that at the present moment Germans were consumed by jealousy of France and hatred for Russia, that they dreamed of being a powerful state, of uniting... but for what purpose?.. if they could have explained why, it would not have been lunacy. [. . .]

... If we renounce our sympathies and antipathies, if we forget what is dear and hateful to us, then we will hardly feel sorrow about what is going on in Europe. The military dictatorships and lawless empires are nearer to ending than the traditional kingdoms and lawful monarchies. Europe will not be bogged down by them, but will be led to a common denominator... or it will rot through, and, either by means of peace or war, come upon a terrible void. And this void will be the grave of all that is obsolete.

Proudhon—with a terrible lack of humanity—once reproached Poland because "it does not wish to die."[4] We could say this more justly of *old* Europe. It is clinging to life with all its strength, but illness and death are coming closer and closer. Consciousness, thought, science and all its applications long ago outgrew the Gothic and bourgeois forms of the old governance. The spirit is at odds with a body which is worn out, limited, and racked with ailments, and which keeps the soul in chains. The French revolution of 1789 feared this already and for that reason went astray with politics and war; it was happy to have an external occupation, and from the "rights of man" it developed the code of *bourgeois rights.*

No matter how unsteady and pale the revolution of 1848, it raced powerfully to continue the interrupted political regeneration, and here is where the final battle began for the dying old man who had outlived his days, armed with an entire arsenal of ancient weapons, against an adolescent made strong by a single thought, a single belief, a single truth, who in the first clash released his sling and did not fall. It seems that it could have gone better: the Old Goliath was victorious, but he, and not the adolescent, is dying.

[. . .] Ideas are not sown in the earth. Science and thought are not *glebae adscripti,* are not tied to the soil...

...There was no place for the Gospel in Judea, so it was carried to Rome and preached to the barbarians; there is no room for a young worker in his father's house and his native fields, so he sets off for America... I do not know where...

We have said this not for the first time, but we think it necessary to sometimes repeat it, and especially necessary to repeat it now, when everything is covered with dark clouds and has so quickly become gloomy.

II

[. . .] Only two nations—among those who have entered the main channel—enjoy special rights in history and are oriented differently toward the future.

Their task is a simpler one.

Their situation is less complex.

They are not troubled at present by "an unnecessary recollection and an unresolved quarrel."[5]

Nothing needs to be done on behalf of the North American union, for it is going full sail, *au large*.[6]

Russia could find its own channel even more easily, but it has lost its way in some kind of fog. It has dreamed up a compulsory past, drowned its old ships, and has cast stones into its own sea, but then is afraid to strike them with an oar.

Strength and time are being lost to no purpose.

The government lacks *understanding*, and we lack *faith*.

The success of our reactionary movement—newly baked from stale European flour—is based on this.

To explain anything to the government is a major feat, which we will not undertake; it would sooner come across it by blind instinct, or find it by touch, than comprehend anything.

We wish for something else: to cleanse our primary question from all the rubbish and silt and say to our friends whose faith is faltering what Sieyès said to his colleagues after Mirabeau's famous "*Allez dire*": "We are the same people today that we were yesterday—let us continue."[7]

...A few months ago I talked for a long time with an old man.[8] He has spent *half* of his more than sixty years in prison; his entire life he has been persecuted, and he is being persecuted now, not just by his enemies but by his own people. This man, forgotten in prison, emerged in 1848 from the graves of Mont Saint-Michel like an apparition amidst the jubilation of the February revolution, and when they expected him to offer a joyful greeting, a shout, and delight, he said loudly: "We are drowning," and the crowd which had let him out of jail moved away, as if from a villain, a holy fool, or someone infected with the plague... "*And it is you who are drowning us, not our enemies,*" he continued. He was imprisoned once again, and, taking advantage of his incarceration, he made slanderous remarks about it, and *the republic drowned, and they were the ones who drowned it.*

For another fifteen years he watched from inside the prison walls at the destruction of all the initiatives and all the hopes; gray as the moon, he emerged again from prison; the old man was met by the former hatred, the former spite, and physically broken, in terrible poverty, completely alone, he disappeared into the mountains, away from his native land.

This old man is *Auguste Blanqui.*

[. . .] He depressed me, and something dark arose in my soul. A book lay on the table;[9] I took it up, sure that I would find lies, filth, and slander, and I could not put it down: once more a series of martyrs, tireless activists, and young and old fighters rose before me. This official *Vilna* literature had erected a remarkable monument *to the Polish emigration. . . .* From 1831 to 1866 they labor on, and their work is destroyed; they begin anew, and it is once more destroyed; again they begin [. . .] from every place they *return* to their homeland, bearing in their chest an unquenchable faith in the liberation to come and a readiness to fall in battle for it.

Why do we have so *little* faith, why is our faith so weak? Why have so many of us hung our heads and lost heart at the first sign of failure, at the first unfortunate attempts, *not even realizing that they may have been carried out mistakenly?*

Is it possible that to believe *with great faith* a desperate situation or a mystical lunacy is required?

[. . .] Our battle is just beginning, and its lines are just being drawn.

The reactionary period has been ongoing for less than *five years.* [. . .]

Everything that has happened is sad, and half of it was not even needed from *their* point of view. But could one really have expected that *this* government, the last fruit cultivated in the hothouses of the Winter Palace, would act sensibly and dispassionately, that it would act wisely and humanely? Could one really have expected that a society consisting of people who were raised in the depravity of manor house life, having become accustomed from their childhood years to arbitrariness and slavery, to the spectacle of suffering and torture, that a society raised on bribes and slander, in government offices and Shemyakin courts, consisting of characters out of Ostrovsky, from the menagerie of the "dark kingdom," would act wisely and humanely?[10] That, like Saul, it would be blinded as a scoundrel and recover his sight as an apostle?

One should not have expected that Alexander Nikolaevich, having fallen asleep while reading *What Is to Be Done?* or *The Bell,* would wake up with a zealous desire to return land to the people and set up workshops for women and men in the Winter Palace.[11]

Then there would be no need for a struggle, as a miracle would be sufficient. [. . .]

In Russian government life one new element has developed recently, and we value it highly—it is the tsar's tongue, which is constantly chattering, the police, who go about satisfying their needs with a rattle in their hands, the literary *dikasteria,*[12] who uphold on an hourly basis tsarist grandeur and Orthodox sanctity, freelance journalism on a temporary contract, which defends the throne and the fatherland...

It is a step in the mud—a huge step forward.

The mud will dry up and remain, but it is impossible to keep silent. The coarse and ignorant destruction of honest organs is a shame, but it would be twice the shame if these disgraceful organs were abolished.

It is not so important *what* the government says, but why it is speaking. It is speaking because it *lacks faith.* It feels the need to convince not only others, but itself, that it is as *powerful* as before, very *powerful.* If it possessed the Nicholaevan self-assurance, it would begin to strike out without opening its mouth. It speaks because *it is afraid.* In the dumb silence surrounding it, something is not right, is not what it used to be; you can hear the mouse-like bustle of history...

And we remain silent, consumed in our turn by unbelief and fear.

It is necessary to get out of this awkward situation. Afraid of the sea, we suffer from the rocking motion, holding on to one spot in an impossible equilibrium. We are fortunate that our ship is not going backward, and is not running aground.

"Well, what is to be done? Speak more definitely, and make a formulation"...

The demand made of us, that we formulate our thoughts about the case of Russia, is repeated fairly often. It is surprising, and causes us to involuntarily smile at the naive proof of that inattention and carelessness with which people generally read. All of our activity, all our life has been nothing but *a formulation of one thought, one conviction,* and, namely, the one about which people ask. One can say that we have been mistaken our entire life, one can say that our idea is disastrous and our conviction absurd, but *one cannot* say that we *have not formulated* our point of view, with the logic common to mankind and the memories in our head.

Perhaps by "formulas," our friends, like the French, have in mind prescriptions, i.e., drugs and orders, given in advance about how to act in this case or that. Indeed, we do not have those kinds of formulas. And there is no need for them. Serious prescriptions are improvised on the general principle of science and on the investigation of a given circumstance. [. . .]

History is what differentiates man from the animals: its character, in contrast to animal development, consists of the application of more or less conscious efforts for the organization of his way of life, for the hereditary, generic refinement of instinct, understanding, and reason with the help of memory. [. . .]

In the middle of the night following the 14th of December and the Polish rebellion of 1831, in the midst of the amazing ease with which the Nicholaevan yoke crushed all the new shoots, the first people to cry out for "land" were the Moscow Slavophiles, and although they stood on actual soil with their left legs,[13] they were still the first.

They understood our socioeconomic uniqueness in the allotment of land, in the repartition of land, in the rural commune and communal landholdings; but, having understood one side of the question, they neglected the other side—the *freedom* sought by the individual enslaved by the village, tsar, and church. The admirers of the good old days—out of spite for the Petrine order—the true nationalists and *premeditated* Orthodox believers, with ingratitude forgot that it was the West that had given them an all-saving civilization, in the light of which they found a treasure house in the land, which they began to examine.

Europe, where bourgeois liberalism was going full sail, had no concept of how a mute Russia was living on the sidelines; the most educated of Russians prevented them from seeing anything other than poor copies of their own paintings.

The first pioneer who set off to discover Russia was Haxthausen.[14] Having by chance come upon the traces of the Slavic communal system somewhere on the banks of the Elbe, the Westphalian baron set off for Russia and, fortunately, addressed himself to Khomyakov, K. Aksakov, the Kireevskys, et al. Haxthausen was genuinely one of the first to tell the Western world about the Russian rural commune and its profoundly autonomous and social principles—and when was that?

It was on the eve of the February revolution,[15] i.e., on the eve of the first broad but unsuccessful attempt to introduce social principles into state structure. Europe was very busy, and, because of its own sad fiasco, it failed to notice Haxthausen's book. Russia remained for them an incomprehensible state, with an autocratic emperor at its helm, and with an enormous military that threatened every movement for freedom in Europe.

Our own attempts to acquaint the West with unofficial Russia followed almost directly upon Haxthausen.

For seven whole years we taught about Russia—as much as we could and where we could.[16] Pythagorean theory didn't help very much. We were listened to absentmindedly before the Crimean War, with hatred during it, and inattentively before and after. [. . .]

III

With the death of Nicholas, tongues were loosened. The suppressed, secret, peevish thoughts that had accumulated came to light and told of their daydreams, each in its own way. In Russia at that time there was something completely chaotic, but reminiscent of a holiday, of the morning and springtime.

A remarkable mixture of various ages of mankind, of various directions and views—ones that had long ago exhausted themselves and ones that had barely sprouted—appeared on the scene. It was an opera ball, in which every kind of costume colorfully flashed by, from liberal tailcoats with a collar up the back of the head, as in the time of the first restoration, all the way to democratic beards and hairstyles. The German doctrinaire approach to slavery and absolutism and forgotten platitudes on political economy walked alongside the Russian Orthodox socialism of the Slavophiles and Western social theory "from this world." And this was all reflected not only in public opinion, not only in somewhat uninhibited literature, but in the government itself. [. . .]

All of the Russia that was awakening sincerely craved independent speech—speech not made sore by the censor's collar—yet there was not a single free printing-press to answer this need, except for the one in London. We put the West aside, and turned all our strength to our native cause, toward which we have striven since childhood and throughout our whole life.

The Polestar and *The Bell* appeared when the move and the rearrangement of furniture were at their height, at that exciting time of endless ferment, in which each word could become an embryo and a point of departure. Having brought on ourselves the responsibility of the first free Russian speech, what in fact did we say? With what did we appear before the giant who was still wiping his eyes?

The entire positive and creative part of our propaganda comes down to those same two words which you will find on the pages of our first publications and in the most recent issues—*Land and Liberty*, the development of the idea that there is no *Liberty without Land* and that the *Land is not secure without Liberty*. [. . .]

Right alongside the emancipation of the serfs we persistently demanded *the emancipation of the word* as the condition and the atmosphere without which there can be no popular advice about the common cause. Only open discussion and the press can replace the class-free assembly that was impossible before the emancipation of the serfs; only a lively *representation* of the word—not bound by any forms or censorship—can clarify issues and point out what has actually matured in popular understanding and to what extent.

All around were private struggles and private incidents, issues arose from events and events took place which mixed up all the maps, provoking passionate rejections and attractions, but, while breaking away from the path, we constantly returned to it and constantly held onto our two fundamental ideas.

And that is why, when the sovereign recognized in principle the emancipation of the serfs *with land*, without the slightest inconsistency and with complete sincerity we said: "You have conquered, Galilean!" for which we received reprimands from both sides.[17]

We will say in passing that neither the doctrinaires of loyalty nor the puritans of demagogy wanted to understand our unpretentious attitude toward the government. The oppositional and denunciatory character of our propaganda was a matter of practical necessity and not a goal or a foundation; strong in our faith, we had no fear of any kind of *pacification,* and, changing our weapon with ease, we continued the very same battle. It was impossible for us to lose our way. [. . .]

The idea of a bloodless coup was dear to us; everything that has been said of us to the contrary is just as much a lie as the statement that *we* assured the Poles that Russia was on the point of an uprising in 1862. There is, however, nothing fantastic in that; in Russian life there are none of the irreconcilable, stubborn, mutually destructive forces which have led Western life from one bloody conflict to another. If such irreconcilability did exist, then it is between the peasants and the landowners, but it was settled peacefully, and would have been settled without any blood at all if the cowardly government and its agents, who are enemies of the peasant cause, had not strained the situation for no reason.

Our imperial system and our gentry have no roots and they know it. They had prepared to take the last rites in 1862 and came to life only when the Petersburg fire, Katkov's slander, and the Polish uprising came to their rescue. The people love the tsar as the representative of defense and justice (a common factor in all undeveloped peoples); they do not love the emperor. The tsar for them is an ideal, and the emperor is the antichrist. Imperial power is maintained by the military and by the bureaucracy, i.e., by machines. The military will beat anyone on orders, without distinction, and the bureaucracy will copy out and fulfill the will of the leadership without argument. That kind of government cannot be felled with an axe, but at the first spring warmth it will melt into the life of the people and drown in it.

We were firmly convinced of the latter. The landowning class was being wiped out before our eyes, and, like vanishing pictures, was turning pale and being transformed into various pale deformities. The Russian imperial system has external political goals of self-preservation and it has tremendous power, but it has no principles; the same can be said of the environment surrounding it, and this has been the case since Peter himself. Between the day Nicholas died and his funeral, the court and the general staff were able to turn themselves into liberals "superficially, hypocritically." But who said that before this they were deep and sincere absolutists?

The Russian government was on the path to some kind of transformation, but, having taken fright, sharply turned off it. Our primary mistake was a mistake in timing, and, more than that, in imagining all the conditions and forces we forgot one of the most powerful forces—*the force of stupidity*. The old ways used it to gain strength.

The emancipation of the serfs, the grumbling of the landowners, the mood of society, of journalism, and of certain government circles... all of this inexorably led *to the first step,* i.e., the creation of a duma or an assembly. The experiences of the Moscow and Petersburg nobility obviously demonstrate this, but, as befits landowners, they were too late. When they raised their voices, the sovereign had been crowned a second time in all his autocracy by European threats and popular ovations.

We did not foresee the power of popular reaction. The animated spirit of 1612 and 1812 was only raised at a time of genuine danger to the fatherland; there was none this time but there was a desire for some kind of demonstration, and the mute made use of their tongues.

We looked upon the reaction as a day's misfortune and proceeded foremost with an analysis and consideration of the economic and administrative coup in the very spirit and direction of *Russian socialism.*

Keeping in the forefront the right to land, we advocated the development of elected self-government from the village to district, from the district to the region, and from the region to the province—we went no further, *and did not need* to—on the one hand, we pointed to the disgrace of personal arbitrariness, of the military-bureaucratic governance of the country, the excesses of the seraglio, and landowner brutality; on the other hand, we pointed to the assembly that could be seen in the distance, which would be chosen by a free alliance of provinces to discuss the *land question.*

One of the most difficult questions—not by its content but by the incorrigibility of prejudices defending the opposing view—was the question of "communal ownership of land."

[. . .] By *Russian socialism* we mean socialism that proceeds from the land and from the peasant way of life, from the factual allotment and existing repartition of fields, from communal possession and communal governance—and we advance together with the workers' cooperatives toward that economic *justice* for which socialism strives in general and which is affirmed by science.

This title is all the more necessary because, alongside our doctrine, a purely Western socialist doctrine has developed—with great talent and understanding—namely in Petersburg. This division is completely natural, stemming from the concept itself, and constitutes no kind of antagonism. We wound up complementing each other.

The first representatives of social ideas in Petersburg were the *Petrashevtsy*. They were even tried as "Fourierists." Behind them stood the strong personality of Chernyshevsky. He did not belong to any one social doctrine, but offered a profound social idea and a deep criticism of the contemporary order. Standing alone, a head taller than all the others, amidst the ferment in Petersburg over issues and forces, amidst the chronic vices and the incipient gnawing of conscience, amidst the youthful wish to live differently and to break loose from the usual filth and untruth, Chernyshevsky decided to grab the helm and try to point out to those who were thirsting and striving *what they should do*. [. . .]

Chernyshevsky's propaganda was an answer to *current* suffering, a word of comfort and hope to those who were perishing in the harsh grip of life. It showed them a way out. It set a tone for literature and drew a line between the *actual* young Russia and the one that pretended to be that Russia, a bit liberal, while still slightly bureaucratic and serf-owning. Its ideals lay in joint labor, in the organization of workshops, and not in an empty hall in which the Sobakeviches and Nozdrevs[18] would play at being "bourgeois gentry" and landowners in opposition.

The tremendous success of the social doctrine among the younger generation, and the school that it stimulated, led not only to literary echoes and outlets, but the beginnings of practical applications with historical significance. The emancipation of the serfs with an acknowledgment of their right to land, with the preservation of the commune and the conversion to socialism by young and active minds which had not yet been corrupted by life nor confused by doctrinaire thought, served as irrefutable proof of the benefits of our continual faith in the character of Russian development.

At the same time we followed step by step the debates inside the editorial commission and the introduction of the Statutes of February 19th; we examined the statutes themselves, as we sought to introduce to the rural revolution institutions closest to our views, while in Petersburg, Moscow, and even the provinces, phalanxes of young people were preaching in word and deed the general theory of socialism, of which the rural question presented itself as a *particular case.* [. . .]

The serf reform, with all its contradictions and incompleteness, immediately led to its own economic, administrative, and judicial consequences, with the introduction of the zemstvo[19] institutions, the new court system, etc. These were syllogisms, which were impossible to avoid.

All the reforms, beginning with emancipation, were not only incomplete but were deliberately distorted. In not one of them could be found that breadth and candor, that passion for destruction and creation with which great men and great revolutions have done their breaking down and building up; *in all of them* the worthlessness and bankruptcy of the old government of *edicts and arbitrary rule* could be recognized; but all of them contained an embryo, whose development was delayed, and perhaps deformed, but which was *alive.* [. . .]

Until the year 1863 we were still trying, despite the muddy spring roads at home, to follow the unwieldy old government carriage, and the louder we rang the bell, the more it lost its way. If the coachmen did not listen, the crowd surrounding them listened and, heaping abuse on us, did a portion of what we had been talking about. Then they went deaf as well. Since then energetic speech has had to yield for a time to cries of denunciation and indignation, which provoked a society wallowing in blood and filth, along with a *shallow, heartless, and faithless* government.

The government retreated in all areas, and, with all this, its retreat had neither a serious justification nor a serious character. If it really thought by means of frivolous arrests and indiscriminate exile to stop *history* and an already unmasked national development, it would be boundlessly to be pitied, but we think that the Winter Palace's vision did not extend that far. The palace, maintained in fear and trembling by its eunuchs and rhetors, did not fear *history,* but something lurking in the corner, and this was at a time when it said publicly and loudly that the government had never felt itself to be more powerful and popular as it did then. It's no wonder. Patriotism made people forget all that was humane in their heart and everything that was *inhumane* in the imperial system; the newspapers were full of loyal liturgies... the serfs, free of the landowners, and the landowners, free of their status, the Old Believers and the Jews, the Cossacks and the Germans—all of them by word of mouth rushed to support the throne and the altar... It was expected that benefits would follow and an expansion of rights, but the government pointed with horror to several articles and several young people and answered the upsurge of loyalty with an upsurge of persecution and brutality. What exactly they were afraid of, they did not say.

There was something crazy in all of this, and that is the way it ended—*with the shot on the 4th of April.*

Those who had been *hopeful* became embittered at their unfulfilled *hopes.* The first fanatical character, full of a gloomy religious belief, grabbed a pistol.

The revenge did not succeed, but the pretext was established and seized upon with savage joy, the reaction was justified, and the tsarist scarecrows were justified. Nevertheless, if the revenge did not succeed, the *terror also did not succeed.* Having begun on false premises, it got confused and was bogged down in dirty tricks by the police.

What did Muravyov's roundup accomplish, and what did his royal trumpeter Katkov proclaim? Where is the universal conspiracy in which all the dark forces of this world—the English, bankers, emigrants in Switzerland, Mazzini's emissaries and missionaries,[20] the Poles, us and not us, and, finally some kind of "worldwide revolutionary committee," unknown to the rest of the world?

From this entire affair only a corpse remains, a mute witness to nasty tsarist revenge and some unfortunate people, exiled *without a trial or any defense,* accused of *not wanting* a regicide...

To kill several people, some with a ready noose, others with long terms in prison, is not difficult; a locomotive can kill, so can the plague and a rabid dog. Terror reaches further: it is not enough to kill people, it wants to kill thoughts, ideas, and beliefs...

[. . .] The echo of Karakozov's shot exposed a terrifying vacuum in the Winter Palace, the sad absence of serious thought and deliberation... and it was so on all our "mountaintops."

[. . .] It is not our business whether they understand or not, and what they understand; the question for us is to find out what exactly they are moving against, what they fear, the way that Catholics fear Protestantism, the way that French monarchists fear revolution. The great enemy, the antichrist, the final judgment that they fear and against which they move is socialism.

And isn't that a great step forward?

And does this mean bringing history to a halt and moving backward?

They are afraid... not of a constitution, not of a republic, not of democracy... they are afraid of socialism mixed up with some sort of nihilism.

Did they ever stop to think what—aside from blue glasses and short hair—is meant by this word?

We will have more to say about *nihilism*, but here we just want to turn the attention of people of good conscience who, like parrots, repeat a word without knowing its meaning [. . .] to them we say that *nihilism* in its serious sense means *science and doubt, research in place of faith, and understanding in place of obedience.*

Revealing itself in opposition to popular well-being and human thought, socialism and reason, the government has come out for barbarity, serfdom, and stupidity...

The most recent terror killed it more than it killed other people. It killed the moral significance of the government; walking unsteadily and talking nonsense, it descended from the platform on which it has paraded since the death of Nicholas, arm in arm with Osip Nikolaevich Komissarov-Kostromsky.[21]

Further action will take place *outside it, without it.*

Power which takes nothing into account can do a great deal of harm, but *it cannot* in fact stop a movement which it fears and which will carry the mainland away to another destiny. It will move along, inadvertently, unconsciously, like a man asleep on a ship.

And is it advancing? And are we as a whole advancing?

[. . .] The reaction is absurd and repulsive, yes, yes, a thousand times yes... but where is the mighty brake that would stop the movement? Are they really going to take land away from the peasants and exclude them from elections? Doesn't the investigation into the Karakozov case demonstrate that among Moscow youth there was an idea for propaganda among the peasant factory workers, the first attempt at an organic combination of these two social levels that we were talking about?

"Yes, but they grabbed the young people and exiled them. It's a pity, but the places of the exiled will not remain empty."

Let us remember what it was like under Nicholas... and wasn't it during his time that the volcanic and bloody underground work began, which came into the light when he left this earth?

During the past five years we have become a little spoiled and a little undisciplined, forgetting that what we were given were not *rights, but indulgences.* It is time once again to focus.

It is vexing that history moves along such muddy and isolated country roads, but only *conscious thought* takes a direct route. Not changing our program, we will also take history's path, maneuvering with it, pressing along together with it. And how could it be otherwise, when the reaction solemnly recognized our program, which it actually became, according to the expression of the Brussels *Echo*, *"the banner that stands against the banner of the Winter Palace."*[22]

We will hold up this banner, or others will replace us—that is not the point—our banner, the banner of "Land and Liberty" taken up *by us, has been acknowledged* by the enemy camp.

Notes

Source: "Poriadok torzhestvuet!" *Kolokol*, l. 230, December 1, 1866 (I); l. 231–32, January 1, 1867 (II); l. 233–34, February 1, 1867 (III); 19:166–99, 427–31.

The opening epigraph is French for "Order reigns in Warsaw": words from a speech by France's minister of foreign affairs, Horace Sebastiani, at a meeting of the French parliament concerning the suppression of the Polish uprising.

1. In 1853, in conversation with the British ambassador, Hamilton Seymour, Nicholas I called Turkey the "sick man." Seymour reported back to Westminster, where the alarm was raised at possible Russian plans to carve up the Ottoman Empire.

2. Here, as elsewhere in the essay, Herzen indulges in puns that fail to translate. The adjective *ugolovnyi* (criminal) contains the same root as the noun *golova* (head).

3. Marc Caussidière (1808–1861) was in opposition to the July monarchy in France and, when that regime fell, briefly served as prefect of police in the provisional government before going into exile in England.

4. Pierre-Joseph Proudhon (1809–1865) stated this negative attitude toward national autonomy in chapter 6 of an 1863 treatise, "Si les traits de 1815 on cessé d'exister? Actes du futur congrès."

5. Herzen has translated the followed verses from a poem by Goethe about America: "Dich stort nicht im Innern / Zu lebendiger Zeit / Unnützes Erinnern / Und vergeblicher Streit."

6. Out into the open sea.

7. These statements were made on June 23, 1789, at a meeting of the Etats Générales, when deputies of the third estate (commoners), who had declared themselves the National Assembly on June 17, continued to meet despite the king's order for them to disperse. Count Honoré Mirabeau (1749–1791) informed the official who asked them to vacate the room that he should "go and tell" his master that they were there by the will of the people, after which the Abbé Emmanuel-Joseph Sieyès urged them to return to the subject of their meeting.

8. Herzen met with Blanqui in October 1866 in Freiburg.

9. The book in question is *Polish Emigration Before and During the Last Uprising: 1831–1863*, by Vasily F. Rach, published anonymously in Vilna in 1866.

10. "Shemyakin courts" is a proverbial expression, dating from a fifteenth-century prince of Galicia, and implies arbitrary judgments. Alexander N. Ostrovsky (1823–1886) was a prolific playwright, who most famously depicted the life of the merchants in Moscow and the Volga regions; "the dark kingdom" refers to the setting and atmosphere of Ostrovsky's plays and to an influential 1859 essay about it by the radical critic Nikolay Dobrolyubov.

11. Herzen turns frequently to the issue of land, while Chernyshevsky's novel is centered on the advantages of workshops.

12. In ancient Athens, a judicial body made up of volunteers.

13. This phrase implies they were on the wrong side, coming to this conclusion from incorrect principles.

14. Baron August Haxthausen (1792–1866), an economist, traveled through Russia in 1843–44 and wrote a three-volume study based on his travels, which was published between 1847 and 1852.

15. 1848.

16. Herzen lists the following works: *Von anderen Ufer* (1850), *Du développment des idées revolutionaries en Russia* (1851), *Le socialisme et le people russe, lettre à Jules Michelet* (1851), and articles in *L'Homme,* a periodical published in Jersey.

17. This phrase was used by Herzen in a number of earlier essays.

18. Sobakevich and Nozdrev are characters in Gogol's *Dead Souls.*

19. The introduction of the zemstvo in 1864 transferred responsibility in areas such as taxation, medical care, education, and road repair to local councils. Widely believed—except by Russian revolutionaries—to have been one of the more successful reform measures, its powers were restricted between 1890 and 1905.

20. Herzen knew and admired Giuseppe Mazzini (1805–1872), a leading Italian nationalist, democrat, and active participant in European revolutionary circles, from Mazzini's several periods of exile in London.

21. Komissarov (1838–1892) is the peasant credited with saving Alexander II from the assassination attempt in 1866 (Doc. 80).

22. Baron Fedor I. Firks (1812–1872), under the pseudonym Skedo-Ferroti, was the Brussels publisher of the newspaper *L'Echo de la Presse Russe,* which came out in Russian, French, and German between 1861 and 1867.

÷ 93 ÷

The Bell, Nos. 233–234, February 1, 1867. Herzen greeted the New Year in Nice, "lying in bed with Prince Dolgorukov's *Notes*" (*Let* 4:336). He added the final two paragraphs to the piece below to encourage the author, who had seen and disliked the first version. The review provoked a negative reaction from the Russian revolutionary Serno-Solovyovich, who despised Herzen's "liberal" tolerance of the Russian aristocracy. This article makes a similar point to de Custine's *Letters from Russia in 1839,* that the Russian aristocracy bears little resemblance to other European elites.

A NEW "VELVET BOOK" OF RUSSIAN NOBLE FAMILIES
[1867]

A new "velvet book" of Russian noble families has been published in Geneva under the modest title *The Notes of Prince Peter Dolgorukov.*[1] The first volume, like the Book of Genesis and the Acts of the Apostles of the highest levels of the gentry, appears at a very appropriate time. Genealogical trees in Russia were always prepared like fir trees before Christmas... depending on how much you paid, that's how many golden apples you got. But recently, in light of the imminent and not entirely honest end of serf-owning, people have begun to invent not separate trees, but an entire forest, a kind of *valiant noble history,* honorable in the present, honorable in the past, patriotic, historical, etc. In the past we used to hear from gray-haired butlers and various hangers-on: "Now that was *a genuine Russian gentleman,*[2] a Russian gentleman in the full sense of the word"... But in our day these expressions have been elevated from the servants' hall to the *front hall* of literature and therefore it is very interesting to find out what was a *genuine Russian gentleman,* and what *full sense* of this word our government and gentry scribes on aristocratic affairs are talking about.

The first volume of the *Notes* of Prince Dolgorukov, a representative of one of our most ancient princely families, is completely devoted to an enumeration of the principal families who surrounded the imperial throne at the beginning of the 18th century and helped to rule Russia. It amounts to just facts, detailed facts, carefully gathered and almost without commentary, ending with the regency of Biron, thus it takes in the *honeymoon* of the new empire. Reading this horrendous, frenzied, criminal *carmen horrendum,*[3] sometimes you have to set the book aside to recover from the horror and loathing. Here you abandon the human world: these are other creatures, other reptiles devoid of anything human except their talent for denunciation, kowtowing, stealing, and harming their fellow creatures. It is not the number of innocent victims, the rivers of blood and tears, or the torture and hard labor that depress the reader... all chronicles are full of blood and injustice, [. . .] but in the *childhood and youth of the gentry* there is a whiff of meanness, the absence of any conviction, shame, or honor, the cynicism of servility, and the consciousness of transgressions. A Dominican with strong faith burning a heretic,[4] or an Asian slave with his religion of obedience, is a thousand times more a human being than this entire gang of *aristocrats*—scoundrels, who sold themselves as a group to get serfdom, and individually for power and money.

And it is these informers, pimps, telltales and executioners, who tortured friends and family, who were beaten, flogged and spat upon by Biron, embezzlers, bribe takers, monsters toward their peasants, monsters toward their subordinates—these make up the basis of the *genuine Russian gentlemen.* And their descendants now dare to throw stones at the Polish gentry. The Polish gentry had the terrible vices of their time, they were savage and proud, they oppressed and robbed the people, but for all that they possessed the valor of feudal lords—not one king beat them with a stick, and not a single court favorite ran the gauntlet, like our lackeys with St. Andrew ribbons, thieves in princely cloaks, and all the highwaymen of the Guards' terror squads, who alternate between serving in the State Council and at hard labor. History has seen nothing like this: the same way that the filth from the London sewers formed a special layer at the mouth of the Thames, with a special population of infusoria,[5] so from Russian life a layer of *genuine Russian gentry—strata petropolitana*[6]—has come to the surface and developed, thanks to a false civilization and thorough depravity. It should be covered with earth as soon as possible to be redeemed by a renewed life and a series of human actions, and not summoned from a muddy grave, or summoned—as Pr. P. V. Dolgorukov has done—in a way that exposes it mercilessly to shame and embarrassment.

The sins of the fathers do not fall on their descendants only when the descendants do not pride themselves on their origins. A coat of arms comes with certain obligations and serves as a reminder: whoever holds it dear cannot sever ties with family legend; sometimes the light of past glory burns out... and the stains of past disgrace always show themselves.

We impatiently await the second installment of this great unmasking and exposure of our aristocratic servants and at that time we will make extracts from the extraordinarily interesting *Notes* of Prince Dolgorukov.

We have seen the great-grandfathers of our Petersburg and Moscow matadors—and we will see their grandfathers... and we sincerely ask the author to acquaint us with the fathers as soon as possible.

Notes

Source: "Novaia 'barkhatnaia kniga' russkikh dvorianskikh rodov," *Kolokol,* l. 233–34, February 1, 1867; 19:218–20, 441–42.

1. *Mémoires du Prince Pierre Dolgoroukow* (Geneva, 1867), vol. 1. Herzen ironically compares Dolgorukov's critical work with an official genealogy of the most prominent noble families compiled at the end of the seventeenth century by a specially established office for genealogical affairs. The book issued at that time had a crimson velvet cover.

2. *Barin.*

3. A song or verse that horrifies those who hear it (Lat., from Livy). In Livy, this phrase characterized the punishment announced for a young man who had killed his sister; Herzen previously used it in reference to the investigation of the Decembrists.

4. Members of the Franciscan and Dominican orders were involved in the courts of the Inquisition.

5. Minute aquatic creatures.

6. The Petersburg layer.

✣ 94 ✤

The Bell, Nos. 233–234, February 1, 1867. The first part of this article is based on notes sent by an anonymous correspondent. The title and editorial comments were added by Herzen.

OUR SYSTEM OF JUSTICE
[1867]

All of the accused in the well-known case of the armed uprising in Kazan[1] have been condemned by the Kazan criminal court to hard labor for the following period of time:

Ten years:
Vladimir Polinovsky (arrested at the beginning of May 1863)
Alexander Sergeev (arrested at the beginning of May 1863)
Semen Zhemanov (arrested at the end of April 1863)
Alexey Shcherbakov (arrested September 1, 1863)[2]
Arkady Biryukov (arrested at the beginning of May 1863)

Eight years:
Ivan Krasnopyorov (arrested at the beginning of March 1863)
Nikolay Orlov (arrested at the beginning of June 1863)
Vasily Dernov (arrested at the beginning of June 1863)

Six years:
Egor Krasnopyorov (arrested at the beginning of June 1863)
Petr Allev (arrested in the middle of September 1863)

Four years:
Rudolf Mitterman (arrested at the beginning of May 1863)
Viktor Lavrsky (arrested at the beginning of June 1863)

The State Senate, *despite the petition of the criminal chamber for a lessening of the punishment,* INCREASED THE DURATION OF THE PUNISHMENT in the following manner:

For the first two, sentenced by the chamber to ten years of hard labor, the Senate fixed a period of 14 years.

For the two who escaped and one who remains (in the same category)—12 years of hard labor.

For those the chamber sentenced to eight and six years—the Senate fixed on 10.

Those who got four years—now get six.[3]

What's going on? Have the sons of the fatherland completely lost their minds and their conscience?

In December, *Mitrofan Podkhalyuzin*, a Cossack from the nobility, was shot in Warsaw for his part in the Polish uprising, more than a year after the suppression and *pacification*. Seeing this, Russian journalists still have no shame in pointing out the cruelty of Turkish rule. Where have the Turks executed someone a year after an offense? *Austria betrayed* Podkhalyuzin![4] There's character for you!

...I am Rosslav on the throne, and I am Rosslav in shackles...[5]

Russia is being beaten and beaten... it's all black eyes, bruises, and rags, the provinces and its reputation are being lost little by little, and everything is as vile as before, people are being handed over for punishment as in Bakunin's time[6] ... only then there were no executions.

Russian newspaper further inform us that in Ryazan *Yurlov and Obnovlensky* have been sentenced to death ... That in Omsk they shot the peasant *Portnyagin, "who did not confess to the killing and who WAS NOT FOUND with the stolen belongings of the deceased,* but clues in the case demonstrate that the murder *must have been* committed by him."

What a Hercules column of cruelty, dullness, stupidity, and heartlessness!

In Orenburg the soldier *Arkhip Mayorov* was shot for impertinence toward a superior who was planning to flog him, for what reason the newspapers failed to say.

In the matter of the Polish outrage in eastern Siberia,[7] the military field court in Irkutsk decided on death sentences for 7 men from the first category, namely Artsimovich (Kvyatkovsky), Sharamovich, Tselinskii, Illyashevich, Bronsky, Reymer, and Kotkovsky, and, along with that, 19 more by a throw of the dice (one out of every ten) from the second and third categories. An additional 194 were sentenced to one hundred strokes of the lash and an unlimited period of time working in the mines; 92 men, accused of consorting with the rebels, were sentenced according to statutes 199 and 830 relating to exiles; 133 remained under suspicion; 260 were freed outright and four were turned over to a civilian court (*The Moscow Gazette,* December 15, 1866, No. 264).

Notes

Source: "Nashe pravosudie," *Kolokol,* l. 233–34, February 1, 1867; 19:221–23, 442–45.

1. The investigation into the insurrection began in 1863; its leaders were tried by a military court and executed. The sentences passed down for the remaining defendants

by the Kazan criminal court were affirmed—and the number of years increased—by the Senate in June 1866.

2. Herzen: "Zhemanov and Shcherbakov escaped in November 1866." The two young men were members of the Kazan branch of Land and Liberty, which conducted propaganda among the peasants. After their escape, both eventually made their way to Switzerland, and introduced themselves to Herzen and Ogaryov.

3. Herzen's additional comments begin at this point.

4. Podkhalyuzin was accused of deserting his regiment in 1863 to help the Poles, then hiding under an assumed name in Austria, until his 1865 arrest.

5. Herzen is paraphrasing the words of Rosslav from Knyazhnin's tragedy of the same name.

6. Austria handed Bakunin over to Russian authorities in 1851. In 1861, Bakunin escaped from Siberian exile and made his way east, eventually reaching Herzen and Ogaryov in London.

7. In 1865, Polish exiles staged an uprising in Siberia. Of the 680 people turned over to the military court, only 95 did not receive additional sentences.

⇥ 95 ⇤

Moscow—Our Mother and Stepmother
[1867]

IT IS NOT FOR YOU, NOT FOR YOU[1] to hoist the banner for liberation—first cleanse yourselves, repent, acquire one language and one standard, or openly remain the slaves that you are; in this status you can be the "scourges of Providence" but *not liberators*. A person who selfishly wants freedom for himself and others like him, and at the same time puts his neighbor in stocks, is unworthy of freedom. That is what it was like for Christianity—at the beginning a great thing—and then for the great revolution of 1789 (about which our pygmies now speak condescendingly); if they did not save and liberate the entire world, all the same they did believe in general salvation and liberation, and summoned everyone to their side without the bestial hatred of one species for another, without zoological biases and antipathies.

It is possible at one and the same time to be *a loving mother and an evil stepmother,* but then you cannot complain that in the eyes of any honest person your unjust love calls forth if not hatred, then revulsion.

For that reason we present the following two extracts from *Moscow.* Speaking of a spiritual-revolutionary demonstration (with which we fully sympathize) that took place in a Greek monastery in Moscow, the editor observes:

But this very requiem involuntarily summons us to melancholy reflection. We have heard that the fulfillment of such a simple and natural desire, like the desire to collectively remember in church martyrs who loved their fellow man and loved Christ, involved unanticipated difficulties, and it was necessary to get permission in Petersburg. How can that be! Even *in order to gather together in an Orthodox church* and pray for Orthodox believers, who have died for the sake of their faith, *society must request permission from the authorities?* In order to perform such a religious ritual, will the local spiritual authorities have to take into account diplomatic considerations and find out whether such an action is in agreement with the political views of the ministry, and the reaction in Petersburg? One cannot fail to regret the dependent state of the clergy and the strange *confusion* of rights and responsibilities by society and the government!

What is the result of such confusion? Society, adopting for itself the government's point of view, *quite often takes upon itself the responsibilities of the Third Department* and by this narrows its circle of activities and deviates from its calling. The government "reforms the function" of society, exceeding the limits where it, the government, is called upon to act and where it can be powerful, and extends itself to such areas of life where the external tools of state power cannot reach, and where the government, against its will, must seem ineffective... It weakens society, keeping it forever in swaddling clothes and on a leash.[2]

Alongside this sensible, intelligent speech *of a mother,* wouldn't it be a good idea to hear the endearments *of a stepmother,* wouldn't it be good to look at her nasty spite, which intoxicates a mind that nothing can satisfy—not the fact that she beat her stepchildren within an inch of their lives, not the fact that while covered with blood and bruises "they are still breathing and dare to speak their own language." Here it is!

A permanent resident of Kiev can't help noticing—says a *Moscow* correspondent—that recently Polish speech has begun to resound *more boldly* in Kiev: it is heard on the street, in restaurants, and in all public places, and that's not all—this Polish speech is accompanied—in relation to Russians—*by that brazen, provocative glance* which the high-born Pole is so good at. It is obvious that our Poles have raised their heads: the Goluchowski phenomenon and all sorts of chimeras have turned their heads. They say that in districts of Volynia that border Galicia, noble Polish landowners have recently begun to speak provocatively—in relation to Russian matters—with a very Polish naïveté: "Just wait," they threaten local authorities, "come spring and Goluchowski will arrive with Napoleon, and they will chase you right out of here."[3]

Gentlemen of the police, assert your rights.

What terrible and lasting depravity has come from three years of government-sponsored patriotism. People with no connection either to the police or *The Moscow Gazette* so easily make or spread denunciations, like Katkov, resting on his sky-blue laurels.[4]

Why should Poles have to *whisper* in Polish? Why should they look lovingly at the Russians? Only our grandfathers and forefathers kissed the hand that beat them on the mouth and flogged them on the back.

The lethargic state which the editor of *The Day* has been enjoying has restored his strength although it has not sobered him,[5] but at one time—along with the sacred objects in the Faceted Palace and the Kremlin—didn't he hold dear the rights of man and not the hateful hand of the government, which was invading the last strongholds of the individual, shaming it with violence, shaving the beard of the gray-haired Khomyakov, knocking the ancient cap off his head, and forbidding, as *indecency,* our native peasant coat?..[6]

It is fortunate that, except for the Russian consul, nobody knows or reads *Moscow* in Turkey, because if Sadyk Pasha showed his pious sultan the newspaper, and the latter began, for the love of Turkey and Mohammed, to exterminate not only people, but also the Greek language and dress,[7] and began to persecute points of view and punish clothing...

[. . .] Before you liberate others, begin with yourself, take a good steaming in the bathhouse, use a couple of birch twigs: you have too much from the Petrine and Arakcheev eras stuck on you. [. . .]

What can be said about the government when society, when *free* public opinion denounces Poles for speaking Polish and not casting loving glances at Russian officials?

This is the brake that is holding Russia back and keeping it from racing toward the great future that is being thrust upon it, preventing it from atoning for old sins and pushing fresh crimes into the background... No, it is not for you to hoist the banner of liberation: your love is filled with hatred!

Notes

Source: "Moskva—mat' i machekha," *Kolokol,* l. 235–36, March 1, 1867; 19:224–26, 445–46.

1. Once again paraphrasing Psalm 113/115, Herzen criticizes the newspaper *Moscow* for the campaign—by Ivan Aksakov, Metropolitan Filaret, and others—in support of

uprisings by Orthodox Christians against the Turks on Crete, and in Serbian and Bulgarian territories. He was also irritated by Aksakov's anti-Polish polemic in *The Day*.

2. This citation is from an editorial by Aksakov in the January 11, 1867, issue of *Moscow*, which was devoted to the January 8, 1867, service in memory of those killed on Crete. This editorial led to a government warning to *Moscow* for its sharp views on the relations between church and state. Aksakov answered the warning in the January 22 edition, and Herzen reprinted this answer in the March 15 issue (no. 237) of *The Bell*.

3. Herzen quotes from a letter from Kiev published in *Moscow* on January 13, 1867. Count Agenor Goluchowski was appointed governor-general in Galicia in 1866 by Austria. He sought to increase Polish influence in the region and decrease that of Russia.

4. Katkov was of course known for his denunciations in print. The gendarme uniform was sky-blue.

5. Aksakov was forced to suspend publication of *The Day* from mid-December 1865 until the beginning of January 1867.

6. In 1849 Yuri Samarin and Ivan Aksakov were briefly held under arrest. In April 1849, the minister of the interior, on the tsar's authority, ordered the gentry to refrain from having beards, since it could interfere with wearing uniforms. The Slavophiles saw this as a general prohibition on traditional Russian dress, which was worn as a sign of support for Russian principles. The police were vigilant in making sure that the Aksakov brothers observed the ban on beards. The garments Herzen refers to are, respectively, the *murmolka* and *poddëvka*.

7. Sadyk Pasha was the Turkish name of Mikhailo Czaikovsky (Michal Czajkowski, 1804–1886), who fought for Poland in 1831–32, after which he fled to Paris and then to Turkey, where he converted to Islam, organized a Cossack brigade to fight the Russians during the Crimean War, and eventually accepted amnesty from Alexander II, converted to Orthodoxy, and lived in Ukraine from 1872 until his death.

⇥ 96 ⇤

The Bell, No. 239, April 15, 1867. The title makes obvious references to the large, non-functioning bell and cannon in the Kremlin, as well as to Herzen's newspaper.

———

RIVALS OF THE BIG BELL AND THE BIG CANNON
[1867]

A correspondent for *Le Nord*, talking about his three-week stay in Moscow, points out—like two great rarities—not the large bell and not the large cannon, but Filaret, the 84-year-old chief prelate, and *Katkov*, the much younger, but no less great, chief publisher.[1] Before the decline of one of

Katkov's predecessors, the emperor Nicholas, some American fool lied to the extent that he called the two lead bullets that Nicholas used for eyes as "mild," to the great delight of *Punch*. That is what Katkov is experiencing now. The correspondent visited him—as if crawling into Saltychikha's cage—and couldn't get over his admiration for the graciousness and meekness of the passionate editor-inquisitor. Is the great career of Muravyov's Homer coming to an end? He's growing a little paler and less visible, and the Belgian correspondents are beginning to exaggerate his importance, and, what is much worse, the nasty *News* accuses him not only of rivaling the big bell, but the *smaller one*, that is, us. One huntsman for the gentry is beginning to think that *The Moscow Gazette* and *The Bell* have a single editorial staff (quite a compliment for us!) and calls Katkov's articles *chimes*.[2]

[. . .] It is clear that the abyss into which he pushed Russia on a daily basis has begun to terrify Katkov; he has stumbled at the very edge, and has found people who are more Katkov than he himself is.

But it is also impossible to turn back, Serafim-Abadonna, and he is forced to "wander sadly through the past," and, blushing for the present, receive from his fellow diggers insults and kicks.[3]

It's a bad business to be a *renegade*.

Notes

Source: "Soperniki bol'shogo kolokola i bol'shoi pushki," *Kolokol*, l. 239, April 15, 1867; 19:241, 454–55.

1. *Le Nord* was a political daily (1855–92), published in Brussels and subsidized by the Russian government. The report in question appeared in the March 28, 1867, issue under "Chronique de Moscou." The author spoke with reverence of the clarity of Filaret's mind and the sanctity of his way of life. Katkov was praised for the independence of his views and his position as the first genuine Russian commentator.

2. The reactionary *News* took issue with Katkov over the question of land reform; Herzen was naturally amused by squabbles between two basically like-minded periodicals.

3. The image of Serafim-Abadonna wandering sadly through the past, repenting his sins, comes from the first part of the German poet Friedrich Klopstock's epic poem "Der Messias."

⇥ 97 ⇤

The Bell, No. 242, June 1, 1867. Conditions were worsening in Russia, although Herzen does not appear to be as shocked as his correspondent.

The Right to Congregate—New Restrictions
[1867]

We received this from Petersburg:

> Why have you omitted the outrageous measures that have placed
> every sort of gathering under police surveillance? According to the
> new law, not only secret political and non-political meetings are con-
> sidered "illegal," but in general *any kind of meeting* with any sort of
> goal that does not receive preliminary permission. The police are
> ordered to seek out criminal societies everywhere, harsh punish-
> ments are set for participants, and, finally, there is a promise of
> *forgiveness and all kinds of leniency for informers.*

Only that? Isn't there any payment, by the number of societies, or per
person?

All this is vile, all this is pure Valuev and genuine Shuvalov, so why is the
correspondent surprised? Don't these measures belong to a series of vile
measures from the past five years? And before that did we really have some
kind of right of assembly—*droit de reunion?*... Enough!

Notes

Source: "Pravo sobirat'sia—novye stesneniia," *Kolokol*, l. 242, June 1, 1867; 19:265, 469.

⇒ 98 ⇐

The Bell, No. 243, June 15, 1867. A Polish émigré, Anton Berezovsky, a veteran of the
1863 uprising against Russian rule, took a shot at Alexander II in Paris on June 6, 1867,
a crime for which he was given a life sentence by the French courts. Herzen delayed a
trip to Nice to respond in print to this new assassination attempt. He wrote to a friend
that "my head is spinning—news, gossip, bullets, tsars, horses—but I have to keep my
wits about me and write" (*Let* 4:419). He was likely unaware that the tsar's young mis-
tress, Katya Dolgorukaya, had also traveled to Paris and that Alexander II ignored considerations of safety to secretly visit her. Herzen's disapproval of Karakozov's attempt
the previous year to kill the tsar damaged the writer's relations with young Russian
revolutionaries abroad, but he did not waver in his rejection of such acts of individual
terror which only led to further repression, and he believed that his views would be better understood in the future.

THE SHOT OF JUNE 6
[1867]

Once more a shot rings out. We will not go on about it at great length. Our opinion about people who take such a path is well known, and neither the howl of crazy loudmouths,[1] nor abuse by the powerful of this world will cause us to extol this type of attempt, which brings with it terrible calamities, nor to pronounce words of judgement on the martyrs who condemn themselves to death and whose conscience is clear for the very reason that they are fanatics.

It goes without saying that the June 6 shot will exert no influence on the spirit of our publication. Our convictions were formed a long time ago, and no chance event can bend them to the right or to the left.

There is a great lesson for Russia in this.

Berezovsky will be judged in open court, not in a secret torture chamber the way Karakozov was judged, and he will be tried by judges, not by specially selected generals.

The first investigator, looking at the poor-quality pistol Berezovsky used, noted that in all likelihood, he had no accomplices.[2] Hundreds of young people were brought into the Karakozov case, although their innocence was known. Just the mention by Limayrac in *Le Constitutionnel* about a moral connection between the shot and cries of "Long live Poland!" provoked a cry of disapproval not only in liberal journals but in those with a monarchist or religious point of view.[3]

In closing, we turn our readers' attention to Shuvalov's police trickery, in asking Berezovsky whether he had corresponded with his father.[4] That is, he tried to entangle relatives, acquaintances, their relatives and their acquaintances—in both Poland and Russia—in this business, which so clearly stood on its own!

This should be a genuine cause for contemplation.

Notes

Source: "Vystrel 6 iiunia," *Kolokol*, l. 243, June 15, 1867; 19:269, 472–74.

1. Herzen had received anonymous letters of abuse after his article "Irkutsk and Petersburg" (Doc. 80).

2. The accused had pawned his coat in order to purchase this cheap weapon, which wound up injuring him instead of the tsar.

3. Paulin Limayrac, the chief editor of the newspaper, made note of pro-Polish demonstrators in Paris during the days leading up to the 6th of June.

4. Chief of gendarmes Shuvalov, who had accompanied Alexander to Paris, took part in the first round of interrogations.

↦ 99 ↤

The Bell, No. 243, June 15, 1867. A decade earlier, Herzen had begun what he expected to be a continuing series about trips taken by members of the tsar's family (Doc. 11). "Venerable Travelers (Part Two)" has much more in common with the themes that interested him in 1867 than it has with his earlier satirical travelogue. Herzen started writing this article about the tsar's journey to Paris before the Berezovsky story broke, and completed it afterward. Bakunin thoroughly approved of this piece, which he said reminded him of the young Alexander Herzen, "whose wise and fresh laughter had such a powerful and beneficial impact on Russia... Remain our powerful Voltaire. In this lies your truth and your power" (*Let* 4:425). Herzen's comment that in the age of the telegram one need only travel for amusement—and never for business—remains remarkably fresh after 150 years.

Venerable Travelers (Part Two)
[1867]

> Nous sommes aujourd'hui ce que nous
> avons été hier... continuons.
> —Sieyès, 1789

We faced a question à la Shpekin,[1] *to print* or *not to print* our report on the first part of the sovereign's journey after the June 6th shot. The question was decided by the fact that, after the shot, the journey continued even more pleasantly than before. The genuine success of the journey began at that point: ovations, speeches, and open carriages. In addition, they are all military men—and what sort of *military man* worries the next day about a bullet that did not hit him, but hit the ear of a horse ridden by Mocquard's son-in-law?[2]

It is time, however, to stop shooting, or else a future Karamzin will have to deal with a new history so full of bullets, double-barreled pistols, and a nonsensical amount of speeches and telegrams, that he will have to ask Turgenev for the right to name it *Stories About Unsuccessful Hunters*.[3]

June 10

I. The Sovereign in the Avenue Marigny

But where is *the first part?* In the first issue of *The Bell*, it appeared exactly *ten years* ago on the occasion of a journey by the "widowed empress-mother." Ten years later we are called upon to say a few words about the travels of the obviously "not widowed emperor." There is something mystical in this: between us and the great traveler there is a mysterious connection, about which we will definitely consult with Hume.[4] We were both in Vyatka in 1837,[5] and in Paris he is staying on the same street where we lived in 1847,[6] so that the sovereign could write a *final* "Letter from Avenue Marigny" for *The Contemporary* if Valuev had not shut it down.[7]

But now to business. You are familiar with the beginning of the journey, or, as Russian newspaper disciplinarians say, of "the imperial procession," but what about its goal?

"It is not known!"

"Would you be interested in knowing?"

"Very much so."

"How can there not be any?"

First of all, we absolutely do not believe that the sovereign came to Paris *on business.* No one goes anywhere on business these days: with ministers and correspondence, with counts and telegrams,[8] one can take care of not only every kind of business, but also every kind of idleness. Alexander Nikolaevich wanted to have a good time, and Napoleon wanted to show off a pièce de résistance like the tsar—see, he says, "who we are entertaining"... And with Turkey, what will be will be[9]—it was not accustomed to fatalism.

Second... we find the first reason sufficient, and, according to Leibniz, where one reason is sufficient, there is no point in looking for others.[10]

Alexander Nikolaevich did Napoleon a good deed, and unburdened himself of the tedium of Petersburg. The Byzantine-Darmstadt piety[11] had reached the point of suffocation in the Winter Palace, and instead of amusements, there were Austrian and Turkish Slavs, with whom one had to speak *German*[12] in order to understand their Russian feelings and their conversations with the devout subjects of Her Majesty. No matter how incredibly pious an autocrat might be, there is only so much piety he can take. Life was unbearable.

The French got angry in vain that the sovereign did not bring the esteemed empress with him—it was a bit of good luck and a tactful move. Let her pray for his health and preservation from all of France's intrigues and ailments, while he was able to relax a little in freedom. He had some masculine concerns to attend to... and he did not waste a second. [. . .]

The sovereign, to be fair, wanted—in the image and likeness of the late Alexander Pavlovich—to enter Paris on horseback.[13] At the final station it seems he was already seated on his horse. It was, however, explained to him that Alexander I captured Paris with military troops, while now Paris was conquering Alexander II with kindness, so it followed that it was for Paris to approach him on horseback, but the numbers did not allow for that. There was nothing to be done, the emperor made haste, and a closed carriage raced to the Avenue Marigny. [. . .]

From the theater it was a short walk home. The next day it was off to the exhibition—here the Russian horses bore witness to the degree of perfection achieved by their parents in this profession,[14] and Russian stones spoke in favor of geological cataclysms in the earth, under the special direction of the ministry of state property.[15] From the stables the sovereign led Napoleon to an inn to have a bite to eat; all the food was Russian, even the champagne, which they say was brought for this purpose from Tver.

[. . .] Poles, for the most part, have left Paris, with Czartoryski[16] *en tête;* one of them even left vertically, taking off in a hot-air balloon. That gave us the wonderful idea of starting a campaign in Siberia to get everyone— young and old alike, mullah and shaman, Votyak and Ostyak—to agitate for the sovereign to favor them with a visit. And then maybe the authorities would order all *the Poles to leave.*

II. A La Porte![17]

In the peaceful era prior to the year 1848, Nikolay Pavlovich, who loved to travel around various lands and amaze the Germans with his waistline, his elkskin pants, and his splendidly polished jackboots, was once in Vienna.[18] At that time there ruled in Austria not the present sovereign, who so successfully began his reign by hanging captured generals who had surrendered to Paskevich, but his foolish and sickly predecessor.[19] There was a parade. No matter where Nicholas went, no fewer than fifty thousand people were rounded up. Regiment after regiment marched by, and finally there was the Kaiser Nicholas regiment; the Austrian emperor was dozing on an enormous gray horse, with his Hapsburg lip sticking out even further than usual—suddenly there was a noise: having seen his regiment, Nicholas, with his characteristic bravery, stood before them, received the report, skillfully led the toy soldiers, and went at full speed to inform the emperor that everything was in good order. In Austria things are done quietly and one rushes on foot. The dozing Ferdinand opened his eyes and was stupefied: Nicholas was racing toward him "with a gloomy and severe face,"[20] and with a bared saber—closer and closer. Ferdinand turned his horse and gave it the spur for the first time and took to his heels. Nicholas, turning pale with disgust, took off after him along the streets of Vienna. "*Bruder,*" he cried out, "don't be afraid, *treue Schwesterliebe widmet dir mein Herz.*"[21] Finally he caught up with Ferdinand, who did not go back to the parade, but returned to his palace and went to bed. [. . .]

Who could have imagined that twenty-five years later the son of the late Nikolay Pavlovich would play out just such a scene on a more peaceful field, namely in the Palais de Justice, the palace *of retribution*. The sovereign came to the courthouse not on business, but to see whether everything was in order. Some of the lawyers raised the cry "*Vive la Pologne!*" They did this more as a compliment, knowing that in all manifestos and in various decrees the sovereign speaks of his love for Poland and his truly parental care for it. The guards—those preservers of decorum—did not like this cry and they shouted to the friends of Poland: "*A la porte!*" The sovereign, imagining that "*à la porte!*" referred to him and probably recalling that he too was a friend of Poland, turned and left with his entire suite [. . .] galloping to another place where they would also shout "*Vive la Pologne!*"[22]

[. . .] The sooner he gets out of Poland, the sooner he would be able to peacefully stroll around the exhibition. Only not by means of such tricks like the Verzhbolovo customs amnesty. But how could they come up with something sensible when they still spend their time going through suitcases? Evil tongues have said that this is not an amnesty, but a visa for Paris. That is how the French understood it.[23]

P.S. On the 12th the newspapers said that on the way to Versailles there were more cries of "Long live Poland!" as Alexander II and Napoleon rode by. Napoleon said: "They are incorrigible," and the sovereign answered: "That is proof that they must be stopped." Then he requested (and this does him great honor) that they release the people who had been arrested for shouting this slogan. In Russia and Siberia there are thousands of Poles, who never shouted but had merely thought "Long live Poland!" We propose that they be liberated as well, since the tsar's opinion cannot change as a result of latitude and longitude.

Notes

Source: "Avgusteishie puteshestvenniki (Stat'ia vtoraia)," *Kolokol*, l. 243, June 15, 1867; 19:280–85, 481–86.

Regarding the opening epigraph, see Doc. 92, Part II for information about Abbé Sieyès. Herzen is using the quote above to emphasize his unchanging position toward autocracy, and to point out Alexander II's inability to draw the appropriate lessons from French revolutionary history.

1. Shpekin played the postmaster in Gogol's play *The Inspector General;* in act 5, scene 8, he must decide whether to open a letter or not. Herzen plays on the similarity of the Russian roots of the words *pechatat'* (to print) and *raspechatat'* (to unseal).

2. Napoleon III's equerry Ramboud, son-in-law of the French ruler's late personal secretary Mocquard, noticed Berezovsky with a gun and rode up to shield the emperor; the shot hit his own horse.

3. In a June 8, 1867, letter to Turgenev, author of *Notes of a Hunter,* Herzen jokingly suggested a title for a history of Alexander II's reign, with two botched assassination attempts to date: *Notes of Unsuccessful Hunters by Successful Ones* (*Zapiski durnykh okhotnikov khoroshimi*).

4. Hume was an English spiritualist who visited St. Petersburg in the mid-1860s.

5. Herzen was in exile in Vyatka from May 1835 through December 1837; the heir to the throne visited the town on May 18–20, 1837, during his get-acquainted trip around Russia. As a result of this visit and the efforts of the poet Zhukovsky, who accompanied Alexander as a tutor, Herzen was transferred to Vladimir. Herzen described this meeting in letters and in *Past and Thoughts.*

6. During his stay, from May 20 (June 1) until May 30 (June 11), Alexander was given the use of an apartment in the Elysée Palace on Avenue Marigny, where Herzen lived from April to October 1847.

7. Installments of Herzen's *Letters from the Avenue Marigny* appeared in two different issues of *The Contemporary* for 1847. The journal was banned in May 1866.

8. *Grafy, telegraphy.*

9. The announced purpose for the tsar's trip to Paris was to attend the World Exposition, but rumor said that there were to be talks about getting French help in pressing Turkey to quit the Slavic regions of Europe. As Herzen predicted, little was accomplished in the diplomatic arena.

10. Herzen jokingly refers to the "principle of sufficient reason" credited to the German philosopher and mathematician Gottfried Leibniz (1646–1716).

11. This is a reference to the devout posture of Empress Maria Alexandrovna, who converted to Orthodoxy upon her arrival in Russia in 1840. Herzen saw as hypocritical the combination of barbaric state policy and imperial piety.

12. On May 14, 1867, in Tsarskoe Selo, Alexander had received a delegation of Slavs who had come to Russia for the Moscow Ethnographic Exposition.

13. After the defeat of Napoleon and the surrender of the French, Alexander I made a triumphal entry into Paris on March 19/31, 1814.

14. The achievements of Russian horse breeding were displayed at the exhibition, and on June 3, 1867, Alexander II was awarded a gold medal for improvements in this field.

15. Herzen appears to be referring, ironically as always, to the theft of state salt stores and landslides in the salt-mining region of Nizhny Novgorod.

16. Prince Czartoryski (1828–1894) was the leader of the Polish aristocracy in emigration.

17. Get out of here!

18. Nicholas visited Vienna in 1833 and 1835. During the first visit, the emperor made the tsar head of a regiment of hussars. The episode related here took place during the second trip.

19. In 1848, Emperor Ferdinand I abdicated in favor of his nephew Franz Joseph. The latter began with a bloody suppression of the Hungarian uprising, with the aid of Russian forces led by Prince Paskevich. On August 13, 1849, nine Hungarian generals were executed on orders of Franz Joseph.

20. The ironic paraphrase of a line from Pushkin's ballad about a pale knight.

21. "Brother, my heart pledges to you a sister's true love." Herzen places a paraphrase of lines from Schiller's ballad "The Knight of Toggenburg" in the mouth of Nicholas I.

22. Parisian newspapers reported that similar demonstrations greeted the tsar at the Musée de Cluny, Notre Dame, and at a parade in the tsar's honor in front of the Grand Opéra.

23. On Alexander's way to France, an order was given "at the highest level" to finish up with all political cases connected to the Polish uprising and return home all exiled natives of the Kingdom of Poland who had behaved well, in the opinion of local authorities. European public opinion saw this as simply a way to assure the tsar a peaceful journey.

⇥ 100 ⇤

The Bell, Nos. 244–245, July 1, 1867. Herzen began to think about halting publication of *The Bell* for six months. A number of factors made it more difficult to carry on: reaction appeared to be triumphing in Russia, as progressive voices—including those who had supplied *The Bell* with information—were silenced, the newspaper's audience was greatly reduced, and there were tensions with Russian revolutionaries in Europe. Bakunin was one of the loudest voices raised in favor of continuing as before, writing to Herzen that readership had picked up again at home, and that even 500 copies could wield significant influence. He advised Herzen to change not the direction but the tone of the paper; there should be no further letters to the tsar and less caustic humor (*Let* 4:405). The Western and Russian reactionary press saw any hiatus as proof of the defeat of Herzen's ideas, a conclusion that is refuted below. As the title suggests, it is a summary of the most significant period of Herzen's publishing activity, and, beyond that, of a "national project" that had begun in the 1830s, in a circle of friends from Moscow University (Root, *Gertsen i traditsii,* 229).

This issue of *The Bell* included another excerpt from *Past and Thoughts;* although it refers to the year 1862, it is evocative of many moments in Herzen's life. The folklore reference to Ilya Muromets had been used before to characterize Alexander II in 1858, when he was moving to the right and away from the path toward "development, liberation, construction" (Doc. 18). Here it is Alexander Herzen himself who is unsure about the next step.

> Like the knights in fairy tales who have lost their way, we had stopped at the crossroads. If you went to the right, you would lose your horse, but survive. If you went to the left, the horse would be fine but you would perish. If you went straight ahead, everyone would abandon you, and if you went back... but that was no longer possible, that road was overgrown with grass. If only some magician or hermit monk appeared, who could relieve us of the burden of this decision... (*Kolokol,* 8–9:2002)

Believing that the remaining audience for his journalism was European, a French edition, *Le Kolokol,* with a Russian supplement, was published from January to December 1868. Herzen died in January 1870 and was buried beside his wife in Nice on a hill overlooking the sea.

1857–1867
[1867]

On July 1, 1857 the *first* issue of *The Bell* was published in London. The current issue marks our tenth anniversary.

Ten years! We have stood firm, and, most importantly, we have stood firm *for the past five years,* which were very difficult.

Now we want to take a breath, wipe away the perspiration, and gather new strength, and, for that reason, we will stop publication for *six months.* The next issue of *The Bell* will come out on January 1, 1868, and with that we will begin *a second decade.*

Now we wish calmly, without the diversion of urgent work, to take a close look at what is going on at home, where the waves are headed and where the wind is pulling, and we want to check in which areas we were correct and in which we were mistaken.

We have taken a backward glance too often, especially in recent times, to have to repeat yet again our creed and the bases of the view that we have taken in *The Bell;* they were immutable, and at least our official *enemies* never doubted this. *The Bell* was and will be more than anything else an organ of *Russian socialism and its development*—socialism of the farm and the workers' cooperative, of the countryside and the city, of the state and the province.

For us, everything is subordinate to the social development of Russia: forms and individuals, doubts and mistakes—but since it is impossible without freedom of speech and assembly, without general discussion and counsel, with all our strength we called for and will continue to call for an *Assembly of the Land.* In it we see no more than a gateway, but an open gateway, and that is most important—until now Russian development has had to secretly come in over the fence, while the watchman was not looking or slept...

All the rest is mud and dust on the road, logs and stones under the wheels; all the rest could be left in the shade to decay on its own, if only these logs and stones did not crush the best people, if they didn't drown in this swamp the intrepid sowers of the early morn as they went out to work. For that reason, together with the "general part" there will again be a section on unmasking abuses.

What our pause will mean to us is that it makes it possible to measure to what extent interest in *The Bell* is great or weak, alive or dead, and how much its absence will be noticed... However, toward the end of the year we intend once more to remind readers about ourselves, and to publish, *if pos-*

sible, a series of new articles in a special publication called *A Bell Almanac.*[1] It will also contain a program for our journal in 1868.

Perhaps, by the time we return, or during our home leave, younger and fresher activists will test their strength. It is time for young talents to break their seal of silence. Conditions in Russia for uncensored publication are terrible, the best journals have been crushed, and the best newspapers face the constant threat of warning and suspension. Why is so little published abroad? Our press and several others offer a genuine opportunity. We would happily welcome any Russian publication. We will not feel crowded—there are plenty more fish in the sea.

P.S. If any compelling reasons, events, communications, or corrections cause us to interrupt our silence, we will publish a supplement no later than August 1st.[2]

Notes
Source: "1857–1867," *Kolokol,* l. 244–245, July 1, 1867; 19:286–87, 486–88.

1. Herzen dropped the idea of an almanac later that year as he concentrated his efforts on articles for the periodical itself when it resumed publication.

2. A supplementary leaflet was issued on the occasion of *The Bell*'s tenth anniversary (*Let* 4:430).

CRITICAL ESSAY

ALEXANDER HERZEN: WRITINGS ON THE MAN
AND HIS THOUGHT

Robert Harris

In a number of important aspects, the literary career of Alexander Ivanovich Herzen (1812–1870) gained a renewed impetus with his arrival on British soil in 1852, and culminated in the decade from 1857 to 1867, Herzen's *Bell* years. His writings during this fifteen-year period exhibit a mixture, and at times a synthesis, of the two major components in his development: the period of roughly fifteen years in Russia during which Herzen studied and wrote on philosophy and social thought, and the following decade during which he lived in the West, where he was exposed firsthand to European culture and practice, people and institutions, popular views and public opinion.

After leaving Russia in early 1847 and spending over five stormy and eventful years on the Continent (France, Switzerland, and Italy), Herzen relocated to London in the summer of 1852, residing there for the following twelve and a half years. Within six months he had established the Free Russian Press, which would become the focus of his endeavors until his final years.

Many of Herzen's most subtle and intriguing concepts are formulated in *The Bell* (*Kolokol*), coedited by Herzen and, after the first two issues, by his close friend N. P. Ogaryov (1813–1877). In just over a decade, a total of 245 issues were produced, not great numbers at first blush, but significant for the genre, establishing the publication as one of the longest-running émigré journals in nineteenth-century Europe. This success was in part due to Herzen's established reputation as a writer, his deft skills as an administrator of the press, and, not least, his ability to fund the operation out of his personal fortune. Rising to a peak circulation of 2,500 copies, and passed on to many more than that number, *The Bell* holds the distinction of being the first revolutionary organ to gain wide distribution within Russia, clandestinely smuggled across its borders, disseminated illegally to intelligentsia and agitators, and, it is rumored, read secretly in the highest offices of government—even the palace.[1] Considering the obstacles involved, which included the organization of Russian-language authors and typesetters, the great distance and difficulties in shipping the contraband issues to Russia and evading its border controls and censorship, the controversial and sometimes incendiary nature of the content, and the palpable effect of Herzen's publications on public opinion inside Russia, his printing activities constitute a remarkable, if not singular achievement in the annals of dissident protest in the face of an autocratic and hostile regime. Herzen's flagship journal, *The Bell*, remains one of the great legacies of Russian social and political thought.

The availability in English of Herzen's texts of the 1850s and 1860s fills a significant void. Despite the duration of Herzen's stay in England, and the influence of *The Bell* and its parent publication, *The Polestar* (*Poliarnaya zvezda*), this later period in Herzen's life has not received sufficient attention, particularly in comparison with Herzen's pre-1852 activity and thought. There are several reasons for this lacuna. Herzen's first forty years have attracted a good deal of research. In the 1830s Herzen became deeply engaged in German philosophy and French social thought, and intellectual historians take much interest in this early period, when a young, idealistic Herzen passionately sought answers to life's complexities in grand philosophical systems. More poignantly, in the late 1840s and early 1850s Herzen crystallized his doctrine of revolutionary socialism, considered to be his monumental contribution to Russian history, and one which was decisive in influencing the path of Russia's political development through to the 1917 revolution and beyond. For many historians, these years comprise the "useful" Herzen, at least in terms of the impact of his doctrine on the course of world history.

Biographers also tend to focus on the same period, beginning with Herzen's departure from Russia in early 1847, his arrival in Paris in late March, and his witnessing of the 1848 revolts and the reactions and disillusion that followed, culminating in Louis-Napoleon's coup d'état in 1851 and arrogation of the title emperor in 1852. Herzen produced a number of classic essays and several cycles of "letters" reporting these extraordinary events and his travels during this time, and these were gathered in popular volumes that set forth his doctrine of Russian socialism.[2] The early 1850s also brought a series of personal crises and tragedies, Herzen's "family drama," which has sparked much interest in Herzen's personal life. In sum, Herzen's 1847–52 period, years of Sturm und Drang, of exuberant hopes and shattered ideals, has been a magnet for writers and academics.

When, in mid-1852 Herzen left for the foggy calm of England, it appeared that the most fascinating and productive years of his life were behind him. Moreover, it is generally held that Herzen did not take warmly to London and he did not develop many contacts there.[3] In his memoirs,

Herzen only encourages this perception, writing of his "hermit's life" in one of the town's more remote areas.[4] A review of Herzen scholarship from the late nineteenth century to the current day is instructive in tracing the changing understanding of the significance of his life and thought.

Until the last decade of the twentieth century, Russian scholars had to overcome a number of impediments and obstacles in their writing on the man and his thought. Generally, there has hardly been a time when these scholars could write about Herzen in an entirely unhindered way. Twice arrested and banished within his homeland because of his alleged political views and orientation, Herzen finally left Russia and was forced to remain in exile. During most of the tsarist period, his works were banned outright, though some secondary literature on the man, comprising mainly non-ideological, biographical sketches, was published.[5] In 1900 this injunction was removed, though it took a few years for the effects of the ban to dissipate and for serious Herzen scholarship in Russia finally to emerge.[6] In 1905 Herzen's works began to be printed in Russia, and by 1908 Vetrinsky, who had been arrested and exiled for his participation in a student circle, published a substantial monograph tracing Herzen from childhood to his last days, with the text divided between Herzen's life in Russia and his years abroad.[7]

As a historian, journalist, and pedagogue, P. N. Milyukov (1859–1943) was notable among the pioneering Russian scholars of Herzen. Regarded as a "Moscow liberal with leftward aspirations,"[8] Milyukov, like Herzen, could not be pigeonholed into standard rubrics and categories. Steering clear of nationalistic conservatives and doctrinaire socialists, he maintained a distinct ideological tension, attempting to blend liberalism and socialism without being dragged into the camp of either nationalistic conservatives or doctrinaire socialists. In 1900 Milyukov published a short essay, "In Memory of Herzen,"[9] on the occasion of the thirtieth anniversary of his passing. Milyukov regarded Herzen as Russia's greatest writer,[10] and he, in turn, was compared to Herzen in terms of the importance of his publicistic endeavors on behalf of Russia's opposition movement.[11] On the centenary of Herzen's birth, Lenin, in his own "In Memory of Herzen" tribute, claimed Herzen for the cause of the revolution.

From 1907 to 1920, Ivanov-Razumnik[12] (1878–1946) produced over fifteen major studies, including an eight-part history of Russian social thought that includes a fine chapter on Herzen.[13] During roughly the same period, he wrote a series of small but valuable essays on Herzen, beginning with his 1905 article on Herzen and the Russian populist Mikhailovsky.[14]

In *On the Meaning of Life*, Ivanov-Razumnik describes two "objectivist" doctrines—positivist and religious, both with a fixed historical "aim" or grand vision—and a third doctrine, "immanent subjectivism," of which Herzen is presented as founding father and most exemplary exponent.[15]

Despite the burst of essays and monographs on Herzen that appeared during the first two decades of the twentieth century, in his 1918 monograph K. Levin complained that this scholarship had generated more misunderstandings than accurate appraisals, and was riddled with conflicting images and portrayals of the man.[16] This assessment can be attributed in part to the relative newness of Herzen research in Russia, and to the fact that a complete critical edition of his writings was still not available.[17] Scholarly efforts were significantly facilitated by the 22-volume edition of Herzen's collected works, edited by Mikhail Konstantinovich Lemke (1872–1923), and issued as a foundation of the revolution's noble heritage and intellectual pedigree by the People's Commissariat for Education. This work, completed in 1925, remained the principal point of departure for all Herzen scholarship for the next forty years. Other works appearing in this period include Bogucharsky's running biography, virtually devoid of notes or supporting material, which covers the last thirteen years of Herzen's life in less than forty pages,[18] and a pamphlet-sized popular biography by Steklov first published in 1920.[19]

As the new Soviet order was established, Herzen scholarship was forced to take a sharp turn. Formerly the bête noir of the tsarist regime, Herzen was now accorded a central position on the podium of Russian socialist ideologues and elevated to the pantheon of national heroes. While this encouraged writing on Herzen, it also meant that interpretation was made to conform to strict guidelines and received understanding; a figure of such importance was to be defined within the tight ideological framework that Lenin had imposed.[20]

The typical Soviet-era study begins with Lenin's famous dictum, his epigraphic image of Herzen as dissident voice and peasant advocate.[21] The main body of such research is replete with quotations from Herzen, frequently laid out in a cut-and-paste fashion,[22] interlaced with fact-filled commentary, and thickly cross-referenced with Lenin's writings (it is not unusual to find pages that include more Lenin than Herzen). Analysis is often couched in Soviet ideological terminology, premised on a causal relationship between economic structures and literary and intellectual phenomena, as well as aesthetics and values. Herzen's democratic ethos is reduced to having paved the way for the vanguard of Russian Marxism[23]—quite an irony, considering Herzen's profound dislike for much of Marx's writings—and his teaching is viewed as an intermediate stage on the path of Marxist-Leninist aesthetics.[24] One author somewhat anachronistically reads this alleged intermediacy back into Herzen's own understanding, attributing his personal or "spiritual" tragedy to his being caught in the middle of "the revolutionism of bourgeois democracy, which was already dying in Europe, and the revolutionism of the socialist proletariat, which had not ripened."[25] These studies often draw to a close not with the author's considered thoughts or findings, but with several more quotations from Lenin which are seen to sum up all that can (or should) be derived from Herzen's work.

One of the few Russian monographs specifically to treat Herzen's *Bell* closely follows this formula, quoting Lenin so often that on some pages the author no longer bothers to supply a reference. Indicative of the general gist of such scholarship, the first page of the bibliography guides the reader interested in understanding more about Herzen to two works by Marx and seventeen by Lenin.[26] Another monograph expands this list somewhat to include Engels.[27]

Tatarinova's volume on Herzen, published in a series on "revolutionary democratic publicists," contains a section on the Free Russian Press, though the interpretation relies heavily not only on Lenin but on Plekhanov, who views Herzen as an early contributor to the stream of socialist materialism.[28] Monographs on Herzen's social philosophy[29] and historical views[30] follow a similar approach. Overall, much of Soviet scholarship on Herzen tends to be descriptive—often painstakingly so, with great effort on detail and documentation—but with a restrictive or circumscribed analytic or critical range.

The above does not in any way suggest that the literature of the Soviet period should be dismissed or ignored. Over the course of seven decades, a considerable corpus of studies on a wide variety of aspects and angles of Herzen and his works was produced. A number of literary projects were carried out that would have been difficult to orchestrate and finance in the West. The most significant of these is the definitive thirty-volume edition of his collected writings, with extensive notes and critical apparati.[31] This opus, which took over a decade to complete, remains the standard reference work in the field. Also of note is the five-volume chronology of Herzen's life, which provides a detailed diary-like account of Herzen's movements and activities.[32]

There is another intriguing aspect to Soviet Herzen scholarship. Among some writers, the choice of Herzen as a subject may indicate something other than simple endorsement of Leninist doctrine. As the theme of one work, entitled *Herzen Against Autocracy*,[33] suggests, Herzen set a model for the expression of free thought against the background of a repressive regime—a luxury not easily afforded the Soviet author documenting this very topic.[34] The irony of this circumstance could not entirely have been lost among readers. The subversive aspect of Herzen scholarship in Soviet secondary literature is a worthy topic in itself.[35]

In the resurgence of essays and monographs on Herzen emanating from Russia during the last two decades one can detect new approaches with innovative methods and means of analysis employed to elucidate the man and his doctrine in a fresh light.[36]

Growing interest in Herzen in the West may be seen in the context of the broader fascination with Russia during the first decades of the twentieth century. This was marked by a spurt of publications that ventured into a creative arena situated somewhere between romance and scholarship, in which a search was conducted for the "soul" or "spirit" of Russia as represented by its great nineteenth-century literary figures and its innovative Silver Age poets and artists. In England, attention turned to Russian art and literature, while Continental studies included T. G. Masaryk's tour de force *Russland und Europa* (1913), a wide-ranging survey of Russian history, literature, and philosophy. Masaryk allocates several important subchapters to Herzen, depicting him with much admiration and empathy. The author, however, worked from the limited corpus of Herzen's texts available before the First World War.

The upheavals of 1917–19 and the assumption of power by Lenin, who, as noted above, accorded Herzen a central role as the ideological progenitor of Russian socialism, piqued the curiosity of those wishing to better understand the monumental events taking place.

In part a result of Russia's dramatic political and ideological transformation and in part due to the production of Lemke's important reference work, Herzen scholarship began to move forward with quickening pace. In France, Labry produced two in-depth studies in the 1920s, with the majority of the research focused on Herzen's ideological development within Russia and the impact of French thought upon his doctrine.[37] In the English-speaking world, the publication of Garnett's pocketbook translations of *My Past and Thoughts* (*Byloe i dumy*), Herzen's most popular work, helped bolster interest in the man and his thought.[38] By the early 1930s, E. H. Carr (1892–1982) was working on the first significant English-language study of Herzen. Based in part on *My Past and Thoughts,* Carr's work, *The Romantic Exiles,*[39] is largely biographical. It is well written, engaging, and entertaining, but it does not attempt to grapple with the intellectual streams of Herzen's doctrine.

By the end of the Second World War, the Soviet Union had reestablished itself as a major power, and as the Cold War emerged and intensified, the

Eastern bloc became a significant focus of concern in the West. With scholars and commentators expressing polarized views on the Soviet regime and communist doctrine, discussion extended to the influences that led to the current situation, one which pitted Western democracies against an ideological system whose antecedents stretched back into the previous century. It was only natural, given Herzen's important role in Russia's intellectual heritage, socialist doctrine, and revolutionary movement, that scholarship in the West on this important figure should launch in earnest.

The fortuitous constellation of man and moment occurred when a rising academician of Russian origin, with a specialty in philosophy and a penchant for the history of ideas, was appointed to serve at the British embassy in Moscow for a brief spell in autumn 1945. With his keen interest in Russian thought and literature, and having written a significant monograph on Marx, Isaiah Berlin (1909–1997) was well apprised of the historical pillars on which modern Russia rested. However, in his brief encounter with the grim, stark reality of Stalin's regime, Berlin became acquainted firsthand with a wholly different Russia than that which he had come to admire through its literature. He was deeply touched by his conversations with Russian intellectuals, and these exchanges contributed to his desire to promote an alternative vision of Russia that had strong roots in the past and offered hope for the future.

In a Foreign Office memorandum entitled "A Note on Literature and the Arts in the Russian Soviet Federated Socialist Republic in the Closing Months of 1945,"[40] Berlin distinguishes between two visions of Russia. One was manifest in revolutionary Leninist doctrine and Stalin's autocratic rule; the other, stifled to a trembling silence, was the underlying "Russian genius" which had long sought to be liberated from the oppressive grip of state control and censorship. While it was the totalitarian image that was gaining hold in the West, Berlin was a devotee of an entirely different vision of Russia, a liberal, humanist current that he would chronicle and examine in some of his most famous essays.

Berlin's Moscow memorandum was confidential, and could offer no succor to its muted subject, Russia's literary intelligentsia. Given the political climate and palpable danger in Stalinist Russia of publicizing links with foreigners, Berlin could not write candidly about Russian contemporaries. It appears, however, that he soon arrived at a solution to this dilemma. In Herzen, Berlin found a perfect surrogate, a homegrown Russian figure, lauded as a hero by the Soviets themselves, who could "speak out" for those who could not, without risk or fear of reprisal. In the following two years Berlin's central motif contrasting two opposing forces in Russian history gestated and crystallized as he crafted his first essay in which Herzen would take center stage.[41]

While Berlin was far too sophisticated to invoke the "soul" or "spirit of Russia" phrase that had become popular in previous decades, he developed a thesis that does share some elements with earlier romantic notions which contemplate an indigenous body of thought spawned by a particular national group or people. The Soviet worldview hearkened back to Marx, a product of the West; Berlin, however, indicates that the historical voice of Russia can be heard by turning to its writers, poets, artists, and intelligentsia, particularly those of the nineteenth century.[42] It is this enlightened humanist stream that Berlin uses as a foil against what he perceives to be the perversions of Russian tradition under Stalinist Marxism. At the heart of the freethinking, anti-authoritarian current in Russian intellectual history and political thought was Herzen, who became something of a poster boy, the standard-bearer of a rich and variegated Russian legacy that was being smothered both in ideological and concrete terms. Berlin popularized an image of Herzen as not only central in the development of Russia's intellectual, socialist, and revolutionary heritage, but also as the most outstanding representative of an authentically Russian brand of liberal thought. Moreover, Herzen could serve as a beacon not only for Russia, but for the West, which had succumbed to the "dangerous" and "sinister" notions lurking in the "political ruminations" of German and French romanticism.[43]

Berlin's flowing, erudite, and supremely crafted essays were instrumental in directing scholarly and popular attention to Herzen and his thought.[44] In championing Herzen, Berlin offered an alternative view of Russia as he chose to focus on the freedom-loving heritage that was suppressed under the Soviet regime. Berlin regarded Herzen as a remedy to the malaise of Western thought,[45] the dangerous seed that had grown into Nazi fascism on the one hand, and Marxist-Leninist doctrine and Stalinist repression on the other.[46] Berlin's portrayal of Herzen deserves close scrutiny, and, arguably, a monograph on this subject alone could be written. E. H. Carr is reported to have suggested that Berlin understood himself in the tradition of Herzen, and this leaves open the possibility that, conversely, Berlin may have been inclined to fashion Herzen to some extent in his own image.[47] Through his essays and by dint of the scholars he coached, advised, and inspired, Berlin influenced a key group of Herzen scholars in the West, and his particular approach set the tone for further research.[48]

It was only in the 1950s that Herzen scholarship in the West began to come into its own, dovetailing with the interest of certain scholars in non-Marxist formations of Russian thought. This research offered an alternative representation of Russia and its ideology to that which had been crystallizing during the Cold War era and the McCarthy years. In 1951 Richard Gilbert Hare (1907–1966) (who had also worked in the Foreign Office) published *Pioneers of Russian Social Thought,* which offered fuller vignettes of several of the figures that Berlin had surveyed in his 1948 article. Hare accorded more space to Herzen than any other figure in the monograph, although he cites little secondary literature. In a similar vein, Eugene Lampert (1914–2004), a Russian cultural and intellectual historian, completed *Studies in Rebellion* (1956), a survey of Russian revolutionary thought, featuring essays on three nineteenth-century non-Marxist Russian thinkers. Lampert devotes more space to Herzen than to any other subject in his book. In his analysis, Lampert concentrates on Herzen's ideology and moral theory, less so on Herzen as a concrete political figure.

Franco Venturi (1914–1994) opens his classic study, *Roots of Revolution,* which first appeared in Italian in 1952, with a chapter on Herzen, whom he dubs "the true founder of Populism."[49] Venturi regards Herzen's influence on the movement as largely due to his force of personality—his personal experiences, and comments which were conveyed in his memoirs, in which "autobiography constantly intrudes on politics"—rather than in the production of a unified doctrine. He further maintains that Herzen looked back with a degree of nostalgia to his parents' generation, late eighteenth-century gentry who strove, albeit somewhat unsuccessfully, after the values of enlightenment and an emerging notion of social responsibility. These values, embodied to some extent in the Decembrists, were fundamental in inspiring Herzen's worldview. Venturi notes the influence of Saint-Simon, Proudhon, and Fourier, and tracks Herzen's absorption of their thought in a narrative outline which, in a brief chapter, takes the reader to 1848. After treating Bakunin, Venturi returns to Herzen, with an equally brief but helpful chapter on *The Bell.* In doing so, Venturi produced one of the first studies in the West to draw attention to *The Bell* and its significance in the rise of populism. However, the author's primary concern, as the book's original title, *Il populismo russo,* makes clear, is to trace the history of the populist movement as it coalesced with other streams of thought to produce the circumstances required for the Russian revolution. Herzen and his publications are of interest to Venturi mainly in regard to their instrumentality in providing the basis for certain fundamental elements of the populist movement of the 1860s.

Marc Raeff, a fine scholar of eighteenth- and nineteenth-century Russia, emerged out of the same scholarly zeitgeist of the postwar era. In 1950 he completed his dissertation, and similar to the research bent of Berlin, Venturi, Hare, Lampert, and Malia (see below), it was on a theme that highlighted a softer, non-Marxist version of Russian socialism, stressing liberal rather than authoritarian or determinist elements.[50]

By the end of the 1950s the time was ripe for a full-length English-language monograph on Herzen, and the study of Martin Malia (1924–2004), published in 1961 but over a decade in gestation, filled this gap admirably. To this day, Malia's monograph is often regarded as the first port of call, if not the standard reference on the subject. Though dated and subject to the inevitable errors, flaws, and biases that are uncovered with time and exposure to criticism, *Alexander Herzen and the Birth of Russian Socialism: 1812–1855* remains the best single intellectual biography written on Herzen's first forty years, though it is just as much (if not more) a history of the development of Russian socialism during the reign of Nicholas I, with Herzen emblematic as the main protagonist.

Trained as a cultural historian and social scientist, Malia delves into the realm of the "social psychology" of ideas, devoting much energy to Herzen's intellectual development in Russia, the formative years in which he absorbed European thought. According to Malia, Herzen's socialism was largely developed before he ever left Russia's borders. Malia's study effectively ends in 1852, the very year Herzen arrived in England. In accord with several authors cited above, Malia was convinced that Herzen was not integrated into English life, and "largely ignored the English, as they did him."[51] He allocates little space to Herzen's activities after his arrival in London, or to his writings of that period.[52] There is only fleeting reference to Robert Owen, for example, and J. S. Mill is only mentioned once in the entire monograph of nearly 500 pages. This, despite the fact that Herzen was influenced by both thinkers, and, moreover, Herzen's essay on Owen is considered one of his finest. *The Bell,* among Herzen's greatest achievements, hardly figures in Malia's narrative.[53]

In not addressing Herzen's final eighteen years, two-thirds of which were spent in London, Malia's study stops short and does not embrace the full span, and arguably most intriguing period, of Herzen's thought. Clearly, there is much work to be done on this period in Herzen's life, and an understanding of his *Bell* writings is essential to the appreciation of Herzen at his most sophisticated.

Aileen Kelly, who encountered Isaiah Berlin during her days as a graduate student at Wolfson College in the late 1960s, writes in the solid tradition of the esteemed master, tracing the rich and variegated interweaving of Russian and European ideas to which Herzen was exposed. She has strong reservations regarding certain aspects of Malia's portrayal, which she rightly asserts has been a dominant influence for the understanding of

Herzen in the West. Kelly also notes that the "standard Soviet interpretation, based on Lenin's view that Herzen represents a transitional stage between utopian socialism and Russian Marxism," has meant that "his place in Russian thought, like that of many other thinkers mangled by Soviet ideologists, has yet to be properly assessed."[54]

One of the few scholars to seriously and consistently address the issue of Herzen's London period has been Monica Partridge. She unearths connections, contacts, and associations which were previously not known, places Herzen frequented in London, and figures with whom he associated. Partridge earned a reputation for uncovering unpublished memoirs and letters; however, she employs these mainly to supplement Herzen's biography, and she does not tend to weave these materials into the broader scheme of Herzen's intellectual development or with his written pieces during these years. Be that as it may, Partridge highlights the significance of Herzen's London years as "the most settled and successful period of his life."[55] She strongly makes the case that Herzen's English period has been unjustifiably neglected, and is full of promise for further research.[56]

Edward Acton aims to construct a "unified picture" of Herzen's development. He maintains that "the different aspects of his life and thought were inextricably intertwined," and attempts to demonstrate this by "tracing the impact of public events and private tragedy upon his political thought and activity."[57] Following in the footsteps of his doctoral supervisor E. H. Carr, Acton's framework is primarily biographical, and through this tangled skein he explores the development of Herzen's thought. Acton devotes a full chapter to "The Tragedy" and asserts that Herzen's personal crisis profoundly impacted his "political and ideological development" and "triggered off a basic shift in his outlook and activity."[58]

Acton's findings are worthy of note, in that he detects a palpable turn in Herzen's thought. Acton traces this "change in the tone of his writings" to the summer of 1852, the very time that Herzen moved to England. Indeed, after 1852 Herzen was prompted to reconsider and reassess many of his positions. It is Herzen's experience in England, his strong bonds with journalists and political activists as demonstrated by Partridge's research, his witnessing firsthand the town hall meetings and evolving parliamentary system, his exposure to the thought of Owen and Mill, as demonstrated in his writings—in sum, a long period of residency in a non-revolutionary, civil, and relatively prosperous and successful society—that contributed to Herzen's fundamental reorientation.

A decade after the appearance of Acton's biography, Judith Zimmerman published a monograph focusing on the transitional nature of Herzen's first years in the West, from 1847 to 1852, a period in which Herzen struck a new balance between his Russian heritage and European ideals. Although Malia's work extends to these years, Zimmerman contends that it does not properly address Herzen's transformation during this period. She asserts that Malia views Herzen's development in Russia as both formative and decisive, that he "had little interest in the mature [post-1847] Herzen," and that, in consequence, Malia's section on Herzen in the West is "truncated and inaccurate in detail."[59]

Approaching Herzen with a sociological emphasis, Zimmerman explores "the process by which Herzen became an effective political actor." According to her research, Herzen's development of a revolutionary émigré identity was facilitated by his integration into a revolutionary community that lent his efforts a stamp of legitimacy and provided a "supportive milieu" and a "viable tradition" within which he could operate.[60] These contacts also played a large role in Herzen's reformulation of his positions.[61] This process was so thorough that "by 1852 Herzen had emerged [. . .] to make a new life and a new career for himself." This newly formed man then left the Continent and moved to England, where "he [. . .] found a community in which he could function—the world of exiles as it crystallized in London during the 1850s." Zimmerman, however, does not tell us anything more about this next stage, as this is beyond the parameters of her research. "The present work ends at the brink of this new life, with Herzen in England. [. . .]" As Zimmerman notes, commenting on Malia's work, which she feels is solid on Herzen only up until 1847, "there is no similar substantial study of the mature Herzen." Zimmerman brings Herzen's biography five years forward, but no further. By her own criteria of analysis, one would expect that Herzen, now surrounded by a new set of close acquaintances in London, and a different "supportive milieu" and "tradition," would have been open to further change and integration of new perspectives and approaches, beliefs, and values. Indeed, Zimmerman felt Herzen's post-1852 period merited attention, and vowed to write another volume, a sequel to *Midpassage*, but this project never materialized.[62]

Abbott Gleason's monograph covers the development of Russian socialism, populism, and radicalism of the 1850s and 1860s, including a chapter on "the new era and its journalists." Herzen's *Bell* is treated, however, as a section within a chapter, and not an attempt at a major evaluation.[63] As noted above, several scholars have pointed to the relative lack of study of Herzen's London years and his contributions to *The Bell*, with some biographers vowing to one day fill that gap. Russian researchers have also noted the absence of research in this area. Lomunov maintains that "in international Herzen scholarship the English connections are studied much less than, for example, his French, Italian, or German connections."[64]

There are several excellent studies by historians of philosophy and Russian political thought that contain important sections on Herzen. In the late 1940s and early 1950s, the surveys of Russian philosophy of N. O. Lossky (1870–1965) and V. V. Zenkovsky (1881–1962), both Russian Orthodox philosophers in exile, were published. Lossky rejects the "typical bolshevik tendency" of Lenin and others who claim Herzen for themselves and interpret his writing as a forerunner of materialist doctrine. However, Lossky himself tends to slot thinkers into either what he considers to be mainstream Russian philosophy, which he regards as religious or spiritual, or that which is outside this category. Consequently, Herzen, an unbridled critic of organized religion, receives scant treatment. Lossky attempts to justify the short shrift he gives Herzen by noting that Herzen's efforts were more in the field of practical political thought than philosophy per se.[65]

Zenkovsky observes that Herzen lacked any formal system and did not expound his doctrine in a purely philosophical manner. He points out that it is this feature of Herzen's discourse that complicates the task of the scholar, who must sift and separate passages of pure abstract thought and speculation from off-the-cuff comments, artistic expressions, and simple opinion. However, he does see a fair amount of internal cohesiveness in Herzen's thought, and devotes a section to investigating his doctrine. While most scholars have considered Herzen an atheist, or at least agnostic,[66] Zenkovsky identifies another Herzen who, in the 1830s, departed from analysis and rationalism and gave free rein to religious passion. Influenced by Saint-Simon's *Nouveau Christianisme,* Herzen saw in this doctrine the basis of moral renewal, a "new order" in Europe and Russia. While Herzen, ever the iconoclast, was a critic of the church as an institution, according to Zenkovsky's reading he espoused particular aspects of the Christian ethos as represented in scripture, and even gravitated toward aspects of mysticism. This aspect of Herzen's life and thought—Zenkovsky goes so far as to call Herzen an "essentially religious figure"—has yet to be explored in any depth.[67]

Sergei Vasilievich Utechin (1921–2004), who also came under the influence of Berlin during his time at Oxford, considers Herzen "the father of the modern Russian political emigration."[68] He recognizes that Herzen moderated his radical revolutionary position during his later years, and attributes matters of revolutionary strategy and tactics more to Ogaryov than to Herzen himself.

The Jesuit priest Frederick Copleston (1907–1994) wrote one of the great histories of Western philosophy of the last century. His *Philosophy in Russia* benefits greatly from his comparative perspective. Tracing Herzen's movement from Schelling to Hegel, Hegel to Feuerbach, and on to positions akin to positivism, Copleston notes that the writings of Herzen and most other Russian thinkers belong more properly to the category of ideological thinking, social theory, or practical philosophy, rather than pure philosophy; however, any attempt to untangle and rationalize these various strands would be artificial, providing only a "caricature of his thought." Herzen was aware of discrepancies between his personal beliefs and those of the schools he studied and sometimes adopted.[69] He had to live with such inconsistencies, but live with them he did, rather than trying artificially to reconcile them in a perfect and complete philosophical system. Along these lines, which recognize Herzen's complex interweaving of rational and incisive thought with his personal experience and constitution, Copleston does acknowledge the changes in Herzen's beliefs and positions in his later years, that is, during the *Bell* period.

Most significantly, and counter to the many accounts of Herzen as the committed revolutionary (a moniker which was true, of course, in his earlier days), Copleston notes what appears to be a fundamental change in Herzen's understanding of the progress of history. Man has limited ability to affect history, which has its own pace and direction. Regime change, in today's vulgar terminology, is a shallow, ill thought-out concept. The development of the consciousness of the people will do more to move society forward than a sudden, radical overthrow of the existing order, which may only result in external, cosmetic alterations. Real change must come from within. It is perhaps in part Herzen's profound emphasis on the inner life, the human spirit, that Copleston, a man of the cloth, finds so appealing (despite Herzen's critique of organized religion), leading him to laud Herzen as "one of the most attractive figures among the Russian radical thinkers."[70]

Andrzej Walicki, one of the finest scholars of Russian thought to publish in the last third of the twentieth century, devotes several brief but important chapters to Herzen. Walicki situates Herzen's doctrine within the context of larger Russian and European currents, particularly the fascination with Hegel that dominated the Moscow salons in the 1830s and 1840s. Herzen proved to be something of a philosophical dissident, kicking up his heels at those who were "reconciled with reality" and who rejected any call for action in the real world. Using Hegel against the Hegelians themselves, Walicki details how Herzen decried the "cult of historical reason" and argued for a synthesis of empiricism (materialism) and idealism, especially in its capacity to generate dialectics, which allowed for a fluid, mobile, and multidimensional approach to major issues. Herzen showed the same tendency toward synthesis in his consideration of the positions of Slavophiles and Westerners (particularly Belinsky and Kavelin). He adopted and expanded the Slavophile's championing of "indigenous" or "authentic" Russian principles; however, he accorded primacy to the rights of the individual over the claims of authority and tradition, these latter two notions constituting cardinal pillars of the Slavophile position. Walicki also notes that Herzen integrated key arguments, such as the concept of Russia's "lack of history," from Chaadaev, a thinker who is difficult to slot into either category.[71] Walicki examines Herzen's positions on this issue in greater detail in his *Slavophile Controversy*, where he considers Herzen as the "natural link" between the Slavophiles and Westerners of the 1840s and the populists of the 1860s and '70s.[72] Perhaps more than any other scholar, Walicki has noted a major shift in Herzen's positions in his mature years. Referring to a letter that Herzen wrote in 1868, the very end of the *Bell* period, Walicki writes: "This document shows that Herzen's ideas had changed significantly."[73] Indeed, Herzen evolved and transformed during his years in England; his doctrine, as expressed in *The Bell*, furnished a bridge to the thought and activism of the following decades.

The above studies, which devote entire sections to Herzen, should be supplemented by a number of other works in the broader field of Russian intellectual history that shed light on important aspects of Herzen's thought. These include works on the Russian intelligentsia in general.[74]

Herzen has also been analyzed from a literary or stylistic perspective. While he did write a number of fictional pieces, Herzen did not earn his fame through his artistic talents, and many histories of Russian literature contain scant reference to him. Belinsky, analyzing Herzen's novel, *Who Is to Blame? (Kto vinovat?* 1845–47), suggests that Herzen is really more of a philosopher than a poet.[75] Despite such lukewarm assessments, Herzen has been analyzed as a belles-lettrist, [76] a literary critic,[77] and an interlocutor in dialogue or debate with other literary figures.[78] His creative works have been examined in the context of the literature of the period,[79] and these, along with his other writings, have attracted the critical attention of Chernyshevsky, Dobrolyubov, Pisarev, Plekhanov, Gorky, Lunacharsky, and a host of others.[80]

Most notably, there have been serious literary examinations of his *Past and Thoughts*. Earlier research recognized that there was more to this work than meets the eye, allowing for several layers of analysis and interpretation. Chukovskaya's small monograph suggests that Herzen's great work is "to no less degree a self-portrait than an autobiography."[81] The best studies are those that detect Herzen's subtle but complex interweaving of biographical details with world history. Höffler-Preissmann's monograph asserts that Herzen aimed to construct a narrative in which contemporary history is embodied within literary portraits, resulting in "a perfect fusion of life with his artistic imagination."[82] Schmid focuses on the personal dimension of *Past and Thoughts*, arguing that Herzen's intention was to represent "Weltgeschichte als Familiendrama," a skilled interlacing of global events and autobiography.[83] In a modern paraphrase of Herzen's own comments, Ginzburg notes that *Past and Thoughts* eludes the usual categories of classification. Neither pure literature, nor straight history or autobiography, it is rather a distinctive fusion of several genres, a memoir imbued with a deliberate, studied, and conscious historicism.[84] Along similar lines, Paperno examines how Herzen links "intimacy" and "history" by employing literary structures and Hegelian models.[85] Other investigations have considered Herzen in terms of the literary schools that influenced his writing,[86] as well as his relationship with other authors.[87] Aside from literary studies, general works on nineteenth-century Russian journalism invariably include a section on Herzen.[88]

It may be argued from the above survey that there are, broadly speaking, three major trends in Herzen scholarship. The biographical genre is fueled by material from Herzen's celebrated memoirs, his correspondence, and archival documents which include the observations of those who met or knew Herzen. Works of intellectual history attempt to trace influences and tease a coherent philosophy or worldview out of Herzen's largely topical, publicistic writings. Literary studies explore Herzen's transition from romanticism to naturalism in the 1830s and 1840s, and finally to the development of his own groundbreaking style of confessional prose in the 1850s.

Beyond the above rubrics, an intriguing parallel developed between Herzen scholarship in Soviet Russia and, mutatis mutandis, in the West after World War II. Both were dominated for some time by a larger-than-life, authoritative commentator who has influenced much of later scholarship. During the Soviet era, Lenin's interpretation had to be heeded or, at the very least, cunningly worked around, even while quoting him de rigueur at every possible juncture. Admittedly of a different nature and degree, it may be argued that a fair amount of Herzen scholarship in the West has been inspired by Berlin's interpretation and approach, not only by dint of the essays which treat Herzen and his circle,[89] but in a much subtler yet more pervasive sense. In the last sixty years, a number of key Western scholars who wrote some of the most important studies on Herzen's thought were directly influenced by Berlin, and corresponded with him on the subject throughout his life.[90] Berlin's influence was not restricted to those in the

West. Russian scholars such as Elsberg have considered Berlin's analysis of Herzen as emblematic of the contemporary "ideological battle over Herzen's legacy."[91] To Elsberg, as Berlin, an "authentic" understanding of Herzen could be used to support or critique contemporary worldviews, political systems, and regimes. The debate over the interpretation of Herzen went beyond mere literary analysis.

———

There have been studies that have examined Herzen in regard to particular years or stages in his life,[92] or the cities in Russia in which he resided.[93] A number of monographs have been based on Herzen's nexus of interactions and associations with certain European nations.[94] Herzen's English period has still to attract comparable dedicated studies, and the publication of a selection of his essays, with commentary and explanation, is a long-awaited and significant contribution to Herzen scholarship which will allow English readers for the first time to appreciate Herzen's landmark essays and subtle discourse. A study of Herzen's writings during his *Bell* years shows him in all his brilliance, complexity, and, indeed, inconsistencies, as an idealistic, non-compromising, engaged émigré, straddled between the immaculate structures of pure philosophy, the soaring ideals of a lofty social, egalitarian morality, and the exigencies and limitations of a terribly imperfect world.

Herzen's years in the West solidified and crystallized his belief that Russia had to follow its own path in finding solutions to its distinctive problems. Picking up on a line of argument that had already been suggested in one form or other in the 1830s and 1840s, Herzen asserted that Russia's isolation from the West could play in its favor, allowing it to bypass the deleterious features of an ill and declining Western civilization, which was hampered by alien conventions such as Roman contracts and codes created to regulate European individualism. Antipodal to this conception of a decadent West was Herzen's central image of an idealized *mir*, the Russian peasant village or commune. The *mir*, which became the keystone of Herzen's mature thought and his great hope for an indigenous, egalitarian solution to Russia's problems, became so attractive to Herzen in part due to his pressing need to find an organic, nonviolent answer to issues that Europe itself could not fully solve.

In this regard, England provided a useful model—an island that had followed its own course in a gradual manner, over the span of centuries, from the Magna Carta to the development of an elected parliament and independent judiciary, with a long tradition of civic duty, a vigorous free press, and a relatively high degree of personal liberty. In this environment Herzen was allowed to operate, unencumbered by government, authorities, or censorship, despite Russia's pleas to shut him down. Moreover, during his years in London Herzen became apprised of the very different perspective of English intellectuals on events occurring on the Continent, especially those of 1848.[95]

In the ideational realm, during his *Bell* years, Herzen was profoundly influenced by two English thinkers, J. S. Mill and Robert Owen. Mill's writings, especially on liberty, struck a chord with Herzen, who agreed with much of Mill's critique on herd-like behaviour of the contented masses, the sameness, banality, and lack of individual expression that was increasingly characterizing modern European society. Herzen found in Mill the perfect support for the argument that Russia could not rely on Western solutions, because the West itself was ill, exhausted, and in decline. Herzen utilized Robert Owen, whom he regarded as an exemplary champion of socialism, in a similar fashion. It was not the authorities who caused Owen's plans to founder, but the lack of support and understanding from the broad masses, whose Western, bourgeois individualism made them numb to higher ideals and the rewards of social solidarity.

It is precisely at this stage of his life, witnessing the wide berth of civic freedom allowed to both individuals and groups in England, yet observing the inability of society to advance further and capitalize on the possibilities at hand, that Herzen developed his theory on the cardinal importance of educating the people, a vital requirement without which real progress could not be made. External changes in the system were not enough, and there was little to be gained by simply altering the structure of government and allowing the masses to do as they pleased. Herzen learned during his London years that, if anything, the English were more conformist and less likely to speak out than those on the Continent, precisely because of the fact that they already enjoyed a fair degree of personal freedom, and required little more from life than the illusion that they were exercising their freedom, or, at least, could do so if they desired.[96] In Mill and Owen, Herzen found both champions and foils for his own doctrine of liberty and socialism, with both figures demonstrating the pitfalls of Western society in its inability to provide a proper vehicle for the ideals they espoused. Paradoxically, Herzen enlisted Mill to counter the aspirations of Russia's liberals, who hoped that reforms would lead to a bourgeois Western model. Herzen, via Mill, and through his own experience in the West, pointed out the shallowness and futility of such limited aspirations.

Herzen believed a fitting vehicle for both individual freedom and social equality should be searched for not in the decadent West but in a specifically Russian institution and structure. Ensconced deep in the Russian countryside, immune to the maladies of the West, was the peasant commune. Instead of the West providing solutions for Russia, Russia would provide for itself, and perhaps even suggest a model for the West as well. Herzen's views coalesced into a doctrine that combined the romantic, folk, communal image of the *mir* with a program of advancing the people to a state of conscious recognition so that they could take hold of their own destiny.[97] In 1861, at the height of the influence of *The Bell*, Herzen first uttered the catchphrases which became the battle cries of the next generation, "zemlia i volia" ("land and freedom") and "V narod!" ("To the people!"). During Herzen's English period he also adopted the biological, evolutionary theory that was just beginning to influence modern patterns of thought.

During Herzen's years in England he significantly modified his earlier views and integrated his personal observations on English society, the theory of English philosophers and social thinkers—especially Mill and Owen—and new scientific paradigms. In England, with his new set of liberal contacts, and under the influence of a socialism that was evolving in a public forum, Herzen fully developed a custom-made theory for progress and development in Russia, one that influenced the *narodniki* (populists) of the following decades.

After a series of painful and stormy years on the European continent, Herzen arrived at a new and profound understanding of his life and the world around him in England. This period, essentially the last major chapter of both literary and practical achievement in his life, represents the consummation and fulfillment of all parts of his character, an integrated Herzen who, for the first time, was able to bring his idealist, utopian visions closer to the ground, and who managed to complement his writings with concrete activity in the West, establishing a landmark publishing enterprise which had a profound impact on Russia itself. Gurvich-Lishchiner maintains that Herzen strove "to reconstruct a harmonious integrity of vision of the person and the world."[98] For Herzen, this was both a literary endeavor, in the form of an original style of memoir, *Past and Thoughts,* begun in earnest almost immediately upon his arrival in England, and a practical effort to engage with the world and the movement of history, as was done through the Free Russian Press. Both enterprises mark a new and important phase in Herzen's varied and winding career, and both projects are inextricably entwined. In his mature years (post 1852), Herzen moved closer to the view that real social change begins first with individual development, inner strength, and the construction of character, *Bildung.*[99] His experience of England only served to strengthen this notion, particularly in regard to Mill's inner aesthetic, which sought to defend individuality and the "integrity of self against the homogeneity of Western industrial democracies."[100]

Herzen's extended exposure to English life, culture, and thought, a sojourn on English soil which comprised the longest amount of time he was to spend in any foreign land,[101] may be regarded as the culmination of a lifelong search for a harmony between one's inner, spiritual life, practical deeds in the world, and the relationship with one's community and nation. The fruits of this search are expressed most clearly and eloquently in *The Bell*, essays and articles of a particular era that address the eternal questions of self and humanity.

Notes

1. Rambaud writes of issues of *The Bell* "spread out" on the emperor's table: "Les numéros proscrits pénétraient cependant par milliers en Russie et, étalés sur la table de l'empereur, lui dénonçaient les iniquités les plus cachées." Alfred Rambaud, *Histoire de la Russie depuis les origines jusqu'à l'année 1877* (Paris: Hachette, 1878), 677.

2. *S togo berega* (*From the Other Shore*), widely regarded as Herzen's chef d'oeuvre, first appeared in German as *Vom anderen Ufer: Aus dem Russischen Manuskript* (Hamburg: Hoffmann und Campe, 1850); in 1855 Herzen's London press published the Russian text under his pseudonym Iskander. Herzen wrote "letters" of his experiences in the West, beginning with his "Letters from Avenue Marigny," published in Nekrasov's *Contemporary* in 1847. These and other such letters from the 1847–52 period were published as *Pis'ma iz Frantsii i Italii* (*Letters from France and Italy*) (London: Trübner, 1855).

3. "He did not like London. He spoke English very badly; he made few acquaintances there; and he writes with some asperity of the people and their habits." J. D. Duff, foreword to *The Memoirs of Alexander Herzen* (New Haven, Conn.: Yale University Press, 1923), xiii. These contentions persisted. "As for the English, he met few among them . . . On the whole, little attention was paid to him in England, and he responded with mingled admiration and dislike for his hosts." Isaiah Berlin, introduction to Alexander Herzen, *From the Other Shore*, trans. M. Budberg (London: Weidenfeld and Nicolson, 1956), xii.

4. "Takogo otshel'nichestva ia nigde ne mog naiti, kak v Londone." A. I. Gertsen, *Sobranie sochinenii v tridtsati tomakh* (Moscow: Izdatel'stvo Akademii nauk SSSR, 1954–66), 11:10.

5. In 1894 Milyukov delivered six public lectures, which included mention of the Decembrists and Herzen. Within months he was dismissed from teaching and sent into exile for two years. Undeterred, Milyukov set to work in Ryazan and published a series of sympathetic feuilletons on the romantic and emotional life of the "idealists" of the 1830s: Stankevich, Belinsky, and Herzen. See P. Miliukov, "Liubov' u idealistov tridtsatikh godov," *Russkiia vedomosti* 34 (issue numbers 276, 282, 289, 305, 335, 345) (1896).

6. As late as 1904, Boborykin, in his article on the Russian intelligentsia, still does not allow himself to mention Herzen by name, but instead refers to him as the "publisher of *The Bell* and *From the Other Shore*." P. Boborykin, "Russkaia intelligentsiia," *Russkaia mysl'* 25, no. 12 (1904): 82.

7. Ch. Vetrinskii (Vasilii Evgrafovich Cheshikhin-Vetrinskii), *Gertsen* (St. Petersburg: Svetoch, 1908).

8. P. N. Miliukov, *Vospominaniia (1859–1917)*, ed. M. M. Karpovich and B. I. El'kin, vol. 1 (New York: Izdatel'stvo Imeni Chekhova, 1955), 145.

9. P. Miliukov, "Pamiati Gertsena," *Mir Bozhii*, 9, no. 2, section 2 (February 1900): 17–21.

10. Paul N. Miliukov, *Russia To-Day and To-Morrow* (New York: Macmillan, 1922), 359.

11. See Iv. Il. Petrunkevich, *Iz zapisok obshchestvennogo deiatelia: Vospominaniia*, ed. A. A. Kizevetter (Prague, 1934; Berlin: Petropolis-Verlag), 337.

12. His real name was Razumnik Vasil'evich Ivanov.

13. Ivanov-Razumnik, *Istoriia russkoi obshchestvennoi mysli* (1907), 3rd ed. (St. Petersburg: M. M. Stasiulevich, 1911), 365–414.

14. Ivanov-Razumnik, "Gertsen i Mikhailovskii," in *A. I. Gertsen* (1905; Petrozavod: Kolos, 1920), 46–76. Ivanov-Razumnik exemplifies the hazards of the scholar who dared write in a free and unhindered way during the first years of the Bolshevik regime. He published studies on Herzen, Chernyshevsky, Lavrov, and Mikhailovsky, and favored populism over Marxism. With the consolidation of the new order, he soon found himself blacklisted, and then incarcerated for periods between 1921 and 1941.

15. See Ivanov-Razumnik, "O smysle zhizni," 2nd ed. (St. Peterburg, 1910). For more on Ivanov-Razumnik's writings on Herzen, see N. V. Kuzina, "A. I. Gertsen v sochineniiakh i tvorcheskom soznanii R. V. Ivanova-Razumnika 1910–1920 gg.," in *Gertsenovskie chteniia* (Kirov: Dept. kul'tury i iskusstva Kirovskoi oblasti, 2002), 12–17.

16. See Kirik Levin, *A. I. Gertsen: Lichnost', ideologiia* (Moscow: Dennitsa, Tipografiia Voennogo Komissariata Moskovskoi oblasti, 1918; 2nd ed.: Gosudarstvennoe Izdatel'stvo, 1922), v.

17. An edition of Herzen's writings in ten small volumes began to be published in the West five years after his death, but this represented only a fraction of his total output. Herzen's *Bell* essays are almost completely absent, and sections of other texts are missing. See *Sochineniia A. I. Gertsena s predisloviem (Oeuvres d'Alexandre Herzen)* (Geneva: H. Georg, 1875–79).

18. See V. Ia. Bogucharskii, "Poslednii period zhizni (1857–1870 gg.)," in *Aleksandr Ivanovich Gertsen* (Moscow: Gosudarstvennoe Izdatel'stvo, 1920/1921), 124–62.

19. Iurii M. Steklov, *A. I. Gertsen (Iskander): 1812–1870* (Moscow: Gosudarstvennoe Izdatel'stvo, 1920; 2nd ed., Gosudarstvennoe Izdatel'stvo, 1923).

20. See, for example, the treatment of Herzen in general historiographical overviews such as Nikolai L. Rubinshtein, *Russkaia istoriografiia* (Moscow: OGIZ/Gospolitizdat, 1941), 204–8.

21. Lenin's laudatory pronouncement declares that Herzen's *Bell* "broke the slavish silence" and "valiantly championed the liberation of the peasants." V. I. Lenin, "Pamiati Gertsena," *Sotsial-Demokrat*, no. 26, May 8 (April 25), 1912.

22. A striking example of this genre is the work of A. I. Volodin (1933–2004), which is essentially a composite of selected passages followed by tendentious interpretation in which he "reveals" the "dialectical materialism" ensconced in Herzen's outlook. See Aleksandr I. Volodin, *Gertsen* (Moscow: Mysl', 1970).

23. See Aleksei T. Pavlov, *Ot dvorianskoi revoliutsionnosti k revoliutsionnomu demokratizmu (ideinaia evoliutsiia Gertsena)* (Moscow: Izdatel'stvo Moskovskogo universiteta, 1977), 114.

24. See Ia. El'sberg, "Esteticheskie vzgliadi A. I. Gertsena," in *A. I. Gertsen: 1812–1870*, ed. I. G. Klabunovskii and B. P. Koz'min (Moscow: Gosudarstvennyi Literaturnyi muzei, 1946), 22.

25. Ioann S. Novich (Fainshtein), *Dukhovnaia drama Gertsena* (Moscow: Khudozhe-stvennaia literatura, 1937), 16.

26. See Zinaida P. Bazileva, *"Kolokol" Gertsena (1857–1867 gg.)* (Moscow: Gosudar-stvennoe Izdatel'stvo politicheskoi Literatury, 1949), 289. Another such work examines the atheistic outlook of Herzen and Ogaryov in *The Bell,* focusing on their discussion of freedom of conscience, and their critiques of religion, clericalism, and the social position of the Orthodox church. This brief study, too, is composed largely of a patchwork of excerpts and extended passages from the two authors, and begins and ends with Lenin's words. See Valentina S. Panova, *"Kolokol" Gertsena i Ogar'eva ob ateizme, religii I tserkvi* (Moscow: Mysl', 1983).

27. See "Kratkaia bibliografiia sochinenii Gertsena i literatury o nem," in *A. I. Gertsen: Seminarii,* by M. I. Gillel'son, E. N. Dryzhakova, and M. K. Perkal' (Moscow: Pros-veshchenie, 1965), 119–21.

28. See Liudmila E. Tatarinova, *A. I. Gertsen* (Moscow: Mysl', 1980), 86–181.

29. See Zinaida V. Smirnova, *Sotsial'naia filosofiia A. I. Gertsena* (Moscow: Nauka, 1973). Indicative of many such studies, the chronological chapters of Smirnova's work focus largely on the development of Herzen's thought in the 1830s and 1840s, culminating in his reactions to the 1848 revolutions.

30. Natal'ia M. Pirumova, *Istoricheskie vzgliady A. I. Gertsena* (Moscow: Gosudar-stvennoe Izdatel'stvo polit. Lit-y, 1956).

31. A. I. Gertsen, *Sobranie Sochinenii v tridtsati tomakh* (Moscow: Izdatel'stvo akademii nauk SSSR, 1954–66). The work (herein: *Sobranie sochinenii*) comprises 33 separate books, plus index.

32. *Letopis' zhizni i tvorchestva A. I. Gertsena (1812–1870),* vols. 1–5 (Moscow: Nauka, 1974–90).

33. Natan Ia. Eidel'man, *Gertsen protiv samoderzhaviia: Sekretnaia istoriia Rossii XVIII–XIX vekov i Vol'naia russkaia pechat'* (Moscow: Mysl', 1973). See also the collection of Eidelman's essays on the issue of freedom of speech and Herzen's efforts with the Free Russian Press: N. Ia. Eidel'man, *Svobodnoe slovo Gertsena* (Moscow: Editorial URSS, 1999). This volume contains several essays on *The Bell,* including "Anonymous Corre-spondents of *Kolokol,*" originally published as "Anonimnye korrespondenty 'Kolokola'" in *Problemy izucheniia Gertsena* (Moscow: ANSSSR, 1963), 251–79; and "Secret Corre-spondents of *Polestar,*" originally published as *Tainye korrespondenty "Poliarnoi zvezdy"* (Moscow: Mysl', 1966).

34. Herzen could only find one justification for the pain of his self-imposed exile, and this was the absolute necessity to live in an environment of free speech and the impera-tive to fight for those who lacked it. See *S togo berega,* in *Sobranie sochinenii,* 6:13–14. Not long after his arrival in London, Herzen realized his most momentous achievement, the establishment of his press. One of its first products was a small pamphlet addressed to his Russian brethren, a tiny manifesto declaring Herzen's deepest tenets and values. At the heart of it lies Herzen's maxim: "Without freedom of speech, man is not free." "Vol'noe russkoe knigopechatanie v Londone: Brat'iam na Rusi" (February 1853), Doc. 2 in this collection.

35. This theme transcends the Soviet era. A few years after the collapse of the Soviet Union, interest revived in Herzen and Ogaryov's multi-pronged campaign against the "official" version of history presented in Baron Modest Korf's rendition of the Decem-brist revolt and the accession to the throne of Nicholas I. Herzen had refuted what he

branded Korf's "servile" and "slavish" account in a notice appearing in *The Bell* 1, no. 4 (January 10, 1857), in a separate article, and a book: *14 dekabria 1825 i imperator Nikolai* (London: Trübner, 1858). A reprint of the latter, along with introduction, notes, and analysis, appeared as *14 dekabria 1825 goda i ego istolkovateli* (Gertsen i Ogarev protiv barona Korfa), ed. E. L. Rudnitskoi, prepared by A. G. Tartakovskii (Moscow: Nauka, 1994).

36. See, for example, the creative approaches and new directions taken in Elena N. Dryzhakova, *Gertsen na zapade: V labirinte nadezhd, slavy i otrechenii* (St. Petersburg: Akademicheskii proekt, 1999) (this work devotes only 39 pages to Herzen's 1855–64 period); Vasilii F. Antonov, *A. I. Gertsen: Obshchestvennyi ideal* (Moscow: Editorial URSS, 2000); and Ruslan Khestanov, *Aleksandr Gertsen: Improvizatsiia protiv doktriny* (Moscow: Dom intellektual'noi knigi, 2001).

37. Raoul Labry, *Herzen et Proudhon* (Paris: Bossard, 1928); Raoul Labry, *Alexandre Ivanovic Herzen, 1812–1870: Essai sur la formation et le développement de ses idées* (Paris: Éditions Bossard, 1928).

38. Alexander Herzen, *My Past and Thoughts: The Memoirs of Alexander Herzen*, trans. Constance Garnett, 6 vols. (London: Chatto and Windus, 1924–27).

39. Edward Hallett Carr, *The Romantic Exiles: A Nineteenth-Century Portrait Gallery* (London: V. Gollancz, 1933; reprint: Harmondsworth, Eng.: Penguin, 1968).

40. Originally a restricted document, the report was published in its entirety as "The Arts in Russia Under Stalin," in *The Soviet Mind: Russian Culture Under Communism*, ed. Henry Hardy (Washington, D.C.: Brookings Institution, 2004).

41. "Russia and 1848" highlights Herzen's central role in the development of the Russian intelligentsia as a counterforce to the oppressive regime of Nicholas I. Berlin traces the emergence of a distinct Russian "native social and political outlook" against the backdrop of "the gigantic strait-jacket of bureaucratic and military control." It is this formation of a flank of moral opposition, spearheaded by Herzen, that Berlin identifies as a heroic Russian liberal voice in the face of repressive measures. See Isaiah Berlin, "Russia and 1848," *Slavonic Review* (*Slavonic and East European Review*) 26 (1948): 341, 359.

42. Berlin considered Marx to be the most influential of all nineteenth-century thinkers, though he took issue with several of his basic positions and tenets, such as his negative regard for nationalism. A decade after completion of his study on Marx, Berlin can be seen as offering the alternative refrain of Herzen, a socialist of strong national convictions: "In the 1950s Berlin went on to reveal to English and American readers the riches of nineteenth-century Russian populism and liberalism as represented by Herzen . . . and to argue something we need to remember today more than ever, that nationalism can be and has been an ally of liberalism." Alan Ryan, introduction to Isaiah Berlin, *Karl Marx: His Life and Environment* (1939), 4th rev. ed. (New York: Oxford University Press, 1996), xvi.

43. See Isaiah Berlin, "The First and the Last: My Intellectual Path," *New York Review of Books*, May 14, 1998, pp. 10–11.

44. Berlin's activities stretched far beyond the halls of academia. Regarding Berlin's direct influence on Tom Stoppard's "Coast of Utopia" trilogy, see "The Coast of Utopia," *Lincoln Center Theater Review* 43 (2006). One critic writes that English Herzenism, led by the Berlin school, projects Herzen as "a post-war liberal in nineteenth-century clothing." Thomas Harlan Campbell, "Restaging the Gercen 'Family Drama': Tom Stoppard's Shipwreck and the Discourse of English 'Herzenism,'" *Russian Literature* 61, no. 1–2 (January 1–February 15, 2007): 207–43.

45. "To the analytical antinomies he addressed, Berlin affixed the dyad of East and West as he sought in the exertions of 19th century Russian writers a counterweight to the exaggerated pursuit of perfection emblematic of the Enlightenment. . . . Turgenev, Tolstoy, and Herzen, Berlin believed, were expositors of an alternative, corrective, vision, sources for redress and repair for what ails the West's record of ideas. Herzen was his favorite. Berlin appreciated Herzen because he declined to pursue a singular coherent doctrine, and for his open temperament." Ira Katznelson, "Isaiah Berlin's Modernity," *Social Research* 66, no. 4 (1999): 1087–88.

46. In the mid-1950s, having witnessed the fruits of Stalinism, Nazism, and the escalating Cold War, Berlin writes: "On the whole, it is Herzen's totalitarian opponents both of the Right and of the Left that have won." Isaiah Berlin, introduction to Herzen, *From the Other Shore*, trans. Budberg, xx.

47. " 'Lampert sees Herzen as Lampert writ large,' I remember Berlin telling me, when I was embarking on a doctorate on Herzen. Carr's retort, when I recounted this to him, was that 'Berlin sees Berlin as Herzen writ large.' " Edward Acton, "Eugene Lampert: Distinguished Scholar of Russian History" (obituary), *Guardian*, September 10, 2004, p. 29. In a letter of August 1938, Berlin writes: "Oh dear, Herzen. There is no writer, & indeed no man I shd like to be like, & to write like, more" [sic]. *Flourishing: Letters, 1928–1946*, ed. Henry Hardy (London: Pimlico, 2005), 279.

48. Offord comments that Berlin "established a hagiographic tradition" and that this, in part, accounts for the lack of critical examination of Herzen by later scholars. Derek Offord, "Alexander Herzen and James de Rothschild," *Toronto Slavic Quarterly* 19 (Winter 2007): 1.

49. Franco Venturi, *Roots of Revolution* (1952; London: Weidenfeld and Nicolson, 1960).

50. See Marc Raeff, "The Peasant Commune in the Political Thinking of Russian Publicists: Laissez-Faire Liberalism in the Reign of Alexander II" (Ph.D. thesis, Harvard University, 1950). Also in this vein, in 1951 V. Pirozhkova completed a dissertation that considered the "collapse" of Herzen's utopian vision. Her dissertation was later published as Vera Piroschkow [Vera Aleksandrovna Pirozhkova], *Alexander Herzen: Der Zusammenbruch einer Utopie* (Munich: A. Pustet, 1961).

51. Martin Malia, *Alexander Herzen and the Birth of Russian Socialism: 1812–1855* (Cambridge, Mass: Harvard University Press, 1961), 393.

52. Malia conceives of Herzen as a figure influenced to a great degree by the ideational and aesthetic constructs he formed in Russia. "The liberal institutions of England . . . so utterly failed to impress him." Martin E. Malia, "Schiller and the Early Russian Left," in *Russian Thought and Politics*, vol. 4, ed. H. McLean, M. Malia, and G. Fischer (Cambridge, Mass.: Harvard University Press, 1957), 197.

53. This omission was noted in Hare's review: "A study of Herzen's contribution to Russian socialism should surely take into account the most mature and influential period of his life, when after the death of Nicholas I (1855), he fascinated the new Emperor and a large Russian reading public through the pages of his London-published journal *The Bell*." Richard Hare, review of *Alexander Herzen and the Birth of Russian Socialism, 1812–1855*, by Martin Malia, *Russian Review* 21, no. 2 (April 1962): 191–92.

54. Aileen M. Kelly, "Herzen and Proudhon: Two Radical Ironists," in *Views from the Other Shore* (New Haven, Conn.: Yale University Press, 1999), 84.

55. Monica Partridge, *Alexander Herzen: 1812–1870* (Paris: Unesco, 1984), 83.

56. See Monica Partridge, "Alexander Herzen and the English Press," *Slavonic and East European Review* 36, no. 87 (June 1958): 453; and Monica Partridge, "Alexander Herzen and England," in *Alexander Herzen: Collected Studies*, 2nd ed. (Nottingham: Astra, 1993), 115.

57. Edward Acton, *Alexander Herzen and the Role of the Intellectual Revolutionary* (Cambridge, Eng.: Cambridge University Press, 1979), ix.

58. Acton argues that Herzen's "private ordeal" "did more than predispose him emotionally" in his thought and attitude. The "personal catastrophe" "touched him at the deepest level" and impacted "his basic approach to historical development." Acton, *Alexander Herzen*, 105–8.

59. Judith E. Zimmerman, *Midpassage: Alexander Herzen and European Revolution, 1847–1852* (Pittsburgh, Pa.: University of Pittsburgh Press, 1989), xv.

60. Ibid., xii–xiii.

61. In earlier research, Zimmerman writes of Herzen: "I discovered that personal relations were far more important in determining political position than was pure ideology." Judith E. Zimmerman, "Herzen, Herwegh, Marx," in *Imperial Russia 1700–1917: State, Society, Opposition; Essays in Honor of Marc Raeff*, ed. E. Mendelsohn and M. Shatz (DeKalb: Northern Illinois University Press, 1988), 298.

62. Zimmerman, *Midpassage*, xii, xv, 222, 225.

63. See Abbott Gleason, *Young Russia: The Genesis of Russian Radicalism in the 1860s* (New York: Viking, 1980), 84. Citations are pulled almost entirely from secondary sources. For example, the references to *The Bell* are all sourced from Bazileva's 1949 monograph, and there are no citations in the chapter directly from Herzen's works.

64. K. N. Lomunov, "A. I. Gertsen v londonskii period ego zhizni," in *Alexander Herzen and European Culture*, ed. Monica Partridge (Nottingham: Astra, 1984), 1.

65. See N. O. Lossky, *History of Russian Philosophy* (New York: International Universities Press, 1951), 57.

66. Zernov writes: "Herzen was the only leader of the intelligentsia who was more an agnostic than a dogmatic atheist and for this reason he remained on the fringe of the movement. He was never accepted whole-heartedly as their teacher by its more radical members." Nicolas Zernov, *The Russian Religious Renaissance of the Twentieth Century* (New York: Harper and Row, 1963), 20.

67. See V. V. Zen'kovskii, *Istoriia russkoi filosofii* (Paris: YMCA, 1948), 278, 285–86.

68. "Herzen was not the first Russian political émigré . . . but Herzen was the first to look on emigration as a base from which one could try to influence intellectual and political developments at home." S. V. Utechin, *Russian Political Thought: A Concise History* (London: J.M. Dent, 1963), 117, 119.

69. For example, Herzen believed that action was necessary to realize social goals, and that this presupposes the existence of freedom of will and action. However, the positivists that Herzen so admired tended to regard human freedom as an illusion, a chimera which has no basis in scientific observation or knowledge.

70. Frederick C. Copleston, *Philosophy in Russia* (Notre Dame, Ind.: University of Notre Dame Press, 1986), 1–5, 93–99.

71. Andrzej Walicki, *A History of Russian Thought from the Enlightenment to Marxism* (1973; Stanford, Calif.: Stanford University Press, 1979), 115–34, 162–80.

72. The notion of Herzen either as a liminal or transitory figure is expressed by a number of scholars. Offord writes that "the émigré Herzen occupied political space

somewhere between the liberals . . . and the militant young thinkers." Derek Offord, *Nineteenth-Century Russia: Opposition to Autocracy* (London: Pearson, 1999), 54. Schapiro points out that although Herzen's positions of the 1850s are "reminiscent of the Slavophiles," Herzen was a Western-oriented, rationalist, revolutionary atheist, all of which was anathema to the Slavophiles. Leonard Schapiro, *Rationalism and Nationalism in Russian Nineteenth-Century Political Thought* (New Haven, Conn.: Yale University Press, 1967), 82–83.

73. Andrzej Walicki, *The Slavophile Controversy: History of a Conservative Utopia in Nineteenth-Century Russian Thought* (1964; Oxford: Clarendon, 1975), 173, 580.

74. See *Russkaia intelligentsia: Istoriia i sud'ba,* compiled by T. B. Kniazevskaia (Moscow: Nauka, 1999); *Rossiia* 2, no. 10 (1999) (Russkaia intelligentsiia i zapadnyi intellektualizm: Istoriia i tipologiia); *Russian Intelligentsia,* ed. Richard Pipes (New York: Columbia University Press, 1961); and Marc Raeff, *Origins of the Russian Intelligentsia* (New York: Harcourt Brace and World, 1966).

75. See V. G. Belinskii, "Vzgliad na russkiu literaturu 1847 goda," in *Sobranie sochinenii,* vol. 8 (Moscow: Khudozhestvennaia literatura, 1982), 381.

76. See Lev. A. Plotkin, "Gertsen-belletrist," in *O russkoi literature: A. I. Gertsen, I. S. Nikitin, D. I. Pisarev* (Leningrad: Khudozhestvennaia literatura, 1986), 7–55.

77. See Ivan G. Pekhtelev, *Gertsen-literaturnyi kritik* (Moscow: Prosveshchenie, 1967).

78. See Leonid S. Radek, *Gertsen i Turgenev: Literaturno-esteticheskaia polemika* (Kishinev: Shtinnitsa, 1984).

79. See V. A. Rutintsev, *Gertsen: Pisatel',* 2nd ed. (Moscow: ANSSSR, 1963); Sof'ia D. Gurvich-Lishchiner, *Tvorchestvo Gertsena v razvitii russkogo realizma serediny XIX veka* (Moscow: Nasledie, 1994).

80. See *A. I. Gertsen v russkoi kritike,* intro. essay and notes by V. A. Putintsev (Moscow: Gosudarstvennaia Khudozhestvennaia literatura, 1953).

81. Lidiia K. Chukovskaia, *"Byloe i dumy" Gertsena* (Moscow: Khud. lit-a, 1966), 143. Elizavetina asserts that Herzen crafted his particular "memoir-autobiographical genre" in order to impart more knowledge and understanding than other available literary forms. Galina G. Elizavetina, *"Byloe i dumy" A. I. Gertsena* (Moscow: Khudozhestvennaia literatura, 1984), 154.

82. See Ulrike Höffler-Preissmann, *Die Technik des literarischen Porträts in Alexander Herzens "Byloe i dumy"* (Mainz: Liber, 1982), 1–2, 140–41.

83. See Ulrich Schmid, *Ichentwürfe: Die russische Autobiographie zwischen Avvakum und Gercen* (Zürich: Pano-Verlag, 2000), 327–69.

84. See Lidiia Ia. Ginzburg, *O psikhologicheskoi proze,* 2nd ed. (Leningrad: Khudozhestvennaia literatura, 1977), 251–52.

85. See Irina Paperno, "Intimacy and History: The Gercen Family Drama Reconsidered," *Russian Literature* 61, no. 1–2 (January 1–February 15, 2007): 1–65.

86. Gurvich-Lishchiner examines the influence of German writers, including Schiller, Goethe, and Heine. See Sof'ia D. Gurvich-Lishchiner, *Tvorchestvo Aleksandra Gertsena i nemetskaia literatura: Ocherki i materialy* (Frankfurt am Main: Peter Lang, 2001).

87. S. Rozanova, *Tolstoi i Gertsen* (Moscow: Khudozhestvennaia literatura, 1972).

88. A standard treatment may be found in "Zhurnal'no-izdatel'skaia deiatel'nost' A. I. Gertsena i N. P. Ogareva: 'Poliarnaia zvezda' i 'Kolokol,'" in *Istoriia russkoi zhurnalistiki: XVIII–XIX vekov,* ed. A. V. Zapadov (Moscow: Vysshaia shkola, 1963), 279–304.

89. Berlin wrote the introductions not only to translations of Herzen's writings but to the English translation of Venturi's *Roots of Revolution* and Raeff's *Russian Intellectual History*.

90. Malia began his doctoral thesis in 1949, the year that Berlin came to Harvard as a visiting lecturer, and the very time that the latter was developing his ideas on Herzen and the Russian intelligentsia. Lampert began corresponding with Berlin in 1950, and soon the theologian was drawn into his orbit, as was S. V. Utechin, who arrived at Oxford the same year, and who later made efforts to publish Berlin's writings in Russia. Andrzej Walicki met Berlin in early 1960, writing that their first encounter became "the foundation of the moral and intellectual bond" that developed between them. Aileen Kelly wrote her doctoral dissertation under Berlin's supervision and coedited and introduced Berlin's *Russian Thinkers*.

91. See Ia. E. El'sberg (Shapershtein), "Ideinaia bor'ba vokrug naslediia Gertsena v nashe vremia," in *Problemy izucheniia Gertsena* (Moscow: ANSSSR, 1963), 432–48. Elsberg wrote a monograph on Herzen, referred to widely, that has gone through several editions (1948, 1951, 1956, 1963), the last revision topping 700 pages.

92. Novich's study surveys Herzen's early years (primarily during the 1830s). See Ioann S. Novich (Fainshtein), *Molodoi Gertsen: Iskaniia, idei, obrazy, lichnost'* (Moscow: Sovetskii pisatel', 1980). We have already noted Zimmerman's *Midpassage,* which covers the 1847–52 period. Linkov focuses on Herzen's pro-Polish activities with the Land and Liberty movement: Iakov I. Linkov, *Revoliutsionnaia bor'ba: A. I. Gertsen i N. P. Ogarev i tainoe obshchestvo "Zemlia i volia" 1860–kh godov* (Moscow: Nauka, 1964).

93. Perkal's pocket-size monograph covers Herzen's years in St. Petersburg (1839–41 and 1846) with relatively little scholarly apparatus. See Mark K. Perkal', *Gertsen v Peterburge* (Leningrad: Lenizdat, 1971). See also the popular booklet by Viktor G. Smirnov, *Gertsen v Novgorode* (Leningrad: Lenizdat, 1985).

94. See Eberhard Reissner, *Alexander Herzen in Deutschland* (Berlin: Akademie-Verlag, 1963); Ulrike Preissmann, *Alexander Herzen und Italien* (Mainz: Liber Verlag, 1989); Nadja Bontadina, *Alexander Herzen und die Schweiz: Das Verhältnis des russischen Publizisten und Aristokraten zur einzigen Republik im Europa seiner Zeit* (Bern: P. Lang, 1999); L. P. Lanskii, "Gertsen i Frantsiia," *Literaturnoe nasledstvo* 96, "Gertsen i zapad," ed. S. A. Maklashin and L. P. Lanskii (Moscow: Nauka, 1985): 254–306.

95. See, for example, F. B. Smith, "The View from Britain: Tumults Abroad, Stability at Home," and J. H. Grainger, "The View from Britain: The Moralizing Island," in *Intellectuals and Revolution: Socialism and the Experience of 1848,* ed. Eugene Kamenka and F. B. Smith (London: E. Arnold, 1979), 94–120, 121–30.

96. "Robert Ouen," *Poliarnaia zvezda* 6 (1861): 286.

97. Yarmolinsky argues that Herzen's conception of the *obshchina* was a "fantasy-laden . . . social myth" created by "an expatriate who had never been close to the actualities of Russian rural life." Avrahm Yarmolinsky, *Road to Revolution: A Century of Russian Radicalism* (London: Cassell, 1957), 172.

98. S. Gurvich-Lishchiner, "Chaadaev-Gertsen-Dostoevskii: K probleme lichnosti i razuma v tvorcheskom soznanii," *Voprosy literatury* 3 (2004): 221.

99. See Lina Steiner, "Gercen's Tragic *Bildungsroman:* Love, Autonomy, and Maturity in Aleksandr Gercen's *Byloe i dumy,*" *Russian Literature* 61, no. 1–2 (January 1–February 15, 2007): 139–73.

100. See Colin Heydt, *Rethinking Mill's Ethics: Character and Aesthetic Education* (London: Continuum, 2006). On Mill's exploration of "the sphere of imagination, self-culture, personal aesthetics" and that which is necessary "to secure to the individual an area within which his individuality may be exercised to the full," see Alan Ryan, "On Liberty: Beyond Duty to Personal Aesthetics," in *The Philosophy of John Stuart Mill* (London: Macmillan, 1970), 233. In his mature years, Herzen recognized that the element of inner freedom of conscience was of at least equal importance as that of freedom from the coercion of the state.

101. Of Herzen's approximately 30 years of literary activity, 23 years were spent abroad, with over half of those years spent in England.

BIBLIOGRAPHY

Acton, Edward. *Alexander Herzen and the Role of the Intellectual Revolutionary*. Cambridge, Eng.: Cambridge University Press, 1979.

Afanas'ev, Akensandr. *Russian Fairy Tales*. Translated by Norbert Guterman. New York: Pantheon, 1973.

Alekseyeva, Ludmila. *U.S. Broadcasting to the Soviet Union: A Helsinki Watch Report*. New York: Helsinki Watch Committee, 1986.

Alekseyeva, Ludmila, with Paul Goldberg. *The Thaw Generation: Coming of Age in the Post-Stalin Era*. Boston: Little, Brown, 1990.

Annenkov, P. V. *The Extraordinary Decade: Literary Memoirs*. Translated by Irwin Titunik. Edited by Arthur P. Mendel. Ann Arbor: University of Michigan Press, 1968.

———. *Literaturnye vospominaniia*. Introductory essay by V. I. Kuleshov. Commentary by A. M. Dolotova, G. G. Elizavetina, Iu. V. Mann, et al. Moscow: Khudozhestvennaia Literatura, 1983.

Antonov, V. F. *A. I. Gertsen: Obshchestvennyi ideal anarkhista*. Moscow: Editorial URSS, 2000.

Autour de l'Alexandre Herzen: Révolutionnaires et exiles du XIXe siècle: Documents inédits. Edited by Marc Vuilleumier, Michel Aucouturier, et al. Geneva. Librairie Droz, 1973.

Bakhtin, M. M. *Rabelais and His World*. Translated by Hélène Iswolsky. Bloomington: Indiana University Press, 1984.

———. *Speech Genres and Other Late Essays*. Translated by Vern McGee. Edited by C. Emerson and M. Holquist. Austin: University of Texas Press, 1986.

Bazileva, E. P. *"Kolokol" Gertsena (1857–1867 gg.)*. Moscow: OGIZ Gosudarstvennoe Izdatel'stvo Politcheskoi literatury, 1949.

Beliavskaia, I. M. *A. I. Gertsen i pol'skoe natsional'no-osvoboditel'noe dvizhenie 60–x godov XIX veka*. Moscow: Izdatel'stvo Moskovskogo Universiteta, 1954.

Belinskii, V. G. "Vzgliad na russkuiu literaturu 1847 goda." In *Sobranie sochinenii*, vol. 8. Moscow: Khudozhestvennaia literatura, 1982.

Berlin, Isaiah. "The First and the Last: My Intellectual Path." *New York Review of Books*, May 14, 1998, pp. 10–11.

———. *Flourishing: Letters 1928–1946*. Edited by Henry Hardy. London: Chatto and Windus, 2004.

———. *Karl Marx: His Life and Environment* (1939). 4th rev. ed., with an introduction by Alan Ryan. Oxford: Oxford University Press, 1996.

———. *The Power of Ideas*. Edited by Henry Hardy. Princeton, N.J.: Princeton University Press, 2000.

———. *The Proper Study of Mankind*. Edited by Henry Hardy and Roger Hausheer. New York: Farrar, Straus and Giroux, 1998.

————. *Russian Thinkers*. Edited by Henry Hardy and Aileen Kelly. Introduction by Aileen Kelly. New York: Penguin, 1979.

————. *The Soviet Mind: Russian Culture Under Communism*. Edited by Henry Hardy. Washington, D.C.: Brookings, 2004.

Billington, James, *Mikhailovsky and Russian Populism*. Oxford: Clarendon, 1958.

Billington, James, and Kathleen Parthé. *The Search for a New Russian National Identity: Russian Perspectives*, 2003. Available as pdf file from www.loc.gov.

Boborykin, Petr D. "Russkaia intelligentsia," *Russkaia mysl'*, 25, no. 12 (1904).

————. *Vospominaniia*. 2 vols. Moscow: Izdatel'stvo Khudozhestvennaia literatura, 1965.

Bogucharskii, V. Ia.. "Poslednii period zhizni (1857–1870 gg.)." In *Aleksandr Ivanovich Gertsen*, 124–62. Moscow: Gosudarstvennoe Izdatel'stvo, 1920/1921.

Bontadina, Nadja. *Alexander Herzen und die Schweiz: Das Verhältnis des russischen Publizisten und Aristokraten zur einzigen Republik in Europer seiner Zeit*. Bern: P. Lang, 1999.

Bradley, Joseph. *Voluntary Associations in Tsarist Russia: Science, Patriotism, and Civil Society*. Cambridge, Mass.: Harvard University Press, 2009.

Bulgakov, Sergei N. *Dushevnaia drama Gertsena*. Kiev: Izdatel'stvo Knizhnyi magazin S. I. Ivanova, 1905.

Campbell, Thomas Harlan. "Restaging the Gercen 'Family Drama': Tom Stoppard's Shipwreck and the Discourse of English 'Herzenism.'" *Russian Literature* 61 (January 1–February 15, 2007): 207–43.

Carr, E. H. *The Romantic Exiles*. Harmondsworth, Eng.: Penguin, 1968.

Chamberlain, Lesley. *Motherland: A Philosophical History of Russia*. London: Atlantic, 2004.

Choldin, Marianna Tax. *A Fence Around the Empire: Russian Censorship of Western Ideas Under the Tsars*. Durham, N.C.: Duke University Press, 1985.

Christoff, Peter K. *An Introduction to Nineteenth-Century Russian Slavophilism: A Study in Ideas*, vol. 3, *K. S. Aksakov: A Study in Ideas*. Princeton, N.J.: Princeton University Press, 1982.

Chukovskaia, Lidiia. *"Byloe i dumy" Gertsena*. Moscow: Khudozhestvennaia literatura, 1966.

————. *Zapiski ob Anne Akhmatovoi*, vol. 1, 1938–1941. Paris: YMCA, 1976. Vol. 2, 1952–1962. Paris: YMCA, 1980.

————. *Zapiski ob Anne Akhmatovoi v trekh tomakh*. Moscow: Soglasie, 1997.

Confino, Michael, ed. *Daughter of a Revolutionary: Natalie Herzen and the Bakunin-Nechayev Circle*. Translated by Hilary Sternberg and Lydia Bott. Introduction by Michael Confino. LaSalle, Ill.: Library, 1973.

Copleston, Frederick C. *Philosophy in Russia*. Notre Dame, Ind.: University of Notre Dame Press, 1986.

Crichtlow, James, *Radio Hole-in-the-Head: Radio Liberty, An Insider's Story of Cold War Broadcasting*. Washington, D.C.: American University Press, 1995.

de Custine, Astolphe. *Letters from Russia*. Translated and edited by Anka Muhlstein. New York: New York Review of Books, 2002.

Derzhavin, N. S. *A. I. Gertsen: Literaturno-khudozhestevnnoe nasledie*. Moscow: ANSSSR, 1947.

Dobroliubov, Nikolai A. "Literaturnye melochi proshlogo goda." In *Sobranie sochinenii v deviati tomakh*, 4:48–112, 433–45. Moscow: Khudozhestvennaia literatura, 1962.

———. *Polnoe sobranie sochinenii*, vol. 6. Moscow, 1939.

Dostoevsky, Fyodor. *A Writer's Diary*, 2 vols. Translated and annotated by Kenneth Lantz. Introductory study by Gary Saul Morson. Evanston, Ill.: Northwestern University Press, 1993.

———. *A Writer's Diary*. One-volume abridged edition. Translated and annotated by Kenneth Lantz. Edited and with an introduction by Gary Saul Morson. Evanston, Ill: Northwestern University Press, 2009.

Dryzhakova, Elena N. *Gertsen na zapade: V labirinte nadezhd, slavy i otrechenii*. St. Petersburg: Akademicheskii proekt, 1999.

Eidel'man, Natan Ia. *Gertsen protiv samoderzhaviia: Sekretnaia istoriia Rossii XVIII-XIX vekov i Vol'naia russkaia pechat'*. Moscow: Mysl', 1973.

———. *Svobodnoe slovo Gertsena*. Moscow: Editorial URSS, 1999.

Elizavetina, Galina G., *"Byloe i dumy" A. I. Gertsena*. Moscow: Khudozhestvennaia literatura, 1984.

El'sberg [Shapirshtein], Iakov Efimovich. *A. I. Gertsen: 1812–1870*. Edited by I. G. Klabunovskii and B. P. Koz'min. Moscow: Gosudarstvennyi Literaturnyi muzei, 1946.

———. *Gertsen: Zhizhn' i tvorchestvo*. 4th rev. ed. Moscow: Khudozhestvennaia Literatura, 1963.

———. "Ideinaia bor'ba vokrug naslediia Gertsena v nashe vremiia." In *Problemy izucheniia Gertsena*, 432–48. Moscow: ANSSSR, 1963.

Evgen'ev-Maksimov, V. *Sovremennik pri Chernyshevskom i Dobroliubove*. Leningrad: Khudozhestvennaia Literatura, 1936.

Figes, Orlando. *Natasha's Dance: A Cultural History of Russia*. New York: Metropolitan Books, 2002.

Frank, Joseph. *Dostoevsky: The Stir of Liberation 1860–1865*. Princeton, N.J.: Princeton University Press, 1986.

Frieden, Nancy Mandelker. *Russian Physicians in an Era of Reform and Revolution, 1856–1905*. Princeton, N.J.: Princeton University Press, 1981.

Gertsen, A. I. *Polnoe sobranie sochinenii i pisem*. 22 vols. Edited by M. Lemke. Petrograd, Gosudarstvennoe izdatel'stvo, 1915–25.

———. *Sobranie sochinenii v tridtsati tomakh*. 33 vols. Moscow: ANSSSR, 1954–66.

———. *Sochineniia A. I. Gertsena s predisloviem (Oeuvres d'Alexandre Herzen)*. Geneva: H. Georg, 1875–79.

Gillel'son, Maksim Ivanovich. *A. I. Gertsen: Seminarii: Posobie dlia studentov*. Leningrad: Prosveshchenie, 1965.

Ginzburg, L. *O psikhologicheskoi proze*, 2nd. ed. Leningrad: Khudozhestvennaia literatura, 1977.

Gleason, Abbott. *Young Russia: The Genesis of Russian Radicalism in the 1860s*. Chicago: University of Chicago Press, 1983.

Grainger, J. H. "The View from Britain: The Moralizing Island." In *Intellectuals and Revolution: Socialism and the Experience of 1848*, edited by Eugene Kamenka and F. B. Smith, 121–30. London: E. Arnold, 1979.

Gray, John. *Gray's Anatomy: Selected Writings*. London: Allen Lane/Penguin Books, 2009.

Gurvich-Lishchiner, Sof'ia D. "Chaadaev-Gertsen-Dostoevskii: K probleme lichnosti i razuma v tvorcheskom soznanii." *Voprosy literatury* 3 (2004): 173–221.

———. "Gertsen i russkaia 'intellektual'naia proza.'" *Voprosy literatury* 4 (1976): 172–95.

————. *Tvorchestvo Aleksandra Gertsena i nemetskaia literature: Ocherki i materialy.* Frankfurt am Main: Peter Lang, 2001.

Hamburg, G. M. *Boris Chicherin and Early Russian Liberalism 1828–1866.* Stanford, Calif.: Stanford University Press, 1992.

Hare, Richard. Review of *Alexander Herzen and the Birth of Russian Socialism,* by Martin Malia. *Russian Review* 21, no. 2 (April 1962): 191–92.

Herzen, Alexander. *Childhood, Youth, and Exile.* Translated by J. Duff. Introduction by Isaiah Berlin. Oxford: Oxford University Press, 1980.

————. *Ends and Beginnings.* Translated by C. Garnett. Translation revised by H. Higgens. Selected and edited with an introduction by Aileen Kelly. Oxford: Oxford University Press, 1985.

————. *From the Other Shore and The Russian People and Socialism.* (No translator listed.) Introduction by Isaiah Berlin. Cleveland, Ohio: Meridian, 1963.

————. *Letters from France and Italy.* Translated and edited by Judith Zimmerman. Pittsburgh, Pa.: University of Pittsburgh Press, 1995.

————. *My Past and Thoughts,* 4 vols. Translated by Constance Garnett. Revised by Humphrey Higgens. Introduction by Isaiah Berlin. London: Chatto and Windus, 1968.

————. *My Past and Thoughts.* A one-volume version of the 1968 edition. Abridged, with a preface and notes by Dwight Macdonald. Berkeley: University of California Press, 1982.

————. *Selected Philosophical Works.* Translated by Lev Navrozov. Moscow: For. Langs. Publ. House, 1956.

————. *Who Is to Blame? A Novel in Two Parts.* Translated, with an introduction by Michael Katz. Ithaca, N.Y.: Cornell University Press, 1984.

Herzen, Natalie. *Daughter of a Revolutionary: Natalie Herzen and the Bakunin-Nechaev Circle.* Translated by Hilary Sternberg and Lydia Bott. Edited, with an introduction by Michael Confino. LaSalle, Ill.: Library, 1973.

Heydt, Colin. *Rethinking Mill's Ethics: Character and Aesthetic Education.* London: Continuum, 2006.

Höffler-Preissmann, Ulrike. *Die Technik des literarishcen Porträts in Alexander Herzens "Byloe i dumy."* Mainz: Liber, 1982.

Hopkins, Mark. *Russia's Underground Press: The Chronicle of Current Events.* Foreword by Andrei Sakharov. New York: Praeger, 1983.

Ianov, Aleksandr. "Alternativa." *Molodoi kommunist* 1 (1974): 70–77.

————. "Otkuda v samoderzhavnoi Rossiii vzialsia Gertsen?" *Znanie-sila* (2009): 1–3. See also Yanov.

Inber, Vera. *Pochti tri goda.* Leningrad: Sovetskii pisatel', 1946.

Istoriia Moskvy, vol. 3. Edited by N. M. Druzhinin and M. K. Rozhkova. Moscow: ANSSSR, 1954.

Ivanov-Razumnik. "Gertsen i Mikhailovskii." In *A. I. Gertsen* (1905). Petrozavod: Kolos, 1920.

————. *Istoriia russkoi obshchestvennoi zhizni* (1907). 3rd ed. St. Petersburg: M. M. Stasiulevich, 1911.

————. *O smysle zhizni.* 2nd ed. St. Petersburg, 1910.

Ivanova, F., ed. *A. I. Gertsen v russkoi kritike: Sbornik statei.* 2nd rev. ed. Introduction and notes by V. Putintseva. Moscow: Khudozhestvennaia Literatura, 1953.

Jahanbegloo, Rami. *Conversations with Isaiah Berlin: Recollections of a Historian of Ideas.* London: Phoenix, 1993.

Kamenev, L. V. *Ob A. I. Gertsene i N. G. Chernyshevskom.* Petrograd: "Zhizn' i znanie," 1916.

Kelly, Aileen. Introduction to *Ends and Beginnings,* by Alexander Herzen, vii–xvi. New York: Oxford University Press, 1985.

———. *Toward Another Shore: Russian Thinkers Between Necessity and Chance.* New Haven, Conn.: Yale University Press, 1998.

———. *Views from the Other Shore: Essays on Herzen, Chekhov, and Bakhtin.* New Haven, Conn.: Yale University Press, 1999.

Khestanov, Ruslan. *Aleksandr Gertsen: Improvizatsiia protiv doktriny.* Moscow: Dom intellektual'noi knigi, 2001.

Kirpotin, V. "Aleksandr Ivanovich Gertsen (K 75–letiiu so dnia smerti)." *Krasnoe znamia,* January 1945. An undated newspaper clipping found in Herzen's collected works; accompanying articles are dated Jan. 23 and 25.

Klabunovskii, I., and Koz'min, B., eds. *A. I. Hertsen 1812–1870: Sbornik statei.* Moscow: Gosudarstevnnyi Literaturnyi Muzei, 1946.

Kniazhevskaia, T. B., comp. *Russkaia intelligentsia: Istoriia sud'by.* Moscow: Nauka, 1999.

Kolokol: Izdanie A. I. Gertsena i N. P. Ogareva 1857–1867. Vols. 1–11. Moscow: ANSSSR, 1962–64.

Kolokol: Izdanie A. I. Gertsena i N. P. Ogareva 1857–1867: Sistematicheskii rospis' statei i zametok. Moscow: Izdatel'stvo vsesoiuzhnoi knizhnoi palaty, 1957.

Kolokol (La Cloche). Facsimile edition. 11 vols. Moscow: Nauka, 1979.

Krestovskii, Vsevolod V. *Krovavyi Puf, Panurgovo stado.* Moscow: "EKSMO," 2007.

Kul'tura. December 2001. Unsigned obituary of Viktor Astaf'ev.

Kunka, Françoise. *Alexander Herzen and the Free Russian Press in London 1852 to 1866.* Saarbrücken: Lambert Academic Publishing, 2011.

Kuzina, N. V. "A. I. Gertsen v sochineniiakh i tvorcheskom soznanii R. V. Ivanova-Razumnika 1910–1920 gg." In *Gertsenovskie chteniia.* Kirov: Dept. kul'tury i isskustva Kirovskoi oblasti, 2002.

Labry, Raoul. *Alexandre Ivanovic Herzen, 1812–1870: Essai sur la formation et le développement de ses idées.* Paris: Éditions Bossard, 1928.

———. *Herzen et Proudhon.* Paris: Bossard, 1928.

Lampert, Evgenii. *Studies in Rebellion.* London: Routledge and Kegan Paul, 1957.

———. *Sons Against Fathers: Studies in Russian Radicalism and Revolution.* Oxford: Clarendon, 1965.

Landmarks: A Collection of Essays on the Russian Intelligentsia 1909. Translated by Marian Schwartz. Edited by Boris Shragin and Albert Todd. New York: Karz Howard, 1977.

Lanskii, L. P. "Gertsen i Frantsiia." *Literaturnoe nasledstvo,* vol. 96, "Gertsen i zapad," 254–306. Edited by S. A. Maklashin and L. P. Lanskii. Moscow: Nauka, 1985.

Lenin, V. I. "Pamiati Gertsena." *Sotsial-Demokrat,* no. 26, May 8 (April 25), 1912.

Letopis' zhizni i tvorchestva A. I. Gertsena

———. Vol. 1. 1812–1850. Edited by G. G. Elizavetina, L. P. Lanskii, A. M. Malakhova, and V. A. Putintsev. Moscow: Nauka, 1974.

———. Vol. 2. 1851–1858. Edited by L. P. Lanskii and I. G. Ptushkina. Moscow: Nauka, 1976.

———. Vol. 3. 1859–1864. Edited by I. G. Ptushkina and S. D. Gurvich-Lishchiner. Moscow: Nauka, 1983.

———. Vol. 4. 1864–1867. Edited by S. D. Gurvich-Lishchiner. Moscow: Nauka, 1987.

———. Vol. 5. 1868–1870. Edited by S. D. Gurevich-Lishchiner and L. R. Lanskii. Moscow: Nauka, 1990.

Levin, Kirik. *A. I. Gertsen: Lichnost', ideologiia.* Moscow: Dennitsa, Tipografiia Voennogo Komiteta Moskovskoi oblasti, 1918 (2nd ed., Gosudarstvennoe Izdatel'stvo, 1922).

Lilla, Mark, Ronald Dworkin, and Robert Silvers. *The Legacy of Isaiah Berlin.* New York: New York Review of Books, 2001.

Lindstrom, Thaïs. *A Concise History of Russian Literature,* vol. 1, *From the Beginnings to Chekhov.* New York: New York University Press, 1966.

Linkov, Iakov L. *Revoliutsionnaia bor'ba: A. I. Gertsen i N. P. Ogarev i tainoe obshchestvo "Zemlia i volia" 1860–kh godov.* Moscow: Nauka, 1964.

Lishchiner, S.: see Gurevich-Lishchiner, S.

Literaturnoe nasledstvo, vols. 39–40 (1941), 61 (1953), 62 (1955), 63 (1956), 64 (1958).

Lomunov, K. N. "A. I. Gertsen v londonskoi period ego zhizni." In *Alexander Herzen and European Culture,* edited by Monica Partridge. Nottingham: Astra, 1984.

Lossky, N. O. *History of Russian Philosophy.* New York: International Universities Press, 1951.

Lunacharskii, Anatolii Vasil'evich. "Aleksandr Ivanovich Gertsen." In *Sobranie sochinenii v vos'mi tomakh,* 1:129–51. Moscow: Khudozhestvennaia Literatura, 1963.

Maksimova, M. K. "Traditsionnaia metafora v iazyke proizvedenii A. I. Gertsena." In *Voprosy razvitiia grammatiki i leksiki russkogo iazyka,* 297–310. Leningrad: Pedagogicheskii Institut Imeni Gertsena, Uchenye zapiski, volume 373, 1968.

Malia, Martin. *Alexander Herzen and the Birth of Russian Socialism.* New York: Universal Library, 1965.

———. "Schiller and the Early Russian Left." In *Russian Social Thought and Politics,* vol. 4, edited by H. McLean, M. Malia, and G. Fischer. Cambridge, Mass.: Harvard University Press, 1957.

Masaryk, Thomas Garrigue. *The Spirit of Russia: Studies in History, Literature, and Philosophy,* 2 vols., translated by Eden Paul and Cedar Paul. London: George Allen and Unwin, 1961.

Maynard, John. *Russia in Flux Before the October Revolution.* New York: Collier, 1962.

McKenzie, Kermit E. "The Political Faith of Fedor Rodichev." In *Essays on Russian Liberalism,* edited and with an introduction by Charles E. Timberlake, 42–61. Columbia: University of Missouri Press, 1972.

McLean, Hugh. *Nikolai Leskov: The Man and His Art.* Cambridge, Mass.: Harvard University Press, 1977.

McReynolds, Louise. "V. M. Doroshevich: The Newspaper Journalist and the Development of Public Opinion in Civil Society." In *Between Tsar and People: Educated Society and the Quest for Public Identity in Late Imperial Russia,* edited by Edith Clowes, Samuel Kassow, and James West, 233–47. Princeton, N.J.: Princeton University Press, 1991.

Meshcherskii, Kniaz'. *Vospominanii.* Moscow: Zakharov, 2001.

Miliukov, P. N. "Pamiati Gertsena." *Mir Bozhii,* 9, no. 2 (February 1900): 17–21.

———. *Russia To-Day and To-Morrow.* New York: Macmillan, 1922.

———. *Vospominaniia (1859–1917)*, vol. 1, edited by M. M. Karpovich and B. I. El'kin. New York: Izdatel'stvo Imeni Chekhova, 1955.

Miller, Martin. *The Russian Revolutionary Emigres 1825-1870.* Baltimore: The Johns Hopkins University Press, 1986.

Monas, Sidney. "The Twilight Middle Class of Nineteenth-Century Russia." In *Between Tsar and People: Educated Society and the Quest for Public Identity in Late Imperial Russia,* edited by Edith Clowes, Samuel Kassow, and James West, 28–37. Princeton, N.J.: Princeton University Press, 1991.

Morson, Gary Saul. *The Boundaries of Genre: Dostoevsky's "Diary of a Writer" and the Traditions of Literary Utopia.* Austin: University of Texas Press, 1981.

———. "Editor's Introduction: The Process and Composition of a *Writer's Diary.*" In Fyodor Dostoevsky, *A Writer's Diary,* one-volume abridged edition, translated and annotated by Kenneth Lantz, xix–lxii. Evanston, Ill.: Northwestern University Press, 2009.

———. "Introductory Study: Dostoevsky's Great Experiment." In Fyodor Dostoevsky, *A Writer's Diary,* 2 vols., translated and annotated by Kenneth Lantz, 1–117. Evanston, Ill.: Northwestern University Press, 1993.

Moser, Charles. *Antinihilism in the Russian Novel of the 1860s.* The Hague: Mouton, 1964.

Moss, Walter G. *Russia in the Age of Alexander II, Tolstoy and Dostoevsky.* London: Anthem, 2002.

Mosse, W. E. *Alexander II and the Modernization of Russia.* London: I. B. Tauris, 1992.

Novich, Ioann [Fainshtein]. *A. I. Gertsen: Stenogramma publichnoi lektsii, prochitannoi 4 aprelia 1947 goda v Dome Soiuzov v Moskve.* Moscow, 1947.

———. *Molodoi Gertsen: Iskaniia, idei, obrazy, lichnost'.* Moscow: Sovetskii pisatel', 1980.

Offord, Derek. "Alexander Herzen and James de Rothschild." *Toronto Slavic Quarterly* 19 (Winter 2007).

———. *Nineteenth-Century Russia: Opposition to Autocracy.* London: Pearson, 1999.

———. "Perilous Voyage: Alexander Herzen and the Legacy of the Russian Intelligentsia." *TLS* 5688 (April 6, 2012): 14–15.

———. *Portraits of Early Russian Liberals: A Study of the Thought of T. N. Granovsky, V. P. Botkin, P. V. Annenkov, A. V. Druzhinin and K. D. Kavelin.* Cambridge, Eng.: Cambridge University Press, 1985.

Orlova, Raisa. *Memoirs.* Translated by Samuel Cioran. New York: Random House, 1983.

———. *Poslednii god zhizni Gertsena.* New York: Chalidze, 1982.

Panaev, I. I. *Literaturnye vospominaniia.* Edited by N.L. Brodskii, F. V. Gladkov, et al. Leningrad: Khudozhestvennaia Literatura, 1950.

Pantin, I. K. "A. I. Gertsen: Nachalo liberal'nogo sotsializma." *Voprosy filosofii* 3 (2006): 118–31.

Paperno, Irina. "Introduction: Intimacy and History: The Gercen Family Drama Reconsidered." *Russian Literature* 61 (January 1–February 15, 2007): 1–65.

———. *Stories of the Soviet Experience: Memoirs, Diaries, Dreams.* Ithaca, N.Y.: Cornell University Press, 2009.

Parthé, Kathleen. "Putin Should Consider a Nineteenth-Century Blogger." *The Moscow Times,* March 30, 2012.

———. *Russia's Dangerous Texts: Politics Between the Lines.* New Haven, Conn.: Yale University Press, 2004.

Partridge, Monica. *Alexander Herzen: 1812–1870*. Paris: UNESCO, 1984.

———. "Alexander Herzen and England." In *Alexander Herzen: Collected Studies*, 2nd ed. Nottingham: Astra, 1993.

———. "Alexander Herzen and the English Press." *Slavonic and East European Review* 36, no. 87 (June 1958): 453.

Pavlov, Aleksandr. *Ot dvorianskoi revoliutsionnosti k revoliutsionnomu demokratizmu (ideinaia evoliutsiia Gertsena)*. Moscow: Izdatel'stvo Moskovskogo universiteta, 1977.

———. "Polovina knigi ob Aleksandre Gertsene." In Martin Malia, *Aleksandr Gertsen i proiskhozhdenie russkogo sotsializama 1812–1855*, translated by Aleksandr Pavlov and Dmitrii Uzlaner, 7–31. Moscow: Izdatel'skii dom "Territoriia budushchego," 2010.

Pekhtelev, Ivan G. *Gertsen-literaturnyi kritik*. Moscow: Prosveshchenie, 1967.

Perkal', M. K. *Gertsen v Peterburge*. Leningrad: Lenizdat, 1971.

Perlina, Nina. "Vozdeistvie gertsenovskogo zhurnalizma na arkhitektoniku i polifonicheskoe stroenie *Dnevnika pisatelia* Dostoevskogo." *Dostoevsky Studies* 5 (1984): 142–55.

Pervukhin, Natalia. "Alexander Herzen and Vladimir Pecherin in Their Literary Memoirs." In *Life Lines: Perspectives on Russian and European Culture, Society, and Politics: A Festschrift for Professor Raymond T. McNally*, edited by Nicholas Racheotes and Hugh Guilderson, 108–27. Boulder, Colo.: East European Monographs, 2001.

Petrunkevich, E. I. *Iz zapisok obshchestvennogo deiatelia: Vospominaniia*. Edited by A. A. Kizevetter. Prague, 1934; Berlin: Petropolid-Verlag.

Pipes, Richard, ed. *Russian Intelligentsia*. New York: Columbia University Press, 1961.

Piroschkow, Vera [Vera Aleksandrovna Pirozhkova]. *Alexander Herzen: Der Zusammenbruch einer Utopie*. Munich: A. Pustet, 1961.

Pirumova, N. M. *Aleksandr Gertsen—Revoliutsioner, myslitel', chelovek*. Moscow: Mysl', 1989.

———. *Istoricheskie vzgliady A. I. Gertsena*. Moscow: Gosudarstvennoe Izdatel'stvo politicheskoi Literatury, 1956.

Plekhanov, Georgii. *Sochinenii*. 24 vols. Moscow: Gosudarstvennoe Izdatel'stvo, 1923–1928.

Plotkin, Lev A. "Gertsen-belletrist." In *O russkoi literature: A. I. Gertsen, I. S. Nikitin, D. I. Pisarev*. Leningrad: Khudozhestvennaia literatura, 1986.

Polonsky, Rachel. *Molotov's Magic Lantern: A Journey in Russian History*. London: Faber and Faber, 2010.

Porokh, I. V. "Gertsen o Rossii." In *V razdum'iakh o Rossii (XIX vek)*, edited by E. L. Rudnitskaia, 230–42. Moscow: "Arkheograficheskii tsentr," 1996.

Prawdin, Michael. *The Unmentionable Nechaev: A Key to Bolshevism*. New York: Roy, 1961.

Preissmann, Ulrike. *Alexander Herzen und Italien*. Mainz: Liber Verlag, 1989.

Putintsev, V. A., ed. *A. I. Gertsen v russkoi kritike*, 2nd rev. ed. Moscow: Khudozhestvennaia literatura, 1953.

———. *Gertsen v vospominaniiakh sovremennikov*. Moscow: Khudozhestvennaia Literatura, 1956.

Radek, Leonid S. *Gertsen i Turgenev: Literaturno-esteticheskaia polemika*. Kishinev: Shtinnitsa, 1984.

Raeff, Marc. *Origins of the Russian Intelligentsia*. New York: Harcourt Brace and World, 1966.

————. "The Peasant Commune in the Political Thinking of Russian Publicists: Laissez-Faire Liberalism in the Reign of Alexander II." Ph. D. thesis, Harvard University, 1950.

Rambaud, Alfred. *Histoire de la Russie depuis les origins jusqu'à l'année 1877*. Paris: Hachette, 1878.

Reikhel', Mar'ia K. [Ern]. *Otryvki iz vospominanii M. K. Reikhel' i pis'ma k nei A. I. Gertsena*. Moscow: Izdanie L. E. Bukhgeim, 1909.

Reiser, S. A. *Letopis' zhizni i deiatel'nosti N. A. Dobroliubova*. Moscow: Kul'turno-prosvetitel'naia literatura, 1953.

Reissner, Eberhard. *Alexander Herzen in Deutschland*. Berlin: Akademie-Verlag, 1963.

Root, Andrei. *Gertsen i traditsii Vol'noi russkoi pressy*. Kazan: Izdatel'stvo Kazanskogo universiteta, 2001.

Rossiia 2, no. 10 (1999). [Russkaia intelligentsia i zapadnyi intellektualizm: istoriia i tipologiia].

Rozanov, V. V. *The Apocalypse of Our Time and Other Writings*. Translated by Robert Payne and Nikita Romanoff. Edited by Robert Payne. New York: Praeger, 1977.

————. *Izbrannoe*. Edited by E. Zhiglevich. Munich: A. Neimanis, 1970.

Rozanova, S. *Tolstoi i Gertsen*. Moscow: Khudozhestvennaia literatura, 1972.

Rubinshtein, Nikolai L. *Russkaia istoriografiia*. Moscow: OGIZ/Gospolitizdat, 1941.

Rutintsev, V. A. *Gertsen: Pisatel'*, 2nd ed. Moscow: ANSSSR, 1963.

Ryan, Alan. "On Liberty: Beyond Duty to Personal Aesthetics." In *The Philosophy of John Stuart Mill*. London: Macmillan, 1970.

Safran, Gabriella. *Wandering Soul: The Dybbuk's Creator, S. An-sky*. Cambridge, Mass.: Harvard University Press, 2010.

Salisbury, Harrison. *The 900 Days: The Siege of Leningrad*. New York: Harper and Row, 1969.

Samoilov, D. S., and L. K. Chukovskaia. *Perepiska 1971–1990*. Edited by G. I. Medvedeva-Samoilova, E. T. Chukovskaia, and Zh. O. Khavkina. Moscow: Novoe literaturnoe obozozrenie, 2004.

Schapiro, Leonard. *Rationalism and Nationalism in Russian Nineteenth-Century Thought*. New Haven, Conn.: Yale University Press, 1967.

Schmid, Ulrich. *Ichentwürfe: Die russische Autobiographie zwischen Avvakum und Gercen*. Zürich: Pano-Verlag, 2000.

Semenov, V. *Aleksandr Gertsen*. Moscow: "Sovremennik," 1989.

Serge, Victor. *Memoirs of a Revolutionary 1901–1941*. Translated and edited by Peter Sedgwick. Oxford: Oxford University Press, 1967.

Service, Robert. *Trotsky: A Biography*. Cambridge, Mass.: Belknap/Harvard University Press, 2009.

Shklovskii, Viktor Borisovich. *Povesti o proze: Razmyshleniia i razbory*, vol. 2. Moscow: Khudozhestvennaia literatura, 1966.

Shlapentokh, Dmitry. *The French Revolution in Russian Intellectual Life 1865–1905*, with a new introduction by the author. New Brunswick, N.J.: Transaction, 2009.

Smirnov, Viktor G. *Gertsen v Novgorode*. Leningrad: Lenizdat, 1985.

Smirnova, Zinaida V. *Sotsial'naia filosofiia A. I. Gertsena*. Moscow: Nauka, 1973.

Smith, F. B. "The View from Britain: Tumults Abroad, Stability at Home." In *Intellectuals and Revolution: Socialism and the Experience of 1848,* edited by Eugene Kamenka and F. B. Smith, 94–120. London: E. Arnold, 1979.

Solzhenitsyn, Aleksandr. *The First Circle.* The restored text, translated by Harry T. Willetts. New York: Harper, 2009.

———. *Invisible Allies.* Translated by Alexis Klimoff and Michael Nicholson. Washington, D.C.: Counterpoint, 1995.

———. "Ne obychai degtem shchi belit', na to smetana." *Literaturnaia gazeta,* Nov. 4, 1965. Translated by Donald Fiene in *Russian Literature Triquarterly* 11 (1975): 264–69.

———. *Publitsistika v trekh tomakh,* vol. 1, *Stat'i i rechi.* Yaroslavl: Verkhne-Volzhskoe Knizhnoe izdatel'stvo, 1995.

Steiner, Lina. "Gercen's Tragic *Bildungsroman:* Love, Autonomy, and Maturity in Aleksandr Gercen's *Byloe i dumy.*" *Russian Literature* 61, no. 1–2 (January 1–February 15, 2007): 139–73.

Steklov, Iu. *A. I. Gertsen (Iskander) 1812–1870 g.* Moscow: Gosudarstvennaia Izdatel'stvo, 1920.

Strakhov, N. N. "Gertsen." *Bor'ba s zapadom v nashei literature: Istoricheskie i kriticheskie ocherki,* kniga pervaia. Kiev: Tipografiia Choklova, 1897; rpt. The Hague/Paris: Mouton, 1969.

Struve, P. B. *Patriotica: Politika, kul'tura, religiia, sotsializm.* Moscow: Izdatel'stvo "Respublika," 1997.

Tatarinova, Liudmila E. *A. I. Gertsen.* Moscow: Mysl', 1980.

Tatishchev, S. S. *Imperator Aleksandr II, Ego Zhizn' i Tsarstvovanie.* 2 vols. St. Petersburg: Izdatel'stvo A. S. Suvorova, 1903.

Tertz, Abram [Andrei Sinyavsky]. *The Trial Begins* and *On Socialist Realism.* Translated by Max Hayward and George Dennis. Berkeley: University of California Press, 1982.

Tikhomirov, Vladimir. "Gertsen-200. Bereg levyi, bereg pravyi." *Literaturnaia gazeta,* April 4, 2012.

Tolstaya, Tatyana. *Pushkin's Children: Writings on Russia and Russians.* Translated by Jamie Gambrell. New York: Houghton Mifflin, 2003.

Tolstoi, Lev Nikolaevich. *Sobranie sochinenii v dvadtsati tomakh,* vols. 18, 20. Moscow: Khudozhestvennaia literatura, 1965.

Tompkins, Stuart Ramsay. *The Russian Intelligentsia: Makers of the Revolutionary State.* Norman: University of Oklahoma Press, 1957.

Trifonov, Iurii. "Kak slovo nashe otzovetsia. . . (Beseda s kritikom L. Anninskim, 1980)." In *Kak slovo nashe otzovetsia,* 307–19. Moscow: Sovetskaia Rossiia, 1985.

Tucker, Robert. "The Image of Dual Russia." In *The Transformation of Russian Society: Aspects of Social Change Since 1861,* edited by Cyril Black, 587–605. Cambridge, Mass.: Harvard University Press, 1960.

———. *Political Culture and Leadership in Soviet Russia: From Lenin to Gorbachev.* New York: W. W. Norton, 1987.

Ulam, Adam B. *Ideologies and Illusions: Revolutionary Thought from Herzen to Solzhenitsyn.* Cambridge, Mass.: Harvard University Press, 1976.

Usakina, T. I. "Stat'ia Gertsena 'VERY DANGEROUS!!!' i polemika vokrug 'Oblichitel'noi literatury' v zhurnalistike 1857–1859 gg." In *Revoliutsionnaia situatsiia v Rossii v 1859–1861 gg.,* edited by M. V. Nechkina et al. Moscow: ANSSSR, 1960.

Utechin, S. V. *Russian Political Thought: A Concise History*. New York: Frederick A. Praeger, 1964.

Venturi, Franco. *Roots of Revolution*. Translated by Francis Haskell. Introduction by Isaiah Berlin. New York: Universal Library, 1966.

Verhoeven, Claudia. *The Odd Man Karakozov: Imperial Russia, Modernity and the Birth of Terrorism*. Ithaca, N.Y.: Cornell University Press, 2009.

Vetrinskii, Ch. *Gertsen*. St. Petersburg: Svetoch, 1908.

———. "*Kolokol* i krest'ianskaia reforma." In *Velikaia reforma*, Anniversary Edition in six volumes, 4:194–219. Moscow: Sytin, 1911.

Volodin, Aleksandr I. *Gertsen*. Moscow: Mysl', 1970.

Walicki, Andrzej. *A History of Russian Thought from the Enlightenment to Marxism*. Stanford, Calif.: Stanford University Press, 1979.

———. *Legal Philosophies of Russian Liberalism*. Oxford: Oxford University Press, 1987.

———. *Russia, Poland, and Universal Regeneration*. Notre Dame, Ind.: University of Notre Dame Press, 1991.

———. *The Slavophile Controversy: History of a Conservative Utopia in Nineteenth-Century Russian Thought*. Translated by Hilda Andrews-Rusiecka. Notre Dame, Ind.: University of Notre Dame Press, 1989.

Woehrlin, William F. *Chernyshevskii, the Man and the Journalist*. Cambridge, Mass.: Harvard University Press, 1971.

Wortman, Richard, *The Development of Russian Legal Consciousness*. Chicago: University of Chicago Press, 1976.

———. *Scenarios of Power: Myth and Ceremony in Russian Monarchy*, vol. 1, *From Peter the Great to the Death of Nicholas I*, Princeton, N.J.: Princeton University Press, 1995; vol. 2, *From Alexander II to the Abdication of Nicholas II*, Princeton, N.J.: Princeton University Press, 2000.

Yanov, Alexander, *The Origins of Autocracy: Ivan the Terrible in Russian History*. Translated by Stephen Dunn. Berkeley: University of California Press, 1981. See also Ianov.

Yarmolinsky, Avrahm. *Road to Revolution: A Century of Russian Radicalism*. London: Cassell, 1957.

Zakharov, V. "'Do dna svobodnyi genii' (K 175–letiiu so dna rozhdeniia A. I. Gertsena)." *Oktiabr'* 3 (1987): 181–89.

Zamyatin, Yevgeny. *A Soviet Heretic*. Translated and edited by Mirra Ginsburg. Chicago: University of Chicago Press, 1970.

Zen'kovskii, V. V. *Istoriia russkoi filosofii*. Paris: YMCA, 1948.

Zernov, Nicolas. *The Russian Religious Renaissance of the Twentieth Century*. New York: Harper and Row, 1963.

Zhelvakova, Irena A. *Dom v Sitsevom Vrazhke*. Moscow: Moskovskii rabochii, 1982.

———. *Gertsen (Zhizn' zamechatel'nykh liudei)*. Moscow: Molodaia gvardiia, 2010.

———. "Literaturnyi obraz v publitsistike A. I. Gertsena ('Kolokol' 1857–1867 gg.)." In *Revoliutsinionnaia situatsiia v Rossii v 1859–1861 gg*, edited by M. V. Nechkina et al., 2:505–18. Moscow: ANSSSR, 1962.

———. *Ot devich'ego polia do eliseiskikh polei: Poiski i nakhodki, vstrechi i vpechatleniia*. Moscow: Znak, 2005.

"Zhurnal'no-izdatel'skaia deiatel'nost' A. I. Gertsena i N. P. Ogareva: 'Poliarnaia zvezda' i 'Kolokol.'" In *Istoriia russkoi zhurnalistiki: XVIII-XIX vekov*, edited by A. V. Zapadov, 279–304. Moscow: Vysshaia shkola, 1963.

Zimmerman, Judith E. "Herzen, Herwegh, Marx." In *Imperial Russia 1700–1917: State, Society, Opposition; Essays in Honor of Marc Raeff,* edited by E. Mendelsohn and M. Shatz. DeKalb: Northern Illinois University Press, 1988.

———. *Midpassage: Alexander Herzen and European Revolution, 1847–1852.* Pittsburgh, Pa.: University of Pittsburgh Press, 1989.

Zubok, Vladislav. *Zhivago's Children: The Last Russian Intelligentsia.* Cambridge, Mass.: Harvard/Belknap, 2009.